INDEPENDENT DIRECTORS IN ASIA

The rise of the independent director in Asia is an issue of global consequence that has been largely overlooked until recently. Less than two decades ago, independent directors were oddities in Asia's boardrooms. Today, they are ubiquitous. *Independent Directors in Asia* undertakes the first detailed analysis of this phenomenon. It provides in-depth historical, contextual and comparative perspectives on the law and practice of independent directors in seven core Asian jurisdictions (China, Hong Kong, India, Japan, Singapore, South Korea, Taiwan) and Australia. These case studies reveal the varieties of independent directors in Asia, none of which conform to its original American concept. The authors develop a taxonomy of these varieties, which provides a powerful analytical tool for more accurately understanding and effectively researching independent directors in Asia. This new approach challenges foundational aspects of comparative corporate governance practice and suggests a new path for comparative corporate governance scholarship and reform.

DAN W. PUCHNIAK is Director of the National University of Singapore (NUS) Centre for Asian Legal Studies, the Editor-in-Chief of the *Asian Journal of Comparative Law* and an Associate Professor at NUS Law. He specialises in corporate law with an emphasis on comparative corporate law in Asia and has published widely on comparative, Asian, Singaporean and Japanese corporate law and governance.

HARALD BAUM serves as Senior Research Fellow and Head of Japanese Department at the Max Planck Institute for Comparative and International Private Law in Hamburg and as Professor of Law at the University of Hamburg. He is the executive founding editor of the *Journal of Japanese Law* and has authored and edited numerous books and articles on business law, corporate governance and capital market regulation in Germany, the EU, Japan and the US.

LUKE NOTTAGE is Associate Director of the Centre for Asian and Pacific Law at the University of Sydney and Founding Director of the Australian Network for Japanese Law and Japanese Law Links. He specialises in corporate governance, foreign investment regulation, arbitration, contract law and consumer product safety law, with a particular interest in Japan and the Asia-Pacific. His other publications include *Corporate Governance in the 21st Century: Japan's Gradual Transformation* (2008) and *Foreign Investment and Dispute Resolution Law and Practice in Asia* (2011).

CAMBRIDGE UNIVERSITY PRESS

International Corporate Law and Financial Market Regulation

Corporate law and financial market regulation have major implications for how the modern economy is organized and regulated and for how risk is managed and distributed – domestically, regionally and internationally. This Series seeks to inform and lead the vibrant scholarly and policy debate in this highly dynamic area by publishing cutting-edge, timely and critical examinations of the most pressing and important questions in the field.

INDEPENDENT DIRECTORS IN ASIA

A Historical, Contextual and Comparative Approach

Edited by

DAN W. PUCHNIAK

National University of Singapore

HARALD BAUM

Max Planck Institute for Comparative and International Private Law

LUKE NOTTAGE

University of Sydney

CAMBRIDGE
UNIVERSITY PRESS

CAMBRIDGE
UNIVERSITY PRESS

University Printing House, Cambridge CB2 8BS, United Kingdom

One Liberty Plaza, 20th Floor, New York, NY 10006, USA

477 Williamstown Road, Port Melbourne, VIC 3207, Australia

4843/24, 2nd Floor, Ansari Road, Daryaganj, Delhi – 110002, India

79 Anson Road, #06-04/06, Singapore 079906

Cambridge University Press is part of the University of Cambridge.

It furthers the University's mission by disseminating knowledge in the pursuit of education, learning, and research at the highest international levels of excellence.

www.cambridge.org
Information on this title: www.cambridge.org/9781107179592
DOI: 10.1017/9781316819180

First published 2017

Printed in the United Kingdom by Clays, St Ives plc

A catalogue record for this publication is available from the British Library.

Library of Congress Cataloging-in-Publication Data
Names: Puchniak, Dan W., 1976– editor. | Baum, Harald, editor. | Nottage, Luke, editor.
Title: Independent directors in Asia : a historical, contextual and comparative approach / edited by Daniel William Puchniak, National University of Singapore, Harald Baum, Max-Planck-Institut für ausländisches und internationales Privatrecht, Luke Nottage, University of Sydney.
Description: Cambridge, United Kingdom ; New York, NY : Cambridge University Press, 2017. | Series: International corporate law and financial market regulation | Includes bibliographical references and index.
Identifiers: LCCN 2017033143 | ISBN 9781107179592 (hardback : alk. paper)
Subjects: LCSH: Directors of corporations – Asia. | Directors of corporations – Legal status, laws, etc. – Asia. | Corporations – Asia. | Corporation law – Asia.
Classification: LCC HD2891.85 .I53 2017 | DDC 338.6095–dc23
LC record available at https://lccn.loc.gov/2017033143

ISBN 978-1-107-17959-2 Hardback

CONTENTS

FIGURES

TABLES

CONTRIBUTORS

FADY AOUN, Lecturer of Law, University of Sydney Law School.

BRUCE ARONSON, Professor of Law, Hitotsubashi University, Graduate School of International Corporate Strategy.

VIVIENNE BATH, Professor of Chinese and International Business Law, University of Sydney Law School; Director of the Centre for Asian and Pacific Law and Chair of the China Studies Centre Research Committee, The University of Sydney.

HARALD BAUM, Senior Research Fellow, Max Planck Institute for Comparative and International Private Law, Hamburg; Professor of Law, University of Hamburg.

HSIN-TI CHANG, Professor of Law, National Taipei University.

KYUNG-HOON CHUN, Associate Professor, Seoul National University School of Law.

GEN GOTO, Associate Professor, Graduate Schools for Law and Politics, University of Tokyo.

VIKRAMADITYA KHANNA, William W. Cook Professor of Law, University of Michigan Law School.

KON SIK KIM, Professor, Seoul National University School of Law.

SOUICHIROU KOZUKA, Professor of Law, Gakushuin University, Tokyo.

LUH LUH LAN, Associate Professor, National University of Singapore Business School and Faculty of Law.

YU-HSIN LIN, Assistant Professor, City University of Hong Kong School of Law.

MANABU MATSUNAKA, Associate Professor, Nagoya University Graduate School of Law.

LUKE NOTTAGE, Professor of Law, University of Sydney Law School.

DAN W. PUCHNIAK, Associate Professor, National University of Singapore, Faculty of Law; Director, National University of Singapore Centre for Asian Legal Studies.

WOLF-GEORG RINGE, Professor of Law and Economics and Director of the Institute of Law and Economics, University of Hamburg; Visiting Professor, University of Oxford.

XIN TANG, Professor, Tsinghua University School of Law.

YING-HSIN TSAI, Associate Professor of Law, National Taiwan University.

UMAKANTH VAROTTIL, Associate Professor, National University of Singapore, Faculty of Law.

ACKNOWLEDGEMENTS

The editors would like to gratefully acknowledge and sincerely thank Professor Souichirou Kozuka, Tokyo, for the important role he played in this book project. Beginning with the organisation of panel sessions for the 2nd East Asian Law and Society Association conference in Seoul and then the Law and Society Association annual conference in Honolulu, his contribution in laying the foundation for this project has been critical to its development. In addition, throughout the project, Professor Kozuka played a key role in shaping its direction. This project would not have been the same without his important input and significant efforts.

The editors gratefully acknowledge the generous financial support for the research project from the Max Planck Institute for Comparative and International Private Law, Hamburg, the Japanese-German Center Berlin, German Fritz Thyssen Foundation and the National University of Singapore (NUS) Centre for Asian Legal Studies and the NUS EW Barker Centre for Law & Business for sponsoring two major later conferences – in Berlin and Singapore respectively – which were foundational in this book project. The editors also gratefully acknowledge grants from the Legal Scholarship Support Fund at Sydney Law School and funding from the Centre for Asian and Pacific Law at the University of Sydney for a smaller related symposium.

The editors would like to extend special thanks to Samantha Tang from the NUS Centre for Asian Legal Studies for her skilful and diligent research assistance, which significantly benefited this book project in myriad ways. The editors would also like to specially thank Marcel Wong and Zou Lingyi Laura from NUS Law for their skilful and diligent research assistance in the final editorial stages of this project. The editors are also grateful for the enormous help and research assistance from students at the University of Chicago Law School (especially, Hannah Loo), NUS Law (especially, Ho Jun Yee Lester, Irina Golovkovskaya, Srruthi Ilankathir, Hita Kumar and Jesslyn Zeng) and Sydney Law School (especially, various CAPLUS student interns including Min Jung Esther Choi, Michael Power and Mariko Kadota, as well as Ganesh Vaheisvaran and Kirsten Gan).

The editors were fortunate to be able to present and receive enormously helpful feedback on various parts of the book at forums around the world. In particular, the editors would like to thank ETH Zurich Center for Law and Economics, Hitotsubashi ICS, the Japanese Ministry of Justice, the Institute of Comparative Law in Japan (Chuo University), the Inter-Pacific Bar Association, Kyushu University Graduate School of Law, London School of Economics, Mori Hamada and Matsumoto, Oxford University Commercial Law Centre, Seoul National University Law School, University College London Centre for Commercial Law, the University of Chicago Law School, University of Tokyo Faculty of Law and Politics and Vanderbilt Law School for generously organising venues to present and receive helpful feedback on various parts of this book project.

In addition, many thanks to John Armour, Gary Bell, Marco Becht, Margaret Blair, Brian Cheffins, Weitseng Chen, Paul Davies, Jean du Plessis, Michael Dowdle, Luca Enriques, Carsten Gerner-Beuerle, Louise Gullifer, Gerard Hertig, Alan K. Koh, Suzanne Le Mire, Curtis Milhaupt, Masafumi Nakahigashi, Jennifer Payne, Ian Ramsay, Arad Reisberg, Mathias Siems, Holger Spamann, Zhong Xing Tan and Kristin van Zwieten for providing insightful feedback and suggestions on various parts of this book. Of course, any errors or omissions remain our own.

Last, but not least, the editors would like to sincerely thank Cambridge University Press for its support for this book project and editorial efforts.

ABBREVIATIONS

2001 Code	2001 Code of Corporate Governance (Singapore)
2005 Code	2005 Code of Corporate Governance (Singapore)
2012 Code	2012 Code of Corporate Governance (Singapore)
2013 Act	Companies Act, 2013 (India)
ABIT	ABIT Computer Corporation
ACGA	Asian Corporate Governance Association
ACSI	Australian Council of Superannuation Investors
AEC	ASEAN Economic Community
AICD	Australian Institute of Company Directors
AIMA	Australian Investment Managers' Association
APRA	Australian Prudential Regulation Authority
ASX	Australia Stock Exchange
AUS	Australian Dollar
BBK Survey	survey conducted by Balasubramanian, Black and Khanna (India)
CAPCO	China Association for Public Companies
CAMAC	Corporations and Markets Advisory Committee (Australia)
CCGC	Collection of Corporate Governance Codes
C/E	'comply and explain' approach
CEO	chief executive officer
CFO	chief financial officer
CGC	Corporate Governance Committee (Singapore)
CII	Confederation of Indian Industry
CPA	Certified Public Accountant
CSMAR	China Stock Market and Accounting Research
CSR	corporate social responsibility
CSRC	China Securities Regulatory Commission
DIDD	Database of Independent Director Definitions
D&O insurance	Directors and Officers Liability Insurance
DPJ	Democratic Party of Japan
EMCA	European Model Company Act
EU	European Union
FSA	Financial Services Agency (Japan)

FSC	Financial Supervisory Commission (Taiwan)
GEM	Growth Enterprise Market (China)
HIH	HIH Insurance Ltd
HKEx	Hong Kong Exchanges and Clearing
HKD	Hong Kong Dollar
ID	independent director
IMF	International Monetary Fund
INED	independent non-executive director
IT	information technology
KCC	Korean Commercial Code
KFTC	Korea Fair Trade Commission
KONEX	Korea New Exchange
KOSDAQ	Korean Securities Dealers Automated Quotations
KOSPI	Korea Composite Stock Price Index
LDP	Liberal Democratic Party
MAS	Monetary Authority of Singapore
MBCA	Model Business Corporations Act (US)
METI	Ministry of Economy, Trade and Industry (Japan)
MOF	Minister for Finance (Singapore)
MOJ	Ministry of Justice (Japan)
MoM	majority of the minority vote
MOPS	Market Observation Post System (Taiwan)
MORC	Memorandum of Regulatory Cooperation
MSIL	Maruti Suzuki India Limited
NASDAQ	National Association of Securities Dealers Automated Quotations
NCLT	National Company Law Tribunal (India)
NED	non-executive director
NTD	New Taiwan Dollar
NTS	National Tax Service (Korea)
NTU	National Taiwan University
NYSE	New York Stock Exchange
OD	outside director
OECD	Organisation for Economic Co-operation and Development
OROA	adjusted operating return on assets
OTC	over-the-counter
PAP	People's Action Party (Singapore)
PRC	People's Republic of China
RMB	Renminbi (China)
S&P	Standard & Poors
SEA	Securities and Exchange Act (Taiwan)
SEC	Securities and Exchange Commission (US)
SEBI	Securities and Exchange Board of India

SFIPC	Securities and Futures Investors Protection Center
SFC	Hong Kong Securities and Futures Commission
SFO	Securities and Futures Ordinance (Hong Kong)
SGX	Singapore Exchange
SOE	state-owned enterprise
SME	Small and Medium-Sized Enterprise Board (China)
SMEs	small and medium enterprises
SZSE	Shenzhen Stock Exchange
TIDD	Temasek Independent Director Database (Singapore)
TSE	Tokyo Stock Exchange
TWSE	Taiwan Stock Exchange
UK	United Kingdom
UK Code	Combined Code of Corporate Governance (UK)
US	United States of America
USD	United States Dollar

Introduction

DAN W. PUCHNIAK, HARALD BAUM AND LUKE NOTTAGE

I The Rise of the Independent Director in the West and Asia

The rise of the independent director in Asia is remarkable. Merely two decades ago, independent directors were oddities in Asia's boardrooms. Today, as this book reveals, they are ubiquitous. Indeed, Asian companies and jurisdictions that lack a significant cadre of independent directors are now seen as outliers – and, more importantly, as being at risk of corporate governance failures. This stands in stark contrast to the 1980s, when Japan's lifetime-employee-dominated boards, which lacked even a scintilla of independence, were the role model for Asia and much admired in the West.[1]

The concept of the independent director and its related model of the 'monitoring board of directors' were, however, not an Asian invention. The concept originated in the United States (US) from the 1970s onwards, as explained by *Baum* in Chapter 1. Today, in their place of origin, the US, the reliance on independent directors as a panacea for various corporate governance ills has reached its zenith. Over the last several decades, the primary legislative and judicial response to almost every major corporate scandal in the US has been to increase the reliance on independent directors. In 2013, in US public companies, 85 per cent of directors were independent, and so-called 'super-majority-boards' with only *one* remaining inside director – normally the CEO – were widespread.[2]

[1] D. W. Puchniak, 'The 2002 Reform of the Management of Large Corporations in Japan: A Race to Somewhere?', *Australian Journal of Asian Law*, 5(1) (2003), 42. See also L. Nottage, 'Japanese Corporate Governance at a Crossroads: Variation in "Varieties of Capitalism"?', *North Carolina Journal of International Law and Commercial Regulation*, 27 (2001), 255; for a general discussion, see H. Baum, 'Emulating Japan?' in H. Baum (ed.), *Japan: Economic Success and Legal System* (De Gruyter, 1997), 1.

[2] U. Velikonja, 'The Political Economy of Board Independence', *North Carolina Law Review*, 92 (2014), 855, 857.

Around 25 years ago, the concept of independent directors was adopted and refined in the United Kingdom (UK). During the 2000s, the UK situation came to mirror that in the US in some respects. About 90 per cent of directors in UK public companies were independent.[3] From the UK, the faith in independent directors further migrated to Continental Europe. Today, no sophisticated European jurisdiction can do without a UK-style 'comply or explain' corporate governance code, which in turn must deal with independent directors in one way or another to be considered credible. Accordingly, the European Model Company Act of 2015 recommends an 'appropriate balance of independent non-executive directors'.[4]

These trends are also reflected on the supranational level. The Organisation for Economic Co-operation and Development (OECD) recommends in its *G20/OECD Principles of Corporate Governance* of 2015 that important tasks should be assigned to independent board members which 'can contribute significantly to the decision-making of the board'.[5] Similarly, the OECD report *Better Policies for Board Nomination in Asia* of 2013 emphasises the importance of independent directors in the nomination (and other) committees in Asian companies.[6]

This is all the more surprising as there is scarce empirical support for the assumption that independent directors are efficient monitors, as *Ringe* shows in Chapter 2. Only fairly recently, in the wake of the Global Financial Crisis of 2008, has the concept of the independent director come under closer and critical scrutiny – but mainly in Europe.[7]

The precipitous rise of independent directors from obscurity to ubiquity in Asia is as such noteworthy. All of Asia's leading economies appear to have transplanted, or at least claim to have transplanted, the concept of the independent director either directly from its US origin or indirectly via the UK model. However, at least at first sight, this rise

[3] The number has somewhat decreased since then: see Chapter 1 at IV. 1.

[4] European Model Company Act Group, *The European Model Company Act (EMCA) Draft 2015*, Sec. 5, available at http://law.au.dk.

[5] *G20/OECD Principles of Corporate Governance* (OECD Publishing, 2015), available at http://dx.doi.org/10.1787/9789264236882-en.

[6] *Better Policies for Board Nomination in Asia* (OECD Publishing, 2013), available at http://dx.doi.org/10.1787/9789264204386-en. For a basic overview of some of the rules regarding independent directors in many Asian jurisdictions, see generally, ACGA, 'Rules and Recommendations on the Number of Independent Directors in Asia' (2010), available at www.acga-asia.org/. Special thanks to the ACGA for providing useful information for this chapter and book project.

[7] See Chapter 2 at II for a detailed discussion of the growing scepticism of independent directors.

appears to merely mirror an international trend – perhaps suggesting that a book on independent directors *in Asia* may be unwarranted. What we suggest does warrant a book, however, is the fact that Asia's independent directors, in a myriad of complex and intriguing ways, as this book demonstrates, are markedly different from what their Anglo-American origins would suggest. As shown by *Puchniak and Kim* in Chapter 3, a comparison of the jurisdiction-specific chapters in this book reveals that *none* of Asia's leading economies have adopted the American concept of the independent director in form and function. To add to the complexity, within Asia, the form and function of 'independent directors' varies, sometimes significantly, from jurisdiction to jurisdiction. This is because the form independent directors take and the function they fulfil are substantially influenced by each jurisdiction's unique shareholder ownership structures, legal origins, types of shareholders, functional substitutes, political economy and cultural norms. In short, the specific details of so-called 'legal transplants' and local context matter – a lot.

These findings are salient in several ways. From a theoretical perspective, as explained by *Puchniak and Kim* in Chapter 3 and elaborated on in Chapter 13 by *Kozuka and Nottage*, the fact that Asia's independent directors depart in form and function so markedly from their places of origin has at least three important implications for comparative corporate law and governance. First, it provides a poignant example of how even in today's globalised world legal transplants are fraught with difficulty and, at least in some cases, may arguably be impossible to achieve in substance at all. Second, it provides a powerful reminder that in spite of the proliferation of common legal terminology and concepts, the global convergence of corporate law and governance may be much further away than is often assumed by the persistent trend in comparative corporate law scholarship to provide grand universal theories to solve the world's corporate governance problems.[8] Third, and perhaps most importantly, the rise of the independent director in Asia illustrates how local context is critically important for accurately understanding corporate law and governance in Asia (and, we suspect, everywhere else).[9] Somewhat

[8] See D. W. Puchniak and H. Baum, 'The Derivative Action in Asia: Some Concluding Observations' in D. W. Puchniak, H. Baum and M. Ewing-Chow (eds.), *The Derivative Action in Asia: A Comparative and Functional Approach* (Cambridge University Press, 2012), 398 ff., for a similar observation regarding the derivative action, another legal transplant in many Asian jurisdictions.

[9] For a similar conclusion see, D. W. Puchniak, 'Multiple Faces of Shareholder Power in Asia: Complexity Revealed' in R. Thomas and J. Hill (eds.), *Shareholder Power* (Edward

surprisingly, Asia has largely (and erroneously) been ignored so far in comparative corporate law in general and particularly with respect to the independent director.

From a practical perspective, it is important to realise that it is a flawed assumption to believe that independent directors in Asia are essentially tantamount in form and function to those in the US or the UK. However, as shown by *Puchniak and Kim* in Chapter 3, the modus operandi of most prominent institutional investors, proxy advisory firms and international financial organisations assumes just that. This is of critical practical importance because enormous faith and fortune hinge on this belief. As highlighted hereafter, the potential consequences of this flawed assumption are magnified by the seismic shift of economic power towards Asia. An accurate understanding of independent directors in Asia, which this book aims to provide, is therefore an issue of both Asian and global consequence.

II Why Asia Matters[10]

The rise of Asian companies, stock exchanges and economies over the last 50 years has been extraordinary and the shift in economic power towards Asia can no longer be ignored.[11]

The first Asian economy to achieve unimaginable economic success was Japan. Starting in the late 1950s, Japan accomplished what Nobel Laureate economist Michael Spence has identified as unthinkable: developing an economy that doubled in size in less than a decade.[12] What makes Japan's accomplishment even more remarkable is that it repeated this feat several times over from the 1960s to the 1980s. As a result, by the late 1980s, Japan's stock market was the largest in the world. Its companies dominated numerous global industries and, by some measures, it was the richest country in the world. Interestingly, however, in the context of this book, Japan accomplished this with a corporate governance system

Elgar, 2015). See also, L. A. Bebchuk and A. Hamdani, 'The Elusive Quest for Global Governance Standards', *University of Pennsylvania Law Review*, 157 (2009), 1263.

[10] A significant portion of the section was based on Puchniak, 'Multiple Faces of Shareholder Power in Asia' which can be consulted for detailed citations and additional sources.

[11] For a political analysis of the power shift towards Asia, see G. Rachman, *Easternization: War and Peace in the Asian Century* (The Bodley Head, 2016).

[12] D. H. Brady and M. Spence, 'The Ingredients of Growth', *Stanford Social Innovation Review*, available at ssir.org.

that was almost entirely devoid of independent directors. In fact, Japan's lifetime-employee-dominated boards – in which independent directors were almost non-existent – were a hallmark of its world-leading companies, capital markets and economy. Notwithstanding the burst of the economic bubble in 1990 and the infamous ensuing two 'lost decades', Japan has maintained its status as one of the world's three largest economies.

Japan's outstanding economic success provided a model for other Asian countries. Starting from the 1960s, Asia's so-called 'tiger economies' each followed in Japan's footsteps by building economies that doubled in size in under a decade. All of these repeated this feat several times over in the decades that followed. As a result, by the late 1990s, Asia's tigers all had developed economies, which produced companies and capital markets that were competitive with (and, in some cases, superior to) those in the West. Moreover, in the 1990s, Singapore and then Hong Kong overtook Japan in terms of Gross Domestic Product (GDP) per capita, with the other Asian tigers following their lead.

Importantly, in the context of this book, as in Japan, the economic success in these economies was largely accomplished *without* the aid of independent directors. Rather, and in so far distinct from Japan, these successful Asian economies were built on a foundation of companies controlled by large-block family and/or state controlling shareholders, whose dominance over corporate governance appeared to be the key to their extraordinary economic development.[13]

Although the Asian Financial Crisis (Crisis) from 1997 to 1999 rocked the foundation of Asia's tiger economies, one of the greatest untold stories of Asia's economic rise is what has occurred in its tiger economies in the 15 years *following* the Crisis. During this time, Singapore has led the way by continuing its phenomenal growth, which has catapulted it to now having a GDP per person that is double Japan's and, indeed, higher than any G7 country. It is also recently ranked as having the world's best economy, topping global charts in terms of economic competitiveness. In a similar vein, the GDP per person in Hong Kong now exceeds Japan and the United States, and its stock exchange has led the world in initial public offerings in five of the past eight years.[14] Moreover, Taiwan's GDP per person now exceeds Japan's, and Korea now has a GDP per person roughly equivalent to Japan's and most developed Western countries. In

[13] See the comparative analysis in Chapter 3 at III.
[14] 'Hong Kong Exchanges and Clearing: Down Market?', *The Economist*, 24 June 2017, available at www.economist.com.

the process, all of the tiger economies have produced world-leading companies in myriad industries.[15]

Last, but certainly not least, China and India are in the midst of their own economic growth miracles and, with over two billion people, have already transformed themselves into the world's most important engines for economic growth. Just two decades ago, Chinese companies were virtually non-existent on the global stage. Today, China has more Fortune Global 500 Companies than any other country in the world aside from the United States.[16] In this regard, merely two decades ago, China's stock exchanges were in their infancy. Today, they are poised to challenge the Western stock exchanges for global supremacy. After struggling to keep up with China, India now appears to be possibly the next rising star of Asia. Its economy, capital markets and companies have more recently risen from obscurity to being a focal point for international investors. Indeed, India now is one of the ten largest economies in the world and is projected to be in the top five by the end of this decade. Further, attention should be accorded to the increasingly tight integration within the Asian economies, which are presently underpinned by an ever-growing number of multilateral, regional and bilateral investment treaties, including the launch of the ASEAN Economic Community (AEC) in 2016.[17]

In sum, the net result of the last half century of Asia's economic development is clear: the West's domination of the world economy is in all likelihood phasing out. By 2020, three of the world's four largest economies will be in Asia (China (1), Japan (3) and India (4)). In 2010, Asian stock exchanges captured 66 per cent of the capital raised globally through initial public offerings, up from 12 per cent in 1999. In 2013, for the first time, there were more Fortune Global 500 Companies in Asia than in either North America or Europe (see Table 1.1).[18]

This remarkable development is what makes the examination of the independent director in Asia so timely, important and interesting. For the purposes of this book, we concentrate on Asia's seven most important and

[15] Puchniak, 'Multiple Faces of Shareholder Power in Asia'.

[16] *Ibid.*

[17] See, for example, V. Bath and L. Nottage, 'Asian Investment and the Growth of Regional Investment Agreements' in C. Antons (ed.), *Routledge Handbook of Asian Law* (Routledge, 2017); M. Kawai and G. Wignaraja (eds.), *Asia's Free Trade Agreements: How Is Business Responding?* (Edward Elgar, 2011).

[18] Puchniak, 'Multiple Faces of Shareholder Power in Asia'.

Table I.1 Economic and Corporate Governance Developments Across Asia

Jurisdictions	Total population (million), 2015	Nominal GDP (million USD) and world ranking, 2015	GDP per capita based on Purchasing Power Parity (IntD),[a] 2015	Market capitalisation of listed domestic companies (million USD), 2015[b]	Doing Business Ranking, 2015[c]
Japan	127.0	4,123,258 (3)	37,321	4,894,919.1	34
South Korea	50.6	1,377,873 (11)	34,549	1,231,199.8	4
China	1,371.2	10,866,444 (2)	14,238	8,188,019.3	84
Taiwan[d]	23.5	523,006 (–)	46,833	–	11
Hong Kong	7.3	309,929 (33)	56,719	3,184,874.2	5
Singapore	5.5	292,739 (37)	85,208	639,955.9	1
India	1,311.1	2,073,543 (7)	6,088	1,516,216.7	130

[a] The data in this column is denominated in International Dollars (IntD), where 'an international dollar would buy in the cited country a comparable amount of goods and services a US dollar would buy in the US'. See World Bank, 'What Is an "International Dollar"', available at datahelpdesk.worldbank.org.

[b] Data for this and the preceding two columns is from the World Bank Databank, available at data.worldbank.org. Data in this column has been rounded up to the nearest third decimal place.

[c] N. A. Chakra et al., 'Doing Business 2016: Measuring Regulatory Quality and Efficiency' (World Bank, 2015), available at www.doingbusiness.org.

[d] Data for Taiwan for the first three columns is taken from the International Monetary Fund's World Economic Outlook Database, available at www.imf.org. No data on Taiwan is available for the 'market capitalisation of listed domestic companies' indicator that is comparable to the other jurisdictions.

dynamic economies out of Asia's more than 45 countries: China, Hong Kong, India, Japan, Singapore, South Korea and Taiwan. Collectively, these seven jurisdictions account for approximately 80 per cent of Asia's economic output and are home to its nine largest stock exchanges.[19] After the United States, China and Japan are, respectively, the world's second and third largest economies and, India and South Korea are, respectively, the third and fourth largest economies in Asia. Hong Kong, Singapore and Taiwan regularly rank among the most competitive and dynamic economies in the world.[20]

In addition, these jurisdictions represent the most populous and economically influential economies in the region. They also are diverse in terms of stages of development, competitiveness, capital markets and the extent to which independent directors have been encouraged or required – although independent directors have been on the rise in all seven jurisdictions. These jurisdictions involve a variety of legal traditions, so this variable can also be brought into the picture in comparing and assessing the regional evolution and impact of independent directors. They also display interesting variability in terms of the structure and type of shareholders – although concentrated shareholding, family firms and state-owned enterprises are prominent. Additionally, Australia is included as a separate chapter in this book for comparative reasons, as it has extensive economic relations throughout Asia, and its jurists have longstanding links with the common law countries in Asia.

III The Independent Director Defined

Before proceeding any further, for the purpose of this book, there is a critical conceptual point that must be clarified: who qualifies as an 'independent director'?[21] At first blush, the answer to this question appears intuitively simple: an independent director is a person on a company's board who is not dependent on *someone* or *something* related to the company. A comparative analysis, however, quickly shows that no universal

[19] D. W. Puchniak, 'The Complexity of Derivative Actions in Asia: An Inconvenient Truth' in D. W. Puchniak, H. Baum and M. Ewing-Chow (eds.), *The Derivative Action in Asia: A Comparative and Functional Approach* (Cambridge University Press, 2012), 98.

[20] *Ibid.*, 98.

[21] See Chapter 1 at I. 3 and Chapter 2 at III. 2 for an extensive discussion of the complex issue; see also D. C. Clarke, 'Three Concepts of the Independent Director', *Delaware Journal of Corporate Law*, 32 (2007), 73.

definition of 'independence' exists. Regulatory standards across countries generally employ various definitions using different combinations of criteria according to what the jurisdiction's legislature or other governing body regarded as imperative in the particular context.[22] The lack of a shared understanding comes as no surprise if one considers the fact that independent directors exist within boards that have a multiplicity and diversity of functions.[23] These will vary depending on the particular agency problems that are most acute in a given jurisdiction's unique corporate governance environment.[24] In other words, the context in which independent directors operate in each jurisdiction is highly path dependent.[25]

However, as explained by *Puchniak and Kim* in Chapter 3, leading corporate governance advisory firms, entire areas of comparative corporate governance research and prominent organisations (e.g., the World Bank) have often assumed that there is a singular definition of independence – most often based on the American concept of the independent director. In this respect, we depart from this approach for the reasons given above and in the individual chapters that follow.

Independence is not an end in itself, but instead, constructed to serve a pre-defined goal. If the main task assigned to the independent directors is to monitor management as a solution to the classic agency conflict between managers and dispersed shareholders as owners, independence from the entrenched Chief Executive Officer (CEO) of the stereotypical US Berle-Means corporation seems to be the most important criterion. If, on the other hand, the primary function of such directors is to protect minority shareholders against a controlling blockholder in an archetypical Continental European or most Asian companies, independence from the latter will be the decisive characteristic.

[22] For a general discussion, see, for example, P. L. Davies and K. J. Hopt, 'Boards in Europe: Accountability and Convergence', *American Journal of Comparative Law*, 61 (2013), 301, 317 ff.

[23] For the purpose of this book, we only deal with public listed companies and non-financial companies.

[24] See, for example, R. B. Adams, B. E. Hermalin and M. S. Weisbach, 'The Role of Directors in Corporate Governance: A Conceptual Framework and Survey', *Journal of Economic Literature*, 48 (2010), 58.

[25] For an up-to-date overview of different corporate governance arrangements in major economies, see, for example, K. J. Hopt, 'Comparative Corporate Governance: The State of the Art and International Regulation', *American Journal of Comparative Law*, 59 (2011), 1.

As such, for the purpose of this book, we suggest the following working definition: an independent director is a non-executive outside director who is not in some way affiliated with management, a major shareholder and/or the company in a way that compromises his or her independence. However, merely having independence from management (but not the controlling shareholder) will satisfy the requirements for being described as an 'independent director' in the context of this book. To do otherwise would be to exclude the American concept of the independent director. This would not make sense as conventional (yet erroneous) wisdom suggests the American definition has become the global standard. As empirically proven by *Puchniak and Lan* in Chapter 9, this is clearly not the case as the vast majority of countries around the world have not adopted the American definition of the independent director. As in Asia, these countries have defined independence as being independent from management *and* significant shareholders.

IV Organisation of the Book

The *first part* of the book is made up of three general chapters. The first two deal with the origins, the theoretical foundations and the economic efficiency of the concept of the independent director. The third presents the comparative and theoretical findings of the jurisdictional chapters and develops a taxonomy of independent directors in Asia.

Chapter 1 provides a historical and comparative analysis of the rise of the concept of the independent director in, first, the US and later on, the UK. The corporate board as a management organ in the modern sense sprung to life in the seventeenth century. When joint-stock companies flourished in the UK during the eighteenth and nineteenth centuries and attracted an ever-increasing number of average citizens as investors, managerial powers started to shift gradually from the boards in their entirety to professional managers acting as executive directors – the classical corporate agency conflict arose. In the first half of the twentieth century, a managerialist model of corporate governance dominated both economies. It was not until the 1970s that the concept of the independent director and the related model of the 'monitoring board' first appeared in the US. Today, as mentioned above, the reliance on independent directors has reached its zenith in the US. In the early 1990s, the concept of independent directors was adopted and refined in the UK. From there it migrated to Continental Europe. The reluctant acceptance and only gradual implementation of this legal transplant in Germany is taken as an example to illustrate the difficulties of adopting the US-style concept in a sharply different corporate governance environment, with controlling shareholders, which is also typical for almost all of the Asian jurisdictions analysed in this book.

Chapter 2 develops a theoretical framework for and to re-evaluate the Western corporate governance concept of 'board independence', in order to prepare the ground for its evaluation in the Asian context. Independent directors have long been perceived as an essential tool to improve the monitoring role of the board in Western economies. Yet, the Global Financial Crisis of 2008 shed doubt on the effectiveness of independence as the primary requirement for directors: it has become clear that independent directors did not prevent firms' excessive risk taking. In general, as is discussed in depth in the chapter, the empirical support for staffing boards with independent directors remains surprisingly shaky given the ubiquitous reliance on them. The chapter further reveals that under the surface of seemingly unanimous consensus about board independence in Western jurisdictions, a surprising theoretical disharmony prevails about the justification, extent and purpose of independence requirements. These considerations lead one to question the benefits of the current system. Consequently, the chapter calls for a reflection on the inherent purpose of director independence and proposes a new, 'functional' concept of board independence, overcoming its deficiencies by addressing the challenge to strike a more effective balance between independence and dependence.

Chapter 3 chronicles the meteoric rise of the independent director in Asia. It reveals a reality which is the opposite of what conventional wisdom suggests: many of Asia's leading economies have surpassed those in the West in terms of the proportion of 'independent directors' on corporate boards and the strictness of the laws promoting 'independent directors'. The chapter explains why the meteoric rise of the 'independent director' in Asia is complex. Although the label 'independent director' has been transplanted precipitously from the US (in some cases via the UK) throughout Asia, who is labelled an 'independent director' (i.e., the 'form' that independent directors take) and what independent directors do (i.e., the function they perform) in Asia differ significantly from the American concept of the independent director. To add to the complexity, the form and function of 'independent directors' vary within Asia from jurisdiction to jurisdiction. As such, in reality, there are 'varieties of independent directors in Asia' – none of which conform to the American concept of the independent director. This challenges the widely held assumption that independent directors are universally similar, and complicates interjurisdictional comparisons. The chapter attempts to overcome this comparative hurdle by identifying six factors that have driven the evolution of diverse, jurisdiction-specific, varieties of independent directors in Asia: (1) shareholder ownership structures; (2) legal origins; (3) types of shareholders; (4) functional substitutes; (5) political economy; and (6) cultural norms. These factors provide a basis for constructing a 'loose taxonomy' of the varieties of independent directors in Asia, which provides a useful tool for identifying which interjurisdictional comparisons are likely to yield significant insights and which are likely to mislead. It concludes with a discussion on how an understanding of the varieties of independent directors in Asia can advance corporate governance practice and contribute to comparative corporate governance theory. The conclusion reminds readers that while this chapter extracts the important comparative lessons from the jurisdiction-specific chapters in this book, to gain an accurate understanding of independent directors in Asia the details in each of the jurisdiction-specific chapters are essential.

The *second part* of this book contains the seven Asian jurisdiction-specific chapters. The order in which the Asian jurisdiction-specific chapters are presented in this book is based on the jurisdictions' respective geographies (north-east to south-west), legal traditions (civil law to common law) and the strength of historical and cultural linkages between the jurisdictions. As such, the Asian jurisdiction-specific chapters are presented in the following order: Japan, South Korea, China, Taiwan, Hong Kong, Singapore and India.

The survey starts in Chapter 4 with *Japan*, whose resistance to the global rise of independent directors has drawn considerable attention locally and abroad. Even today, Japan still has no compulsory law for having even one independent director on the board of a listed company. In a unique and highly gradual reform process, Japan only began to consider transplanting the Anglo-American monitoring board model, and consequently independent directors, from the early 2000s – more than a decade after its economic bubble burst, which brought about the first 'lost decade'. Since the 2002 reform, Japanese companies have been able to opt for a one-tier board with committees, which are required to be composed of a majority of outside (but not necessarily independent) directors. In 2009, the Tokyo Stock Exchange amended its Listing Rules requiring at least one independent (and not merely outside) director or statutory auditor (*kansayaku*). In 2014, Japan amended its Companies Act, which promoted, but did not require, companies to adopt independent directors.

In 2015, Japan adopted a UK-style 'comply or explain' Code, which recommends that two or more independent directors be on the board of a listed company. The political dynamics behind the 2014/2015 reforms were not, as is often assumed, the major corporate scandals uncovered in Japan a few years earlier. Rather, the fundamental change in the shareholding structure of listed Japanese companies (i.e., roughly one-third of their shares are now held by foreigners) and the government's desire to attract foreign investment appear to have been the impetus for the reforms. Japanese business lobby groups, however, are still sceptical about the advantages of having independent directors. What is exceptional about Japan's approach is perhaps not necessarily the slow speed of its progress towards an independent monitoring board, but rather, the fact that change has taken place without significant external shocks.

Chapter 5 presents the somewhat unexpected experiences in *Korea* after adopting an IMF recommendation to require all large listed companies to fill a majority of their board seats with directors who are independent from management *and* major shareholders. This mandatory regime was designed to enhance the monitoring function of the boards in large listed Korean companies. Arguably, making independent directors mandatory has increased diversity and transparency in Korean boardrooms and, in turn, improved the monitoring function of Korean boards. After 15 years in operation, however, a unique reality concerning independent directors in Korea appeared. Increasingly, companies fill their independent director quota with retired government officials, such as high-ranking prosecutors or tax officers. While professors and lawyers are increasingly being tapped to become independent directors, it is becoming progressively more difficult to find businessmen or career bankers serving as independent directors in large listed companies. This is strikingly different from Western jurisdictions, where most of the independent or non-executive directors in large listed companies are CEOs, Chief Financial Officers, or high-level executives of other large companies. This trend in Korea may suggest that many companies want their independent directors to play a 'relational role', especially in terms of providing a channel of communication with the government. The prohibition on legal lobbyists under Korean law appears to have created a market for independent-director-cum-lobbyists – a role for independent directors that was certainly not anticipated by the legislature.

China implemented independent director requirements for listed companies in 2001. As Chapter 6 explains, the driving force for the reform was the country's securities market regulator. It introduced the reform with the objective of raising the level of corporate governance in public listed companies. Presently, almost all of China's 2,500 listed companies have made at least one-third of their management board members 'independent'. Considering the unique features of China's capital market environment and corporate governance system, it seems doubtful, however, whether independent directors can monitor effectively on their own (i.e., without strong support from other institutions and/or monitoring mechanisms). Further, it is an open question how independent China's 'independent' directors are in practice and how they function given that all listed companies are required to have a supervisory board – in addition to 'independent directors' on the management board. The chapter proposes reforms to three areas of Chinese corporate law to improve the effectiveness of independent directors as monitors: the nomination system for independent directors; the system for disciplining errant independent directors; and the compensation system for properly incentivising independent directors.

Chapter 7 examines the challenges and problems that have occurred with respect to the use of independent directors during *Taiwan's* watershed regulatory transition from a double board to a one-tier board system. A fundamental corporate governance reform in 2006 granted public companies the ability to choose between a one-tier or the previously mandatory double board structure – with the former requiring 'independent directors'. Subsequent reforms promoted the use of one-tier boards and thus, consequently, independent directors. The chapter examines the definition of 'independence' under the current law, revealing that the present regulatory regime only provides a nominal *ex ante* check on independence. Ultimately, it concludes that with the absence of *ex post* substantive judicial review of director independence, independent directors in Taiwan are at risk of being manipulated by controlling shareholders and used as conduits for the extraction of private benefits of control – while ostensibly appearing to protect minority shareholders from such abuse. Given the lack of *ex post* judicial review of director independence in Taiwan, social ties are likely to continue to hinder the impartiality of 'independent directors'.

Hong Kong was one of the first Asian jurisdictions to introduce independent directors on a listed company board, in as early as 1993, as Chapter 8 reveals. Since 2012, at least one-third of the board of directors must be independent non-executive directors. The major corporate governance issue for Hong Kong companies has been the dominance of controlling shareholders. Companies listed in Hong Kong are often majority or factually controlled either by a family group or, in the case of many significant Chinese companies, a majority state-owned enterprise. There is therefore significant potential for conflicts of interest between the controlling shareholder and the minority shareholders in relation to company operations. Views on the success of independent directors in relation to the controlling shareholder issue are mixed. Doubts have been voiced as to whether independent directors, originally designed to monitor management in companies with dispersed shareholdings, are an effective method of dealing with the controlling shareholder problem. The high level of minority protection in Hong Kong is accordingly deemed to be due to a superior judicial system rather than the use of 'independent directors'.

Singapore implemented a UK-inspired Code of Corporate Governance, which required the adoption of American-style independent directors on a 'comply or explain' basis in 2001. Chapter 9 demonstrates that this embrace of American-style independent directors made Singapore a corporate governance outlier. Although the vast majority of listed companies in Singapore have highly concentrated block-shareholding structures, the new rules did not demand that independence included independence from significant shareholders – as is the rule in most other jurisdictions with concentrated shareholders. However, a surprising 98 per cent of Singapore's listed companies embraced these American-style independent directors – which according to classic agency theory should have been functionally irrelevant. As such, the rise of the independent director in Singapore raised three puzzles: (1) why would Singapore's highly skilled regulators deviate from the seemingly logical path of other controlling-shareholder-dominated jurisdictions by transplanting American-style independent directors into its controlling-shareholder environment?; (2) why did listed companies in Singapore embrace seemingly functionally irrelevant American-style independent directors, and what role (if any) have these directors played in Singapore corporate governance?; and (3) why, after more than a decade of near-perfect compliance and plaudits from ranking agencies, did Singapore decide to abandon American-style independent directors? The chapter offers solutions to these three puzzles and in doing so explores the comparative corporate law lessons that can be derived from this intriguing tale of the rise of independent directors in Singapore.

Board independence has become a critical centrepiece in *India's* corporate governance debate. Chapter 10 emphasises that the traditional distinction between controlled and dispersedly held firms is likely too coarse for the purpose of evaluating, and even defining, board independence as not all controllers are the same: they could range from single controllers to groups consisting of multi-generational family members or non-family members to firms where the state is the controller. Board independence likely operates differently in each scenario. In India, concentration of shareholdings in public companies is the norm. Mostly these are family groups, but also state-owned enterprises continue to play an important role. This chapter explores how the concept of board independence came to India and how the different ownership and institutional conditions in India may influence the functioning and value of board independence. The Companies Act of 2013 introduced a new governance regime that provides extensive powers and responsibilities and imposes significant liabilities on independent directors that transform their role to one that emphasises monitoring. Interestingly, this transformation in India was not the result of international developments, but a reaction to internal systemic shocks due to local corporate governance scandals.

The *third part* of this book deals with alternative perspectives and conclusions. Chapter 11 provides a comparative view on *Australia*. The chapter argues that the surprisingly large number of non-institutional blockholders in companies listed on the Australian Securities Exchange (ASX) impacted the roles and composition of boards. A major criterion for assessing independence is accordingly whether the director has links with a 'substantial' (5 per cent +) shareholder. The shift away from executive boards towards 'monitoring' boards, with fewer members and more independent directors, began in the early 1990s in Australia but this transition was neither rapid nor particularly smooth. Only after a wave of serious corporate failures from the early 2000s, the ASX implemented in 2004 a requirement for listed companies to adopt a majority of independent directors on an 'if not, why not' basis. More stringent standards followed from 2014 onwards. There is only weak empirical evidence in Australia of positive effects stemming from independent directors. A controversial econometric study published in 2013 concluded that over AUS $69 billion in corporate value had been destroyed from 2003 to 2011 by the 'if not, why not' ASX requirement for a majority of independent directors on listed company boards.

The ensuing Chapter 12 provides a 'micro-perspective' on independent directors in Asia by presenting *case studies* from six Asian countries to examine the actual functioning of independent directors at specific companies in these jurisdictions. The purpose of this chapter is to draw lessons about the functionality of independent directors from these individual case studies and thus provide an additional lens to better understand independent directors in Asia. In sum, the case studies indicate that independent directors in Asian jurisdictions can and do play a positive role, although not necessarily the role assumed by the US model. Instead, the presence of controlling shareholders and other local conditions have encouraged independent directors to adapt and, for example, to contribute to monitoring functions without being directly in charge of such functions. More importantly, independent directors have acted creatively to earn the trust of controlling shareholders and help them to adapt to changing social demands on businesses through advice and mediation between the company and outsiders. Such a role for independent directors is a logical reaction to local context, even if not predicted by the US model, and also constitutes a positive contribution to corporate governance in Asia.

Chapter 13 concludes this book by highlighting theoretical lessons and practical implications. The expansion of independent director regimes in the Asian region, combined with significant diversity in their specific requirements, raises intriguing implications in the longstanding debate on convergence in corporate governance. These developments demonstrate the limits of legal convergence, and remind practitioners of 'functional' comparative law to be open-minded when defining the specific functions of independent directors in various jurisdictions. Further, the 'transplantation' of independent director requirements in the Asian region (including the intriguing migration of a substantial shareholder exclusion from an Australian reform proposal to the Hong Kong listing rules) suggests that economic, social and political factors played a key role in shaping the timing and features of the divergences associated with the rise of the independent director in Asia. This chapter goes on to consider the motivations behind the implementation of such independent director requirements, the relative success of such 'transplants' and their implications for leading theories on legal transplants. The 'transplantation' of the independent director across Asia suggests that for the foreseeable future, the process of formulation, de-contextualisation and storage in the global reservoir of corporate governance tools, followed by re-contextualisation to adapt to the local market, will continue in Asia. Instead of convergence in the narrow sense, we will witness continued reform of corporate governance involving constant adjustment of independent director requirements, continued and perhaps even greater variety (rather than straightforward convergence) and occasional intercourse between global and local ideas. This will remain a dynamic process with no distinct common objective, although the persistent influence of Anglo-American institutional investors means that some independent director requirements will likely remain.

This book ends with *two appendices*. The first appendix supplies *timelines* of major developments relating to the independent director requirements in each of the jurisdictions covered in the book. Together, the timelines provide a comparative picture of the evolution of the independent director in Asia – which reveals the underlying dynamics, potential drivers and mutual influences of this evolution. The second appendix provides the *key provisions* from statutes, regulations, corporate governance codes and listing rules from each of the Asian jurisdictions (translated into English where necessary). This should be useful for comparative scholars and lawyers as no such resource currently exists. The reader can easily check the regulatory background for each chapter without having to turn to external resources.

PART I

Theoretical Framework

1

The Rise of the Independent Director in the West

Understanding the Origins of Asia's Legal Transplants

HARALD BAUM*

I Introduction

1 Why Origins Matter

Independent directors have precipitously risen from obscurity to ubiquity in Asia as a corporate governance tool. All Asian jurisdictions discussed in this book have transplanted, or at least claim to have transplanted, the concept of the independent director from the United States (US) and/or United Kingdom (UK). However, as this book demonstrates, independent directors in Asia are not only markedly different than independent directors from their US-UK place of origin, but also are markedly different from jurisdiction to jurisdiction, and even within each jurisdiction in Asia. This is because the role that independent directors play is influenced significantly by each jurisdiction's unique shareholder structure, functional substitutes, institutions, regulators, courts, history and culture.[1] To determine the extent to which independent directors

* Professor Dr, Senior Research Fellow and Head of Japanese Department, Max Planck Institute for Comparative and International Private Law, Hamburg; Professor, University of Hamburg; Research Associate, European Corporate Governance Institute, Brussels. The author thanks Bruce Aronson, Marco Becht, Souichirou Kozuka, Luke Nottage and Wolf-Georg Ringe for valuable criticism and insights; special thanks go to Dan Puchniak for a most fruitful dialogue throughout the project. All remaining errors are mine.

1 For a discussion of the importance of the given social and cultural context, see A. N. Licht, 'Culture and Law in Corporate Governance' in J. Gordon and W.-G. Ringe (eds.), *The Oxford Handbook of Corporate Law and Governance* (Oxford University Press, forthcoming).

in Asia are different from their US-UK origin, it is imperative to have a clear understanding of the latter. As such, in order to make the origin of Asia's independent directors clear, this chapter provides a concise historical and comparative analysis of the rise of the independent director in the US and UK. In addition, this chapter examines how the independent director has migrated from its US-UK origin to Continental Europe. Understanding this phenomenon is important as it provides a point of comparison for determining the extent to which the rise of the independent director in Asia is distinctly 'Asian', or otherwise distinct from the rise of the independent director in the West.

2 *Independence as a Magic Cure*

Essentially – and allowing for some simplification – the concept of independent directors and the related model of a 'monitoring board of directors' originated in the US in the 1970s, and underwent some modifications thereafter. Around 25 years ago, the concept of independent directors was adopted and refined in the UK. From there, the concept of the independent director began its conquest of the European Union as a fundamental corporate governance principle and a 'must have' corporate governance tool. The final draft in 2015 of the European Model Company Act provides in Section 5 that 'the board [of a traded company] should comprise an appropriate balance of independent non-executive directors'.[2]

On the supranational level, the Organisation for Economic Co-operation and Development (OECD) recommends that important tasks should be assigned to independent board members who 'can contribute significantly to the decision-making of the board' in its *G20/OECD Principles of Corporate Governance* of 2015.[3] Similarly, the OECD report *Better Policies for Board Nomination in Asia* of 2013 emphasises the importance of independent directors in nomination (and other) committees in Asian companies.[4] In a similar vein, a report compiled by the Asian Corporate Governance Association (ACGA) of 2010 recommends the nomination of a sufficient number of independent directors

[2] European Model Company Act Group, *The European Model Company Act (EMCA) Draft 2015*, available at http://law.au.dk.

[3] *G20/OECD Principles of Corporate Governance* (OECD Publishing, 2015), 50, available at http://dx.doi.org/10.1787/9789264236882-en.

[4] *Better Policies for Board Nomination in Asia* (OECD Publishing, 2013), available at http://dx.doi.org/10.1787/9789264204386-en.

to Asian boards.[5] Independent directors obviously have become global players.

Today, in their place of origin, in the US, the reliance on independent directors as a panacea for various corporate governance ills has reached its zenith. In 2013, in US public companies, 85 per cent of directors were independent and 60 per cent of boards had only one non-independent director – the Chief Executive Officer (CEO).[6] Over the past decades, the primary legislative and judicial response to almost every major corporate scandal has been to increase their reliance on independent directors. Current levels of independence, however, cannot be equated solely to a legislative push, because there is no legal requirement in the US for boards to have more than a majority of independent directors. In other words, independence has increasingly been embraced by US public companies in an unregulated space.[7] In this sense, the faith in independent directors in the US appears to have achieved an almost cult-like status as a magic cure for a variety of corporate governance ills.[8]

During the 2000s, the UK situation came to mirror that in the US as about 90 per cent of directors in UK public companies were independent.[9] From the UK, the faith in independent directors migrated to Continental Europe. Today, no sophisticated European jurisdiction can do without a UK-style 'comply or explain' corporate governance code, which in turn must deal with independent directors in one way or another in order to be considered credible. In short, at least until very recently, independent directors were a largely unquestioned prescription for a panoply of corporate governance problems in Europe as well. The American cult of the independent director appears to have become ingrained in parts of Europe's corporate governance DNA.

As discussed in greater detail below, however, the Global Financial Crisis appears more recently to have produced some disenchantment in Europe with taking independence to US extremes. This being said, even post-Crisis, the faith that Europe has in independent directors has

[5] ACGA, 'Rules and Recommendations on the Number of Independent Directors in Asia', available at www.acga-asia.org.

[6] U. Velikonja, 'The Political Economy of Board Independence', *North Carolina Law Review*, 92 (2014), 855, 857 f. with further references.

[7] For the rationale behind this strategy, see *infra* III.5.

[8] See the telling title of a critical article by U. Rodrigues, 'The Fetishization of Independence', *Journal of Corporation Law*, 33 (2008), 447.

[9] Heidrick & Struggles, *Corporate Governance Report 2009: Boards in Turbulent Times* (2009), 45; the number has somewhat decreased since then. See *infra* IV.1.

persisted as UK boards remain reliant on having a majority of independent directors to make decisions, and in the rest of Europe, independent directors remain as an entrenched feature on the boards of public companies.

3 *Who Is Independent?*

Before proceeding any further, for the purpose of this chapter (and indeed for the entire book) there is a critical concept that must be clarified: who qualifies as an 'independent director'?[10] At first blush, the answer to this question appears intuitively simple: a director on a company's board who is not dependent on *someone* or *something* that is related to the company is independent. In the abstract, this definition sounds compelling. In practice, however, this abstract definition is vexed with uncertainty: precisely *who* or *what* is the *someone* or *something* from which an independent director must be independent? A myriad of possibilities spring to mind, some more readily than others:

- The CEO of the company (or even her immediate family, extended family and/or friends)?
- Other board members or the entire senior management of the company (or even their immediate families, extended families and/or friends)?
- The company itself (or even its parent company, subsidiary companies or companies that are part of its corporate group)?
- The controlling shareholder (or even a *de facto* controlling shareholder or a significant shareholder)?
- Other corporate stakeholders (such as creditors, suppliers or employees)?
- Other interest groups (such as environmentalists, organised labour or potential corporate acquirers)?
- A specific corporate transaction in which the director has an interest (and, therefore, is in fact the one to be monitored and not the one to be monitoring)?

Obviously, the definition of 'independence' depends on the context or, more precisely, on the *function* that the director is supposed to fulfil. Independence is not an end in itself, but is instead constructed to serve a pre-defined goal. If the main task assigned to the independent

[10] See also the discussion in Chapter 2 at III.2.

directors is to monitor management as a means to solving the classic agency conflict between managers and dispersed shareholders (owners), independence from the entrenched CEO of the stereotypical US Berle-Means corporation seems to be the most important criterion. If, on the other hand, the directors' task is defined predominantly as protecting minority shareholders against a controlling blockholder in an archetypical Continental European or many Asian companies, independence from the latter will be the decisive characteristic.[11] Even if directors qualify *ex ante* as formally independent based on both of these parameters, they may not actually be in a position to provide a substantially objective judgement of a related party transaction involving a conflict of interest if they have a personal interest in that business transaction, and thus are themselves conflicted.

Accordingly, there is no universal definition of 'independence'. Regulatory standards across countries generally employ various definitions using different combinations of the abovementioned criteria according to what the jurisdiction's legislature or other governing body regard as imperative in the given context.[12] Independence is mostly defined *ex ante* in a somewhat formalistic way with reference to the *status* of the directors in relation to various criteria, often formulated in negative terms that describe the absence of certain relationships as a prerequisite for assuming independence. In some cases, however, only positive examples of independence are provided. Courts are sometimes more flexible, and focus on the *transaction* in question instead, considering whether the director involved was a substantially disinterested one as an alternative to the question whether the director was formally independent of the parties involved in the transaction.

This lack of a shared understanding comes as no surprise if one considers the fact that independent directors exist within boards that have a multiplicity and diversity of functions. This suggests that independent

[11] See, for example, Chapter 9 (Singapore) at IV; Chapter 10 (India) at II (for the discussion about different kinds of controlling shareholders in India).

[12] For an overview, see P. L. Davies and K. J. Hopt, 'Boards in Europe: Accountability and Convergence', *American Journal of Comparative Law*, 61 (2013) 301, 317 ff.; P. L. Davies et al., 'Boards in Law and Practice: A Cross-Country Analysis in Europe' in P. L. Davies et al. (eds.), *Boards in Law and Practice* (Oxford University Press, 2013), 28 ff.; see also D. Ferreira and T. Kirchmaier, 'Corporate Boards in Europe: Size, Independence and Gender Diversity' in M. Belcredi and G. Ferrarini (eds.), *Boards and Shareholders in European Listed Companies: Facts, Context and Post-Crisis Reforms* (Cambridge University Press, 2013), 191 ff.

directors are likely to play a variety of roles depending on the primary functions of the board,[13] which may themselves vary depending on the particular agency problems that are most acute in a given jurisdiction's unique corporate governance environment.

In other words, the context in which independent directors operate in each jurisdiction is highly path-dependent.[14] The only common denominator in all of the various conceptions of the *independent director* seems to be the fact that the directors in question have to be *non-executive* ones, meaning that they are not part of a company's management team.[15] However, it goes without saying that being a non-executive director is not equivalent to being an independent one. Even an *outside director*, someone who is not an employee of the company nor retained by it (other than in his or her capacity as director), is by no means an independent one *per se*. The prototypical member of a German supervisory board,[16] for example, is an outside director not involved in managing the company, but who usually has financial or business affiliations with the company or a major shareholder, or represents one of these.

The theoretical and practical discussions do not always consider these nuances when analysing the concept of the independent director or the conditions which may support independence.[17] Given the ubiquity of the concept in statutes, listing rules and corporate governance codes, it is surprising how little theoretical consideration has been given to the nature of 'independence'.[18] A fundamental, although often ignored, paradox

[13] See, for example, R. B. Adams, B. E. Hermalin and M. S. Weisbach, 'The Role of Directors in Corporate Governance: A Conceptual Framework and Survey', *Journal of Economic Literature*, 48 (2010), 58.

[14] For an up-to-date overview of different corporate governance arrangements in major economies, see, for example, K. J. Hopt, 'Comparative Corporate Governance: The State of the Art and International Regulation', *American Journal of Comparative Law*, 59 (2011), 1; and the various contributions in: A. M. Fleckner and K. J. Hopt (eds.), *Comparative Corporate Governance: A Functional and International Analysis* (Cambridge University Press, 2013); for a general discussion regarding the complexity of a meaningful comparison of corporate law, see also D. C. Clarke, '"Nothing but Wind"? The Past and Future of Comparative Corporate Governance', *American Journal of Comparative Law*, 59 (2011), 75.

[15] D. C. Clarke, 'Three Concepts of the Independent Director', *Delaware Journal of Corporate Law*, 32 (2007), 73, 79; see also L. M. Fairfax, 'The Uneasy Case for the Inside Director', *Iowa Law Review*, 96 (2010), 127 ff.

[16] Germany adheres to the two-tier board system. See *infra* IV. 3.

[17] Clarke, 'Three Concepts of the Independent Director', 73.

[18] Notable exceptions are S. Le Mire and G. Gilligan, 'Independence and Independent Company Directors', *Journal of Corporate Law Studies*, 13 (2013), 443; and Clarke, 'Three Concepts of the Independent Director'; one of the extremely rare discussions of the

is that 'independence actually creates dependence', as the independent director has to rely on company insiders for information.[19] Rather, the role of independent directors is most often *assumed* to be monolithic, fixed and even universal – with the addition of more independent directors often being deemed to axiomatically improve corporate governance. How these improvements occur is rarely scrutinised and rather, as it seems, accepted on blind faith alone. From this flawed perspective, the discussion surrounding independent directors is often reduced to a myopic consideration of the appropriate proportion of independent directors that should be on boards.[20] Only fairly recently, in the wake of the Global Financial Crisis of 2008, has the concept of the independent director come slowly under closer and critical scrutiny in Europe.[21] In America, however, aside from a small but growing number of corporate governance 'heretics',[22] independent directors still seem to be regularly accepted as the panacea for all kinds of corporate governance shortcomings.

With a clearer understanding now of what an 'independent director' is, or perhaps more accurately, what an independent director can be, we can now delve into the rich history that forms the foundation of the rise of the independent director in the West. Inevitably, the start of such an inquiry must begin with a brief historical examination of the origins of the board of directors itself, which is explored in section II. Thereafter, a detailed consideration of the historical rise of the independent director in the US,

concept of independence as such and in all of its aspects was written by Swiss company law expert J. N. Druey, 'Unabhängigkeit als Gebot des allgemeinen Unternehmensrechts' in S. Kalss, C. Nowotny and M. Schauer (eds.), *Festschrift Peter Doralt* (Manz, 2004), 151 ff. A fundamental comprehensive analysis of the concept can be found in a recent German publication by C. Kumpan, *Der Interessenkonflikt im deutschen Privatrecht* (Mohr Siebeck, 2014), 138 ff., 158 ff.

19 Druey, 'Unabhängigkeit', 163, 169.

20 Davies and Hopt, 'Boards in Europe', 317 f.

21 See Chapter 2 at II for a detailed discussion of the growing scepticism; see further M. Gutiérrez and M. Sáez, 'Deconstructing Independent Directors', *Journal of Corporate Law Studies*, 13 (2013), 63.

22 See, for example, Rodrigues, 'The Fetishization of Independence'; Fairfax, 'The Uneasy Case for the Inside Director'; E. J. Pan, 'Rethinking the Board's Duty to Monitor: A Critical Assessment of the Delaware Doctrine', *Florida State University Law Review*, 38 (2011), 209, 225; R. S. Karmel, 'Is the Independent Director Model Broken?' (Brooklyn Law School Legal Studies Research Papers, Accepted Paper Series, Research Paper No. 348, July 2013), available at http://ssrn.com/abstract=1972057; J. R. Brown, Jr, 'The Demystification of the Board of Directors' (University of Denver Sturm College of Law, Legal Research Paper Series, Working Paper No. 14–37, 2014), available at http://ssrn.com/abstract=2474394.

which is the birthplace of the concept itself, will be undertaken in section III. Then, in section IV, the focus of our historical inquiry will shift to the UK, which has played a role in refining and, especially, exporting the concept of the independent director around the world. In addition, the migration of independent directors from the UK to Continental Europe will be considered briefly, with a particular focus on the transplantation of independent directors to civil law jurisdictions. This analysis seeks to provide a useful point of comparison for similar developments in Asia, which will be discussed in detail in Chapter 3. Finally, to streamline the European analysis, the focus in Continental Europe will be on the recent developments in European Community law and Germany will be used as a case study to illustrate European Community law in a member state. Indeed, the German example is a fascinating one as it has a long history of rigid separation between executive and non-executive directors, which was introduced as early as 1861. Now, let us step back in time and explore the origins of the Western transplant, which has ostensibly proliferated throughout Asia.

II Historical Origins of the Board of Directors

1 Medieval Guilds and Chartered Companies

Today in almost every jurisdiction, regulation demands or assumes that public companies are managed by a board, or at least under the direction of a board of directors. This is quite remarkable because the worldwide spread of the board system is a comparatively new development, replacing other successful models such as the merchant house in pre-Meiji Japan. It is even more remarkable because complaints about the ineffectiveness of boards have been voiced universally for as long as company boards have existed.[23] Making a caricature of the very concept of the corporate board, companies with dispersed ownership typically seem to be run in practice by the executive management team or the CEO, and companies with concentrated ownership are often actually run by the dominant shareholder, with the board playing only a peripheral role in both cases. So how did the idea that the board of directors should play a central role in

[23] F. A. Gevurtz, 'The European Origins and the Spread of Corporate Board of Directors', *Stetson Law Review*, 33 (2004), 925, 926 f.

corporate management achieve widespread popularity, and from where did it originate?

The use of a body of representatives as a tool for collective governance can be traced back to the medieval guilds and political institutions in the late Middle Ages in Western Europe.[24] Some guilds developed into regulated companies, such as the British Company of Merchant Adventurers in the sixteenth century,[25] which had by charter a governor and an elected board of 'assistants' taking care of the company's governance.[26] Though these governing boards were familiar with the practice of collective governance, they did not have much else in common with modern boards.[27] Its members were active merchants who traded on their own accounts, and not passive investors like the modern private shareholder. The board's main tasks were to resolve disputes among the members and to set up rules regulating the members' behaviour.[28]

2 *The First Joint-Stock Companies*

Though the British trading companies, like the East India Company, had started as chartered companies, they were subsequently structured with features similar to the modern joint-stock company during the seventeenth century:[29] members were no longer allowed to trade on their own

[24] *Ibid.*, 946 ff.

[25] For the evolution of the stock company in general, see M. Schmitthoff, 'The Origin of the Joint-Stock Company', *The University of Toronto Law Journal*, 3 (1939), 74 (discussing the competing theories); for an institutional perspective, see P. Lipton, 'The Evolution of the Joint Stock Company to 1800: A Study of Institutional Change' (Monash University, Department of Business Law and Taxation, Working Paper No. 19, 2009), available at http://ssrn.com/abstract=1413502; for historical developments in the UK, see in general P. L. Davies, *Gower's Principles of Modern Company Law*, 6th edn (Sweet and Maxwell, 1997), 18 ff.

[26] Gevurtz, 'The European Origins', 945 f.; for an overview of the historical antecedents of corporate directors and officers, see C. O'Donnell, 'Origins of the Corporate Executive', *Bulletin of the Business Historical Society*, 26 (1952), 55, 60 f.

[27] Y. Zhao, *Corporate Governance and Directors' Independence* (Kluwer Law International, 2011) 11, which provides an excellent concise historical overview of the evolution of the board of directors and the independence of directors at 9–36.

[28] Gevurtz, 'The European Origins', 946.

[29] Schmitthoff, 'The Origin of the Joint Stock Company', 90 f.; for a historical overview over the legal developments regarding the East India Company, see R. Harris, 'The English East India Company and the History of Company Law' in E. Gepken-Jager, G. van Solinge and L. Timmerman (eds.), *VOC 1602–2002: 400 Years of Company Law* (Kluwer Legal Publishers, 2005), 217 ff.

under the company's franchise, and voting rights increasingly depended on the amount invested by a member in the company's permanent joint stock.[30] Such companies started to trade on their own accounts, and boards, elected by members, began to manage the affairs of companies and to take business decisions in their best interests, acting as the members' representatives. This marked the birth of the corporate board as a management organ in the modern sense.[31] With benefits in the form of economic returns and voting rights dependent on the capital paid into the company's common fund, the former 'confederation of merchants' was transformed into a 'vehicle for passive investment by the general public'.[32]

In these early days, the monitoring capacities of the board did not yet play a significant role in their own right, and a modern understanding of the different roles of management and the board of directors had yet to be developed.[33] Most members of the board were heavily invested in the company and thus, in effect, managed the company in their own interests. They were elected because other investors assumed that they were trying their best for the company in enlightened self-interest, thus making a monitoring board unnecessary.[34]

A parallel development of joint-stock companies and accordingly corporate boards took place in Continental Europe.[35] A famous example is the Dutch East India Company, which was founded two years after its English counterpart.[36] Other examples include the corporate boards that developed as tools of governance for Hanseatic merchant societies. In the US, the operation of boards of directors in early American corporations was unsurprisingly rooted in the English tradition. A prominent example is the 1791 charter of the first Bank of the United States, which

[30] Gevurtz, 'The European Origins', 944; some claim that by the mid-seventeenth century these companies already had developed most of the main characteristics of a modern company; see also Lipton, 'The Evolution of the Joint Stock Company', 16 with further references.

[31] Zhao, *Corporate Governance and Directors' Independence*, 11.

[32] Gevurtz, 'The European Origins', 944; see also Harris, 'The English East India Company', 234 ff.

[33] Zhao, *Corporate Governance and Directors' Independence*, 12.

[34] *Ibid.*; O'Donnell, 'Origins of the Corporate Executive', 70.

[35] For a brief overview, see F. A. Gevurtz, 'The Historical and Political Origins of Corporate Board of Directors' (2004), 30 ff., available at http://ssrn.com/abstract=546296.

[36] Schmitthoff, 'The Origin of the Joint-Stock Company', 93 ff.; for a historical overview over the legal developments regarding the Dutch East India Company, see Paul Marie Louis Frentrop, *A History of Corporate Governance 1602–2002* (Deminor, 2003), 49 ff.

was modelled in parts based on the Bank of England's 1694 charter.[37] In general, former European colonies usually adopted their mother countries' institutions to a large degree. In accordance with this custom, the board of directors as a corporate organ and governance tool spread to a multitude of jurisdictions.[38] Even a country like Japan, which was never colonised, regarded the modern joint-stock corporation with its board as a superior form of enterprise for establishing and conducting business. Immediately after the Meiji Restoration of 1868, the Japanese government began to promote the introduction of a company system, and in 1876, the first Japanese banks had to be organised as joint-stock companies by decree.[39]

3 *The Rise of the Executive Director and the Split of the Board*

During the eighteenth and nineteenth centuries, joint-stock companies flourished as a business model in Britain.[40] They constituted the successful British 'landmark of the early capitalist society'.[41] The separate legal personality of the company – and the accompanying creation of limited liability that provided a financial shelter for its shareholders[42] – made this form of enterprise highly attractive for an ever-increasing number of average citizens. The attraction persisted, notwithstanding recurrent scandals, such as the South Sea Bubble in 1720 and others. In his famous treatise on the wealth of nations published in 1776, Adam Smith complained that one could not expect directors of a joint-stock company, 'being the managers rather of other people's money than their own … [to] watch over it with the same anxious vigilance with which the partners in a private copartnery frequently watch over their own'.[43]

37 Gevurtz, 'The Historical and Political Origins', 16 ff.

38 Gevurtz, 'The European Origins', 935 f.

39 H. Baum and E. Takahashi, 'Commercial Law and Corporate Law in Japan: Legal and Economic Developments after 1868' in W. Röhl (ed.), *A History of Law in Japan since 1868* (Brill, 2005), 330, 341 ff.

40 Lipton, 'The Evolution of the Joint Stock Company to 1800', 16; Davies, *Gower's Principles of Modern Company Law*, 22 ff.

41 Zhao, *Corporate Governance and Directors' Independence*, 13.

42 This was fully acknowledged in Britain by the Limited Liability Act of 1855; see R. R. Formoy, *The Historical Foundations of Modern Company Law* (Sweet and Maxwell, 1923), 114 ff.; Davies, *Gower's Principles of Modern Company Law*, 40 ff.

43 Adam Smith, *An Inquiry into the Nature and Courses of the Wealth of Nations*, ed. Edwin Cannan (Modern Library, 1937); for a discussion of Smith's general scepticism towards joint stock companies see A. M. Fleckner, 'Adam Smith on the Joint Stock Company'

The broader the investing circle of shareholders became, the wider the gap between the shareholders and the companies' directors, with the latter taking charge of managing the companies' affairs.[44] With this, the separation of ownership and control became apparent. Lawmakers and courts acknowledged, or at least assumed, that the board of directors would manage companies. In reality, however, managerial power had started to shift gradually from the boards in their entirety to professional managers acting as executive directors. This shift was caused by the growth and diversification of the joint-stock companies. This delegation of power increasingly deprived the boards of directors of their managerial role, and the boards became segmented between those running the company and those 'invited to sit on the board for non-managing purposes'.[45] In Britain, it became customary to hire members of the nobility as non-executive directors to create a veneer of respectability and to use their names as bait for the investing public;[46] in the US, retired generals and film stars were later preferred as board members instead to entice investors.[47]

The German regulation of stock companies in the Commercial Code of 1861 (*Allgemeines Deutsches Handeslgesetzbuch*) was probably the first law to acknowledge these developments legally.[48] The split between a supervisory board and a management board became mandatory. Members of the management board were not – and still are not – allowed to act simultaneously as members of the supervisory board. Thus, at least in principle, a clear separation between executive and non-executive functions was introduced, although the law allowed more powers to be assigned to the supervisory board in the articles of incorporation beyond what was required to perform its mandatory supervisory functions. Thus, in practice, the distinction was somewhat blurred. A strict exclusion of

(Max Planck Institute for Tax Law and Public Finance Working Paper 2016–01, 2016), available at www.tax.mpg.de.

44 Zhao, *Corporate Governance and Directors' Independence*, 15 f.

45 *Ibid.*, 17 f.

46 A vivid critical analysis of this practice can be found with H. B. Samuel, *Shareholders' Money* (Pitman, 1933), 111 ff.

47 Zhao, *Corporate Governance and Directors' Independence*, 18 f.

48 M. Roth, 'Corporate Boards in Germany' in P. L. Davies et al. (eds.), *Boards in Law and Practice* (Oxford University Press, 2013), 253, 276 f.; R. Wiethölter, *Interessen und Organisation der Aktiengesellschaft im amerikanischen und deutschen Recht* (C. F. Müller, 1961), 271.

the supervisory board from the management of the company came with the Stock Corporation Act of 1937.[49]

III From 'Shirtsleeve' Directors to Independent Directors: Developments in the US

1 The Era of Inside Directors

A famous article published in 1934 in the *Harvard Law Review* had the telling title 'Directors Who Do Not Direct'.[50] The author, William O. Douglas, criticised the widespread corporate scandals in the US in the 1920s and 1930s that were made possible by, among other factors, the almost complete passivity of directors. He especially warned that a board staffed with 'shirtsleeve' directors who are close to management would prove to be an illusionary form of protection in companies with a wide diffusion of stock ownership, where the boards are the only means of protecting shareholders against management.[51] In this way, managers 'came to be their own supervisors, and the stockholders were moved into a position of effective subservience to those who by tradition and law were their servants'.[52] This is an early – if dramatic – description of the classic agency conflict between managers and shareholders as owners of widely held public companies. Douglas was amongst the first to discuss the different tasks that directors should fulfil and to propose some rudimentary version of a monitoring board, where directors who were independent from management should play a prominent role.[53] An early legislative attempt to install a certain portion of independent directors on the boards of special corporations – in this case, funds – can be found in the Investment Company Act of 1940. This type of regulation, however, remained an outlier for several decades.

[49] Roth, 'Corporate Boards in Germany', 277; for a comprehensive historical overview see, for example, M. Lutter, 'Der Aufsichtsrat im Wandel der Zeit: von seinen Anfängen bis heute' in W. Bayer and M. Habersack (eds.), *Aktienrecht im Wandel*, Vol. 2: *Grundsatzfragen des Aktienrechts* (Mohr Siebeck, 2007), 389 ff.; for developments in Germany, see *infra* at IV.3.

[50] W. O. Douglas, 'Directors Who Do Not Direct', *Harvard Law Review*, 47 (1934), 1305; the heading was also used a year earlier for a chapter in Samuel, *Shareholders' Money*, 111.

[51] Douglas, 'Directors Who Do Not Direct', 1307.

[52] *Ibid.*, 1308.

[53] L. E. Mitchell, 'The Trouble with Boards' in F. C. Kieff and T. A. Paredes (eds.), *Perspectives on Corporate Governance* (Cambridge University Press, 2010) 17, 25.

In reality, inside directors – from within the company's rank and file and employed by it full time – dominated the corporate boards for the first half of the twentieth century. And even outside directors on the boards – those non-executive directors who were not employees of the company – who increasingly started to outnumber inside directors during the second half of the twentieth century were, until fairly recently, not independent; rather, they were affiliated with the company and its management by interlocking directorships or on the basis of financial or other business relationships.[54] A managerialist model of corporate governance dominated in the mid-twentieth century and especially the 1950s.[55] Boards played a passive role; their members were chosen and dominated by the CEO and had little or no incentive to challenge him.[56] In short, the CEO got 'exactly the kind of boards he want[ed]'.[57] The CEO regularly also held the position of the chairman of the board of directors. In this model, public corporations resembled some kind of bureaucratic hierarchy controlled by professional managers, while boards of directors acted as mere figureheads and shareholders were mostly ignored.[58] From a comparative perspective, it is surprising how weak the position of the shareholder in US joint-stock companies was then and is still now.[59] Responsibility for the company lies squarely with the board and, as a rule, shareholders traditionally cannot even propose directors to be elected to the board.

The 1950s was a time of stakeholder capitalism in the US: management's objective was not focused exclusively on profit-making but also on balancing the different stakeholder interests while assuming a role as a central planner of the large corporations.[60] A 1961 survey among

[54] An analysis of the different types of outside directors in US corporations in the 1960s can be found in M. L. Mace, *Directors: Myth and Reality* (Division of Research, Graduate School of Business Administration, Harvard University, 1971), 86 ff.

[55] For detailed description see A. D. Chandler, *The Visible Hand: The Managerial Revolution in America*, 16th edn (Belknap Press of Harvard University Press, 2002).

[56] J. N. Gordon, 'The Rise of Independent Directors in the United States, 1950–2005: Of Shareholder Value and Stock Market Prices', *Stanford Law Review*, 59 (2007), 1465, 1511; Mace, *Directors: Myth and Reality*, 86.

[57] Mace, *Directors: Myth and Reality*, 78.

[58] S. M. Bainbridge, 'Director Versus Shareholder Primacy in New Zealand Company Law as Compared to U.S.A. Corporate Law' (2014), available at http://ssrn.com/abstract_id=2416449.

[59] M. Roth, 'Unabhängige Aufsichtsratsmitglieder', *Zeitschrift für das gesamte Handels- und Wirtschaftsrecht*, 175 (2011), 605, 611.

[60] Gordon, 'The Rise of Independent Directors in the United States', 1511.

executive managers of large corporations showed that over 80 per cent of them regarded it as their task not to act in the interest of shareholders alone, but also in the interest of employees and consumers.[61] This understanding of the senior management team allocating the firm's rents among its various stakeholders fits the role of the board of directors as an *advisory* board staffed with insiders and affiliated outsiders, such as bankers, suppliers, lawyers, etc.[62] At best, these boards served as sources of advice and counsel to the CEO without providing any monitoring, and thus the famous study titled *Directors: Myth and Reality* published in 1971 stated that they 'were found *not* to perform the classical and generally accepted roles that are attributed to them'.[63] A monitoring board would have been simply an irritant in such a setting.

2 *The Battle of the 1970s*

Two watershed events sparked a dramatic change in the 1970s.[64] The first event involved two corporate scandals, which is unsurprising as corporate scandals have a storied history of sparking corporate law reform. The second event was an academic publication, which is somewhat surprising as, depressingly, academic publications rarely drive reforms. The initial corporate scandal was the sudden and completely unexpected financial collapse of Penn Central, a major railway company, in 1970. As it turned out, the company's directors did not have the slightest idea about the company's financial troubles before its implosion; even worse, they obviously had not even tried to gather any relevant information about the financial state of the company.[65]

A second corporate scandal came when it was revealed in the course of the Watergate hearings that hundreds of companies had made 'questionable payments', namely illegal campaign contributions, as well as outright bribes in and outside of the US.[66] This scandal swept the issue of the role

[61] *Ibid.*, 1512 with further references.

[62] *Ibid.*, 1513.

[63] Mace, *Directors: Myth and Reality*, 86.

[64] For a detailed historical analysis see B. Cheffins, 'Corporate Governance since the Managerial Capitalism Era', *Business History Review* (forthcoming) (University of Cambridge Faculty of Law Research Paper No. 39/2015, 2015), available at http://ssrn.com/abstract=2618480.

[65] An investigation by the SEC unearthed these and other troubling findings. *SEC Staff Study of the Financial Collapse of the Penn Central Co.: Summary* (1972–73 Transfer Binder), Fed. Se. L. Rep. (CCH) ¶ 78,931 (1972).

[66] Gordon, 'The Rise of Independent Directors in the United States', 1516 f.

of the corporation as an institution into the highly controversial political debate of the day.[67] The movement for corporate social responsibility was spearheaded by (among others) the consumer rights activist Ralph Nader, the co-author of the then-famous book *Taming the Giant Corporation*,[68] which made the corporation, and particularly the unrestrained powers of its management, responsible for various social ills.[69] This created additional pressure for company law reform as Nader placed part of the blame on the dysfunctional boards of directors. However, Nader's proposal to create a cadre of full-time professional directors whose members should be exclusively allowed to sit on boards went nowhere.[70]

Nevertheless, these pressures led to a profound re-conceptualisation of the board's role and structure.[71] The academic publication that presented the 'monitoring model' of the board of directors and paved the way for its gradual rise was Melvin Eisenberg's influential book *The Structure of the Corporation*, published in 1976.[72] According to Eisenberg, the board's essential function was to monitor senior management – more precisely, to select, monitor and remove the members of the chief executive's office.[73] This was exactly what had *not* happened in the past. Eisenberg regarded all other functions of the board, such as advising the CEO or authorising major corporate decisions, as being of minor importance or as being merely pro forma.[74] In his view, the board needed to be truly independent from the executives it was supposed to monitor in order to fulfil its monitoring task, and it needed to be in a position to obtain all the information necessary for this task.[75]

By the end of the 1970s, after a prolonged, intense and sometimes vicious discussion, business circles finally accepted the inevitability of

[67] S. M. Bainbridge, *Corporate Governance after the Financial Crisis* (Oxford University Press, 2012), 51.

[68] R. Nader, M. Green and J. Seligman, *Taming the Giant Corporation* (Norton, 1976).

[69] *Ibid.*, 62 ff.

[70] Bainbridge, *Corporate Governance*, 52. But, interestingly, a comparative idea with respect to professionalism was promoted in 2014: permitting firms to provide board services as professional 'board service providers'. S. M. Bainbridge and M. T. Henderson, 'Boards-R-Us: Reconceptualizing Corporate Boards', *Stanford Law Review*, 66 (2014), 1051.

[71] Gordon, 'The Rise of Independent Directors in the United States', 1518 ff.

[72] M. A. Eisenberg, *The Structure of the Corporation: A Legal Analysis* (Little, Brown and Co., 1976).

[73] *Ibid.*, 162 ff.

[74] *Ibid.*, 157 ff.

[75] *Ibid.*, 170; Eisenberg discussed the two-tier board system as an alternative governance structure: *Ibid.*, 177 ff.

a monitoring board at least partly staffed with independent directors.[76] The Securities and Exchange Commission (SEC) had endorsed the model from the start and requested in 1976 that the New York Stock Exchange (NYSE) amend its listing requirements to include an audit committee composed of independent directors, which it did in 1977. The controversy about the role of independent directors in corporate governance flamed up again with all its intensity in 1982 when the American Law Institute published the first tentative draft of its planned *Principles of Corporate Governance*. Eisenberg was the reporter for the first sections of the Principles that, among other ideas, envisioned an extended role for independent directors.[77] In the end, the final Principles retained the basic division between the monitoring and the managing functions of the board though under different terminology, whereas the initially proposed mandatory rules for the composition of the boards were changed into mere recommendations.[78] Nevertheless, the Principles became highly influential, and the monitoring board model evolved into being part of best corporate practice.

The outcome of the corporate governance reforms of the 1970s was mixed: managerial elites made significant concessions, but at the same time, they were able to hold onto the important managerial prerogative over the composition and actual functioning of the board.[79] While the new rhetoric of monitoring independent directors was widely accepted, real change in the habits and practices of the board had just begun.[80] There is also another, somewhat darker interpretation of the changes. In this reading, from the beginning of the discussion, business circles were interested only in making use of the monitoring board as a shield to protect directors from serious threats of legal liability, a plan that ultimately succeeded.[81]

3 *Success of the Monitoring Model*

When a wave of hostile takeovers re-shaped the corporate landscape in the US in the 1980s by making use of the market for corporate control, the Delaware courts, where most of the takeover-related court proceedings took

[76] For an excellent and concise analysis of the political debate about Eisenberg's proposals, see Mitchell, 'The Trouble with Boards', 34–53.

[77] Bainbridge, *Corporate Governance*, 54 f. with further references.

[78] *Ibid.*, 57 with further references.

[79] Gordon, 'The Rise of Independent Directors in the United States', 1519.

[80] *Ibid.*

[81] Mitchell, 'The Trouble with Boards', 34 f., 44 f., 52 f., 59.

place, were quick to make use of the fact that the majority of large companies by then had embraced the monitoring model with outsider-staffed boards.[82] Now, the protective side effect of the model became clear. In a string of decisions throughout the 1980s, the Delaware courts established the practice of looking *only* at the process of decision making in the target company but *not* into the substance of the deal. Thus, a properly composed board that behaved in accordance with the model and exercised at least a formally independent judgement was allowed to 'just say no' to a hostile bid that would favour the target's shareholders without having to fear any liability.[83] This is an outcome that would be unthinkable in the corporate governance world of the UK, where the target's board is supposed to be neutral and not to frustrate the decision of the shareholders in any way.[84] The hostile takeover movement in the US focused attention on shareholder value as the ultimate management objective. The managerial elite that was previously critical of independent directors started to welcome them as an essential part of shareholder capitalism.[85]

4 *Scandals, Crises and Reforms after 2000*

The focus on the maximisation of shareholder value and the independent board became characteristic of the corporate world in the 1990s. The time of stakeholder capitalism and insider-dominated boards was gone for good. By 2000, 78 per cent of the directors of US public companies were already independent and 23 per cent of the companies had a non-executive chairman.[86] The monitoring model obviously had taken root in the corporate world, but it was far from being a cure-all as the collapse of Enron, WorldCom and other corporate failures were brought to the awareness of a shocked public at the beginning of the new millennium. A cynical observer might be tempted to note that the circumstances leading to the implosion of these firms eerily resembled those of the collapse

[82] For a detailed analysis of the role the Delaware courts played in promoting the role of independent directors see B. R. Cheffins, 'Delaware and the Transformation of Corporate Governance' (The University of Cambridge Faculty of Law Legal Studies Research Paper Series, Paper No. 64/2014, November 2014), 39 ff., available at: http://ssrn.com/abstract=2531640.

[83] Mitchell, 'The Trouble with Boards', 55 with further references; another critical analysis can be found with Pan, 'Rethinking the Board's Duty to Monitor'.

[84] General Principle 3, Takeover Code.

[85] Gordon, 'The Rise of Independent Directors in the United States', 1526.

[86] Velikonja, 'Political Economy of Board Independence', 857 with further references.

of Penn Central some 30 years earlier; but only this time the board of directors, which again obviously had no idea what was going on in the companies they were expected to monitor, was not composed of a mix of inside and some affiliated outside directors but mostly of *independent* directors.[87] Though a major part of the blame for the scandals can be attributed to the failure of the gatekeepers, especially the accountants, the events showed the deficits of the governance system developed in the 1990s with the independent monitoring board at its core.[88]

The US lawmaker's answer was more of the same: increasing the level of independence within company boards. The vehicle for this was the Sarbanes-Oxley Act of 2002, at the centre of which stood the monitoring model, which was thus in effect codified.[89] As a result of the reform, boards of listed companies have to be composed of a majority of independent directors, and the audit committee must be fully independent. The standards of director independence were also raised. Later, the Dodd-Frank Act of 2010 – which was the legislative reaction to the 2008 Global Financial Crisis (amongst other things) – further enhanced the role of independent directors by demanding that compensation committees be composed entirely of independent directors.

It is important to note that these enhanced standards were made applicable to diffusely held public companies *only*, but *not* to controlled companies in which a shareholder (or a coordinated group of shareholders) holds more than 50 per cent of the voting rights.[90] In this sense, the US has clearly made the decision that the primary function of independent directors is to monitor management on behalf of *dispersed* shareholders who are – unlike a controlling shareholder – prevented from doing so themselves as a result of their own collective action problems.

5 *Super-Majority Boards*

Interestingly though, by the time the legal changes came into force, most companies had already adapted to these standards. Furthermore, without

[87] The head of Enron's audit committee was a professor of accounting at Stanford University whom one might regard as highly qualified for the job. Bainbridge, *Corporate Governance*, 92.

[88] Gordon, 'The Rise of Independent Directors in the United States', 1535, 1538.

[89] Bainbridge, *Corporate Governance*, 59 f.

[90] § 303 A, NYSE Listed Company Manual available at http://nysemanual.nyse.com/lcm.

being forced to do so by law, regulations or listing rules, by the early 2010s a multitude of companies had installed so-called 'super-majority boards' with only one remaining inside director who was not independent, normally the CEO. In 2013, approximately 60 per cent of the public companies had such super-majority boards and, in general, 85 per cent of all directors were independent.[91]

This comes as a surprise given the decade-long apprehension on the side of management surrounding independent boards. At first blush, the fact that business circles seem to embrace and to gain faith in independent boards appears to be shareholder friendly. The true reasons, however, may be less so. Adopting independent nominating committees helps to avoid regulation that would empower shareholders – an anathema to corporate management – in the nomination process.[92] Adopting super-majority boards actually helps the CEO, who usually serves as chair, to steer the flow of information about the company. Independent directors lack a material relationship with the company. Accordingly, they do not have independent access to information about the company's internal matters. Once there are no inside directors left on the board, the independent directors have no real alternative but to rely more or less exclusively on information supplied by the CEO.[93] In this way, in-dependency creates dependency.[94]

6 *The Arrival of Agency Capitalism and Shift to a Shareholder-centric System?*

This leads us to the observation that the discussion in the US about the benefits and detriments of independent boards is framed by the wider and more general discourse about the balance of power between boards and shareholders as a group.[95] While some propose to empower shareholders and increase their role in corporate governance,[96] others object

[91] Velikonja, 'Political Economy of Board Independence', 857 f. with further references.

[92] Gordon, 'The Rise of Independent Directors in the United States', 1539; Velikonja, 'Political Economy of Board Independence', 860.

[93] Brown, 'The Demystification of the Board of Directors', 35 ff.

[94] Druey, 'Unabhängigkeit', 163, 169.

[95] K. Greenfeld, 'The Third Way: Beyond Shareholder or Board Primacy', *Seattle University Law Review*, 37 (2014), 749.

[96] One of the leading proponents of shareholder empowerment is L. Bebchuk. See, for example, L. Bebchuk, 'The Case for Increasing Shareholder Power', *Harvard Law Review*, 118 (2005), 833.

and insist on (continuing) director primacy.[97] This discourse in turn has to be seen in the context of a major change in the shareholder structure of US corporations. Whereas unsophisticated observers often still associate the US stock market with widely dispersed individual (household) ownership that matches the pattern described by Berle and Means in the 1930s,[98] the reality now is different: an increasing re-concentration of institutional ownership. Over the past three decades, a shift of shareholdings from individual owners to concentrated institutional owners in the form of financial intermediaries could be observed, something that has been aptly described as the 'rise of agency capitalism'.[99] By 2009, the top 1,000 largest US corporations had an average institutional holding of 73 per cent.[100]

Some interpret the re-concentration of institutional ownership in the US as a paradigmatic shift from a manager-centric to a shareholder-centric system.[101] Whereas in a manager-centric environment the major agency conflict is between managers and dispersed shareholders, the prominent agency conflict in a shareholder-centric system is instead between shareholders and creditors.[102] According to this view, the former agency conflict is by and large solved, though less by law than through changes in the market and corporate practices such as shareholder concentration and activism, and changes in managerial compensation, board composition and other things.[103]

97 The leading advocate for director primacy is S. M. Bainbridge. See, for example, S. M. Bainbridge, 'Director Primacy and Shareholder Disempowerment', *Harvard Law Review*, 119 (2006), 1735.

98 A. A. Berle and G. C. Means, *The Modern Corporation and Private Property* (Commerce Clearing House, 1932).

99 R. J. Gilson and J. N. Gordon, 'The Agency Costs of Agency Capitalism: Activist Investors and the Revaluation of Governance Rights', *Columbia Law Review*, 113 (2013), 863. One of the first analyses of this change was R. C. Clark, 'The Four Stages of Capitalism: Reflections on Investment Management Treatises', *Harvard Law Review*, 94 (1981), 561. See also P. Edelman, R. Thomas and R. Thompson, 'Shareholder Voting in the Age of Intermediary Capitalism', *Southern California Law Review*, 87 (2014), 1359.

100 Gilson and Gordon, 'Agency Capitalism', 875 with further references.

101 E. B. Rock, 'Adapting to the New Shareholder-centric Reality', *University of Pennsylvania Law Review*, 161 (2013), 1907.

102 The third classical agency conflict is between controlling and non-controlling shareholders, see R. Kraakman et al., *The Anatomy of Corporate Law: A Comparative and Functional Approach*, 2nd edn (Oxford University Press, 2009), 36.

103 Rock, 'New Shareholder centric Reality', 1909 f., 1917–1926, showing in great detail how the various corporate ills from empire building to captured boards and the undermining of hostile takeovers through staggered boards etc. are mostly problems of the past.

In this view, managers and directors are now regarded as largely 'think[ing] like shareholders'.[104]

If this is the case, then today's governance problems in the US corporate world are possibly not those that are likely to be solved alone, or perhaps even primarily by the independent monitoring board. In this vein, some critics argue that board independence serves only the political goal of deflecting substantive regulation that might limit rent-seeking that favours managers and shareholders alike while putting other stakeholders at a disadvantage.[105] Accordingly, independent boards are seen, at best, as a weak constraint on the ability of managers to impose negative externalities on stakeholders other than shareholders.[106]

7 *Too Much of a Good Thing?*

Other critics articulate fundamental doubts about whether the board system as an institution, especially in the form of the monitoring board, is and can structurally be more than 'façade corporate governance' providing a 'false sense of security for all those dependent upon the corporation' in the light of the complexity of the modern corporation.[107] Before the establishment of the monitoring board, people at least 'knew that the top corporate officers were the center of corporate power'.[108] One of the possible solutions arising from the context of this discussion is a 'return to boards with real managerial powers'.[109]

Stephen Bainbridge, a leading proponent of 'director primacy' – as a third alternative to manager primacy and shareholder primacy[110] – criticises the present US practice on similar grounds. Though an ardent supporter of the board system who regards group decision makers as superior to individual decision makers, he is highly sceptical of over-emphasising the board's monitoring function and its mandatory independence.[111] In

[104] *Ibid.*, 1910.
[105] Velikonja, 'Political Economy of Board Independence', 860 f.
[106] *Ibid.*, 862.
[107] Mitchell, 'The Trouble with Boards', 59 f.
[108] *Ibid.*, 60.
[109] *Ibid.*, 61; others, however, claim that greater board independence leads to more rigorous CEO monitoring. See L. Guo and R. W. Masulis, 'Board Structure and Monitoring: New Evidence from CEO Turnover', *Review of Financial Studies*, 28 (2015), 2770.
[110] Bainbridge, 'Director Versus Shareholder Primacy', 3 ff., with further references.
[111] Bainbridge, *Corporate Governance*, 75.

his view, the monitoring model suffers from a crucial deficit: the erroneous assumption that monitoring and management can be separated in any sensible way that improves performance.[112] This criticism challenges essential parts of the corporate revolution that Eisenberg's analysis shaped some 40 years ago. US corporate governance might have arrived at a crossroads regarding independent monitoring. Nevertheless, at least so far, for the majority in the US, the independent director appears to still be seen as a panacea which is well-suited to address a panoply of corporate governance ills.

We now turn in a much briefer fashion to Europe and begin with an analysis of the UK, which drew somewhat different lessons regarding independent boards from the corporate failures in the wake of the recent Financial Crisis than the US.

IV The Rise of Independent Directors in Europe

1 *The UK: Taking the Lead*

Shareholdings in UK listed companies are normally not concentrated but 'semi-dispersed' with international investors, the majority of which are probably also institutions now holding over 50 per cent and domestic institutional shareholders holding another 40 per cent of the shares.[113] A similar shift from individuals to institutional investors can be observed in the US.[114] The institutional and regulatory setup in both jurisdictions is, however, completely different. First, the balance of power between shareholders and boards of directors is in favour of boards in the US.[115] In the UK, shareholders are in a more powerful position as they can, among other things, propose directors for nomination or remove serving directors as well as install a new board independent of the intentions

[112] *Ibid.*, 63 ff. In the collapse of the once famous Canadian network supplier Nortel in 2009, some credit was given to the fact that its board was stuffed with independent directors with no experience of the company's specific business: see P. M. Vasudev, 'Independent Directors Sank Nortel', *Financial Post*, 22 October 2014, available at http://business.financialpost.com.

[113] For figures for 2012, see P. L. Davies, 'Shareholders in the United Kingdom' (ECGI Working Paper No. 280/2015, 2015); P. L. Davies, 'Corporate Boards in the United Kingdom' in P. L. Davies et al. (eds.), *Boards in Law and Practice* (Oxford University Press, 2013), 713, 714 f., both with further references.

[114] See *supra* text accompanying notes 99 f.

[115] See *supra* text accompanying notes 95 ff.

of the incumbent board.[116] From a US perspective, this balance of power is perceived as 'shareholder-centric'.[117]

Second, whereas the US uses mandatory law to regulate corporate governance via federal securities regulation and the corporation law of the individual states, in the UK, rules made by statutory bodies are much more important than legal ones.[118] Accordingly, the Companies Act 2006 provides little mention of the structure, composition and function of boards; it assumes the existence of a single tier board without even mandating it.[119] The central piece of regulation in the area of corporate governance is the UK Corporate Governance Code, which is currently administered by the Financial Reporting Council.[120] It embraces the independent monitoring board model and provides explicit rules on board composition. However, as the Code adheres to the 'comply or explain' principle that had its genesis in an earlier version of the Code, companies may deviate from these rules if they provide an explanation for doing so. The 'comply or explain' principle is enforced by the listing rules of the London Stock Exchange.

The UK's adoption of the monitoring board model is fairly recent.[121] As in the US, the typical British board of the 1950s was an advisory board composed of insiders and framed by a managerialist governance system. The dramatic events that shaped corporate governance in the US during the 1970s and 1980s were largely absent in the UK (as in the rest of Europe). It was industry, and not the government, that first promoted the concept of monitoring by non-executive (though at first not necessarily independent) directors in the early 1980s.[122] Things started to change with the report of the Committee on Financial Aspects of Corporate Governance in 1992. The Committee was set up by the financial industry

[116] P. L. Davies and S. Worthington, *Gower and Davies' Principles of Modern Company Law*, 9th edn (Sweet and Maxwell, 2012), 436.

[117] Rock, 'New Shareholder-centric Reality', 1978. A shared problem is that institutional shareholders are rather passive owners. For the US and the UK respectively, see Gilson and Gordon, 'Agency Capitalism', 876; Davies, 'Shareholders in the United Kingdom', 14 ff.

[118] Davies, 'Corporate Boards in the United Kingdom', 716.

[119] *Ibid.*, 716 f.

[120] Financial Reporting Council, *The UK Corporate Governance Code* (September 2014), available at http://frc.org.uk.

[121] For a detailed historical analysis see B. R. Cheffins, 'The Rise of Corporate Governance in the UK: When and Why', *Current Legal Problems*, 68 (2015), 387, available at http://dx.doi.org/10.1093/clp/cuv006.

[122] Zhao, *Corporate Governance and Directors' Independence*, 30 f.

in 1991 after a series of corporate scandals became public and was chaired by Sir Adrian Cadbury.[123]

The Committee's so-called Cadbury Report soon attracted much international attention.[124] It was the beginning of the British corporate governance movement.[125] The Committee had identified the domination of many companies by a single highly powerful CEO as a central corporate governance problem.[126] Accordingly, the Cadbury Code of Best Practices proposed a board staffed with a sufficient number of non-executive directors. A majority of these were suggested to be independent – with three non-executive directors regarded as a minimum requirement.[127] Some core elements of the conception of an independent monitoring board were without doubt 'imported' from the US, who was the 'first mover' in establishing norms of 'good' corporate governance.[128]

The Cadbury Code of Best Practices was reviewed six years later by the Hampel Committee, which suggested in 1998 to combine these recommendations with those of the Greenbury Committee on directors' remuneration of 1995.[129] The resulting Combined Code was subsequently revised in 2006, following the recommendation of the Higgs Report of 2003. The British government had initiated this report in the wake of the Enron and other scandals in the US. The 2006 revision of the Combined Code recommended that half of the board members of large companies should be independent non-executive directors. In the years between 2001 and 2009, the number of independent directors on the boards of companies listed in the UK oscillated around the high benchmark of 90 per cent.[130]

In 2010, the Combined Code was transformed into the present UK Corporate Governance Code. Interestingly, the strong emphasis on independent non-executive directors as an antidote to an individual or a small group of individuals dominating the board[131] was changed to the recommendation that 'the board and its committees should have the

[123] B. R. Cheffins, 'The History of Corporate Governance' (ECGI Law Working Paper No. 184/2012, 2012), 19 f., available at http://ssrn.com/ abstract=1975404; Cheffins, 'The Rise of Corporate Governance in the UK'.

[124] C. Jordan, 'Cadbury Twenty Years On', *Villanova Law Review*, 58 (2013), 1.

[125] Davies and Worthington, *Principles of Modern Company Law*, 424.

[126] *Ibid.*, 424 f.

[127] Davies, 'Corporate Boards in the United Kingdom', 738.

[128] Cheffins, 'The Rise of Corporate Governance in the UK', 3.

[129] For the history of the various codes see Davies and Worthington, *Principles of Modern Company Law*, 425 f.; Cheffins, 'The Rise of Corporate Governance in the UK'.

[130] Roth, 'Unabhängige Aufsichtsratsmitglieder', 616 with further references.

[131] Main Principle A3, Combined Code 2006.

appropriate balance of skills, experience, independence and knowledge of the company to enable them to discharge their respective duties and responsibilities effectively'.[132] It comes as no surprise that by 2011, the number of independent directors on the boards of companies listed in the UK had shrunk to 61 per cent in response to this change.[133]

The major regulatory change has to be seen in connection with the Walker Review, which was published in 2009 in the wake of the Global Financial Crisis.[134] The Review recommended that financial firms in need of expertise need not be bound by the Code's recommendation of having their boards composed half of independent directors. This is an instructive example of how expertise is presently gaining ground in comparison to independence when it comes to board composition.[135]

The post-crisis reform shows a significant discontinuity from the US concept of strict independence that has resulted in the dominance of super-majority independent boards.[136] In general, it has been observed that the average European Union corporate board increasingly resembles the average US board in two aspects: size and gender diversity, where the European companies have been gaining ground.[137] However, regarding board independence, the gap between the US and the European Union has always been visible on average (though until recently less so for the UK) but did dramatically increase between in 2000 and 2010 from 19 per cent to around 40 per cent.[138]

Three other characteristic features of the UK Corporate Governance Code are: (1) that the CEO and the chair of the board should not be exercised by the same individual as both roles are regarded as being distinct;[139] (2) that the chairman should hold meetings with the independent

[132] Main Principle B, Corporate Governance Code 2014. The Principle is the same in the 2010, 2012 and 2014 editions of the Corporate Governance Code.

[133] Roth, 'Unabhängige Aufsichtsratsmitglieder', 616.

[134] Sir David Walker, *A Review of Corporate Governance in UK Banks and Other Financial Industry Entities* (2009), available at www.hm-treasury.gov.uk.

[135] Davies, 'Corporate Boards in the United Kingdom', 739; S. M. Le Mire, 'Independent Directors: Partnering Expertise with Independence', *Journal of Corporate Law Studies*, 16 (2016), 1.

[136] G. Ferarini and M. Filippelli, 'Independent Directors and Controlling Shareholders around the World' (ECGI Law Working Paper No. 258/2014, 2014), 7, available at http://ssrn.com/ abstract=2443786.

[137] Ferreira and Kirchmaier, 'Corporate Boards in Europe', 198.

[138] *Ibid.*

[139] Principle A.2.1, Corporate Governance Code 2014; Davies and Worthington, *Principles of Modern Company Law*, 428.

non-executive directors without executive directors being present;[140] and (3) that the board should appoint one of the independent non-executive directors to be the senior independent director who will be available as a contact person for the chair, the other independent directors and the shareholders who would like to contact the board (i.e., there should be a 'lead independent director').[141] A new additional feature came with a revision of the UK listing rule in 2014. Since then, in premium listed companies that have a controlling shareholder, a dual voting process is required for the election or re-election of independent directors. This process provides minority shareholders with an increased voice in the election of independent directors in listed companies with a controlling shareholder.[142]

The UK Corporate Governance Code puts the decision of whether a director qualifies as independent in the hands of the board.[143] The board should determine whether the director is independent in character and judgement and whether there are relationships or circumstances which are likely to affect, or could appear to affect, the director's judgement.[144] Furthermore, the board should state its reasons if it determines that a director is independent notwithstanding the existence of relationships or circumstances which may appear relevant to its determination.[145]

It is noteworthy that, being a representative of a significant shareholder as a rule excludes independence.[146] Here again, we see a stark contrast to the US regulatory regime of board composition, where a relationship with a major shareholder does *not* exclude independence. To the contrary, as explained previously, US companies with a majority block shareholder are exempt from the requirement that listed companies must have a majority of independent directors on their board.[147]

[140] Principle A.4.2, Corporate Governance Code 2014.

[141] Principle A.4.1, Corporate Governance Code 2014; Davies and Worthington, *Principles of Modern Company Law*, 429; in the US, exchange listing standards require the appointment of an independent lead director if the CEO chairs the board. Bainbridge, *Corporate Governance*, 104 f.

[142] UK Listing Rule 9.2.2A R and 9.2.2E R.

[143] Davies, 'Corporate Boards in the United Kingdom', 740.

[144] Principle B.1.1, Corporate Governance Code 2014.

[145] *Ibid.*

[146] For a major critique of this rule, see J. L. Hansen, 'Active Owners and Accountable Directors' in H. S. Birkmose, M. Neville and K. E. Sørensen (eds.), *Boards of Directors in European Companies: Reshaping and Harmonising Their Organisation and Duties* (Kluwer Law International, 2013), 241, 250 ff.

[147] See *supra* text accompanying note 90.

The shift from independence to competence and expertise was a quick and pragmatic reaction to the Global Financial Crisis. This shift reinforces the observation that the pro-active and business-oriented stance regarding non-executive directors and subsequently independent non-executive directors in Britain is probably the main reason for the international success of the flexible British model of corporate governance.[148] This contrasts with the rather grudging acceptance of the corporate reforms in the US under public, administrative and federal pressures. Though the UK was late to embrace the independent monitoring model pioneered by the US, it was able to make considerable refinements to the independent monitoring model.

2 *The EU: Building on the UK Experience*

For better or worse,[149] the Cadbury Report set corporate governance standards in the European Union. A corporate governance code with its 'comply or explain' principle is, with slight variations, now ubiquitous in the Member States. The concept of having at least some independent non-executive directors on the board also became, though somewhat hesitantly, a European standard.

The European Commission dealt with the role of non-executive or supervisory directors in general in 2005, in the form of a non-binding Recommendation.[150] The Recommendation closely follows the former UK Combined Code, by recommending the adoption of 'an appropriate balance of executive/managing and non-executive/supervisory directors such that no individual or small group of individuals can dominate decision making'.[151] The number of independent non-executive or supervisory directors elected to the (supervisory) board of companies should be sufficient to ensure that any material conflict of interest involving directors can be properly dealt with.[152] The Recommendation provides the following definition of independence:

[148] Zhao, *Corporate Governance and Directors' Independence*, 35; for a much less benign view on the achievements of the Cadbury Report, see Hansen, 'Active Owners and Accountable Directors', 249: 'Rather than seeing the Cadbury Report as state-of-the-art regulation, it was in fact a rear guard action to avoid legislative encroachment on the status quo.'

[149] Hansen, 'Active Owners and Accountable Directors', 249.

[150] Commission Recommendation (2005/162/EC) of 15 February 2005 on the role of non-executive or supervisory directors of listed companies and on the committees of the (supervisory) board, OJ L 52/51 [hereinafter 'European Commission Recommendation'].

[151] Section 3.1, European Commission Recommendation; for the former corresponding British rule, see *supra* text accompanying notes 129 f.

[152] Section 4, European Commission Recommendation.

> [a] director should be considered to be independent only if he is free of any business, family or other relationship, with the company, its controlling shareholder or the management of either, that creates a conflict of interest such as to impair his judgment.[153]

The decision as to whether a director qualifies as independent is assigned to the board, as in the UK.[154] Annex II to the Recommendation sets out a list of negative criteria that would threaten a director's independence.

In response to the Global Financial Crisis, European Union legislation became more stringent. A Directive of 2014 makes a majority of independent directors and an independent chair mandatory for audit committees of public-interest companies.[155]

Largely independently of the European Commission, a group of European scholars drafted a European Model Company Act (EMCA). The final draft of the Act was published in 2015.[156] Section 5 of the Act recommends that the board of a traded company should comprise an appropriate balance of independent non-executive directors. The EMCA does not provide a definition of independence of its own, but instead refers to the 2005 Recommendation of the European Commission and thus, in effect, to the Combined Code of the UK.[157]

3 *Germany: Quick on Outside Directors, Slow on Independent Ones*

As mentioned, Germany was probably the first jurisdiction to establish a formalised separation between management and supervision in as early as 1861.[158] Since then, the German corporate governance system has been characterised by the two-tier board structure.[159]

153 Section 13.1, European Commission Recommendation.

154 Section 13.2, European Commission Recommendation.

155 Directive 2014/56/EU of the European Parliament and of the Council of 16 April 2014 amending Directive 2006/43/EC on statutory audits of annual accounts and consolidated accounts, [2014] OJ L158/196. This Directive modifies, *inter alia*, Art. 39 of the EU Accounting Directive.

156 European Model Company Act Group, *The European Model Company Act (EMCA) Draft 2015*. An earlier Pan-European project was the *Corporate Governance Principles and Recommendations* published in 2000 by the European Association of Securities Dealers which recommended that there 'should be a sufficient number of board members … who are independent of management, influential shareholders and other conflicting interests' (Recommendation VI.1.b).

157 See *supra* text accompanying note 151.

158 See *supra* text accompanying notes 48 f.

159 For a comparative discussion in English see K. J. Hopt, 'The German Law of and Experience with the Supervisory Board' (ECGI Working Paper No. 305/2016, 2016),

The management board is exclusively staffed with executive directors. It has to serve the 'interest of the company', but has wide discretion on how to achieve this objective.[160] The interest of the company in fact encompasses a plurality of interests: those of shareholders, labour and the public interest (*Gemeinwohl*). The interests of (other) specific stakeholders, such as creditors or suppliers, are not included. Increasing shareholder value is *not* an exclusive objective, though it has probably become the most important as traditional debt financing became less and the capital markets became more important; details are disputed depending on the political preferences of the proponents.[161]

By contrast, from the beginning, the law required the supervisory board to be composed exclusively of outside non-executive directors.[162] The tasks of the supervisory board are usually regarded as twofold: *ex post* monitoring of the management board and *ex ante* advising on business strategy. Arguably, the latter is in substance a form of proactive or preventative monitoring, which makes it impossible to separate the two functions into two distinct watertight compartments.[163]

Being an outside director does, of course, not mean the same thing as being an independent director. Rather, the non-executive directors staffing the supervisory board were – and to some extent still are – typically either affiliated with the company and its management or were

2, available at http://ssrn.com/abstract=272270; Roth, 'Corporate Boards in Germany'; J. J. du Plessis et al., 'An Overview of German Business or Enterprise Law and the One-Tier and Two-Tier Board Systems Contrasted' in J. J. du Plessis et al. (eds.), *German Corporate Governance in International and European Context*, 2nd edn (Springer, 2012), 1 ff. For a comparative analysis of the German and the British board models, see P. C. Leyens, 'Aufsichtsrat: Terra incognita des englischen Gesellschaftsrechts?' in S. Grundmann et al. (eds.), *Unternehmen, Markt und Verantwortung. Festschrift für Klaus J. Hopt zum 70. Geburtstag am 24. August 2010*, Vol. 2 (De Gruyter, 2010), 3135 ff.

160 Section 76, Stock Corporation Act (*Aktiengesetz*).

161 H. Merkt, 'Germany: Internal and External Corporate Governance' in A. M. Fleckner and K. J. Hopt (eds.), *Comparative Corporate Governance: A Functional and International Analysis* (Cambridge University Press, 2013), 521, 536 f. with further references.

162 The regulation is presently found in Section 105, Stock Corporation Act of 1965 (*Aktiengesetz*). For an English overview over the composition and function of the supervisory board, see Hopt, 'The German Law of and Experience with the Supervisory Board'; J. J. du Plessis and I. Saenger, 'The Supervisory Board as Company Organ' in J. J. du Plessis et al., *German Corporate Governance*, 91 ff.

163 A brief discussion can be found in U. Hüffer and J. Koch, *Aktiengesetz*, 11th edn (C. H. Beck, 2014) at § 111 marginal notes 5 ff.; for a detailed analysis see K. J. Hopt and M. Roth, at § 111 marginal notes 52 ff., in K. J. Hopt and H. Wiedemann (eds.), *Großkommentar Aktiengesetz*, 2nd edn (De Gruyter, 2005).

constituency directors representing major shareholders. Accordingly, the traditional structure has been aptly described as an 'insider system' of corporate governance.[164] This pattern corresponded with the widespread block-holding structure until the partial dissolution of what was dubbed 'Germany Inc.' from the late 1990s onwards.[165] But even today, we see a prevailing strong presence of group affiliation and block-holding families amongst listed companies. The latter feature is also characteristic of many Asian companies.[166]

Since the introduction of enterprise co-determination in 1976, half of the supervisory board members of large companies are, by law, constituency directors representing labour, with a mix of directors coming from the company's workforce as well as from the industrial unions – a rather unusual institutional setting internationally speaking.[167] Whether these can be regarded as 'independent' continues to be a hotly debated topic. Since the beginning of 2016, listed companies subject to co-determination are further legally bound to (gradually) introduce a 30 per cent minimum of female supervisory board members.[168]

Germany still has one of the lowest proportions of independent non-executive (supervisory) directors in Europe. In 2011, only 21 per cent of the supervisory directors were independent, 49 per cent were employee representatives, 5 per cent were former executive directors, 8 per cent were shareholder nominees and 19 per cent were other non-independent supervisory directors.[169] The idea of independent monitoring by outsiders still meets much scepticism that is rooted in the persistently strong presence of family-controlled and dependent companies.[170] Accordingly, the concept of independence only slowly gained ground and was introduced in two distinct

[164] K. J. Hopt, 'Law and Corporate Governance: Germany within Europe', *Journal of Applied Finance*, 27 (2015), 8. Another (in)famous insider corporate governance system can be found in Japan, see Chapter 4 (Japan).

[165] W.-G. Ringe, 'Changing Law and Ownership Patterns in Germany: Corporate Governance and the Erosion of Deutschland AG' (University of Oxford, Legal Research Paper No. XX/2014, 2014), available at http://ssrn.com/abstract=2457431.

[166] See Chapter 3 at III.2.

[167] For an English overview see O. Sandrock and J. J. du Plessis, 'The German System of Supervisory Codetermination by Employees' in J. J. du Plessis et al., *German Corporate Governance*, 149 ff.

[168] For the background to this legislation, see U. Seibert, 'Frauenförderung durch Gesellschaftsrecht – Die Entstehung des Frauenfördergesetzes', *Neue Zeitschrift für Gesellschaftsrecht* (2016), 1.

[169] Roth, 'Corporate Boards in Germany', 303 f. with further references.

[170] Hopt, 'Law and Corporate Governance', 10; for the German discussion on corporate governance see (in English), J. J. du Plessis and I. Saenger, 'An Overview of the

steps.[171] The first step came in the form of independence from management in 2002 and the second step came in the form of independence from a significant blockholder in 2012.[172] Germany has been slow in increasing the independence of its boards, but the same is true of other European jurisdictions, such as the Scandinavian countries with block-holding structures.[173]

The Stock Corporation Act has no general provision on independence, but provides a few mandatory requirements for supervisory directors. As mentioned, the supervisory board has to be exclusively composed of outside non-executive directors.[174] Furthermore, a member of the supervisory board may neither be a legal representative of a subsidiary nor may she hold an interlocking directorship.[175] Listed companies must have at least one independent director on the supervisory board, and if one is established, on the audit committee.[176] This regulation was triggered by European Union law.[177]

Independence is predominantly dealt with in the German Corporate Governance Code[178] established in 2002.[179] It is based on the 'comply or explain' principle in the British model, a legal transplant into German law. That principle is given legal force by the Stock Corporation Act and not, as in the UK, by listing rules. Listed companies have the statutory duty to publish annually a declaration of compliance with the Code

Corporate Governance Debate in Germany' in J. J. du Plessis et al., *German Corporate Governance*, 15 ff.

171 A concise critical overview can be found in M. Hoffmann-Becking, 'Unabhängigkeit im Aufsichtsrat', *Neue Zeitschrift für Gesellschaftsrecht* (2014), 801.

172 See Chapter 9 (Singapore) for comparative developments in that jurisdiction.

173 Hansen, 'Active Owners and Accountable Directors'; for a general discussion see P. Lekvall (ed.), *The Nordic Corporate Governance Model* (sns förlag, 2014).

174 Section 105, Stock Corporation Act: 'A member of the supervisory board must not simultaneously be a member of the managing board'. For an English overview of the composition and function of the supervisory board see Hopt, 'The German Law of and Experience with the Supervisory Board'; du Plessis and Saenger, 'The Supervisory Board as Company Organ', 91 ff.

175 Section 100 para. 2 nos. 2 and 3, Stock Corporation Act (*Aktiengesetz*).

176 Section 100 para. 5, Section 107 para. 4, Stock Corporation Act (*Aktiengesetz*).

177 Art. 41 para. 1 of the European Commission Directive on statutory audits of annual accounts and consolidated accounts, Directive 2006/43/EC of the European Parliament and of the Council of 17 May 2006.

178 Government Commission for the German Corporate Governance Code, *German Corporate Governance Code* (as amended on 5 May 2015), available at www.dcgk.de; for a German commentary on this topic, see H. M. Ringleb et al. (eds.), *Kommentar zum Deutschen Corporate Governance Kodex*, 5th edn (C. H. Beck, 2014).

179 The history of the Code is discussed in du Plessis and Saenger, 'An Overview'.

where they have to disclose whether they comply or, if not, explain to what extent and why they are not complying with the Code.[180]

The Code suggests that the 'Supervisory Board has to be composed in such a way that its members as a group possess the knowledge, ability and expert experience required to properly complete its tasks'.[181] This recommendation obviously reflects the pertinent rule in the UK Corporate Governance Code.[182] Furthermore, the Code recommends that the 'Supervisory Board shall include what it considers an adequate number of independent members'.[183] Thus, it is up to the supervisory board to decide what composition fits its company best. The board has wide discretion in deciding the precise number of independent members that it believes is 'adequate'; there is no objective criterion to rely on.[184] In general, the Code emphasises expertise rather than independence.[185]

There is no positive definition of independence in the Code. It only supplies an exemplary short catalogue of criteria, which may cause a substantial and not merely temporary conflict of interest and thus exclude independence.[186] The Code's list of negative criteria is less strict than those recommended by the European Commission.[187]

It was only after a heated discussion that the list of criteria was extended in 2012, to include a relationship with a controlling shareholder (or an enterprise associated with her) as excluding independence.[188] Given that the historical legislator of the Stock Corporation Act conceived the Supervisory Board as a representative organ of the *shareholders* – to compensate them for a loss of direct influence over the management – it may indeed appear to be slightly irritating that, today, being a shareholder or having a relationship with a shareholder is a possible indicator for disqualification from serving as a member of that Board or a committee thereunder.[189] Critics have emphasised that representatives of controlling

[180] Section 161, Stock Corporation Act; see Chapter 11 (Australia) at III. 2 for a comparable 'if not, why not' approach in Australia.
[181] No. 5.4.1, German Corporate Governance Code.
[182] See text accompanying notes 134 ff.
[183] No. 5.4.2 (1), German Corporate Governance Code.
[184] Ringleb et al., *Kommentar*, marginal note 1023.
[185] Roth, 'Corporate Boards in Germany', 306.
[186] No. 5.4.2 (2), German Corporate Governance Code.
[187] See *supra* note 153.
[188] T. Florstedt, 'Die Unabhängigkeit des Aufsichtsratsmitglieds vom kontrollierenden Aktionär', *Zeitschrift für Wirtschaftsrecht* (2013), 337.
[189] Hoffmann-Becking, 'Unabhängigkeit im Aufsichtsrat', 806. By contrast, the Swedish Corporate Governance Code takes a positive view of the role the company's major

shareholders have the incentives and probably the expertise to monitor the management board efficiently.[190] Reflecting these considerations, the Government Commission for the German Corporate Governance Code issued a critical comment on the 2014 Draft for the OECD Principles of Corporate Governance,[191] complaining about a perceived tendency – originating from the Anglo-American world – to assign important tasks in principle exclusively to independent directors instead of taking the more flexible approach of dealing with conflicts of interest on a case by case basis.[192]

As a concluding remark regarding the German regulation of independent directors, a recent legal change of banking law is worth mentioning. Since January 2014, the reformed Banking Act requires that supervisory (non-executive) directors of financial institutions not only be independent but must also have sufficient *expertise* and *experience* as well as sufficient time to be able to fulfil their tasks properly.[193] The change was triggered by the implementation of the Capital Requirements Directive in German banking law. The new emphasis on expertise is certainly necessary. A recent study showed a systemic underperformance of the German state-owned banks – which hold nearly half of all bank assets in the country – during the 2008 Global Financial Crisis in comparison with private banks.[194] This could be traced back to a 'statistically highly significant and qualitatively large' difference in boardroom competence.[195] Independent, but financially 'illiterate' supervisory board members, often from a political background, were unable to fully understand the risks of the financial business they were expected to monitor. All German banks that were in financial trouble due to the Global Financial Crisis were publicly owned.[196]

shareholder may play in corporate governance, see Hansen, 'Active Owners and Accountable Directors', 260 with further references.

190 N. Paschos and S. Goslar, 'Unabhängigkeit von Aufsichtsratsmitgliedern nach den neuesten Änderungen des Deutschen Corporate Governance Kodex', *Neue Zeitschrift für Gesellschaftsrecht* (2012), 1361, 1362; Hoffmann-Becking, 'Unabhängigkeit im Aufsichtsrat', 807.

191 OECD, 'OECD Principles of Corporate Governance, Draft for Public Comment – November 2014' (OECD, 2014/2015), available at www.oecd.org.

192 Press comment of 26 January 2015 by the Regierungskommission Deutscher Corporate Governance Kodex, available at www.dcgk.de/.

193 Section 25d of the Banking Act (*Kreditwesengesetz*).

194 H. Hau and M. Thum, 'Sub-Prime Crisis and Board (In-)Competence: Private Versus Public Banks in Germany', *Economic Policy*, 24 (2009), 701.

195 *Ibid.*, 705.

196 *Ibid.*, 703; this reflects international observations, see Chapter 2 at IV.2.

The findings above show that in Germany, the concept of the independent director has developed an increasing attraction for policymakers notwithstanding the fact that its regulatory framework (still) puts a lot of emphasis on the expertise of the members of the supervisory board. Even though Germany has been resistant to independent directors for quite some time, it has now adopted them and they appear to be in Germany for the long run – for better or worse.

V Should the West's Independent Director Migrate East?

Where does this *tour d'horizon* through the Western evolution of the independent director leave us? The ubiquitous repetitive history of corporate calamities and scandals, in spite of a century-long effort to get the function and composition of the board 'right', offers a cautionary lesson. This scepticism is reinforced by the fact that the empirical support for staffing boards with independent directors remains surprisingly shaky, which is explored in Chapter 2.[197] These findings are hard to accommodate with the faith and fortune placed in the West on board independence, and the corresponding enthusiasm of policymakers to promote or enforce it.

Since the beginning of the joint stock corporation, a board of directors with some type of monitoring function has existed, although it has also been obviously flawed. This suggests that the concept of the monitoring board may, like democracy, only be a second-best option – yet better than any other alternative. All problems notwithstanding, the collective decision making and some kind of control, however imperfect, seem to have been proven over time to be more useful than other institutional arrangements. This being said, it seems equally clear, as our journey has shown, that the process of improving and adapting the concept of the independent director and monitoring board to an ever-changing corporate reality has been far from perfect. Certainly, we see no 'end of history'[198] for the model and function of the board of directors in the West. Rather, there seems to be a greater need for further thought and a healthy scepticism of the concept of the independent director, at least if taken to the extreme. In this spirit, two central lessons might be drawn from

[197] See Chapter 2 at IV.2; see also Chapter 10 (India) at IV.1 and Chapter 11 (Australia) at V for the pertinent discussions in India and Australia, respectively.

[198] Cf. H. Hansmann and R. Kraakman, 'The End of History for Corporate Law', *Georgetown Law Journal*, 89 (2001), 439.

history, which we hope may serve as valuable points for comparison with the more recent rise of the independent director in Asia.

The first and obvious lesson is that policymakers in the US conceived the independent board as a corporate governance tool with the aim of addressing the classic agency conflict between managers and owners in a Berle-Means corporation with dispersed ownership. It was *not*, however, designed to solve the agency problems between minority shareholders and a controlling shareholder in a corporation with concentrated ownership. Whether independent directors *can* actually fulfil a meaningful monitoring role in such a setting is an entirely open question.[199] The heated discussion in Continental Europe – where concentrated ownership is commonplace[200] – is telling. As far as we can see, there are practically no empirical studies dealing with this question. In Asia, we frequently find corporate structures with concentrated shareholders, be they family members or the state. The question of conceptual suitability and the possible need for institutional adaptation seem to be of utmost importance.

The second lesson became clear in the aftermath of the 2008 Global Financial Crisis: independence as such is *not* sufficient to guarantee good monitoring. This explains the recent shift from the more or less exclusive focus on independence to a more nuanced concept including competence and experience in the UK. In Germany, the emphasis was traditionally placed on competence rather than independence. Future developments will probably bring a more flexible[201] and *competence-oriented* board composed of a 'competent' mix of directors with *ex post* and *ex ante* monitoring functions. 'Competence' will include sufficient independence from key players involved in the company (however defined), material disinterest (no conflict of interest),[202] expertise and experience

[199] Gutiérrez and Sáez, 'Deconstructing Independent Directors', 63 (sceptically observing that directors lack the mandate, the incentives, and the ability to properly monitor insiders under such circumstances); see also Hansen, 'Active Owners and Accountable Directors', 250 ff.; Hoffmann-Becking, 'Unabhängigkeit im Aufsichtsrat', 807.

[200] F. Barca and M. Becht, *The Control of Corporate Europe* (Oxford University Press, 2001).

[201] The optimal balance of board composition for a given company depends on a number of exogenous factors and will possibly differ during the firm's lifespan; for the specific problems boards are supposed to solve within small and medium-sized companies (SMEs), see M. Neville, 'The Many Roles of Boards in SMEs' in H. S. Birkmose et al. (eds.), *Boards of Directors*, 241.

[202] Some claim that rather than being formally independent, the directors' impartiality, trustworthiness and disinterestedness should be secured; see Gutiérrez and Sáez, 'Deconstructing Independent Directors', 83 f.

as well as motivation and optimal personal authority.[203] Chapter 2 in this book explores this issue in greater detail.

In comparison, the *super-majority independent monitoring* board we can observe today in the US may be a dead end. This kind of excessive independence actually creates a new dependence on corporate insiders, namely the CEO, with respect to the all-important issue of gaining the necessary information for sound monitoring. Asian policymakers should beware of this pitfall.

[203] For the latter, see Le Mire and Gilligan, 'Independence and Independent Company Directors'.

2

Independent Directors

A Theoretical Framework

WOLF-GEORG RINGE*

I Introduction

The concept of board independence has become one of the most successful exports of United States (US) corporate governance.[1] The theoretical concept of having outside, disinterested members joining corporate boards is an innovation of 'good governance' in post-war US board practice, which has gradually increased over time.[2] From there, the concept has conquered the world to become accepted in many other jurisdictions. In most Western legal systems, independent or outside directors were seen as an essential corporate governance tool to improve the monitoring role of the board,[3] and legal rules mandating independence have become increasingly popular worldwide.[4] As this book documents, Asian countries are no exception to this rule, with the legal transplant of board independence being ubiquitous in Asian best practices, listing rules and legal requirements – for better or worse.[5]

* This contribution is an extended and updated version of my previous paper 'Independent Directors: After the Crisis', *European Business Organization Law Review*, 14 (2013), 401, available at http://ssrn.com/abstract=2293394.

[1] K. J. Hopt, 'Comparative Corporate Governance: The State of the Art and International Regulation', *American Journal of Comparative Law*, 59 (2011), 1, 25–26; see Chapter 1 for a comprehensive historical overview; a prominent Asian example is Singapore's adoption of the US model in 2001, see Chapter 9 (Singapore) at II.

[2] J. N. Gordon, 'The Rise of Independent Directors in the United States, 1950–2005: Of Shareholder Value and Stock Market Prices', *Stanford Law Review*, 59 (2007), 1465.

[3] In this contribution we speak of 'the board', largely for simplicity – knowing that some countries use a two-tier board system. In these two-tier jurisdictions, we would refer to the supervisory board.

[4] J. Armour et al., 'Shareholder Protection and Stock Market Development: An Empirical Test of the Legal Origins Hypothesis', *Journal of Empirical Legal Studies*, 6 (2009), 343, 362.

[5] See Chapter 3 for a comparative analysis of the major Asian jurisdictions dealt with in this volume.

However, at least in the West (with the exception of the US), unqualified faith in independent board members is currently losing ground. The 2007–2008 Global Financial Crisis highlighted a number of serious shortcomings in the system. Independent directors have in no way prevented firms' excessive risk taking; further, they have sometimes shown serious deficits in understanding the business they were supposed to control, and have remained rather passive in addressing structural problems. In short, it is clear now that independent directors had severe shortcomings and that boards can have 'too much' independence.[6] Yet, regulators continue to develop more stringent and comprehensive independence standards.

A closer look reveals that under the surface of seemingly unanimous consensus about independence in Western jurisdictions, a surprising disharmony prevails about the justification, extent and purpose of independence requirements. This prompts us to re-evaluate the entire concept of independence. This chapter explores the idea of independence for corporate directors across Western jurisdictions. By exploring the weaknesses of the concept over the past decades, and recent insights which came to light during the Global Financial Crisis, this chapter proposes a 'functional' concept of board independence. This would include directors that are independent of the firm's controller, but at the same time more accountable to (minority) shareholders.

The chapter is structured as follows. Section II discusses the role of independent directors in the Financial Crisis and reviews current commentary and regulatory initiatives. Sections III and IV go back to the roots of 'independence' by exploring the justification for independence across jurisdictions and raising four challenges to the soundness of the instrument. Section V presents a proposal to move closer to a functional concept of independence, both to make independence more operational and to mitigate the problems and challenges presented earlier. Section VI concludes.

II Independent Directors and the Financial Crisis

The concept of board independence originated in the US.[7] US case law has long encouraged independent and non-employee directors, while US

[6] See recent empirical contributions, for example, R. B. Adams, 'Governance and the Financial Crisis', *International Review of Finance*, 12 (2012), 7; A. Beltratti and R. M. Stulz, 'The Credit Crisis around the Globe: Why Did Some Banks Perform Better?', *Journal of Financial Economics*, 105 (2012), 1; D. H. Erkens, M. Hung and P. Matos, 'Corporate Governance in the 2007–2008 Financial Crisis: Evidence from Financial Institutions Worldwide', *Journal of Corporate Finance*, 18 (2012), 389.

[7] See Chapter 1 for a comprehensive historical overview.

exchange rules require that company boards include a majority of independent directors and that key committees be composed of a majority, or entirely, of independent directors.[8]

Regulation is often scandal-driven or responds to economic crises. In response to a number of major corporate and accounting scandals, including those affecting Enron and WorldCom, the Sarbanes-Oxley Act reformed large parts of US corporate law and capital market regulation. This included strengthening of board independence: *inter alia*, the Sarbanes-Oxley Act required publicly traded companies to have wholly independent audit committees with the power and the duty to select outside auditors.[9]

In a similar way, the Global Financial Crisis of 2007–2008 re-opened the debate around corporate governance and risk management.[10] Again, independent directors were partly blamed for the major failures of 'checks and balances'.[11] Academic research claims that financial institutions with more independent directors performed worse during the Financial Crisis.[12] The account that the Financial Crisis was, if not caused, at least facilitated by idiosyncratic and institutional deficits in board-level corporate governance has become ever more popular in the financial press.[13] Further, a number of academic papers have sought to

[8] For empirical data on the rise of independent ('outside') directors in the United States, see Gordon, 'The Rise of Independent Directors in the United States', 1465; M. Kahan and E. Rock, 'Embattled CEOs', *Texas Law Review*, 88 (2010), 997, 1023–1025.

[9] E. M. Fogel and A. M. Geier, 'Strangers in the House: Rethinking Sarbanes-Oxley and the Independent Board of Directors', *Delaware Journal of Corporate Law*, 32 (2007), 33; Hopt, 'Comparative Corporate Governance', 1, 25.

[10] Numerous publications on this subject have already been published. See, for example, S. M. Bainbridge, *Corporate Governance after the Financial Crisis* (Oxford University Press, 2012); C. Mayer, *Firm Commitment: Why the Corporation Is Failing Us and How to Restore Trust in It* (Oxford University Press, 2013); OECD, *Corporate Governance and the Financial Crisis: Key Findings and Main Messages* (OECD, June 2009).

[11] The iconic American investor Carl Icahn claims that the Financial Crisis was caused by the failure of a 'significant set of checks and balances – ultimately ending with the boards of directors'. See C. Icahn, 'Corporate Boards That Do Their Job', *Washington Post*, 16 February 2009, A 15.

[12] Erkens et al., 'Corporate Governance in the 2007–2008 Financial Crisis'; H. Mehran, A. Morrison and J. Shapiro, 'Corporate Governance and Banks: What Have We Learned from the Financial Crisis?' (Federal Reserve Bank of New York Staff Reports No. 502, June 2011).

[13] J. Schnatter, 'Where Were the Boards? Accountability Shouldn't End with the CEO', *The Wall Street Journal*, 25 October 2008, A 11; D. Goldman, '"Goodbye and Good Riddance" AIG Directors!', *cnnmoney.com*, 30 June 2009, available at http://money.cnn.com; J. R. Finlay, 'Outrage of the Week: Leadership Fiddles While Bear Stearns Burns' (blog entry, 14 March 2008), available at http://finlayongovernance.com.

confirm the account that boards not only failed, but failed in a way that contributed to or exacerbated the Financial Crisis and the resulting losses at banks and in the real economy.[14] This line of scholarship often suggests that boards of banks failed to conduct proper risk oversight at their institutions in the years leading up to the Financial Crisis.[15] Similarly, other scholars have noted that boards made poor decisions with respect to compensation, operations and investment at financial institutions.[16] In sum, these accounts view the Financial Crisis and poor bank performance as a function of corporate governance failure, particularly of monitoring boards.[17]

As might be expected, this stream of the literature has led to deeper critiques of board performance, particularly the performance of independent directors. For those who had previously thought that independent directors were of questionable value, this may provide confirmation. But those who believe independent directors can play a significant role in the management of general firm performance have sought to rehabilitate these directors by pointing to their remediable deficits. According to them, directors failed, for example, at risk management because they lacked appropriate incentives, expertise or information.[18] Alternatively, they did not have the power, tools or advisors to properly supervise and assess risk. As for any bad decisions, again this was largely due to informational failures and asymmetries, failed incentives or other fixable deficits at director

[14] Boards of directors in general are said to have 'played an abysmal role'. L. L. Dallas, 'Short-Termism, the Financial Crisis, and Corporate Governance', *Journal of Corporation Law*, 37 (2012), 265, 352.

[15] M. E. Murphy, 'Assuring Responsible Risk Management in Banking: The Corporate Governance Dimension', *Delaware Journal of Corporate Law*, 36 (2011), 121.

[16] See, for example, J. C. Coffee, Jr., 'What Went Wrong? An Initial Inquiry into the Causes of the 2008 Financial Crisis', *Journal of Corporate Law Studies*, 9 (2009), 1; R. Sprague and A. J. Lyttle, 'Shareholder Primacy and the Business Judgment Rule: Arguments for Expanded Corporate Democracy', *Stanford Journal of Law, Business and Finance*, 16 (2010), 1, 31–32.

[17] The narrative finds mixed support in the available empirical evidence. B. R. Cheffins, 'Did Corporate Governance "Fail" during the 2008 Stock Market Meltdown? The Case of the S&P 500', *Business Lawyer*, 65 (2009), 1; see also R. Stulz and R. Fahlenbrach, 'Bank CEO Incentives and the Credit Crisis', *Journal of Financial Economics*, 99 (2011), 11.

[18] E. J. Pan, 'Rethinking the Board's Duty to Monitor: A Critical Assessment of the Delaware Doctrine', *Florida State University Law Review*, 38 (2011), 209, 225–231; L. A. Cunningham, 'Rediscovering Board Expertise: Legal Implications of the Empirical Literature', *University of Cincinnati Law Review*, 77 (2008), 465; R. M. Jones and M. A. Welsh, 'Toward a Public Enforcement Model for Directors' Duty of Oversight', *Vanderbilt Journal of Transnational Law*, 45 (2012), 343.

level.[19] Often, these critiques revert to the argument that had boards been even more independent of management they might have been more questioning of executives and successful in both their monitoring role and – depending on the legal system – their managerial role.[20]

Somewhat surprisingly, these accounts often arrive at the same solution: to enhance the influence of independent directors and to strengthen their independence and accountability. In short, 'more of the same, just better'. Thus, academics have proposed revisions to legal standards to exert pressure on independent directors to provide closer supervision over risk management[21] and to have some level of expertise in such matters.[22] Legal liability standards should be similarly enhanced to incentivise boards to conduct prudent oversight.[23] Other accounts have argued for greater regulatory intervention to ameliorate behavioural deficits of boards and directors.[24]

1 *The Regulatory and Quasi-Regulatory Push for Independence*

Similar arguments have largely driven corporate governance regulatory responses (and preludes to them) since the Financial Crisis. A good illustration is the so-called Walker Report, introduced by Sir David Walker in 2009 to examine corporate governance in the banking industry after the crisis.[25] His report is almost entirely focused on board failures and board-related remedies. The most relevant passage reads:

> The most critical need is for an environment in which effective challenge of the executive is expected and achieved in the boardroom before decisions are taken on major risk and strategic issues. For this to be achieved will require close attention to board composition to ensure the right mix of both financial industry capability and critical perspective from high-level experience in other major business. It will also require a materially

[19] N. F. Sharpe, 'Rethinking Board Function in the Wake of the 2008 Financial Crisis', *Journal of Business and Technology Law*, 5 (2010), 99, 110; see also L. A. Bebchuk and H. Spamann, 'Regulating Bankers' Pay', *Georgetown Law Journal*, 98 (2010), 247.

[20] See, for example, J. Manns, 'Building Better Bailouts: The Case for a Long-Term Investment Approach', *Florida Law Review*, 63 (2011), 1349, 1392.

[21] Pan, 'Rethinking the Board's Duty to Monitor', 225–231.

[22] Cunningham, 'Rediscovering Board Expertise'.

[23] Jones and Welsh, 'Toward a Public Enforcement Model for Directors' Duty of Oversight'.

[24] K. N. Johnson, 'Addressing Gaps in the Dodd-Frank Act: Directors' Risk Management Oversight Obligations', *University of Michigan Journal of Law Reform*, 45 (2011), 55, 66. These board-centred responses form the lion's share of reform proposals outside the realm of enhanced prudential regulation.

[25] Sir David Walker, *A Review of Corporate Governance in UK Banks and Other Financial Industry Entities* (2009), available at www.hm-treasury.gov.uk.

> increased time commitment from non-executive directors (NEDs), from whom a combination of financial industry experience and independence of mind will be much more relevant than a combination of lesser experience and formal independence. In all of this, the role of the chairman is paramount, calling for both exceptional board leadership skills and ability to get confidently and competently to grips with major strategic issues. With so substantial an expectation and obligation, the chairman's role will involve a priority of commitment that will leave little time for other business activity.[26]

The Walker Report thus focuses on fundamental aspects of board composition, leadership and commitment. Beyond these structural aspects, it subsequently points to the need for increased board oversight of risk management[27] and compensation practices,[28] as well as board engagement with long-term shareholders.[29]

Other examples are more concerned with bank governance and the specific problems of financial institutions. For example, the Basel Committee on Banking Supervision of the Bank for International Settlements recommended, in its 2010 *Principles for Enhancing Corporate Governance*, that banks should have a formal written policy for dealing with conflicts of interests of board members as well as an objective compliance process for implementing this policy.[30] In a similar vein, the European Commission's 2010 *Green Paper on Corporate Governance in Financial Institutions* emphasised the importance of board independence and called for improving recruitment practices and strengthening measures intended to prevent conflicts of interests within the board and within the financial institution in general.[31] The Commission picked up this topic one year later in its second Green Paper, dealing with corporate governance in general, in particular in the context of remuneration policies.[32] The Swiss Financial Market Supervisory Authority went as far as

[26] *Ibid.*, 9.

[27] *Ibid.*, 78–89.

[28] *Ibid.*, 90–106.

[29] *Ibid.*, 60–77.

[30] Basel Committee on Banking Supervision, *Principles for Enhancing Corporate Governance* (2010), paras. 55–56, available at www.bis.org.

[31] European Commission, *Green Paper: Corporate Governance in Financial Institutions and Remuneration Policies* (COM (2010) 284), 11, available at http://ec.europa.eu.

[32] European Commission, *Green Paper: The EU Corporate Governance Framework* (COM (2011) 164), 5, 9, 14, available at http://ec.europa.eu. See also on this the recommendations of the European Corporate Governance Forum, *Statement of the European Corporate Governance Forum on Director Remuneration* of 23 March 2009, in particular para. 6, available at http://ec.europa.eu.

to suggest that banks should have at least one-third independent board members.[33]

US regulation in the wake of the Global Financial Crisis has also followed the trend towards emphasising the role of the board and bolstering independence.[34] For example, the Dodd-Frank Act provides for the creation of risk committees to ensure proper management of risk at financial and non-financial firms; these must consist of independent directors and must include at least one expert in risk management.[35] It further requires compensation committee members to be fully independent.[36] Similarly, European Union (EU) post-crisis legislation mandates for audit committees of public-interest firms to have a majority of independent directors and an independent chair.[37]

The post-Financial Crisis board-related reform agenda will not be detailed here, but overall, board-centred reform enhancing the power of independent directors has become a commonly used regulatory technique by lawmakers, regulators and the stock exchanges globally.[38] This trend has continued in post-crisis reforms. The result is that directors, especially independent directors, have emerged as a potentially more powerful and autonomous monitoring organ in post-Financial Crisis corporate governance.[39]

However, the overwhelming and uncritical support for independence is by no means a universal standard. Consider the example of Japan, where no

[33] Swiss Financial Market Supervisory Authority (FINMA), *Board of Directors of Banks and Securities Dealers* (28 August 2012), 2, available at www.finma.ch.

[34] L. M. Fairfax, 'The Uneasy Case for the Inside Director', *Iowa Law Review*, 96 (2010), 127, 136.

[35] § 165, Dodd-Frank Wall Street Reform and Consumer Protection Act, Pub. L. No. 111–203, H.R. 4173.

[36] § 952, Dodd-Frank Act.

[37] Directive 2014/56/EU of the European Parliament and of the Council of 16 April 2014 amending Directive 2006/43/EC on statutory audits of annual accounts and consolidated accounts, [2014] OJ L158/196. This Directive modifies, *inter alia*, Art. 39 of the EU Accounting Directive.

[38] See, for example, § 301, Sarbanes-Oxley Act of 2002, Pub. L. No. 107–204, 116 Stat. 745 (requiring audit committees comprised of independent directors); § 165(h), Dodd-Frank Act (requiring certain public financial companies and bank holding companies to have risk committees comprising independent directors).

[39] P. Rose, 'Regulating Risk by "Strengthening Corporate Governance"', *Connecticut Insurance Law Journal*, 17 (2010), 1. But see the claim by Velikonja, according to whom board independence reforms were solely undertaken to delay or to avoid further, more structural reform. U. Velikonja, 'The Political Economy of Board Independence', *North Carolina Law Review*, 92 (2014), 855.

independent directors were recommended at all until recently.[40] Even the government's modest plan to introduce a mandatory requirement for firms to appoint at least one independent director was too much for conservative business circles. In the end, a watered-down version of the original legislative proposal, which used a 'comply or explain' approach, was passed.[41] Japan's recent Corporate Governance Code now recommends that listed companies appoint at least two independent board members, but this is not a mandatory requirement.[42]

2 *Scholarly Criticism*

The regulatory developments described so far are in stark contrast to most academic comment. We have already seen that empirical evidence of the positive effects of board independence is, at best, mixed.[43] A number of observers claim that the concept of independent directors 'might have been pushed too far'.[44] Others go further by positing that post-crisis corporate governance rules are 'quack corporate governance', reflecting political ideals and ignoring empirical evidence.[45] This is particularly true for § 952 of the Dodd-Frank Act, as seen above, which requires that each member of an issuer's compensation committee be independent. This rule goes against all available evidence. Most empirical studies have strongly rejected the claim that independent compensation committees are positively correlated with firm performance or with improved CEO compensation practices.[46]

40 On the background, see S. Deakin, 'What Directors Do (and Fail to Do): Some Comparative Notes on Board Structure and Corporate Governance', *New York Law School Law Review*, 55 (2010/11), 525, 538–540.

41 'Back to the Drawing Board', *The Economist*, 3 November 2012, 68. For more details on the recent reform of Japanese corporate law, see Chapter 4 (Japan) at II.1.c.

42 'Winds of Change: The Prospects for Shaking Up Japanese Firms Have Never Looked So Good', *The Economist*, 6 June 2015. For details, see Chapter 4 (Japan) at II.1.d.

43 See above notes 12 ff. For an overall perspective, see R. B. Adams, B. E. Hermalin and M. S. Weisbach, 'The Role of Boards of Directors in Corporate Governance: A Conceptual Framework and Survey', *Journal of Economic Literature*, 48 (2010), 58.

44 G. Kirkpatrick, 'The Corporate Governance Lessons from the Financial Crisis', *OECD Journal: Financial Market Trends*, 96 (2009), 61, 81–82.

45 S. M. Bainbridge, 'Dodd-Frank: Quack Federal Corporate Governance Round II', *Minnesota Law Review*, 95 (2011), 1779, relying on the terminology previously used by Roberta Romano when describing the corporate governance rules implemented by the 2002 Sarbanes-Oxley Act. See also R. Romano, 'The Sarbanes-Oxley Act and the Making of Quack Corporate Governance', *Yale Law Journal*, 114 (2009), 1521.

46 For an overview, see I. Anabtawi, 'Explaining Pay without Performance: The Tournament Alternative', *Emory Law Journal*, 54 (2005) 1557, 1582–1583.

Further, research by the Organisation for Economic Co-operation and Development (OECD) suggests that independence has mainly been implemented by setting up 'negative lists' of undesirable criteria, and that this might have led to qualifications (i.e., a 'positive list') or suitability being only of secondary importance.[47] To this end, the OECD recommends that such a negative list should be complemented by positive examples of director qualities that would increase independence.[48] Moreover, they note that 'the issue is not just independence and objectivity but also capabilities'.[49] Other researchers emphasise that regulation itself may have contributed to the failure of independent directors.[50] That is, independence criteria prescribed by regulatory standards often exclude those very people that used to work at the firm, thus excluding key experts on the subject matter of the firm's business.[51] In this vein, empirical studies that predominantly focus on the special case of banks have suggested that board independence is positively related to lower performance during the Financial Crisis or even to the likelihood of a bank bailout.[52] The reason for increasingly independent boards of banks could well be due to country-specific regulation.[53]

This 'question mark' behind independence will be developed further in the following sections. The next section explores the roots of board independence, after which four fundamental challenges to the concept are discussed. This then leads us to our 'more functional' account of board independence, which overcomes its ostensible weaknesses.

3 *Lawmakers' 'Obsession' with Independence*

The contrasting views between regulators and scholars beg the question of why independence as a regulatory tool has been so popular in the wake

47 Kirkpatrick, 'The Corporate Governance Lessons from the Financial Crisis', 81–82.

48 *Ibid.* See also *G20/OECD Principles of Corporate Governance* (2015), 40, 51–52, available at www.oecd.org.

49 Kirkpatrick, 'The Corporate Governance Lessons from the Financial Crisis'.

50 J. Winter, 'The Financial Crisis: Does Good Corporate Governance Matter and How to Achieve It?' in E. Wymeersch, K. J. Hopt and G. Ferrarini (eds.), *Financial Regulation and Supervision: A Post-Crisis Analysis* (Oxford University Press, 2012), 368, 376 para. 12.15.

51 *Ibid.*

52 Adams, 'Governance and the Financial Crisis'; B. A. Minton, J. P. A. Taillard and R. Williamson, 'Financial Expertise of the Board, Risk Taking and Performance: Evidence from Bank Holding Companies', *Journal of Financial and Quantitative Analysis*, 49 (2014), 351.

53 D. Ferreira, T. Kirchmaier and D. Metzger, 'Boards of Banks' (ECGI Finance Working Paper No. 289/2010, 2010), available at http://ssrn.com/abstract=1620551.

of the Financial Crisis. In other words, it is surprising that lawmakers and regulators worldwide appear to have ignored academic critiques of independent directors in favour of strengthening independence standards.[54]

There are several explanations for this obsession, against better advice, with board independence. The starting point is that post-crisis legislation is often misconceived and flawed. Lawmakers are frequently under public pressure, and force reforms through the legislative process in a great hurry.[55] Many corporate governance reforms were not a result of careful deliberation, but instead enacted following limited legislative debate, and during a media frenzy seeking answers to one of the biggest crises of modern financial history.[56]

Further, it appears that strengthening independence standards is a regulatory response that has a number of advantages in post-crisis situations. First, such reforms arguably do not do great harm, even if they are ineffective. At the same time, they allow politicians to demonstrate to their constituents that they are actively resolving the crisis and 'are doing something'. From this perspective, these developments would be more symbolic than substantial.[57]

Secondly, drafting stricter independence criteria is a comparatively low-cost regulatory alternative: it does not create significant costs for both regulators and the regulated parties. This is in part because the concept of independence is already well established, and the costs of adaptation to stricter standards are low. Path dependence theory may even suggest that remaining within the pattern of once-established governance standards is to be preferred over dramatic course changes.

Thirdly, a related point is that insisting on a continuation of the same regulatory concept can act as a form of self-assurance and provides support for earlier views. Abruptly changing course and introducing an entirely different regulatory tool would be an indirect admission of previous failures. By continuing with an (albeit stricter) form of director independence, politicians can essentially say that they had been right all

[54] See also on this aspect F. Clarke and G. Dean, *Indecent Disclosure: Gilding the Corporate Lily* (Cambridge University Press, 2007), 44 ff.

[55] Romano, 'The Sarbanes-Oxley Act and the Making of Quack Corporate Governance', 1528 (on SOX); Bainbridge, 'Dodd-Frank: Quack Federal Corporate Governance Round II' (on Dodd-Frank).

[56] There is an immense body of literature discussing the impact of bubbles (and their bursts) on lawmaking; see, for example L. E. Ribstein, 'Bubble Laws', *Houston Law Review*, 40 (2003), 77.

[57] M. Kahan and E. Rock, 'Symbolic Corporate Governance Politics', *Boston University Law Review*, 94 (2014), 1997.

the time, and previous solutions only need to be strengthened. Thus, a 'more of the same' approach is preferred to a rethinking of the general framework.

Finally, these explanations may coincide with or correspond to a much simpler explanation: directors' organisations lobbying for legislative changes favourable to them, especially the well-established non-executive board associations.[58]

III Why Do We Have Independent Directors?

In order to understand the conclusions we can draw from the crisis, we need to go back to the origins of the concept of directors' independence. In order to establish whether anything has 'failed' or should be modified, we need to understand why independence was seen as desirable in the first place.

1 *Improving the Board's Performance*

Traditionally, the principle of director independence has been justified by the proper role of boards: to provide effective and unbiased monitoring.[59] As one of the key roles of the board is to monitor the executive management, this task can be carried out best if those who monitor are independent of those who are supervised. Fundamentally, there is a conflict of interest dimension: independence is seen as a primitive precondition for ensuring *ex ante* that board decisions are not tainted by arbitrary considerations.[60]

This rationale is confirmed by the fact that the importance of independence has been emphasised in particular areas within the board where such conflicts of interests are potentially salient. In this sense,

[58] See, for example, the US National Association of Corporate Directors (NACD), the Organization for Non-Executive Independent Directors (ONEID, a subgroup of the powerful Institute of Directors), the Financial Times Non-Executive Directors' Club or Itnea, the Association for Non Executive Directors and Chairmen – NEDs & Independent Directors.

[59] See Chapter 1 at I.3 and III.2.

[60] See on this, R. Nolan, 'The Legal Control of Directors' Conflicts of Interest in the United Kingdom: Non-Executive Directors Following the Higgs Report' in J. Armour and J. McCahery (eds.), *After Enron: Improving Corporate Law and Modernising Securities Regulation in Europe and the US* (Hart Publishing, 2006), 367. See also Armour et al., 'Shareholder Protection and Stock Market Development', 343, 355 (classifying independent directors as a shareholder protection tool).

most regulatory initiatives over the past decades that have refined the concept place special emphasis on independence for board committees, such as the remuneration committee, the nomination committee and the audit committee. Potential conflicts are exacerbated in these areas: for example, the audit committee is the key body evaluating the performance of the management. The temptation to let personal connections prevail over objective criteria is substantial. To this end, most regulators around the world have enhanced independence criteria for these or similar committees.

Our intuition is supported by a brief survey of justifications usually cited. For example, the requirements of the New York Stock Exchange state that '[r]equiring a majority of independent directors will increase the quality of board oversight and lessen the possibility of damaging conflicts of interest'.[61]

Academic scholarship has refined the theoretical foundations of independence in various ways. One of the classic academic articles dealing with the problem emphasises that independent directors 'act as shareholder surrogates to assure that the company is run in the long-term best interests of its owners'. This quote, incidentally, sounds as if it is from the current debate on 'shareholder short-termism'; yet it comes from a 1991 article by Ronald J. Gilson and Reinier Kraakman.[62] The important implication (and extension to the basic monitoring role) is that the ultimate goal of independence is to further the interests of the shareholders, and that it is not an end in itself.[63] From this perspective, independent directors are seen as a 'trustee' for shareholders, to mitigate managerial agency costs.[64]

But independent directors have been considered as a tool with much wider objectives, even as a panacea for almost every corporate law problem.[65] Thus, independent directors are said to prevent self-dealing by examining transactions involving conflicts of interest; they should monitor management to detect and prevent managerial fraud. Further,

[61] § 303 A.01, NYSE Listed Company Manual, available at http://nysemanual.nyse.com.

[62] R. J. Gilson and R. Kraakman, 'Reinventing the Outside Director: An Agenda for Institutional Investors', *Stanford Law Review*, 43 (1991), 863, 873.

[63] Gilson and Kraakman note that this statement still does not explain how independent directors effectively carry out their role. *Ibid.*, 873–874.

[64] L. Enriques, H. Hansmann and R. Kraakman, 'The Basic Governance Structure: The Interests of Shareholders as a Class' in R. Kraakman et al. (eds.), *The Anatomy of Corporate Law*, 2nd edn (Oxford University Press, 2009), 64 ('trusteeship strategy').

[65] See Chapter 1 at I.2.

independent directors are supposed to examine corporate affairs and thus to prevent managerial mismanagement. Some even go as far as to say that independent directors serve the interests not just of the shareholders, but of all stakeholders, if not of society as a whole.[66]

Jeffrey Gordon, in a 2007 article, advanced the idea of a connection between the role of independent directors and the development of the stock market, in particular addressing the problem of directors who are less informed and familiar with the company.[67] His argument is that increasingly sophisticated and efficient stock markets permit companies to retain more independent directors, since the more informative share price serves as a signal for them and makes up for the lack of business understanding.[68] Thus, Gordon argues, independent directors are more valuable than insiders since they are more distant from management. The more developed and informed the stock market is, the easier it is for independent directors to monitor the management and, consequently, the more functional it is to have independent directors on the board, avoiding reliance on explicit expertise.

2 *Criteria of Independence*

These theoretical accounts give a comprehensive picture and provide ample justification for having independent directors on the board. Yet, the precise criteria for determining whether a director is truly 'independent' are surprisingly unclear.[69]

Some regulators try to define independence by providing an abstract, general description. This strategy has predominantly been used by international bodies that try to combine approaches applicable across jurisdictions. Thus, for example, the Basel Committee finds that the 'key characteristic of independence is the ability to exercise objective, independent judgement after fair consideration of all relevant information

[66] On this discussion, see P. Beleya et al., 'Independent Directors and Stakeholders Protection: A Case of Sime Darby', *International Journal of Academic Research in Business and Social Sciences*, 2 (2012), 422.

[67] Gordon, 'The Rise of Independent Directors in the United States', 1465.

[68] *Ibid.*, 1541–1563. See, for criticism, Bainbridge, *Corporate Governance after the Financial Crisis*, 99–100.

[69] For a recent overview, see P. L. Davies and K. J. Hopt, 'Corporate Boards in Europe: Accountability and Convergence', *American Journal of Comparative Law*, 61 (2013), 301, 317–326; M. Roth, 'Unabhängige Aufsichtsratsmitglieder', *Zeitschrift für das gesamte Handels- und Wirtschaftsrecht (ZHR)*, 175 (2011), 605; see also Chapter 1 at I.3.

and views without undue influence from executives or from inappropriate external parties or interests'.[70]

At the national level, many regulatory instruments give a list of criteria which attempt to describe what does not constitute independence. For example, both the United Kingdom (UK) Corporate Governance Code[71] and the NYSE Listed Company Manual[72] provide a relatively similar negative catalogue of criteria that would normally exclude a specific director's independence, such as where the director

- has been an employee of the company or a connected entity within the past years;
- is or has been connected with the company's auditors, advisors, directors or senior employees;
- has received additional remuneration from the company apart from the director's remuneration;
- has had a material business relationship with the company; or
- represents a significant shareholder (UK only).

Some jurisdictions have gone further by increasing the level of detail and the complexity of such lists, thus making them very complex to apply.[73]

An example of a compromise solution may be found in the German Corporate Governance Code.[74] The German Code provides a (short) list of criteria, but qualifies them in the following way: a director is not deemed independent 'if he/she has personal or business relations with the company, its executive bodies, a controlling shareholder or an enterprise associated with the latter *which may cause a substantial and not merely temporary conflict of interests*' (emphasis added).[75] This appears to be a middle ground between the two extreme models described above: at

[70] Basel Committee, *Principles for Enhancing Corporate Governance*, para. 38.

[71] Section B.1.1., Financial Reporting Council, *The UK Corporate Governance Code* (September 2014), available at http://frc.org.uk.

[72] § 303 A.02, NYSE Listed Company Manual.

[73] See, for example, Section 3.2 of the Danish Corporate Governance Code, May 2013 (updated November 2014), available at http://corporategovernance.dk/english. On board independence in Nordic company law, see the excellent article by J. L. Hansen, 'On the Independence of Directors in the Nordic Countries: Where the Shareholder Is King' in P. Krüger Andersen, N. Jul Clausen and R. Skog (eds.), *Shareholder Conflicts* (Thomson, 2006), 69. See also Chapter 3 at II.3 for a comparative analysis of the concept of independence in the major Asian jurisdictions discussed in this volume.

[74] German Corporate Governance Code (2015), available at www.dcgk.de/en/code.html; see Chapter 1 at IV.3 for a brief overview over the German corporate governance structure.

[75] *Ibid.*, section 5.4.2.

first, providing a list of substantial criteria – which, however, only count if there is a substantial, long-term conflict of interests.

The EU Recommendation of 2005 on this subject[76] almost resignedly states that '[i]t is not possible to list comprehensively all threats to directors' independence; the relationships or circumstances which may appear relevant to its determination may vary to a certain extent across Member States and companies, and best practices in this respect may evolve over time'. Nevertheless, the Recommendation then goes on to give a very detailed list of criteria.[77]

Do all of these differences matter? It is submitted that the specific phrasing of these regulations is of less importance than the actual substantial differences. Indeed, substantial differences do exist. There is a surprising divergence as to the relevance of independence from controlling shareholders: for example, this criterion is included in the UK definition of independence, but not in its US counterpart as listed above.[78] Germany introduced this criterion recently, but will only consider it relevant if it involves a substantial and long-term conflict of interests.[79] Another area of divergence is the situation of employee representatives on the board, where Germany differs from most other legal systems, due to its system of co-determination.[80] More generally, the various instruments presented here do not just differ in regulatory style or substance, but also, and fundamentally, in who ultimately determines if the board members of a particular company fulfil the independence criteria or not.[81] For example, the US approach is mandatory in the sense that the NYSE listing authority will scrutinise its own criteria objectively. By contrast, many other jurisdictions leave the final decision on what constitutes independence to

[76] European Commission, Recommendation of 15 February 2005 on the role of non-executive or supervisory directors of listed companies and on the committees of the (supervisory) board, [2005] OJ L52/51.

[77] *Ibid.*, Annex II.

[78] See, in more detail, Enriques et al., 'The Interests of Shareholders as a Class', 66 n. 60.

[79] The 2012 revision of the German Corporate Governance Code included the criterion of personal or business relationship with a controlling shareholder in the list in section 5.4.2. For further details on this provision, see T. Florstedt, 'Die Unabhängigkeit des Aufsichtsratsmitglieds vom kontrollierenden Aktionär', *Zeitschrift für Wirtschaftsrecht (ZIP)* (2013), 337. The first court case on this provision concerns Thyssen Krupp AG, and is now pending before the German courts. D. Fockenbrock, 'Strengers Kampf für Unabhängigkeit', *Handelsblatt*, 22 February 2013, 22.

[80] K. J. Hopt, 'Corporate Governance of Banks after the Financial Crisis' in Wymeersch, Hopt and Ferrarini (eds.), *Financial Regulation and Supervision*, 337, 360, para. 11.52; see also Chapter 1 at IV.3.

[81] Hopt, 'Comparative Corporate Governance', 1, 36.

the board itself. This is the case not only under the EU Recommendation, but also in the UK, where the board determines whether each director is independent in character and judgement.[82] The above-mentioned criteria are then only non-binding guidelines for the board, which is free to deviate under the well-known 'comply or explain' principle. This approach ultimately leaves the question to the market to judge.

In summary, it appears that a closer look at the legal systems of Western economies demonstrates a large divergence in the understanding of 'independence' of board members. This is true for both the regulatory justification of the concept and the precise criteria that are relevant for determining independence.

IV Challenges to Independence

The starting point for this chapter has been the unequalled triumph of the concept of director independence in Western corporate governance over the past decades. Following this, we have seen that the notion of 'independence' is ambiguous and is interpreted differently across countries. This section puts forward a number of challenges to the concept and prepares the ground for a functional account of board independence in Part V.

Challenges to the concept of board independence include inherent weaknesses of the concept and more recent empirical and doctrinal insights. Four challenges may helpfully be distinguished: the fundamental problem of matching 'independence' with industry and ownership structures; questionable empirical evidence of the benefits of the concept; incentive problems; and substitutes in the legal system. We will consider each of these points in turn.

1 *Matching Independence with Industry and Ownership Structure*

The review of different 'independence' criteria undertaken above illustrates a surprising arbitrariness of the relevant criteria and substantial uncertainty as to whether the chosen criteria are actually useful in a given context.

[82] Section B.1.1., UK Corporate Governance Code: 'The board should identify in the annual report each non-executive director it considers to be independent. The board should determine whether the director is independent in character and judgement and whether there are relationships or circumstances which are likely to affect, or could appear to affect, the director's judgement. The board should state its reasons if it determines that a director is independent notwithstanding the existence of relationships or circumstances which may appear relevant to its determination, including ...'.

It would be an oversimplification to require all jurisdictions to define independence along the same lines. On the contrary, independence does and should mean fundamentally different things depending on the shareholder structure and industry structure in which it operates.[83] This has already been recognised by the OECD Principles of Corporate Governance, which state that '[t]he variety of board structures, ownership patterns and practices in different countries will thus require different approaches to the issue of board objectivity'.[84] A functional perspective on board independence would thus attempt to match the precise definition of independence of the particular jurisdiction to the particular needs that arise from the concrete ownership structure.

Consider the basic agency conflicts in corporate governance. In concentrated ownership systems, the main intra-company conflict lies between controlling shareholders and minority shareholders; and the predominant objective of corporate law is to mitigate the costs resulting from this conflict. Thus, independent directors are one tool in the larger toolkit for dealing with shareholder conflicts; it follows that *independence from the controlling shareholder* is an essential criterion when determining whether a particular person is independent.[85] By contrast, in dispersed ownership structures, where managerial agency costs tend to be high, this criterion is largely irrelevant, if not counterproductive. To illustrate the implications of both scenarios in practice, consider the following two examples. The recent extension of the German independence definition to include independence from controlling shareholders was a sensible step in the right direction, as German corporate structure is traditionally dominated by strong blockholders.[86] By contrast, the UK is well-known for its dispersed shareholder ownership structure. Its insistence that independence within the meaning of the UK Corporate Governance Code includes the absence of any links with a significant shareholder is surprising, to put it lightly.[87]

[83] D. Johanson and K. Østergren, 'The Movement toward Independent Directors on Boards: A Comparative Analysis of Sweden and the UK', *Corporate Governance: An International Review*, 18 (2010), 527; Davies and Hopt, 'Corporate Boards in Europe', 323–324.

[84] Section VI.E, OECD Principles of Corporate Governance.

[85] M. Gutiérrez and M. Sáez, 'Deconstructing Independent Directors', *Journal of Corporate Law Studies*, 13 (2013), 63; see also Chapter 9 (Singapore) at III and Chapter 10 (India) at II, respectively, for the pertinent discussion in Singapore and India.

[86] On this change, see H. M. Ringleb et al., 'Die Kodex-Änderungen vom Mai 2012', *Neue Zeitschrift für Gesellschaftsrecht* (2012), 1081, 1087–1088; see also Chapter 1 at IV.3.

[87] Section B.1.1., UK Corporate Governance Code.

Similarly, different industry structures might call for different instruments of corporate governance.[88] For example, Gordon's analysis linking director independence to the information provided by the stock market may work well in highly developed equity markets like the United States.[89] To the extent that stock markets are efficient, independent directors can rely on the signals received from the share price. However, this implies, *a contrario*, that board independence in jurisdictions with less developed stock markets should be careful when transposing the same legal instrument into their domestic law. For example, in jurisdictions where the corporate sector relies more on bank financing or workers' skills, like Japan and Germany, independent directors must necessarily perform a different function.[90]

It is submitted that independence is frequently used without further consideration, such that these basic parameters are forgotten. We will return to this issue below, but for now, it is important to make the point that *there is no universal definition of 'independence'*. This follows from the distinct function that independence has to perform in a given jurisdiction, depending on shareholder structure, industry structure and regulatory goals.[91] Comparing the concept of 'independence' in two countries is like comparing apples and oranges. This conclusion has implications for any global attempt to harmonise or even conceptualise standards through instruments developed by the likes of the OECD, the Basel Committee and the EU.[92] If and where such international instruments or guidelines try to make recommendations for a multitude of jurisdictions, they risk becoming so broad and generalised that the result is vague and of little concrete value.[93] An example is the OECD Code of Governance, which

88 P. A. Hall and D. Soskice (eds.), *Varieties of Capitalism: The Institutional Foundations of Comparative Advantage* (Oxford University Press, 2001); W. Carlin and C. Mayer, 'Finance, Investment and Growth', *Journal of Financial Economics*, 69 (2003), 191; M. Blair and L. Stout, 'A Team Production Theory of Corporate Law', *Virginia Law Review*, 85 (1999), 247.

89 See note 67 above and accompanying text.

90 On data supporting these different factors for industry structures, see Carlin and Mayer, 'Finance, Investment and Growth', 204–208.

91 Johanson and Østergren, 'The Movement toward Independent Directors on Boards', 535, observing that there are merits in understanding independence as a 'global principle of corporate governance'. However, they insist that the practical meaning of independence differs across jurisdictions.

92 For a sceptical account of harmonisation attempts in corporate law, see L. Enriques, 'EC Company Law Directives and Regulations: How Trivial Are They?', *University of Pennsylvania Journal of International Economic Law*, 27 (2006), 1.

93 An example is the discussion on the benefits of a possible EU-wide corporate governance code. Weil, Gotshal & Manges LLP, *Comparative Study of Corporate Governance Codes*

tries to provide an internationally valid statement, yet cannot help being more descriptive than helpful:

> In many instances objectivity requires that a sufficient number of board members not be employed by the company or its affiliates and not be closely related to the company or its management through significant economic, family or other ties. This does not prevent shareholders from being board members. In others, independence from controlling shareholders or another controlling body will need to be emphasised, in particular if the *ex ante* rights of minority shareholders are weak and opportunities to obtain redress are limited. This has led to both codes and the law in some jurisdictions to call for some board members to be independent of dominant shareholders, independence extending to not being their representative or having close business ties with them. In other cases, parties such as particular creditors can also exercise significant influence. Where there is a party in a special position to influence the company, there should be stringent tests to ensure the objective judgement of the board.[94]

2 *Empirical Evidence*

The second challenge to independence is the mixed empirical support it has received in recent years. Essentially, scholars have tried to evaluate whether independent directors improve firm performance, and have come up with overall mixed results.[95] There is thus uncertainty about the merits of the entire concept of independence.

For example, in two ground-breaking studies, US scholars Bhagat and Black reach the conclusion that the number of independent directors on the board is negatively correlated with firm performance.[96] A European study arrives at similar conclusions by measuring the impact of independent directors on compensation levels.[97] Recent research even

Relevant to the European Union and Its Member States: Final Report (2002), 81–83, available at http://ec.europa.eu.

[94] Section VI.E, OECD Principles of Corporate Governance.

[95] For recent overviews, see L. A. Bebchuk and M. S. Weisbach, 'The State of Corporate Governance Research', *Review of Financial Studies*, 23 (2010), 939, 943–945; Adams et al., 'The Role of Boards of Directors in Corporate Governance: A Conceptual Framework and Survey', 80–86; see also Chapter 10 (India) at IV and Chapter 11 (Australia) at V, respectively, for the pertinent discussion in the Indian and the Australian contexts.

[96] S. Bhagat and B. Black, 'The Uncertain Relationship between Board Composition and Firm Performance', *Business Lawyer*, 54 (1999), 921; S. Bhagat and B. Black, 'The Non-Correlation between Board Independence and Long-Term Firm Performance', *Journal of Corporation Law*, 27 (2002), 232.

[97] N. Fernandes, 'EC: Board Compensation and Firm Performance: The Role of "Independent" Board Members', *Journal of Multinational Financial Management*, 18 (2008), 30.

quantifies the dramatic welfare losses that result from the regulatory requirement to have a majority of independent directors.[98]

By contrast, a 2007 study analysing independent directors in British firms is more optimistic about their impact on firm performance.[99] Other studies conclude that legal rules that mandate independence criteria for board members can even yield positive returns for firms.[100]

More recent scholarly work looks at the performance of independent directors specifically during the Financial Crisis. Anecdotal evidence suggests that they did not perform well during the crisis,[101] and empirical scholarship for banks finds that banks with a higher number of independent directors performed worse during the crisis.[102] Indeed, a recent expert report calls on the European Commission to re-evaluate the concept of independent directors and 'identify whether their role is satisfactory and whether independence criteria should not be revisited'.[103] The Commission is currently considering further steps.[104] Some experts have gone further, opining that independent directors were 'too independent

[98] S. Gay and S. C. Denning, 'Corporate Governance Principal-Agent Problem: The Equity Cost of Independent Directors' (Working Paper, 2014), available at http://ssrn.com/abstract=2468942; P. L. Swan and D. Forsberg, 'Does Board "Independence" Destroy Corporate Value?' (Working Paper, 2014), available at http://ssrn.com/abstract=2312325. However, Swan's paper should be treated with caution, see the discussion in Chapter 11 (Australia) at V.

[99] J. Dahya and J. McConnell, 'Board Composition, Corporate Performance, and the Cadbury Committee Recommendation', *Journal of Financial and Quantitative Analysis*, 42 (2007), 535.

[100] B. Black and W. Kim, 'The Effect of Board Structure on Firm Value: A Multiple Identification Strategies Approach Using Korean Data', *Journal of Financial Economics*, 104 (2012), 203.

[101] Reflection Group on the Future of EU Company Law, Report of 5 April 2011, available at http://ec.europa.eu/, section 3.1.6: 'it can be noted that the role played by (independent) directors in the crisis period has not necessarily been convincing and that sometimes even a certain level of distrust in independent directors and their level of knowledge relevant to the company of which they are a director, can be identified'.

[102] Erkens et al., 'Corporate Governance in the 2007–2008 Financial Crisis', 389; Mehran et al., 'Corporate Governance and Banks: What Have We Learned from the Financial Crisis?'.

[103] Mehran et al., 'Corporate Governance and Banks: What Have We Learned from the Financial Crisis?', 50–51.

[104] The Report was discussed at a public conference in Brussels on 16 and 17 May 2011. The Commission then launched a public consultation to seek views from all stakeholders on European company law from 2012 onwards. See 'Consultation on the Future of European Company Law', *European Commission*, available at http://ec.europa.eu. See also European Commission, *Green Paper: The EU Corporate Governance Framework*, section 2.7.2 and Q 22.

to understand the complexities of the businesses they nominally directed' (i.e., too independent of the company they were supposed to monitor)[105] or that the concept of board independence 'might have been pushed too far'.[106] In short, '[r]egulation may actually have contributed to the lack of meaningful involvement of non-executive directors'.[107] By contrast, the International Monetary Fund in its 2014 Global Stability Report concluded that board independence was generally associated with lower risk taking in banks.[108]

Some recent work and policy initiatives have emphasised that the key problem is a lack of expertise rather than the independence of directors.[109] Pure independence without expertise relating to the company's business is clearly undesirable.[110] The latest empirical research on financial institutions shows that banks with more independent board members that lacked financial expertise performed worst during the crisis.[111]

These accounts all have far-reaching implications for the benefits associated with board independence. Taken together, the empirical studies show that board independence will at least not always be helpful in improving company performance. This raises the question of why regulators (and, indeed, companies themselves) have continued to add more independence criteria. It is conceivable that diminishing marginal returns mean that the optimal number of independent directors, at least for US companies, may have already been exceeded.

105 D. Nordberg, 'Corporate Governance and the Board' in S. O. Idowu and C. Louche (eds.), *Theory and Practice of Corporate Social Responsibility* (Springer, 2011), 39, 51; see also Hansen, 'On the Independence of Directors in the Nordic Countries', 79.

106 Kirkpatrick, 'The Corporate Governance Lessons from the Financial Crisis', 81–82.

107 Winter, 'The Financial Crisis: Does Good Corporate Governance Matter and How to Achieve It?', 376, para. 12.15.

108 International Monetary Fund, *Global Financial Stability Report: Risk Taking, Liquidity, and Shadow Banking – Curbing Excess While Promoting Growth* (October 2014), 122.

109 Davies and Hopt, 'Corporate Boards in Europe', 322–323 with further references; K. J. Hopt, 'Corporate Governance of Banks and Other Financial Institutions after the Financial Crisis', *Journal of Corporate Law Studies*, 13 (2013), 219, 248 f. See also Deakin, 'What Directors Do (and Fail to Do): Some Comparative Notes on Board Structure and Corporate Governance', 525.

110 But see the arguments developed by Gordon, 'The Rise of Independent Directors in the United States'.

111 Ferreira, Kirchmaier and Metzger, 'Boards of Banks'. See also H. Hau and M. P. Thum, 'Subprime Crisis and Board (In-)Competence: Private Versus Public Banks in Germany', *Economic Policy*, 24 (2009), 701.

3 *Incentive Problems*

Another problem might be that independence in itself is not enough; scholars have recently placed a greater focus on the proper incentive structure for independent directors.[112] This intuitively makes sense, given the numerous tasks we assign to independent directors and the almost superhuman results we expect from them: they are supposed to guard against self-dealing by examining conflict of interest transactions; we expect them to actively oversee management and to detect and prevent fraud; further, independent directors are supposed to examine corporate affairs and thus prevent managerial mismanagement.[113] All of this is to be done within the limited time that such directors can devote to their job – outside directors are usually not employed full-time by the firm.[114]

A lot is asked of independent directors.[115] In particular, we expect independent directors to speak out and to take a proactive role in monitoring. What, other than possibly reputational or moral constraints, can incentivise them to take up this challenge? What, as some have described it, can encourage them to 'fight the battle' instead of taking a laid-back approach to monitoring?[116]

Consider the Olympus scandal of 2011 in Japan where faulty accounting was covered up for years.[117] Given the scarcity of independent board members

112 But see E. B. Rock, 'The Logic and (Uncertain) Significance of Institutional Shareholder Activism', *Georgetown Law Journal*, 79 (1991), 445, 505.

113 See *supra* section III.

114 L. E. Ribstein, 'Market vs. Regulatory Responses to Corporate Fraud: A Critique of the Sarbanes-Oxley Act of 2002', *Journal of Corporation Law*, 28 (2002), 1, 26; L. Lin, 'The Effectiveness of Outside Directors as a Corporate Governance Mechanism: Theories and Evidence', *Northwestern University Law Review*, 90 (1996), 898, 914–915; M. Lipton and J. W. Lorsch, 'A Modest Proposal for Improved Corporate Governance', *Business Lawyer*, 48 (1992), 59, 64; Gilson and Kraakman, 'Reinventing the Outside Director: An Agenda for Institutional Investors', 884; L. D. Solomon, 'Restructuring the Corporate Board of Directors: Fond Hope – Faint Promise?', *Michigan Law Review*, 76 (1978), 581, 585.

115 A. M. Pacces, 'Controlling the Corporate Controller's Misbehaviour', *Journal of Corporate Law Studies*, 11 (2011), 177, 211: 'Both empirical and theoretical analyses suggest that independent directors may be simply asked too much'.

116 P. L. Davies and S. Worthington, *Gower and Davies' Principles of Modern Company Law*, 9th edn (Sweet and Maxwell, 2012), para. 14–76.

117 For more details on the Olympus scandal, see (briefly) Chapter 4 (Japan) at III.2.a at n. 120; and extensively B. E. Aronson, 'The Olympus Scandal and Corporate Governance Reform: Can Japan Find a Middle Ground between the Board Monitoring Model and Management Model?', *Pacific Basin Law Journal*, 30 (2012), 93. For an analysis of other recent corporate governance scandals in Japan, see Chapter 12 at IV.

in Japan, Olympus stood out amongst Japanese firms by actually having three independent members on its board. However, none of them intervened or prevented the management from misbehaving. Opponents to greater independence on Japanese boards have pointed to the Olympus scandal to support their claim that (the lack of) independence was not the problem, nor will increasing independence help solve the problem.[118] Rather, it seems that the independent directors did not dare speak out: former Olympus president Michael Woodford described them as acting like 'children in a classroom' when they were asked to consider ousting the chairman at the time.[119] Further, it seems doubtful that reputational constraints really work.[120]

Lawmakers have suggested obvious solutions, such as enhancing liability standards or to financially incentivise directors. Empirical studies have been sceptical about the effectiveness of classical liability standards and enforcement against directors.[121] Nevertheless, it is clear that this aspect of the debate – to consider the incentives available – has reached the mainstream policy discussion. It has too often been neglected in the traditional debate.

4 *Substitutes for Independence*

Independence – as a regulatory tool – may not be the only mechanism for achieving the particular objective for a specific situation; indeed, it may well be that lawmakers prefer alternative avenues and mechanisms. This aspect is frequently overlooked in the policy debate. However, it is fundamental to any meaningful legal comparison. For example, in a transnational comparison, observers frequently point out the notable absence of independent directors in Japanese companies, as already noted above.[122] This superficial analysis does not take into account that Japanese law has strict independence requirements for statutory auditors, at least half of whom must be independent.[123] They may (potentially) fulfil some of the functions of independent directors in other jurisdictions though this may in itself be a simplified assumption.

118 See *The Economist*, 'Olympian Depths', 3 November 2012, 13; see also discussion in Chapter 4 (Japan) at II.1.c and III.2.a.

119 *The Economist*, 'Back to the Drawing Board'.

120 Bainbridge, *Corporate Governance after the Financial Crisis*, 95–97. But see R. W. Masulis and S. Mobbs, 'Independent Director Incentives: Where Do Talented Directors Spend Their Limited Time and Energy?', *Journal of Financial Economics*, 111 (2014), 406.

121 B. Black, B. Cheffins and M. Klausner, 'Outside Director Liability', *Stanford Law Review*, 58 (2006), 1055.

122 See *supra* II.2.

123 Enriques et al., 'The Interests of Shareholders as a Class', 65. See C. Liu, J. Liu and K. Uchida, 'Do Independent Boards Effectively Monitor Management? Evidence from

Germany is another example of a country with a certain reluctance to introduce far-reaching independence requirements. This certainly has to do with the jurisdiction-specific issue of worker representation on the (supervisory) board of large companies, as well as with the concentrated shareholder environment. Following our rationale developed above, we would expect independent directors, as necessary counterweight, to voice the concerns of minority shareholders.[124] And yet, as deplored by the European Commission,[125] German law does not specify strict independence standards and only has the vague requirement for the supervisory board to include 'what it considers an adequate number of independent members'.[126] Criticism of the vagueness of this requirement often does not take into account the substitutes for minority protection offered by German statutory law. Above all, Germany's legal regime for corporate groups provides for a statutory system of compensation or damages for minority shareholders in situations involving corporate groups.[127] Further protection for minority shareholders is provided through the strict requirements for the 'equal treatment of shareholders' in German law,[128] and individual shareholders have the ability to challenge the validity of shareholder resolutions.[129] Regulators have been criticised for insisting on Anglo-American standards of independence in German company law, in that this approach is founded on a fundamental misunderstanding of the underlying concepts of German law.[130]

Japan during the Financial Crisis' in W. Sun, J. Stewart and D. Pollard (eds.), *Corporate Governance and the Global Financial Crisis: International Perspectives* (Cambridge University Press, 2011), 188. With regards to the role of statutory auditors see Chapter 4 (Japan) at I, II.1.a and II.1.b.

124 See *supra* IV.1; Chapter 1 at IV.3.

125 Commission Staff Working Document, Report on the Application by the Member States of the EU of the Commission Recommendation on the Role of Non-executive or Supervisory Directors of Listed Companies and on the Committees of the (Supervisory) Board, 13 July 2007, SEC(2007) 1021, 7.

126 Section 5.4.2, German Corporate Governance Code.

127 §§ 15–18 and 291–317, Stock Corporation Act (*Aktiengesetz*). L. Enriques, G. Hertig and H. Kanda, 'Related-Party Transactions' in Kraakman et al., *The Anatomy of Corporate Law*, 176–178; P. Hommelhoff, 'Protection of Minority Shareholders, Investors and Creditors: The Strengths and Weaknesses of German Corporate Group Law', *European Business Organization Law Review*, 2 (2001), 61; Forum Europaeum Corporate Group Law, 'Corporate Group Law for Europe', *European Business Organization Law Review*, 1 (2000), 165.

128 § 53a, Stock Corporation Act (*Aktiengesetz*); L. Enriques, H. Hansmann and R. Kraakman, 'The Basic Governance Structure: Minority Shareholders and Non-Shareholder Constituencies' in Kraakman et al., *The Anatomy of Corporate Law*, 96–99.

129 §§ 241–249, Stock Corporation Act (*Aktiengesetz*).

130 M. Peltzer, 'Für einen schlankeren Kodex! Kritische Evaluierung der Stellungnahme des Handelsrechtsausschusses des Deutschen Anwaltsvereins zu den Reformvorschlägen

Finally, consider the situation in the UK where, according to our rationale, independent directors should have a role in representing shareholders' interests against management.[131] Although this situation resembles the starting point in the US, research shows that UK boards employ significantly fewer independent directors than their US counterparts.[132] A superficial comparison, therefore, would conclude that UK boards should generally increase the proportion of independent directors. However, this disregards the much stronger rights of shareholders to remove and appoint board members.[133] In the UK, shareholders can remove directors at will with a 50 per cent majority requirement. Arguably, this power (and already the threat of using it) makes management much more accountable to shareholders than US law. Further, the role of board decision making differs somewhat between both jurisdictions. This is exemplified by the operation of hostile takeovers: whilst the spotlight in the US is on the hands of the board and *ex post* judicial scrutiny is focused on the board's negotiations with the bidder, takeovers are subject to greater institutional oversight in the UK, sidelining the target board and granting ample powers to the Takeover Panel, an independent body and market watchdog.[134] The functional need for independent voices on the board is more salient in the US than the UK.

In conclusion, we see that the mere number of independent members on the board *as such* is not a meaningful basis for comparative analysis.

V Towards a Functional Understanding of Board Independence

The insights developed above now allow us to develop a concept of 'functional independence' of directors. Central to this theory is the understanding that independence is not a panacea, and certainly not an end in itself. Rather, it is submitted, *independence is a tool for solving a specific problem.* On a very general and abstract level, it is a procedural instrument to protect weak groups within the company and to mitigate agency

der DCGK für den Kodex', *Neue Zeitschrift für Gesellschaftsrecht* (2012), 368, 370; N. Paschos and S. Goslar, 'Unabhängigkeit von Aufsichtsratsmitgliedern nach den neuesten Änderungen des Deutschen Corporate Governance Kodex', *Neue Zeitschrift für Gesellschaftsrecht* (2012), 1361, 1362.

131 See *supra* IV.1.

132 L. A. Bebchuk, 'The Case for Increasing Shareholder Power', *Harvard Law Review*, 18 (2005), 833, 847–850.

133 Section 160, Companies Act, 2006, c.50 (Singapore).

134 P. Davies and K. J. Hopt, 'Control Transactions' in Kraakman et al., *The Anatomy of Corporate Law*, 225.

costs. As we have seen, it might work to the benefit of shareholders in general (dispersed shareholder environment) or minority shareholders, as opposed to controlling shareholders (concentrated shareholder environment). The important point is that independence needs to be designed in accordance with the corporate environment and the specific purpose it is designed for in a given jurisdiction. This allows us to develop the following cornerstones for a functional understanding of director independence.

1 *Improving Independence*

First, independence should be *functional in respect to its purpose.*[135] Lawmakers availing themselves of the instrument of board independence should carefully consider what role the concept should play in their jurisdiction. This should include taking into account the typical or prevailing shareholder structure and industry structure in the jurisdiction. As we have emphasised, one fundamental (yet coarse) distinction is the traditional divide between concentrated and dispersed ownership, where the focus of independence should lie on strengthening, respectively, minority shareholders or shareholders generally.[136] This will have far-reaching implications for the relevant definition of independence, particularly whom the director should be independent from (majority shareholder versus board). At the same time, as we have shown, lawmakers should respect and/or complement pre-existing equivalent substitutes. If adequate safeguards are already in place, additional independence standards will not be necessary and may even be counterproductive. In this vein, we emphasise the importance of independence in situations where conflicts of interest are salient, for example, in the appointment or removal of managers, when setting executive pay, or when auditing executive performance.

Against this background, we can predict the usefulness of different independence criteria for specific situations in any given jurisdiction. Recent changes in the German Corporate Governance Code to include 'independence from a controlling shareholder' can be said to be a step in the right direction (the technical details are still under debate).[137] By

[135] See Chapter 3 at II.3 and II.4.

[136] See *supra* IV.1. Note, however, that the distinction between 'concentrated' and 'dispersed' shareholder structure is a simplification; in practice, many mixed situations or variants exist, see R. J. Gilson, 'Controlling Shareholders and Corporate Governance: Complicating the Comparative Taxonomy', *Harvard Law Review*, 119 (2006), 1642; see also Chapter 10 (India) at II for a discussion about the distinction between different types of controlling shareholders.

[137] The 2012 amendment of the German Corporate Governance Code revised its section 5.4.2 in this sense. See note 75 and accompanying text.

contrast, the fact that the UK Code lists as one of its independence criteria the absence of any links with a significant shareholder is surprising, given the highly dispersed ownership structure in this country.[138]

Secondly, in order for independence to be functional, it needs to *address its very own weaknesses*. As recent empirical research has shown, independence is often associated with ignorance.[139] Lawmakers should therefore ensure that independence is accompanied and supplemented with proper expertise or appropriate ongoing training. This could, for example, be monitored through regular external control. Apart from expertise, avenues that regulators should explore could include raising the accountability of independent directors to shareholders or minority shareholders – this argument is further developed below.[140] Alternatively, monetary or non-monetary incentives could be introduced by law, for example, specific target benchmarks. These measures should address the low incentives to engage with the company that we currently see among directors.

2 *Combining* Independence *with* Dependence

Thirdly, lawmakers should think about *coupling independence with dependence*. What sounds like a contradiction is designed to achieve the following: independence is usually framed as a negative criterion – independence from some group or person, for example. The downside to this approach is that 'independence' is ambiguous as such: a passive concept, bare of any positive, proactive element. The policy discourse would benefit from more experimenting with 'dependent' or 'accountable' directors who would represent the constituency which the legal rules intend to protect.

To make this more concrete: minority shareholders in a concentrated ownership system are currently very much at the mercy of independent directors with low incentives. If, however, such independent directors were at the same time associated with a specific constituency, they would have a more meaningful, positive role. For example, a director could at the same time be independent of a controlling shareholder, but accountable to minority shareholders. This is what is intended by minority appointment rights, as exist in, for example, Italy. Italian company law mandates board representation for minority shareholders in listed companies through an elaborate system of board lists.[141] Since 2007, all listed companies are

[138] Section B.1.1, UK Corporate Governance Code; see also IV.1 above.
[139] Beltratti and Stulz, 'The Credit Crisis around the Globe'.
[140] See *infra* V.2.
[141] Article 147-ter, Consolidated Law on Finance, available at www.consob.it.

required to 'reserve' at least one board seat for candidates drawn from slates submitted by minority shareholders; consequently, even investors holding a comparatively small block of shares can have access to the board.[142] It is encouraging that the European Commission, in its latest Green Paper on Corporate Governance, mentions the Italian system as a good example of making the board more accountable to minority shareholders.[143]

Another example is the recent revision of the UK listing rules concerning companies with a controlling shareholder.[144] A number of governance disasters prompted the UK Listing Authority to revise its rules on the 'premium listing' of the London Stock Exchange.[145] The new rules, which came into effect in May 2014, require that proposed independent directors need to be appointed by two shareholder votes: one is the traditional vote by all shareholders, and the second is a separate vote by minority shareholders only.[146] Where these two votes do not yield agreement, the proposed directors can, after a 90-day cooling off period, be elected in the traditional way with a simple majority.[147]

A related strategy is the well-known and much-discussed German system of employee representation on the board. Similarly to how Italian law or the UK listing rules protect minority shareholders, the German regime takes care of employees. It is important to note, however, that these employee representatives have duties and liabilities like any other director, including the duty to act in the interests of the company as a whole. Nevertheless, their position as appointed representatives of a certain group facilitates information flows between the company or management and the represented group in both directions, and helps ensure

[142] B. E. Eckbo et al., 'Efficiency of Share-Voting Systems: Report on Italy' (ECGI Law Working Paper No. 174/2011, 2011), available at http://ssrn.com/abstract=1431733; M. Belcredi, S. Bozzi and C. Di Noia, 'Board Elections and Shareholder Activism: The Italian Experiment' in M. Belcredi and G. Ferrarini (eds.), *Boards and Shareholders in European Listed Companies* (Cambridge University Press, 2013), 365, 378 ff.

[143] European Commission, *Green Paper: The EU Corporate Governance Framework*, section 2.7.1.

[144] Financial Services Authority, 'Enhancing the Effectiveness of the Listing Regime and Feedback on CP12/2: Supplementary Consultation on Proposed Changes to the Listing Rules Resulting from the Implementation of the Alternative Investment Fund Managers Directive' (CP12/25, October 2012); Financial Conduct Authority, 'Feedback on CP12/25: Enhancing the Effectiveness of the Listing Regime and Further Consultation' (CP13/15, November 2013).

[145] This concerned in particular companies from emerging markets which were listed in London; see G. Varriale, 'What New London Listing Rules Mean for EM Companies', *International Financial Law Review*, 12 (2013), 24.

[146] Rule 9.2.2A and Rule 9.2.2E, UK Listing Rules.

[147] Rule 9.2.2F, UK Listing Rules.

that the concerns of this group are at least heard and considered at board level, thus raising awareness of their positions and encouraging discussions. This is in line with the 'mediating hierarch' theory of corporate governance, which considers the board as an institution that brokers relationships between the company's various constituencies.[148]

Transferring this line of reasoning to the US/UK context of corporate governance, where ownership is typically more dispersed,[149] independent directors should not just be independent of management, but, to some extent, be accountable to the body of shareholders as well. This approach has been proposed in the past, but is not reflected in the current legislative framework.[150] Indeed, some argue that boards should be more accountable to shareholders, relying on empirical data from the Financial Crisis.[151] Even where shareholders are rationally apathetic, new activist shareholders (such as hedge funds, for example), could penetrate into the power vacuum and seek board representation.[152]

Moreover, improving the representation of shareholders or minority groups on the board would have positive side effects. Considering the weaknesses of the typical current independent director as discussed above,[153] there is a good chance that, for example, group representatives would have substantial expertise – simply because the minority group would put forward a candidate who best represents their interests in a sophisticated manner. Similarly, we can expect that the incentive problem will be mitigated: directors who directly represent a specific constituency will have much stronger incentives to pursue a certain agenda than the 'hollow', disinterested director. It is hoped that this will result in an open, fresh dialogue between members of the board: the goal would be for representative directors to present new arguments and possible strategies to their fellow independent directors, informing and inspiring the entire board, and ultimately benefiting the entire company.

[148] M. Blair and L. Stout, 'Director Accountability and the Mediating Role of the Corporate Board', *Washington University Law Quarterly*, 79 (2001), 403; and Blair and Stout, 'A Team Production Theory of Corporate Law'.

[149] This does not prevent these jurisdictions from introducing specific rules for companies with a controlling shareholder. See the recent reforms by the UK Listing Authority at text accompanying note 144.

[150] Gilson and Kraakman, 'Reinventing the Outside Director', 865.

[151] B. B. Francis, I. Hasan and Q. Wu, 'Do Corporate Boards Matter during the Current Financial Crisis?', *Review of Financial Economics*, 21 (2012), 39, 50–51.

[152] On activist hedge funds, see L. Bebchuk, A. Brav and W. Jiang, 'The Long-Term Effects of Hedge Fund Activism', *Columbia Law Review*, 115 (2015), 1085; M. Kahan and E. B. Rock, 'Hedge Funds in Corporate Governance and Corporate Control', *University of Pennsylvania Law Review*, 155 (2007), 1021 (specifically on their role in corporate governance).

[153] See *supra* IV.

On the other hand – *μηδὲν ἄγαν* ('nothing in excess'). There would be fatal consequences if the board was only composed of representatives of certain interest groups. This could lead to overprotection and over-representation of (potentially different) minority groups and activists, blocking an effective organisation of and decision making by the board. The consequence would be 'trench warfare' and decision deadlock.[154] Moreover, it appears beneficial to have a proportion of truly independent outsiders on the board to overcome groupthink and bring in new, fresh ideas. A good balance is essential and a mixture of all of these groups is desirable. The ultimate tenet must be the one from the former Combined Code,[155] which insists that an appropriate balance of directors is essential, 'such that no individual or small group of individuals can dominate the board's decision taking'.[156] These simple words aptly describe the objective of board composition better than many lengthy articles.

In sum, this chapter proposes that board *independence* should be combined with a balanced *dependence* on (or accountability towards) specific constituencies and stakeholders. This approach has the following benefits. First, having a representative on the board will allow the protected group (minority shareholders, for example) to voice their concerns and raise awareness of their positions. Secondly, certain weaknesses that independent directors have shown during the Financial Crisis may be overcome, notably expertise deficits and incentive problems. Appointing representatives with a clear agenda on the board will ensure that these individuals are better incentivised and experienced. Thirdly, an indirect impact may be expected on the incentives of the other, non-appointed directors. Being exposed to new, clearly formulated arguments and (sometimes contrasting) positions within the board dialogue will stimulate debate, improve the quality of dialogue and raise the general standard of discussion. This will enhance the overall standard of board activity, to the benefit of the company as a whole. Fourthly, representative board members could improve information access to their constituents – even if they cannot always do so by virtue of their position, they can raise awareness of the views of minority groups. Conversely, they can also improve access to information by

[154] In this spirit, the recent revision of UK Listing Rules discussed in text accompanying notes 144–147 emphasises that they seek to improve 'minority protection, not minority control'. See Financial Conduct Authority, 'Feedback on CP12/25: Enhancing the Effectiveness of the Listing Regime and Further Consultation', paras. 1.5, 2.16 and 6.19.

[155] The Combined Code of Corporate Governance is the predecessor of the present UK Corporate Governance Code.

[156] Section B.1, UK Corporate Governance Code.

reporting back to their constituents on board deliberations, thereby raising transparency within the company.

VI Conclusion

The dismal performance of many companies during the Financial Crisis has reopened the debate on corporate governance, and in particular on the long-established element of director independence. The objective of current initiatives, legislative initiatives and policy discussions appear to be the enhancement of independence standards; this simply amounts to 'more of the same'. By contrast, this chapter calls for critical reflection on the inherent purpose of director independence and develops a 'functional' notion of director independence so as to overcome its deficiencies.

This is against the background that 'independence' is often used in an undifferentiated way, lacking a clear, unambiguous definition. This complicates cross-border comparisons. This chapter suggests that it is necessary to analyse not only the *notion* but also the *concept* of independence. Thus, independent directors are considered as an avenue to control management and mitigate agency costs by protecting minority groups. The specific role that independent directors have to play depends on the specific jurisdiction, especially the business environment, shareholder structure and industry characteristics. It is therefore crucial to determine which directors should be independent.

However, this chapter argues that independence as such is not enough. The second step is that independence should be carefully balanced with a certain amount of *dependence*. This refers to accountability of directors to certain minority groups which they should protect. Strengthening the accountability of directors promises to overcome certain weaknesses that they have displayed over the past years, most notably expertise and incentive problems. Minority shareholder appointment rights in Italy or election rights in the UK are good examples of a useful concept in a concentrated ownership environment. The corresponding tool for a more dispersed ownership scenario would be a director directly appointed by the shareholders.

Overall, the challenge is to find the right balance between independence and dependence. Independence from the 'controller' (management and/or majority shareholder) should be guaranteed, but a certain accountability to the underrepresented group would be an equally important component in motivating and stimulating the board to perform a meaningful role.

3

Varieties of Independent Directors in Asia

A Taxonomy

DAN W. PUCHNIAK AND KON SIK KIM*

I Introduction

At first blush, the rise of the independent director in Asia appears to be a straightforward example of a significant legal transplant from the United States (US) to Asia. A few decades ago, independent directors, which are an American legal invention,[1] were virtually non-existent in Asia.[2] Today, as this book reveals, they are ubiquitous throughout Asia.

* The authors would like to thank the National University of Singapore (NUS) Centre for Asian Legal Studies (CALS) and EW Barker Centre for Law & Business (EWBCLB) for providing funding to support this research. A substantial part of this chapter was shaped during the period when the second author was visiting NUS Law as a Visiting Research Professor at CALS and EWBCLB in 2016. The second author would like to particularly express his gratitude for the generous invitation by CALS and EWBCLB to facilitate this joint research at NUS Law. We would also like to extend our special thanks to Harald Baum for detailed discussions, insights and feedback, which significantly improved earlier drafts of this chapter. In addition, we would like to thank Hitotsubashi University, Tokyo University and the University of Chicago for organising forums to present earlier drafts of this chapter, which were important in its development. In addition, we would like to thank Bruce Aronson, Gen Goto, Souichirou Kozuka, Curtis Milhaupt, Luke Nottage, Zenichi Shishido, Holger Spamann and Umakanth Varottil for valuable feedback and discussions related to earlier drafts of this chapter. Finally, we are grateful to Samantha Tang for her diligent and skilful research assistance, which exceeded our high expectations. As always, any errors remain our own.

[1] See Chapter 1 at III for a brief history of the American origins of the independent director.

[2] See, for example, Chapter 4 (Japan) at I (Japan's apparent resistance against the adoption of independent directors); Chapter 5 (South Korea) at III.1.b (Korea first enacted statutory requirements for independent directors in 2000); Chapter 6 (China) at II.2 (first Chinese company to adopt independent directors did so in 1993 to comply with the listing rules of the Hong Kong Stock Exchange); Chapter 7 (Taiwan) at II.1 (Taiwan Stock Exchange first enacted listing rules for independent directors in 2002); Chapter 8

Even for those familiar with corporate governance in Asia, the evidence in this book demonstrating the extent to which Asian jurisdictions have promoted and adopted 'independent directors' will likely surprise. A recent report from the leading American proxy advisory firm Institutional Shareholder Services (ISS) claims that over 70 per cent of listed companies in China now have a board comprising a majority of 'independent directors' – ranking China far ahead of Australia and the United Kingdom (UK) in terms of its percentage of boards with a majority of 'independent directors'.[3] For over a decade, Singapore has reported that a majority of all of the directors in its listed companies are 'independent', and that 98 per cent of its listed companies comply with the 'independent director' provisions in its 'comply or explain' Code of Corporate Governance – a higher compliance rate than in the UK, where the 'comply or explain' model was invented.[4] In 2000, South Korea made

(Hong Kong) at II.4 (Hong Kong Stock Exchange first enacted listing rules for independent directors in 1993); Chapter 9 (Singapore) at III.1 (Singapore first enacted statutory requirements for independent directors in 1989); Chapter 10 (India) at III (Securities and Exchange Board of India first enacted listing requirements for independent directors in 2000). See also C. H. Tan, 'Corporate Governance and Independent Directors', *Singapore Academy of Law Journal*, 15 (2003), 355, 365.

[3] The ISS Report found that approximately 50 per cent of listed companies in Australia and the UK have boards composed of a majority of independent directors. See T. Gopal, 'Japan: A Closer Look at Governance Reforms' (ISS, 2015), available at www.issgovernance.com. No information was provided in this report as to the definition of 'independent directors' used, or the method used to collect the information presented in the report. For further discussion on the report's shortcomings in its classification of China's board architecture, see note 75 below. Email clarification was sought from the author of the report on 2 June 2016, but no response was forthcoming as of the publication of this book.

[4] By 2006, 98 per cent of all Singapore-listed companies reported full compliance with the recommendation in Singapore's Code of Corporate Governance that one-third of the board be composed of independent directors, and the majority of directors in listed companies were reportedly independent. See Chapter 9 (Singapore) at I; H. Tjio, *Principles and Practice of Securities Regulation in Singapore*, 2nd edn (LexisNexis, 2011), 326. By contrast, compliance with the recommendation in the UK's 2010 Code of Corporate Governance and 2012 Code of Corporate Governance that at least half of the board be composed of independent non-executive directors for companies listed on the Financial Times Stock Exchange 350 Index ranged from 80 per cent in 2011 to 92 per cent in 2015. See Financial Reporting Council, 'Developments in Corporate Governance and Stewardship 2015' (Financial Reporting Council, 2016), available at www.frc.org.uk; Financial Reporting Council, 'Developments in Corporate Governance and Stewardship 2011: The Impact and Implementation of the UK Corporate Governance and Stewardship Codes' (Financial Reporting Council, 2011), available at www.frc.org.uk. Given that the recommended proportion of independent directors on the board for Singapore and the UK were different (one-third and half respectively), a strict comparison of these compliance rates may not be perfectly accurate, but nevertheless provides a useful guide. For a detailed explanation of the 'comply or explain' model, see Chapter 1 at IV.1.

it *mandatory* for all large listed companies to have a board composed of at least half 'independent directors'.[5] Additionally, since 2004, such boards have been required to have a majority of 'independent directors'[6] – which on its face is a stricter requirement than in any major jurisdiction in the European Union, where the regulation of 'independent directors' generally takes the form of non-mandatory recommendations.[7] In 2000, India made it mandatory for publicly listed companies to have a board with at least one-third 'independent directors', and if the board chair is also an executive of the company then the board must be at least half 'independent directors'[8] – which again appears to be a stricter requirement than in most leading Western countries.[9] In as early as 1993, Hong Kong made it mandatory for all listed companies to have a board with at least two 'independent directors', and more recently made it mandatory for at least one-third of such boards to be composed of 'independent directors'.[10]

These facts reveal a reality which is the opposite of what conventional wisdom suggests: many of Asia's leading economies have surpassed those in the West in terms of the proportion of 'independent directors' on their corporate boards.[11] In a similar vein, many of the laws and regulations in Asia's leading economies appear to do more to promote or require 'independent directors' on the boards of listed companies than those in many leading Western economies.[12] The reality that most leading listed companies in Asia now have a significant number (or, in fact, in many cases a majority) of 'independent directors' on their board is a striking development that has been largely overlooked.[13]

[5] See Chapter 5 (South Korea) at III.1.b.

[6] See Chapter 5 (South Korea) at III.1.b.

[7] P. L. Davies and K. J. Hopt, 'Boards in Europe: Accountability and Convergence', *American Journal of Comparative Law*, 61 (2013), 301, 319.

[8] See Chapter 10 (India) at III.

[9] Davies and Hopt, 'Boards in Europe'.

[10] See Chapter 8 (Hong Kong) at II.1.

[11] Conventional wisdom suggests that the boards of Asian companies are often dominated by insiders. See S. Claessens and J. P. H. Fan, 'Corporate Governance in Asia: A Survey', *International Review of Finance*, 3 (2002), 71, 82; C. L. Ahmadjian, 'Corporate Governance and Business Systems in Asia' in G. Redding and M. A. Witt (eds.), *The Oxford Handbook of Asian Business Systems* (Oxford University Press, 2014), 342–343.

[12] See Chapter 4 (Japan) at II.1.b–c; Chapter 5 (South Korea) at III; Chapter 6 (China) at III.2; Chapter 7 (Taiwan) at II.1; Chapter 8 (Hong Kong) at II; Chapter 9 (Singapore) at II.4; Chapter 10 (India) at III; Chapter 11 (Australia) at III.

[13] As South Korea requires all large listed companies to have their board composed of a majority of independent directors, all large listed Korean companies now have a majority of independent directors on their boards. See Chapter 5 (South Korea) at III.1.b. Another prominent example is in Singapore where all of the directors on the board of

To be clear, this does not suggest that 'independent directors' have been vigorously promoted and widely adopted in every jurisdiction in Asia. In fact, until recently, a majority of listed companies in Japan had no 'independent directors'[14] and about one-third of listed companies in Taiwan still have none.[15] Even in Japan and Taiwan, however, recent legal reforms have driven significant increases in the number of 'independent directors' on corporate boards – a trend that appears likely to continue in both countries.[16] In several important[17] but often overlooked developing Asian countries, such as Bangladesh,[18] Indonesia,[19] Malaysia,[20] the Philippines, Thailand and Vietnam,[21] unbeknownst to most comparative corporate

Temasek (the holding company for Singapore's Government-Linked Companies), except for the CEO, are non-executive independent directors. In addition, 64.87 per cent of the directors in the 23 listed Government-Linked Companies – which comprise the vast majority of the most prominent listed companies in Singapore – are independent directors. See Chapter 9 (Singapore) at III.3. It is also noteworthy that independent directors constitute at least half of the boards of many of the most prominent Asian companies such as Lenovo (7 out of 11), Samsung (5 out of 9), Tencent (4 out of 8), Sony (9 out of 12), Tata Steel (6 out of 12), Acer Group (4 out of 7) and DBS Group Holdings (7 out of 9). See, for example, Lenovo, 'Corporate Governance: Board of Directors', available at www.lenovo.com; Samsung, 'Board of Directors', available at www.samsung.com; Tencent, 'Board', available at www.tencent.com; Sony, 'Corporate Governance', available at www.sony.com; Tata Steel, 'Board of Directors', available at www.tatasteel.com; Acer Group, 'Corporate Governance', available at www.acer-group.com; DBS Group Holdings, 'Annual Report 2015: Board of Directors', available at www.dbs.com.

[14] G. Goto, 'The Outline for the Companies Act Reform in Japan and Its Implications', *Journal of Japanese Law*, 35 (2013), 13, 19.

[15] See Chapter 7 (Taiwan) at II.2.a: 'As of 2014, 66.34 per cent of TWSE-listed and OTC-traded companies have independent directors on their boards.'

[16] Political and regulatory support for independent directors has driven their gradual adoption by companies in Japan and Taiwan. See Chapter 4 (Japan) at IV; Chapter 7 (Taiwan) at IV.

[17] Collectively, these five countries – Bangladesh (158 million), Malaysia (30 million), Thailand (67 million), Indonesia (252 million) and the Philippines (100 million) – have an estimated total population of 607 million. See UNData, 'Data', available at data.un.org.

[18] Emerging Markets Committee of the International Organization of Securities Commissions, 'Corporate Governance Practices in Emerging Markets' (2007), available at www.iosco.org.

[19] M. Prabowo and J. Simpson, 'Independent Directors and Firm Performance in Family Controlled Firms: Evidence from Indonesia', *Asian Pacific Economic Literature*, 25 (2011), 121.

[20] H. Ibrahim and F. A. Samad, 'Corporate Governance Mechanisms and Performance of Public-Listed Family-Ownership in Malaysia', *International Journal of Economics and Finance*, 3 (2011), 105.

[21] D. Vo and T. Phan, 'Corporate Governance and Firm Performance' (2013), available at www.murdoch.edu.au.

governance experts, 'independent directors' have become a mainstay in corporate boardrooms.[22] As such, it is now indisputable that the 'independent director' is a ubiquitous feature of corporate governance throughout Asia – and its rise appears to have no immediate end in sight.[23]

As explained in section II of this chapter, however, the meteoric rise of the 'independent director' in Asia is considerably more complex than it appears. A comparison of the jurisdiction-specific chapters in this book reveals that although the *label* 'independent director' has been transplanted precipitously from the US (in some cases via the UK) throughout Asia, who is labelled an 'independent director' (i.e., the 'form' that independent directors take)[24] and what independent directors do (i.e., the 'function' they perform)[25] in Asia differ significantly from the American concept of the independent director. To add to the complexity, the form and function of 'independent directors' vary *within Asia* from jurisdiction to jurisdiction.[26] As such, in reality, there are *varieties* of independent directors in Asia – none of which conform to the American concept

22 For a basic overview of some of the rules regarding independent directors in many Asian jurisdictions, including Indonesia, Malaysia, the Philippines and Thailand, see generally, ACGA, 'Rules and Recommendations on the Number of Independent Directors in Asia' (2010), available at www.acga-asia.org/.

23 Most of the jurisdictions surveyed in this book predict a potential increase in the number of independent directors in their respective jurisdiction. See Chapter 4 (Japan) at IV; Chapter 7 (Taiwan) at IV; Chapter 8 (Hong Kong) at IV; Chapter 9 (Singapore) at V; Chapter 10 (India) at VII.

24 The precise requirements for independence may differ across jurisdictions, which may take the form of a positive definition of independence consisting of a broadly framed standard, or negative definition of independence in the form of a list of disqualifications, or both. See, for example, Chapter 4 (Japan) at II.1 (a broadly-framed standard of independence with a list of disqualifications); Chapter 5 (South Korea) at III.2.b (a list of disqualifications); Chapter 8 (Hong Kong) at II.2 (a broadly-framed standard of independence with a list of situations in which the director's independence is more likely to be questioned).

25 The primary purpose of the 'American-style' independent director is to monitor management on behalf of dispersed shareholders – as such they are required to be independent from management (but not significant shareholders). See U. Velikonja, 'The Political Economy of Board Independence', *North Carolina Law Review*, 92 (2014), 855, 863–864; B. R. Cheffins, 'The History of Modern U.S Corporate Governance: Introduction' in B. R. Cheffins (ed.), *The History of Modern U.S. Corporate Governance* (Edward Elgar, 2012); J. Gordon, 'The Rise of Independent Directors in the United States, 1950–2005: Of Shareholder Value and Stock Market Prices', *Stanford Law Review*, 59 (2007), 1465.

26 Independent directors in the jurisdictions surveyed in this book may possess idiosyncratic skills that allow them to perform particular roles in their specific jurisdiction. See *infra* III.4 and III.5. See also Chapter 5 (South Korea) at IV.4 (observing the increasing preference in South Korea for appointing former government officials as independent directors, possibly to act as a communication channel between the listed company

of the independent director. This challenges the widely-held assumption that 'independent directors' are universally similar[27] and follow the American concept of the independent director.[28] It also complicates interjurisdictional comparisons of 'independent directors' within Asia, which is a core objective of this book.

and the government); Chapter 6 (China) at II.3; Chapter 7 (Taiwan) at II.2.b; Chapter 9 (Singapore) at III.2 and III.3 (opining that independent directors in Singapore family companies are likely to operate as mediators and advisors to family members; also opining the independent directors in Singapore Government-Linked Companies are appointed to fill the managerial-monitoring gap created by Singapore's unique regulatory environment); Chapter 10 (India) at IV.2 (observing that former government officials or politicians are often appointed as independent directors; also noting that academics are often appointed as independent directors in South Korea, China, Taiwan and India respectively). Other commentators have also made similar observations. See, for example, D. W. Puchniak, 'Multiple Faces of Shareholder Power in Asia: Complexity Revealed' in J. Hill and R. Thomas (eds.), *Research Handbook on Shareholder Power* (Edward Elgar, 2015), 514, 525–526 (observing that in Asia's controlling shareholder environment independent directors may be a mechanism for amplifying the block shareholder's controlling power or a signalling device for 'good' corporate governance; also noting that in Japan outside directors have sometimes served to reinforce *keiretsu* and cross-shareholding links, and in China some have suggested that 'independent' directors may be puppets for the government); D. C. Clarke, 'Independent Director in Chinese Corporate Governance', *Delaware Journal of Corporate Law*, 31 (2006), 125, 207–208 (noting that a survey of 500 listed companies in China found that 45 per cent of independent directors were university professors or researchers from institutes, and observing that the common stereotype of independent directors was a well-meaning but ineffectual academic or celebrity appointed for their prestige and possibly to satisfy regulatory requirements).

27 The assumption that independent directors are the same regardless of their jurisdiction of origin is common in much of the leading research in the field. See, for example, B. S. Black et al., 'Corporate Governance Indices and Construct Validity' (ECGI Finance Working Paper No. 483/2016, September 2016), 27 Table 2, available at https://papers.ssrn.com/sol3/papers.cfm?abstract_id=2838273; D. Katelouzou and M. Siems, 'Disappearing Paradigms in Shareholder Protection: Leximetric Evidence for 30 Countries, 1990–2013', *Journal of Corporate Law Studies*, 15 (2015), 127; B. S. Black et al., 'Does Corporate Governance Predict Firms' Market Values? Evidence from Korea', *Journal of Law, Economics and Organisation*, 22 (2006), 366. Similar assumptions also appear to have been made in other corporate governance surveys and rankings. See N. A. Chakra et al., 'Doing Business 2017: Equal Opportunity for All' (World Bank, 2016), available at www.doingbusiness.org; N. A. Chakra et al., 'Doing Business 2016: Protecting Minority Investors' (World Bank, 2015), available at www.doingbusiness.org; N. A. Chakra and H. Kaddoura, 'Doing Business 2015: Measuring Business Regulations, Protecting Minority Investors in [Name of Economy]' (World Bank, 2014), available at www.doingbusiness.org; L. A. Bebchuk and A. Hamdani, 'The Elusive Quest for Global Governance Standards', *University of Pennsylvania Law Review*, 157 (2009), 1263, 1302–1304, 1311.

28 This is implicit in the literature surveyed at note 27 above, given that it did not occur to any of the authors to explicitly draw a distinction between US-style independent directors and independent directors as an umbrella concept.

Section III of this chapter attempts to overcome this significant hurdle for comparative analysis by offering an explanation for why distinct varieties of independent directors have emerged throughout Asia. At first blush, this question is perplexing. All of Asia's leading economies claim to have either explicitly adopted or been heavily influenced by the American and/or 'Anglo-American' independent director model.[29] With a common model, one would expect to find a high degree of uniformity among independent directors in Asia – not diverse varieties. However, a comparative analysis of the jurisdiction-specific chapters in this book reveals six principal factors that have driven independent directors in Asia to evolve in a variety of unique jurisdiction-specific ways: (1) shareholder ownership structures; (2) legal origins; (3) types of shareholders; (4) functional substitutes; (5) political economy; and (6) cultural norms. Understanding how these factors have driven distinct varieties of independent directors to emerge and evolve in Asia's leading economies allows us to construct a loose taxonomy of the varieties of independent directors in Asia. This taxonomy provides a useful tool for identifying which interjurisdictional comparisons are likely to yield significant insights, and which are likely to mislead.

Section IV of this chapter concludes by highlighting how an understanding of the varieties of independent directors in Asia can advance corporate governance practice and contribute to comparative corporate governance theory. The conclusion illuminates the importance of jurisdiction-specific knowledge for accurately understanding the rise and functions of independent directors in Asia. However, while this chapter extracts the important comparative lessons from the jurisdiction-specific chapters in this book, the details in each of the jurisdiction-specific chapters remain essential.

II Varieties of Independent Directors in Asia: Diversity Revealed

1 *The Myth of the Monolithic 'Anglo-American' Independent Director*

Counting the number of 'independent directors' on corporate boards has become a key metric for comparing the quality of corporate governance across countries and companies around the world. Leading corporate

[29] See Chapter 4 (Japan) at II.1.a; Chapter 5 (South Korea) at II.4; Chapter 6 (China) at II.1; Chapter 7 (Taiwan) at I; Chapter 8 (Hong Kong) at II.4; Chapter 9 (Singapore) at II.3; Chapter 10 (India) at III. The roots of the 'Anglo-American' concept of the independent director are explained below at II.1 and II.2; the 'American' concept of the independent director is explained below at II.3.

governance advisory firms, which influence the allocation of trillions of dollars of global capital, have developed multijurisdictional comparative indices that treat the number of 'independent directors' on corporate boards as a critical factor for measuring 'good' corporate governance.[30] The World Bank uses the requirement for 'independent directors' to be on corporate boards as one of the metrics in its influential 'Ease of Doing Business Index', which ranks the business regulatory environments of 190 economies each year.[31] The number of 'independent directors' on corporate boards is a key variable in several of the most influential corporate governance research indices that drive entire areas of comparative corporate governance scholarship.[32]

All of these influential comparative corporate governance measures make the same assumption: that the term 'independent director' universally refers to people who meet the same criteria and perform the same corporate governance function. Indeed, the assumption that independent directors universally take the same form and perform the same function is the foundation upon which many multijurisdictional policy initiatives and leading academic research that focus on independent directors are built.[33] Obviously, if the criteria for labelling a person an 'independent director' and/or the function that a person labelled as an 'independent director' performs differ significantly from jurisdiction to jurisdiction, then comparing 'independent directors' across jurisdictions is essentially an exercise in comparing 'apples and oranges'.

Based on a comparative analysis of the jurisdiction-specific chapters in this book, it appears that the form and function of independent directors in Asia's leading economies differ significantly from the American concept of the independent director. Although there are important similarities in the form and function of 'independent directors' within Asia, there are also significant intra-Asia jurisdictional differences. While intra-Asia comparisons of 'independent directors' may have more utility than Asia–US comparisons, jurisdictional differences in the form and

[30] See, for example, ISS, 'Board Independence at a Glance' (2016), available at www.isscorporatesolutions.com; MSCI, 'ESG Ratings', available at www.msci.com.

[31] See, for example, Chakra et al., 'Doing Business 2017: Equal Opportunity for All'; Chakra et al., 'Doing Business 2016: Protecting Minority Investors'; Chakra and Kaddoura, 'Doing Business 2015: Measuring Business Regulations, Protecting Minority Investors in [Name of Economy]'.

[32] See, for example, Katelouzou and Siems, 'Disappearing Paradigms in Shareholder Protection', 127; Black et al., 'Does Corporate Governance Predict Firms' Market Values?', 366.

[33] See notes 27 and 28 above.

function of independent directors within Asia must also be recognised and accounted for in comparative analyses.

In sum, the comparative evidence in this book reveals that the label 'independent director' masks the reality that the form and function of 'independent directors' in Asia depart significantly from the American concept of the independent director. This monolithic label obscures the reality that jurisdictional differences in the form and function of 'independent directors' within Asia may be significant. Most importantly, the label conceals interesting intra-Asia jurisdictional similarities that provide valuable opportunities for tailored and insightful comparative analyses. The balance of this section of the chapter will explain how 'independent directors' in Asia depart significantly from the American concept of the independent director, as well as highlight important similarities and differences in the form and function of independent directors in leading Asian economies.

2 *The Independent Director in Asia: Untangling Its Anglo-American Roots*

The genesis of the independent director as a global corporate governance mechanism can be traced to the 1970s in the US.[34] Since then, the primary function of independent directors in American corporate governance has been clear: to monitor management on behalf of dispersed shareholders, who are hindered by collective action problems from monitoring management themselves.[35] This managerial-monitoring function is at the core of the American corporate governance model, which for decades has been focused on solving the primary governance problem in companies with dispersed shareholders: functionally autonomous managers taking advantage of their unchecked power to enrich themselves at the expense of dispersed shareholders.[36]

Despite the fact that independent directors account for the vast majority of directors on American boards, there is still considerable debate about whether American independent directors are effective managerial-monitors.[37] It is, however, uncontroversial that the 'independent director'

[34] See Chapter 1 at I.2; Chapter 2 at II; Chapter 9 (Singapore) at II.1.

[35] Gordon, 'The Rise of Independent Directors in the United States', 1490.

[36] See Chapter 9 (Singapore) at II.1; B. R. Cheffins, 'The History of Corporate Governance' in M. Wright et al. (eds.), *Oxford Handbook of Corporate Governance* (Oxford University Press, 2013).

[37] See Chapter 1 at III.7; Chapter 2 at II and IV; Chapter 10 (India) at IV.

in the US was (and still is) designed to function as a corporate governance mechanism primarily to monitor management on behalf of dispersed shareholders.[38] As such, it makes perfect sense that the NYSE and NASDAQ definitions of 'independence' focus on ensuring that independent directors are independent from the managers of the corporation on whose board they sit.[39]

It is also uncontroversial that in the US, independent directors were not (and are not) primarily designed to be a mechanism for monitoring controlling shareholders.[40] On the contrary, at least based on the theory that underlies the American corporate governance model, independent directors become functionally redundant in companies with a controlling shareholder. As the theory goes, in controlled companies, controlling shareholders are fully capable of either monitoring management or managing the company themselves – rendering nugatory the problem of unchecked self-interested managers, which is the primary corporate governance concern in companies with dispersed shareholders that independent directors in the US are designed to fix.[41]

This theory is evident in the NYSE and NASDAQ listing rules, which explicitly exempt companies with a controlling shareholder from the otherwise mandatory requirement that boards of listed companies must have a majority of independent directors.[42] It is also clear that the definition of 'independence' employed in the NYSE and NASDAQ listing rules do not prohibit significant shareholders or those connected with significant shareholders from qualifying as 'independent directors'.[43] Instead,

[38] See Chapter 1 at I.2 and III; Chapter 2 at II.

[39] § 303A.02, NYSE Listed Company Manual, available at http://nysemanual.nyse.com/lcm; § 5605(a)(2), NASDAQ Listing Rules, available at http://nasdaq.cchwallstreet.com.

[40] See Chapter 1 at III.4; Gordon, 'The Rise of Independent Directors in the United States', 1508 at n. 168; B. M. Ho, 'Restructuring the Boards of Directors of Public Companies in Hong Kong: Barking up the Wrong Tree', *Singapore Journal of International and Comparative Law*, 1 (1997), 507, 518–524.

[41] B. M. Ho, 'Restructuring the Boards of Directors of Public Companies in Hong Kong', 527.

[42] Weil, Gotshal & Manges LLP, 'Public Company Advisory Group, Requirements for Public Company Boards: Including IPO Transition Rules' (2013), 2, 13, 15, available at www.weil.com; Wachtell, Lipton, Rosen & Katz, *Compensation Committee Guide* (2014), 3 n. 3, 73, available at www.wlrk.com. See also § 303A.02, NYSE Listed Company Manual; § IM-5615-5, NASDAQ Stock Market Rules.

[43] In fact, the NYSE and NASDAQ listing rules go a step further by exempting controlled companies from the requirement that their nomination committee and remuneration committee must be composed entirely of (American-style) independent directors. See US Securities Exchange Commission, 'NASD and NYSE Rulemaking: Relating to

in the US, share ownership by independent directors is often viewed as an effective way to align their interests with dispersed shareholders and incentivise them to monitor management more effectively on behalf of dispersed shareholders.[44]

Given this context, it is unsurprising that in the 1990s, the American concept of the independent director became a core feature of the UK's Combined Code of Corporate Governance (UK Code).[45] It is well recognised that the US and UK share the unique distinction of having a high proportion of listed companies with dispersed shareholders.[46] As such, it is understandable that the original definition of 'independence' in the UK Code focused on ensuring that independent directors were independent from the company's management, without any restriction on significant shareholders qualifying as independent directors – wholly embracing the American managerial-monitoring concept of the independent director.[47] Moreover, the UK provided a corporate governance architecture similar to the US within which its American-style independent directors could function, as the typical UK listed company had (and still has) a one-tier board with sub-committees for nomination, remuneration and audit.

In sum, it is clear that the inaugural UK Code did more than merely transplant the 'independent director' *label* from the US to the UK. It transplanted the form of the American independent director (i.e., directors who are independent from management only) to perform the function of the American independent director (i.e., monitoring management on behalf of dispersed shareholders) into a corporate governance architecture similar to the US (i.e., a one-tier board with committee system). From this perspective, it appears that the American concept of the independent director was indeed transplanted into the inaugural UK Code, arguably creating the concept of the 'Anglo-American' independent director. In this context, UK–US comparisons of the independent director are more akin to 'twins separated at birth' than 'apples and oranges'.

Corporate Governance' (Release No. 34-48745, 2003), available at www.sec.gov; Findlaw, 'SEC Approves NYSE and NASDAQ Proposals Relating to Director Independence' (23 March 2006), available at http://corporate.findlaw.com.

44 D. C. Clarke, 'Three Concepts of the Independent Director', *Delaware Journal of Corporate Law*, 32 (2007), 73, 91.

45 See Chapter 1 at IV.1; Chapter 9 (Singapore) at II.1.

46 See Chapter 1 at III.6, IV.1.

47 See Chapter 1 at IV.1; Chapter 9 (Singapore) at II.1.

This is not to suggest that the UK independent director has *remained* true to its American origins. The American-style definition of independence in the inaugural UK Code was amended in 2003 to require independent directors to be independent from both the management *and* significant shareholders.[48] The UK also amended its rules in 2014 for electing independent directors in premium-listed companies[49] with controlling shareholders to give minority shareholders a non-binding vote over their election – aiming to make independent directors a more effective mechanism for monitoring controlling shareholders.[50] Moreover, since the Global Financial Crisis, the UK has decreased its emphasis on the independence of directors, while the US has moved in the opposite direction.[51] In sum, it appears that the form and function of the UK independent director has evolved away from its US origins.

In addition, longstanding differences in UK–US corporate law and governance suggest that it is likely that independent directors in the UK and US had different functions even at the time of transplantation. The importance US corporate law places on independent directors as gatekeepers for hostile takeovers and derivative actions contrasts sharply with the UK, where independent directors play a peripheral role in such critical matters.[52] The absolute right under UK company law to remove (independent) directors at any time[53] in public companies is diametrically

[48] Section 1(A.3.1), The Combined Code on Corporate Governance (Financial Reporting Council, 2003), available at www.ecgi.org. This was at the recommendation of D. Higgs, 'Review of the Role and Effectiveness of the Non-Executive Directors' (2003), available at www.ecgi.org.

[49] Premium-listed companies are required to comply with UK-specific rules that are higher than the European Union minimum requirements. See London Stock Exchange, 'Listing Regime', available at www.londonstockexchange.com.

[50] Where a premium-listed company has a controlling shareholder, the election and re-election of independent directors is subject to approval by the: (1) shareholders as a whole; and (2) independent (i.e., minority) shareholders. If the company fails to obtain the necessary approvals, it may propose a special resolution that: (1) must be voted on within a period of 90 to 120 days from the original vote; and (2) must be approved by the shareholders as a whole. See Listing Rule 9.2.2.AR, 9.2.2.ER and 9.2.2.F; Financial Conduct Authority, 'PS 14/8: Response to CP13/15: Enhancing the Effectiveness of the Listing Regime' (May 2014), available at www.fca.org.uk.

[51] See Chapter 2.

[52] See Chapter 1 at III.3; Chapter 2 at IV.4.

[53] A director may be removed at any time without cause pursuant to an ordinary resolution passed by the company's shareholders: see section 168(1), Companies Act 2006, c. 46 (UK). Similar provisions are present in other jurisdictions: see section 152, Companies Act, 2006, c. 50 (Singapore); section 462, Companies Ordinance, c. 622

opposed to a history of staggered boards in listed US companies.[54] The mandatory approach of regulating independent directors in the US contrasts sharply with the UK's hallmark 'comply or explain' regulatory regime.[55] Such differences in UK–US corporate law and governance suggest that upon closer examination, even at the time of transplantation, references to an 'Anglo-American' concept of the independent director may have masked important differences.

Ultimately, although the core concept of the American independent director – a managerial-monitor director, on a one-tier board, in a company with dispersed shareholders – was transplanted into the inaugural UK Code, it is clear that the UK independent director has evolved in its own way. Moreover, even at the time of transplantation, distinct aspects of UK–US corporate law and governance required UK–US independent directors to perform different functions in different regulatory environments. This realisation does not comport with the widely held assumption of a universal concept of the independent director or even an 'Anglo-American' concept of the independent director.

For at least three reasons, this nuanced understanding of the American concept of the independent director and its evolution in the UK are essential for understanding the rise of the independent director in Asia. First, all of Asia's leading economies claim to have either explicitly adopted or been heavily influenced by the American and/or 'Anglo-American' independent director models.[56] As such, to evaluate these claims and understand their historical roots requires a clear understanding of the history of the independent director in the UK and US. Second, the clear differences that have emerged between the UK–US independent director models suggest that varieties in the form and function of the independent director in Asia should be expected. Indeed, the fact that the UK and US – two common law, English speaking, Western countries, with similar corporate board and shareholder ownership structures – have developed different concepts of the independent director suggests that

(Hong Kong); Art. 339, para. 1 and Art. 341, Company Law, Art No. 86 of July 26, 2005 (Japan).

[54] R. Kraakman et al., *The Anatomy of Corporate Law: A Comparative and Functional Approach*, 2nd edn (Oxford University Press, 2009), 60–61.

[55] See Chapter 1 at IV.1.

[56] See Chapter 4 (Japan) at II.1.a; Chapter 5 (South Korea) at II.4; Chapter 6 (China) at II.1; Chapter 7 (Taiwan) at I; Chapter 8 (Hong Kong) at II.4; Chapter 9 (Singapore) at II.3; Chapter 10 (India) at III.

diversity, rather than uniformity, among independent directors in Asia should be expected; the opposite of what conventional wisdom suggests.[57] Third, differences between UK–US independent directors and the evolution that has occurred in the UK concept suggest that claims that Asian jurisdictions have modelled their systems on the US, UK and/or 'Anglo-American' concept of the independent director should be scrutinised.

3 *The Form of Independent Directors in Asia: Decisively Un-American and Surprisingly Diverse*

A comparison of the jurisdiction-specific chapters in this book reveals that none of Asia's leading economies (i.e., China, India, Hong Kong, Japan, Singapore, South Korea and Taiwan) have adopted the American concept of the independent director in form and function. In its thinnest conception, the form that 'independent directors' take can be considered to be the object of their independence (i.e., what they are designed to be independent from). Based on this conception, the thinnest form of the American independent director is to be a director who is independent from the company's management – but not from the company's significant shareholders.[58]

Considering the US origins of the independent director and the conventional wisdom that the American concept of the independent director has become a global phenomenon,[59] it is surprising that *none* of Asia's leading economies currently use the American concept of the independent director, even in its thinnest form. Today, independent directors in all of Asia's leading economies are designed to be independent from the company's management *and* significant shareholders.[60] In fact, in China, India, Hong Kong, South Korea and Taiwan it has always been this way

[57] For further discussion on convergence in corporate governance, see H. Hansmann and R. Kraakman, 'The End of History for Corporate Law', *Georgetown Law Journal*, 89 (2001), 439; Chapter 13 at II.

[58] See Chapter 1 at I.2 and III.

[59] B. R. Cheffins, 'Corporate Governance Reform: Britain as an Exporter' in David Hume Institute, *Hume Papers on Public Policy: Corporate Governance and the Reform of the Company Law* (Edinburgh University Press, 2000); D. C. Langevoort, 'The Human Nature of Corporate Boards: Law, Norms, and the Unintended Consequences of Independence and Accountability', *Georgetown Law Journal*, 89 (2001), 797, 798; see also Chapter 9 (Singapore) at II.

[60] See Chapter 4 (Japan) at II.1.a, II.1.b and II.1.c; W. Tanaka, 会社法 [Company Law] (2016), 212–216; Chapter 5 (South Korea) at III.2.b; Chapter 6 (China) at III.3; Chapter 7 (Taiwan) at II.1; Chapter 8 (Hong Kong) at II.2; Chapter 9 (Singapore) at II.3; Chapter 10 (India) at III.

(i.e., none of these jurisdictions have ever used the American concept of the independent director, even in its thinnest form).[61]

Japan and Singapore stand out as two leading Asian economies that, at one time in their histories, have utilised or claimed to utilise the American concept of the independent director in its thinnest form. Japan's situation is somewhat complex. In 2002, Japan amended its company law to *ostensibly* provide the option of adopting an 'American-style board' with 'American-style independent directors'.[62] However, upon closer examination, these so-called 'American-style independent directors' were in fact defined in such a way that they were not actually required to be independent from either management or significant shareholders. In reality, these directors were only required to not work for the company or its subsidiaries (i.e., to be 'outside directors').[63] Most importantly, these so-called 'independent directors' were legally permitted to have personal connections with management and/or to be employed by significant shareholders (i.e., they did not even need to satisfy the American concept of the independent director in its thinnest form).[64] Starting in the late 2000s, the definition of independence was gradually tightened by successive amendments to the Tokyo Stock Exchange listing rules, which required independent directors to be independent from management *and* significant large-block shareholders.[65] Finally, Japan's recently amended Companies Act expanded the definition of 'outside directors' to require them to be independent from corporate management *and* large-block shareholders.[66]

Singapore stands out among Asia's leading economies as the only jurisdiction that has enthusiastically embraced the American concept of the independent director, at least in its thinnest form.[67] In 2001, Singapore

[61] See Chapter 5 (South Korea) at III.2.b; Chapter 6 (China) at III.3; Chapter 7 (Taiwan) at II.1; Chapter 8 (Hong Kong) at II.2; Chapter 10 (India) at III.

[62] D. W. Puchniak, 'The 2002 Reform of the Management of Large Corporations in Japan: A Race to Somewhere?', *Australian Journal of Asian Law*, 5 (2003), 42; R. J. Gilson and C. J. Milhaupt, 'Choice as Regulatory Reform: The Case of Japanese Corporate Governance', *American Journal of Comparative Law*, 53(2) (2005), 343; P. Lawley, 'Panacea or Placebo? An Empirical Analysis of the Effect of the Japanese Committee System Corporate Governance Law Reform', *Asian-Pacific Law and Policy Journal*, 9 (2007), 105.

[63] See Chapter 4 (Japan) at II.1.a.

[64] See Chapter 4 (Japan) at II.1.a.

[65] See Chapter 4 (Japan) at II.1.b.

[66] See Chapter 4 (Japan) at II.1.c.

[67] See Chapter 9 (Singapore) at II.4 and III.1.

explicitly designed its independent director to be independent from management, but not from significant shareholders.[68] In 2005, the Singapore government considered seriously a proposal to amend its definition of independence to require independence from management *and* significant shareholders, but this proposal was ultimately rejected.[69] It was not until the latest version of Singapore's Corporate Governance Code went into force in 2015, that its definition of independence was expanded to ostensibly require independence from management *and* significant shareholders.[70] This recent shift in Singapore's approach has moved Asia's most enthusiastic adopter of the American form of the independent director away from it.

A thicker conception of the form that 'independent directors' may take would include the position that 'independent directors' occupy within a jurisdiction's corporate governance architecture and the legal nature of such a position. According to the American concept, 'independent directors' hold positions as directors on one-tier boards with nomination, audit and remuneration committees. These positions are secured by mandatory law, which currently requires independent directors to compose a majority of board members and all board-committee members in listed companies.[71]

An examination of the positions that 'independent directors' occupy in the diverse corporate governance architectures of Asia's leading economies reveals a significant departure from this thicker conception of the form of the American independent director – with China arguably providing the clearest example. All listed companies in China have a 'double board'[72] structure (i.e., a 'management board' composed of shareholder representatives who make management decisions and a 'supervisory

[68] Corporate Governance Committee, *Consultation Paper* (2000), 5, available at www.mas.gov.sg; Corporate Governance Committee, *Report of the Committee and Code of Corporate Governance* (2001), 8, available at www.acra.gov.sg; see also Chapter 9 (Singapore) at III.1.

[69] The Council on Corporate Disclosure and Governance, *Consultation Paper on Proposed Revisions to the Code of Corporate Governance* (2004), 7–9, available at www.acga-asia.org.

[70] Code of Corporate Governance, Art. 2.3(e)–(f), 4 n.2 (defining '10% shareholder'), 5 n.6 (defining 'directly associated'); see also Chapter 9 (Singapore) at IV.1.

[71] See Chapter 1 at III.4.

[72] For clarity, we refer to the two-tier board in China and Taiwan as a 'double board'. The 'double board' is distinct from the German two-tier board for a number of reasons, especially since China and Taiwan do not permit the supervisory board to appoint the management board. See Chapter 6 (China) at II.2; Chapter 7 (Taiwan) at II.1.

board' composed of shareholder and employee representatives who supervise the management board and senior managers).[73] This 'double board' structure has no equivalent in American corporate governance.[74] In turn, the nature of the positions held by 'independent directors' in listed companies in China and the US are different, which is problematic for comparative analyses. Some comparative research considers all of the directors on the supervisory board of a Chinese listed company to be 'independent directors';[75] other comparative research only considers directors on the management board of a Chinese listed company who meet the Chinese definition for independence to be 'independent directors'.[76] This confusion is understandable as the Chinese and American board structures differ substantially and, therefore, the positions that 'independent directors' adopt in each jurisdiction are distinct – with no formal (or functional)[77] equivalence. This makes comparisons difficult and potentially misleading when it is assumed – which is often the case – that the nature of the positions that Chinese and American independent directors occupy are equivalent.[78]

Comparisons of independent directors in Japan and the US confront a similar problem.[79] Japan's new Companies Act allows listed companies to adopt a one-tier board, 'double board'[80] or hybrid board – each having

[73] Chapter 6 (China) at II.2.

[74] The 'double board' structure is derived from the German corporate governance system. See Chapter 1 at IV.3; Chapter 6 (China) at II.2; Chapter 7 (Taiwan) at II.1.

[75] This assumption appears to have been made in a report issued by ISS: Gopal, 'Japan: A Closer Look at Governance Reforms'. It is unclear if supervisory board members were deemed to be independent directors for jurisdictions with two-tier boards in 'Exhibit 3: Global Comparison of Board Independence' provided in the report. A distinction should be made between supervisory board members and independent directors, especially in the case of China, where independent directors were introduced to perform the monitoring functions that supervisory board members were unable to provide. See Chapter 6 (China) at II.2. Email clarification was sought from the author of the report on 2 June 2016, but no response was forthcoming as of the publication of this book.

[76] Clarke, 'The Independent Director in Chinese Corporate Governance', 150–151; Z. Yuan, 'Independent Directors in China: The Path in Which Direction?', *International Company and Commercial Law Review*, 22 (2011), 352, 354–357.

[77] See II.4 below.

[78] See note 75 above.

[79] An ISS report on Japan's 2014 reform of its independent director regime directly compares the average percentage of board independence in Japan and the US without further elaboration on the material difference between the two regimes: Gopal, 'Japan: A Closer Look at Governance Reforms'.

[80] Japan's 'double board' is distinct from the German two-tier board system, as the board of statutory auditors is not allowed to appoint or dismiss directors. A shareholder resolution is required to elect and dismiss directors (and statutory auditors): Arts. 329 and

distinct types of directorial positions and roles for independent directors.[81] As the vast majority of listed companies in Japan have adopted a 'double board', which is staffed by *kansayaku* (statutory auditors), the independent directors in Japan and the US occupy different types of positions. An influential school of thought suggests that members of Japan's 'supervisory board' (i.e., *kansayaku*) are essentially similar to American independent directors and, therefore, should be counted as such in multijurisdictional comparisons.[82] The more common view, however, is that only members of the 'management board' who meet the Japanese definition for independence should be considered to be 'independent directors'.[83] However, directors on the 'management board' are monitored by the 'supervisory board' staffed by *kansayaku*, which by definition makes their position and responsibilities distinct in form from American independent directors.[84]

In Taiwan, the company law has recently been amended to require large companies to abandon the 'double board' and adopt a one-tier board by the end of 2017.[85] As such, from 2018, the nature of the position held by independent directors in Taiwan will be broadly comparable to American independent directors, at least in this one aspect. Similarly, listed companies in

339, Companies Act; see also Gilson and Milhaupt, 'Choice as Regulatory Reform', 343, 348.

[81] Goto, 'The Outline for the Companies Act Reform in Japan and Its Implications', 17–19; Chapter 4 (Japan) at II.1; Chapter 12 at IV.1.

[82] B. E. Aronson, 'Japanese Corporate Governance Reform: A Comparative Perspective', *Hastings Business Law Journal*, 11 (2015), 85, 98–102. That foreign investors fail to understand this is a frequent lament amongst Japan insiders. In a provocative article, Matsunaka argues that the *kansayaku* have evolved over time to resemble directors so much that they have effectively lost their independent identity, leading to an 'identity crisis'. M. Matsunaka, '監査役のアイデンティティ・クライシス' [The Kansayaku's Identity Crisis], 商事法務, 1957 (2012), 4. See alsoシンポジウム　監査役制度の正しい理解のために [Panel Discussion on Correctly Understanding the *Kansayaku* Regime], '各界から見た日本のコーポレート・ガバナンスと監査役制度' [The *Kansayaku* Regime and Corporate Governance in Japan from the Perspectives of Different Interest Groups], 月刊監査役, 613 (2013), 4, which featured representatives from the University of Tokyo, *Keidanren*, ISS, Tokyo Stock Exchange, Toyota and the professional association representing *kansayaku*. However, *kansayaku* are distinct from American independent directors for multiple reasons, including their inability to vote at board meetings and participate in decisions regarding the appointment and removal of managers. See Chapter 4 (Japan) at III.2.a.

[83] See Chapter 4 (Japan) generally, which adopts the conventional approach that statutory auditors are *not* independent directors.

[84] See Chapter 4 (Japan) at II.1.a.

[85] See Chapter 7 (Taiwan) at II.3.

Hong Kong, India, Singapore and South Korea have one-tier board structures, making independent directors in these jurisdictions also comparable to American independent directors, at least in this one aspect of their forms.

A second aspect of this thicker conception of the form of independent directors is the legal nature of their positions. In the US, mandatory law requires independent directors to compose a majority of board members and all board-committee members in listed companies.[86] In Asia's leading economies, Japan represents the other extreme as it is the only leading Asian economy in which mandatory law does not require *any* independent directors in listed companies.[87] In contrast, South Korean company law mandates that all large listed companies have a majority of independent directors on their boards.[88] India and Taiwan's regulatory approaches have evolved in a similar way over time: they both first introduced the independent director on a 'comply or explain' basis; and later implemented mandatory law for a minimum number/proportion of 'independent directors' after optional law did not achieve the level of independence the government desired.[89] Singapore evolved in the opposite direction: it first introduced minimal mandatory requirements for the number of independent directors; and later implemented a UK-style 'comply or explain' code to increase the number of 'independent directors' to a level that the government desired.[90]

Finally, the thickest conception of the form of the independent director may include the personal characteristics that the typical independent director in a jurisdiction brings to the position. Again, there appears to be significant differences between independent directors in the US and Asia's leading economies based on this thickest conception of form. In the US, the vast majority of independent directors are corporate executives from other companies.[91] In China, however, historically almost half of all directors on the boards of listed companies have

[86] § 303A.01, § 303A.04–06 NYSE Listed Company Manual; § IM-5605-1, § IM-5605-4, § IM-5605-5, § IM-5605-6, § IM-5605-7 NASDAQ Stock Market Rules.

[87] However, Japan recently strengthened its promotion of independent directors by changing its purely optional regulation of independent directors to a UK-style 'comply or explain' regime, which requires companies to explain if they have no independent directors. See Chapter 4 (Japan) at II.1.c.

[88] See Chapter 5 (South Korea) at III.2.a.

[89] See Chapter 7 (Taiwan) at II.1; Chapter 10 (India) at V.3.

[90] See Chapter 9 (Singapore) at II.4 and IV.2.

[91] R. J. Gilson and R. Kraakman, 'Reinventing the Outside Director: An Agenda for Institutional Investors', *Stanford Law Review*, 43 (1991), 863, 872; S. Ferris et al., 'Too Busy to Mind the Business? Monitoring by Directors with Multiple Board Appointments', *Journal of Finance*, 58 (2003), 1087.

been university professors – a trend which is also prevalent, but less pronounced, in South Korea, Taiwan and India.[92] For China, Singapore and South Korea, the formal and informal connections that independent directors have with the government tend to be more pronounced than in other jurisdictions, but for different reasons in each jurisdiction.[93] In Japan, independent directors tend to be lifetime employees and to have connections with other companies in *keiretsu*-affiliated firms.[94] In Singapore, informal connections that independent directors in family firms have with family controllers tend to be a defining characteristic in such firms – which also likely plays an important role in most other leading Asian economies as family controlled corporations make up a large portion of listed firms in most jurisdictions (with the notable exception of Japan).[95]

The proportion of the board of listed companies that is composed of independent directors is also a critically important aspect of the thickest conception of the form of independent directors. Today, the typical board of a listed company in the US is composed entirely of 'independent directors', except for the CEO.[96] As suggested above, due to the diversity in definitions for independence and varieties of positions held by directors who may be considered to be 'independent directors', statistics reporting the number of 'independent directors' in Asia's leading economies vary considerably depending on the criteria used by the surveyor for identifying which directors should be counted as being 'independent directors'. For example, in China, the ISS survey, which appears to have counted supervisory board members as independent directors, reported that almost 70 per cent of boards in China had a majority of independent directors;[97] another survey by the Asian Corporate Governance Association, which appears to only count members of the management board designated as independent directors, reported that approximately 20 per cent of boards in China had a majority of independent directors.[98]

92 See Chapter 5 (South Korea) at IV.4; Chapter 7 (Taiwan) at II.2.b; Chapter 10 (India) at IV.2.

93 See Chapter 6 (China) at II.3; Chapter 9 (Singapore) at III.3; Chapter 5 (South Korea) at IV.4.

94 Lawley, 'Panacea or Placebo?', 105, 135.

95 S. Claessens et al., 'The Separation of Ownership and Control in East Asian Corporations', *Journal of Financial Economics*, 58 (2000), 81, 102–103; Chapter 9 (Singapore) at III.2.

96 Velikonja, 'The Political Economy of Board Independence', 857.

97 Gopal, 'Japan: A Closer Look at Governance Reforms'.

98 ACGA and KPMG, *Balancing Rules and Flexibility* (2014), available at www.accaglobal.com.

Even in the face of this uncertainty, however, there are no statistics suggesting that any of Asia's leading economies have approached US-levels of having (or even labelling) the entire board, except for the CEO, as independent directors.

At least on a self-reporting basis (i.e., without definitional differences being scrutinised) and if the supervisory board members are not considered to be 'independent directors', it appears that the level of board independence varies widely across Asia's leading economies. On this basis, the typical board of a large listed company in India, Singapore and South Korea tends to report having a majority of 'independent directors'; in China and Hong Kong the typical board reports having one-third to half 'independent directors'; and in Japan and Taiwan the typical board reports having one or two 'independent directors'.[99]

In sum, there is a significant difference in the forms that 'independent directors' take in the US and Asia's leading economies. This difference is seen in the thinnest conception of form, as the American form focuses on independence from management; whereas, the form that has emerged in Asia's leading economies focuses on independence from management *and* significant shareholders. Magnifying this difference is the fact that the very nature of the positions that independent directors in Asia's leading economies occupy are in some jurisdictions fundamentally different than in the US. Moreover, the use of (or even complete reliance on, in the case of Japan) non-mandatory regulation of independent directors in many of Asia's leading economies is distinct from the reliance on mandatory regulation in the US. Finally, the unique and diverse characteristics and skills of independent directors and the smaller proportion of independent directors on boards further distinguish the form (and, as explained below, also the function) of the 'independent director' in Asia's leading economies from the US.

Perhaps more interesting is that there are important similarities and differences in the forms of the 'independent director' *within* Asia. The most salient intra-Asia similarity is that all of Asia's leading economies have gravitated towards a concept of the independent director designed to be independent from management *and* significant shareholders – which is clearly distinct from the American concept.[100] Despite this core

[99] *Ibid.*; Gopal, 'Japan: A Closer Look at Governance Reforms'.

[100] As Puchniak and Lan confirm empirically in Chapter 9 (Singapore) at II.2, the trend towards an 'un-American' form of the independent director is a global phenomenon that has been largely overlooked.

similarity, what has been almost entirely overlooked are the diverse varieties of forms of the 'independent director' in Asia, at least based on a thicker conception of form. In jurisdictions that mandate one-tier boards (i.e., Hong Kong, India, Singapore and South Korea) the positions occupied by independent directors are broadly comparable to the American form, at least in this aspect. However, in jurisdictions that permit non-one-tier boards (Japan, China, and Taiwan until 2018) the distinct nature of these positions complicates any direct comparison. There is also intra-Asia diversity in the non-mandatory (Japan), mandatory (China and South Korea) and hybrid mandatory/non-mandatory (Hong Kong, India, Singapore and Taiwan) approaches that exist in terms of implementing and regulating independent directors. Finally, there are similarities in the prominent characteristics and skills of independent directors among some of Asia's leading jurisdictions (e.g., in China, India, South Korea and Taiwan academics make up a sizable portion of independent directors), but not others – further highlighting varieties in the thicker conception of the form of independent directors in Asia's leading economies.

4 *The Functions of Independent Directors in Asia: Diverse Expectations Revealed*

There is an obvious link between the form that independent directors take and the function that they perform. As such, the significant differences between the forms of independent directors in Asia's leading economies and the US suggest that there are likely to be differences in their functions. Similarly, the diversity in the forms of independent directors among Asia's leading economies suggests that there is also likely to be functional diversity among independent directors within Asia. It cannot be assumed, however, that merely because independent directors have the same form that they will perform the same function, or that independent directors that have different forms will perform different functions. Indeed, as explained below, the unique and diverse contexts in each of Asia's leading economies suggest that the relationship between form and function is complex and highly jurisdiction-specific.

It is also important to remain cognisant of the difference between the function that independent directors are *expected* to perform and how independent directors *actually* function in practice. Although these two aspects of functionality are distinct, they are also interrelated. How independent directors are expected to function, may influence how they actually function and vice versa. For analytical purposes, however, it makes sense to bifurcate our comparative analysis by first examining the expected functions and then the actual functions of independent directors in Asia's leading economies and the US.

As explained above, since the genesis of the American independent director in the 1970s, the primary expected function of independent directors in the US has been clear: to monitor management on behalf of dispersed shareholders, who are hindered by collective action problems from monitoring management themselves.[101] By contrast, the primary expected function of independent directors in most of Asia's leading economies is to monitor controlling shareholders on behalf of minority shareholders, in order to mitigate the risk of the former extracting private benefits of control from the company.[102]

In China, India, Hong Kong, South Korea and Taiwan, the expectation that independent directors would primarily act as monitors of controlling shareholders is evident in the policy discussions and academic commentaries surrounding the adoption of independent directors in each jurisdiction.[103] This expectation is also evident in the inaugural definitions that these jurisdictions adopted for 'independence' which, as explained above, all generally provide that independent directors should be independent from significant shareholders.[104] Thus, although there are claims that some of these jurisdictions were inspired by the US concept of the independent director,[105] this inspiration appears to have had little or no influence on the actual details of the policy discussions and/or legislative drafting in terms of the

[101] See Chapter 1 at III.2.

[102] 'Private benefits of control (i.e., benefits that the controlling shareholder receives as a result of their controlling power, which are not provided to the minority shareholders). A common example of private benefits of control is when a controlling shareholder causes the company to sell a piece of its property, at below market value, to a company the controlling shareholder wholly owns. In such a case, the private benefit that the controlling shareholder receives increases proportionally as the percentage of the controlling shareholder's equity stake in the company decreases. In this common example, the controlling shareholder can be seen to have used her controlling power to extract a financial benefit from the company that was greater than the proportion of her equity stake.' Puchniak, 'Multiple Faces of Shareholder Power in Asia', 527. See also R. J. Gilson and J. N. Gordon, 'Controlling Controlling Shareholders', *University of Pennsylvania Law Review*, 152 (2004), 785.

[103] See Chapter 5 (South Korea) at III.1 and III.2.b; Chapter 6 (China) at II.1; Chapter 7 (Taiwan) at III.3.a; Chapter 8 (Hong Kong) at II.2 and II.4, Chapter 10 (India) at V.1 and V.2.

[104] See Chapter 5 (South Korea) at III.2.b; Chapter 6 (China) at III.3; Chapter 7 (Taiwan) at II.1; Chapter 8 (Hong Kong) at II.2; Chapter 10 (India) at V.2.

[105] See Chapter 7 (Taiwan) at I.

function that independent directors were (and are) expected to actually perform in these jurisdictions.

In this context, Japan and Singapore are outliers among Asia's leading economies as independent directors in both countries have *not* historically been expected to play almost any role in monitoring controlling shareholders. This is clear in the policy discussions and academic commentaries surrounding the adoption of independent directors in both countries.[106] Also, as explained above, notably in both countries the inaugural definitions for 'independence' did *not* require independence from significant shareholders.[107] In fact, in Singapore, the policy committee and regulatory authority made it explicitly clear that the primary expected function of independent directors was to act as managerial-monitors – but not monitors of controlling shareholders.[108]

The policy debates surrounding the adoption of independent directors in Singapore suggest that another important reason for their adoption was to send a signal to international investors that Singapore has 'good' corporate governance.[109] It appears that in several of Asia's leading economies there was (and still is) an expectation among government officials and companies that the adoption of independent directors will function as an important signal of 'good' corporate governance to domestic and international investors.[110] For reasons explained in section III below, however, it appears that this function of independent directors was likely of greater importance in Singapore and lesser importance in Japan, at least in comparison to other leading Asian economies.

Further, some civil law jurisdictions adopted independent directors to address the specific shortcomings of the supervisory board or its local equivalent under their respective corporate law regimes. In China and Taiwan, where double boards are permitted, the primary motivation for the adoption of independent directors was to address the perceived failure of their supervisory boards.[111] In South Korea, the inaugural mandatory independent regime replaced the traditional statutory auditors with an audit committee composed primarily of independent directors in large

[106] See Chapter 4 (Japan) at III.1; Chapter 9 (Singapore) at II.3 and II.4.

[107] See Chapter 4 (Japan) at III.1; Chapter 9 (Singapore) at II.3 and II.4.

[108] See Chapter 9 (Singapore) at II.4.

[109] See Chapter 9 (Singapore) at II.4.

[110] See Chapter 4 (Japan) at III.1; Chapter 5 (South Korea) at III.1; Chapter 8 (Hong Kong) at II.4; Chapter 10 (India) at V.1.

[111] See Chapter 6 (China) at II.2; Chapter 7 (Taiwan) at II.1.

listed companies.[112] In Japan, independent directors were expected to address the perceived failure of the board of statutory auditors to effectively monitor traditional lifetime-employee-dominated 'management boards' in large Japanese companies. Japan's inaugural independent director system encouraged companies to adopt an 'American-style' one-tier board with sub-committees, under which a board of statutory auditors was not (and is still not) permitted.[113] By contrast, in China, independent directors are expected to function as members of the management board who act as complementary monitors (and not substitute monitors) to the supervisory board – with the supervisory board still monitoring the independent directors and the other members of the management board.[114]

Another important driver of the adoption and reforms of Japan's independent director system has been the government's desire to signal its effective management of Japan's economic malaise.[115] There is considerable evidence in other leading Asian economies (and the US and EU) that governments – especially in the wake of poor economic performance and/or a financial crisis – often implement legislation with the aim of encouraging independent directors to signal effective political governance.[116] Although governments in several of Asia's leading economies (and the US and EU) have implemented and reformed their independent director regimes with the expectation that they will function as a signal of effective political governance, for reasons explained below, this expected function appears to have been particularly salient in the evolution of Japan's independent director system.[117]

Finally, it is important to note that Japan and Singapore have recently reformed their independent director systems with the expectation that one of the functions of their independent directors will be to monitor

[112] See Chapter 5 (South Korea) at III.1.b; K. S. Kim, 'Transplanting Audit Committees to Korean Soil: A Window into the Evolution of Korean Corporate Governance', *Asian-Pacific Law and Policy Journal*, 9 (2007), 163, 164.

[113] See Chapter 4 (Japan) at II.1; Puchniak, 'The 2002 Reform of the Management of Large Corporations in Japan', 49–56; Gilson and Milhaupt, 'Choice as Regulatory Reform', 352–353.

[114] See Chapter 6 (China) at II.2 and III.4.d; J. Zhao, 'Comparative Study of U.S. and German Corporate Governance: Suggestions on the Relationship between Independent Directors and the Supervisory Board of Listed Companies in China', *Michigan State Journal of International Law*, 18 (2010), 495, 506–507, 507 n. 76 (observing that the functions of independent directors in this context are 'more operable and direct').

[115] See Chapter 4 (Japan) at III.2.

[116] See Chapter 2 at II; Chapter 5 (South Korea) at III.1; Chapter 8 (Hong Kong) at II.4; Chapter 9 (Singapore) at II.4.

[117] See Chapter 4 (Japan) at III.2.

controlling shareholders.[118] Although the reforms in both countries have been cautious and limited,[119] they suggest a movement towards Asia's other leading economies (and away from the US) as independent directors are increasingly being seen as a corporate governance mechanism which is expected to monitor controlling shareholders.[120]

In sum, it appears that the expected functions of independent directors in Asia's leading economies differ significantly from the US. The main point of divergence is that in most of Asia's leading economies the primary expected function of independent directors is to monitor controlling shareholders, whereas in the US this is not the case. Within Asia, jurisdictions that currently allow or previously allowed double boards, have expected independent directors to either complement or substitute for ineffective supervisory boards – distinguishing them from common law jurisdictions which historically have had one-tier board structures. Finally, although the expectation that independent directors will function as a signal of 'good' corporate governance and/or political effectiveness appears to exist in many of Asia's leading economies, the importance of these functions appears to vary from jurisdiction to jurisdiction in Asia (and, we suspect, elsewhere).

5 *The Actual Functions of Independent Directors in Asia: Empirical Ambiguity and Contextual Idiosyncrasy*

Determining whether the expected functions of independent directors are actually put into practice is extremely difficult and complex. At the most general level, the question that is often asked to determine whether independent directors have fulfilled their expected functions has been similar in most jurisdictions: do independent directors improve corporate performance? Despite the widespread adoption of 'independent directors' and a litany of empirical studies, there is a surprising absence of clear empirical evidence in the United States, the EU and Asia that independent directors actually improve corporate performance.[121]

118 See Chapter 4 (Japan) at II.1.c and Chapter 9 (Singapore) at IV.2.

119 See Chapter 9 (Singapore) at IV.2 (observing that the Singapore's definition of 'independence' is likely to bring about a functional rather than substantive change).

120 See Chapter 9 (Singapore) at V.

121 See, for example, Chapter 1 at V; Chapter 2 at II.2 and IV.2; Velikonja, 'The Political Economy of Board Independence', 855, 859–860, 868–872; S. Bhagat and B. S. Black, 'The Non-Correlation between Board Independence and Long-Term Firm Performance', *Journal of Corporation Law*, 27 (2002), 231, 239; Y. Miwa and J. M. Ramseyer, 'Who Appoints Them, What Do They Do? Evidence on Outside Directors from Japan', *Journal of Economics and Management Strategy*, 14 (2005), 299.

In Asia, on balance, most of the empirical evidence has failed to find a definitive link between independent directors and corporate performance.[122] However, there are a few empirical studies in Japan,[123] Hong Kong[124] and South Korea[125] that suggest that independent directors, in certain situations, may improve corporate performance.[126] Considering that the extensive empirical research on independent directors in the US has been unable to produce clear evidence that independent directors improve corporate performance, it is unsurprising that such evidence remains elusive in Asia. Moreover, as explained above, the diversity in the form and function of 'independent directors' within Asia suggests that any interjurisdictional attempt to evaluate the impact of independent directors across Asia will be fraught with methodical problems and compromised by the interjurisdictional diversity in the form and function of independent directors.[127]

It should be noted that most of the research that considers the effectiveness of independent directors has examined their impact at the firm level – but not the jurisdictional level.[128] There has been little

[122] See Chapter 9 (Singapore) at II.1; Chapter 10 (India) at IV.1; see also A. K. Garg, 'Influence of Board Size and Independence on Firm Performance: A Study of Indian Companies', *Vikalpa*, 32 (2007) 39; Ibrahim and Samad, 'Corporate Governance Mechanisms and Performance of Public-Listed Family-Ownership in Malaysia'; Prabowo and Simpson, 'Independent Directors and Firm Performance in Family Controlled Firms: Evidence from Indonesia'.

[123] See Chapter 4 (Japan) at III.1.

[124] See Chapter 8 (Hong Kong) at III.4; A. Lei and D. Deng, 'Do Multiple Directorships Increase Firm Value? Evidence from Independent Directors in Hong Kong', *Journal of International Financial Management and Accounting*, 25(2) (2014), 121; see also F. Cheng, 'Corporate Governance in Hong Kong: An Empirical Study of the Effects of Independent Non-Executive Directors on Voluntary Corporate Disclosures and Adoption of Best Corporate Governance Practices' (City University of Hong Kong Institutional Repository, 2011) available at http://dspace.cityu.edu.hk; B. Jaggi and J. Tsui, 'Insider Trading Earnings Management and Corporate Governance: Empirical Evidence Based on Hong Kong Firms', *Journal of International Financial Management and Accounting*, 18(3) (2007), 192.

[125] B. S. Black et al., 'Methods for Multicountry Studies of Corporate Governance: Evidence from the BRIKT Countries', *Journal of Econometrics*, 183 (2014), 230.

[126] See Chapter 4 (Japan) at III.1; Chapter 5 (South Korea) at IV.1.

[127] See II.3 and II.4 above.

[128] See, for example, Bhagat and Black, 'The Non-Correlation between Board Independence and Long-Term Firm Performance', 231–274 (surveying 934 of the largest US firms from 1985 to 1995); Gordon, 'The Rise of Independent Directors in the United States', 1465–1568 (reviewing overall trends in board composition in US public companies from 1950 to 2005).

empirical analysis on whether adopting independent directors, which may improve the image of a jurisdiction's corporate governance, has a positive macroeconomic impact. In addition, there has been limited analysis on whether the use of regulations promoting independent directors as a signal of good political governance is actually an effective political strategy.[129]

Perhaps even more interesting are the idiosyncratic and unanticipated functions that independent directors have come to perform in Asia's leading economies. Partially as a result of pressure from the IMF following the Asian Financial Crisis, South Korea adopted mandatory legislation, which now requires the boards of all large listed companies to have a majority of independent directors.[130] There has been an increasing trend to fill these mandatory independent director positions with ex-government officials so that they can function as government lobbyists.[131] It is suggested that a reason that independent directors may be increasingly fulfilling this function in South Korea is because Korean law strictly prohibits companies from retaining professional government lobbyists – driving companies to fill the mandated 'independent director' positions with clandestine government lobbyists.[132]

In Japan, there is evidence that when the inaugural independent director system was adopted that the loose definition for independence allowed companies in *keiretsu* groups to fill 'independent director' positions with senior management from other *keiretsu*-affiliated companies. The reason suggested for this behaviour was that it allowed *keiretsu*-affiliated companies to signal 'good' corporate governance, while at the same time reinforcing their corporate group links.[133] This is the direct opposite of the role that scholars and policymakers in other jurisdictions expect independent directors to play in group companies.[134]

[129] See, for example, Chapter 2 at II.3; Chapter 4 (Japan) at III.2; Velikonja, 'The Political Economy of Board Independence', 855, 892–915 (arguing that reforms directed at improving board independence has displaced substantive reform following corporate crises or scandals).

[130] See Chapter 5 (South Korea) at III.2.

[131] See Chapter 5 (South Korea) at IV.4.

[132] See Chapter 5 (South Korea) at IV.4.

[133] Lawley, 'Panacea or Placebo?', 117–119, 135.

[134] This was precisely the intended role for independent directors in respect of South Korea's *chaebols* (i.e., corporate groups): Chapter 5 (South Korea) at III.1.a and III.1.b; A. C. Pritchard, 'Monitoring of Corporate Groups by Independent Directors', *Journal of Korean Law*, 9 (2009), 1, 18–19 (opining that independent directors should constrain the power of controlling shareholders in South Korea's *chaebols*).

In Singapore, there is empirical evidence that its inaugural American-style definition of independence allowed family-controlled firms (Family Firms) to systematically appoint family friends as independent directors. This allowed Family Firms to signal their compliance with 'good' corporate governance, while effectively preserving the status quo of family controllers dominating the corporate governance in such firms.[135] However, there is qualitative evidence that suggests that these family-friendly directors have in some cases served a valuable function in Family Firms by acting as trusted mediators between family member block shareholders in family-shareholder disputes.[136] Conversely, in Singapore's Government Linked Companies, independent directors appear to play a purely managerial-monitoring role as Singapore's unique institutional architecture has purposefully limited the ability of the government to exercise its full powers as a controlling shareholder.[137] This demonstrates that even within a single jurisdiction independent directors may function differently in companies with different types of shareholders – something which there is also evidence of in India.[138]

There are more examples in this book of unique, jurisdiction-specific, functions that independent directors have come to play in each of Asia's leading economies. What these examples make clear, is that there is a litany of diverse, idiosyncratic, jurisdiction-specific functions that are carried out by 'independent directors' in Asia's leading economies. These functions would have been beyond the wildest dreams of Professor Eisenberg, the 'founding father' of the (American) independent director in the 1970s.[139] Interestingly, the actual functions that 'independent directors' in Asia's leading economies now perform are a far cry from Eisenberg's conception of independent directors as monitors of management on behalf of dispersed shareholders.[140]

[135] See Chapter 9 (Singapore) at III.2; Y. T. Mak and T. Ng, 'Independent Directors: A Well-Functioning Market', *Business Times*, 16 September 2010.

[136] See Chapter 9 (Singapore) at III.2; W. Ng and J. Roberts, '"Helping the Family": The Mediating Role of Outside Directors in Ethnic Chinese Family Firms', *Human Relations*, 60 (2007), 285.

[137] See Chapter 9 (Singapore) at III.3.

[138] See Chapter 10 (India) at II

[139] M. A. Eisenberg, *The Structure of the Corporation: A Legal Analysis* (Little, Brown and Co., 1976).

[140] See Chapter 1 at III.2; Chapter 9 (Singapore) at II.1.

III Understanding the Diverse Varieties of Independent Directors in Asia: A Taxonomy

1 Building the Foundation for a Loose Taxonomy of Independent Directors in Asia

The revelation that *none* of Asia's leading economies have adopted the American concept of the independent director in form and function calls into question some of the most influential comparative corporate governance indices and research, which assume the opposite to be true.[141] An awareness of the varieties in the forms and functions of independent directors *within* Asia is an important reminder that local context is central to corporate governance, which undermines a prominent movement in comparative corporate governance to develop universal theories.[142] However, it is easier to demonstrate that an American-centric (universal) understanding of the 'independent director' in Asia is flawed, than to explain why diverse (un-American) varieties of independent directors have developed. Nevertheless, understanding this development is important as it provides an avenue for improving comparative analyses of independent directors in Asia which, as explained below, has significant practical and theoretical value.

An in-depth comparative analysis of the jurisdiction-specific chapters in this book reveals that there are six principal factors that help explain the evolution of independent directors in Asia (which are ranked generally in their approximate order of importance): (1) shareholder ownership structures; (2) legal origin; (3) types of shareholders; (4) functional substitutes; (5) political economy; and (6) cultural norms. Understanding how each of these factors has shaped the development of independent directors in Asia illuminates the similarities among certain aspects in the forms and functions of independent directors in Asia, and provides meaningful avenues for comparative analyses. Conversely, examining these six factors also highlights the distinct nature of the varieties

[141] See note 27 above.

[142] See, for example, Chapter 13 at II (explaining how the development of independent directors in Asia challenges the 'convergence in corporate governance' theory); D. W. Puchniak, 'The Complexity of Derivative Actions in Asia: An Inconvenient Truth' in D. W. Puchniak et al. (eds.), *The Derivative Action in Asia: A Comparative and Functional Approach* (Cambridge University Press, 2012), 124–127; D. W. Puchniak, 'The Derivative Action in Asia: A Complex Reality', *Berkeley Business Law Journal*, 9 (2013), 1, 24–28. See also, P. Legrand, 'Noted Publications: Puchniak, Dan W., Harald

of independent directors in Asia; this helps to explain why comparisons between independent directors in the US and Asia often have limited value, and why nuanced comparisons between independent directors among certain Asian jurisdictions on particular issues may produce useful insights.

These six factors provide an explanation for the evolution of varieties of independent directors in Asia and the foundation for developing a loose taxonomy of independent directors in Asia. This taxonomy, which is described in more detail below, allows for tailored interjurisdictional comparisons, which focus on categories (or subcategories) of the different varieties of independent directors in multiple Asian jurisdictions that share similar forms and/or functions – thus lending themselves to more meaningful comparative analyses. Ultimately, as illustrated below, systematic identification of comparable varieties of independent directors in Asia results in comparative research that produces more accurate and insightful results, which is one of the goals of this book.

2 *The Six Principal Factors Driving the Varieties of Independent Directors in Asia*

The first factor, which appears to have played the strongest role in the un-American evolution of independent directors in Asia, is the difference in the shareholder ownership structures between listed companies in the US and Asia's leading economies.[143] As explained above, the managerial-monitoring model of the independent director in the US was created to address the collective action problems which are inherent in companies with dispersed shareholders.[144] In the context of American corporate governance, the evolution of the managerial-monitoring model of the independent director makes perfect sense as public companies with dispersed shareholders have traditionally predominated in the US.[145]

Baum and Michael Ewing-Chow (eds.). The Derivative Action in Asia. Cambridge, Cambridge University Press, 2012', *Journal of Comparative Law*, 7 (2012), 347.

143 Most of the jurisdictions surveyed in this book are dominated by companies with concentrated ownership. See Chapter 5 (South Korea) at II.3; Chapter 6 (China) at I and II.1; Chapter 7 (Taiwan) at II.4; Chapter 8 (Hong Kong) at II.4; Chapter 9 (Singapore) at I; Chapter 10 (India) at II.3.

144 See II.2 above.

145 However, the increased involvement of institutional investors complicates this characterisation: R. J. Gilson and J. N. Gordon, 'The Agency Costs of Agency Capitalism: Activist Investors and the Revaluation of Governance Rights', *Columbia Law Review*, 113 (2013), 863.

However, in all of Asia's leading economies – with the notable exception of Japan[146] – most companies have a concentrated shareholder structure.[147] This reorients the primary agency problem in listed companies from managerial rent seeking to block shareholders extracting private benefits of control.[148] Most policymakers in Asia's leading economies appear to be acutely aware of this difference between corporate governance in the US and Asia, and have clearly recognised the function of the independent director as a monitor of controlling shareholders in their respective jurisdictions.[149]

The US independent director was neither intended nor designed to address agency problems arising from concentrated shareholder ownership.[150] This raises a critical question: are independent directors well-suited to function as a mechanism for monitoring significant shareholders to mitigate private benefits of control? It is difficult for an independent director to be an independent monitor of the very shareholders who can appoint and remove her. Ensuring that independent directors are actually independent from majority and/or controlling shareholders is a common issue raised in most of the jurisdiction-specific chapters[151] – illustrating the value of interjurisdictional comparisons of independent directors *within* Asia as a method for identifying and analysing critical issues that may improve their effectiveness.

Taiwan is the only Asian jurisdiction examined in this book that has attempted to address this problem directly by requiring mandatory cumulative voting, but it appears that this has been largely ineffective in creating meaningful independence from the controlling shareholders.[152] Given the flaws inherent in majority shareholder rule, it is curious that Taiwan has been the only jurisdiction to make a serious attempt at finding an alternative mechanism for appointing independent directors.[153]

146 See Chapter 4 (Japan) at II.3.

147 See Chapter 5 (South Korea) at II.3; Chapter 6 (China) at II.1; Chapter 7 (Taiwan) at II.4; Chapter 8 (Hong Kong) at II.4; Chapter 9 (Singapore) at I; Chapter 10 (India) at II.

148 Kraakman et al., *The Anatomy of Corporate Law*, 307–309.

149 See note 103 above.

150 See Chapter 1 at V.

151 See Chapter 6 (China) at III; Chapter 7 (Taiwan) at IV; Chapter 8 (Hong Kong) at III.2; Chapter 10 (India) at II.

152 See Chapter 7 (Taiwan) at II.3.

153 The corporate statutes of South Korea do require cumulative voting, but allow a firm to opt out of it by putting a provision in the articles of incorporation (Korean Commercial Code Art. 382-2(1)). An overwhelming majority of listed firms have opted out of cumulative voting.

Unfortunately, the reasons behind Taiwan's failure to effectively reform its shareholder voting system are still unclear – suggesting that future comparative research on this issue would be valuable.[154]

The second factor that appears to have driven the evolution of varieties of independent directors in Asia is the legal origins of Asia's leading economies and, perhaps more importantly, the origins of the specific provisions regulating each jurisdiction's particular independent director regime (which often appear to be distinct from the jurisdiction's general legal origin or 'legal family'). As explained above, board structure impacts significantly the forms that independent directors take and functions that they perform.[155] All of Asia's leading economies with civil law origins (i.e., China, Japan, South Korea and Taiwan) have historically permitted non-one-tier boards; whereas, all of Asia's leading economies with common law origins (i.e., Hong Kong, India and Singapore) have traditionally required (and still require) one-tier boards.[156] At first blush, this suggests that it may make sense to bifurcate comparative analyses according to the jurisdiction's civil law and common law origins.

However, a more in-depth analysis suggests that such an approach would be flawed. The importance of the *general* origins of a jurisdiction's legal system and/or company law are often usurped by the legal origin of the *specific* corporate governance provision and/or reform being examined. US law had a clear influence on reforms to implement one-tier boards in Japan (optional, from 2003),[157] South Korea (mandatory, from 2000)[158] and Taiwan (mandatory, from 2018).[159] Post-reform, the form and function of independent directors in these historically civil law jurisdictions became more comparable with independent directors in historically common law jurisdictions.[160] In a similar vein, as might be expected, the use of a UK-style code of corporate governance, which employs an optional 'comply or explain' approach, was first adopted in Asia's leading economies with Commonwealth origins (i.e., Hong Kong

[154] One possible solution would be to grant a third-party *locus standi* to nominate directors: Tan, 'Corporate Governance and Independent Directors', 385–386.
[155] See II.3 above.
[156] See Chapter 8 (Hong Kong) at I; S. Mehrotra, 'Corporate Board Structure in the United States and India: A Comparative View', *Indian Journal of Corporate Governance*, 8 (2015), 166, 167.
[157] See Chapter 4 (Japan) at II.1.a.
[158] See Chapter 5 (South Korea) at III.1.b.
[159] See Chapter 7 (Taiwan) at II.1.
[160] See Chapter 4 (Japan) at II.1.a; Chapter 5 (South Korea) at II.1 and II.4; Chapter 7 (Taiwan) at IV.1.

(from 2005) and Singapore (from 2001)).[161] However, in 2015, Japan – a country with a civil law legal origin and no strong historical connection to the Commonwealth – adopted a code of corporate governance based on the UK 'comply or explain' model.[162]

In sum, although the civil law and common law legal origins of Asia's leading economies are not irrelevant, classifying independent director regimes for the purpose of comparison solely along these lines would be misguided. However, it appears that there is value in tracing the origins of a *specific* provision back to its source. Such a tailored approach may provide useful grounds for comparison with the source provision (e.g., comparing the effectiveness of 'comply or explain' codes for promoting independent directors in Japan and the UK) and/or with other jurisdictions that also trace the origin of a specific provision to the same source (e.g., comparing the effectiveness of 'comply or explain' codes for promoting independent directors in Hong Kong, India, Singapore and, now, Japan).

The third factor that appears to have driven the evolution of varieties of independent directors in Asia are the different types of shareholders that exist in Asia's leading economies.[163] In all of Asia's leading economies – with the notable exception of Japan – a significant portion of listed companies are Family Firms, where family members are the controlling shareholders.[164] There is empirical evidence from Singapore that independent directors in Family Firms tend to be family friends.[165] However, qualitative evidence suggests that these family friends often use their unique position as trusted non-family members to play a valuable role mediating intra-family shareholder disputes.[166] The uniqueness of the expected and/or actual function of independent directors in Family Firms may be amplified by the sometimes different incentives for family-member controlling shareholders compared to other controlling shareholders (e.g., family-controllers may want to pass on a successful business to future generations – something often particularly prized in Asian cultures – which may mitigate the risk of excessive private benefits of control).[167] This suggests

[161] See Chapter 8 (Hong Kong) at II.4; Chapter 9 (Singapore) at II.4.

[162] See Chapter 4 (Japan) at II.1.c.

[163] Puchniak, 'Multiple Faces of Shareholder Power in Asia', 514.

[164] See Chapter 5 (South Korea) at II.3; Chapter 7 (Taiwan) at II.4; Chapter 8 (Hong Kong) at II.4; Chapter 9 (Singapore) at III.2; Chapter 10 (India) at II.

[165] See Chapter 9 (Singapore) at III.2.

[166] See note 136 above.

[167] W. Ng and J. Roberts, '"Helping the Family": The Mediating Role of Outside Directors in Ethnic Chinese Family Firms', 285, 287, 307; Puchniak, 'Multiple Faces of Shareholder

that further research on the role of independent directors in Family Firms may be particularly valuable for Asia's leading economies.

A prominent feature in China, Hong Kong, India and Singapore, which distinguishes these jurisdictions from the US and other leading Asian economies, is the importance of listed companies that have the government as their controlling shareholder (Government Controlled Companies – GCCs).[168] In GCCs, there is the additional agency problem of the state trying to use its controlling shareholder power for political gain. This creates the conundrum of how 'independence' should be defined in GCCs, as excluding otherwise competent independent directors on the basis of their political affiliations would seem unworkable, and may often be undesirable (as shown in the Singapore chapter).[169] There is no evidence that China, Hong Kong, India or Singapore have attempted to *directly* address this unique agency problem or even consider whether independent directors should (or could) play an effective role in limiting political meddling in board decisions in GCCs. Singapore appears to have successfully addressed this agency problem indirectly by creating an institutional architecture that limits the government's power as a controlling shareholder – a model which China has considered transplanting.[170] This suggests that further comparative research on the function that independent directors should (or could) play in jurisdictions with GCCs may produce valuable insights for several of Asia's leading economies.

Foreign shareholders are another type of shareholder that has influenced the evolution of the independent director in Asia's leading economies. Several jurisdiction-specific chapters note the desire to attract foreign investors as an impetus for adopting independent directors to signal 'good' corporate governance.[171] The influence of foreign shareholders appears to be at least partially contingent on the size and developmental

Power in Asia', 530–531. It should be noted that in many non-Asian cultures there is a strong cultural norm to pass businesses onto children. However, increasingly there are prominent examples in the US where the opposite norm seems to be emerging – with the efforts by Warren Buffett and Bill Gates to encourage wealthy individuals to pass on most of their wealth to charity (and not their children) as perhaps the most prominent example. The question is whether this cultural norm is stronger in Asia's leading economies with Family Firms and, if so, what the implications may be.

168 See Chapter 6 (China) at II.1; Chapter 8 (Hong Kong) at II.4; Chapter 9 (Singapore) at III.3; Chapter 10 (India) at II.3.

169 See Chapter 9 (Singapore) at III.3.

170 C. H. Tan et al., 'State-Owned Enterprises in Singapore: Historical Insights into a Potential Model for Reform', *Columbia Journal of Asian Law*, 28 (2015) 61, 62–63.

171 See Chapter 4 (Japan) at II.1.c; Chapter 5 (South Korea) at III; Chapter 8 (Hong Kong) at II.4; Chapter 9 (Singapore) at II.4 and IV.1.

state of the respective economy – with the smaller and less developed economies appearing to respond more to their influence.[172]

Finally, the use of cross-shareholding and pyramid structures appears to have a significant impact on the function of independent directors in Japan and South Korea respectively – adding an important and unique element to their respective independent director regimes. Based on a purely empirical analysis, the shareholding structure of Japan's large public companies is as dispersed as the UK and US.[173] However, as a result of stable/cross-shareholding networks, lifetime-employee manager-directors who have indirect control over large blocks of shares, have dominated the governance of most public listed companies in post-war Japan.[174] This has created a unique corporate governance environment, which suggests that the role of independent directors in Japan's empirically dispersed shareholder environment is not only clearly different from the US, but also likely distinct from Asia's other leading economies.[175] The use of pyramid shareholding structures in South Korea has created a situation where cash flow and control rights are perhaps more unbalanced than in any of Asia's other leading economies.[176] This type of shareholding may also present unique challenges for its independent directors – something that could benefit from comparative analysis with other jurisdictions that have pyramidal ownership structures.[177]

The fourth factor that has driven the evolution of the varieties of independent directors in Asia is the functional substitutes for independent directors that vary across Asia's leading economies and distinguish them from the US and UK. Perhaps the most discussed functional substitute in Asia's leading economies is the board of statutory auditors (*kansayaku*) in Japan. As mentioned above, it has been argued that *kansayaku* essentially fulfil the same function as independent directors – a point that has

[172] Compare Singapore's embrace of independent directors to signal compliance with global corporate governance norms, with Japan's considerably more gradual acceptance of independent directors: Chapter 4 (Japan); Chapter 9 (Singapore).

[173] Kraakman et al., *The Anatomy of Corporate Law*, 29; Puchniak, 'Multiple Faces of Shareholder Power in Asia', 523–524.

[174] Lawley, 'Panacea or Placebo?', 135.

[175] Gilson and Milhaupt, 'Choice as Regulatory Reform', 360–362.

[176] See Chapter 5 (South Korea) at II.3; K. Kim, 'Dynamics of Shareholder Power in Korea' in J. Hill and R. Thomas (eds.), *Research Handbook on Shareholder Power* (Edward Elgar, 2015), 536–540 (a short description of unique aspects of ownership structure in South Korea).

[177] Claessens et al., 'The Separation of Ownership and Control in East Asian Corporations', 81–112 (comparing shareholding structures in South Korea to other Asian jurisdictions).

been made with some success by various interest groups as a rationale for resisting mandatory requirements for independent directors in Japan.[178] A similar argument could be made in Asia's other leading economies, which have historically permitted or required non-one-tier boards (i.e., China, South Korea and Taiwan).[179] However, for various reasons, this argument has been less persuasive in these other jurisdictions: in China, mandatory legislation requiring independent directors was implemented in 2001, despite companies having supervisory boards;[180] in South Korea, strict mandatory independent director requirements were implemented in 2000 for large listed companies, replacing statutory auditors which could have been maintained as a possible functional substitute for independent directors;[181] and in Taiwan, one-tier boards with independent directors will be mandatory for listed companies from 2018, extinguishing the option for companies to have boards of statutory auditors as a functional substitute for independent directors.[182]

Another interesting functional substitute, which was mentioned above, is Singapore's institutional architecture that is designed to constrain the government's power as a controlling shareholder in GCCs. This institutional architecture has largely succeeded in preventing the government from using its controlling shareholder power to extract private benefits or influence GCCs for short-term political gain.[183] This success helped Singapore justify its use of the American definition of independence (i.e., requiring independence from management, but not significant shareholders) despite having a highly concentrated shareholder environment – while simultaneously increasing its reputation for 'good' corporate governance.[184]

It is clear that the *existence* of functional substitutes has had jurisdiction-specific effects, which magnify the diversity among the varieties of independent directors in Asia. In addition, the *absence* of well-recognised functional substitutes and complements for independent directors also distinguishes independent director regimes in Asia from the

178 See note 82 above.

179 See Chapter 5 (South Korea) at II.4; Chapter 6 (China) at II.2; Chapter 7 (Taiwan) at II.1.

180 See Chapter 6 (China) at II.2.

181 See Chapter 5 (South Korea) at III.1.

182 See Chapter 7 (Taiwan) at II.1 (stating that all listed companies must appoint at least two independent directors by 31 December 2017).

183 See Chapter 9 (Singapore) at III.3. It should be noted that the classic explanation of 'private benefits of control' arguably does not fit well in the context of GCCs. For a detailed explanation of this issue see, Puchniak, 'Multiple Faces of Shareholder Power in Asia', 526–532.

184 See Chapter 9 (Singapore) at III.2.

US and UK. According to the (Anglo)American-cum-global norms of 'good' corporate governance, the existence of hostile takeovers, shareholder litigation and proxy contests are commonly seen as corporate governance mechanisms that complement independent directors.[185] The relative weakness or absence of these complementary corporate governance mechanisms in Asia's leading economies suggests that independent directors may be even more crucial to attain 'good' corporate governance in Asia than in the US or UK.[186]

However, evidence from this chapter demonstrates that such reasoning is likely misguided, as it erroneously assumes that the functions of independent directors in Asia and the UK–US are the same – when, as demonstrated in this chapter, they are clearly not. Although hostile takeovers, shareholder litigation and proxy contests may be seen to complement the managerial-monitoring function, which is of paramount importance for independent directors in the US and UK, the importance of managerial-monitoring in Asia's controlling-shareholder dominated corporate governance environment is not as acute. This suggests that while there may be meaningful comparative lessons to draw from certain functional substitutes based on targeted comparisons within Asia, comparing functional substitutes between Asia and the UK–US may be of limited value or even misleading.

The fifth factor that has driven the evolution of varieties of independent directors in Asia is the unique and diverse political economies that exist in Asia's leading economies. In South Korea, strict mandatory legislation requiring half of the boards of large companies to be independent was a condition of an IMF bailout – which, in the 1990s, South Korea desperately required as a result of the Asian Financial Crisis.[187] Interestingly, however, it is suggested in the Korean chapter that the Korean government was more supportive of the strict mandatory requirement 'imposed' by the IMF than what may have been assumed. Indeed, it appears that there 'were factions in the government that may have wanted to use the political capital provided by the IMF to curtail the power of the *chaebol*, which would have been unthinkable prior to the financial crisis'.[188]

In several of Asia's leading economies, there appear to be political struggles between the government, corporate lobbyists and sometimes

[185] Puchniak, 'Multiple Faces of Shareholder Power in Asia', 512, 516.
[186] *Ibid.*, 515–520.
[187] See Chapter 5 (South Korea) at III.1.a.
[188] See Chapter 5 (South Korea) at III.1.b.

other interest groups, situations which often have unique jurisdiction-specific effects on how each jurisdiction's independent director regime evolves.[189] Perhaps one of the most interesting and complex examples is the domestic politics which uniquely shaped the independent director's evolution in Japan. As described in the Japan chapter, the ambitions of political operatives and parties, the informal custom of requiring consensus on government committees and powerful business lobbies resulted in a battle over whether to require a single independent director on the boards of listed companies.[190] In the end, Japan's political economy provides valuable insight into why mandatory legislation requiring even a single independent director was unattainable and a watered-down 'comply or explain' code of corporate governance was eventually adopted.[191]

Although the effects of each jurisdiction's political economy vary, there are interesting common trends that can be distilled from the jurisdiction-specific chapters. It appears that in most of Asia's leading jurisdictions (with the notable exception of South Korea), stock exchanges have been heavily involved in lobbying the government to implement more stringent independent director requirements.[192] This makes sense as exchanges may benefit from signalling to the world that they are in compliance with (Anglo)American-cum-global norms of 'good' corporate governance.[193] In addition, it appears that incumbent political parties often initiate or support proposals to strengthen independent director legislation, especially in the wake of a financial crisis.[194] This may be motivated by the fact that implementing 'independent director' requirements is normally a relatively inexpensive and straightforward way for the government to signal that it is taking action to strengthen the economy without actually fundamentally changing the system.[195] Conversely, it appears that business lobbyists in most jurisdictions tend to oppose strengthening independent director regulation as they may remove power from the

[189] See Chapter 4 (Japan) at II.1 and III.2; Chapter 5 (South Korea) at III.1; Chapter 8 (Hong Kong) at II.4; Chapter 9 (Singapore) at II.4.

[190] See Chapter 4 (Japan) at III.2.

[191] See Chapter 4 (Japan) at III.2.b.

[192] See Chapter 4 (Japan) at II.1.b; Chapter 6 (China) at II.2; Chapter 7 (Taiwan) at II; Chapter 8 (Hong Kong) at II.4; Chapter 10 (India) at III.

[193] See Chapter 4 (Japan) at II.1.b; Chapter 6 (China) at II.2; Chapter 7 (Taiwan) at II; Chapter 8 (Hong Kong) at II.4; Chapter 10 (India) at III.

[194] Velikonja, 'The Political Economy of Board Independence', 855, 892–893, 899.

[195] See Chapter 4 (Japan) at II.1.d; Chapter 6 (China) at II.2; Chapter 7 (Taiwan) at II; Chapter 8 (Hong Kong) at II.4; Chapter 9 (Singapore) at II.4; Chapter 10 (India) at III.

corporate management and/or controlling shareholders, which are the groups represented by the lobbyists.[196]

The sixth factor that has driven the evolution of the varieties of independent directors in Asia is cultural norms. In Japan, the post-war insider-dominated lifetime-employee corporate culture has likely played an important role in its outlier position as the only jurisdiction with no mandatory law regulating independent directors, and in corporate Japan's long resistance to having any independent directors on corporate boards.[197] In Singapore, the cultural norm in the ethnic Chinese business community of preserving wealth for future generations appears to limit family controllers' extraction of private benefits of control – potentially providing a functional substitute for or complement to the monitoring function of independent directors in Family Firms.[198] In China, India, South Korea and Taiwan, the deep culture of respect for teachers may provide some explanation for the high percentage of professors among independent directors on corporate boards.[199]

These examples suggest that cultural norms have played a role in the evolution of independent directors in Asia and that their impact may vary across jurisdictions – making the varieties of independent directors in Asia even more diverse. There are, however, at least two cultural norms that appear to be present in all of the diverse cultures of Asia's leading economies, which may present challenges for the effectiveness of independent directors: the centrality of informal relationships in business which makes finding and identifying truly independent directors particularly difficult in Asia; and the avoidance of direct confrontation, especially with people in positions of authority and in public, which may limit the effectiveness of independent directors on boards.[200] A more systematic examination of these and other potential cultural norms on the function of independent directors in Asia appears to be a particularly rich and understudied area for future research.

[196] See Chapter 4 (Japan) at III.2.b; Chapter 5 (South Korea) at III.1.b (observing that, under the cover of the IMF, the Korean government was able to push through reforms that might have met with resistance from the *chaebol*). For a short description of the political environment surrounding corporate governance in Korea, see, e.g., K. Kim, 'Corporate Law and Corporate Law Scholarship in Korea: A Comparative Essay' in J. O. Haley and T. Takenaka (eds.), *Legal Innovations in Asia* (Edward Elgar, 2014), 257–258.

[197] See Chapter 4 (Japan) at III.2.a, IV and V (examples of resistance to independent directors).

[198] See Chapter 9 (Singapore) at III.2.

[199] See Chapter 5 (South Korea) at IV.4; Chapter 6 (China) at II.3; Chapter 7 (Taiwan) at II.2.b; Chapter 10 (India) at IV.2.

[200] See Chapter 7 (Taiwan) at III.2.b; Chapter 8 (Hong Kong) at III.3 and IV.

3 Operationalising the Six Principal Factors to Create a Loose Taxonomy

The six principal factors discussed above provide valuable insights into why varieties of independent directors exist in Asia and what has caused them to adopt their forms and functions. In addition, an understanding of these six factors provides the foundation for developing a 'loose taxonomy' of the varieties of independent directors in Asia. Such a taxonomy allows us to classify Asia's leading economies into subsets of comparable jurisdictions with respect to particular issues and then systematically examine these issues through targeted comparative analysis. Ultimately, we suggest that this approach will improve our understanding of independent directors in Asia and illuminate new areas for meaningful comparative research.

A few brief examples illustrate how the six factors can be operationalised under our 'loose taxonomy'. To start, let us consider how the first factor, shareholder structure, can be used to classify a subset of Asia's leading economies and illuminate useful areas for comparison within this subset. In all of Asia's leading economies, except for Japan, listed companies generally have a controlling shareholder structure. This highlights a key issue for comparison: how do independent directors, which were invented to solve the dispersed shareholding problem in the US, function in controlling shareholder dominated jurisdictions? One interesting observation is that all of the jurisdictions in this subset have departed from the American concept of the independent director by requiring independence from significant shareholders in their definitions of independence. However, all jurisdictions in this subset, except for Taiwan, still allow independent directors to be elected by majority shareholder vote. This raises intriguing questions for future research: why would these jurisdictions mandate independence from majority shareholders in their definitions of independence, but then implicitly allow majority shareholders to control the appointment and removal of these 'independent directors'? On this note, why was Taiwan unsuccessful in its attempt to remedy this apparent problem by mandating cumulative voting?

Another illustration of our 'loose taxonomy' can be found in our examination of legal origins. As explained above, Asia's leading civil law economies (i.e., China, Japan, South Korea and Taiwan) comprise a subset of jurisdictions which have allowed companies to adopt a non-one-tier board. An interesting question that arises in these jurisdictions is how independent directors, which were invented in the US to operate in a one-tier board environment, fit into non-one-tier board regimes.

In addition, all of the jurisdictions in this subset have or had corporate organs (i.e., statutory auditors or supervisory boards) that perform similar functions to independent directors.[201] This raises the issue of how these jurisdictions will coordinate the functions of these two overlapping mechanisms. A more targeted use of the legal origins factor may classify subsets of jurisdictions for comparison based on the historically traceable origins of a *particular* feature within a jurisdiction's independent director regime. For example, as explained above, the fact that Japan's 'comply or explain' regime was modelled on the UK's Code provides a rational basis for comparing Japan on this issue with the UK and also with Hong Kong and Singapore (which are the two other leading Asian jurisdictions that also currently have a UK 'comply or explain' model). This example illustrates how tracing the legal origins of particular provisions in a jurisdiction's independent director regime can reveal subsets of jurisdictions for a meaningful comparative analysis of an important issue.

Yet another example can be found in our examination of specific types of shareholders. In China, India and Singapore, the government is the controlling shareholder in a substantial portion of companies. As suggested above, a potential issue for future research is whether such jurisdictions should require independent directors in government-controlled companies to be independent from the government or ruling party. A strict policy of excluding independent directors based on political affiliation may significantly reduce the talent pool for independent directors without necessarily avoiding many meaningful conflicts of interest.[202] In all of Asia's leading economies, with the notable exception of Japan, similar issues arise as to how independence should be defined with respect to Family Firms. This subset of jurisdictions could benefit from further research on this issue as there is evidence that friends of the controlling family can perform a valuable mediating role as independent directors in Family Firms.[203]

These examples merely scratch the surface of the potential uses of the six principal factors as a way to identify salient issues for comparison in particular subsets of jurisdictions, which share common characteristics among their independent directors on particular issues. This methodological approach for comparison is diametrically opposed to the prevailing approach of assuming that independent directors are universally similar and thus universally comparable in all aspects for every issue

[201] Large listed firms in South Korea historically had statutory auditors, but now have an audit committee instead of statutory auditors.

[202] See Chapter 9 (Singapore) at III.3.

[203] See note 136 above.

across all jurisdictions.[204] The fact that independent directors possess unique attributes in different jurisdictions should be cause for inspiration rather than resignation: indeed, the varieties of independent directors in this book have revealed fertile areas for further study.

IV Conclusion: Implications of Varieties of Independent Directors in Asia

If there is one main point that emerges from this chapter and book, it is this: there is no single concept of the independent director in Asia. There are varieties of independent directors in Asia that take on different forms and perform different functions. This discovery has important practical and theoretical implications for at least three reasons.

First, corporate governance indices, which influence the allocation of trillions of dollars of investment capital and define entire sub-fields of corporate governance research, implicitly assume that independent directors around the world take the same form and perform the same function.[205] An in-depth comparison of the jurisdiction-specific chapters in this book demonstrates that this assumption is false. Indeed, it does not hold true even within Asia.

Second, it is misleading to point to the rise of the independent director in Asia as evidence of corporate governance convergence towards the American (or Anglo-American) corporate governance model. This chapter demonstrates that much of the 'convergence' that has occurred with the independent director in Asia is often only skin deep. The body of comparative evidence in the jurisdiction-specific chapters reveals the significant divergence in form and function within Asia – and even more so between Asian jurisdictions and the US–UK. This should not surprise as recent developments even suggest divergence of the concept of the independent director between the US and UK.

Third, the discovery of varieties of independent directors in Asia highlights the importance of drilling-down in comparative corporate governance research beyond common labels – which may be increasingly more abundant in our internet age. This presents a serious challenge to interjurisdictional empirical research, which tends to rely heavily on labels or law on the books for its primary data. The importance of 'labels' also raises an interesting question about their strategic value as signalling devices. The

[204] See II.1 above.

[205] See, for example, Katelouzou and Siems, 'Disappearing Paradigms'; Black et al., 'Does Corporate Governance Predict Firms' Market Values'; A. O. Santos, 'Integrated

fact that 'mere' labels have been able to influence important corporate governance indices and influential research suggests that more research should be devoted to why this is the case and how this may be used or abused.

If there is a second main point that emerges from this chapter and book, it is that although corporate governance is jurisdiction-specific and complex, targeted and nuanced comparative analysis can produce valuable practical and theoretical results. Producing such results, however, requires the type of in-depth jurisdiction-specific analysis that is contained in the jurisdiction-specific chapters of this book – which is diametrically opposed to the macro-empirical analysis that has increasingly driven policymakers and the academic literature in the field of comparative corporate governance.[206] A specific example of this is how we demonstrate in this chapter that legal origins do in fact matter – but in a localised way that focuses on the *specific* historically verifiable origins of *particular* legal provisions in *each specific* jurisdiction, rather than vague (and often inaccurate) notions of legal origins of an entire system examined at the jurisdictional level.[207] Perhaps, most importantly, the loose taxonomy of the independent director in Asia that we have created lays a foundation for exploring this critical issue more accurately and systematically in the future.

Admittedly, this chapter raises more questions for future research than definitive answers. However, hopefully the loose taxonomy of the forms, functions and issues that together define the varieties of independent directors in Asia will provide a path for further exploration of this fascinating issue for years to come.

Ownership and Control in the GCC Corporate Sector' (International Monetary Fund Working Paper, 2015), available at www.imf.org; C. Aoyagi and G. Ganelli, 'Unstash the Cash! Corporate Governance Reform in Japan' (International Monetary Fund Working Paper, 2014), available at www.imf.org; Technical Committee of the International Organisation of Securities Commissions, 'Board Independence of Listed Companies: Final Report' (2007), available at www.iosco.org; Emerging Markets Committee of the International Organisation of Securities Commissions, 'Corporate Governance Practices in Emerging Markets' (2007), available at www.iosco.org; OECD, 'Corporate Governance: A Survey of OECD Countries' (OECD, 2004), available at www.oecd.org.

206 See, for example, Gopal, 'Japan: A Closer Look at Governance Reforms'; OECD, 'Corporate Governance Factbook 2015' (OECD Publishing, 2015), available at www.oecd.org; Puchniak, 'Multiple Faces of Shareholder Power in Asia', 520 (describing GovernanceMetric International's global corporate governance ratings); M. Siems, 'Shareholder Protection around the World ("Leximetric II")', *Delaware Journal of Corporate Law*, 33 (2008), 111; Technical Committee of the International Organisation of Securities Commissions, 'Board Independence'.

207 See II.2 above.

PART II

Asian Jurisdiction-Specific Chapters

4

Japan's Gradual Reception of Independent Directors

An Empirical and Political-Economic Analysis

GEN GOTO, MANABU MATSUNAKA AND SOUICHIROU KOZUKA*

I Introduction: The Untold Story of Japan's Unique and Gradual Reform

To many outside observers, Japan appears to be an outlier in terms of its resistance to allowing independent directors into its corporate boardrooms. During the 1990s, the emerging trend around the world was to promote the adoption of independent directors. Japanese corporate law reforms, however, remained focused primarily on strengthening its autochthonous *kansayaku* (statutory auditors) system.[1] In 2002, when

* Sections III.1 and III.2 of this chapter were first drafted by Matsunaka and Goto respectively, while the remaining sections were first prepared by Kozuka. Although Goto served at the Ministry of Justice of Japan as a part-time officer from March 2010 to July 2013 and participated in the reform project of the Companies Act, this chapter does not represent the views of the Ministry of Justice. The authors would like to thank Andreas Fleckner, Saburo Sakamoto, Masakazu Shirai, Zenichi Shishido and Yueh-Ping (Alex) Yang for their valuable comments and advice. The research for this article was financially supported by the JSPS Research Grant No. 24330027 (for Kozuka and Matsunaka) and the JSPS Postdoctoral Fellowship for Research Abroad and Grants-in-Aid for Scientific Research (A) No. 24243001 (for Goto).

[1] As explained in detail below, a *kansayaku* is someone who is not an employee who has the responsibility to audit a company's activities to ensure the legality of the acts of directors, officers and employees. *Kansayaku* may be regarded as a kind of director in the sense that they are not employees and are appointed at the shareholders' meeting. In large companies, the auditing of financial statements is primarily undertaken by a professional accountant, and the *kansayaku* merely review the former's audit report. In this case, the *kansayaku*'s main responsibility is to audit the company's day-to-day activities to find indicia of illegal acts. Aronson argues that *kansayaku* is functionally a 'quasi-compliance officer'. B. E. Aronson, 'The Olympus Scandal and Corporate Governance

Japan created the option of adopting a one-tier Anglo-American board structure to promote the appointment of outside directors to the boards of large companies, only a handful of companies opted for this new board structure.[2] More recently, in 2014, the attempt to make just a *single* independent director mandatory under the Companies Act ultimately failed after much debate. As a result, today, Japan still does not have any compulsory rule for having even a *single* independent director on the board of a listed company.[3] Based on these events, the view of outsiders that Japan has consistently resisted the adoption of independent directors appears to have some basis in reality.

However, this outsider view, which is based largely on failed attempts to promote independent directors through reforms to the Companies Act, tells only part of the story. Notably, in 2009, the Tokyo Stock Exchange (TSE) amended its listing rules to require listed companies to adopt either an independent director or independent *kansayaku* – a clear move towards introducing greater independence into the boardrooms of Japan's most powerful companies. Outsiders have often overlooked this point. Similarly, in 2012, following the Olympus scandal,[4] the TSE introduced a rule urging listed companies to adopt independent *directors* rather than independent *kansayaku*. Perhaps most importantly, Japan adopted the Corporate Governance Code in 2015,[5] which requires listed companies either to appoint two or more 'independent directors' or to provide reasons for not doing so. By adopting a corporate governance code, based on the now ubiquitous 'comply or explain' approach, Japan has followed in the footsteps of many other jurisdictions around the world that have implemented 'comply or explain' regimes to promote the adoption of independent directors in listed companies.[6]

Reform: Can Japan Find a Middle Ground between the Board Monitoring Model and Management Model?', *Pacific Basin Law Journal*, 30(1) (2012), 93, 141. For more information on the operations of *kansayaku*, see T. Yoshii, 'Japan's Corporate Auditor System', *Journal of Japanese Law*, 9 (2004), 39.

2 See *infra* II.1.a.

3 For a detailed analysis of the 2014 amendments to the Companies Act, see S. Kozuka, 'Reform after a Decade of the Companies Act: Why, How, and to Where?', *Journal of Japanese Law*, 37 (2014), 39.

4 On the Olympus scandal and its implications for corporate governance, see Aronson, 'The Olympus Scandal and Corporate Governance Reform'; see also Chapter 12 at IV.5.

5 The Council of Experts Concerning the Corporate Governance Code, Japan's Corporate Governance Code [Final Proposal] (2015).

6 'Japan's Corporate Governance Code', *Japan Exchange Group*, available at www.jpx.co.jp; see, e.g., Chapter 7 (Taiwan) at II.1; Chapter 8 (Hong Kong) at II; Chapter 9 (Singapore) at II.3; Chapter 11 (Australia) at III.2.

These recent developments suggest that Japan is making gradual changes to its corporate boards. Such changes must be viewed in the context of changes occurring in the wider picture of Japan's corporate governance and economic reforms over the last few decades. On the other hand, it is also apparent that the changes in Japanese boards are extremely gradual – especially when viewed from a comparative perspective. As suggested above, the proposed single independent director requirement in the recent reforms to the Companies Act caused substantial controversy and was ultimately defeated. As such, it is interesting to examine why the move towards independent monitoring boards has been so gradual in Japan, and why such comparatively modest reforms have sparked such fierce debate. To answer these questions, it is necessary to examine the political context surrounding the reforms and identify the particular interests which have driven this debate.

The remainder of this chapter will proceed as follows. Section II describes the reforms that have affected boards of Japanese listed companies over the last two decades, as well as examining the evolving composition of Japanese boards and the seismic change in Japan's shareholding structure – which is integral to understanding the context in which Japanese boards operate. Section III analyses the 2014 reform to the Companies Act through the lenses of empirical and political analyses. Section IV introduces some thoughts on the developments until now and future outlook based on them. Section V then concludes with lessons drawn from the case of Japan.

II Background: Changes over the Last Two Decades

1 Reforms to the Law and Listing Rules

a The Genesis of the Monitoring Board in Japan

Independent directors are at the core of the monitoring model of corporate boards.[7] According to the monitoring model, non-executive directors monitor management, and the independence of such non-executive monitors enhances their effectiveness. Thus, without independent directors it would be difficult to classify a board as falling into the classic (Anglo-American) definition of a monitoring board.

[7] M. A. Eisenberg, *The Structure of the Corporation* (Little, Brown and Company, 1976), 139–185. For further background information on the monitoring model, see Chapter 1 at III.2.

Japan's first encounter with the monitoring board model came in 2002 as a result of reforms to its company law.[8] The amendments gave large companies the option[9] of adopting a board with committees which, at least according to its formal board structure, appeared to be similar to a typical one-tier Anglo-American board structure.[10] If a company opts for the 'committee-type board' structure then the traditional *kansayaku* (i.e., board of statutory auditors) may not be appointed. Instead, the board of directors must appoint committees for nomination, audit and compensation – each of which is required to have a majority of outside directors. In practice, this means that companies, which opt for the 'committee-type board' structure, must have at least two outside directors (i.e., the same outside directors can serve on each of the three committees, wherein each committee must have a minimum of three members and a majority of outside directors). The option for companies to select the 'committee-type board' structure was subsequently incorporated into the 2006 Companies Act. As such, today, companies still have the option of whether to adopt the 'committee-type board' structure.

It is noteworthy that in the context of the 'committee-type board', an 'outside director' is defined as a person who is not and who has never been an executive director, officer or employee of the company or its subsidiary. This requirement is intended to avoid the situation in which outside directors are intimidated by executive directors, especially the CEO.[11] When the reform was introduced in 2002, it was the first time that Japan had offered a board structure which, if selected, would make it mandatory for a company to have an outside director on its board.[12]

[8] The reforms were contained in the Act on Special Rules to the Commercial Code Regarding the Audit and Other Matters of Joint Stock Companies (Special Rules Act). This Act was repealed in 2006 after the Companies Act entered into force.

[9] A large company was defined as a company with stated capital of at least 500 million yen or debt of at least 20 billion yen, pursuant to the last balance sheet.

[10] R. J. Gilson and C. J. Milhaupt, 'Choice as Regulatory Reform: The Case of Japanese Corporate Governance', *The American Journal of Comparative Law*, 53(2) (2005), 343; P. Lawley, 'Panacea or Placebo? An Empirical Analysis of the Effect of the Japanese Committee System on Corporate Governance Law Reform' in L. Nottage, L. Wolff and K. Anderson (eds.), *Corporate Governance in the 21st Century: Japan's Gradual Transformation* (Edward Elgar, 2008), 128.

[11] An employee of the parent company would qualify as an outside director because persons from the parent company were deemed to be in a stronger position than the management of the subsidiary and, thus not prone to intimidation from the management of the subsidiary. Similarly, a person from the main bank or the company's major business partners is also qualified to be an outside director.

[12] Corporate law reforms prior to the 2002 amendments to the Special Rules Act focused on enhancing the power of *kansayaku*. In 1993, the Special Rules Act introduced the

However, it should be noted that even if a company adopts the 'committee-type board' structure, it is only required to have outside – but not independent – directors. This fact, as well as the fact that the definition of 'outside' directors was amended in 2014 to bring it closer to the definition of 'independent' directors, has often been overlooked in analyses that compare Japan's 'committee-type board' system with other systems that have come to require independent directors in Asia and around the world.[13]

However, despite only requiring a majority of outside (and not necessarily independent) directors on the three committees and, in turn, two outside directors on the board in total, the 'committee-type board' structure has not gained favour in corporate Japan. In the first round of shareholder general meetings after the reform (i.e., general meetings in 2003), only 71 firms (45 of which were listed companies) – which represented approximately 3 per cent of the companies that were eligible to opt for the 'committee-type board' structure at that time – adopted it.[14] As of July 2014, according to the White Paper on Corporate Governance published by the TSE only 1.7 per cent of listed companies (57 out of 3,414 listed companies) now use the 'committee-type board' structure.[15] This illustrates the continued resistance to the monitoring board model in corporate Japan.

b Gradual Promotion of Independent Directors by the TSE

In 2009, the TSE amended its Listing Rules and required all listed companies to appoint at least one 'independent director or independent *kansayaku*'.[16] The new Rules were introduced after two government reports, produced by the Ministry of Economy, Trade and Industry (METI) and the Financial Services Agency (FSA), affirmed the merits of independent directors for the corporate governance of listed companies. The two reports were prepared in response to the proposals advanced by

requirement for the *kansayaku* in a large company to establish a board of *kansayaku*, with at least one member being an 'outside' *kansayaku*. Later, in 2001, this rule was altered such that half of the board of *kansayaku* had to be composed of outside *kansayaku*.

[13] D. W. Puchniak, 'The 2002 Reform of the Management of Large Japanese Corporations: A Race to Somewhere?', *The Australian Journal of Asian Law*, 5 (2003), 42, 64.

[14] Gilson and Milhaupt, 'Choice as Regulatory Reform: The Case of Japanese Corporate Governance'.

[15] Tokyo Stock Exchange, *TSE-Listed Companies White Paper on Corporate Governance 2015* (2015), 15.

[16] Section 436-2, Listing Rules of Tokyo Stock Exchange.

foreign institutional investors through the Asian Corporate Governance Association (ACGA).[17]

On the one hand, the Listing Rules of the TSE made substantial progress by introducing an 'independence' requirement for directors and *kansayaku*, which is significantly more stringent than the 'outside' requirement used in the Companies Act. Under the Listing Rules, an independent director or *kansayaku* is defined as someone who has no conflict of interest with the general shareholders. The definition of 'independence' is phrased in general terms as opposed to the formalistic definition of 'outside director/ *kansayaku*' in the Companies Act.[18] The TSE further supplements its general definition of 'independence' by providing an enumerated list of categories of people who will generally not be considered to be independent as they would tend to have potential conflicts of interest with the general shareholders.[19]

On the other hand, the impact of the 'independence' requirement in the Listing Rules was compromised because it permitted the appointment of independent *kansayaku*.[20] However, in May 2012, the TSE introduced another provision in its Listing Rules that recommended that companies

[17] ACGA, 'White Paper on Corporate Governance in Japan' (2008), available at www.acga-asia.org, 5, 18–23. For more details on ACGA, see Chapter 1 at I.2.

[18] Art. 2 (15), Companies Act; see Regulatory Appendix.

[19] Specifically, the Listing Rules state that the following people will generally not be considered to be independent directors: executive directors or officers of the parent company or a sister company; an executive director or officer of another company that does business with the company (such as the main bank); a consultant, accountant or lawyer of the company; and immediate family members of the aforementioned people, as well as immediate family members of executive directors or officers of the company or its subsidiary. If the company intends to appoint any of these people as an independent director it must consult the TSE in advance. Guideline III.5. (3)-2 Guidelines concerning Listed Company Compliance, Tokyo Stock Exchange.

[20] In the first year, as of October 2010, 1.514 companies (70.5 per cent of all the listed companies with independent directors or *kansayaku*) appointed independent *kansayaku* but no independent directors. Two hundred and fourteen companies (10 per cent) appointed only independent directors. These include 49 companies with the 'committee-type' structure, which means that 165 companies with *kansayaku* boards appointed independent directors but no independent *kansayaku* (i.e., all of their outside *kansayaku* were not independent). Further, there were 418 companies or 19.5 per cent that appointed both independent directors and independent *kansayaku* (Tokyo Stock Exchange, *TSE-Listed Companies White Paper on Corporate Governance 2011*, 40). The preference seems to have slightly changed in two years. The statistics of October 2012 report that 1.493 companies (65.6 per cent of those with independent director/*kansayaku*) appointed independent *kansayaku* only, while 219 companies (9.6 per cent) appointed only independent directors and 563 (24.8 per cent) appointed both independent directors and

should nominate an independent director rather than an independent *kansayaku*.[21] This provision was further strengthened in February 2014 to *strongly* recommend that listed companies have at least one independent director (as opposed to one independent *kansayaku*).[22] As such, the TSE has methodically and gradually aligned itself with the global trend of endorsing listed companies' introduction of independent members to their boards.

c The 2014 Amendments to the Companies Act

The 2009 Amendments to the Tokyo Stock Exchange Listing Rules were followed by deliberations on statutory reform. When the Legislative Council and its Companies Act Working Group began to consider amendments to the Companies Act in 2010 under the Democratic Party of Japan (DPJ) administration,[23] it was proposed that the appointment of outside directors[24] for all companies be made mandatory. The resulting Outline of Reform,[25] however, did not introduce a mandatory requirement. Instead, it imposed a duty on companies that did not have any

independent *kansayaku* (Tokyo Stock Exchange, *White Paper on Corporate Governance 2013*, 52).

21 Section 445-4, Listing Rules of Tokyo Stock Exchange. The provision, when first introduced in 2012, required listed companies to 'make efforts (努めるものとす) to secure independent director/*kansayaku* by giving due consideration to the meaning of an independent member having a voting right at the meeting of the board of directors'.

22 The current text of Section 445-4, Listing Rules of Tokyo Stock Exchange provides: 'an issuer of listed domestic stocks must make efforts (努めなければならな) to secure at least one independent director as a member of its board of directors'.

23 In Japan, the majority of the bills submitted to the Diet are prepared by governmental agencies and are sponsored by the Cabinet. For reforms of basic private and criminal law, of which the Ministry of Justice (MOJ) is in charge, it is customary for the MOJ to consult with the Legislative Council to provide an outline of the proposed reform, and the MOJ will draft a bill following that outline. It is also customary for the Legislative Council to set up a working group, consisting of law professors, representatives of relevant private interests and government officials, for discussions on a specific consultation. Officials of MOJ serve as the secretariat of the Legislative Council and its working groups. The members, the minutes and the working papers of the Companies Act Working Group are available at www.moj.go.jp.

24 Note that the proposed reforms were not intended to make 'independent' directors mandatory. One possible reason may be that if a certain category of director becomes mandatory under the Companies Act, it must be recorded in the public registry on corporations. Because the registry officer has limited access to the information when accepting the file, it is difficult to codify an elusive qualification like 'independence' into the Companies Act.

25 On the outcome of the deliberations at the Legislative Council, see G. Goto, 'The Outline for the Companies Act Reform in Japan and Its Implications', *Journal of Japanese Law*,

outside directors to disclose in their respective annual reports the reasons why they believed it was inappropriate for them to appoint at least one outside director.[26] Furthermore, in December 2012, the Liberal Democratic Party (LDP) (which returned to power after deliberations at the Legislative Council were concluded) introduced a new provision in the Reform Bill, which imposed a duty on all listed companies without outside directors to give reasons at their respective annual shareholders' meetings for their failure to have even a single outside director.[27]

These requirements adopted a 'comply or explain' approach which, as mentioned above, has become the standard approach for regulating independent directors around the world.[28] Given the difficulty for any company to explain its refusal to appoint even *one* outside director, the pressure to comply with this 'optional' minimal requirement may be seen to be particularly strong in the Japanese context – as few countries have explicitly set such a low bar for compliance.[29] The 2014 Amendments to the Companies Act therefore entrenched Japan's position that the appointment of at least one outside director is generally perceived to be beneficial for listed companies, and companies may refuse to do so only in exceptional circumstances.

Two other important changes were also initiated by the 2014 Amendments. First, a third type of board structure was introduced.[30] Similar to the 'committee-type board' structure, companies choosing this new option are not allowed to appoint *kansayaku*. However, unlike the 'committee-type board' structure, which requires the establishment of three committees, the new option only requires one compulsory committee – the 'audit and supervisory committee'. The 'audit and supervisory committee'[31] must have a majority of outside directors. In this new

35 (2013), 13. The resulting amendments almost reflected the report of the Legislative Council, though one important addition was made, as described in the text. See Kozuka, 'Reform after a Decade of the Companies Act: Why, How, and to Where?', 39.

26 Art. 124, para. 2, Ministerial Order for Implementation of the Companies Act.

27 Art. 327-2, Companies Act. Disclosure in documents for the general assembly is also required. Art. 74-2, Ministerial Order to implement the Companies Act.

28 See Chapter 2 at III.2, for further information on the creation of this concept in the UK.

29 Saburou Sakamoto et al., '平成二六年改正会社法の解説（I）' [Official Commentary on the 2014 Amendments to the Companies Act], 商事法務, 2040 (2014), 28, 36. See also, Art. 124, para. 3, Ministerial Order for Implementation of the Companies Act (stating that appointment of two or more outside *kansayaku* is not a sufficient reason for not appointing an outside director).

30 Arts. 399-2–399-14, Companies Act.

31 The name of the committee in Japanese is 監査等委員会 (*kansa-to i'inkai*), the literal translation of which is 'the committee for audit and other matters'. Nevertheless,

optional 'audit and supervisory committee' board structure, nomination and remuneration committees are optional and are not subject to the majority outsider director requirement.

Second, the definition of 'outside' director or *kansayaku* has been amended such that directors or employees of the parent or sister company are not permitted to take on such positions.[32] Other types of interests, such as a business relationship between the company employing the person who is subsequently appointed director or *kansayaku* at the other company, are not excluded. Nevertheless, this new definition indicates a shift in regulatory policy towards a concept of independence, and away from the previous rationale of reducing the risk that outside directors and *kansayaku* might be 'intimidated' by management. Both amendments demonstrate the gradual acceptance of the monitoring model in Japan, though Japan has done so in a uniquely hybrid and tepid manner.[33]

The motivation of the reform is as noteworthy as its content. Contrary to speculation by foreign observers,[34] the Olympus scandal was not the primary driving force of the reform. It is important to note that the Olympus scandal was uncovered in October 2011, which is a year and a half after reform discussions began in February 2010.[35] The Global Financial Crisis did not affect the discussions either, not least because it had a limited impact on the Japanese financial industry. The difference between the resulting 2014 Amendments to the Companies Act and the Dodd-Frank Act in the US was also clear: the latter's concern with controls on excessive risk taking by management is absent from Japan's amendments.

this article chose to use the name 'audit and supervisory' committee (監査監督委員会 (*kansa kantoku i'inkai*)), which was the name used during the deliberations at the Legislative Council, to better reflect its meaning.

32 Art. 2(15) and (16), Companies Act, see Regulatory Appendix.

33 The potential for this hybrid approach was suggested in Aronson, 'The Olympus Scandal and Corporate Governance Reform'.

34 See, for example, W. G. Ringe, 'Independent Directors: After the Crisis', *European Business Organization Law Review*, 14(3) (2013), 401, 408.

35 Prior to the Olympus scandal, Japan's leading car manufacturer, Toyota, encountered widespread accusation for the alleged defects in its cars causing unintended acceleration. While some argued that the incident revealed problems with the Toyota's corporate governance, see B. E. Aronson, 'Learning from Toyota's Troubles: The Debate on Board Oversight, Board Structure, and Director Independence in Japan', *Journal of Japanese Law*, 15(30) (2010), 67; see also Chapter 12 at IV.5. It should be noted that this argument did not gain much support within Japan, and no intervention to that end was taken pursuant to the deliberations at the Legislative Council.

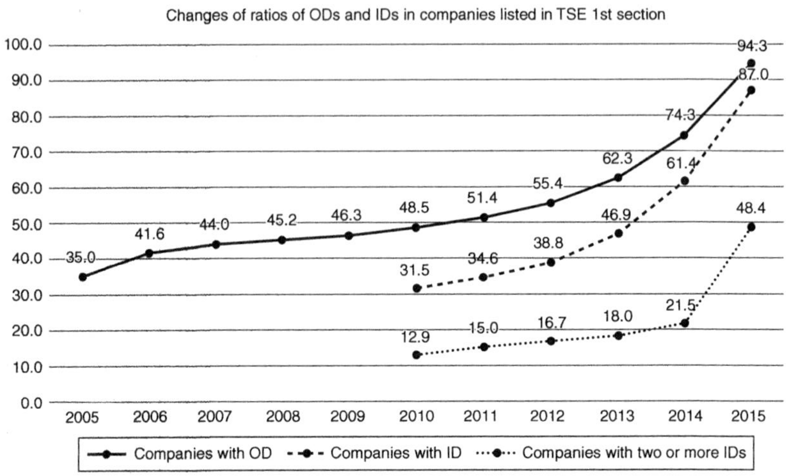

Figure 4.1 Changes of Ratios of ODs and IDs in Companies Listed in TSE First Section

requirements for independent or outside directors were proposed. The proportion of listed companies in the First Section of the TSE grew from 45.2 per cent in 2008 to 48.5 per cent in 2010, and then to 55.4 per cent in 2012. After the Outline of Reform for the 2014 Amendments to the Companies Act was published, the proportion of listed companies rose to 62.3 per cent in 2013, 74.3 per cent in 2014 and then to 94.3 per cent in July 2015.[47] The proportion of TSE First Section companies, which appointed two or more independent directors, has also risen from 12.9 per cent in 2010 to 21.5 per cent in 2014, and then to 48.4 per cent in 2015.[48]

Further, the White Paper of the TSE sheds light on the attributes of people appointed as independent directors.[49] Nearly two-thirds (64.2 per cent) of the independent directors appointed by companies with *kansayaku* boards are from other companies.[50] Out of the total

47 'Appointment of Outside Directors by TSE-Listed Companies [Confirmed report]', Tokyo Stock Exchange, Inc., 29 July 2015, available at www.jpx.co.jp. See also Tokyo Stock Exchange, *White Paper on Corporate Governance 2015*, 23.

48 'Appointment of Outside Directors by TSE-Listed Companies [Confirmed report]', Tokyo Stock Exchange, Inc.

49 Tokyo Stock Exchange, *White Paper on Corporate Governance 2015*, 31.

50 By contrast, note the figures for Korea or Taiwan are substantially different. See Chapter 5 (South Korea) at IV.4, and Chapter 7 (Taiwan) at II.2.b, respectively.

number of independent directors, attorneys make up 14.0 per cent, academics 10.8 per cent, certified public accountants 4.9 per cent and tax accountants 1.1 per cent. If one focuses instead on the proportion of independent people in the total number of outside directors/*kansayaku* in each category, the picture changes.[51] Academics are the most likely to qualify as 'independent', as 87.6 per cent of academics serving as outside directors/*kansayaku* are listed as 'independent'. Certified public accountants (CPAs) (78.9 per cent) and lawyers (76.3 per cent) have a similar degree of independence, whereas only 53.5 per cent of people from other companies serving as outside directors/*kansayaku* are listed as independent.

These results suggest that Japanese companies tend to have a limited pool of business people from which they may elect independent directors and/or that firms expect that outside directors/*kansayaku* from the business world will play different roles. Professionals such as academics, attorneys and CPAs are less likely to have conflicts of interest, and therefore are more likely to qualify as independent directors/*kansayaku*. However, it is worth considering whether such persons are indeed able to effectively monitor management.

3 *Background Changes in Shareholding Structure*

The political dynamics involved during the 2014 Amendments might be difficult to understand if one holds the traditional view that the LDP is a conservative party that supports the interests of big businesses. However, Japan's economic structure has undergone significant changes following the post-war period, which inevitably led to a shift in the relative power of various interest groups.

The most conspicuous change is in Japan's shareholding structure, with higher levels of foreign ownership and greater pressure on large public companies from foreign investors to improve their corporate governance. Before the 1990s, extensive cross-shareholding was prevalent in

[51] Tokyo Stock Exchange, *White Paper on Corporate Governance 2015*, 53. Note that the numbers in the text above are those for the proportion of independent people in the total number of both outside directors and outside *kansayaku*. Data for the proportion of independent directors to outside directors is not available.

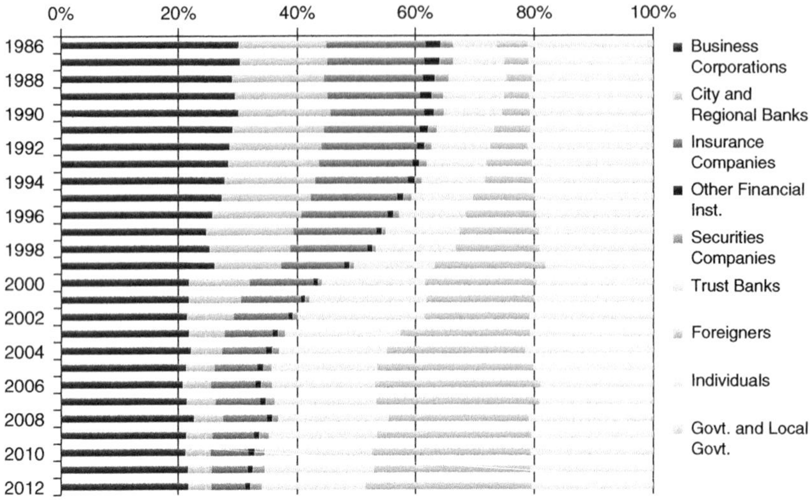

Figure 4.2 Transition of Share-Ownership Distribution of Listed Corporations in Japan

Japan.[52] Since the late 1990s, however, cross-shareholding has gradually unwound, as Figure 4.2 shows.[53]

Figure 4.2[54] shows the share-ownership distribution by investor category of all listed corporations in Japan on an aggregate basis over time. The three categories of investors on the left side of each row, namely non-financial business corporations, banks and insurers, are 'insider

[52] 'Cross-shareholding', which refers to the situation in which two corporations hold each other's shares, has been said to be one of the characteristics of Japanese corporate governance. According to Z. Shishido, 'Japanese Corporate Governance: The Hidden Problems of Corporate Law and Their Solutions', *Delaware Journal of Corporate Law*, 25 (2000), 189, 210–211: '[t]he Japanese method of stabilizing management is through cross-shareholding. An implicit agreement is made between two companies to hold ownership in the other partners' stock, usually around one percent by nonfinancial firms and up to five percent by banks. Each company makes the same type of implicit agreements with, for example, twenty companies. Consequently, a spider web of mutual stockholding among inside shareholders is created, thereby stabilizing majority stock ownership.' In this chapter, however, the term cross-shareholding is used to include other forms of shareholding relationships that have a similar effect, such as circular shareholdings among three or more corporations or unilateral shareholding by a mutual insurance company.

[53] The following analysis is largely based on G. Goto, 'Legally "Strong" Shareholders of Japan', *Michigan Journal of Private Equity and Venture Capital Law*, 3(2) (2014), 125.

[54] Figure 4.2 is based on data from the '2012 Share Ownership Survey, Share Distribution Survey § 2–5', Tokyo Stock Exchange, available at www.tse.or.jp.

shareholders' that tend to support incumbent management. These investors can be approximated to shareholders in a cross-shareholding relationship. The three categories on the far-right side of the graph, namely individuals, foreigners and trust banks,[55] are 'outsider shareholders' that may support hostile bidders or activist investors, depending on the situation.

The percentage of shares held by insider shareholders, which was as high as 61.8 per cent in 1986, has decreased to 31.2 per cent in 2012 as cross-shareholding has become unwound. The largest period of decline took place in the late 1990s and was largely a result of the banking crisis of 1997–1998 and subsequent regulation[56] forcing banks to sell their shares in other corporations.[57] Insurers that were in a similarly distressed situation also sold their shares,[58] although they were not subject to the regulation noted above. Correspondingly, the ratio of outsider shareholders has increased to 65.9 per cent as of 2012, with foreign investors and trust banks increasing their holdings. Although the unwinding of cross-shareholding relationships seems to have stopped or largely slowed since 2005,[59] cross-shareholding relationships are no longer commonplace.

It must be noted, however, that Figure 4.2 tends to over-emphasise the number of corporations with large market capitalisations, as it is based on the aggregate data of all listed corporations calculated based on the market share price. Research on a corporation-to-corporation basis has shown that the unwinding of cross-shareholding and the increase of foreign investment is taking place primarily in large public corporations, while small and medium-sized listed corporations still

[55] Shareholding by trust banks consists of shareholding for beneficiaries, such as investment trusts (mutual funds), private pension trusts, and other domestic investment funds, and shareholding for trust banks' own account. Although the exact proportion of these two categories is unknown, it is reasonable to assume that the ratio of shares held for trust banks' own account has been considerably low in recent years, since the restrictions on shareholdings by banks apply only to the shares held for trust banks' own account. Art. 2(1) 2, Cabinet Office Ordinance on the Restriction of Shareholdings by Banks.

[56] Art. 3, para. 1, The Act on Restriction of Shareholdings by Banks.

[57] H. Miyajima and F. Kuroki, 'The Unwinding of Cross-Shareholding in Japan: Causes, Effects, and Implications' in M. Aoki, G. Jackson and H. Miyajima (eds.), *Corporate Governance in Japan* (Oxford University Press, 2007), 79, 90–91.

[58] *Ibid.*, 90.

[59] H. Miyajima et al., '日本型コーポレート・ガバナンスはどこへ向かうのか(上)「日本企業のコーポレート・ガバナンスに関するアンケート」調査から読み解く' [Where Is the Japanese Corporate Governance Oriented?: Analysing the Results of 'Questionnaire on Corporate Governance of Japanese Corporations' (1 of 2)], 商事法務, 2008 (2013), 4, 9.

seem to have a relatively high ratio of cross-shareholdings and a lower percentage of shareholding by foreign investors.[60] As foreign ownership of large public companies is comparatively higher, such companies face greater pressure from foreign investors to improve their corporate governance as compared to the small and medium-sized listed corporations.

III Recent Reform: 2014 Amendments to the Companies Act

This section evaluates the recent debate on whether the Companies Act should make it mandatory for listed companies to appoint outside directors. As mentioned earlier, even the modest proposal to make just one outside director mandatory was rejected in favour of a 'comply or

[60] W. Tanaka, '株式保有構造と会社法: 「分散保有の上場会社のジレンマ」を越えて' [Share-Ownership Structure and Corporate Law: Beyond the Dilemma of Dispersedly-Held Listed Corporations], 商事法務, 2007 (2013), 30, 31–32. There are a few reasons for this diversification between large corporations and small and medium corporations with respect to the degree of cross-shareholding unwinding.

First, when banks were forced to sell their shares of other corporations, they began with those of corporations with larger market capitalisation and higher market valuation, while refraining when possible from selling those of smaller corporations in order to avoid giving the market a negative impression that a corporation is being abandoned by its bank. Miyajima and Kuroki, 'The Unwinding of Cross-Shareholding in Japan: Causes, Effects, and Implications', 99, 102; H. Miyajima and K. Nitta, '株式所有構造の多様化とその帰結' [Diversification of Share-Ownership Structure and its Consequences: Unwinding and 'Revival' of Cross-Shareholdings and the Role of Foreign Investors] in H. Miyajima (ed.), 日本の企業統治: その再設計と競争力の回復に向けて [Corporate Governance in Japan: Toward Redesigning Corporate Governance and Recovering Competitiveness] (Toyo Keizai, 2011), 105, 122. It is also worth noting that corporations that had their shares sold by banks tended to sell the shares of those banks within the same or following year. Miyajima and Kuroki, 'The Unwinding of Cross-Shareholding in Japan: Causes, Effects, and Implications', 104.

Second, foreign investors tend to prefer to invest in larger corporations with higher proportions of overseas sales and higher returns on assets, presumably because they are more familiar with them, thereby replacing banks as shareholders of such corporations. Miyajima and Nitta, '株式所有構造の多様化とその帰結', 135; see also Miyajima and Kuroki, 'The Unwinding of Cross-Shareholding in Japan: Causes, Effects, and Implications', 86–88. Such replacement of banks by foreign investors is occurring at a slower pace in small and medium corporations.

Third, there was a limited revival of cross-shareholding among non-financial business companies after 2005. The stunted return of cross-shareholding was especially pronounced among cash-rich corporations that were targeted by activist hedge funds. Miyajima and Nitta, '株式所有構造の多様化とその帰結', 117, 125–130.

The unwinding of cross-shareholdings might develop in the coming years, as the Corporate Governance Code requires listed companies to disclose their policy for the cross-shareholdings. Its impact will need further examination.

explain' approach. The first subsection examines the possible impacts of the (rejected) mandatory outside director proposal and the (accepted) 'comply or explain' solution by drawing on empirical studies on board composition in Japanese companies. The second subsection analyses the political process to highlight the identity and motivations of the actors involved. Together, they shed light on the overall landscape of the reform and its significance for Japan.

1 *Insights from Empirical Research*

Section III.1.a surveys empirical studies examining how independent directors affect firm value in Japan. Section III.1.b follows with a survey of empirical studies on board compositions in Japanese firms. As these empirical studies themselves form part of the background to recent reforms in Japan, an appreciation of the trends in these studies is necessary to fully understand trends in Japanese corporate governance. Drawing inferences from the previous two sections, section III.1.c discusses the possible impacts of the 'comply or explain' approach implemented in the 2014 reform and the rejected mandatory outside director requirement. Even if empirical studies show that appointing independent directors improves efficiency in general, it does not follow that every firm must have the same number of independent directors. It also does not mean that having more independent directors always leads to higher firm value. Recent studies by economists agree that the optimal number (or ratio) of independent directors varies among firms.[61] The ideal is for firms to appoint independent directors only when doing so improves efficiency. Since differing approaches toward increasing the number or proportion of independent directors will affect different types of firms, we discuss whether the end (i.e., appointing independent directors) is itself desirable, as well as whether the means adopted for the purposes of this end are proper.

a Effect of Independent Directors on Firm Value

Anglo-American advocates of independent directors often argue that independent directors protect the interests of shareholders in general

[61] R. B. Adams, B. E. Hermalin and M. S. Weisbach, 'The Role of Boards of Directors in Corporate Governance: A Conceptual Framework and Survey', *Journal of Economic Literature*, 48(1) (2010), 58, 60–62.

vis-à-vis managers. If independent directors were useful in this respect, one might think that there should be empirical evidence showing a positive correlation between the appointment of a specific number of independent directors and corporate performance.[62] The simplest possible methods to determine whether appointing an outside director or directors improves firms' performance are to compare firms with and without outside directors, or to test whether a number or a proportion of outsiders in a board correlates with performance.

In 2005, Miwa and Ramseyer provided the first empirical study to ascertain the general relationship between firm performance and outside directors in Japan. Using data from the 1,000 largest listed firms in Japan from 1986 to 1994, Miwa and Ramseyer found an absence of any positive correlation between the appointment of outside directors and firm performance.[63] It should be noted, however, that the boards of Japanese firms have undergone significant changes since the time period analysed in this study.

A simple comparison of firms with and without outside directors (or comparing firms with more and fewer outside directors) would suffer from severe endogeneity problems.[64] For example, it is possible that it is not the appointment of independent directors that affects firm value, but rather that the firm value affects whether and how many independent directors are appointed. Accordingly, recent studies have adopted more sophisticated research methods.[65] The first approach is to investigate the conditions or specific attributes of firms that are associated with the effectiveness of outside directors. In other words, this approach discards

[62] For a survey of empirical studies in Japan, see K. Uchida, '日本企業の取締役会の進化と国際的特徴' [Development and Characteristics of Board of Directors of Japanese Firms in the International Context], 商事法務, 2007 (2013), 41–48; for a general discussion of empirical studies in the US and UK see Chapter 2 at IV.2; for empirical studies in Australia, see Chapter 11 (Australia) at V.

[63] Y. Miwa and J. M. Ramseyer, 'Who Appoints Them, What Do They Do?: Evidence on Outside Directors from Japan', *Journal of Economics and Management Strategy*, 14(2) (2005), 299, 326–332, 328–29, Table VI.

[64] For endogeneity problems in corporate governance studies, see B. E. Hermalin and M. S. Weisbach, 'Boards of Directors as an Endogenously Determined Institution: A Survey of the Economic Literature', *Federal Reserve Bank of New York Economic Policy Review*, 9(1) (2003), 7.

[65] R. Duchin, J. G. Matsusaka and O. Ozbas, 'When Are Outside Directors Effective?', *Journal of Financial Economics*, 96(2) (2010), 195. This is the general trend of empirical studies on board composition. For the trend of empirical studies, see Adams et al., 'The Role of Boards of Directors in Corporate Governance: A Conceptual Framework and Survey'.

the assumption that independent directors affect firms in the same way, and recognises that independent directors may raise firm value in specific types of firms, but not in others.[66]

Saitō's 2010 study covered 483 firms in the Nikkei 500 listed on the TSE during 1996–2006.[67] First, he showed that the stock market reacts favourably to the initial appointment of an outside director(s).[68] However, the market did not respond in the same way when firms increased the number of outside directors.[69] Further, Saitō showed that the appointment of the first outside director for a firm led to an improvement in operating performance,[70] but subsequently increasing the number of outside directors did not. In a more recent study, Saitō confirmed that operating performance significantly improves in the three years following the initial appointment of an outside director(s).[71]

Regarding the relationship between managerial-monitoring performance and outside directors, Saitō's study showed that the CEO turnover rate is significantly higher in underperforming firms with outside

[66] Other than studies introduced here, Miyajima and Ogawa shows that firms with outside directors perform better compared to firms without outside directors when limited to firms with lower cost of gathering information in Japan. H. Miyajima and R. Ogawa, '日本企業の取締役会構成の変化をいかに理解するか?：取締役会構成の決定要因と社外取締役の導入効果' [Understanding Change in Board Composition: Determinants of Board Composition and Effects of Outside Directors] (RIETI Policy Discussion Paper Series 12-P-013, 2012), available at www.rieti.go.jp.

[67] The refined version of his research (in Japanese) is T. Saitō, '日本企業による社外取締役の導入の決定要因とその効果' [Determinants of Appointment of Outside Directors and Their Effects in Japanese Firms] in H. Miyajima (ed.), 日本の企業統治：その再設計と競争力の回復に向けて [Corporate Governance in Japan: Toward Redesigning Corporate Governance and Recovering Competitiveness] (Toyo Keizai, 2011), 181–231.

[68] T. Saitō, 'Boards with and without Outside Directors: An Empirical Comparison' (Working Paper, 2010), 25–26 and 53 Table 7, panel A. In precise, sample firms mark statistically significant positive short-term cumulative abnormal return (CAR) when they appoint outside director(s) for the first time, but not for increasing the number of outside directors.

[69] *Ibid.*, 26–27 and 53 Table 7, panel A. In order to handle the problem of anticipation of the event by market, he estimates two-stage CAR and obtains similar results. *Ibid.*, 53 Table 7, panel B.

[70] *Ibid.*, 17–25 and 50–52 Tables 4–6. The operative performance, measured by industry and performance adjusted operating return on assets (OROA), is improved after an initial appointment of outside director(s), but not after an increase in the number of outside directors.

[71] Saitō, '日本企業による社外取締役の導入の決定要因とその効果', 207–208, Tables 4–6.

directors than in those without,[72] and that the CEO turnover rate generally rises in underperforming firms, especially when outside directors are present.[73]

A 2012 study by Uchida based on data from all listed firms from 2002 to 2011 showed a significant positive correlation between the presence of an outside director and the performance of firms with specific attributes,[74] but found no significant correlation between the ratio of outside directors and firm performance.[75] It also showed that firms with a high ratio of cross-shareholding and/or low foreign ownership experienced high firm performance when the proportion of outside directors was increased.[76] Taken together, Uchida suggested that these results showed that outside directors do not replace, but rather complement, Japanese-style corporate governance.[77]

[72] Saitō, 'Boards with and without Outside Directors: An Empirical Comparison', 30–31 and 58 Table 12. However, empirical results on the effect of outside directors to the replacement of CEOs are mixed. Besides Saitō ('Boards with and without Outside Directors'), Liu and Uchida report a positive correlation between outside directors and CEO turnover rate. C., Liu, J. Liu and K. Uchida, 'Do Independent Boards Effectively Monitor Management? Evidence from Japan during the Financial Crisis' in W. Sun, J. Stewart and D. Pollard (eds.), *Corporate Governance and the Global Financial Crisis: International Perspectives* (Cambridge University Press, 2011), 188–214. In contrast, as referred to in detail below, Miyajima and Ogawa, '日本企業の取締役会構成の変化をいかに理解するか?： 取締役空き構成の決定要因と社外取締役の導入効果' denies this correlation. See *infra* notes 86–87 and accompanying text.

[73] To be precise, although the CEO turnover rate is significantly and negatively associated with OROA in the previous year, interaction term of OROA in the previous year and outside director dummy is also significantly and negatively correlated with the turnover rate. Saitō, 'Boards with and without Outside Directors: An Empirical Comparison', 58 Table 12.

[74] K. Uchida, '社外取締役割合の決定要因とパフォーマンス' [Determinants of Ratio of Outside Directors on Firms' Board and Their Performance], 証券アナリストジャーナル, 50(2) (2012), 8–18, 11.

[75] Tobin's Q is commonly used in empirical studies of this area. See, for example, Adams et al., 'The Role of Boards of Directors in Corporate Governance: A Conceptual Framework and Survey'.

[76] The interaction term of outside director ratio and cross-shareholding ratio is significantly and positively related with Tobin's Q. Uchida, 社外取締役割合の決定要因とパフォーマンス, 15–17 and 16 Table 2. The author also tests whether the relationship holds when considering the effect of foreign shareholdings by using the interaction term of outside director ratio and a proxy for a traditional Japanese shareholding structure (which is generated by synthesising 1-foreign shareholding ratio and cross-shareholding ratio) and finds similar result. *Ibid.*, 14 panel B. This fact reinforces the robustness of the result shown in the text.

[77] *Ibid.*, 17.

b Determinants of Board Composition

The results of the empirical studies discussed above seem to support the argument that the optimal structure for each company may vary, given that different companies have different attributes. We now turn to empirical studies examining the relationship between a firm's various attributes and board composition. This enables us to ascertain whether and where there are any inefficiencies in board composition.[78]

Miwa and Ramseyer in their seminal 2005 study argued that board composition in Japan varies according to the firm's attributes, and is therefore optimal.[79] However, they did not determine whether firms have an optimal board composition for monitoring management. This is because the attributes Miwa and Ramseyer focused on as explanatory variables for board composition[80] (e.g., the industrial sector in which the firm is located, whether the firm has a parent company and the firm's level of financial distress), do not reflect the necessity or the cost of monitoring by outsiders.

In 2011, Saitō conducted a more comprehensive study on board composition using panel data of 511 firms in the Nikkei 500 and showed that Japanese firms do not always appoint outside directors even when it is efficient to do so.[81] Although firms with higher monitoring costs are more likely to appoint outside directors,[82] firms with higher private benefits for managers are less likely to appoint outside directors (i.e., board composition is not optimal in a different aspect in each case).[83]

[78] In addition to the following studies, Uchida also shows that the composition of Japanese listed firm's board is partially efficient but partially inefficient. *Ibid.*, 14–15.

[79] Miwa and Ramseyer, 'Evidence on Outside Directors from Japan', 314–322, 333.

[80] *Ibid.*, 316–17, Table III.

[81] There is another study reporting that although board size of firms is partially optimal, the independence of their boards (measured by ratio of outside directors) for 1,531 firms listed on the TSE during 2003–2007 is not optimal. H. Aman and P. Nguyen, 'The Size and Composition of Corporate Boards in Japan', *Asian Business and Management*, 11(4) (2012), 425. The difference between T. Saitō, 'The Determinants of Board Composition When Managers Control Director Selection: Evidence from Japan' (Working Paper, 2011) may be due to differences in the sample firms and/or explanatory variables.

[82] Other variables used as a proxy of monitoring costs (market to book ratio, risk and a synthesised variable of the three variables) are not found to have significant correlation with board composition.

[83] Saitō, 'The Determinants of Board Composition When Managers Control Director Selection', 19–22, 37–38 Tables 6 and 7. The private benefit for managers is proxied by free cash flow or synthesised variable of free cash flow and Lerner index.

In 2012, a study by Miyajima and Ogawa also found that board composition may be inefficient in some respects. Their analysis demonstrated that firms with a greater need for monitoring, especially firms with anti-takeover measures, were more likely to appoint independent directors, which indicated that board composition in such firms was optimal. They, however, also demonstrated that firms were less likely to appoint independent directors where information asymmetry (i.e., the cost of gathering information by independent directors) was low,[84] and that firm performance improves with the presence of, and an increase in the number of, independent directors (but only where the cost of obtaining information on such firms was low).[85] These findings indicate that firms that can be easily monitored by outsiders may appoint too few independent directors; conversely, firms that may not fully benefit from outsider monitoring due to high informational costs may appoint too many independent directors.

However, Miyajima and Ogawa rejected the proposition that the appointment of independent directors has an impact on CEO turnover rates. There is no significant correlation between the appointment of independent directors and CEO turnover rates whether in general or when the specific attributes of firms are taken into account.[86] In addition, they suggest that firms with high foreign shareholdings tend to appoint too many independent directors, which leads to lower performance.[87]

c Conclusions

Except for Miwa and Ramseyer's 2005 study, recent empirical studies tend to suggest that even though the appointment of independent directors may not improve corporate performance in general, there are certain circumstances where the appointment of outside directors does improve performance.[88] However, the extent to which they do so depends on the context, and the precise situations in which corporate performance is improved by the appointment of outside directors are unclear. Further,

[84] Miyajima and Ogawa, '日本企業の取締役会構成の変化をいかに理解するか?：取締役会構成の決定要因と社外取締役の導入効果', 13–15 and 39–40 Tables 4 and 5. The information asymmetry is proxied by research and development intensity, market to book ratio, volatility of stock return and ratio of intangible assets.

[85] *Ibid.*, 22 and 45 Table 10. The firm performance is measured by industry adjusted return on assets.

[86] *Ibid.*, 23–25 and 46 Table 11.

[87] *Ibid.*, 18–19, 43 Table 8, 22 and 45 Table 10.

[88] Compare this result with the findings of empirical studies for the US / UK and for Australia: see Chapter 2 at IV.2 and Chapter 11 (Australia) at V.

these studies conclude that the board composition of Japanese firms may be suboptimal in some respects. Firms that are likely to benefit from monitoring by outsiders tend to appoint too few outside and/or independent directors, but firms that are unlikely to benefit from such monitoring often appoint too many. Further, firms that would benefit from more stringent monitoring by outsiders (such as firms where managerial private benefits are high) are less likely to appoint outside directors.[89]

These results suggest a basis for legal or other types of regulatory intervention (such as stock exchange rules) regarding board composition.[90] Ideally, regulatory intervention should be targeted only at firms with suboptimal board compositions (i.e., intervention should affect only firms that 'inefficiently have no IDs', and not firms that 'efficiently have no IDs' (as depicted in Figure 4.3a)). It is important to recognise that the optimal number of independent directors may differ for individual firms,[91] and that the optimal number of independent directors might be zero for some firms (as shown in Figure 4.3a).

The following question then arises: do these empirical studies justify the recent corporate reforms in Japan? We note that the 'comply or explain' approach adopted in the reforms may not improve the overall situation. This approach encourages firms without any outside directors to appoint at least one such director, as companies failing to comply will have to incur the additional cost of disclosing and explaining their non-compliance to shareholders. The precise cost of this disclosure will again differ depending on the demands of the shareholders.

Foreign investors may be less friendly towards management and therefore impose more stringent demands, whereas management-friendly shareholders such as cross-shareholders are likely to be less demanding. Firms with a high proportion of management-friendly investors are therefore likely to face lower disclosure cost, which in turn reduces their

89 However, it should be noted that Saitō, 'The Determinants of Board Composition When Managers Control Director Selection', and Miyajima and Ogawa, '日本企業の取締役会構成の変化をいかに理解するか?： 取締役会構成の決定要因と社外取締役の導入効果' [Understanding Change in Board Composition: Determinants of Board Composition and Effects of Outside Directors], report contrasting results for firms with a higher extent of managerial private benefits. This may be due to a difference in their research design: the latter includes whether the sample firms adopt anti-takeover defences in their independent variables as one of the proxies for the necessity of monitoring, but the former does not.

90 For problems associated with deriving implications for law from the results of these empirical studies, see W. Tanaka, '立法事実と実証分析の利用：齋藤報告へのコメント' [An Empirical Analysis of Board Structure of Japanese Firms: Comment on Saitō], ソフトロー研究, 20 (2012), 43–51.

91 See *supra* note 61 and accompanying text.

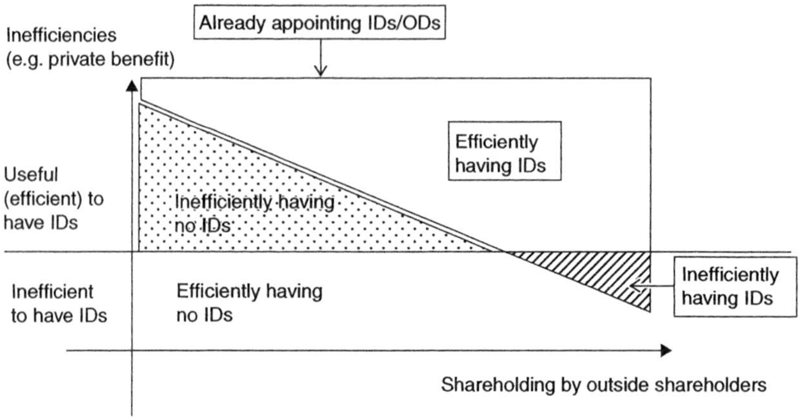

Figure 4.3a ID's Effects on Efficiencies

incentive to comply with outside director requirements. Yet, precisely because management-friendly shareholders are unlikely to act as an effective check against management, these firms require outsider monitoring. Under the 'comply and explain' model, these firms have little incentive to appoint outside directors – often resulting in less than optimal outcomes.

In contrast, firms with substantial foreign ownership are likely to have higher disclosure costs due to the demands of foreign investors and therefore have a significant incentive to comply with the outside director requirements. However, given that such firms are already subject to stringent monitoring from foreign investors and therefore require fewer additional outside directors, the 'comply or explain' model often incentivises the firms to appoint more outside directors than is optimal. This relationship between shareholding structure and the appointment of independent directors is depicted in Figure 4.3a.

In sum, a 'comply or explain' model may not provide the right incentives to listed firms in general. The firms that would benefit from outsider monitoring have a low incentive to appoint outside directors, and therefore appoint too few (see 'benefit of "comply to explain" (C/E)' in Figure 4.3b). Instead, the 'comply or explain' model raises disclosure costs for firms with substantial foreign ownership, which require fewer outside directors but nevertheless have a high incentive to 'comply' due to the demands of their respective foreign investors (see 'cost of C/E' in Figure 4.3b).[92]

[92] There is an underlying assumption in this argument that foreign institutional investors cannot easily judge whether an individual firm really needs outsiders on its board of

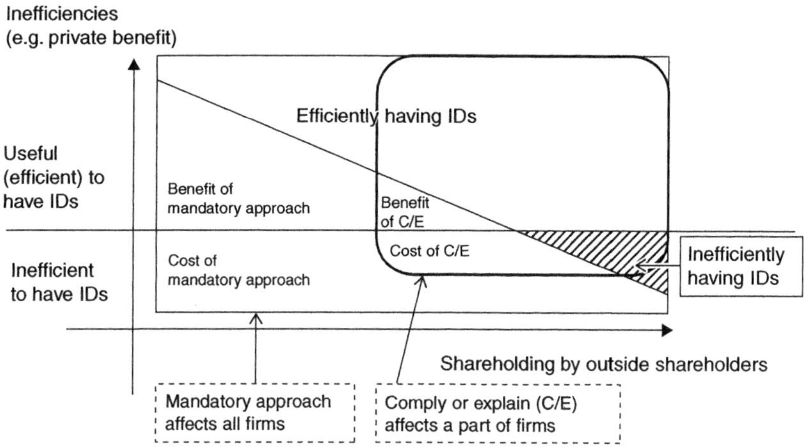

Figure 4.3b Comparison of Approaches for Promoting Appointments of IDs

However, we believe that a mandatory outside director requirement is not necessarily better than the 'comply or explain' approach currently adopted in Japan. Given that there are firms where the optimal number of outside directors is zero, a mandatory outside director requirement would require such firms to appoint one, resulting in suboptimal outcomes. However, where the optimal number of outside directors for a firm is at least one, and such firms have not appointed any outside directors, imposing a mandatory outside director requirement would result in optimal outcomes for these firms. Both the costs and the benefits of the mandatory outside director requirement therefore exceed those of the 'comply or explain' approach (see Figure 4.3b).

Determining which approach is superior depends on the overall distribution of firms in Japan. Where a large number of firms have a less than optimal number of outside directors and fail to comply with the outside director requirements under the 'comply or explain' approach, a mandatory outside director requirement should be adopted.[93] Further, if it were optimal for most companies to have at least one outside director

directors, or how many of them firms need. Since they tend to apply their voting policies uniformly to firms in which they invest, this may be a plausible assumption – but this entirely depends on the cost of gathering information and voting.

93 The justification will be stronger if most firms who do not need outside directors face serious difficulties in explaining the reason under the 'comply or explain' approach, since the cost of both approaches does not differ materially under this condition, although we note that the mandatory approach provides more substantial benefits.

(i.e., if the line dividing 'efficient/inefficient to have IDs' in Figure 4.3b moves downwards), a mandatory outside director would result in more optimal outcomes than the 'comply or explain' approach. In contrast, the 'comply or explain' approach is preferable where it correctly incentivises firms with a suboptimal number of outside directors to appoint more outside directors by raising disclosure costs for such firms, and reducing disclosure costs for firms where it is not optimal for such firms to appoint outside directors. However, the 'comply or explain' approach adopted in Japan and the proposed (and rejected) mandatory director requirement both require directors to appoint at least one outside director. The difference between these options is more likely to be theoretical than real unless the two options provide for a different number of outside directors.

2 *Political Dynamics Behind the Legal Reforms*

As discussed in section II, Japan's corporate governance system has been gradually changing over the past few decades. This is exemplified by the 2014 Amendments to the Companies Act. First, although the Legislative Council implicitly took the position that the outside directors are beneficial for companies, it merely introduced regulations for the appointment of outside directors using a 'comply or explain' approach, instead of a mandatory outside director requirement. Second, while the LDP intervened to modify the reform bill based on the Outline of Reform provided by the Legislative Council, it stopped short of introducing a mandatory outside director requirement, and chose to strengthen the existing 'comply or explain' approach instead. Arguably, the minor changes effected by the LDP could herald major ones in the long run.

To analyse the implications of Japan's corporate reforms, this section examines the 2014 Amendments from a political perspective. Specifically, it will address two questions: (1) how did the Companies Act Working Group of the Legislative Council decide on the proposed outside director provisions in the Companies Act, and why did it decide not to enact a mandatory outside director requirement?; and (2) why did the ruling LDP party modify the Reform Bill, but only make slight changes to it?

a How Did the Working Group Reach Its Conclusion?

Overview of the Discussions at the Working Group

To determine the approach taken by the Companies Act Working Group towards the proposed outside director provisions in the Companies Act, this section begins with an overview of the Working Group's discussions. To start, the proposal for a mandatory outside director requirement was not motivated by any corporate scandal or the 2008 Global Financial Crisis.

Rather, the driving forces behind this proposal were the low long-term performance of the Japanese stock market, and the lack of confidence[94] of foreign investors in Japanese corporate governance.[95]

Opponents to the mandatory outside director requirement, especially the representative from *Keidanren*, made two main arguments:[96] (1) they posited that it was unclear that outside directors were necessary when outside *kansayaku* were part of a company's governance structure and could, in turn, act as managerial-monitors;[97] and (2) they suggested that there is no 'one size fits all' board structure for 'good' corporate governance, and, in turn, each company should have their own discretion to choose the structure that suits them best.[98]

The first argument gave rise to extensive discussions regarding the functions that could be performed by outside directors, but not by outside *kansayaku*.[99] The key statutory difference is that the former can vote at the board of directors' meetings, whilst the latter cannot. As such, unlike outside directors, outside *kansayaku* cannot participate in decisions regarding the appointment and dismissal of management. In turn, supporters of the mandatory outside director requirement argued that outside *kansayaku* were unable to act as effective managerial-monitors.

The second argument that there is no 'one size fits all' board structure[100] is called into question by recent empirical studies. These studies suggest

[94] This view was most clearly expressed by a member of the Working Group representing the Pension Fund Association (Kigyō Nenkin Rengō-kai), the largest private pension fund in Japan. 法制審議会　会社法制部会 第 1 回会議議事録 [The Minutes of the 1st Meeting of the Companies Act Working Group of the Legislative Council], held on 28 April 2010, 24, available at www.moj.go.jp.; 法制審議会　会社法制部会 第 2 回会議議事録 [The Minutes of the 2nd Meeting of the Companies Act Working Group of the Legislative Council], held on 26 May 2010, 2–6 (both remarks by Mr Hamaguchi), available at www.moj.go.jp.

[95] The Minutes of the 2nd Meeting of the Companies Act Working Group of the Legislative Council, 6 (remark by Mr Hamaguchi), and 6–10 (remark by Mr Ishida).

[96] *Keidanren* (Japan Business Federation) is the most influential business organisation in Japan, consisting of major companies and industrial associations (see, www.keidanren.or.jp/en/).

[97] 会議議事録 [The Minutes of the 4th Meeting of the Companies Act Working Group of the Legislative Council], held on 25 August 2010, 16 (remark by Mr Hachioji), available at www.moj.go.jp.

[98] The Minutes of the 2nd Meeting of the Companies Act Working Group of the Legislative Council, 16–17; 法制審議会 会社法制部会 第 3 回会議議事録 [The Minutes of the 3rd Meeting of the Companies Act Working Group of the Legislative Council], held on 23 June 2010, 37–38 (both remarks by Mr Hachioji), available at www.moj.go.jp.

[99] The Minutes of the 4th Meeting of the Companies Act Working Group of the Legislative Council, 27–49.

[100] Presumably inspired by existing literature on the effect of board composition on firm performance in the United States (such as S. Bhagat and B. S. Black, 'The Non-Correlation between Board Independence and Long-Term Firm Performance', *Journal*

that while the optimal board structure for each individual company may differ, the appointment of outside directors in Japan seemed to be decided based on managerial self-interest rather than shareholder interests. As such, the appointment of the *first* outside director impacts the company's return on assets positively.[101]

Interestingly, however, some representatives of shareholder interests who were generally assumed to be in favour of monitoring by outside directors, opposed the introduction of a mandatory outside director requirement. The representative of the Pension Fund Association acknowledged the usefulness of requiring listed companies to have an outsider-*majority* board. However, he noted that the mandatory outside director requirement might be harmful if companies were merely required to appoint only one or two outside director(s) – such tepid reforms might be used as an excuse to abandon future corporate governance reforms.[102] Further, a guest speaker from Institutional Shareholders Services feared that a mandatory outside director requirement might result in mere formalistic compliance, which would in turn hinder further corporate governance reforms.[103] In addition, two law professors expressed their doubts about the effect of a mandatory outside director requirement and their preference for a 'comply or explain' approach.[104]

Decision by Unanimity

Formally, the decisions of the Working Group are made by a simple majority vote of the members attending the meeting, and when the vote

of Corporate Law, 27 (2002), 231), *Keidanren* asserted that it should be carefully examined whether the mandatory appointment of outside directors would lead to strengthening competitiveness of Japanese companies. See also The Minutes of the 4th Meeting of the Companies Act Working Group of the Legislative Council, 31 (remark by Mr Hachioji).

101 法制審議会 会社法制部会 第 9 回会議議事録 [The Minutes of the 9th Meeting of the Companies Act Working Group of the Legislative Council], held on 26 January 2011, 3–5 (remark by Professor Tanaka, introducing papers of Professor Takuji Saitō), available at www.moj.go.jp. For a detailed discussion of the relevant empirical studies, see section III.1 of this chapter.

102 The Minutes of the 4th Meeting of the Companies Act Working Group of the Legislative Council, 36 (remarks by Mr Hamaguchi).

103 The Minutes of the 2nd Meeting of the Companies Act Working Group of the Legislative Council, 9–10 (remarks by Mr Ishida).

104 The Minutes of the 4th Meeting of the Companies Act Working Group of the Legislative Council, 47 (remarks by Professor Tanaka) and The Minutes of the 9th Meeting of the Companies Act Working Group of the Legislative Council, 18 (remark by Professor Fujita).

is evenly divided, the chairman has the casting vote.[105] After intensive discussions, the members of the Working Group took very different positions. It would be fair to say that it was very difficult to predict if the mandatory outside director requirement would have been adopted if the issue was put to a vote.

Unfortunately, this vote never came to pass. The proposed mandatory outside director requirement was dropped from the first draft of the Outline of Reform prepared for the 23rd meeting of the Working Group by the MOJ, and was substituted with a 'comply or explain' approach.[106] Presumably, this decision was made due to the lack of consensus on the mandatory outside director requirement in the Working Group,[107] since it is customary for the Legislative Council and its Working Groups to make decisions unanimously on private law matters.[108] This practice seems to give considerable bargaining power to each member, especially those from related interest groups such as *Keidanren*.[109]

Why does this practice exist? In-depth historical research would be necessary for a comprehensive answer, but some hints may be found in the nature of governmental councils.[110] Governmental councils are established partly to separate policymaking from the democratic political process, so as to give attention to views that might not be fully reflected in the latter and

[105] Art. 7, paras. 2 and 3, Ordinance on the Legislative Council (Hōsei Shingi-kai Rei), Cabinet Order No. 134 of 1949. Sub-members do not have votes.

[106] 会社法制の見直しに関する要綱案（第一次案）[The First Draft of the Outline for the Companies Act Reform], 1, available at www.moj.go.jp.

[107] 法制審議会 会社法制部会 第 23 回会議議事録 [The Minutes of the 23rd Meeting of the Companies Act Working Group of the Legislative Council], held on 18 July 2012, 2 (remark of Mr Shizuka), available at www.moj.go.jp.

[108] On the other hand, it is not rare for a decision to be made by majority vote for matters related to criminal law, as the members from bar associations tend to oppose such decisions. For example, at the 152nd meeting of the Council (7 February 2007), two reports regarding criminal law issues were decided by majority votes while three reports regarding private law issues were decided by unanimous votes. See, 法制審議会 第 152 回会議 議事概要 [The Summary of the Discussions at the 152nd Meeting of the Legal Council], available at www.moj.go.jp. Also, it has been noted that corporate law issues were also decided by majority vote during the 1960s and 1970s, as there were fundamental disagreements among members. Y. Yamada, 'ステイク・ホルダーと会社法' [Stakeholders and Corporate Law] in M. Nakahigashi and H. Matsui (eds.), 会社法の選択–新しい社会の会社法を求めて [Choices Made by the Corporate Law: In Search of the Corporate Law for the New Society] (Shōji Hōmu, 2010), 31, 103 n. 178.

[109] S. Kozuka and J. Lee, 'The New Japanese Insurance Act: Comparisons with Europe and Korea', *Journal of Japanese Law*, 14(28) (2009), 73, 77, 87.

[110] This preference for a unanimous decision is not unique to governmental councils in Japan. For example, a committee of an international organisation drafting conventions may try to achieve unanimity in order to induce future ratification by as many countries as possible. Further, it is possible that Japan has a greater preference for unanimous

to facilitate balanced decision making.[111] From this perspective, as Professor Akira Morita argues in a book based on his experience of serving on many governmental councils, unanimity is the source of authority of a governmental council's report; therefore, a decision by a majority vote is only a second-best solution.[112]

Further, the officials at the MOJ were reluctant to put the issue to a vote in the face of strong industry opposition. First, corporate law reforms are a repeat game, and the MOJ and industry players are participants in a repeat game from a game theory perspective. To obtain industry support for future law reforms, it would be unwise for the MOJ to overlook strong industry opposition in the absence of substantial political support. Second, it is important to note that the Council is not the only legislative channel for corporate law reform.[113] Industry players may also lobby politicians to propose a bill serving their interests, or modify a bill proposed by the MOJ that is against their interests.[114] Such events would not be pleasant for the MOJ, or for the career prospects of the officials in charge.

Opposition of *Keidanren*

With the practice of unanimous decision making, the enactment of the proposed mandatory outside director requirement – which was strongly opposed by *Keidanren* – was very difficult, if not impossible, to achieve. Although by 2010, the number of listed corporations that appointed one or more outside directors was gradually increasing,[115] there were still

decisions than other countries due to Japan's cultural preference for harmony, but this has yet to be confirmed.

111 Another benefit of governmental councils would be simply to take advantage of the knowledge of diverse experts.

112 A. Morita, 会議の政治学 [Politics of Governmental Councils] (Jigaku-sha, 2006), 9–10 and 43–46.

113 H. Morita, 'Reforms of Japanese Corporate Law and Political Environment', *Journal of Japanese Law*, 37 (2014), 25. Professor Morita notes that bargaining power of the industry against academics on corporate law reforms increased after the 1997 reform regarding deregulation of stock options, which was drafted by members of LDP without consulting the Council.

114 It should be noted, however, that it is unclear to what extent the option in the text above was available for industry in mid-2012, as the relationship between the DPJ government and *Keidanren* was reported to be not a good one. Further, although the LDP, which traditionally had strong ties with *Keidanren*, is expected to return to power in the next election, the LDP could be more reluctant to relax monitoring requirements for corporate managers, as it would face greater public criticism than when it intervened to enable the use of stock options in 1997.

115 'Appointment of Outside Directors by TSE-Listed Companies [Confirmed report]', Tokyo Stock Exchange, Inc.

several significant corporations that did not have any outside directors.[116] Importantly, some of these 'holdout corporations' were influential members of *Keidanren*, which made it difficult for *Keidanren* to support any mandatory requirement for outside directors.

In addition, it was important for *Keidanren* to defend the principle that decisions on governance structure should be left to the discretion of each individual corporation. This was the case as doing so would likely guard against the gradual escalation towards increasingly outsider-dominated boards in Japanese listed companies. *Keidanren*'s fear was that if it buckled on the mandatory requirement for a single outside director, this may open the door to further calls to increase the number of outside directors – for example, from one to one-third or even to the majority of the board. Although such future amendments would merely bring Japan in line with most other jurisdictions in Asia and around the world,[117] it would be an unwelcome watershed change for many of Japan's most powerful companies that are the core members of *Keidanren*.

Why then did *Keidanren* agree to the 'comply or explain' approach adopted by the 2014 Amendments?[118] Indeed, initially, the *Keidanren* representative opposed the 'comply or explain' approach on the basis that it would have substantially the same effect as a mandatory requirement. However, the *Keidanren* representative eventually compromised. One possible reason is the repeat game situation (mentioned above) that existed between the MOJ and *Keidanren*. *Keidanren* might have let the MOJ score points on this issue because it had attracted substantial public attention, knowing that it would be important for the MOJ and its officials to achieve results once the reform process had begun. Further, as there were other important issues for the *Keidanren* (e.g., proposals regarding the introduction of a derivative suit by shareholders of a parent corporation against the directors of its subsidiary, and the liability of a parent corporation against its subsidiary and its enforcement via derivative suit by minority shareholders of the subsidiary)[119] it is conceivable that *Keidanren* decided to use its bargaining power to achieve desirable

[116] For example, Toyota, Nippon Steel and Sumitomo Metal Corporation, and Canon did not appoint any outside director as of August 2012. These are the companies from which the chairmen of *Keidanren* were elected during the last two decades.

[117] See, for example, Chapter 5 (South Korea) at III.1.b; Chapter 8 (Hong Kong) at II.1; Chapter 9 (Singapore) at III.1.

[118] See *supra* II.1.e.

[119] Goto, 'The Outline for the Companies Act Reform', 31–36.

results on these other issues instead of a complete victory on the issue of monitoring by outside directors.

Effect of the Olympus Scandal

One might be surprised to find out that the Olympus scandal, which raised serious concerns as to the opacity and inward-looking culture of Japanese corporations,[120] did not affect the outcome of the Working Group discussions. As the problems at Olympus involved the detection and correction of financial losses and the cover-up of such losses by management, which could be addressed by outside *kansayaku*, outside directors were not necessarily the best solution to the problems brought to light by the Olympus scandal.[121] Further, expert governmental councils generally refuse to make rash populist regulations. This is arguably a virtue, rather than a vice.

b Why Did the LDP Intervene to Modify the Bill, But Then Only Make Slight Changes?

Considering the lukewarm 'comply or explain' approach proposed by the Working Group, the LDP decided to modify the bill based on the Outline of Reform provided by the Legislative Council, but stopped short of introducing a mandatory outside director requirement. This raises the following questions: (1) why did the LDP intervene at this stage?; and (2) why did it not go further by introducing a mandatory outside director requirement?

[120] The Olympus scandal involved the concealment of huge investment losses by top managers for more than a decade, which became public after Michael Woodford, a foreigner CEO, who was investigating the problem, was suddenly dismissed by the board of directors under the lead of the Chairman Tsuyoshi Kikukawa who was the former CEO and had been involved in the concealment. For more details, see Aronson, 'The Olympus Scandal and Corporate Governance Reform', 102–104, 106–114. In relation to the debate on appointment of outside directors, Olympus had been appointing three outside directors, which was well beyond the average of Japanese companies. As these outside directors were not able to detect the loss concealment and they all approved of the dismissal of the CEO, some asserted that this scandal exemplified the uselessness of outside directors. It must be noted, however, that two of these outside directors were affiliated with a recipient of donations by Olympus or a newspaper that had been receiving advertisement fees from Olympus and were not 'independent' enough. On the other hand, although Woodford did not qualify as an outside director as he was the CEO and had been a long-time employee, he was an 'outsider' in a sense that he did not share a culture of blind obedience to the former CEO. This may suggest the usefulness of having an 'outsider' within the board of directors.

[121] For a critique of various legislative efforts to use independent directors as a regulatory tool in response to corporate scandals, see Chapter 2 at II.3.

Why Did the LDP Intervene Despite the Low Political Salience of Corporate Governance Issues?

Law reforms that strengthen corporate governance are often political reactions to corporate scandals. These are situations where the political salience (i.e., the importance of a particular issue to the average voter) of corporate governance issues is high.[122] Based on this insight, one might suspect that the intervention by the LDP was caused by the high political salience of corporate governance issues following the Olympus scandal.

This intervention, however, took place in late 2013,[123] two years after the Olympus scandal was brought to light in October 2011.[124] At this time, various political issues had higher political salience, including the liability and reconstruction of the Tokyo Electric Power Company after the Fukushima Nuclear Power Plant disaster. Hence, it would be fair to say that the political salience of the Olympus scandal had diminished significantly by late 2013. The question then becomes: why did the LDP intervene at this point in time?

Professor Hatsuru Morita proposes an explanation for the LDP's intervention using the median voter theory, and asserts that the emergence of a two-party system, which was a result of the change of electoral rules to a single-member district system, motivated the LDP to appeal to stakeholders on corporate governance issues.[125] This argument, however, overlooks the fact that the Japanese political situation in 2013 did not reflect a two-party system, which had declined dramatically in December 2012 with the striking defeat of the DPJ and the LDP's return to power.[126] Even if the median voter theory was applicable at that point of time, it is quite difficult to imagine that a median voter would appreciate the corporate governance reforms initiated by

[122] P. D. Culpepper, *Quiet Politics and Business Power: Corporate Control in Europe and Japan* (Cambridge University Press, 2011), 4–7.

[123] Sakamoto et al., '平成二六年改正会社法の解説（I）', 29–30.

[124] It also took nearly two years from the Lehman shock in September 2008 until the enactment of the Dodd-Frank Act in July 2010, but it would be fair to say that the aftermath of the Financial Crisis remained one of the US's primary concerns in 2010.

[125] Morita, 'Reforms of Japanese Corporate Law and Political Environment', 35–36. It must be noted that Professor Morita's concern is with the LDP's sudden change in direction, as opposed to the question of why the LDP did so at this particular point in time.

[126] K. E. Kushida and P. Y. Lipscy, 'The Rise and Fall of the Democratic Party of Japan' in K. E. Kushida and P. Y. Lipscy (eds.), *Japan under the DPJ: The Politics of Transition and Governance* (The Walter H. Shorenstein Asia Pacific Research Center, 2013), 3–4.

the LDP's intervention, which were limited in their extent and complicated in their form.[127]

This chapter offers a different perspective by exploring the motivations of individual politicians,[128] rather than the parties themselves.[129] For parties or politicians in general, there are few, if any, benefits to strengthening corporate governance where it has low political salience. However, for an individual politician with a personal interest in corporate governance, there might be 'political salience' on an individual level with that particular politician's political base.

The politicians who were active in the legislative process for the 2014 Amendments – Representative Yasuhisa Shiozaki[130] from the LDP, and Councillor Tsutomu Okubo[131] and Representative Takeshi Shina[132] from the DPJ – had previously advocated for stronger corporate governance. The problem for these politicians, however, was the difficulty in gaining support from other politicians and parties when the political salience at the party level for corporate governance issues was low. The peculiarity of the 2014 Amendments was that Representative Shiozaki happened to be one of the six acting chairpersons of the Policy Research Council of the LDP. As the approval of the Policy Research Council is required for

127 Discussions at the Diet between Representative Shiozaki and Minister Sadakazu Tanigaki, in which the Reform Act was described as imposing a 'virtual obligation' on listed companies to appoint an outside director, could be understood as an attempt by members of the LDP to ease this incomprehensibility and to (over-) emphasise their achievement to voters.

128 In theory, there is also a possibility that an individual officer of the MOJ with a special incentive takes an initiative on a particular issue to the extent of his power. In the 2014 amendments, however, no individual officer in charge played a particular role as those played by individual politicians described in this section. Note that this view might be biased, as one of the authors was himself involved in the reform as a part-time officer of the MOJ.

129 Existing political science literature on corporate governance tends to focus on the extent of the influence of political parties and their interactions with interest groups. See, for example, J. W. Cioffi, *Public Law and Private Power: Corporate Governance Reform in the Age of Finance Capitalism* (Cornell University Press, 2010), 2–3, 8–11; Culpepper, *Quiet Politics and Business Power*, 180–192.

130 Representative Shiozaki worked at Bank of Japan before being elected as a member of the Diet in 1993. He was also the Chief Cabinet Secretary for the 1st Abe administration from 2006 to 2007, and is the Minister of Health, Labour and Welfare since September 2014.

131 Councillor Okubo worked at Morgan Stanley Japan before being elected as a member of the Diet.

132 Representative Shina was a banker and an in-house lawyer at Shinseki Bank before being elected as a member of the Diet.

the LDP to support a bill,[133] Representative Shiozaki was able to request modifications to the Bill based on the Outline of Reform put forward by the Legislative Council as a condition for his approval.[134]

One might argue that the promotion of corporate governance as a measure to promote investment and economic growth was not only a matter of concern for Representative Shiozaki, but was also a key policy in the LDP's political platform. Indeed, the LDP government went on to publish Japan's Corporate Governance Code.[135] Although it is true that Prime Minister Shinzo Abe has emphasised the importance of corporate governance,[136] it was Representative Shiozaki who played the lead role in the promotion of corporate governance through the 2014 Amendments, as it seems that Prime Minister Abe was content with the original Outline of the Legislative Council.[137]

Why Did the LDP Stop Short of a Mandatory Outside Director Requirement?

In light of the above, why did the LDP – or more precisely Representative Shiozaki – not go further to demand the introduction of a mandatory outside director requirement?[138] This is even more puzzling because, in April 2012 in response to the Olympus scandal, several divisions of the

[133] Art. 42, para. 2, The Constitution of the Liberal Democratic Party (*Jiyū Minshutō Tōsoku*), available at www.jimin.jp.

[134] Approval of the Policy Research Council must be made through the Policy Deliberation Committee (*Seichō Shingi-kai*), which consists of the chairperson and vice-chairpersons of the Policy Research Council. Art. 45, para. 2 and para. 4, The Constitution of the Liberal Democratic Party.

[135] See *supra* II.1.f.

[136] Shinzo Abe, 'A New Vision from a New Japan' (Speech at World Economic Forum 2014 Annual Meeting, 22 January 2014), available at japan.kantei.go.jp.

[137] At a governmental meeting on 2 April 2013, Prime Minister Abe ordered Minister of Justice Tanigaki to proceed with the Companies Act reform in order to promote corporate governance, in response to Minister Tanigaki's explanation of the original Outline. See the instruction of the Prime Minister titled 'Policies for the Present Based on the Discussions at the 4th and the 5th Meetings of the Industrial Council', item 3; 第 4 回 産業競争力会議議事要旨 [The Summary of the Discussions at the 4th Meeting of the Industrial Competitiveness Council], held on 15 March 2013, 5–6, available at www.kantei.go.jp.

[138] A related question is, why Representative Shiozaki did not wait for the discussion for the Corporate Governance Code and bothered to intervene only to make a slight change. One possibility is that it was important for his reputation as a 'tough' politician who would not just rubber-stamp bills arranged by bureaucrats. In this regard, it is worth noting that Representative Shiozaki played an important role in the aftermath of the banking crisis in 1998 regarding financial and banking law reform, which was done 'outside the traditional policymaking nexus of LDP leaders and MOF bureaucrats'. J. A. Amyx, *Japan's Financial Crisis, Institutional Rigidity and Reluctant Change* (Princeton

Policy Research Council of the LDP jointly proposed the introduction of a mandatory requirement to appoint multiple independent directors.[139] In contrast, in April 2012, the DPJ merely suggested the need for outside directors to take a more active role,[140] but subsequently in April 2014 submitted a competing bill to introduce a mandatory requirement for listed companies to appoint at least one outside director.[141]

These policy shifts are understandable if one matches the respective policy positions of the LDP or DPJ to when they were in power.[142] The LDP's limited intervention in late 2013 appears to have been due to its deference to the 'comply or explain' approach proposed by the Legislative Council. Even though the Legislative Council's consultation and report were made under the previous DPJ administration, it was presumably difficult for the LDP as the ruling party to completely override the Legislative Council's decision, because it was a unanimous decision made independent of the political process.[143] In April 2012, the LDP, which was still the opposition party, and Representative Shiozaki were not under any such constraints.

University Press, 2004), 205–206. Another possibility is that Representative Shiozaki thought that even a slight change was important to ensure that the reform at the next forum (in this case the Corporate Governance Code) could go a little further, as corporate governance reforms in Japan seldom take a huge leap.

139 Jiyū Minshu-tō (Liberal Democratic Party) (2012), Hoōmu Bukai, Zaimu Kinyū Bukai, Keizai Sangyō Bukai, Kigyō/Shihon-shijyo Hōsei Purojekuto Chi-mu and Kigyō-Kaikei Shō-i'inkai (Judicial Affairs Division, Treasury and Finance Division, Economy, Trade and Industry Division, Project Team on Corporate and Capital Market Law and Working Group on Corporate Accountings), 企業統治改革案について[On Reform Plan of Corporate Governance], 1 April 2012, available at /www.y-shiozaki.or.jp.

140 Nihon Keizai Shinbun, '民主、社外取締役の積極活用提言　義務化明記せず' [DPJ Proposes Active Use of Outside Directors, Does Not Clearly State Introduction of Mandatory Appointment], 12 April 2012, available at www.nikkei.com. The fact that the Olympus scandal did not lead to bipartisan reforms for the mandatory appointment of outside directors suggests that the effect of this scandal on Japan did not rise to the level of the Enron scandal or of the Financial Crisis of 2007–2008 in the US, since the Olympus scandal did not involve malfunctioning of a highly-trusted system (as was Enron) or a national economic downturn (as was the Financial Crisis).

141 Bill Submitted by Member of the House of Representatives to the 186th Diet, No. 15, available at www.shugiin.go.jp. This opposing bill was eventually rejected on 23 April 2014.

142 For a brief description of Japan's political situation during this period, see the Timeline.

143 This does not mean that a report of the Legislative Council is always respected. For example, the Council's 1996 report on family law to permit a married couple to use different surnames has not led to a submission of a reform bill to date, as there was a strong opposition from the conservatives. See Hōmushō (Ministry of Justice), 選択的夫婦別氏制度（いわゆる選択的夫婦別姓制度）について[On the Use of Different Surnames by a Married Couple], available at www.moj.go.jp.

In contrast, the DPJ was forced to leave the matter to the ongoing discussions at the Legislative Council because it was the governing party during the Olympus scandal,[144] and had initiated the proceedings at the Legislative Council. After it lost power, the DPJ was no longer obligated to agree with the Legislative Council, and allowed its members to propose a competing bill to appeal to voters by demanding more stringent regulations on big businesses as compared to the LDP.

IV Analysis and Outlook: Where Does Japan Stand, and Whither?

Contrary to the views of some outside observers,[145] Japan has not been completely resistant to adopting independent directors. It is true, however, that Japan greeted the adoption of independent directors with less enthusiasm than its neighbours.[146] As of 2015, Japan has no mandatory requirement for any outside or independent directors. However, in 2015, following in the well-trodden path of a multitude of jurisdictions around the world (with the notable exception of the United States), Japan adopted a 'comply or explain' Corporate Governance Code, which requires all listed companies to adopt two independent directors or explain why they have failed to comply. Moreover, the Companies Act set a lower requirement that all companies must adopt at least one outside director or explain why they have failed to comply. As these requirements are relatively minimal – especially when viewed comparatively – it suggests that the pressure on Japanese companies to meet these minimal requirements may be stronger than in other jurisdictions with more onerous independence requirements. As such, it would clearly be inaccurate to suggest that Japan has completely rejected the use of independent directors in its corporate boards.

Moreover, in our view, what is exceptional about Japan is not necessarily the slow speed of its progress towards an independent monitoring board, but the fact that it has taken place without significant external shocks. The Japanese economy has been suffering from poor performance for two decades, and institutional investors have repeatedly pressed

[144] The difference between the DPJ's situation in April 2012 and that of the LDP in late 2013 depended on whether the Legislative Council had completed its discussions. While the DPJ had to leave the matter completely to the Legislative Council, the LDP was able to make a modification within the framework proposed by the Legislative Council.

[145] See, for example, Ringe, 'Independent Directors: After the Crisis', 408.

[146] See, for example, Korea, Hong Kong or Singapore at Chapter 5 (South Korea) at III.1; Chapter 8 (Hong Kong) at II.4; and Chapter 9 (Singapore) at II.4 respectively.

for corporate governance reforms. However, these driving forces have been weaker than the 2008 Financial Crisis or scandals involving rampant exploitation by controlling shareholders.[147] Though lobbying by foreign institutional investors and pressure through the capital market by institutional investors in general were taken into consideration by the Japanese political and business leaders, such pressures were never decisive in the Japanese context, as compared to some Asian jurisdictions during the Asian Financial Crisis. Therefore, Japan's situation seems comparable to the developments in the US, where the monitoring model with independent directors developed over about two decades, and without strong foreign pressure. In this context, Japan has spent a substantial period of time carefully examining the role of independent directors, as distinguished from the role of the existing autochthonous *kansayaku*.

The gradual adoption of independent directors in Japan emphasises the particular importance in the Japanese context of 'preclearance' or efforts to resolve conflicts amongst the views of opposing parties informally before the issue gets publicly discussed.[148] Although the discussion over the mandatory requirement of outside directors was expressly made at the Legislative Council, the legislative process only began after nearly half of all companies listed in the First Section of the TSE had already appointed outside directors. Moreover, the ultimate outcome of the discussion process was a minimal optional requirement that the remaining listed companies will likely find easy to accept. Such gradual and modest reforms may be partly the cause, and partly the outcome, of the legislative process. The practice of a unanimous decision making process, which is the *de facto* norm at the Legislative Council, in practice grants a veto to every player involved in the process. However, as most of them are repeat players, these vetoes are used, if ever, in a constrained manner.

Nevertheless, it must be noted that gradual changes are nonetheless *changes*, whose cumulative impact over time could be enormous. The political initiatives of LDP politicians may signal such changes, particularly their desire to push business leaders towards accepting independent directors in the boardroom.

[147] See, for example, Chapter 2 at II.3; Chapter 5 (South Korea) at III.1.

[148] J. R. Macey et al., 'Politics, Bureaucracies, and Financial Markets: Bank Entry into Commercial Paper Underwriting in the United States and Japan', *University of Pennsylvania Law Review*, 139 (1990), 369.

LDP politicians are apparently no longer strong allies of established businesses; they now appear to have derogated from the previous practice of 'preclearance' and actively seek to change the attitudes of key players. The emergence of reformers within the LDP coincides with the growth of the DPJ, which is a centre-left party consisting of reformists supported by educated urban residents and labour advocates.[149] The DPJ failed to take a clear position on corporate governance reform, because labour unions, which were one of their supporting organisations, favoured the traditional Japanese stakeholder model and opposed the shareholder-oriented model.[150] The LDP reformers were fortunate in that there was nothing to prevent them from advocating for a shareholder-oriented model. Depending on the progress of labour market reform and its impact on the labour union's political power, there is a high possibility that the Japanese business leaders will move closer to the LDP reformers (and their counterparts in the DPJ) in parting with the old stakeholder model in favour of the shareholder-oriented model (see Figure 4.4).

Although no one can be sure about whether this will come to pass, there can be no doubt that Japan is constantly transforming itself to respond to the changing environment that it faces.[151] The seemingly modest introduction of 'comply or explain' rules on independent directors constitutes a significant development in the course of such gradual, but ongoing, changes.

V Conclusion

Japan is undoubtedly one of the few jurisdictions that have only recently accepted independent members in their boardrooms. Even after introducing the 'comply or explain' regime through legislation and the Corporate

[149] For a history of the DPJ, see P. Koellner, 'The Democratic Party of Japan' in A. Gaunder (ed.), *The Routledge Handbook of Japanese Politics* (Routledge, 2011), 25 and J. A. A. Stockwinn, *Governing Japan: Divided Politics in a Resurgent Economy*, 4th edn (Wiley-Blackwell, 2008).

[150] On the relationship between DPJ and the labour union, see L. E. Carlile, 'The Labor Movement' in A. Gaunder (ed.), *The Routledge Handbook of Japanese Politics* (Routledge, 2011), 172.

[151] The finding is consistent with the more general argument of 'gradual transformation' advanced by L. Nottage, 'Perspectives and Approaches: A Framework for Comparing Japanese Corporate Governance' in L. Nottage, L. Wolff and K. Anderson (eds.), *Corporate Governance in the 21st Century: Japan's Gradual Transformation* (Edward Elgar, 2008), 41–51.

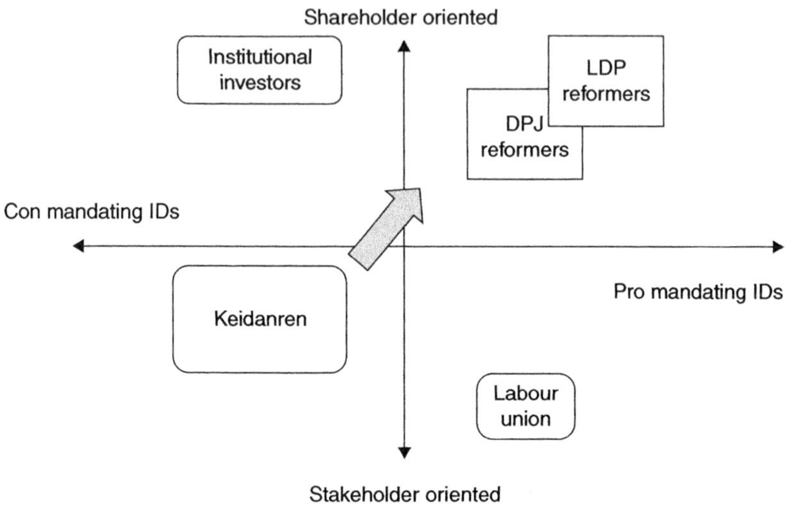

Figure 4.4 Positions of Relevant Actors and the Future Migration

Governance Code, the required number is minimal, respectively one and two. This fact, together with the *kansayaku* system, which has existed for over a century, as well as the well-known post-war practice of lifetime employment in major Japanese businesses, have given many outside observers the impression that Japan has been extremely reluctant to improve its corporate governance practices.

This chapter argues that the truth is somewhat different. Japan has gradually and consistently been engaged in corporate governance reforms over the last two decades. Independent directors became part of the reform agenda in the late 2000s; public consultations followed suit, and general discussions about the functions and purposes of independent directors, including their limitations, permeated business, political and academic circles. At some point, individuals showed strong leadership in influencing the direction of the debates. Nevertheless, this process was gradual and time-consuming, and not aided by scandals, such as the Olympus scandal.

The unique direction of developments in Japan reflects the economic success and political stability it has enjoyed in the last two decades. Until very recently, it was the second largest economy in the world, and even now, it remains a mature economy with a relatively stable political climate. What defines Japan's experience is the absence of external shocks, political turmoil or significant regime changes. Instead, Japan was subject to gradual changes in the global economy, which took the form of changes in its shareholding structure. Market changes brought about corporate governance changes, but only gradually. As long as the market continues to change – which will surely be the case – Japanese corporate governance rules will change as well.

5

Korea's Mandatory Independent Directors

Expected and Unexpected Roles

KYUNG-HOON CHUN

I Introduction

Throughout the world, board independence is regarded as one of the most significant features of 'good' corporate governance. Despite repeated challenges to the 'blind faith' that is often expressed in independent directors,[1] the number of independent directors on the boards of public companies in the United States (US) has been constantly increasing.[2] As highlighted in the other chapters of this book, 'American-style' independent directors have ostensibly been transplanted into many jurisdictions in Asia and around the world.[3] Today, almost every major proposal

[1] *See* for example, U. Rodrigues, 'The Fetishization of Independence', *Journal of Corporation Law*, 33 (2008), 447 (arguing that 'current rules over-rely on independence, transforming an essentially negative quality – lack of ties to the corporation – into an end itself'); L. M. Fairfax, 'The Uneasy Case for the Inside Director', *Iowa Law Review*, 96 (2010), 127 (arguing that 'the value of independent directors has been overstated, while the value of inside directors has been under-appreciated'); U. Velikonja, 'The Political Economy of Board Independence', *North Carolina Law Review*, 92 (2014), 855 (suggesting that 'institutional investors value director independence because it displaces more meaningful reform' and arguing that 'board independence mandates should be retired because they are inefficient at best and damaging at worst').

[2] In 2000, 78 per cent of directors of US public companies were independent, 22 per cent of companies had only one non-independent director and 23 per cent of companies had a non-executive chairman. By 2013, 85 per cent of directors were independent, 60 per cent of boards had only one non-independent director (i.e., the CEO) and 45 per cent had a non-executive chairman. Velikonja, 'Board Independence', 857. For a brief overview of the development of the concept in the US (and in other non-Asian jurisdictions) see Chapter 1 of this book.

[3] It should be noted that although many jurisdictions in Asia and around the world claim to have transplanted 'American-style' independent directors into their corporate governance systems, in reality significant differences often exist between the corporate governance mechanism that has been transplanted by (and among) these

for corporate governance reform includes some measures for enhancing the independence of directors.

In this respect, Korea is no exception. In order to implement the requirements of the International Monetary Fund (IMF) in the aftermath of the Asian Financial Crisis, Korea adopted various measures to reform its corporate governance system. One of the most significant reforms was to enhance board independence. Unlike many other jurisdictions, where corporate governance codes, listing rules or other types of 'soft law' are used to promote the use of independent directors, Korea's statutory company law requires that the boards of all large listed companies and certain financial institutions consist of a majority (or, in the case of smaller companies or financial institutions, at least a quarter) of 'independent directors',[4] who must be independent from the management *and* major shareholders of the company. This mandatory regime was designed to enhance the monitoring function of boards in listed companies and financial institutions in Korea.

It has been 15 years since the adoption of these reforms. Despite the rather long passage of time, there is still considerable debate about whether the mandatory independent director regime is functioning properly. Although many of the detailed regulations governing independent directors are generally in line with those of other leading jurisdictions, we are now witnessing a unique reality concerning independent directors in Korea. Notably, it appears that many independent directors play, and their companies expect them to play, neither 'advisory' nor 'monitoring' roles, but rather, roles related to 'government relations'. This role was not contemplated by the legislature when the mandatory independent director regime was adopted.

jurisdictions and the American concept of the independent director. As Lan and Puchniak highlight in Chapter 9 (Singapore) of this book, this fact has been almost entirely overlooked by policy-makers, pundits and academics around the world. As such, Lan and Puchniak suggest that the commonly held belief that the American concept of the independent director has been transplanted around the world is a myth. In general, as explained in this chapter, Lan and Puchniak's theory largely holds true in the context of Korea.

[4] The Korean terminology corresponding to 'independent director' would be *sawae-isa*. Its direct translation is 'outside director', but since Korean law requires certain criteria for a *sawae-isa* to secure his or her independence from management and major shareholders, 'independent director' would be another possible translation of *sawae-isa* (and there is no other established legal jargon in the Korean language corresponding to 'independent director'). Throughout this chapter, a *sawae-isa* in the Korean law and literature will be referred to as an 'independent director'.

This chapter aims to analyse the legal and regulatory framework, as well as the reality, concerning independent directors in Korea from a comparative perspective. More specifically, it aims to answer the following questions: what was the driving force behind the legislation that brought about mandatory independent directors in Korea and what was the intention of the legislature in passing this legislation?; how does Korean law define 'independence' and what are the similarities and differences between the Korean law and the laws of other major jurisdictions?; are Korea's independent directors functioning in the manner that the legislature intended them to function?; and, if Korea's independent directors are playing an unexpected role, then why are they behaving in an unexpected manner and what are the implications of their unexpected behaviour?

In order to answer these questions, section II briefly describes the general corporate law and governance context in Korea, which sets the stage for an in-depth discussion of Korea's intriguing independent director regime. Section III analyses the laws and regulations governing independent directors in Korea, including the motives and historical context behind this regulatory regime. Section IV discusses the unique reality concerning independent directors in Korea and explores the reasons, as well as the implications, of this unique phenomenon.

II Korean Corporate Governance at a Glance

1 *The Korean Corporate Law*

The modern Korean legal system is normally classified as a civil law system. By far, the most important source of law are statutes enacted by the Korean National Assembly. Amongst those statutes, the Korean Commercial Code (first enacted as Act No. 1212, finally amended as Act No. 14096) (*Sang-beob*, or the 'KCC'), which was enacted in 1962 and amended 25 times thereafter, is the major source of law governing corporations.

One should not, however, underestimate the growing importance of judge-made law, which has grown substantially over time in quantity as well as quality. Judicial precedents are accorded almost as much respect as in common law countries by practitioners and academics,[5] and there

[5] K. H. Chun et al., *Corporations and Partnerships in South Korea* (Wolters Kluwer, 2014), 24.

is a significant body of judicial precedent on corporate law. This development accelerated considerably in the 2000s, as shareholder activists as well as creditor banks increasingly initiated lawsuits in the wake of the Asian Financial Crisis.

2 *Korean Companies and the Capital Market*

At the end of 2015, there were 591,694 companies in Korea. Under Korean law, companies engaging in business can adopt one of five distinct types of corporate forms, namely, *hap-myeong hoesa* (general partnership company), *hapja hoesa* (limited partnership company), *yuhan chaeg-im hoesa* (limited liability company), *yuhan hoesa* (limited company) and *jusik hoesa* (stock corporation). The *jusik hoesa* is by far the most common type of company. Almost 95 per cent of companies (560,639) are incorporated stock corporations.[6] The stock corporation is the only type of company that is eligible to list on a stock exchange in Korea.

As of January 2015, there were 1,899 listed companies in Korea: 769 on the Korea Composite Stock Price Index ('KOSPI'); 1,059 on the Korean Securities Dealers Automated Quotations ('KOSDAQ'); and 71 on the newly launched Korea New Exchange ('KONEX').[7] The KOSPI is generally perceived as a market for established firms, whereas the KOSDAQ – which was modelled on and named after the NASDAQ – is perceived as a market for smaller start-up companies. Technically, both the KOSPI and KOSDAQ are divisions of the Korea Exchange, which is the only stock exchange that operates in Korea. The market capitalisation of the Korea Exchange (i.e., the KOSPI and KOSDAQ combined) was US $1,231 billion as of the end of 2015 – constituting 1.96 per cent of global capitalisation and ranking 14th in the world in terms of its size.[8]

3 *Distinctive Features of Korean Corporate Governance*

There are a few noteworthy features of Korean corporate governance. First, a number of large business groups – commonly known as *chaebol* – dominate the corporate scene in Korea. *Chaebol* is usually defined as a large group of related corporations engaged in diverse lines of business

[6] National Tax Service, *Statistical Yearbook of National Tax* (Seoul, 2016) (available in Korean).

[7] Current numbers are available at http://eng.krx.co.kr/.

[8] Press release of the Korea Exchange (1 February 2016) (available in Korean).

under highly concentrated family or individual control.[9] For example, as of March 2015, the Samsung Group, which is composed of 67 companies[10] (including 17 listed companies) accounted for approximately 26 per cent of the total market capital of the Korean stock market. A few other business groups such as Hyundai Motors, LG, SK, Lotte, Hyundai Heavy Industry and GS also represent a large portion of the Korean economy. As of March 2015, listed companies belonging to the top ten business groups accounted for 60 per cent of the total market capital of the KOSPI (i.e., approximately 54 per cent of the total market capital of the Korean stock market).

Member companies of these business groups are legally independent but tied together by cross-shareholdings, circular shareholdings and pyramidal structures. The strategic use of these structural devices enables the controlling shareholders to exercise voting power over affiliated companies substantially greater than their economic cash flow rights.[11] In these business groups, important business plans and decisions are often made at the group level, rather than at the level of each constituent company. The largest shareholder at the top of such a group structure is usually the founder of the group or his descendants. He is often called a 'chairman' and aided by a well-organised staff of elite employees selected and dispatched by the key constituent companies.

Another noteworthy feature of Korean corporate governance is that even listed companies tend to have controlling shareholders, most of whom being controlling minority shareholders.[12] According to a recent study, around 80 per cent of listed companies had an individual (as opposed to a company) as their largest shareholder (combined with other related persons). On average, in 2012, their shareholding ratio (combined with other related persons) was 22.5 per cent for KOSPI companies and 26.8 per cent for KOSDAQ companies. Table 5.1 shows the shareholding ratio of the largest *individual* shareholders in listed firms in Korea.

[9] H. J. Kim, 'Living with the IMF: A New Approach to Corporate Governance and Regulation of Financial Institutions in Korea', *Berkeley Journal of International Law*, 17 (1999), 63.

[10] Excluding companies established under the laws of foreign countries.

[11] A. C. Pritchard, 'Monitoring of Corporate Groups by Independent Directors', *Journal of Korean Law*, 9(1) (2009), 5.

[12] See O. R. Song, 'The Legacy of Controlling Minority Structure: A Kaleidoscope of Corporate Governance Reform in Korean Chaebol', *Law and Policy in International Business*, 34 (2002), 183.

Table 5.1 Shareholding Ratio of the Largest Individual Shareholders

		2007	2008	2009	2010	2011	2012
KCSPI	Average Shareholding Ratio (per cent)	21.34	21.37	21.84	22.35	23.08	22.47
	No. of Companies with Individual Largest Shareholder	646	645	633	621	588	621
	Total No. of Companies	746	765	770	777	791	784
KOSDAQ	Average Shareholding Ratio (per cent)	25.75	25.14	24.96	25.19	26.75	26.81
	No. of Companies with Individual Largest Shareholder	942	1,005	1,013	931	829	852
	Total No. of Companies	1,023	1,038	1,028	1,029	1,031	1,005

Source: Corporate Governance Service, *Corporate Governance White Book 2012* (in Korean), 97 (available at www.cgs.or.kr).

Despite the presence of controlling shareholders, the remaining shares seem to be quite dispersed in many firms. In 2013, the number of shareholders exceeded 10,000 in 315 listed firms (17.6 per cent of all listed firms) and exceeded 5,000 in 639 listed firms (35.7 per cent of all listed firms). Considering this in combination with the existence of controlling minority shareholders, one may presume that, in a substantial number of listed companies, the interests of dispersed non-controlling shareholders are potentially vulnerable to the opportunistic behaviour of the controlling minority shareholders. Thus, unlike a dispersed ownership structure (i.e., an Anglo-American-style 'Berle-Means' type company), where agency problems primarily arise between the management and dispersed shareholders, agency problems are more likely to be acute between the controlling shareholder and non-controlling shareholders in most listed companies in Korea.

4 *Roles of the Board of Directors in Korea*

In modern companies, the roles of the board of directors are multi-layered. Scholars classify the board's roles based on their different functions,[13] and we may think of four seemingly distinct but closely interrelated roles: managerial role; oversight role; advisory role; and relational role. The managerial role is derived from the somewhat archaic notion that the board should manage the company.[14] The oversight role (or manager-monitoring or supervisory role), highlighted by Professor Eisenberg in his seminal book *The Structure of the Corporation* in 1976, is currently regarded as the most important function of the board in modern corporations – particularly in large public listed companies. Some scholars also highlight the advisory role of the board as a 'friend' (as opposed to a monitor) of management, who advises on strategic matters. The board's function as a communication

[13] For example, Johnson, Daily and Ellstrand classify directors' roles into those of control, service and resource dependence. The control role corresponds to the monitoring role, the service role roughly corresponds to the advisory role, and the resource dependence role refers to the role of 'facilitating the acquisition of resources critical to the firm's success'. J. L. Johnson et al., 'Board of Directors: A Review and Research Agenda', *Journal of Management*, 22(3) (1996), 411.

[14] For example, the Model Business Corporation Act (MBCA) prepared by the American Bar Association, before its revision in 1974, required that 'the business and the affairs of a corporation shall be managed by a board of directors'. The current version of the MBCA provides that 'the business and affairs of the corporation shall be managed by or under the direction, and subject to the oversight, of its board of directors'.

channel with various stakeholders (e.g., employees, creditors, the community and the government) has also been attracting the attention of scholars and managers, and is often referred to as playing the 'relational role' of the board.[15]

Among these roles, the Korean law originally anticipated boards (which follow the one-tier structure)[16] to play a managerial role, and later supplemented this with the expectation that boards would also play a monitoring role. From its initial enactment in 1962, the KCC provides that 'the corporate affairs shall be *managed* by the decisions of the board of directors' (Article 393(1)). Similar to the Model Business Corporations Act in the US before its 1974 revision, this statement describes the managerial function, which was traditionally regarded as the fundamental role of the board. The term 'corporate affairs' may be interpreted broadly to include almost all of the decisions of the company. It is generally accepted, however, that the day-to-day operation of the corporate business is deemed to be delegated to representative directors,[17] even in the absence of an explicit provision in the statute or the articles of incorporation.

In 1984, the KCC was amended to add the provision that 'the board of directors shall *monitor* the performance of the duties of the directors' (Article 393(2)). Some commentators argue that this monitoring role does not fit well with the managerial role described in Article 393(1) above. They suggest that this is particularly the case when the board is composed of the senior executives of the company – which was typical in most Korean companies until the late 1990s (and still is the norm among many small and medium-sized companies). Currently, however, there is a general consensus among commentators that, for a company whose independent directors occupy the majority of board positions, the monitoring role is at the heart of the board's functions. The prevalence

15 The 'relational role' refers to 'the use of board memberships to facilitate the sharing of information and perspectives among corporations and their various stakeholders, such as shareholders, consumers, and the legal and financial community, and to ensure the corporation the continued support of these stakeholders'. L. L. Dallas, 'Developments in US Boards of Directors and the Multiple Roles of Corporate Boards' in J. Sarra (ed.), *Corporate Governance in Global Capital Markets* (UBC Press, 2003), 191–192.

16 Korea is a one-tier board jurisdiction. Thus, it does not have any bicameral system such as a supervisory board and a management board.

17 A representative director is a director (i.e., a board member) who has the authority to act on behalf of the company. Externally, as against third parties, a representative director has full authority to represent and legally bind the corporation in any and all of its business activities. Usually, the CEO takes the position of the representative director.

of independent directors on the board naturally leads to the assumption that 'monitoring of management' will be the board's primary function. Such boards, however, are a fairly new phenomenon in Korea – which is a point that will be elaborated on in greater detail below.

In addition to these general roles, the KCC specifically reserves certain decisions for the board of directors. For example, the following corporate actions are under the sole authority of the board: convening of a meeting of shareholders (Article 362); election and dismissal of a representative director (Article 389); approval of competition of a director with the company (Article 397); approval of self-dealing transactions (Article 398); approval of appropriation of the corporate opportunities by a director (Article 397-2); issuance of new shares (Article 416); issuance of bonds (Article 469); establishment and closure of a branch office (Article 393); and hiring and firing of a general manager (Article 393).

III Rules Governing Independent Directors in Korea

1 *Historical Context*

a The Asian Financial Crisis and the IMF's Bailout Programme

The Asian Financial Crisis, which began in July 1997, severely affected many countries in Asia, including Korea. Stock prices and the value of the Korean Won plummeted, causing a liquidity crisis for businesses and the nation as a whole. In particular, the ability of companies to pay off foreign currency denominated debts was severely damaged. A considerable number of large conglomerates and even some financial institutions went bankrupt or had to undergo serious restructuring. Many financial institutions and companies that survived the crisis were saddled with bad loans, which eventually caused the entire banking system to sink into a quagmire of non-performing loans. The IMF provided emergency financial support to the Korean government in December 1997. A condition of this financial support, however, was that the Korean government would accept the IMF's reform programme.

A Letter of Intent between the IMF and the Korean government was first signed on 3 December 1997, and amended eight times before the final amendment was signed on 12 July 2000. The main points of contention were macroeconomic policies (such as maintaining high interest rates), restructuring of the financial industry and the rehabilitation of financially distressed companies. Further, since the IMF was of the view that Korea's ill-functioning corporate governance and the lack of a proper monitoring system within Korean companies contributed to the crisis, one element of the reform was to increase the transparency and accountability of the management of Korean companies.[18] The reform plan included, among other things, enhancing board independence and establishing an audit committee instead of having an internal statutory auditor.

More specifically, an agreement between the IMF and Korean government entitled 'Korea: Memorandum on Economic Program' was attached to the Letter of Intent dated 7 February 1998. This document required 'listed companies on the Korea Stock Exchange to have at least one independent director'. Thereafter, another document titled 'Updated Memorandum on the Economic Program for the Second Quarterly Review' was attached to the 2 May 1998 Letter of Intent. This document specifically required 'at least one-fourth of the board of directors of listed companies to be outsiders from FY 1999' and the target date for initial compliance was set as 30 June 1998.[19]

These documents raise an intriguing question: why did the IMF make its financial aid conditional on strengthening the independence of directors in listed companies in Korea? It seems that the primary focus of the IMF was the introduction of the audit committee, rather than strengthening the independence of Korean boards. It was felt, however, that if audit committees were to replace internal statutory auditors (*gamsa* in Korean)[20] that it would be essential for boards to have a sufficient number of truly independent directors to make these audit committees function effectively in Korean listed companies. In other words, independent

[18] The 'Memorandum on the Economic Program' attached to the Letter of Intent dated 3 December 1997 states: 'The government recognizes the need to improve corporate governance and the corporate structure. Toward that end, transparency of corporate balance sheets (including profit and loss accounts) will be improved by enforcing accounting standards in line with generally accepted accounting practices, including through independent external audits, full disclosure, and provision of consolidated statements for business conglomerates' (available at www.imf.org).

[19] 'Letter of Intent from the Government of Korea' (2 May 1998), International Monetary Fund, available at www.imf.org.

[20] An internal auditor is also called a statutory auditor or a corporate auditor. It is a concept imported from Japan (*kansayaku*), whose role is to supervise the execution of directors' duties. For more details, see K. S. Kim, 'Transplanting Audit Committees to Korean Soil: A Window into the Evolution of Korean Corporate Governance', *Asian-Pacific Law and Policy Journal*, 9 (2007), 163, 165–168.

directors were seen by the IMF as a prerequisite for well-functioning audit committees – which was the primary focus of the reform.

In addition, there was a widespread belief that the reckless expansion of *chaebol* companies, empowered by extremely high leverage and complicated cross-guarantees, was one of the causes for a series of bankruptcies of large companies in Korea during the Asian Financial Crisis. There was a time when the *chaebol* structure was widely praised as a symbol of Korea's aggressive entrepreneurship, which brought about high levels of economic growth. In the aftermath of the Asian Financial Crisis, however, the *chaebol* structure was blamed for amplifying the magnitude of the crisis and causing the crisis to spread. The deleterious economic effects produced by the *chaebol* structure were posited to be a result of the diversification of *chaebol* into non-core businesses, cross-guarantees made among *chaebol* affiliated companies and cross- or circular shareholdings.[21] The IMF, as well as many Korean policymakers and pundits, believed that a strong and independent board monitoring system, such as an audit committee composed of independent directors, could have prevented *chaebols* from engaging in destructive empire building on such risky foundations. Further, the IMF and Korean policymakers believed that independent audit committees may have prevented wealth tunnelling by controlling *chaebol* families and, in turn, protected minority shareholders and other stakeholders from the Financial Crisis.

b Reforms Pursuant to the IMF Programme

In February 1998, pursuant to the IMF's conditions, the listing rules of the Korea Exchange were amended. This was the first step in a long line of legal changes that eventually led to Korea's current independent director regime. The amendment mandated that at least one-quarter of the directors of companies listed on the Korea Exchange be independent directors, who were required to satisfy a number of specific criteria related to their independence.

The first statutory requirement came with the amendment to the Securities Exchange Act on 21 January 2000 (Act No. 6176, which took

[21] S. J. Chang, *Financial Crisis and Transformation of Korean Business Groups: the Rise and Fall of Chaebols* (Cambridge University Press, 2006) states that 'the intricate web of cross-shareholding, debt guarantees, and vertical integration resulted in extensive cross-subsidization and kept chaebols from shedding unprofitable businesses. … [T]he structure of chaebols later inhibited other adaptations and for all practical purposes became nearly dysfunctional' (p. i).

effect on 1 April 2000). This amendment required all listed companies to have at least a quarter of their board made up of independent directors, who were required to satisfy a myriad of criteria related to their independence. In addition, it required that listed companies with total assets exceeding 2 trillion Won (approximately 1.5 billion Euro) ('*large* listed companies') to have *at least a half* of their boards made up of such independent directors. The large listed companies were also required to establish an 'independent director nomination committee' to nominate candidates for the independent director positions. Under the same statute, large listed companies also became obligated to establish an audit committee with at least two-thirds of its members being independent directors, in lieu of the traditional internal 'statutory auditor'. The KCC was also amended to provide statutory grounds for the audit committee, which was (and still is) optional for *non-listed* companies.

Almost simultaneously, these requirements were expanded to *unlisted* companies in the *financial industry*. The Securities Exchange Act, Bank Act and Insurance Business Act were all amended in 2000 to require, respectively, securities companies, commercial banks and insurance companies to have boards with at least half of their members being independent directors. These requirements applied regardless of whether a financial company was listed or unlisted.

After the successful reforms, the IMF issued a final Letter of Intent dated 12 July 2000 with an attachment titled 'Memorandum on Economic Policies'. It outlined the IMF's 'final review' of Korea's various reforms including corporate governance reforms. This document suggests that the Korean government may have gone even further than what the IMF mandated with respect to strengthening the independence of Korean boards. Specifically, the document states:

> Amendments to the Commercial Code and the Securities Law passed in December 1999 enacted further improvements in corporate governance, including requiring that at least 50 percent of the directors on boards of large companies be outside [independent] directors and the establishment of audit committees of boards of directors in lieu of statutory auditors.[22]

[22] 'Letter of Intent from the Government of Korea' (12 July 2000) International Monetary Fund, available at www.imf.org. The word in the square brackets was added by the author.

This statement illustrates that implementing mandatory rules to create corporate boards with a large contingent of independent directors and an audit committee was recognised as a key element of the post-crisis corporate governance reform by both the IMF and Korean government. Indeed, it appears that, to a certain extent, the legislative initiatives may have been partially driven by the Korean government – with the IMF being the initial impetus and public face behind the changes. In fact, some people involved in the reforms have suggested that there were factions in the government that may have wanted to use the political capital provided by the IMF to curtail the power of the *chaebol*, which would have been unthinkable prior to the Financial Crisis. Further, the cover provided by the IMF may have allowed the government to make such reforms, while leaving the IMF to blame for any later problems or backlash by the politically powerful *chaebol*. Such theories surrounding the reforms are supported only by anecdotal evidence – although additional evidence with respect to the impetus within Korea for the reforms is provided below.

Moreover, in line with this theory, the abovementioned requirements for large listed companies and financial companies were strengthened even further on 1 April 2004. Due to revisions to the relevant statutes, large listed companies and financial companies were required to have the 'majority' (as opposed to 'at least a half') of their board members to be independent directors. Moreover, as a result of the 2004 revisions, at least one of the audit committee members must be an expert in accounting or finance, and the chairperson of the audit committee must be an independent director. Since 2004, there have not been any substantial changes to the rules relating to independent directors, but it is worth noting that the provisions on independent directors were moved from the Securities Exchange Act to the Korean Commercial Code with no significant changes in substance in 2009.

c Reflections on the Historical Context

As discussed above, the Asian Financial Crisis and the subsequent bailout programme of the IMF were the main forces behind the statutory reforms which implemented independent directors in Korea. This dramatic reform was possible only because of the efforts of a number of influential people *within* Korea (including some Korean government officials, politicians, lawyers and scholars), who shared a common belief: that independent directors would perform the monitoring role better than insiders; and that the enhanced monitoring function of boards would result in strong Korean corporations, which would bolster the Korean economy as a whole and help prevent another financial crisis.

There is some evidence which suggests that the pressure from outsiders was not the only driving force behind Korea's adoption of the independent director. Even before the crisis, the Bank Act was amended (on 13 January 1997) to require boards of commercial banks to have a majority of 'non-executive' directors. Although the Bank Act did not specifically require the element of 'independence' at that time, the amendment was based on the belief that a board composed entirely of insiders would not properly perform its monitoring function.[23] Second, the independence requirements were further strengthened (i.e., the requirement was strengthened from 'at least a half' to a 'majority' of the board for large listed companies and financial institutions) even after Korea successfully 'graduated' from the IMF bailout programme and was no longer under any obligation to revise its law.

Admittedly, there has been serious criticism of Korea's mandatory independent director system. Concerns have been expressed about the true independence of many ostensibly 'independent' directors as well as their lack of business experience.[24] Many experts believed (and in fact still believe) that the internal statutory auditor, if properly elected and equipped with sufficient resources, would perform the monitoring function better than independent directors – most of whom are not experts in business and only involved in the corporate affairs of the company on a part-time basis.

In any event, it is fairly evident that, when the IMF, the legislature (i.e., the Korean National Assembly) and the administrative branch of the Korean government adopted the rules governing independent directors, they all expected that independent directors would perform the monitoring role better than corporate insiders. Other functions – such as the managerial role, advisory role and relational role – were not

[23] 'The concept of an outside director was not entirely new to the business community in Korea. ... [B]y the time outside directors were required for listed firms, the business community had at least a minimum understanding of their role in corporate governance.' Kim, 'Transplanting Audit Committees', 164. Of course, there was also strong hostility against the audit committee concept because '[i]ntroducing a foreign institution like the audit committee under outside pressure was somewhat humiliating' (*ibid.*).

[24] B. S. Black et al., 'Corporate Governance in Korea at the Millennium: Enhancing International Competitiveness', *Journal of Corporation Law*, 26 (2001), 537.

contemplated in the early 2000s when the independent director system was initially adopted.

2 *Current Rules*

a Minimum Number of Independent Directors

Following the 2009 revision, the KCC categorises directors into three groups: (1) executive directors (*sanae isa*, translated directly as 'inside directors'); (2) independent directors (*sawae isa*, translated directly as 'outside directors');[25] and (3) non-executive non-independent directors (*gita bisangmu isa*, translated directly as 'other non-executive directors') (Article 317(2)(viii)). The third group refers to directors who are neither full-time employees of the company, nor otherwise engaged in the daily business of the company (and thus are outsiders), but who fail to satisfy the independence requirements. These three categories demonstrate that the KCC clearly distinguishes 'outside-ness' from 'independence'.[26] As a result of these statutory categorisations, at the time of election and registration of a new director,[27] the company must specify which category the new director falls under.

Non-listed companies may choose to have independent directors. However, if a non-listed company decides to establish an audit committee (instead of having a statutory auditor) as its internal monitoring organ, then at least two-thirds of the audit committee members must be independent directors. It is only to this extent that a non-listed company is required to have independent directors.

Under the KCC, with certain narrow exceptions,[28] at least one-quarter of the total number of directors of a listed company must be independent directors (Article 542-8(1)). Moreover, '*large* listed companies' must

[25] See note 4 above.

[26] D. C. Clarke, 'Three Concepts of the Independent Director', *Delaware Journal of Corporate Law*, 32 (2007), 73 highlights 'critical differences between independent, outside, and disinterested directors' and argues that 'these manifestations serve different purposes and should not be confused with each other'. It would be fair to say that the KCC clearly recognises such differences given the statutory categorisation of the directors. Interested/disinterested directors are separately regulated under Articles 391(3), 368(4) of the KCC.

[27] Election, re-election, expiry of term of office, dismissal, resignation, incapacitation or death of a director must be registered with the court's registrar office. The registration must be filed by the company.

[28] For example, venture companies with total assets less than 100 billion Won, insolvent companies under the bankruptcy proceedings or the rehabilitation proceedings, listed

have at least three independent directors that constitute a *majority* of the board. Financial companies – such as a financial holding company, a commercial bank, an insurance company or a securities investment company (functionally similar to an investment bank in the US) – are subject to the same requirements as the large listed companies.

Further, a person may not serve as an independent director of a listed company if he or she is already serving as a director (including an independent director), an executive or a statutory auditor for two companies. Thus, the maximum number of listed companies for which a person may concurrently serve as an independent director is two.

b Independence Requirements

Instead of providing a positive definition of, or qualifications for, an independent director, the KCC and its regulations provide a long list of reasons for disqualification. In other words, the element of 'independence' is specifically required for independent directors, but there is neither a positive definition nor a broad standard to determine whether a director is independent.

This is somewhat different from many other jurisdictions that have adopted a broad definition or standard for independence. For example, the NYSE listing rules provide a general standard (i.e., 'no director qualifies as "independent" unless the board of directors affirmatively determines that the director has no material relationship with the listed company'), followed by a list of specific disqualifications (e.g., 'The director is, or has been within the last three years, an employee of the listed company, or an immediate family member is, or has been within the last three years, an executive officer, of the listed company').[29] The NASDAQ Equity Rules define 'independent director' more clearly as 'a person other than an Executive Officer or employee of the Company or any other individual having a relationship which, in the opinion of the Company's board of directors, would interfere with the exercise of independent judgement in carrying out the responsibilities of a director' and subsequently provides a list of persons who shall not be considered independent.[30] The European Commission Recommendation provides that 'A director should be considered to be independent only if he is free of

companies in their first year of listing, and companies which have resolved to dissolve are exempted from this requirement, even if their shares are traded on the exchange.

[29] § 303A.02, NYSE Listed Company Manual.

[30] NASDAQ Equity Rules 5605.

any business, family or other relationship, with the company, its controlling shareholder or the management of either, that creates a conflict of interest such as to impair his judgment.'[31]

For non-listed companies, the disqualification list under the KCC is as follows (Article 382(3)):

- directors, executives and employees who are engaged in the regular business of the relevant company, or those who were in such positions within the last two years;
- the largest shareholder, his/her spouse, lineal ascendants and lineal descendants;
- in cases where the largest shareholder is a company, its directors, statutory auditors, executives and employees;
- the spouses, lineal ascendants and lineal descendants of the directors, statutory auditors and executives of the company;
- the directors, statutory auditors, executives and employees of a parent or a subsidiary of the company;
- directors, statutory auditors, executives and employees of a corporation which has a significant interest in the relevant company; or
- directors, statutory auditors, executives and employees of another company for which directors, executives or employees of the relevant company serve as directors or executives.

For listed companies, in addition to the foregoing reasons for exclusion, the following list of disqualified persons applies (Article 542-8(2)):

- a person younger than the age of 19;
- a person who was adjudicated bankrupt and has not yet been reinstated;
- a person who, within the past two years, was released or exempted from imprisonment for a criminal violation;
- a person who, within the past two years, was dismissed or removed from their positions for a violation of laws prescribed in the enforcement decree[32] of the KCC;[33]
- 'specially related persons' (as defined in Article 34(4) of the enforcement decree of the KCC, which includes family members within

[31] Commission Recommendation (2005/162/EC) of 15 February 2005, No. 13.1.

[32] Korean statutes including the KCC usually have two types of subregulations: an enforcement decree issued by the President of the Republic of Korea and an enforcement regulation issued by the relevant minister. An enforcement decree has higher force than an enforcement regulation.

[33] This list includes 28 statutes, mainly related to financial and banking matters.

second cousins, directors, executives, employees and affiliate companies) of the largest shareholder;

- shareholders holding 10 per cent or more of the voting rights or exercising *de facto* influence over the important management decisions of the company ('major shareholders');
- spouse, lineal ascendants and lineal descendants of the 'major shareholders'; or
- a party who has entered into 'major business contracts' with the company and the directors, executives, statutory auditors or employees of such parties (including those who were in such positions during the last two years).

The last category in the list above (i.e., 'major business contacts') is further explained in greater detail in the enforcement decree of the KCC. Specifically, without limitation, major business contacts include:

- if the amount of transactions between company A (which is a listed company) and company B during the last three years exceeds 10 per cent of the total assets or total revenue of company A, then company B's directors, executives, statutory auditors or employees (including those who were in such positions during the last two years) may not serve as an independent director of company A;
- if the contract amount between company A (which is a listed company) and company B during the recent business year exceeds 10 per cent of the total revenue of company A, then company B's directors, executives, statutory auditors or employees (including those who were in such positions during the last two years) may not serve as an independent director of company A;
- if the aggregate amount of borrowing, lending or guarantee between company A (which is a listed company) and company B exceeds 10 per cent of company A's legal capital,[34] then company B's directors, executives, statutory auditors or employees (including those who were in such positions during the last two years) may not serve as an independent director of company A;
- lawyers, accountants, consultants and others who are providing consulting services to a company may not serve as an independent director of the company; and

[34] Generally stated, the legal capital corresponds to the amount of par value of the shares multiplied by the total number of issued shares.

- associates or partners of a law firm, an accounting firm or a consulting firm providing consulting services to a company may not serve as an independent director of the company.

It is worthwhile to note that major shareholders and their related persons are considered to not be independent under the KCC. Companies with controlling shareholders are not exempted from the mandatory independent director requirements, and independence from the controlling or major shareholders is believed to be an important qualification of independent directors. This stands in sharp contrast to the US, where most of the independent director requirements are only applicable to diffusely held public companies based on the belief that independent directors are of limited or no value when there are controlling shareholders.[35] This also calls into question the common trope that Korea transplanted 'American-style' independent directors into its corporate governance regime.

In short, under the KCC, independent directors must be independent from the company in all respects including ownership, kinship, employment and business relations. Generally, the disqualification criteria are similar to those found in the listing rules of other jurisdictions – but are notably wider than in the US as they exclude major shareholders (or those related to major shareholders) from being independent.[36] Although the KCC does not define independence in a positive way, the lengthy list of reasons for disqualification (i.e., lack of independence) fulfils a similar purpose. That being said, it is

[35] See Chapter 1 at III.4.

[36] For instance, under the NYSE rules, a director is not independent among others if: (1) the director is, or has been within the last three years, an employee of the listed company, or an immediate family member is, or has been within the last three years, an executive officer, of the listed company; (2) the director has received, or has an immediate family member who has received, during any 12-month period within the last three years, more than $120,000 in direct compensation from the listed company, other than director and committee fees and pension or other forms of deferred compensation for prior service; (3) the director is a current partner or employee of a firm that is the listed company's internal or external auditor; or (4) the director is a current employee, or an immediate family member is a current executive officer, of a company that has made payments to, or received payments from, the listed company for property or services in an amount which, in any of the last three fiscal years, exceeds the greater of $ million, or 2 per cent of such other company's consolidated gross revenues. These requirements are generally similar to the reasons for disqualification under the KCC – except they importantly do not mention anything with respect to major shareholders or those connected to major shareholders.

questionable whether such a purely rule-based laundry list approach, without any positive standard, is optimal. Indeed, an individual who is in substance not independent may technically circumvent the foregoing reasons for disqualification, which surely would be contrary to the legislative intent.

c Nomination Committees

In the case of a large listed company, independent director candidates must be nominated by an 'independent director nomination committee', which is one of the sub-committees of the board of directors (Article 542-8(4)). There must be a majority of independent directors on the nomination committee. As a procedural device to further ensure independence, the nomination committee may supplement the gaps created by the KCC's use of a purely rules-based approach for independence. This is because the nomination committee would not (or, at least, should not) nominate a person who technically passes the KCC's test for independence, but who is in reality not independent. Many commentators, however, criticise the fact that nomination committees are often strongly influenced by the largest shareholder. Finally, independent directors are elected by a majority vote from among the nominees at the general meeting of shareholders – further reinforcing the influence of the largest shareholder.

d Audit Committees

As explained above, the adoption of the mandatory independent director regime in Korea was closely related to the recommendation by the IMF for Korea to adopt audit committees. As such, a brief examination of the rules governing audit committees provides helpful insight into understanding the roles of independent directors in Korea.

Independent directors must constitute at least two-thirds of the audit committee, whether or not the relevant company is listed. The chairperson of the audit committee must also be an independent director. Naturally, the question that arises is whether an audit committee is mandatory for all companies under Korean law.

One would think that the answer to this question is rather straightforward. Unfortunately, it is not. Due to the frequent and piecemeal amendments to the KCC, the issue of whether an audit committee is mandatory for a company is actually fairly complex. First, a non-listed company whose legal capital is 1 billion Won (approximately 0.8 million Euro) or more and a listed company whose total assets are less than 100 billion

Won (approximately 80 million Euro) must have at least one statutory auditor or establish an audit committee composed of at least three directors, with at least two-thirds of the members being independent directors (Articles 409(1)(4), 415-2(1)(2)). In other words, these companies may choose to have a statutory auditor or an audit committee.

Second, a listed company whose total assets are between 100 billion and 2 trillion Won must have at least one full-time statutory auditor or establish a 'qualified' audit committee (Article 542-10(1)).

Third, a listed company whose total assets are 2 trillion Won (approximately 1.5 billion Euro) or more must establish a 'qualified' audit committee (Article 542-11(1)). The members of the 'qualified' audit committee are directly elected by the shareholders from the directors, while members of the ordinary audit committee are elected by the directors amongst themselves.

IV The Reality of Mandatory Independent Directors in Korea

1 *Changes in Board Practices after 2000*

The introduction of the requirement to have independent directors in 2000 – in particular the 'majority requirement' for large listed companies which was adopted in 2004 – resulted in significant changes in the composition as well as operation of the board of directors of listed companies in Korea.

First, the size of boards in listed companies decreased dramatically. Although there are no reliable statistics, large listed firms generally had dozens of board members before the 1997 Financial Crisis. Since board seats were often regarded as honorary positions, which were the culmination of reaching the top of the corporate ladder, it was reasonable to distribute them to as many senior executives as possible. For example, the board of Samsung Electronics was composed of 59 directors in March 1997,[37] most of whom were part of the senior management. Currently, the average number of board members of the large listed companies is between seven and eight, presumably due to practical difficulties in finding a sufficient number of qualified independent directors. For example,

[37] Supreme Court Decision, 28 October 2005, 2003da69638 (a shareholders' derivative suit against directors of Samsung Electronics).

each of Samsung Electronics and Hyundai Motor Corporation has only nine directors (four executive directors and five independent directors).[38]

Second, the presence of independent directors has caused listed companies to operate the board of directors in a more 'formal' or 'proper' manner. Prior to 2000, it was not uncommon for many Korean companies (even large listed ones) to execute minutes of the board meeting by affixing the seals of the directors, without holding an actual meeting. Careful review and active discussion were not commonly part of the board meetings in most companies. The introduction of independent directors and the increasing number of shareholder lawsuits, however, have eliminated this nonchalant attitude towards board meetings. Although independent directors rarely have to personally pay damages out of their own pockets as a result of breaching their directors' duties, they have been named as defendants and held to be technically liable in a number of derivative suits.[39] The risk of personal liability became a real threat, and no independent director would agree to the risky and improper practice of holding board meetings merely on paper. Currently, in listed companies, materials are usually distributed well in advance of the meeting for the directors' deliberation and the directors are provided with the opportunity to question the management about any relevant issues before making important decisions.

It is unclear whether such changes have actually increased firm value. One empirical study, however, has found that Korean firms with 50 per cent independent directors enjoyed an increase in share price of roughly 40 per cent, which suggests that 'greater board independence causally predict[s] higher share prices in emerging markets'.[40] Another empirical study also found a strong positive correlation between the introduction of the independent director requirements and the performance of listed

[38] It is related to another interesting issue of the optimum size of the board and optimum number of outsiders on the board. According to recent research, R&D-intensive firms, for which firm-specific knowledge of insiders is relatively important, have a higher fraction of insiders on the board and, for these firms, Tobin's Q increases with the fraction of insiders on the board. This research challenges the notion that restrictions on board size and management representation on the board enhance firm value. J. L. Coles et al., 'Boards: Does One Size Fit All?', *Journal of Financial Economics*, 87 (2008), 329.

[39] This is so mainly because the other defendants (in most cases, the largest shareholder who was also one of the executive directors) paid the whole amount of the damages.

[40] Black et al., 'Does Corporate Governance Predict Firms' Market Values? Evidence from Korea', *Journal of Law, Economics, and Organization*, 22(2) (2006), 366.

companies in Korea.[41] This is in contrast to studies on companies listed in the US, where the presence of independent directors appears to have had a nominal or even negative impact on firm performance.[42]

2 *Number of Independent Directors*

Virtually every firm listed on the KOSPI has independent directors, and the average number of independent directors per firm was 2.37 in 2010. On the KOSDAQ, around 20 per cent of the firms are exempt from the independent director requirements due to their small size.[43] However, the number of independent directors (per firm and in total) in KOSDAQ companies has been slightly on the rise. Table 5.2 shows the number of independent directors in listed firms in Korea from 2003 to 2010.

As of 31 March 2012, out of the 1,773 companies listed on the KOSPI and KOSDAQ, 1,622 companies (92.6 per cent) had at least one independent director. The number of independent directors was 3,216 in total (2,999 excluding multiple appointments) and 1.96 on average.[44] As explained above, the number of independent directors is much higher in large listed companies.

3 *Monitoring Function Enhanced?*

Although the monitoring role of the board was specified in the 1984 revision to the KCC, it was not regarded as a core function of the board until the 1997 Financial Crisis. After the crisis and subsequent statutory changes, the presence (or prevalence, in the case of large listed firms) of independent directors in the boardroom highlighted the monitoring function of the board. The companies could no longer easily force or nudge

[41] J. J. Choi, S. W. Park and S. S. Yoo, 'The Value of Outside Directors: Evidence from Corporate Governance Reform in Korea', *Journal of Financial and Quantitative Analysis*, 42(4) (2007), 941.

[42] See, for example, S. Bhagat and B. S. Black, 'The Non-Correlation between Board Independence and Long-Term Firm Performance', *Journal of Corporation Law*, 27 (2002), 231 (using 1991 Board and Stock Ownership Data); O. Faleye et al., 'The Costs of Intense Board Monitoring', *Journal of Finance Economy*, 101 (2011), 160 (showing that improved monitoring comes at the expense of corporate performance). See also the discussion in Chapter 2 at IV.2.

[43] Venture companies with total assets less than 100 billion Won are exempted from the requirement to have an independent director.

[44] Korea Listed Companies Association, 'Status of Outside Directors of Listed Companies' (April 2012) (in Korean).

Table 5.2 Number of Independent Directors

	KOSPI				KOSDAQ			
Year	No. of Firms w/ no I.D.	No. of Firms w/ some I.D.	No. of I.D. (total)	No. of I.D. (per firm)	No. of Firms w/ no I.D.	No. of Firms w/ some I.D.	No. of I.D. (total)	No. of I.D. (per firm)
2003	37	650	1,402	2.16	352	516	746	1.45
2004	18	657	1,456	2.22	312	579	813	1.40
2005	15	650	1,450	2.23	327	568	824	1.45
2006	9	657	1,504	2.29	298	628	948	1.51
2007	6	673	1,554	2.31	242	730	1,139	1.56
2008	3	689	1,642	2.38	207	820	1,360	1.66
2009	0	712	1,693	2.38	176	866	1,432	1.65
2010	Not available	710	1,684	2.37	Not available	843	1,331	1.58

Source: Korea Listed Companies Association, 'Analysis of Appointment of Outside Directors', published each year in Korean language. Versions up to 2010 are available on its website (www.klca.or.kr) only in Korean language. The Association, however, ceased to publish this document from 2011.

their boards to approve transactions that were clearly in favour of the largest shareholder (or his family members) and detrimental to the other shareholders – although they could sometimes do so when the board was composed entirely of company insiders. A reduction in the number of board members and improvement in the procedures of board meetings (see above for further explanation) also contributed to enhancing the monitoring function of boards in listed companies.

There are, however, strong objections to this point of view. A survey that examined 341 independent directors of listed companies belonging to Korea's ten largest business groups found that only two out of the 341 independent directors had voted against any item on the board's agenda between May 2012 and April 2013. In a similar vein, in listed companies belonging to Korea's 49 largest business groups, only 25 proposals put before their respective boards were disapproved of out of 6,720 proposals submitted between May 2012 and April 2013. Between May 2013 and April 2014, among the listed companies belonging to Korea's 47 largest business groups, out of 5,718 proposals submitted, only 15 proposals put before their respective boards were disapproved.[45] Based on these statistics, many academics and pundits have complained that the boards of listed companies, even if they are composed of independent directors, are no more than rubber stamps. Social ties between the independent directors and the management of such companies are often pointed to as one of the main factors leading to such an outcome.[46]

The low objection rate, however, does not in and of itself mean that there is a lack of monitoring. In practice, board proposals, along with related materials, are usually distributed to the board members one to two weeks prior to the board meeting. Any serious questions or objections from the directors are usually raised and discussed before the

[45] This data is available in 'Information Disclosure Regarding the Governance of the Large Business Groups' disclosed by the Korea Fair Trade Commission (a government agency in charge of competition and antitrust) every year. The most recent one was disclosed on its website (www.kftc.go.kr) on 22 December 2016. Details are available in Korean only.

[46] Recent research on Korean listed companies found that '87 percent of boards are conventionally independent but that only 62 percent are conventionally and socially independent'. This research also shows that 'firms whose boards are conventionally and socially independent award a significantly lower level of compensation, exhibit stronger pay-performance sensitivity, and exhibit stronger turnover-performance sensitivity than firms whose boards are only conventionally independent'. In this research, social ties were measured by way of regional origin, mutual *alma mater*, military service, and industry. B. H. Hwang and S. Kim, 'It Pays to Have Friends', *Journal of Financial Economics*, 93 (2009), 138.

board meeting. If the management fails to persuade the directors, then the board proposal would most likely be withdrawn or modified. In other words, because significant issues are usually reviewed and sorted out before the board meeting, a low objection rate at the actual board meeting does not necessarily mean that board members are complacent.

4 *Analysis of the Careers of the Independent Directors: Another Function?*

What is more noteworthy than the low objection rate is the change in the career background of independent directors. As Table 5.3 shows, individuals with a business or management background constituted 45.2 per cent of independent directors in 2004, but their proportion continuously decreased until it reached 28.4 per cent in 2011.[47] The sharpest increase occurred in the group of former public officials, which more than tripled from 2.7 per cent in 2004 to 8.9 per cent in 2011. Considering that a significant number of former judges and former prosecutors (as well as other former officials that are members of the bar) were counted as 'lawyers' in Table 5.3, the actual percentage of former officials is likely far greater than what Table 5.3 suggests. Certified public accountants, whose expertise is likely suitable for performing the role of monitoring, constituted 5.4 per cent in 2011 as opposed to 7.1 per cent in 2004. In contrast, interestingly, it appears that professors and lawyers are becoming increasingly popular – with professors making up 24.7 per cent and lawyers making up 12.2 per cent of independent directors in 2011.

This trend is even more pronounced in Korea's large business groups. Based on the public disclosure documents of 255 listed firms (both KOSPI and KOSDAQ firms) belonging to 63 large business groups, 187 firms newly appointed (or re-appointed at the expiry of the term of office) 384 independent directors between 2 January 2013 and 30 October 2013. The breakdown of the 384 independent directors in terms of their career backgrounds is as follows (in descending order):[48]

[47] One reason for such a sharp decrease is the creation of a new category in Table 5.3 in 2009 ('members of industry association'), because people who fall under this new category were likely counted as having a 'business/management' background before 2009. However, even considering such an effect, it is clear that the portion of the independent directors with a business/management background is decreasing.

[48] Corporate Governance Service, *CGS Report*, 45 (January 2014), 6–11 (in Korean). The numbers are cumulative (i.e., if a director was both a professor and former government

Table 5.3 Career Background of the Independent Directors (KOSPI Market)

	2004	2005	2006	2007	2008	2009	2010	2011
Business/Management	640 (45.2%)	630 (43.3%)	622 (41.4%)	635 (40.9%)	636 (38.7%)	540 (31.9%)	525 (30.8%)	491 (28.4%)
Professor	303 (21.4%)	334 (23.0%)	352 (23.4%)	360 (23.2%)	385 (23.4%)	400 (23.6%)	415 (24.3%)	427 (24.7%)
Lawyer	152 (10.7%)	168 (11.6%)	191 (12.6%)	191 (12.3%)	189 (11.5%)	210 (12.4%)	197 (11.6%)	212 (12.2%)
Accountant/Tax attorney	101 (7.1%)	101 (6.9%)	94 (6.3%)	89 (5.7%)	78 (4.8%)	98 (5.8%)	88 (5.2%)	93 (5.4%)
Former public officials	38 (2.7%)	50 (3.4%)	47 (3.1%)	80 (5.1%)	68 (4.1%)	125 (7.4%)	138 (8.1%)	154 (8.9%)
Researcher	31 (2.2%)	24 (1.7%)	28 (1.9%)	25 (1.6%)	25 (1.5%)	52 (3.1%)	46 (2.7%)	39 (2.3%)
Journalist	17 (1.2%)	20 (1.4%)	22 (1.5%)	25 (1.6%)	22 (1.3%)	32 (1.9%)	32 (1.9%)	32 (1.8%)
Members of industry associations	–	–	–	–	–	98 (5.8%)	127 (7.4%)	151 (8.7%)
Others	134 (9.5%)	127 (8.7%)	148 (9.8%)	149 (9.6%)	239 (14.6%)	138 (8.2%)	137 (8.0%)	132 (7.6%)
Total	1,416	1,454	1,504	1,554	1,642	1,693	1,705	1,731

Source: Korea Listed Companies Association, 'White Book for the General Meeting of Shareholders', published each year in Korean language. Versions up to 2011 were available on its website (www.klca.or.kr) only in Korean. The Association, however, ceased to publish this document and even versions up to 2011 are currently no longer accessible on its website.

- 131 professors (28.5 per cent);
- 82 lawyers, including 45 former judges and former prosecutors (17.9 per cent);
- 73 former government officials (15.9 per cent) excluding lawyers;[49]
- 61 businessmen or professional managers (13.3 per cent); and
- 26 accountants (5.7 per cent).

Moreover, according to the public disclosure documents of 93 listed companies belonging to Korea's ten largest business groups, 68 independent directors were newly appointed in 2013 and, among them, 28 individuals (41.2 per cent) were former government officials, including ten from the National Tax Service.[50]

The professional backgrounds of independent directors in Korea's largest listed companies are markedly different than the backgrounds of independent directors on the boards of large listed companies in other jurisdictions. In the US, independent directors are typically chosen on the basis of their business expertise (e.g., CEOs of other companies are more likely than lawyers to serve on the boards of public companies).[51] To provide another comparative perspective, Table 5.4 lists the professional backgrounds of the non-executive board members of some of the world's largest companies. Most of the independent or non-executive directors of these companies are CEOs, CFOs or other high-level executives at large public companies.

This raises an intriguing question: how can we explain the increasing preference in Korea for former government officials to serve as independent directors on the boards of listed companies? One possible theory is that these former government officials draw on their past experiences and expertise as regulators to improve the internal compliance system

official, he is counted twice. The percentage was calculated using this cumulative number as denominator).

[49] This includes: (1) 22 former tax and customs duty officers (4.8 per cent), including five former heads of the National Tax Service (NTS) and ten former heads of the Regional Offices of the National Tax Service; (2) 12 from the Ministry of Finance and Economy; (3) nine from the Korea Fair Trade Commission (KFTC), the competition authority of Korea which is also in charge of regulating large business groups; (4) nine from the Board of Audit and Inspection, a government agency in charge of audit and inspection of the governments; (5) 14 former staff members of the Blue House (the Presidential Office corresponding to the White House in the United States); and (6) six former officials of the Financial Supervisory Service, the regulator of the financial industry and securities markets.

[50] Corporate Governance Service, *CGS Report*, 6–11 (in Korean).

[51] S. P. Ferris et al., 'Too Busy to Mind the Business? Monitoring by Directors with Multiple Board Appointments', *Journal of Finance*, 58 (2003), 1087.

Table 5.4 Career Background of the Non-Executive Directors (Global Fortune Top 10)

Name of Company	No. of Board Members	Career of Non-executive Directors
Royal Dutch Shell	2 Executives 9 Non-executives 1 Company Secretary	(1) Business/management/finance: 5 (2) Lawyer: 1 (3) Public officials: 2 (4) (1)+(3): 1
Wal-Mart Stores	2 Executives 14 Non-executives	(1) Business/management/finance: 10 (2) Public official: 1 (3) Professors: 2 (4) Accountant: 1
Exxon Mobil	1 Executive 12 Non-executives	(1) Business/management/finance: 7 (2) (1) + Public official: 1 (3) Professors: 3 (4) (1)+(3): 1
Total	3 Executives 12 Non-executives	(1) Business/management/finance: 7 (2) Public official: 1 (3) (1)+(2): 3 (4) Professor: 1
British Petroleum	4 Executives 10 Non-executives	(1) Business/management/finance: 6 (2) Public official: 1 (3) Professor: 1 (4) Accountants: 2

Source: websites of each company (as of May 2014).

of the company on whose board they sit. This theory, however, does not sufficiently explain the abnormally high proportion of ex-officials from 'powerful' government agencies such as the NTS, the KFTC and the prosecutors' office who tend to be on the boards of listed companies in Korea. If the companies consider compliance (which is a type of monitoring) as a primary function of independent directors, certified public accountants trained in large accounting firms or corporate lawyers trained in large law firms would appear to be stronger candidates in terms of their expertise and experience. It is quite clear that when companies appoint these ex-officials as independent directors, they expect them to play a relational role rather than a monitoring role (i.e., serving as a communication channel with the government).

In this regard, it is noteworthy that Korea does not have any statutory provision clearly allowing and/or regulating lobbyists. Several attempts to legislate comprehensive acts governing lobbyists have failed, including a bill entitled, 'Lobbyist Registration and Lobbying Disclosure Act' (which was submitted to the National Assembly in 2005). Absent such legislation, any lobbying activity is likely to constitute a violation of the 'Lawyers Act' and be subject to a criminal fine or imprisonment. In the absence of comprehensive legislation governing professional lobbyists, many listed firms may have an incentive to utilise their board members as unofficial resources for communicating with the government.[52]

There is another lingering puzzle regarding the professional backgrounds of independent directors in Korea: why are there such a small number of professional managers and such a large number of professors amongst the independent directors in Korean listed companies? The answer may lie in the ownership structure of Korean companies. As discussed above, most Korean companies have controlling 'individual' shareholders, who dominate the governance of their company and/or corporate group. The founders of the company – or sometimes the founder's sons or grandsons – have themselves made important strategic

[52] Such an incentive is not unique to Korea. There is research that has explored the importance of political connections of board members in the United States. Based on a review of S&P 500 companies, it found 'a positive abnormal stock return following the announcement of the nomination of a politically connected individual to the board'. Interestingly (and naturally), it also reports that the stock price response to the Republicans winning the 2000 presidential election shows an increase in the value of companies connected to the Republican Party and a decrease in value of companies connected to the Democratic Party. E. Goldman et al., 'Do Politically Connected Boards Affect Firm Value?', *The Review of Financial Studies*, 22(6) (2009), 2331.

and managerial decisions and hired/fired senior executives, leaving little room for growth of experienced professional managers. There is only a limited pool of senior businessmen who are widely respected in the Korean business community. Controlling shareholders in Korea also tend to be reluctant to invite senior executives of other companies into their boardrooms, as they believe what goes on in the boardroom must remain confidential. From the perspective of the controlling shareholders and their family members, professors would be far less dangerous to their interests than the senior executives of other companies, because they have fewer conflicts of interest and less knowledge about the actual business or industry.

Yet another puzzle is why the proportion of former government officials abruptly increased in 2009 (from 4.1 per cent to 7.4 per cent). To the author's knowledge, no explanation has been provided for this development by either pundits or professors in Korea. One hypothesis may point towards a supply-side explanation. Following the presidential election in December 2007, the government transformed from a relatively progressive party to a conservative party in February 2008. As is commonplace with a change of government, a number of high-ranking government officials (e.g., ministers, vice-ministers, heads of important government agencies and other senior officials) either voluntarily left their positions or were forced out. This may have created a large pool of high-ranking retired government officials in early 2008, and many of them might have sought new careers and/or have been recruited as independent directors in March 2009.[53] March 2008 was apparently too early for them to become independent directors because of the lengthy process preceding the annual general meeting of shareholders, where directors are appointed (i.e., nomination by the nomination committee, indication of the director candidates in the notice of annual meeting, etc.). Nonetheless, absent an empirical study, this remains merely an educated guess.

V Concluding Remarks

As we have seen, there has been a notable convergence between Korea and other leading jurisdictions in terms of the rise of independent directors

[53] Almost all the Korean companies hold their annual general shareholders meeting in March every year.

and some of the roles that they play in the corporate governance of listed companies.[54] There has also been some important divergence from other jurisdictions, which is evident in the mandatory nature of independent directors in Korean law and the manner in which Korean law defines independence. This being said, many observers agree that the introduction of the requirement to have independent directors in Korea has increased the diversity and transparency of Korean boards, and thereby improved their monitoring function. This is the role that the legislature expected independent directors to play.

However, after 15 years in operation, we are now witnessing a unique reality concerning independent directors in Korea. Increasingly, companies are filling their independent director quota with retired government officials, such as high-ranking prosecutors or tax officers. While professors and lawyers are increasingly being tapped to become independent directors, it is becoming progressively more difficult to find businessmen or career bankers serving as independent directors in large listed companies. This trend is even more pronounced in large business groups. This is strikingly different from other jurisdictions, where most of the independent or non-executive directors in large listed companies are CEOs, CFOs or other high-level executives of other large companies. This trend in Korea may suggest that many companies want their independent directors to play a 'relational role', especially in terms of providing a channel of communication with the government. This is certainly not a role that the legislature expected independent directors would play in Korea.

It is yet to be seen whether this trend will weaken the monitoring function of the boards of listed companies in Korea. It is also unclear whether this trend will end up negatively affecting the performance of Korean companies and their shareholder value. These issues are left for future research. Ultimately, however, the case of Korea is further evidence that the unique political and cultural environment of each country often causes legal transplants to evolve in idiosyncratic and unanticipated ways.

[54] Pritchard, 'Monitoring of Corporate Groups', 17 ('Korea's corporate governance provisions, by and large, have more in common with the requirements in the United States than difference'), 25 ('My focus in this paper has been on the convergence between Korea and the United States on the role of independent directors in corporate governance').

6

Independent Directors in China

Facts and Reform Proposals

XIN TANG*

I Introduction

In 2001, the China Securities Regulatory Commission (CSRC) introduced independent directors to improve corporate governance in Chinese listed companies. Presently, almost all of China's approximately 2,800 listed companies have at least three 'independent' directors on their management boards.[1] Despite the ubiquity of independent directors on the management boards of listed companies in China, most empirical studies have failed to demonstrate that the introduction of independent directors has improved corporate performance.[2] Nevertheless, the CSRC has endorsed independent directors as a way to 'promote the standardised operation of listed companies' and

* Professor, Tsinghua University School of Law, Beijing, China.

1 According to the CSMAR (China Stock Market and Accounting Research) database, which can be accessed at www.gtadata.com/products/plist.aspx. Also see, China Association for Public Companies Research Team on Drafting the Guidelines for Exercise of Duties of Independent Directors of Public Companies, '独立董事作用显著提升空间仍较大' [Effects of Independent Directors Are Significant, While Promotion Space Is Still Big], 中国证券报 [China Securities News], 16 January 2014.

2 W. Xiao, Z. Wang and Y. Duan, '大股东存在下的独立董事对公司业绩的影响: 基于内生视角的审视' [The Impact of Major Stake-Holding, Independent Directors to Company Performance: An Endogenous Perspective], 南开管理评论 [Nankai Business Review], 12(2) (2009), 90–96; L. Yang and R. Lu, '独立董事与高管薪酬———基于中国证券市场的经验证据' [Independent Director and Executive Salary: Empirical Evidences from China's Security Market], 当代财经 [Contemporary Finance and Economics], 5 (2009), 110–114; W. Wang, 'Independent Directors and Corporate Performance in China: A Meta-Empirical Study' (27 March, 2014), available at http://ssrn.com/abstract=2417078. For a general discussion of the dubious empirical support for the independent monitoring board see Chapter 2 at II.2 and IV.2.

to safeguard 'the lawful rights and interests of small and medium shareholders'.[3]

Although the CSRC's decision to introduce independent directors into China may be questioned considering the dearth of empirical evidence supporting their utility, it was (and still is) clear that China's capital markets and legal environment present serious corporate governance challenges that must be addressed. Specifically, the risk of wealth tunnelling looms large in Chinese listed companies as they are typically dominated by a strong controlling shareholder, while institutional investors and activist retail investors remain relatively weak. This situation is exacerbated by the lack of effective public and private enforcement mechanisms to monitor and, if need be, discipline the wrongdoing controlling shareholders and the directors under their control. Moreover, the fact that the largest shareholder in many of the most important Chinese listed companies is the government adds another layer of complexity to mitigating private benefits of control in these companies.[4] In this context, the CSRC's hope that independent directors would (and will) serve as an effective tool to monitor directors on the (management) boards of Chinese listed companies – and to act not solely as strategic advisors – was (and is) entirely understandable.

By the same token, however, the problematic features of China's capital markets and legal environment have created serious doubts as to whether independent directors can indeed serve as effective monitors who ultimately mitigate private benefits of control in listed companies in China.[5]

[3] Preface and Article 1, Guiding Opinions on the Establishment of Independent Director System in Listed Companies (China Securities Regulatory Commission, 2001).

[4] L. Lin and C. J. Milhaupt, 'We Are the (National) Champions: Understanding the Mechanisms of State Capitalism in China', *Stanford Law Review*, 65 (2013), 697; J. Yuan, 'Formal Convergence or Substantial Divergence? Evidence from Adoption of the Independent Director System in China', *Asain-Pacific Law and Policy Journal*, 9 (2007), 71.

[5] D. C. Clarke, 'The Independent Director in Chinese Corporate Governance', *Delaware Journal of Corporate Law*, 31 (2006), 125, 204–217; K. L. A. Lau, J. Jiang and G. An, 'An Overview of the Independent Director System in China', *Company Lawyer*, 34(10) (2013), 321; Y. Niu, 'A Brief Analysis of the Defects and Countermeasures of the Independent Director System in China', *International Journal of Law and Management*, 51 (2009), 260; Z. Yuan, 'Independent Directors in China: The Path in Which Direction?', *International Company and Commercial Law Review*, 22 (2011), 352; G. A. Ferrarini and M. Filippelli, 'Independent Directors and Controlling Shareholders Around the World' (European Corporate Governance Institute (ECGI) Law Working Paper No. 258/2014), 32–33, available at http://ssrn.com/abstract=2443786.

Thus, although there is still a hope that China's existing independent director regime may improve corporate governance in its listed companies, the dearth of empirical evidence supporting their effectiveness and conspicuous corporate governance risks suggest that there is considerable room for reform. As such, following a concise review of the current laws and practice of China's independent director regime, this chapter focuses on proposing reforms in three critical areas: the election, liability and compensation of independent directors in China.

The balance of this chapter proceeds as follows. Section II begins by explaining the ownership structure of listed companies in China, the history and evolution of China's independent director regime and the operation of this regime in practice. Section III considers the various forms and levels that 'independence' may take and proposes reforms to the existing definition of 'independence'. Section IV discusses the risk of liability that independent directors face in Chinese listed companies and proposes reforms to this liability regime. Section V examines the compensation of independent directors and explores the potential corporate governance benefits of reforming this area of the law. Section VI concludes with a general assessment of the current independent director regime in China and prognosticates on the viability of implementing the many proposals for reform presented in this chapter.

II Evolution of China's Independent Director Regime

1 *Share Structure of Chinese Listed Companies*

For historical reasons, most listed companies in China were once state-owned. Consequently, during the 1990s and early 2000s, the largest shareholders of most listed companies were government institutions or state-owned enterprises (SOEs).[6] However, the ownership structure in Chinese companies has undergone major changes in recent years. According to a 2011 survey, while the government remained the *de facto* controlling shareholder in most listed companies in some industries

[6] A survey in 2003 found that the shareholding structure of Chinese listed companies was state-dominant in that 84 per cent of public companies were ultimately controlled by the state, compared with 16 per cent of non-state-controlled ones. See S. Liu, P. Sun and N. Liu, '终极产权论、股权结构及公司绩效' [The Ultimate Ownership and Its Shareholding Structure: Does It Matter for Corporate Performance?], 经济研究 [Economic Research Journal], 4 (2003), 51–61.

(e.g., electric power, gas and hydraulic production and supply), private companies or individuals were the controlling shareholders in more than half of the listed companies in other industries (e.g., agriculture, manufacturing and information technology).[7]

An empirical analysis of the shareholding structure in Chinese listed companies from 2003 to 2008 found that ownership of SOEs and private enterprises was highly concentrated, with institutional investors holding merely 4.87 per cent of shares on average.[8] Despite the many benefits that institutional investors can provide in corporate governance,[9] there are still numerous obstacles that prevent them from participating in the corporate governance of listed companies. Institutional investors are generally minority shareholders, as the CSRC has issued regulations limiting the amount of shares that investment fund management companies may hold in listed companies;[10] this, in turn, makes it difficult for institutional

[7] G. Wu and Y. Ye, '股权集中度、行业特征与企业绩效——基于中国上市公司的实证分析' [Ownership Concentration, Industrial Characteristics and Corporate Performance: Based on Empirical Analysis of China's Listed Companies], 北京工商大学学报（社会科学版） [Journal of Beijing Technology and Business University (Social Science)], 28(5) (2013), 92–93. Corporate ownership is still relevant in China, although the boundary between SOEs and POEs here is sometimes blurred such that classification on the basis of equity ownership alone is problematic. See C. J. Milhaupt and W. Zheng, 'Beyond Ownership: State Capitalism and the Chinese Firm', *Georgetown Law Journal*, 103 (2015), 665, 669.

[8] X. Wu and M. Zhai, '上市公司股权结构对现金股利政策的影响' [Empirical Study on Influence of Ownership Structure on Dividend Policy: Based on Ownership Structure Changes after the Split Share Structure Reform], 山西财经大学学报 [Journal of Shanxi Finance and Economics University], 35(1) (2013), 89–90.

[9] B. S. Black, 'Shareholder Passivity Reexamined', *Michigan Law Review*, 89 (1990), 520; M. J. Roe, 'A Political Theory of American Corporate Finance', *Columbia Law Review*, 91 (1991), 10, 54–62; W. Li and B. Li, '机构投资者介入公司治理效果的实证研究——基于CCGINK的经验研究' [An Empirical Study on the Effect of Institutional Investors Participating in Corporate Governance: Based on the Data of 2004–2006 CCGINK], 南开管理评论 [Nankai Business Review], 1 (2008), 4–14; L. Gao and J. Zhang, '公司治理、机构投资者与盈余管理' [Corporate Governance, Institutional Investors, and Earnings Management], 会计研究 [Accounting Review], 9 (2008), 64–72; Y. Lin and J. Tan, '机构投资者与公司治理: 文献评述与研究框架' [Institutional Investors and Corporate Governance: Literature Review and Research Framework], 会计与经济研究 [Accounting and Economics Research], 5 (2013), 72–73.

[10] A CSRC rule addressing the investment of the publicly raised securities investment funds (a major institutional investor in China) prohibits either the market value of the stocks issued by a single listed company as held by a fund exceeding 10 per cent of the net asset value of the fund, or a listed company's stocks held by all the funds managed by a single fund manager exceeding 10 per cent of such stocks. See Article 32(1), Administrative Measures for the Operation of Publicly-Raised Securities Investment Funds (China Securities Regulatory Commission, 2014).

investors to impose meaningful constraints on the majority's control over their companies. Further, institutional investors are likely to be short-term investors who have little or no incentive to participate in corporate governance.

In China, there has been considerable scholarly discussion regarding the exploitation of minority shareholders in state-owned listed companies by their controlling shareholders. This well-documented exploitation typically involves classic wealth tunnelling by the controlling shareholder causing the company to engage in unfair related party transactions and even sometimes blatant misappropriation.[11]

In a similar vein, the problem also extends to privately owned listed companies in China – an area that has received far less attention especially in the English language literature. A survey of non-financial private-owned companies from 2003 to 2010 showed that the largest shareholder held 34.39 per cent of shares on average and 55.37 per cent of the largest shareholders in listed companies held more than 30 per cent of shares. This survey also indicated that boards under the control of a single dominant shareholder were common among these companies. On average, approximately one-third of the boards of directors in privately owned companies were controlled by the largest shareholders. These majority shareholders have substantial influence over the board of directors, and are therefore capable of exerting control over the management of listed companies.[12] Undue influence from the largest shareholders would also render minority shareholders vulnerable to expropriation in these companies.

Inspired by developments in the West, China's system of independent directors was expected to improve corporate governance by enabling such directors to monitor controlling shareholders and the directors under their control.[13] Around 2000, most independent directors served

[11] R. A. Cole, H. Berkman and J. Fu, 'Expropriation through Loan Guarantees to Related Parties: Evidence from China', *Journal of Banking and Finance*, 33(1) (2009), 141; W. Q. Peng, K. C. J. Wei and Z. Yang. 'Tunneling or Propping: Evidence from Connected Transactions in China', *Journal of Corporate Finance*, 17(2) (2011), 306; G. Jiang, C. Lee and H. Yue, 'Tunneling through Inter-Corporate Loans: The China Experience', *Journal of Financial Economics*, 98 (2010), 1.

[12] J. Tang, Y. Li and J. Lu, '股权结构、董事会特征与大股东掏空——来自民营上市公司的经验证据' [Equity Ownership Structure, the Characteristics of Board and Tunneling: Empirical Evidence from China's Private-Owned Listed Companies], 经济评论 [Economic Review], 1 (2013), 88–89.

[13] S. Shen and J. Jia, 'Will the Independent Director Institution Work in China?', *Loyola of Los Angeles International and Comparative Law Review*, 27 (2005), 223.

in state-owned listed companies. However, following the establishment of the Small and Medium-Sized Enterprise Board (SME) and the Growth Enterprise Market (GEM) at the Shenzhen Stock Exchange (SZSE) in 2004 and 2009 respectively, hundreds of private enterprises have made initial public offerings and listed their shares on these sub-markets.[14] As such, a large number of independent directors have been appointed to the boards of these private-controlled listed companies. That said, recent scholarship suggests that the government may have less direct control over SOEs than some have previously suggested and more control over private-owned enterprises than previously thought – perhaps blurring the distinction somewhat between SOEs and POEs in China.[15]

2 *Introduction of Independent Directors*

China's Company Law provides for two types of companies: (1) a Limited Liability Company, which is similar to a private company; and (2) a Joint Stock Company, which is similar to a public company and also referred to as a 'company limited by shares'. All listed companies have to take the form of a Joint Stock Company.[16]

China adopts a dual board structure (two-tier model) for its Joint Stock Companies, consisting of a management board (board of directors) and a supervisory board (board of statutory supervisors).[17] Both boards are required to report information on their activities to the company's shareholders in its general meeting.[18] While the board of directors is responsible for managing the company, the board of supervisors is supposed to supervise the management board and the senior managers. However, without sufficient functional powers, the board of supervisors seems to play no important role in the companies' corporate governance.[19] Specifically, unlike the supervisory board in Germany, the supervisory board in China lacks the critically important power to select or remove members of the management board, or to demand a working report from

[14] P. Wang, 'Ownership Structure of the Chinese Growth Enterprise Market' (1 December 2012), available at http://ssrn.com/abstract=2223989.

[15] Milhaupt and Zheng, 'Beyond Ownership: State Capitalism and the Chinese Firm'.

[16] Articles 2 and 120, the Company Law of the People's Republic of China, as amended 27 October 2005. The newest version of the Company Law, adopted in 2013 and effective from 1 March 2014, is referred to hereinafter as the Company Law.

[17] Articles 108 and 117, the Company Law.

[18] Articles 99 and 37, the Company Law.

[19] Clarke, 'The Independent Director in Chinese Corporate Governance', 173–175.

the management board. By placing independent directors on the board of directors, it is clear that under China's regime, independent directors are supposed to perform the monitoring functions that the board of supervisors has been unable to execute properly.

Independent directors were first appointed by Chinese SOEs to comply with overseas listing rules. In 1993, Qingdao Brewery Co. Ltd applied to be listed on the Hong Kong Stock Exchange, and the company retained two independent directors to meet the requirements of the Exchange.[20] The CSRC subsequently issued a guideline in 1997, which stipulated that 'the companies *may* establish the independent director system if they consider it necessary'.[21] This encouraged, but did not require, listed companies in China to appoint independent directors. It marked the first mention of independent directors in Chinese government regulations.

The independent director system in China remained in its infancy until mandatory requirements for independent directors were introduced by the Shanghai Stock Exchange and the Shenzhen Stock Exchange in 2000 and 2001 respectively.[22] However, these requirements were self-disciplinary regulations and only applied to companies listed on either exchange. It was only with the promulgation of the CSRC's Guiding Opinions on the Establishment of Independent Director System in Listed Companies (CSRC Guiding Opinions) in 2001 that the independent director requirements were officially established for China's domestic stock market. The CSRC Guiding Opinions mandated all listed companies to appoint independent directors, such that 'by June 30, 2003, independent directors shall comprise at least one third of the total directors on the management board' and '[i]f committees for remuneration, auditing, nomination, etc., are established under the management board of a listed company, (then) independent directors shall constitute half or more of the members of those committees'.[23]

The CSRC Guiding Opinions have been consistently followed within China. Many central government ministries and local governments began to institute regulations on the establishment of the independent director system in enterprises within their respective jurisdictions. Most

[20] Rule 3.10, Listing Rule of the Stock Exchange of Hong Kong Limited (1993).

[21] Article 116, Guidelines for the Articles of Association of Listed Companies (1997).

[22] See Guidelines of the Shanghai Stock Exchange on the Corporate Governance (Shanghai Stock Exchange, 2000); Guidelines on the Independent Director System in Listed Companies (Shenzhen Stock Exchange, 2001).

[23] Articles 1(3) and 5(4), CSRC Guiding Opinions.

importantly, the 2005 revision of the Company Law confirmed that the independent director system forms an integral part of Chinese national law, and provided that 'listed companies shall have independent directors, and detailed measures shall be specified by the State Council'.[24]

In recent years, many important regulations and guidelines concerning independent directors have been issued by Chinese government authorities and organisations. The Chinese central government issued several important memoranda on corporate governance and capital market development that contain mandatory provisions on the responsibilities of independent directors. Recently, in 2014, the China Association for Public Companies (CAPCO) officially released the Guideline for the Exercise of Duties of Independent Directors of Public Companies.[25] The Guideline consisted of 48 articles divided into six chapters, with detailed provisions on the general principles, duties, authorities and exercise of duties of independent directors. Although the Guidelines are not mandatory, they provide useful guidance for companies because they unify, categorise and reiterate articles related to the regulation of independent directors which are spread over various existing laws and regulations.

3 *Independent Directors in Practice*

According to the China Stock Market and Accounting Research (CSMAR) database, there were 10,002 independent directors serving in listed companies on the two national stock exchanges – the Shanghai Stock Exchange and the Shenzhen Stock Exchange – by the end of 2013. On average, an independent director serves 1.39 listed companies, and each company retains 4.02 independent directors. The 953 companies listed on the Shanghai Stock Exchange retained 3,956 independent directors, with each company employing 4.15 independent directors; the 1,536 companies listed on the Shenzhen Exchange retained 6,046 independent directors, with 3.94 independent directors per company. This seems to indicate that there were slightly more independent directors in companies listed in Shanghai.[26] Thus, at least on paper, it appears that

[24] Article 123, the Company Law.

[25] 'Guideline for the Exercise of Duties of Independent Directors of Public Companies', CAPCO, available at www.capco.org.cn (in Chinese).

[26] China Association for Public Companies, Research Team on Drafting the Guidelines for Exercise of Duties of Independent Directors of Public Companies (2014).

independent directors have found broad acceptance in Chinese listed companies.

Looking at the background of independent directors, a survey of companies listed in Shanghai conducted in 2009 by the Listed Companies Association of Shanghai found that 78 per cent of listed companies retained experts from universities and research institutions as their independent directors; 51 per cent employed directors or managers from other enterprises; 46 per cent employed accountants, lawyers and consultants; 19 per cent employed retired government officials; and 10 per cent employed current or retired staff of banks.[27]

In October 2013, as an anti-corruption measure, the Organization Department of the Central Committee of the Communist Party of China issued a notice subjecting former Communist Party leaders and government officers to more stringent approval proceedings if they planned to work or continue working for business organisations.[28] This has made it very difficult for in-service and retired Communist Party leaders and government officers to act as independent directors for listed companies. In turn, since the anti-corruption measure was issued, hundreds of so-called 'leader-directors' (*Guanyuan Dongshi*) have resigned from their companies. The percentage of independent directors with a government background has thus decreased substantially since 2014.[29]

While China's independent director regime is clearly in its infancy, recent literature has demonstrated that this regime benefits corporate governance and minority shareholders' welfare as a whole.[30]

[27] China Association for Public Companies, '上市公司独立董事履职情况报告' [Report of Duty Performance of Independent Directors in the Listed Companies] (16 January 2014), available at www.capco.org.cn.

[28] '关于进一步规范党政领导干部在企业兼职(任职)问题的意见' [Opinion On Further Standardizing the Party and Government Leading Cadres Taking Offices in Enterprise] (19 October 2013).

[29] '独立董事辞职潮再现的背后' [Behind the Reappearance of Resign Tide of the Independent Directors], 中国经济时报 [China Economic Times], 30 October 2014.

[30] W. Li and J. Xu, '董事会独立性、总经理继任与战略变化幅度——独立董事有效性的实证研究' [Board's Independence, CEO Succession and the Scope of Strategic Change: An Empirical Research on the Effectiveness of Independent Directors], 南开管理评论 [Nankai Business Review], 17(1) (2014), 4–13; G. Fang and X. Liu, '董事会结构对行为影响的实证分析' [An Empirical Analysis of the Impact of Board Structure on Board Behaviours], 北京工商大学学报(社会科学版) [Journal of Beijing Technology and Business University (Social Science)], 28(5) (2013), 28–35; C. Liu and J. Yang, '独立董事的社会关系与监管功能' [Social Relation and Supervision Function of Independent Directors: Evidence from Forced CEO Turnover], 财经研究 [Journal of Finance and Economics], 39(7) (2013), 16–26.

A survey conducted by CAPCO in 2013 also indicated that most interviewees agreed that independent directors are playing a positive role with respect to corporate governance and the protection of public investors.[31]

III Independence of Independent Directors

1 *Significance of 'Independence'*

Should independent directors in Chinese listed companies be *advisors* or *monitors*? The answer to this question is related to the perceived function of the board of directors in public listed companies. Under the shadow of the 'supreme' authority of the shareholders' general meeting, the board of directors may exercise a range of powers focused on managing the company.[32] Accordingly, the traditional role of the management board in Chinese corporate governance was by definition 'management' rather than 'supervision'. This is changing, however, as independent directors in listed companies must now make up one-third of the management board and these directors are expected to play a monitoring role.

While a number of independent directors hold the view that their main duty is to provide information and advice to listed companies,[33] laws and regulations require independent directors to 'safeguard the overall interests of the company, especially the interests of the minority shareholders'.[34] Numerous administrative sanctions issued by the CSRC, and disciplinary sanctions issued by the two national Stock Exchanges showed

[31] China Association for Public Companies, 'Report of Duty Performance of Independent Directors in the Listed Companies'. The interviewees here include senior managers, independent directors and investors of the listed companies.

[32] Compare the powers of the board of directors (Articles 46 and 108 (3), the Company Law) and of the shareholders' general meeting (Articles 37 (1) and 99, the Company Law).

[33] According to a survey covering more than 1,600 listed companies and 4,000 independent directors, by April 2009, more people are of the view that independent directors should provide professional knowledge and technical support to the listed companies, compared with those of the view that independent directors should first fulfil the duty of supervising the controlling shareholder and management. See L. Zhao, X. Tang and G. Ding, 走出困境——独立董事的义务、职责和责任 [The Way Out: The Role, Tasks, and Responsibilities of the Independent Director], 法律出版社 (Law Press China, 2010), 39.

[34] Article 1(2), Guiding Opinions on the Establishment of Independent Director System in Listed Companies (China Securities Regulatory Commission, 2001); Article 50, Code of Corporate Governance of Listed Companies (China Securities Regulatory Commission and the National Economic and Trade Commission, 2002); see the Regulatory Appendix.

that if a listed company failed to correctly disclose information, the independent directors who signed the pertinent documents will be deemed to have failed to fulfil their duty of supervision, and will consequently face administrative penalties or self-regulatory organisation disciplinary sanctions.[35] The Chinese courts are unlikely to alter this position.[36] Since independent directors are supposed to be *monitors*, their independence will be critically important to the success of the institution.

2 *Different Levels of Independence*

'Independence' suggests that independent directors shall not be influenced by controlling shareholders, *de facto* controllers, or any other interested persons or institutions (related parties) when performing their duties.[37] In essence, the question of independence turns on whether a director is, for any substantial reason, incapable of making a decision with only the best interests of the corporation in mind. The focus is on the independent director's impartiality and objectivity.[38] In theory, there are at least four levels of independence which are described below.

Level 1: The independent director and/or her relatives have no financial relationships with persons or institutions that may influence the performance of the independent director. These relationships include existing employment, shareholding or other monetary or financial relationships. Of these, it should be noted that shareholder relationships constitute a grey area, since opinions differ on whether an independent director's shareholding in a listed company will undermine their independence.[39]

[35] See *infra* IV.

[36] There are presently no court decisions addressing the range of duties owed by independent directors. An administrative law decision relating to fiduciary duty of outside directors working for listed companies observed that the claimant outside director who did not perform his legal obligations in a fraudulent disclosure should bear the corresponding legal liabilities. *DING Li-ye v. China Securities Regulatory Commission*, Beijing No. 1 Intermediate People's Court [(2008) Yi Zhong Xing Chu Zi No. 553]. 丁力业诉中国证券监督管理委员会行政处罚决定纠纷案判决书 ((2008)一中行初字第553号).

[37] Article 1(2), CSRC Guiding Opinions, see the Regulatory Appendix.

[38] See, for example, *In re Oracle Corp. Derivative Litigation*, 824 A.2d 917, 938 (Del. Ch. 2003).

[39] In China, '(i)ndividual shareholders that directly or indirectly hold one percent or more of the issued shares of a listed company or rank among the top ten shareholders, and their lineal relatives' shall not serve as independent directors in the listed companies. Article 3(2), CSRC Guiding Opinions. In the US, federal laws, the SEC rules and rules

Level 2: Apart from the monetary and financial relationships stated above, independence may also require that a person has no other non-personal relationships, which may weaken her capacity to make objective, independent judgements.[40] An example of such a non-personal relationship could be an independent director who (due to the influence of related parties) may lose her professorship or a possible material business opportunity if she casts an unfavourable vote at a board meeting. Under such circumstances, even without an ongoing direct financial relationship between the independent director and the related parties, there may still be other factors influencing the decision of the independent director.

Level 3: An independent director must not have any personal relationships that will compromise her independence; such relationships go beyond the financial and non-personal relationships enumerated above.[41]

Level 4: Apart from the relationships stated in Levels 1 to 3, independent directors should also be free of 'unconscious bias' that may influence their ability to make objective judgements.[42] However, this standard is hard to meet and harder to prove, since it requires a director to detect biases that she herself may not be conscious of, and would also require a subjective detailed investigation into each director's state of mind.

Any attempt to abstractly classify the complicated factors influencing independence may lead to omissions or ambiguity.[43] The complexity of

of the stock exchanges are of different views, see D. C. Clarke, 'Three Concepts of the Independent Director', *Delaware Journal of Corporate Law*, 32 (2007), 73, 91–94.

40 *Grobow v. Perot*, 539 A.2d at 189 (To challenge the independence of the defendant outside directors 'would require plaintiffs to allege with particularity ... directors were dominated or otherwise controlled by an individual or entity interested in the transaction'); *Aronson v. Lewis*, 473 A.2d 805, 815 (1984) ('There must be coupled with the allegation of control such facts as would demonstrate that through personal or other relationships the directors are beholden to the controlling person').

41 *In re Oracle Corp. Derivative Litigation*, 824 A.2d 917, 938–939 (Del. Ch. 2003); V. Brudney, 'The Independent Director: Heavenly City or Potemkin Village?', *Harvard Law Review*, 95 (1982), 597, 613. Relying on economics and sociology literatures, Hwang and Kim identify five types of shared background that might matter: mutual *alma mater*, military service, regional origin, academic discipline and industry. See B. H. Hwang and S. Kim, 'It Pays to Have Friends', *Journal of Financial Economics*, 93 (2009), 138, 140–141.

42 A. Page, 'Unconscious Bias and the Limits of Director Independence', *University of Illinois Law Review* (2009), 237.

43 There is also a significant divergence in the definition of 'independence' in Western legal systems. See W. G. Ringe, 'Independent Directors: After the Crisis', *European Business Organization Law Review*, 14 (2013), 401, 402.

connections and relationships in Chinese society may make it even more difficult to determine if an independent director is truly independent.[44] In light of this, Level 4 may set an excessively high and impractical standard for independent directors. Even the requirements of Level 3 may still be too strict for emerging markets such as China, because it may diminish the pool of available and qualified candidates. This chapter will therefore focus on 'independence' as defined in Level 1 and Level 2.

3 *Practice in China*

In China, independence is defined by reference to family, social or financial connections with the corporation and/or its controlling shareholders.[45] Current laws and regulations require independent directors to satisfy the above Level 1 requirements at the time of their appointment. In practice, the stock exchanges will screen the candidates proposed by listed companies in advance.[46] However, upon appointment and during their term of service, independent directors do not need to satisfy the Level 2 (or stricter) requirements. There are doubts as to whether independent directors are truly 'independent' upon and after their appointment. Critics argue that when independent directors are nominated and elected by the actual or *de facto* controlling shareholder, or the board of directors under their control, these independent directors will inevitably turn into 'puppets' that are unable to execute their supervisory functions properly.[47]

Indeed, the independence of 'independent' directors nominated and appointed under current procedures is doubtful. The CSRC Guiding Opinions state:

[44] J. Liu, '我国公司法移植独立董事制度的思考' [Thoughts about Chinese Company Law's Transplanting the Institution of Independent Director], 政法论坛 [Tribune of Political Science and Law], 21(3) (2003), 48.

[45] Article 3, CSRC Guiding Opinions: see Appendix. See also Article 11, Working Guidelines for the Filing and Training of Independent Directors of Listed Companies on Shanghai Stock Exchange (Shanghai Stock Exchange, 2010); Article 7, Measures of Shenzhen Stock Exchange for the Record-Filing of Independent Directors (Shenzhen Stock Exchange, 2011).

[46] Articles 3–5, Working Guidelines for the Filing and Training of Independent Directors of Listed Companies on Shanghai Stock Exchange (Shanghai Stock Exchange, 2010); Articles 2, 15, 16, Measures of Shenzhen Stock Exchange for the Record-Filing of Independent Directors (Shenzhen Stock Exchange, 2011).

[47] See, for example, C. Xie, '股份公司独立董事任免制度研究' [Study on the Mechanism of Appointment and Removal of Independent Direction in Stock Corporations], 河北法学 [Hebei Law Science], 22(7) (2004), 3.

> [T]he board of directors or the board of supervisors, or shareholders that solely or jointly holds 1 per cent of the issued shares of a listed company may nominate candidates for independent directors. However, such nominations shall be subject to decision by the shareholders' general meeting.[48]

In companies with concentrated shareholding structures, controlling shareholders can control both the board of directors and the board of supervisors, as well as materially influence the independent directors they nominated before. Institutional investors are seldom active in the governance of listed companies in China. That said, there are some reported cases in which institutional investors have nominated candidates to serve as independent directors.[49] However, even in such cases, it must be remembered that for these nominees to be elected to the board, they must also be supported by the controlling shareholder (unless the company has an effective system of cumulative voting or the *de facto* controlling shareholder does not have voting control and faces a proxy battle – both of which are merely theoretical possibilities as they are highly unlikely to occur in China's current corporate governance environment).[50]

4 *Reform Proposals and Analysis*

Two major reforms have been proposed to safeguard the independence of 'independent' directors: (1) that the rights of controlling shareholders to nominate and elect independent directors should be restricted; and (2) that third parties, such as the CSRC, should be allowed to nominate independent directors. After weighing the pros and cons of these proposals, I argue that neither is feasible in the context of Chinese corporate governance. Instead, ultimately, I propose a different solution: that independent directors should be nominated by minority shareholders with some additional regulations supplementing this proposal.

[48] Article 4(1), CSRC Guiding Opinions.

[49] Capital Market Research Institute of Shanghai Securities Exchange, '年度沪市上市公司治理专题调查和研究报告' [Special Survey and Research Report on Corporate Governance of Companies Listed on Shanghai Securities Exchange 2012], 上海证券报 [Shanghai Securities], 23 October 2013.

[50] When cumulative voting presently is not a compulsory requirement for the election of directors and supervisors (Article 105, the Company Law), current laws and regulations do not make any provisions as to whether the shareholders of joint stock companies can solicit proxies for the shareholders' general meeting. So far, proxy solicitation initiated by shareholders rarely happens in the practice of listed companies.

a Restricting the Rights of Controlling Shareholders

Arguably, the power of the controlling shareholder and the board of directors under its control should be restricted during the nomination and election process for independent directors to ensure their independence.[51] According to China's Company Law, candidates for independent directorships should be nominated by authorised parties prior to voting at the shareholders' general meeting. As it is in the current procedure, the nomination committee of a listed company proposes a list of candidates to succeed incumbent directors. After approval by the board, the list is voted on at a shareholders' general meeting. However, if the incumbent independent directors are not truly independent, or if the management board (as well as the board of supervisors) is controlled by the controlling shareholder, the independence of the candidates nominated would remain questionable. To prevent this, minority shareholders should have the right either to nominate independent directors themselves, or to delegate this right to the nomination committee. Nonetheless, as voting rights are among the most fundamental of shareholder rights, legislators should be slow to restrict the voting rights of controlling shareholders. This accords with the practice in European countries and the United States, where it is uncommon to restrict the voting rights of such shareholders, especially through vote capping.[52] In addition, restricting the voting rights of controlling shareholders may violate the principle of shareholder equality, which is a fundamental feature of Chinese corporate law. Adopting this proposal may therefore be unfeasible in the context of Chinese corporate governance.

b Nomination or Appointment by a Third Party

Another view is that independent directors should be nominated and appointed by an impartial third party in order to overcome the opportunistic behaviour of controlling shareholders. The 'third party' may be a governmental agency such as the CSRC, the newly established China

[51] C. Shi, '独立董事选聘程序的完善——基于代理理论的视角' [Improving the Nomination and Election of Independent Directors: From the Perspective of Agency Theory], 财会通讯 [Communication of Finance and Accounting], 10 (2010), 85–86; J. Li, '论我国独立董事产生机制的重构' [Restructuring the Independent Director Production Mechanism in China], 法律科学 [Legal Science], 2 (2004), 67–72.

[52] L. Enriques et al., 'The Basic Governance Structure: Minority Shareholders and Non-Shareholder Constituencies' in R. Kraakman et al. (eds.), *Anatomy of Corporate Law: A Comparative and Functional Approach*, 2nd edn (Oxford University Press, 2009), 91.

Association for Public Companies (or its Committee of Independent Directors) or a special investor association.[53] In China's political-economic context, such a third party would likely have to be an institution supported by the government, and probably on a monopolistic basis.

It is a basic principle of Chinese corporate governance that independent directors as members of the management board are generally elected at the shareholders' general meeting.[54] Enshrined in the current version of China's Company Law, this principle is clearly contravened where a third party is granted the power to appoint independent directors directly to the board. Further, even if a third party is permitted to nominate candidates, a non-binding nomination is meaningless as the shareholders can disregard the nomination and put forward their own nominees instead. Where the third-party's nomination is binding, there is a risk that these nominees might not be qualified, as corporations in different industries and at different stages of development have different needs for their independent directors. A third party lacking intimate knowledge of the nature of a corporation or its development may therefore nominate candidates without the requisite qualifications or experience to function effectively as independent directors.

In addition, given the large number of listed companies in China, nominating independent directors for every listed company would be a formidable task for any single third party. Finally, even if such a third party were to exist, it would itself need to be an institution which has a well-established, efficient and reputable internal governance system – which is also subject to some form of third-party supervision and has to compete with other similar institutions for its operational funding so that it does not become a rent-seeking monopolistic institution.

c Nomination of Independent Directors by Minority Shareholders

Nomination is the key to appointing independent directors because it determines the pool of available candidates from which the shareholders can choose. Therefore, reforms should grant minority shareholders, instead of the controlling shareholder or the board of directors/supervisors under its control, the right to nominate the first group of independent

[53] P. Shui, '独立董事该由谁委派' [Who Shall Appoint the Independent Directors], 中华工商时报 [China Securities News], 11 May 2006.

[54] Articles 99 and 37, the Company Law. Some of the directors, as the representatives of employees, may be elected by the employees. Article 108(2), the Company Law.

directors. For listed companies that already have independent directors, nomination rights should be granted to the nomination committee of the board of directors, in which independent directors occupy a majority as mandated by the CSRC Guiding Opinions. For listed companies with no nomination committee, current independent directors should have the right to nominate their successors. These reforms will help to ensure that the 'independent' directors remain independent of the company's controlling shareholders and board of directors. Such reforms can be instituted by the CSRC, which can confer the power to nominate independent directors solely upon the minority shareholders.

d Other Suggestions

The current system of appointing directors can be substantially improved in other ways. First, the Company Law, or at least the CSRC's Guidelines for the Articles of Association of Listed Companies, should be amended to require all listed companies to adopt cumulative voting for director and statutory supervisor elections.

Second, the Company Law should be amended to combine elections for directors and statutory supervisors. Directors and non-employee supervisors would be elected simultaneously via a united ballot during the shareholders' general meeting.[55] Thus, when the controlling shareholder seeks to ensure the appointment of its representative(s) to the board of directors, it would have to permit the possibility of minority shareholders' representatives sitting on the board of supervisors because of the compulsory cumulative voting regime.[56]

Third, institutional investors should be encouraged to participate more in corporate governance, and the restrictions on the shareholdings of independent directors should be eased.[57] Investors should be encouraged to nominate their qualified representatives,

[55] The employee supervisors should be elected by the employees. Article 117(2), the Company Law.

[56] There has been a provision in a guideline applicable to Chinese commercial banks that tries to achieve roughly the same outcome by requiring a shareholder shall only nominate a candidate for independent director or external statutory supervisor, and shall not simultaneously nominate an independent director and an external statutory supervisor. See Article 8(2) of the Guidance on Joint-Stock Commercial Banks' System of Independent Directors and External Supervisors (The People's Bank of China, 23 May 2002).

[57] For example, shareholders with less than 10 per cent shareholdings and not within the top ten biggest shareholders, or their related personnel should be permitted to serve as independent directors.

solicit shareholder votes and have access to the management board. It is true that there are overlaps between the functions of the board of supervisors and the independent directors on the management board.[58] Nevertheless, while it is highly unlikely that the institution of the board of supervisors will be removed from the Company Law soon, the Company Law should require at least one-third of the board of supervisors to consist of outside supervisors to secure greater statutory supervisor independence. This would help bolster the ability of the supervisory board to support and supplement the work of the independent directors.[59]

5 *Ensuring Independence during Performance of Duties*

Even if newly elected independent directors can satisfy the initial requirements of independence, there is no guarantee that these directors can maintain their independence throughout their terms of office, which may last for three or six years.[60] Independence may be compromised in many ways. Current laws and regulations in China do not provide legal remedies for independent directors who do not maintain their independence during their tenures. Enforcing a requirement of continuing independence is challenging, but not impossible, and is a task that has been undertaken by foreign courts. For example, the Delaware courts have held that it is crucial for independent directors to be independent *during the performance* of their duties, not merely at the point in time when they were elected.[61] Independence is evaluated *ex post* using a transaction-by-transaction based approach under Delaware corporate law.[62]

[58] J. Zhao, 'Comparative Study of U.S. and German Corporate Governance: Suggestions on the Relationship between Independent Directors and the Supervisory Board of Listed Companies in China', *Michigan State Journal of International Law*, 18 (2010), 495, 506.

[59] L. Liu et al., 选任独立董事与公司治理 [The Election of Independent Directors and Corporate Governance], 元照出版公司 (Angle Publishing Co., 2013), 163–174.

[60] The term of office of an independent director shall be the same with that of other directors of the same listed company, which is three years; the term of office of an independent director may be renewed upon expiry thereof if the director is re-elected, with the extension of the term of office not exceeding six years. See Article 4(4), CSRC Guiding Opinions.

[61] *Aronson v. Lewis*, 473 A.2d 805, 816 (1984); *In re Oracle Corp. Derivative Litigation*, 824 A.2d 917, 938 (Del. Ch. 2003).

[62] 'This contextual approach is a strength of our law, as even the best minds have yet to devise across-the-board definitions that capture all the circumstances in which the

China introduced an independent director regime in response to its under-developed corporate governance culture and exploitation of minority shareholders. However, these objectives cannot be achieved if regulators lack sufficient access to the necessary information and tools for ensuring that independent directors remain truly independent throughout their tenures.

The two national stock exchanges are authorised by the CSRC to render advance rulings on the independence of a director, but the exchanges can only do so on the basis of documents filed by the listed company and its independent director candidates. After a director is appointed to the board, the exchanges are not required to judge the independence of a director during his or her term of office. In fact, even if the exchanges had such a responsibility, neither the CSRC nor the exchanges are sufficiently motivated or possess sufficient resources to police the continued independence of these directors.[63]

Although minority shareholders in listed companies clearly have an incentive to monitor and insist on the independence of the 'independent' directors, they lack the tools with which to enforce these desired outcomes. It is also questionable whether minority shareholders will make claims for damages regarding false statements of independence made by persons nominated as independent directors.[64] Further, it is unclear if shareholders can petition a court to invalidate or set aside board resolutions passed with the support of directors who claim to be independent, but who are in fact not. The same uncertainty applies to resolutions of the shareholders' general meeting with similar defects.[65]

Nevertheless, introducing a system of judicial review to determine and enforce the independence of 'independent' directors may be one of the best options for the future development of the Chinese legal system. To achieve this, much work needs to be done to establish the necessary laws and institutions: fiduciary duties of directors must be clearly defined;[66]

independence of directors might reasonably be questioned.' *In re Oracle Corp. Derivative Litigation*, 824 A.2d 917, 941.

63 Clarke, 'The Independent Director in Chinese Corporate Governance', 210–213.

64 Investors can bring lawsuits against listed companies pursuant to Article 69 of the Securities Law, but need to prove that their damages are caused by the false statement, which could be difficult.

65 Article 22, the Company Law.

66 Z. Ren, '中国董事的勤勉义务标准研究' [A Study on the Criterion of the Director's Duty of Diligence], 中国法学 [China Legal Science], 6 (2008), 89–91.

shareholder derivative litigation should be encouraged;[67] and a discovery procedure should be introduced to grant shareholders greater access to the relevant information.[68]

IV Liabilities of Independent Directors

In China, the duties that directors – including independent directors – owe to listed companies and their shareholders can be found generally in the Company Law and the Securities Law.[69] According to the Company Law, directors and officers have a duty to be faithful and diligent to the company and its shareholders, and breaching this duty leads to liability in damages to both the company and shareholders.[70] The Company Law does not distinguish between listed and unlisted companies when imposing such liability. Under the Securities Law, grounds for legal liability of a listed company, its directors and officers mainly involve information disclosure.[71] Both the Company Law and the Securities Law provide for liability of directors generally, without distinguishing between independent directors and executive directors. In practice, legal liability for the directors and officers of listed companies mostly takes the form of administrative penalties imposed by the CSRC and disciplinary actions made by the stock exchanges. Civil litigation against directors and officers in listed companies is very rare.[72] The same is true for criminal prosecutions.[73]

67 H. Huang, 'Shareholder Derivative Litigation in China: Empirical Findings and Comparative Analysis', *Banking and Finance Law Review*, 27 (2012), 619, 648–653.

68 W. Du, '英美民事证据开示若干问题研析' [Research on the (Evidence) Disclosure Procedure under Anglo-American Law], 证据科学 [Evidence Science], 16(6) (2008), 713–722.

69 In order to concentrate on the main topic of this chapter, it will not consider the director liability rules under the bankruptcy law and labour law.

70 Articles 147–149, 152, the Company Law. An article was added to the Criminal Law in 2011 to the effect that, where a director, supervisor or senior manager of a listed company, fails to comply with her duty of loyalty towards the company and takes advantage of her position to manipulate the company to funnel interests to a third party, thus causing heavy losses to the listed company, she shall be sentenced to fixed-term imprisonment and fines. See Article 169-1 of the Criminal Law of the People's Republic of China (中华人民共和国刑法) as amended by 21 February 2011 [herein after the Criminal Law].

71 Articles 69, 193, the Securities Law. A director, who drives her company to make a public offering fraudulently or makes a listed company disclose fraudulent information may be subject to criminal liabilities, Articles 160, 161, the Criminal Law.

72 Huang, 'Shareholder Derivative Litigation in China', 631.

73 Z. Jin and P. Yu, '上市公司高管犯罪问题研究' [Researches on Crimes of Executives in the Listed Companies], 证券法苑 [Securities Law Review], 10 (2010).

1 *Administrative Penalties*

At present, the CSRC is the main authority supervising the work of independent directors in listed companies. Administrative liability of independent directors mainly takes the form of administrative penalties imposed by the CSRC.

From 1 April 2004 to 31 December 2014, the CSRC issued 75 decisions on administrative penalties concerning independent directors, sanctioning a total of 221 independent directors.[74] Within this group of independent directors, 108 were issued both warnings and fines; another 112 received only warnings. An analysis of the 75 cases shows that almost all administrative penalties involving independent directors relate to violations of information disclosure rules. The statistics also show that independent directors were subject to punishment when they voted in the meetings of the board of directors that approved and signed the legally non-compliant disclosure documents.

The Securities Law establishes the legal basis of the abovementioned sanctions. It provides that the directors, supervisors and senior management of a listed company shall ensure that the information disclosed by the company is truthful, accurate and complete.[75] An issuer or listed company that makes false, misleading statements, or makes statements with material omissions, is subject to penalties (fines and warnings) issued by the CSRC. The supervisory authorities may also issue warnings and fines to the 'executive staff directly in charge' (*Zhijie Fuze De Zhuguan Renyuan*) and the 'other persons directly responsible' (*Qita Zhijie Zeren Renyuan*).[76]

In all cases involving administrative penalties, the independent directors were punished under the category of 'other persons directly liable', along with some other directors and officers who were deemed to have assisted in the unlawful acts. The 'executive staff directly in charge' sanctioned in the same cases by the CSRC are normally the president, chief executive officer, chief financial officer and sometimes the secretary of the board of directors; these are considered to be the primary violators.[77]

[74] These statistics are based on the Decisions on Administrative Penalties published on the official website of the CSRC. See, 'Administrative Sanction Decisions', available at www.csrc.gov.cn/.

[75] Article 68(3), the Securities Law.

[76] Such fines may be from RMB 30,000 to RMB 300,000. See Article 193(1), the Securities Law.

[77] Article 58(2)(3), Measures for the Administration of Information Disclosure by Listed Companies (China Securities Regulatory Commission, 2007).

The CSRC has stated in its penalty decisions on independent directors that 'once the directors sign the periodic reporting documents, they shall ensure the truthfulness, accuracy and completeness of the financial data in the reports'.[78] If these periodic reports and other disclosure documents contain materially false statements, the 'executive staff directly in charge' and 'other persons directly liable', including the independent directors, will face administrative penalties.

Theoretically, if the independent directors perform their duties diligently in reviewing the documents before disclosure, their liability can be reduced or excused accordingly.[79] Independent directors can be excused from administrative penalties, for example, if they make specific objections to the issues involved in the information disclosure subsequently found unlawful, provided that these objections are recorded in the minutes of the board meetings of the company and that they also cast dissenting votes at the meetings.[80] Notwithstanding the fact that many independent directors plead the due diligence defence in an attempt to avoid sanctions,[81] between April 2004 and November 2014, there were only three cases in which independent directors achieved an exclusion from or reduction in their administrative liabilities.[82]

The CSRC has developed a multi-factor test to determine whether a person is responsible for a company's misconduct or fraud, and therefore subject to administrative sanctions. It has stipulated that exemptions from liability are exceptional and will only be granted when: (1) the person made specific objections to the decision which ultimately resulted in the misconduct and voted against the decision; (2) the person is unable to properly perform her duties because of *force majeure*;

78 See, China Securities Regulatory Commission Administrative Sanction Decision ([2009], No. 42); China Securities Regulatory Commission Administrative Sanction Decision ([2014], No. 19).

79 Article 58(1), Measures for the Administration of Information Disclosure by Listed Companies (2007); Article 15, Rules on Determining Administrative Liability for Illegal Information Disclosure (Chinese Securities Regulatory Commission, 2011).

80 Article 21, Rules on Determining Administrative Liability for Illegal Information Disclosure (2011).

81 W. Cai, 'The Dilemmas of Independent Directors in China: An Empirical and Comparative Study', *European Business Organization Law Review*, 18 (2017), 123 (information taken from https://researchbank.rmit.edu.au/view/rmit:43252), available at http://ssrn.com/abstract=2758519.

82 China Securities Regulatory Commission Administrative Sanction Decision ([2010] No. 10); China Securities Regulatory Commission Administrative Sanction Decision ([2011] No. 38); China Securities Regulatory Commission Administrative Sanction Decision ([2014] No. 69).

or (3) where the person is not a principal offender and she has reported the illegal act to the company and the regulators in a timely manner.[83]

Apart from these three exceptional exemptions from liability, there are a few mitigating factors which may warrant a director receiving a lighter punishment as a result of corporate misconduct or fraud which include: (1) before the corporate misconduct is discovered, the person has proactively asked the company to correct it or reported the case to the relevant regulators; (2) after the corporate misconduct came to the director's knowledge, the director voiced her concern to the relevant person in charge or the regulator, and has taken appropriate measures; or (3) the director cooperates with the market regulator's investigation and contributes useful information or services.[84]

In contrast, the following circumstances will *not* be accepted as a basis for the exception of liability for a director in the case of corporate fraud or misconduct: (1) the director is not directly involved in management of the company;[85] (2) the director is incompetent and/or lacks the required professional background to understand the misconduct;[86] (3) the director is unfamiliar with the situation as she has just been appointed as a director;[87] (4) the director relies on opinions and reports produced by professional experts;[88] or (5) the person is controlled by the shareholder or the *de facto* controller, or is subject to other external intervention.[89] Further, having no knowledge of the violation does not provide a basis for an exemption.[90]

83 Article 21, Rules on Determining Administrative Liability for Illegal Information Disclosure (2011).

84 See, Article 20, Rules on Determining Administrative Liability for Illegal Information Disclosure (2011).

85 Article 22(1), Rules on Determining Administrative Liability for Illegal Information Disclosure (2011); China Securities Regulatory Commission Administrative Sanction Decision ([2010] No. 17).

86 Article 22(2), Rules on Determining Administrative Liability for Illegal Information Disclosure (2011); China Securities Regulatory Commission Administrative Sanction Decision ([2013] No. 47).

87 Article 22(3), Rules on Determining Administrative Liability for Illegal Information Disclosure (2011); China Securities Regulatory Commission Administrative Sanction Decision ([2011] No. 48).

88 Article 22(4), Rules on Determining Administrative Liability for Illegal Information Disclosure (2011); China Securities Regulatory Commission Administrative Sanction Decision ([2012] No. 53).

89 Article 22(5), Rules on Determining Administrative Liability for Illegal Information Disclosure (2011); China Securities Regulatory Commission Administrative Sanction Decision ([2011] No. 3).

90 China Securities Regulatory Commission Administrative Sanction Decision ([2011] No. 3).

There are no court decisions reviewing the administrative penalties that may apply to *independent* directors. In the exceptional cases where sanctions have been imposed on *outside* directors, the courts have been inclined to affirm the CSRC's decisions. So far, there were only three cases where outside directors of listed companies sued the CSRC for improper punishment, and all the claimants lost their cases.[91]

In the *DING Li-ye* case, the Beijing First Intermediate People's Court upheld the CSRC's decision to sanction an independent director on the basis that the CSRC followed the procedures for due process as established in the Chinese Securities Law. The Court asserted that according to the Chinese Securities Law, directors of listed companies are obliged to perform their duties, supervise information disclosure and ensure its truthfulness, accuracy and completeness. In this case, the CSRC correctly classified the independent director as a 'person subject to direct liability' and issued a warning and fine of RMB 30,000 (about US $4,392) as the independent director clearly did not fulfil his obligations under the Securities Law. The relevant facts were clearly set out in the CSRC's decision, the law and regulations were correctly applied, the procedures applied were lawful and the penalties imposed were adequate.[92] This marked the first time that a local court substantively addressed and affirmed an administrative penalty imposed by the CSRC.

2 *Stock Exchange Disciplinary Sanctions*

Both the Shanghai Stock Exchange and Shenzhen Stock Exchange regularly circulate Notices of Criticisms and Public Criticisms to discipline negligent independent directors.[93] As of 31 December 2014, 38 independent directors of companies listed on the Shenzhen Stock Exchange have

[91] *LU Jiang-hao v. China Securities Regulatory Commission*, Beijing No. 1 Intermediate People's Court [(2002) Yi Zhong Xing Chu Zi No. 219] 陆家豪诉中国证券监督管理委员会行政处罚纠纷案行政裁定书 (2002) 一中行初字第219号; *HUANG Yong v. China Securities Regulatory Commission*, Beijing No. 1 Intermediate People's Court [(2007) Yi Zhong Xing Chu Zi No. 795] 黄勇诉中国证券监督管理委员会行政处罚纠纷案判决书 (2007) 一中行初字第795号; *DING Li-ye v. China Securities Regulatory Commission*, Beijing No. 1 Intermediate People's Court [(2008) Yi Zhong Xing Chu Zi No. 553] 丁力业诉中国证券监督管理委员会行政处罚纠纷案判决书 (2008) 一中行初字第553号.

[92] *DING Liye v. China Securities Regulatory Commission* [(2008) Yi Zhong Xing Chu Zi No. 553].

[93] The two national Stock Exchanges have two principle categories of regulatory tools at their disposal, namely Disciplinary Sanctions (纪律处分) and Oversight Measures (监管措施). Among the Disciplinary Sanctions, independent directors may be subject to Notices of Criticism (通报批评) or Public Criticisms (公开谴责). A Public Criticism

been subject to Notices of Criticisms and eight independent directors have been subject to Public Criticisms. In a similar vein, at the Shanghai Stock Exchange, 77 independent directors have been subject to Notices of Criticism and 13 independent directors have been subject to Public Criticisms.[94]

These cases, in which independent directors were subjected to disciplinary action, involved facts that are similar to the CSRC administrative cases. All of these cases involved illegal disclosures of information, and the independent directors were punished because they had participated in the relevant board meetings, and had approved and signed the illegal information disclosure documents.

Theoretically, the two stock exchanges only deal with less severe violations by independent directors. In practice, however, there have been cases handled by a stock exchange and the CSRC at approximately the same time.[95] The stock exchanges have issued sanctions based on their self-disciplinary rules, such as the Listing Rules and Guidelines on Standardised Operations of Listed Companies.[96] It is unlikely that the stock exchanges will issue sanctions purely based on violations of the Securities Law or solely on the rules and regulations stipulated by the CSRC.

3 *Analysis and Suggestions*

Under the accountability mechanisms applicable to China's independent directors, administrative sanctions are particularly important. The decisions released by the CSRC in recent years show that the number of sanctions issued per year against independent directors is stable. Most

is more severe than a Notice of Criticism. See 'Supervision Measures', Shanghai Stock Exchange, available at www.sse.com.cn; 'Record of Sanction and Punishment', Shenzhen Stock Exchange, available at www.szse.cn.

94 The Shanghai Stock Exchange only publicly publishes its Notices of Criticism decisions made after 5 September 2013, and Public Criticism decisions made after 11 January 2010. The Shenzhen Stock Exchange publishes all disciplinary action decisions made after 24 February 1998 (including both the Notices of Criticism decisions and the Public Criticism decisions).

95 E.g., Beibuwan Port Company case (China Securities Regulatory Commission Administrative Sanction Decision, [2011] No. 3), ST Danhua Company case (China Securities Regulatory Commission Administrative Sanction Decision, [2010] No. 1), Zhongjie Company case (China Securities Regulatory Commission Administrative Sanction Decision, [2010] No. 31), Sanyou Company case (CSRC Decision, [2011] No. 46).

96 Share Listing Rules of Shanghai Stock Exchange (amended in 2014), Guidelines of the Shenzhen Stock Exchange for the Standardized Operation of Companies Listed on the Main Board (amended in 2015).

of the cases are related to illegal information disclosure, and the major punishments are warnings supplemented by fines.

The CSRC has imposed lighter penalties on independent directors, as compared to the sanctions issued against executive directors and senior officers. From 2004 to 2014, more than half of the independent directors punished were only subject to warnings; amongst all the independent directors subject to fines, more than two-thirds have been fined RMB 30,000 (approximately US $4,500), which is the minimum amount stipulated by law. These penalties are nevertheless substantial, especially considering the CSRC's position that independent directors cannot rely on reports released by professional intermediaries (including audited reports by accountants),[97] the low levels of compensation provided for independent directors[98] and the significant impact of sanctions on independent directors.[99]

China's position on the liability of independent directors is uncommon given that developed markets seldom resort to the imposition of legal liability in their supervision of independent directors. Cases imposing out-of-pocket legal liabilities upon outside directors are rare, as are sanctions by government agencies.[100] The greater the pressure on independent directors, the more likely that other mechanisms will be established in these markets to offset the pressure.[101]

97 Cai, 'The Dilemmas of Independent Directors in China: An Empirical and Comparative Study'.

98 See *infra* V.

99 For example, disciplined independent directors will be subject to public publication of the sanctions, being recorded on a nationally unified Database of Securities and Futures Markets Credibility Archive and the impact of the sanctions extends beyond the stock market, as banks and their regulators may make use of the sanction data for their own purposes. Disciplined independent directors are also required to resign from all the listed companies with which they are serving, they cannot be elected to be an independent director for any other listed companies in the following three years. Thus, the consequences of a public criticism on an individual's reputation can be severe, that is the reason why corporate officers and independent directors frequently attempt to persuade the exchanges to sanction only the company, not them individually. See, B. L. Liebman and C. J. Milhaupt, 'Reputational Sanctions in China's Securities Market', *Columbia Law Review*, 108 (2008), 929, 975.

100 B. S. Black, B. R. Cheffins and M. Klausner, 'Outside Director Liability', *Stanford Law Review*, 58 (2006), 1055, 1138–1141, Cheffins and Black, 'Outside Director Liability', 1475–1477; B. S. Black, B. R. Cheffins and M. Klausner, 'Shareholder Suits and Outside Director Liability: The Case of Korea' in Young-Jae Lim (ed.), *Corporate Governance and the Capital Market in Korea* (Korea Development Institute, 2006).

101 Cheffins and Black, 'Outside Director Liability', 1477.

Developed markets have therefore attempted to encourage independent directors to comply with their duties through alternative mechanisms.[102] Since China's domestic market has begun to scrutinise the reputation of independent directors,[103] regulators may establish reputational incentives to encourage these directors to comply with their duties in the near future. In the context of China's independent director regime, it would be fair to reduce the current legal liability imposed on them. This chapter therefore makes four suggestions for determining the legal liability of independent directors.

First, different standards of diligence and prudence should be adopted based on the specific facts of each case. Independent directors who cause corporate losses by breaching their duty of loyalty, obtaining illegitimate gains from affiliated transactions or intentionally participating in activities which violate laws and regulations should be subject to strict penalties. Independent directors who have allegedly failed to act prudently in reviewing the company's disclosure and other documents containing false or misleading statements should only be subject to administrative liability or disciplinary action pursuant to the normal standard of duty of care (instead of a *de facto* principle of strict liability).

Second, except when independent directors violate their duties intentionally or with gross negligence, the supervisory authorities should assess their liabilities by considering their general work performance. If the independent directors have demonstrated that they generally perform their duties diligently, their liability for failing to prevent the company from disclosing an inaccurate or false financial statement should be reduced or even excused.

Third, stock exchanges should play a major role in the punishment of errant independent directors. The self-disciplinary sanctions issued

[102] B. S. Black, B. R. Cheffins and M. Klausner, 'Outside Director Liability: A Policy Analysis', *Journal of Institutional and Theoretical Economics*, 162 (2006), 5.

[103] There are strict requirements to the qualification of independent directors. Researches show that a vast majority of independent directors are experts, scholars or professionals. Good reputation will provide help in self-recognition, work evaluation and future performance of the independent directors. As indicated by an empirical study on China's public companies, independent directors' career concerns lead them to be more closely aligned with investors than with management because their dissenting behaviour is eventually rewarded in the marketplace in the form of more opportunities for directorships. See W. Jiang, H. Wan and S. Zhao, 'Reputation Concerns of Independent Directors: Evidence from Individual Director Voting' (1 November 2013). (American Finance Association 2014 Philadelphia Meetings Paper), available at http://ssrn.com/abstract=2023146.

by stock exchanges should be lighter than the administrative sanctions issued by the CSRC. In fact, recent studies have found that Public Criticisms issued by the Shanghai and Shenzhen Exchanges have had a significant deterrent effect.[104] The stock exchanges should ensure that the rules governing disciplinary sanctions are concrete, clear, certain and fully disclose the reasons behind their decisions. To date, the stock exchanges have generally not provided detailed explanations for the sanctions they have rendered.

Finally, greater share ownership would encourage independent directors to perform their duties diligently. Since the primary duty of independent directors is to supervise the controlling shareholder, or the *de facto* controller and executive directors, holding non-controlling shares in the company will not undermine their independence – but instead align their interests with the minority shareholders.

V Compensation of Independent Directors

1 Regulatory Foundation

Since China established its independent director regime for listed companies in 2001, the regulations relating to the compensation of independent directors have been extremely basic. The CSRC requires listed companies to:

> Provide appropriate allowances to its independent directors. The preliminary plan for the standards of allowances shall be formulated by the board of directors, deliberated and adopted by the shareholders' general meeting and disclosed in the annual report of the company. Except for the aforesaid allowances, independent directors shall not obtain any extra and undisclosed benefits from the listed company, its principal shareholders, or organisations or individuals that have an interested relationship with the listed company.[105]

This system distinguishes the 'allowance' used as compensation for independent directors from the 'remuneration' applicable to other directors and officers.[106] While corporate and individual performance is a relevant

[104] Liebman and Milhaupt, 'Reputational Sanctions in China's Securities Market', 929.

[105] Article 7(5), CSRC Guiding Opinions.

[106] Unlike executive directors, senior executives, core technicians or business personnel, and other qualified employees, independent directors of a listed company cannot join an 'Equity Compensation Plan' issued by the company and therefore have

consideration for the compensation of executive directors and officers, such considerations do not apply to the compensation of independent directors and statutory supervisors.[107]

2 *Current Practice*

Currently, independent directors in China receive a relatively low allowance, which is only provided in cash.[108] The quantum of allowance is usually determined when independent directors are voted onto the board, and adjustments are rarely made following their appointments. While a few independent directors working with major financial institutions have enjoyed generous compensation, more than half of all independent directors had an annual allowance of below RMB 61,000 (about US $8,500) in 2013.[109] The average annual allowance for independent directors of companies listed on the Shanghai Stock Exchange and Shenzhen Stock Exchange was generally limited and only grew slowly from 2005 to 2013. In that same period, the average remuneration for non-independent directors was much higher, as shown in Figure 6.1.

It is worth noting that only 0.71 per cent of all independent directors in 2013 owned shares of the listed companies in which they were serving. The CSRC's current position is that shareholdings of more than 1 per cent of the outstanding shares will impair the independence of independent directors. This view is questionable. Allowing independent directors to own more shares in the company will align their interests with other shareholders, and encourage independent directors to supervise corporate operations in accordance with shareholders' interests.[110]

no access to the restricted stocks or stock options granted by the companies. See Article 8(1), Circular on Promulgating the Measures for the Administration of Stockholder's Rights Drive of Listed Companies (Trial) (China Securities Regulatory Commission, 2006).

107 Articles 69, 70, 77, 78, Code of Corporate Governance of Listed Companies (China Securities Regulatory Commission and the National Economic and Trade Commission, 2002).

108 According to data from the CSMAR database, in 2013 all listed companies remunerated their independent directors with cash.

109 Data from the CSMAR database.

110 Clarke, 'Three Concepts of the Independent Director', 91.

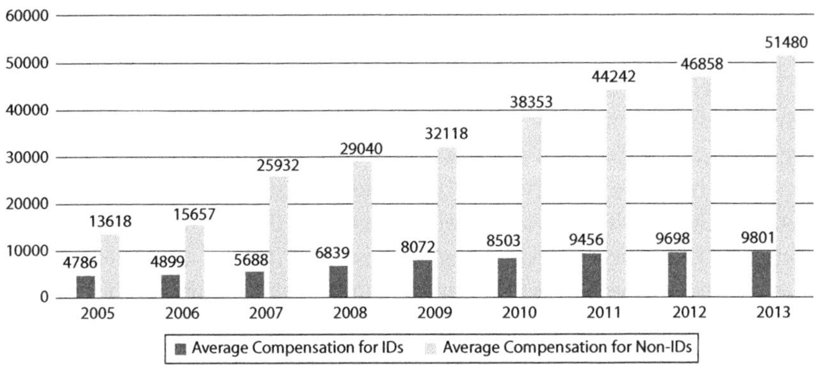

Figure 6.1 Comparison Between the Average Compensation of Independent Directors (IDs) and Non-Independent Directors (Non-IDs) from 2005 to 2013, in US dollars.

Source: Data from the CSMAR database.

3 *Preliminary Analysis*

In general, the low level of compensation for independent directors may lead to the outcome of insufficient incentives to adequately motivate independent directors. Compensation should be competitive so that companies can recruit and retain highly reputable and qualified experts to act as independent directors, and motivate them to improve their job performance.

To achieve this goal, supervisory authorities should encourage companies to pay their independent directors with cash as well as stocks, with the caveat that any stocks issued as compensation to independent directors cannot be sold until a reasonable period (e.g., two years) after the termination of their tenures. Granting compensation in this way is convenient and simple, and has three main advantages: (1) it increases the overall compensation for independent directors; (2) it avoids being overly burdensome for the companies; and (3) it encourages independent directors to focus on long-term stock performance.

On the other hand, it should be noted that since a high percentage of Chinese independent directors are university professors or researchers, they are unlikely to make substantial contributions to corporate management due to time restrictions and lack of business experience. While compensation contingent on corporate performance (e.g., restricted stock or stock options) may be appropriate for entrepreneurial executive directors, such compensation should not be granted to the independent directors.

To determine the amount and form of director compensation, the remuneration committee of a listed company's board of directors must present their proposal to the board. Following the board's approval, the proposal must be approved by the shareholders in the general meeting.[111] Ideally, minority shareholders will be able to monitor director compensation levels by exercising their voting rights at the general meeting. However, given that most listed companies in China have concentrated ownership, it is unclear if minority shareholders, in practice, will be able to successfully monitor or challenge decisions involving director compensation.

Some scholars have recommended an 'indirect' compensation system for independent directors, where a third-party non-profit self-regulatory organisation is responsible for assessing and granting allowances to independent directors.[112] However, it remains to be seen if there is indeed a third-party organisation that has the necessary resources to address the diverse demands of numerous listed companies.[113]

Further, the CSRC requires listed companies to state the total amount of compensation payable to *each* director in their annual reports. This requirement is in addition to the requirement that listed companies must disclose the total amount of remuneration received by *all* the directors and officers.[114] In 2012, the CSRC adopted a stricter requirement for companies listed on the Growth Enterprise Market of the Shenzhen Stock Exchange. According to this stricter requirement, the total pre-tax remunerations (including base salary, bonuses, allowances, subsidies, employee benefits, various insurance premiums, provident funds, annuities and other forms of remuneration) obtained from the company during the reporting period by each incumbent director must be disclosed by the company. The company must also list the names of

[111] Articles 37(1), 99, the Company Law.

[112] J. Guo Jing and N. Wu, '论建立独立董事间接薪酬制度' [On Establishing Rules of Indirect Payment for the Independent Directors], 管理评论 [Management Review], 16(2) (2004), 24–29; Y. Liu, '建立我国独立董事间接薪酬制度的思考' [Deliberation on Establishing Indirect Payment System for Independent Directors in China], 管理科学文摘 [Digest of Management Science], 1 (2005), 46–47.

[113] Q. Li, '对央企控股上市公司实施独立董事间接薪酬制的质疑' [Challenging the Proposed Indirect Payment System for Independent Directors in SASAC Controlled Listed Companies], 经济纵横 [Economic Review], 6 (2011), 110–113.

[114] Article 26, Circular of CSRC on Issuing the Standards for the Contents and Formats of Information Disclosure of Companies Publicly Issuing Securities No. 2 – the Contents

directors and supervisors who do *not* receive remuneration and allowances from the company, and indicate whether they received remuneration and allowances from any entities that are shareholders or other affiliates of the company.[115] Such strict requirements should also apply to all other listed companies.

VI Conclusion

Based on a review of current laws and practices, this chapter proposes reforms to China's 15-year-old independent director regime, which applies to more than 10,000 independent directors in 2,800 listed companies.

Currently, the nomination and election process for independent directors does not appear to safeguard the independence of these directors or to promote good corporate governance. As such, the laws and regulations should be revised so that only the minority shareholders (rather than the controlling shareholder or the board of directors/supervisors under its control) will have the right to nominate the company's initial team of independent directors. A mandatory cumulative voting system to elect directors and a combined model of election of directors and supervisors should also be introduced in listed companies. This new framework would encourage institutional investors to increase their participation in the nomination and voting process. In addition, shareholding limits for independent directors should be eased. Outside statutory supervisors should also be introduced into the board of supervisors to reinforce the role of independent directors as effective monitors of controlling shareholders and executive directors in listed companies.

In terms of public and self-regulatory enforcement, the CSRC's administrative sanctions, and the disciplinary mechanisms used by the two national stock exchanges, pose real difficulties for independent directors

and Formats of Annual Report (China Securities Regulatory Commission, revised in 2005).

115 Article 46(3.2), Rules on the Contents and Formats of Information Disclosure of Companies that Publicly Offer Securities No. 30 – Contents and Formats of Annual Reports of Companies Listed on the Growth Enterprise Market (China Securities Regulatory Commission, revised in 2012); Article 41(3.2), Circular of CSRC on Issuing the Standards for the Contents and Formats of Information Disclosure of Companies Publicly Issuing Securities No. 2 – the Contents and Formats of Annual Report (China Securities Regulatory Commission, revised in 2012).

who have allegedly failed to comply with their duty of supervision. It is suggested that regulators consider the manner in which independent directors have performed their duties, and apply the different standards of diligence and prudence based on the facts of each case when assessing the liability of individual directors. China's stock exchanges should also play a major role in disciplining independent directors who fail to comply with their duties.

Finally, the incentive structure for independent directors in China should be reformed to supplement punitive measures to encourage independent directors to comply with their duties. Currently, independent directors receive a relatively low level of cash compensation, and have been sometimes perceived as cheap decorations, which merely improve the appearance – but not the function – of Chinese corporate governance. As such, listed companies should be encouraged to pay their independent directors with stock in addition to their existing cash compensation. This should be done with a view towards increasing overall compensation levels for independent directors, while avoiding placing too much burden on companies, and encouraging independent directors to focus on the company's long-term stock performance.

7

From Double Board to Unitary Board System

Independent Directors and Corporate Governance Reform in Taiwan

HSIN-TI CHANG, YU-HSIN LIN AND YING-HSIN TSAI

I Introduction

This chapter reviews the regulatory strategies in corporate board reform and analyses the impact of introducing the institution of the independent director into Taiwan's public companies. Taiwan's corporate governance model has been strongly influenced by the German and Japanese models. A primary example of this can be seen in Taiwan's Company Act, which traditionally has followed a double board system: the board of directors constitutes the company decision-making organ, and the statutory supervisor monitors the company. However, in the past decade, Taiwan's corporate governance has also been influenced by the Anglo-American model; consequently, independent directors, along with the unitary board model, have been introduced.

Before February 2013, Taiwan's regulatory authority took a minimalist approach towards the regulation of the internal governance structure of public companies. Generally, Taiwan's public companies could choose to either maintain a double board, switch to a unitary board or adopt a hybrid structure. To enhance board independence, the regulatory philosophy was to mandate the introduction of independent directors in stages, starting with the largest companies. This state of affairs triggered various problems because of the ambiguous distribution of authority between the different corporate organs. On the one hand, the introduction of independent directors was intended to resolve the problem of statutory supervisors' failing to effectively monitor boards of directors. However, on the other hand, independent directors had insufficient incentives to fulfil their duties, and their true independence remains highly questionable without the existence of a corresponding effective system of judicial review.

To further enhance corporate governance and streamline the governance structure of public companies, in December 2013, the Financial Supervisory Commission (FSC) of Taiwan mandated that all public companies with paid-in capital over NTD 2 billion (US $60 million) were to abolish the double board model and switch to the unitary board structure. A decade after the introduction of the institution of independent directors to Taiwan's corporate governance, the government felt that it was necessary to intervene in the internal governance of public companies and took a reformist approach to its corporate board reform. This chapter reviews the reform process since 2002 and critically analyses the challenges of an optional model, along with the legal transplantation process.

Section II introduces the reform of the board structure and presents some statistics regarding the percentage of public companies with independent directors, as well as the occupations of independent directors in Taiwan. In particular, this section analyses the problems with each corporate governance structure, along with the main functions of corporate directors in Taiwan. As of 2014, 66.34 per cent of Taiwan Stock Exchange (TWSE)-listed and Over-The-Counter (OTC)-traded companies have independent directors on their boards. This means that 33.66 per cent of these companies are still resisting this change. According to a new rule promulgated in December 2013, the 33.66 per cent of companies that do not currently have independent directors will be required to introduce at least two independent directors to their respective boards by the end of 2017. The effect of this regulatory policy is yet to be seen. However, it is clear that Taiwan is switching from a double board system to a unitary board system.

Section III builds on this analysis by discussing the incentives that drive independent directors in Taiwan. In particular, it explores the balance that has been struck between the risk of liability and reward of remuneration for the burgeoning class of independent directors in Taiwan. It is noteworthy that Taiwan's Company Act applies the same standard of fiduciary duties to both inside directors and independent directors. However, we have observed that, in some decisions, the court will take into account the position, information, time, knowledge and other factors to reduce or exempt independent directors from liability. Moreover, we observe that to attract highly skilled and qualified people to serve as independent directors, the availability of appropriate Directors and Officers Liability Insurance (D&O insurance) is essential. As of 2014, only 62.51 per cent of TWSE-listed companies provided D&O insurance for their directors. With the introduction of the abovementioned new rule that requires all listed companies to have independent directors by 2017 and the uncertainty of the liability regime, the government should encourage more companies to provide D&O insurance for their directors. With respect to truly independent directors in Taiwan, research studies have shown that substantial social ties exist between controlling shareholders/insiders and independent directors. Absent effective judicial review or an efficient regulatory monitoring mechanism, the impartiality and monitoring function of independent directors will be substantially impaired.

Section IV concludes by asserting that Taiwan has clearly made a formal change in its corporate governance by legislating the adoption of independent directors. It is far less certain, however, whether this formal change has caused a significant shift in how Taiwan's corporate governance actually functions. Ultimately, we suggest that in order for significant functional change to occur, Taiwan must do more than merely ensure that there are independent directors in its boardrooms. Rather, the key to real functional change appears to reside in changing the complimentary institutions that are discussed in this chapter, which are critical in ensuring that independent directors fulfil their intended purpose – but are far too often overlooked.

II Corporate Governance in Taiwan

1 *The Reform of the Board Structure*

The structure of a board is often path dependent in relation to the given country's political and economic conditions. Taiwan's corporate board structure generally follows the Japanese governance structure, which is, in turn, a modified version of the German governance structure.[1] The governance structure in Taiwan and Japan differs from the typical

[1] See Chapter 1 at IV.

German model in that the statutory supervisor position in Japan and Taiwan is weaker than its German counterpart (i.e., the supervisory board). In Germany, the supervisory board has the right to appoint or remove directors; however, in Japan and Taiwan, supervisors are, in principle, nominated by the board and elected by the shareholders. Unlike their German and Japanese counterparts, statutory supervisors in Taiwan do not act collectively as a board; rather, they act individually. To distinguish the Taiwanese model from the German two-tier model, where the supervisory board elects the management board, we use the term 'double board' to describe the board structure in Taiwan throughout this chapter.

Following the enactment of the Sarbanes-Oxley Act of 2002, which relied heavily on independent directors as a means of monitoring US public companies, many Asian countries initiated corporate board reforms to align themselves with the US-style governance structure. Given that there was controversy surrounding the adoption of the US-style unitary board structure among legal scholars in Taiwan, as well as resistance from the business community with regard to increasing board independence, the government authority decided not to invoke drastic reforms of the governance structure, and decided to adopt changes gradually.

The first action was taken by the TWSE in 2002 through the amendment of its listing rules, which required all newly listed companies to have at least two independent directors and one independent statutory supervisor. At that time, the TWSE was still hesitant to apply such requirements to all listed companies, due to the fierce opposition from these companies. The TWSE thus adopted the 'comply or disclose' approach, requiring all listed companies to disclose the TWSE-defined 'independence' of their directors and supervisors. Since then, an increasing number of public companies have voluntarily adopted independent directors and independent supervisors.[2]

The Taiwanese government's proposal for corporate board reform triggered much debate among scholars in Taiwan, the most prominent issue being whether or not Taiwan should introduce independent directors and audit committees and abandon the institution of statutory supervisors. The Taiwanese Congress finally settled the dispute by revising the

[2] Y. H. Lin, *How Public Regulation Changes Corporate Governance Practice: Corporate Board Reform in Taiwan* (Edward Elgar, 2012), 212–213.

Securities and Exchange Act (SEA) in 2006 to give public companies the *option* to have independent directors and the unitary board system.[3]

Paragraph 1 of Article 14-2 of the SEA provides that 'A company that has issued stock in accordance with this Act may appoint independent directors in accordance with its articles of incorporation.' In addition, Paragraph 1 of Article 14-4 of the SEA provides that '[a] company that has issued stock in accordance with this Act shall establish either an audit committee or statutory supervisors'.[4]

Therefore, under existing laws, there are three types of governance structures in Taiwan's public companies: (1) a traditional board, without independent directors, with statutory supervisors (the double board type); (2) a board with independent directors and statutory supervisors (the hybrid type); and (3) a board with independent directors and an audit committee without statutory supervisors (the unitary type).[5] The first two types maintain the double board model, and the last type adopts the unitary model.

In principle, a company can choose from among the three abovementioned types. However, Paragraph 1 of Articles 14-2 and 14-4 of the SEA authorises the competent authority (i.e., the FSC) to, as necessary and in view of the company's scale, shareholder structure, type of operations and other essential factors, require public companies to appoint independent directors of no less than two in number and no less than one-fifth of the total number of directors and to order companies to establish an audit committee in lieu of a supervisor. Based on the belief that independent directors and audit committees are better institutions than statutory supervisors for corporate governance, the FSC is gradually expanding the scope of public companies subject to the compulsory appointment of independent directors and the establishment of audit committees (see Tables 7.1 and 7.2).

Further, to enhance the monitoring of remuneration of directors, statutory supervisors and managerial officers, Taiwan added Article 14-6 of the SEA in November 2010 to compulsorily require all TWSE-listed and OTC-traded companies to establish a remuneration committee to determine salary, stock options and any other substantive incentive

3 *Ibid.*

4 See Regulatory Appendix.

5 Non-public companies in Taiwan may not appoint independent directors and remain a double board structure – that is, a traditional board of directors and a statutory supervisor.

Table 7.1 Public Companies Subject to the Compulsory Appointment of at Least Two Independent Directors in the Board

Date of Promulgation by FSC	Compliance Date	Scope
March 2006[a]	1 January 2007	TWSE-listed and OTC-traded companies with paid-in capital of NTD 50 billion (US $1.6 billion) and public companies in the financial industry
March 2011[b]	22 March 2011 (no later than 31 December 2014)	TWSE-listed and OTC-traded companies with paid-in capital of NTD 10 billion (US $330 million) and public companies in the financial industry
Dec. 2013[c]	31 December 2013 (no later than 31 December 2017)	All TWSE-listed, OTC-traded and public companies in the financial industry

[a] Order No. Financial-Supervisory-Securities-I-0950001615 of the Financial Supervisory Commission, Executive Yuan, 12:60 Executive Yuan Gazette 10601 (28 March 2006).

[b] 19:248 Executive Yuan Gazette 50294.

[c] *Ibid.*

Table 7.2 Public Companies Subject to the Compulsory Establishment of Audit Committees (which shall be composed of the entire number of IDs and shall be no fewer than three in number)

Date of Promulgation by FSC	Compliance Date	Scope
Feb. 2013[a]	20 February 2013	TWSE-listed and OTC-traded companies with paid-in capital of NTD 50 billion (US $1.6 billion) and public companies in the financial industry
Dec. 2013[b]	1 January 2017	1. TWSE-listed and OTC-traded companies with paid-in capital of over NTD 10 billion (US $0.33 billion) and public companies in the financial industry 2. TWSE-listed and OTC-traded companies with paid-in capital of NTD 2 to 10 billion (US $60 to 330 million) should establish an audit committee from 1 January 2017

[a] Order No. Financial-Supervisory-Securities-Corporate-1020004592 of the Financial Supervisory Commission, Executive Yuan, 19:31 Executive Yuan Gazette 6767 (20 February 2013).

[b] 19:248 Executive Yuan Gazette 50294.

measures for directors, supervisors and managerial officers. Members of the remuneration committee have to be either independent directors or non-directors who meet the independence requirements set out in the relevant rules. The committee must have at least three members. Since the old law only requires a minimum of two independent directors on each board, most companies have had to either add additional independent directors to the board, or attempt to retain some independent non-directors to serve on the remuneration committee.

Based on the most recent regulation promulgated by the FSC in December 2013,[6] the boards of all TWSE-listed, OTC-traded companies and public companies in the financial industry (e.g., banks, insurance companies and securities firms), should appoint at least two independent directors. TWSE-listed and OTC-traded companies with paid-in capital of more than NTD 10 billion (US $330 million), as well as public companies in the financial industry, should establish an audit committee. TWSE-listed and OTC-traded companies with paid-in capital of between NTD 2 billion and 10 billion (US $60 to 330 million) should establish an audit committee as of 1 January 2017. In the near future, we can expect that the double board system will be gradually phased out and the unitary board will become the norm in all TWSE-listed and OTC-traded companies.

2 *Empirical Data*

a Public Companies with Independent Directors

In 2005, 612 out of 1,194 (51.26 per cent) TWSE-listed and OTC-traded companies had independent directors on their boards. Around 38.02 per cent of companies had two independent directors, which was in line with Taiwan's regulatory requirements at that time. The percentage of companies that complied with the minimum requirements slowly rose to 41.45 per cent in 2010. In November 2011, the law changed to require at least three independent directors or independent members to be on the remuneration committees for all public companies. As a result, the percentage of companies with two independent directors dropped to 40.09 per cent at the end of 2011, with a corresponding increase in the percentage of companies with three or more independent directors to 18.32 per cent from merely 4.94 per cent in 2005.

[6] Order No. Financial-Supervisory-Securities-Corporate-1020053112 of the Financial Supervisory Commission, Executive Yuan, 19:248 Executive Yuan Gazette 50294 (31 December 2013) [hereinafter '19:248 Executive Yuan Gazette 50294'].

At the end of 2014, the percentage of companies with three or more independent directors rose to 29.43 per cent, with a corresponding decrease in the percentage of companies with only two independent directors to 35.87 per cent. As of 2014, 66.34 per cent of TWSE-listed and OTC-traded companies have independent directors on their boards. The most recent regulation promulgated by the FSC in December 2013 requires all TWSE-listed and OTC-traded companies to appoint independent directors to their boards. As this regulation does not come into effect until the expiration of the three-year term for incumbent directors, we expect the number of independent directors to rise sharply in the next two to three years. Table 7.3 provides the statistics for the number of TWSE-listed and OTC-traded companies that do not have any independent directors, one independent director, two independent directors and three or more independent directors. Table 7.4 provides the percentages for the same.

Figure 7.1 illustrates the trend that more independent directors are being added to the boards of public companies. The total number of companies with independent directors has risen sharply since 2011. The numbers almost doubled in the period from 2005 to 2014. In particular, the number of companies with three or more independent directors has increased sharply, and there has been a decrease in the number of companies that only have one independent director, thereby illustrating a trend towards companies having more independent boards. The curves in Figure 7.1 further demonstrate the power of regulation in shaping the behaviour of firms. For TWSE-listed companies, which are typically large companies, the effect of regulation is even more salient because most reforms were targeted towards larger companies.

Figure 7.2 shows that, in 2013, for the first time the number of TWSE-listed companies that have three or more independent directors exceeded those that have two. This trend has been observed since 2011, and may have arisen due to the new law requiring at least three independent directors or members to be on the remuneration committee, which applies to all public companies. Since the law allows the companies to appoint independent members who are not directors to serve as members of the remuneration committee, as long as the members meet the independence requirement, companies are not required to have three independent directors under the new law. However, we have still seen a surge in the number of companies that have three independent directors since 2011, especially in TWSE-listed companies. This indicates that larger companies are adapting more rapidly than smaller companies in increasing the

Table 7.3 Number of TWSE-Listed and OTC-Traded Companies with Independent Directors

Year	No Independent Directors	One Independent Director	Two Independent Directors	Three or More Independent Directors	Total Number of TWSE and OTC Companies
2005	582	99	454	59	1,194
2006	587	88	476	68	1,219
2007	590	61	512	82	1,245
2008	566	44	529	118	1,257
2009	580	33	531	143	1,287
2010	553	28	548	194	1,322
2011	552	29	560	256	1,397
2012	530	21	562	334	1,447
2013	515	28	557	396	1,496
2014*	518	16	552	453	1,539

Source: Compiled by the authors from the Market Observation Post System of the TWSE.

* The statistics for 2014 are up to October 2014.

Table 7.4 Percentage of TWSE-Listed and OTC-Traded Companies with Independent Directors

	Companies with No Independent Directors	**Companies with One Independent Director**	**Companies with Two Independent Directors**	**Companies with Three or More Independent Directors**
2005	48.74%	8.29%	38.02%	4.94%
2006	48.15%	7.22%	39.05%	5.58%
2007	47.39%	4.90%	41.12%	6.59%
2008	45.03%	3.50%	42.08%	9.39%
2009	45.07%	2.56%	41.26%	11.11%
2010	41.83%	2.12%	41.45%	14.67%
2011	39.51%	2.08%	40.09%	18.32%
2012	36.63%	1.45%	38.84%	23.08%
2013	34.43%	1.87%	37.23%	26.47%
2014*	33.66%	1.04%	35.87%	29.43%

Source: Compiled by the authors from the Market Observation Post System of the TWSE.
* The statistics for 2014 are up to October 2014.

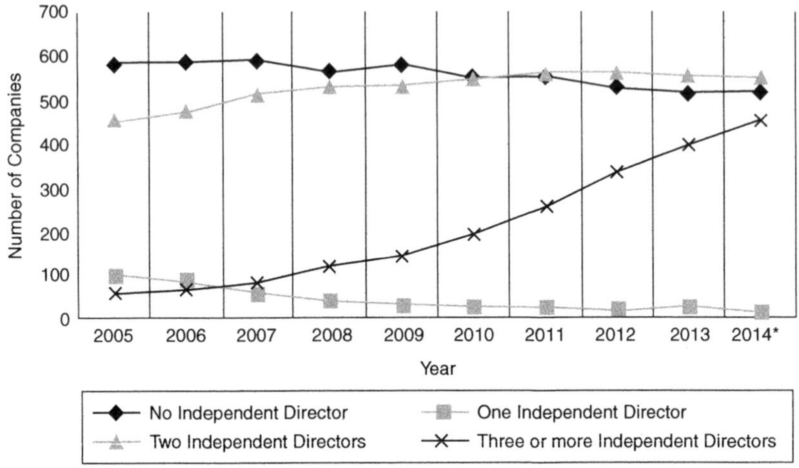

Figure 7.1 Number of TWSE-Listed and OTC-Traded Companies with Independent Directors

Source: Compiled by the authors from the Market Observation Post System of the TWSE.

* The statistics for 2014 are up to October 2014.

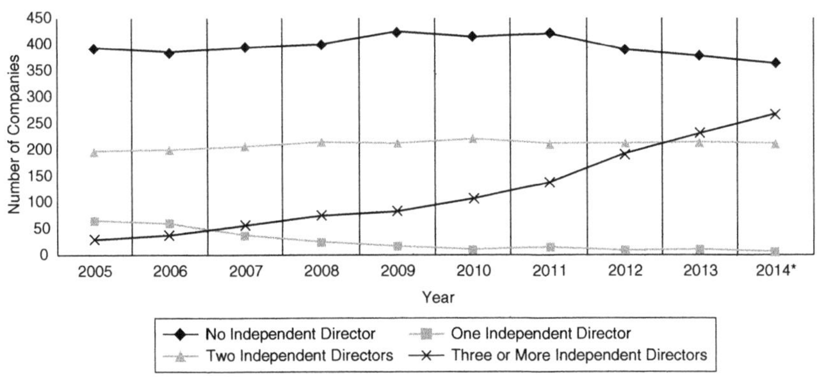

Figure 7.2 Number of TWSE-Listed Companies (Larger Companies) with Independent Directors

Source: Compiled by the authors from the Market Observation Post System of the TWSE.

* The statistics for 2014 are up to October 2014.

number of independent directors and are more willing to enhance the independence of their respective boards.

Another interesting observation is that the number of companies that chose not to have any independent directors in 2005 stayed roughly the same, despite the many reforms in the past decade. Table 7.3 shows that, in 2005, there were 582 companies that had no independent directors. In 2014, the number went down slightly to 518. That means only 10.9 per cent of those companies decided or were forced to introduce independent directors to their boards.

Conversely, for companies that already had one independent director in 2005, 84 per cent of them have since increased their number of independent directors to two or more. There is an apparent resistance from those companies who had no independent directors in 2005 towards the whole concept of having independent directors on the board. The question that arises is: why have companies with no independent directors and companies with one independent director acted differently over the past decade?

From the regulation in March 2011 (see Table 7.1), we can reasonably infer that companies with no independent directors at all are smaller companies with paid-in capital of less than NTD 10 billion (US $330 million) and are not in the financial industry. In addition, these companies are companies who went public before 2002 because all newly-listed companies after 2002 must have at least two independent directors. As such, these companies are smaller companies with a long listing history, and they represent 42.7 per cent of TWSE-listed companies.

The difference between these companies and those with one independent director in 2005 is that these companies resisted the idea of bringing independent directors to the board from the beginning, while those with one independent director embraced the idea of independent directors on a voluntary basis. Those companies resisted having independent directors either because their controlling shareholders did not believe that independent directors would add value to the firm and/or because their controlling shareholders did not want outsiders monitoring them. It would be interesting to see the impact of the December 2013 compulsory requirement to appoint at least two independent directors on these companies, and to test whether these companies are acting rationally in choosing their board structures. While only companies over NTD 2 billion are required to switch to the unitary board model, companies under NTD 2 billion will operate under the hybrid model. The effect of the regulatory choice of the hybrid model over the traditional double board model has yet to be tested.

b The Occupations of Independent Directors

The quality and professional expertise of independent directors are important factors in assessing the effectiveness of this corporate governance mechanism. With the increasing popularity of independent directors, an analysis of their occupations in Taiwan provides a qualitative lens through which policymakers can understand the profiles of these new additions to the board and the functions they might carry out, given their expertise.

In Taiwan, the Market Observation Post System (MOPS) records a description of each independent director's current occupation. Based on this information, the occupation of each independent director can be placed into one of 12 categories The top three occupations of independent directors for both TWSE-listed and OTC-traded companies are the same: (1) corporate directors (31.49 per cent in TWSE-listed and 26.36 per cent in OTC-traded companies); (2) professors (24.69 per cent in TWSE-listed and 22.34 per cent in OTC-traded companies); and (3) managers (7.83 per cent in TWSE-listed and 11.33 per cent in OTC-traded companies) (Table 7.5). When compared to a 2008 study the occupations of independent directors seem to have remained stable for the past six years – in 2008, the top three occupations of independent directors in TWSE-listed companies were the same as in 2014 (i.e., corporate directors (29.03 per cent), professors (24.91 per cent) and managers (12.36 per cent)).[7] In addition, accountants and lawyers consistently have constituted a significant portion of independent directors as they have respectively ranked fourth and fifth in terms of the top occupations of independent directors.

One interesting observation regarding the occupation of independent directors in Taiwan is that professors comprise a significant and important constituency of independent directors – accounting for 24.69 per cent of TWSE-listed companies and 22.34 per cent of OTC-traded companies. This may be because the public image of professors fits well with the concept of 'independence' and professors are generally thought of as experts in their chosen field.[8] However, as professors may not be entirely familiar with the practical aspects of business operations, there is some scepticism about whether they are able to function effectively as independent directors.[9]

[7] Y. H. Lin, 'Overseeing Controlling Shareholders: Do Independent Directors Constrain Tunneling in Taiwan?', *San Diego International Law Journal*, 12 (2011), 363, 398–399.

[8] *Ibid.*, 399.

[9] *Ibid.*, 399–400.

Table 7.5 Occupations of Independent Directors

	TWSE-listed companies		OTC-traded companies	
Occupation	**Number**	**Percentage**	**Number**	**Percentage**
Corporate Director	398	31.49	335	26.36
Professor	312	24.69	284	22.34
Manager	99	7.83	144	11.33
Accountant	93	7.36	119	9.36
Lawyer	72	5.70	68	5.35
Director of NGO	52	4.11	21	1.65
Consultant	40	3.16	27	2.12
CEO, CFO or COO	19	1.51	39	3.07
Physician	7	0.55	4	0.31
Government Official	3	0.24	2	0.16
Politician	2	0.16	3	0.24
Other	167	13.21	225	17.70
Total	1,264	100	1,271	100

Source: Analysed and categorised by the authors based on data from the Market Observation Post System, TWSE (17 December 2014).

3 *Problems with Multiple Corporate Governance Structures in Taiwan*

For double board type companies (i.e., companies which have a traditional board and statutory supervisors) one of the major forces driving the introduction of independent directors and audit committees has been the perceived ineptness of statutory supervisors.[10] Double board type companies continue to face problems increasing the independence and professional competence of their statutory supervisors. The myriad problems and potential reforms to the statutory supervisor system, however, are beyond the scope of this chapter.

For hybrid type companies (i.e., those with both independent directors and statutory supervisors), the roles and functions of independent directors are confusing.

Article 14-3 of the SEA expressly provides that:

> When a company appoints independent directors, the following matters shall be submitted to the board of directors for approval by resolution. Moreover, when an independent director has a dissenting opinion or qualified opinion, it shall be noted in the minutes of the directors meeting for the following matters:
>
> 1. adoption or amendment of an internal control system, pursuant to Article 14-1;
> 2. adoption or amendment, pursuant to Article 36-1, of handling procedures for financial or operational actions of material significance, such as acquisition or disposal of assets, derivatives trading, extension of monetary loans to others, or endorsements or guarantees for others;
> 3. a matter bearing on the personal interest of a director;
> 4. a material asset or derivatives transaction;
> 5. a material monetary loan, endorsement, or provision of guarantee;
> 6. the offering, issuance, or private placement of any equity-type securities;
> 7. the hiring or dismissal of an attesting Certified Public Accountant (CPA), or the compensation given thereto;
> 8. the appointment or discharge of a financial, accounting, or internal auditing officer; and
> 9. any other material matter so required by the Competent Authority.

[10] The ineptness of statutory supervisors has tended to be the result of their lack of independence, lack of professional competence due to family relationships or the manner in which they are elected, the poor performance of their duties as supervisors due to insufficient time and effort and the part-time nature of their position. See Y. Z. Lai, 最新證券交易法解析 [The Newest Analysis of Securities Exchange Act], 2nd edn (2009), 198.

Undoubtedly, the listed items are matters that are relatively material to a company, and the law requires independent directors to have a say in these matters to protect shareholders' interests. However, the listed items are similar to the supervising responsibilities, which were originally performed by statutory supervisors in a double board system. The division of work between independent directors and statutory supervisors is therefore an essential but unsettled issue.

Some scholars have attempted to distinguish between the responsibilities of independent directors and statutory supervisors, viewing them as being distinct in terms of the 'nature' and 'timing' of their supervisory roles. Independent directors are still members of the board of directors and can therefore participate in and vote on business decisions. As such, the nature of their responsibilities is 'internal supervision by participating in board decisions', which constitutes *ex ante* supervision. In contrast, statutory supervisors can attend board meetings and express their opinions, but have no voting rights.[11] As such, their responsibilities consist of 'outside supervision without participating in board decisions', which constitutes *ex post* supervision.[12]

Ideally, this 'dual supervision' by both independent directors and statutory supervisors would have a 'dual effect'. However, it might also have negative effects of redundancy and wasted costs and, more seriously, create incentives for independent directors or statutory supervisors to shirk their responsibilities or to blame each other. Therefore, an unambiguous division of work between independent directors and statutory supervisors is an urgent task for the legislature to resolve.[13]

In the case of companies with unitary boards, at least three problems remain in Taiwan. First, the authority of the audit committee on critical issues is weak as a result of the board's ability in most cases to usurp its authority. Specifically, in most cases, the board can overrule the decision of the audit committee if two-thirds or more of the directors pass a resolution.[14] In cases where the audit committee's decision is essentially disregarded, the only thing it can do is to record the board's reversal

[11] Article 218-2 of the Taiwanese Company Act sets forth that 'Supervisors of a company may attend the meeting of the board of directors to express their opinions.'

[12] L. Y. Liu, '現行上市上櫃公司獨立董事制度之檢討暨改進方案—從實證面觀察' [A Study of the Regime of Independent Directors of Listed Companies in Taiwan. An Empirical Approach], *ChengChi Law Review*, 114 (April 2010), 53, 132.

[13] *Ibid.*, 135. Some scholars suggest the deletion of Article 14-3 from the SEA for type 2 companies so that independent directors are responsible for decision making and execution only and statutory supervisors remain in charge of the supervisory work.

[14] Article 14-5, SEA.

of its decision in the minutes of the directors' meeting and hope that public scrutiny will provide some sanction. This calls into question the effectiveness of the audit committee in companies with unitary boards in Taiwan.

Second, audit committees in Taiwan have a much broader mandate than in other unitary board dominated jurisdictions. This has the potential to interfere in the efficient decision making of companies, because it may allow audit committees to try to interfere with the board's ability to make business decisions. Specifically, Article 14-5 of the SEA provides audit committees with the broad mandate to make decisions on 'all material asset or derivatives transaction', 'all material monetary loans, endorsements, or provision of guarantees' and 'on the offering, issuance or private placement of any equity-type securities'. These types of matters all clearly fall within the scope of business decisions in which the audit committee should not directly be involved.[15] Indeed, the equivalent provisions regulating audit committees of companies listed on the NYSE and LSE do not provide such a broad mandate for audit committees to get involved in business decisions, which should be allocated to the board.

Third, according to Taiwanese law, every independent director on the board automatically becomes a member of the audit committee (i.e., the audit committee is composed of the total number of independent directors on the board).[16] Therefore, the success of the audit committee is highly dependent on who are nominated to be elected as the independent directors. There are two ways to nominate an independent director in Taiwan: (1) nomination by the board of directors; or (2) nomination by minority shareholders who hold 1 per cent or more of the total number of outstanding shares issued by the company.[17] Nevertheless, the relevant laws in Taiwan do not require or even encourage public companies to establish a nomination committee of which all or at least half of

[15] W. R. Tseng, '半套公司治理移植經驗—以審計委員會與特別委員會為例' [An Analysis of Taiwan's Alterations and Misconceptions during Transplantation of Foreign Laws Regarding Corporate Governance: An Exploration of Taiwan's Audit Committee and Special Committee], *Cross-Strait Law Review*, 43 (2014), 33, 36.

[16] Article 14-4, Paragraph 2, SEA.

[17] Article 192-1 of the Taiwanese Company Act provides: 'In case a candidate's nomination system is adopted by a company offering its shares to the public for election of the directors of the company, the adoption of such system shall be expressly stipulated in the Articles of Incorporation of the company; and the shareholders shall elect the directors from among the nominees listed in the roster of director candidates.'

the members are independent directors.[18] As such, the independence and professional competence of both independent directors and audit committees are questionable in Taiwan.[19]

However, Article 198 of Taiwan's Company Act mandates cumulative voting for almost all corporations (except for close corporations at the time of incorporation) to empower minority shareholders in the election of directors.[20] This mechanism might mitigate the concern stemming from the lack of a nomination committee.

4 *The Characteristics of Corporate Ownership in Taiwan*

The corporate ownership of Taiwan's public companies is characterised by its concentrated, family-dominated nature, as well as by the prevalence of business groups. The largest shareholders of non-financial firms in Taiwan control 62.69 per cent of board seats and comprise 49.55 per cent of statutory supervisors. As a result, large shareholders in Taiwan not only own public firms, but also manage and control them.[21] Yeh and Ko found that the average control rights of the largest shareholders in non-financial firms were 29.81 per cent, but the average cash-flow rights were only 22.13 per cent.[22] Before the introduction of independent directors in 2002, many corporate boards in Taiwan conducted 'paper' meetings. Board members were either founding family members or top executives, and family members were usually highly involved in the management of the company.

Another characteristic of Taiwan's corporate ownership structure is the prevalence of business groups. Business groups control most firms in Taiwan and contribute to a large portion of Taiwan's total economic revenue. The top 100 business groups in Taiwan owned more than 7,914 companies in 2013. Among the top ten business groups, eight were in the financial industry.[23] Family businesses continue to dominate Taiwan's economy.[24]

[18] Only two TWSE-listed and OTC-traded companies have voluntarily established a nomination committee. Please see http://mops.twse.com.

[19] Lai, *The Newest Analysis of Securities Exchange Act*, 199.

[20] Article 198 and Article 356-3, Taiwanese Company Act.

[21] Y. H. Yeh, S. L. Tsun and T. Woidtke, 'Family Control and Corporate Governance: Evidence from Taiwan', *International Review of Finance*, 2 (2001), 21.

[22] Y. H. Yeh and C. E. Ko, *The Law and Practice of Independent Directors, Audit Committees and Other Functional Committees in Germany, Japan, the US, and Korea* (Financial Supervisory Commission of Taiwan, 2006), 294–295.

[23] China Credit Information Service Ltd, *Business Groups in Taiwan* (2014).

[24] The major families include: the Tsai family of the Cathay and Fubon groups; the Wu family of the Shin Kong and Tai Shin groups; the Wang family of the Formosa Plastics

With concentrated corporate ownership, the key role of independent directors in Taiwan is to mitigate agency problems that arise between controlling and minority shareholders by monitoring the private benefits of control enjoyed by the controlling shareholders. In the following section, the functions of independent directors in monitoring executive compensation, mergers and acquisitions and self-dealing transactions are explored.

5 *The Role of Independent Directors in Major Board Functions*

The primary role of independent directors in an Anglo-American style unitary board is to mitigate the shareholder-manager agency problem faced by executive directors when performing their monitoring function. Compared to the function of the board of directors in the US, the role of the board of directors in Taiwan is more akin to a management board than a monitoring board. Article 202 of Taiwan's Company Act provides that the 'business operation of a company shall be executed, pursuant to the resolutions to be adopted by the board of directors'.[25] Generally, the board of directors in Taiwan has the power of 'business decision-making'[26] and 'business execution'.[27] Academics have critiqued Article 202 on the basis that it is more suitable for small or medium-sized companies and ignores the needs of large public companies. For small and medium-sized companies, the powers of business decision making and execution are usually linked and are exercised by the board of directors. However, for larger public companies, the board of directors in practice serves more of a monitoring function by establishing functional committees to execute certain decision making and delegating business operations to a chief executive officer or general manager.[28] The introduction

Group; the Gu family of China Trust, Chailease and Taiwan Cement Group; the Kuo family of the Foxconn Group; the Hsu family of the Far Eastern Group; and the Hsu family of the Chi Mei Group. *Ibid.*

25 Article 202 of Taiwan's Company Act states: 'Business operations of a company shall be executed pursuant to the resolutions to be adopted by the board of directors, except for the matters the execution of which shall be effected pursuant the resolutions of the shareholders' meeting as required by this Act or the Articles of Incorporation of the company.'

26 However, allocating the powers of decision making between the meetings of both the board of directors and the shareholders involves the debate between shareholder primacy and director primacy and remains a controversial issue in Taiwan.

27 W. Wang, 公司法論 [Corporate Law], 4th edn (元照 [Yuan Chao], 2008), 539.

28 *Ibid.*

of independent directors to Taiwan's corporate boards has facilitated their transformation from management to monitoring boards. In light of this change, this section reviews how independent directors have been transplanted into Taiwan's corporate governance regime.

The function of the board of directors in Taiwan includes, but is not limited to, the following: appointing and removing top managers (in particular, the CEO); determining the compensation of managers; making decisions concerning corporate strategies; and executing business decisions. In this section, we will address three particular functions and the significant ways in which these functions have evolved over time by emphasising the role that independent directors play in these particular functions.

a Determination of Executive Compensation

For non-public companies, the board of directors has the exclusive authority to determine executive compensation according to Article 29 of Taiwan's Company Act. Since 2010, as previously mentioned, for all TWSE-listed and OTC-traded companies, Article 14-6 of the SEA requires these companies to establish a remuneration committee to determine executive compensation. It is important to note, however, that not all TWSE-listed and OTC-traded companies have independent directors. Therefore, remuneration committees may include independent directors, independent non-directors[29] and corporate insiders.[30]

In addition, as a result of the specific legislation governing remuneration committees,[31] they suffer from the same lack of authority as has been discussed in the case of audit committees. Specifically, the board can overrule the decision of the remuneration committee if two-thirds or more of the directors pass a resolution. In cases where the remuneration committee's decision is essentially disregarded, the board merely needs to specify the circumstances and cause for the difference between

[29] The qualifications and definitions of independent experts are the same as those of independent directors. See Articles 5 and 6, Regulations Governing the Appointment and Exercise of Powers by the Remuneration Committee of a Company Whose Stock Is Listed on the Stock Exchange or Traded Over the Counter.

[30] Such members cannot exceed one-third of the remuneration committee members and may not serve as the convener or as chair of a meeting. See Article 6, Regulations Governing the Appointment and Exercise of Powers by the Remuneration Committee of a Company Whose Stock Is Listed on the Stock Exchange or Traded Over the Counter.

[31] The Regulations Governing the Appointment and Exercise of Powers by the Remuneration Committee of a Company Whose Stock Is Listed on the Stock Exchange or Traded Over the Counter, amended on 27 August 2015.

the remuneration determined by the remuneration committee and its decision. In such a situation, the board's explanation must be publicly announced and reported on a website designated by the regulatory authority.[32] However, the effectiveness of this public shaming tactic is questionable. There is empirical evidence that suggests that the functional effect of the remuneration committee in Taiwan may be weak as a result of its flawed design.[33]

b Control over Mergers and Acquisitions

Taiwan's Business Mergers and Acquisitions Act[34] requires that the board of directors act in the best interest of the company and fulfil its duty of care when conducting a merger or acquisition.[35] Therefore, when making a decision regarding the merger or acquisition of a company, the board of directors has a duty of care to maximise the interests of the company and, in turn, of its shareholders as a whole.

In a recent watershed case, the Chairman of the Yageo Corporation (Yageo) and Kohlberg Kravis Roberts & Co. L.P. launched a management buyout through a tender offer for Yageo and planned to delist it from the TWSE if the tender offer succeeded. Since Yageo was the largest supplier of passive components for electronic products in Taiwan, the government authority raised its concerns about the pricing and fair conduct

[32] Article 7, Regulations Governing the Appointment and Exercise of Powers by the Remuneration Committee of a Company Whose Stock Is Listed on the Stock Exchange or Traded Over the Counter ('Regulation governing remuneration committee') provides that 'If the board of directors will decline to adopt, or will modify, a recommendation of the remuneration committee, it shall require the consent of a majority of the directors in attendance at a meeting attended by two-thirds or more of the entire board, which in its resolution shall give the comprehensive consideration under the preceding paragraph and shall specifically explain whether the remuneration passed by it exceeds in any way the recommendation of the remuneration committee.' Further, '[i]f the remuneration passed by the board of directors exceeds the recommendation of the remuneration committee, the circumstances and cause for the difference shall be specified in the board meeting minutes and shall be publicly announced and reported on the information reporting website designated by the competent authority within two days, counting from the date of passage by the board of directors'.

[33] H. T. Chang, '薪資報酬委員會獨立性與專業性再思考' [Rethinking of the Independence and Expertise Requirements of the Remuneration Committee in Taiwan], *The Taiwan Law Review*, 233 (October 2014), 129–135.

[34] Business Mergers and Acquisitions Act, amended on 8 July 2015.

[35] Article 5 of the Taiwanese Business Mergers and Acquisitions Act provides that '[w]hen a resolution of merger/consolidation or acquisition is passed, the Board of Directors shall, in the course of conducting the merger/consolidation or acquisition, be in the best interest of the company and fulfill its duty of care'.

of the takeover. On 8 April 2011, the Securities and Futures Investors Protection Center (SFIPC)[36] urged Yageo to establish an independent special committee to review the tender offer price and the reasonableness of the takeover plan to protect investors.[37] Yageo then convened a special board meeting and resolved that the tender offer price was within a reasonable range, indicating that the board did not intend to establish a special committee.[38] Although this deal was disallowed due to the lack of approval for the requisite foreign investment by the Investment Committee of the Ministry of Economic Affairs of Taiwan, this case revealed the potential conflict of interest between the board of directors, managers and the shareholders as a whole in the face of a takeover bid.[39]

In July 2012, in response to the above case, Taiwan added Article 14-1 of the Regulations Governing Public Tender Offer for Securities of Public Companies[40] to require the target company to form a review committee to review the fairness and reasonableness of a public tender offer and make recommendations to the target's shareholders, with respect to the present tender offer, when receiving a tender offer from the acquirer.[41] The provision states that the review committee shall have no fewer than three members and shall be composed of independent directors or independent non-directors. All decisions rendered by the review committee require the assent of one-half or more of all the committee members, and the specific assenting or dissenting opinions of the committee members, as well as the reasons for any dissent.

Similarly, the newly amended Article 6 of the Business Mergers and Acquisitions Act requires a public company to establish a special committee before a board resolution regarding a merger or acquisition is

[36] The SFIPC is an organisation that provides consultation on the trading of securities and futures, as regulated by related laws and regulations, the mediation of disputes arising from the trading of securities and futures, and litigation services on behalf of investors. In addition, the Center manages a protection fund to compensate investors if a securities or commodities firm is unable to do so due to financial difficulties. For details, please see www.sfipc.org.tw/english/about/02.asp.

[37] News Release of SFIPC, 8 April 2011, available at www.sfipc.org.tw.

[38] News Release of SFIPC, 14 April 2011, available at www.sfipc.org.tw.

[39] Based on the statistics of the Ministry of Economic Affairs, the numbers of merger and acquisition cases in the past five years in Taiwan are 191 (2011), 186 (2012), 184 (2013), 197 (2014) and 224 (2015), respectively. This shows that the merger and acquisition cases are steadily increasing in recent years. Please see http://gcis.nat.gov.tw/mainNew/subclassNAction.do?method=getFile&pk=126, last visited February 2016.

[40] Regulations Governing Public Tender Offer for Securities of Public Companies, amended on 25 December 2015.

[41] Article 14-1 of the Regulations Governing Public Tender Offer for Securities of Public Companies, which provides that 'After a public company whose securities are being acquired has received the copy of the Public Tender Offer Report Form, the public tender

decided on. The special committee shall review the fairness and reasonableness of a merger or acquisition plan and report the results of the review to the meeting of the board of directors and shareholders.

It is important to note, however, that such a review or special committee in Taiwan does not have the representative authority to negotiate, nor does it have any veto power regarding a takeover bid, merger or acquisition plan. The review or special committee is currently more like an advisor or consultant to the board of directors, and aims to indirectly protect the interests of the minority shareholders. Moreover, the legal consequence of failing to establish a review or special committee has never been clear. The effectiveness of a review or special committee, with respect to substantial controlling conflicts of interest between the board of directors, controlling shareholder and the shareholders, also remains unclear.

c Control over Self-Dealing

The existing literature and history of corporate scandals in Taiwan indicate that wealth tunnelling is a significant threat to Taiwan's corporate governance, and that the major channel for wealth tunnelling is through related party transactions.[42] Taiwan's Company Act essentially allocates to statutory supervisors the power to control self-dealing or tunnelling. Article 223 of Taiwan's Company Act deals with self-dealing by requiring the supervisors to act as the representatives of the company in case of an interested transaction between a director and the company.[43] One of the most controversial issues in such cases is whether statutory supervisors have the authority to determine the terms and conditions of transactions without prior approval from the board of directors, or whether statutory supervisors are merely a rubber stamp representing the company.

The court decisions are split on this issue. Some decisions opine that:

> the legislative purpose of Article 223 of Taiwan's Company Act is to avoid conflicts of interest when a director of a company transacts with the

offer prospectus, and other documents reported and publicly announced by the offer or …, it shall promptly form a review committee, and publicly announce the results of the review within 10 days. The review committee of the preceding paragraph shall review the fairness and reasonableness of the public tender offer conditions and make recommendations to the company shareholders, with respect to the present tender offer.'

42 Lin, 'Overseeing Controlling Shareholders', 383.

43 Article 223 of the Taiwanese Company Act provides that 'In case a director of a company transacts a sale with or borrows money from or conducts any legal act with the company on his own account or for any other person, the supervisor shall act as the representative of the company.'

> company. Considering the friendly relationships among directors and the protection of corporate interests, statutory supervisors can represent the company to transact with a director without the prior approval of the board of directors.[44]

Conversely, other decisions have held that:

> the design of Article 223 is not to empower statutory supervisors to determine the terms and conditions of a transaction between a director and the company ... [and that] ... the business decision-making function of the board of directors cannot be replaced by statutory supervisors. Therefore, before representing a company, statutory supervisors shall obtain the approval of the board of directors regarding such a transaction.[45]

In addition, for public companies, the aforementioned Article 14-5 of the SEA shall apply and thereby make the audit committee responsible for policing self-dealing or wealth tunnelling. Specifically, all related party transactions will be subject to the consent of one-half or more of the audit committee and must then be submitted to the board of directors for a resolution.[46] Despite this system, there is empirical evidence indicating that related party transactions in Taiwan's public companies are common, but are rarely prevented by the audit committee or board. In this sense, it appears that the oversight of independent directors has generally performed ineffectively as a mechanism for preventing deleterious related party transactions in Taiwan's public companies.[47]

III The Incentives and Independence of Independent Directors

1 *Potential of Liability for Independent Directors*

a The Courts' Role in Reducing Liability for Independent Directors for Breaches of Fiduciary Duties

Article 23 of Taiwan's Company Act provides that directors owe their corporations fiduciary duties, including the duties of care and loyalty. In

[44] See, for example, ZuigaoFayuan [Sup. Ct.], Civil Division, 100 Tai-Shang No. 964(21 June 2011) (Taiwan); Taiwan GaodengFayuan [Taiwan High Ct.], Civil Division, 101 Zhong Shang No. 273 (24 September 2013) (Taiwan).

[45] See, for example, Taiwan GaodengFayuan [Taiwan High Ct.], Civil Division, 98 Zhong Su-Geng-Yi No. 121(21 May 2014) (Taiwan); Taiwan GaodengFayuan [Taiwan High Ct.], Civil Division, 97 Zhong-Shang No. 337 (8 October 2008) (Taiwan).

[46] Item (4) of the Article 14-5 of the SEA.

[47] Lin, 'Overseeing Controlling Shareholders', 415.

principle, this provision requires the same standard of conduct for inside directors and independent directors to perform their fiduciary duties. However, we have observed that, in some court decisions, the judge will take into account the position, information, time and knowledge, along with other factors of independent or non-executive directors, to reduce their liability or even exempt them from liability.

This can been seen in the Procomp Informatics case.[48] In this case, the court was of the opinion that the defendant, who was a non-executive director, was not a member of management and had limited information regarding the actual operation, as well as the financial and accounting matters, of the company. Moreover, the court found that the financial statements audited by a CPA were categorised as an 'unqualified opinion' and showed no abnormalities. In turn, the court decided that the defendant non-executive director was not responsible for the false financial statement of Procomp. We suggest that, based on the court's reasoning, it is likely that the defendant would have been found to have breached his fiduciary duties if he was an executive director.

In a similar vein, the court in the Gold Rain Enterprises Corp. case, appears to have lowered the bar for a director to fulfil his fiduciary duties based on factors related to being an independent director.[49] In this case, the court exempted the defendant independent director from liability for making a false financial statement. In arriving at this decision, the court found that the defendant's expertise was in freezing technology and not finance or accounting. Moreover, the court held that the defendant was not a core member of the company and did not actually participate in the decision-making process of the company due to a health condition. Finally, the court reasoned that a CPA audited the financial statements. It appears that the court set a lower standard in this case, which allowed the independent director to effectively discharge his fiduciary duties by simply relying on audited financial statements as he lacked the means of an insider to effectively take any other action.

Nevertheless, it is important to note that the courts have differing opinions on whether defendant directors – regardless of whether they are independent directors – can be exempted from liability by relying on financial statements audited by a CPA in cases involving

[48] Taiwan ShilinDifangFayuan [Shilin Dist. Ct.], Civil Division, 93 Jin No. 3 (11 March 2004) (Taiwan).

[49] Taiwan GaodengFayuan TaichunFenyuan [Taiwan High Ct. Taichung Branch Ct.], Civil Division, 100 Jin-Shang No. 2 (26 February 2013) (Taiwan).

fraudulent financial statements. A vivid example is the case of King's International Multimedia Co.[50] In this case, the court held that a financial statement audited by a CPA was an external supervisory mechanism. In contrast, the court found that the board of directors is in charge of operating the business of the company and making financial statements. In turn, the board of directors has broader powers than merely retaining a CPA to handle financial statements. As such, the court held that the defendant directors (none of whom were non-executive or independent directors) failed to prove that they fulfilled their fiduciary duties.

Based on this limited sampling of court decisions, we cannot definitively conclude that Taiwan's courts have generally or systematically lowered the bar for independent or non-executive directors to satisfy their fiduciary duties. However, it does appear that at least in some cases the courts apply a more lenient standard to independent or non-executive directors than to executive directors in cases involving alleged breaches of fiduciary duties.[51]

b Lower Proportional Liability in Cases of False Financial Statements by the SFIPC

In Taiwan, the Securities Investors and Futures Traders Protection Act (Protection Act),[52] which went into effect on 1 January 2003, authorised the establishment of an institution for the purpose of investor protection.[53] In accordance with the Protection Act, the SFIPC was established in 2003. In addition to consultations and mediations, the SFIPC handles investor complaints, files class-action lawsuits on behalf of investors and manages an investor compensation fund.

One of the main functions of the SFIPC is to file class-action suits for securities fraud cases with 20 or more victims, and it functions as an authorised representative of the victims. Based on the internal

[50] Taiwan Shilin DifangFayuan [Shilin Dist. Ct.], Civil Division, 95 Jin No. 19 (17 December 2013) (Taiwan).

[51] Another possible way to limit the liability of independent directors is to modify the articles of incorporation with a resolution adopted at a meeting of shareholders in advance. This should only be used in the case of slight negligence on the part of the independent director. However, if Article 23 of the Taiwanese Company Act, which provides that directors owe their corporations a fiduciary duty, is recognised as a mandatory rule, a provision of the articles of incorporation that limits the liability of independent directors might conflict with Article 23 and thus be invalid.

[52] Securities Investors and Futures Traders Protection Act, amended on 4 February 2015.

[53] Details regarding the SFIPC are available at www.sfipc.org.tw.

calculation model of the SFIPC, when it refers to the settlement of securities fraud cases with the defendants, including the issuer, and the directors, supervisors, accountants and officers of the issuer, the proportion of liability claimed against the inside directors is higher than the proportion against independent or non-executive directors. In other words, the SFIPC recognises that it should treat inside directors and independent or non-executive directors differently in terms of securities fraud liability to mitigate the responsibility of the latter.

c Directors and Officers Liability Insurance

D&O insurance is an *ex ante* mechanism for directors to insulate themselves against personal liability for breaching their fiduciary duties. As explained above, Taiwan's Company Act formally requires the same standard of conduct for both inside directors and independent directors to perform their fiduciary duties. Therefore, technically, the Act places a heavy burden on independent directors. Even though, as explained above, Taiwan's courts appear to sometimes apply a lower standard of fiduciary duties to independent directors, the uncertainty of this approach makes D&O insurance particularly important for independent directors in Taiwan.

Neither Taiwan's Company Act nor the SEA provide that a company can purchase D&O insurance for its directors. However, Article 39 of the Corporate Governance Best-Practice Principles for TWSE-Listed and OTC-Traded Companies[54] provides that a TWSE/OTC-Listed company may take out D&O insurance for its directors. To do this, Article 39 suggests that a company should either include a provision relating to D&O insurance in its articles of incorporation or pass a resolution at a shareholders' meeting. Although the Corporate Governance Best-Practice Principles are soft law (i.e., not a mandatory rule), they appear to have had a significant impact on the practice of companies as both the number of listed companies providing D&O insurance and the liability limits on D&O coverage provided by insurance policies have increased significantly (see Table 7.6). As such, it is increasingly common for independent directors in Taiwan to have D&O insurance coverage with increasingly higher levels of coverage.

[54] 'Corporate Governance Best-Practice Principles for TWSE-Listed and OTC-Traded Companies', TWSE, available at http://eng.selaw.com.tw.

Table 7.6 D&O Statistics in TWSE-listed and OTC-Traded Companies

	2008	2009	2010	2011	2012	2013	2014
Percentage of TWSE-Listed Companies that Carried D&O[a]	49.2%	52.2%	53.7%	54.9%	57.6%	54.3%	62.51%
Percentage of TWSE-Listed Companies with Independent Director(s)[b]	55.2%	53.7%	57.0%	62.4%	65.0%	69.7%	72.74%
Percentage of OTC-Traded Companies that Carried D&O[c]	45.8%	51.1%	55.5%	56.2%	61.3%	63.7%	64.45%
Percentage of OTC-Traded Companies with Independent Director(s)[d]	79.4%	80.3%	81.8%	81.8%	84.4%	84.5%	87.0%

[a] Market Observation Post System, available at http://mops.twse.com.

[b] *Ibid.*

[c] Market Observation Post System, available at http://mops.twse.com.

[d] *Ibid.*

2 Remuneration of Independent Directors

In Taiwan, the law does not require public companies to disclose each director's individual remuneration. Instead, public companies only have to disclose the range of each director's remuneration and the total amount of all directors' remuneration.[55] According to an academic study, the average annual remuneration of independent directors of TWSE-listed companies was NTD 1 million (approximately US $33,333) in 2007.[56] For companies that have established an audit committee, the average annual remuneration was NTD 4 million (approximately US $133,333), which is markedly different from those that follow the traditional board model. This discrepancy may be due to the fact that in companies with audit committees the company law essentially allocates all of the work that would have been handled by the statutory auditors to the audit committee. As such, the workload of a member of an audit committee is much heavier than that of an independent director of a company that has a statutory auditor. Another reason may be that, in 2007, when the reform just started, most companies that voluntarily opted for the unitary board model were large companies which could afford higher remuneration.

In contrast, the average remuneration of independent directors of OTC-traded companies is far lower than that of those in listed companies (see Table 7.7 and Table 7.8). The average annual remuneration is only NTD 300,000 (approximately US $10,000).[57] Interestingly, this level of

Table 7.7 Average Annual Remuneration of Independent Directors of TWSE-Listed Companies (Thousand NTD)

	2004	2005	2006	2007
Independent Directors	612	801	923	1,173
Non-Independent Directors	–	1,828	1,941	2,146
Audit Committee Members	2,656	3,364	4,440	4,199

55 Art. 10, section 2.C.a., Regulations Governing Information to Be Published in Annual Reports of Public Companies ('The company may opt either to disclose aggregate remuneration information, with the name(s) indicated for each remuneration range, or to disclose the name of each individual and the corresponding remuneration amount').

56 Liu, 'The Regime of Independent Directors', 117.

57 *Ibid.*, 118.

Table 7.8 Average Annual Remuneration of Independent Directors of OTC-Traded Companies (Thousand NTD)

	2004	2005	2006	2007
Independent Directors	223	309	343	353
Non-Independent Directors	595	639	773	745
Audit Committee Members	208	1,734	1,641	344

remuneration also applies to OTC-traded companies that have switched to the unitary board model. One reason for this might be that the average market capitalisation of OTC-traded companies is much smaller than that of TWSE-listed companies. On the one hand, the workload may be less or perhaps such companies may be unable to afford higher remuneration.

3 *The True Independence of Independent Directors*

a The Definition of Independence

In March 2006, the FSC of Taiwan issued regulations governing the appointment of independent directors ('Independent Directors Appointment Rule').[58] The regulations require an independence test, professional qualifications and elections for independent directors. In general, an independent director should have at least five years of work experience in business, law, finance, accounting or another relevant field. In the prior two years and during their tenure, the directors and their immediate family members should not hold substantial shares of the company or maintain employment relationships with the firm, affiliated firms, major shareholders, firms that have substantial business or financial relationships with the firm or firms that provide business, legal, financial, accounting or consultation services to the firm. To ensure adequate participation, an independent director can serve on no more

[58] 'Regulations Governing Appointment of Independent Directors and Compliance Matters for Public Companies', Financial Supervisory Commission, available at http://law.fsc.gov.tw.

than three corporate boards. In response to the criticism regarding the nomination process, and to promote shareholder participation, the rule further provides that any shareholder who holds more than 1 per cent of the shares can submit a nomination list of independent directors to the board.

In an economy where corporate ownership is mostly concentrated, such as Taiwan, the definition of independence should emphasise independence from the controlling shareholders. Hence, the independence test in Taiwan emphasises the relationship between independent directors and the firm's major shareholders. Moreover, the Independent Directors Appointment Rule stipulates that a director shall not qualify as 'independent' if, in the past two years before appointment or during the term of office, he or she was or is:

1. an employee of the company or any of its affiliates;
2. a director or statutory supervisor of the company or any of its affiliates (the same does not apply, however, in cases in which the person is an independent director of the company, its parent company, or any subsidiary in which the company holds directly or indirectly more than 50 per cent of the voting shares);
3. a natural-person shareholder who holds shares, together with those held by the person's spouse or minor children or which are held by the person under others' names, in an aggregate amount of 1 per cent or more of the total number of issued shares of the company or ranking in the top ten in holdings;
4. a spouse, relative within the second degree of kinship, or lineal relative within the fifth degree of kinship of any of the persons in the preceding three subparagraphs;
5. a director, statutory supervisor or employee of a corporate shareholder who directly holds 5 per cent or more of the total number of shares issued by the company or that holds shares ranking in the top five in holdings;
6. a director, statutory supervisor, officer or shareholder holding 5 per cent or more of the shares of a specified company or institution that has a financial or business relationship with the company; or
7. a professional individual who is an owner, partner, director, statutory supervisor or officer of a sole proprietorship, partnership, company or institution that provides commercial, legal, financial, accounting or consultation services to the company or to any affiliate of the company, or a spouse thereof.

Independent directors in Taiwan are only subject to cursory checks. The law defines independence from employment, financial, familial, shareholding and business relationships, but not social and personal relationships. It is inherently difficult to define and exclude social and personal relationships through *ex ante* regulation. *Ex post* judicial review on the true independence of directors in specific transactions should be a better way to address this issue. Absent substantive judicial review of director independence, independent directors could be a tool used by controlling shareholders to eliminate investors' concerns over the potential extraction of private benefits. By introducing independent directors to the board, controlling shareholders can not only improve their company's corporate governance ranking, but also enhance investor confidence.

b Social Ties with Controllers

Lin (2013) surveyed 40 independent directors of Taiwan's public companies to identify and characterise the kinds of personal relationships existing between independent directors and controlling shareholders and to determine whether social ties serve as a useful source of information exchange.[59] Of the 40 independent directors interviewed, 19 used the term 'very close friend' to describe their relationship with controlling shareholders, other directors or CEOs within a given firm, and 14 other independent directors stated that they were personally acquainted with controlling shareholders, other directors or CEOs within a given firm but were not 'very close friends' with these individuals. Only seven of the interviewees had not known the controlling shareholders, other directors or CEOs before being invited to join the board.

The interview results are stunning because almost half of the independent directors described the controlling shareholders, other directors or CEOs of the firms as 'very close friends'. While public companies are required to disclose the financial, familial and business relations among the independent directors, companies and corporate insiders, almost no formal sources of information identify their close personal relationships, even though social ties might hinder the monitoring ability of independent directors. Although it is difficult to generalise from the interview results because of the limited sample,

[59] Y. H. Lin, 'Do Social Ties Matter in Corporate Governance? The Missing Factor in Chinese Corporate Governance Reform', *George Mason Journal of International Commercial Law*, 5 (2013), 39, 60–63.

most interviewees agreed that the majority of independent directors in Taiwan had some degree of social ties with their controlling shareholders or other corporate insiders.

Lin conducted an empirical investigation of the social ties between 505 remuneration committee members (168 independent directors and 337 independent members) and corporate insiders. The findings indicated that around one-third of the members have social ties with insiders.[60] This study further classified social ties into six categories: former insiders; professional consultants; friends; business relationships; academic or social group relationships; and interlocking directors. Of the independent remuneration committee members in Taiwan, 10 per cent are previous employees or managers of the firm and are categorised as prior insiders. Since prior employees were under the supervision of directors, this previous supervisory relationship could impair the independence of 'former insider' independent directors.

The study also casts doubt on the independence of directors who served as professional consultants of the firm. The law only restricts those who served as consultants in the previous two years and contracted with the firm only. This law is, therefore, not applicable to those who served as lawyers or accountants for the chairperson or other directors personally. Finally, the study calls for bans on interlocking directors.[61]

Close relationships between independent directors and controlling shareholders is not a phenomenon unique to Taiwan; rather, it is a common issue that most Asian countries face. In Taiwan, as in many other Asian countries (e.g., China, India, Japan and South Korea), a sophisticated system of commercial courts and a complementary legal system do not exist to provide the kind of *ex post* judicial review that is found in the US.[62] For example, shareholder derivative suits are almost unheard of in Taiwan, due to the various procedural hurdles that exist in the country's

60 Y. H. Lin, '公開發行公司經營者薪酬決定機制之實證分析—兼論薪資報酬委員會新制' [Shareholder Primacy or Director Primacy? Who Decides Director and Executive Compensation in Taiwanese Public Companies?], *Academia Sinica Law Journal*, 14 (2014), 245, 284.

61 *Ibid.*, 294–295.

62 R. J. Gilson and C. J. Milhaupt, 'Choice as Regulatory Reform: The Case of Japanese Corporate Governance', *American Journal of Comparative Law*, 53 (2005), 343, 369–372; U. Varottil, 'Evolution and Effectiveness of Independent Directors in Indian Corporate Governance', *Hastings Business Law Journal*, 6 (2010), 281. (presenting survey and interview data revealing that the general practice of nominating independent directors in Indian listed companies has been for the promoters to identify people known to them or with whom they have significant comfort levels).

corporation law.[63] As a result of these local conditions, *ex post* judicial review of director independence does not exist in Taiwan's current legal system and is unlikely to become a reality in the near future.

In addition, Taiwan's legal system has yet to recognise the role of independent committees in resolving conflicts of interest, and this, in turn, limits the function of independent directors and the value that they can create. Therefore, corporate insiders generally lack incentives to hire truly independent directors not only because no one would review the substantive independence of these directors, but also because corporations would not benefit from having truly independent directors.[64] This is the problem that arises when attempting to transplant an isolated legal mechanism into a different legal system that lacks complementary institutions.

IV Conclusion

The issue of whether Taiwan should abandon the institution of the statutory supervisor and consequently deprive corporations of their autonomy to choose a different corporate governance structure is highly controversial. Nevertheless, the transition from the double board to the unitary board structure has been an established direction in Taiwan, given the competent authority's ruling at the end of 2013.

However, challenges remain regarding the adoption of the independent director mechanism in Taiwan. For example, given the concentrated ownership structure, most independent directors are nominated by controlling shareholders or top executives. Therefore, the establishment of a nomination committee is crucial to ensure the independence of directors. In addition, the overlapping functions of statutory supervisors and independent directors require further clarification, and complementary institutions (e.g., the courts or stock exchanges) need to monitor the true independence of directors.

[63] Y. H. Lin, 'Modeling Securities Class Action Outside the United States: The Role of Nonprofits in the Case of Taiwan', *New York University Journal of Law and Business*, 4 (2007), 143, 164–165; W. R. Tseng and W. Wen, 'Derivative Actions in Taiwan: Legal and Cultural Hurdles with a Glimmer of Hope for the Future' in D. W. Puchniak et al. (eds.), *The Derivative Action in Asia: A Comparative and Functional Approach* (Cambridge University Press, 2012), 215–242. However, in Japan and Korea, a considerable number of shareholder derivative suits are brought. See D. W. Puchniak, 'The Derivative Action in Asia: A Complex Reality', *Berkeley Business Law Journal*, 9 (2013), 1, 4.

[64] D. C. Clarke, 'The Independent Director in Chinese Corporate Governance', *Delaware Journal of Corporate Law*, 31 (2006), 125, 209–210.

The empirical studies discussed in this chapter demonstrate the power of regulation in shaping the 'form' of corporate governance in Taiwan. However, how each corporate governance provision 'functions' still depends on the local conditions. Absent complementary institutions that help each provision fulfil its intended function, regulatory changes over the form of governance measures would not help much. In the past decade, the FSC in Taiwan gradually introduced independent directors and audit committees to Taiwan's public companies, forcing them to transit from a double board to unitary board system. We believe that the regulatory mandate will continue to play an important role in the development of independent directors in the near future. However, more attention should be paid to the true independence and substantive monitoring effect of independent directors in order for them to thrive and function effectively in Taiwan.

8

Independent Directors in Hong Kong

VIVIENNE BATH*

In December 2014, the Hong Kong Stock Exchange (the 'Exchange') was the sixth largest exchange in the world by market capitalisation (with 1752 companies listed on its two boards – the Main Board and the Growth Enterprise Market ('GEM')) and the third largest exchange in Asia behind the Japan Exchange Group – Tokyo and the Shanghai Stock Exchange.[1] The Exchange is a very significant international market, and, in particular, has become a major market for Chinese[2] and China-themed stocks. The Exchange and the Hong Kong Securities and Futures Commission ('SFC') are primarily responsible for securities regulation, although Hong Kong common law and statutory provisions are relevant in a number of areas, particularly in relation to the duties of directors. Companies seeking to list in Hong Kong must show that they satisfy Hong Kong's standards relating to shareholder protection, and must also agree to comply with the Listing Rules of the Exchange, which contain a number of important provisions governing the corporate governance of listed companies.[3]

The initial requirement that a listed company have at least two independent non-executive directors (generally referred to in Hong Kong as

* This chapter was substantially completed in mid 2015.

1 Figures drawn from World Federation of Exchanges, 'Monthly Reports' (last updated December 2014), available at www.world-exchanges.org/statistics/monthly-reports.

2 That is, securities of companies incorporated in the People's Republic of China, not including the Special Administrative Regions of Hong Kong or Macao, or Taiwan.

3 Hong Kong Stock Exchange, 'Rules Governing the Listing of Securities on the Growth Enterprise Market of The Stock Exchange of Hong Kong Limited' (GEM Listing Rules), available at www.hkex.com.hk; Hong Kong Stock Exchange, 'Rules Governing the Listing of Securities on the Stock Exchange of Hong Kong Limited' (Main Board Listing Rules), available at www.hkex.com.hk. Where not otherwise indicated, references to particular rules refer to the Main Board Listing Rules.

'INEDs', but referred to in this chapter as 'independent directors') was introduced into the Listing Rules in 1993. At least one-third of the board of directors must now be independent directors. The scope and significance of the role played by independent directors in Hong Kong listed companies has greatly expanded over time.

This chapter will look at the background to regulation of listed companies in Hong Kong, the content of the independent director requirements in Hong Kong, the history and reasons behind their introduction and development, the debate in Hong Kong surrounding independent directors, the functional alternatives available in terms of corporate regulation and the practical issues that have arisen in relation to the implementation and the operation of the independent director system in Hong Kong.

I Background to Corporate Regulation in Hong Kong

The primary legislative provision in Hong Kong relating to corporate law is the Companies Ordinance,[4] which was originally based on legislation in the United Kingdom, but has been reviewed and significantly modified from time to time in order to deal with Hong Kong circumstances.[5] The Companies Ordinance and its related legislation are administered by the Companies Registry.[6] The most recent changes include clarifications of the scope of directors' duties, conflicts of interest and insider trading.[7]

As noted above, a large number of companies listed on an exchange in Hong Kong are not incorporated in Hong Kong. Nonetheless, the Hong Kong corporate law regime is relevant to their operations in a number of ways, particularly in relation to the filing of information relating to constituent documents, directors and officers, charges and debentures, and, in the case of listed companies, a copy of annual accounts.[8] A non-Hong Kong company is also subject to Part 14 of the Ordinance, which provides for remedies for protection of companies' or members' interests.[9] Registered non-Hong Kong companies are also subject to other aspects of the Hong Kong corporate law regime,

[4] Companies Ordinance, c. 622 (Hong Kong).

[5] For a detailed history, see S. H. Goo, 'Study Report on History of Company Incorporation in Hong Kong' (July 2013), available at www.cr.gov.hk.

[6] *Ibid.*

[7] *Ibid.*, Annex II.

[8] Sections 777 *et seq*, Companies Ordinance c. 622 (Hong Kong).

[9] Section 722(1), Companies Ordinance c. 622 (Hong Kong).

including disqualification of directors, winding-up and orders to cease to carry on business in Hong Kong.[10] Hong Kong company law is also applicable in relation to corporate governance of listed companies, as Hong Kong law, both common law and legislation, is the basis for the standard of corporate regulation and compliance particularly in relation to shareholder protection which is required by the Exchange of a company seeking a listing in Hong Kong.

The primary legislation relating to regulation of securities markets is the Securities and Futures Ordinance (the 'SFO')[11] and its related regulations, which create and regulate the SFC and regulate exchange companies (including both Hong Kong Exchanges and Clearing Limited, the parent company of the Exchange, and the Exchange)[12] and clearing houses, as well as securities intermediaries. The SFO also creates and regulates the Market Misconduct Tribunal, an independent body which is responsible for civil proceedings relating to insider trading, price rigging and other forms of market misconduct,[13] and the Securities and Futures Appeals Tribunal,[14] which deals with regulatory appeals from the SFC and the Hong Kong Monetary Authority. The SFO also gives the SFC power to initiate actions and take steps in relation to investor remedies and compensation.

Control over companies listed on the main board of the Exchange and the GEM is exercised by the Exchange predominantly through the relevant listing rules and their related rules and guidelines, and undertakings to comply with the rules given by the issuer, directors and others prior to listing.

The Companies Registry of Hong Kong[15] acts as the company registrar for Hong Kong companies, registers non-Hong Kong companies in Hong Kong, holds available information held on statutory registers, makes available information and data relating to the above and, in relation to Hong Kong companies, deals with incorporation and deregistration of companies.

[10] Companies (Winding up and Miscellaneous Provisions) Ordinance, c. 32 (Hong Kong).

[11] Securities and Futures Ordinance, c. 571 (Hong Kong).

[12] Hong Kong Exchanges and Clearing Limited, 'About HKEx', available at www.hkex.com.hk.

[13] Market Misconduct Tribunal, 'Home', available at www.mmt.gov.hk.

[14] The Securities and Futures Appeals Tribunal, Financial Services and the Treasury Bureau, 'About Us', available at www.sfat.gov.hk.

[15] Companies Registry, The Government of the Hong Kong Special Administrative Region, 'CR – About Us', available at www.cr.gov.hk.

The SFC was established pursuant to the SFO in 1989. It is an independent statutory body which is responsible for the regulation of securities and futures markets in Hong Kong. The SFC is funded by levies on transactions on the Stock Exchange of Hong Kong and the Hong Kong Futures Exchange as well as fees levied on licence holders.[16] The SFC licenses securities intermediaries, authorises investment products and supervises market operators. It also oversees regulation of takeovers and mergers and stock exchange regulation of listing matters. In conjunction with this, it has the power to set market regulations and to enforce them through investigation of breaches followed by enforcement action. The SFC has a number of memoranda of understanding with other regulatory bodies in Hong Kong in relation to its regulatory functions, as well as a Memorandum of Understanding with the Exchange relating to the coordination of policy and enforcement, which provides the basis for the dual system of enforcement between the Exchange and the SFC.[17]

Hong Kong Exchanges and Clearing Limited ('HKEx')[18] is the holding company for The Stock Exchange of Hong Kong Ltd (the 'Exchange')[19] and the Hong Kong Futures Exchange. The Exchange, largely through the Listing Committee and the GEM Listing Committee, regulates listing and is responsible for the drafting and administration of rules relating to listing and trading, and enforces its rules relating to listing and trading. The listing rules – backed up by signed undertakings – for the main board and GEM (collectively, the 'Listing Rules')[20] are the primary method by which the Exchange regulates the general standard of corporate governance of companies listed in Hong Kong. Corporate standards under the Companies Ordinance are imposed on non-Hong Kong-registered companies both through incorporation by reference in their constituent documents and by the inclusion of specific requirements relating to the

[16] Securities and Futures Commission, 'Our Role | Securities and Futures Commission of Hong Kong', available at www.sfc.hk.

[17] Securities and Futures Commission and The Stock Exchange of Hong Kong Limited, 'Memorandum of Understanding Governing Listing Matters' (January 2003), available at www.sfc.hk. See also Securities and Futures Commission Limited and Hong Kong Exchanges and Clearing Limited, 'Agreed Interpretation of Terms in the MOU for the Purposes of the Commencement of the SFO' (April 2003), available at www.sfc.hk.

[18] Hong Kong Exchanges and Clearing Limited, 'About HKEx', available at www.hkex.com.hk.

[19] Hong Kong Exchanges and Clearing Limited, 'Company Profile', available www.hkex.com.hk.

[20] Hong Kong Stock Exchange, 'GEM Listing Rules'; Hong Kong Stock Exchange, 'Main Board Listing Rules'.

jurisdictions (People's Republic of China ('PRC'), Bermuda and Cayman Islands) which are specifically recognised in the Listing Rules.[21] In the case of companies applying from other jurisdictions the issuer must demonstrate that its jurisdiction of incorporation offers an equivalent standard of shareholder protection to Hong Kong or amend its constituent documents so that it can meet the standard.[22]

II Current Regulatory Regime Relating to Independent Directors: Corporate Governance and the Listing Rules

The Listing Rules regulate corporate governance of companies listed on the Exchange in a number of ways. Pursuant to section 21 of the SFO, the Exchange is required to ensure, as far as reasonably practicable, an 'orderly, informed and fair market' in its securities and must act 'having particular regard to the interest of the investing public'. The Exchange is given a wide power to make rules pursuant to section 23 of the SFO, subject to the approval of the Commission.[23] An issuer and its directors are required to sign undertakings to comply with the requirements of the Listing Rules as a condition to listing.[24] The Listing Committee thus has a range of disciplinary measures available to it that it may take against the issuer or its subsidiaries, directors and senior management under Rules 2A.8, 2A.9 and 2A.10. These include suspension or cancellation of the listing, reprimands, censures, criticism, appointment of an independent advisor, report of the conduct to the SFC or relevant regulator and issue of an order that the breach be remedied.

The provisions relating to independent directors are contained mainly in the following sections of the Listing Rules: Chapter 3 (Authorised

[21] Main Board Listing Rules, appendix 13.

[22] Securities and Futures Commission and The Stock Exchange of Hong Kong Limited, 'Joint Policy Statement Regarding the Listing of Overseas Companies' (27 September 2013), available at www.hkex.com.hk; The Stock Exchange of Hong Kong Limited, 'List of Acceptable Overseas Jurisdictions' (last updated July 2014), available at www.hkex.com.hk.

[23] Section 24, Securities and Futures Ordinance, c. 571 (Hong Kong). There is an exception for rules in a class of rules for which the SFC has agreed that no such approval is required. Under certain circumstances, the SFC may require the Exchange to make certain rules. See Section 23(3), Securities and Futures Ordinance, c. 571 (Hong Kong). The rules so made are not, however, subsidiary legislation. Section 24(8), Securities and Futures Ordinance, c. 571 (Hong Kong).

[24] Main Board Listing Rules, appendix 5.

Representatives, Directors, Board Committees and Company Secretary); Chapter 14A (Connected Transactions); and Appendix 14 (Corporate Governance Code and Corporate Governance Report), although there are other provisions relating to the role of the independent directors throughout the Listing Rules.

In addition to the formal requirements under the Listing Rules, Appendix 14 contains the Corporate Governance Code, which sets out principles of good governance (the 'Principles'). The Code contains both code provisions (the 'Code Provisions') and recommended best practices. Issuers are expected to comply with the Code Provisions, although they may deviate from them and develop their own code of corporate governance in order to comply with the Principles. An issuer which deviates from the Code Provisions must review each Code Provision and provide 'considered reasons' for any deviation in its annual reports, in the Corporate Governance Report required by the Appendix and interim reports. They are also encouraged, but not required, to consider its deviations from the recommended best practices and provide explanations for those as well.

A summary of the provisions relating to independent directors is set out below.

1 *Number and Identification of Independent Directors*

Rule 3.10 requires that the board of a listed company must include at least three independent non-executive directors of whom one must have 'appropriate professional qualifications or accounting or related financial management expertise'. Rule 3.10A provides that independent directors must constitute at least one-third of the board. Pursuant to Rule 3.11, where the numbers fall below three, or the one-third minimum requirement, or the company at any time fails to meet the requirement relating to professional qualifications, the company is required immediately to notify the Exchange and issue a public announcement setting out the details and reasons. Rule 3.12 allows the Exchange to stipulate a minimum number of independent directors which is higher than three if the Exchange considers that circumstances warrant it. Pursuant to Rule 8.10(3), where a new applicant has a controlling shareholder or directors who are engaged in a business which may compete with that of the applicant, the Exchange may 'require the appointment of a sufficient number of independent non-executive directors to ensure that the interests of the general body of shareholders will be adequately represented'.[25]

Principle A.3 of the Corporate Governance Code provides that a board should have an appropriate balance of 'skills, experience and diversity of perspectives' as well as a balance of executive, non-executive and independent directors so that there is a 'strong independent element' on the board, which will allow it to exercise independent judgement. The Principle is not prescriptive in relation to the number of independent directors who should be appointed. It does, however, provide that the independent directors should be of sufficient 'calibre and number' for their views to carry weight.

Code Provision A.3.1 and A.3.2 require that the independent directors be identified in all corporate communications disclosing the names of directors and that a listed company should maintain on its own and the Exchange's website an updated list of directors which identifies their role and function and whether they are independent directors.

2 *Qualifications*

Pursuant to Rule 3.09 every would-be director of a listed company is obliged to satisfy the Exchange that he (or she) 'has the character, experience and integrity and is able to demonstrate a standard of competence commensurate with his position as a director of a listed issuer'. The Exchange may seek further information about the background, business interests, character or experience of such a person. Independent directors must also satisfy the Exchange that he or she has the character, integrity, independence and experience 'to fill his role effectively'. An independent director with accounting or other financial experience is expected to have substantial experience, and to have acted as a public accountant or auditor or have similar experience with internal controls.[26] A person who is appointed as an independent director of a PRC company must also, pursuant to Rule 19A.18(1), 'be able to demonstrate an acceptable

[25] Note that there do not appear to be any Listing Decisions where the Exchange had made such a determination. See Stock Exchange of Hong Kong Limited, 'Listing Decisions', available at www.hkex.com.hk.

[26] Main Board Listing Rules, note to Rule 3.10(2). In a recent decision, the Exchange agreed that a candidate with Chinese accounting qualifications and experience would satisfy that requirement. See Stock Exchange of Hong Kong Limited, 'HKEx Listing Decision HkEx-LD104-1' (September 2010), available at www.hkex.com.

level of competence and adequate commercial and professional experience to ensure that the interests of the general body of shareholders will be adequately represented'. In addition, at least one of the independent directors of a PRC company listed in Hong Kong must be resident in Hong Kong.

An issue which has been particularly controversial is the question of independence. Rule 3.13 sets out a range of factors which the Exchange will take into account in assessing independence, none of which are conclusive. The Exchange is more likely to question the independence of a director in the following situations:

a. the director holds more than 1 per cent of issued share capital of the issuer (including legal and beneficial ownership, convertible shares, options and other interests). The company must satisfy the Exchange prior to the appointment of such a person that he or she is in fact independent. A director who holds more than 5 per cent of the issued capital will normally not be considered to be independent;
b. the director has received securities in the issuer as a gift or in the form of financial assistance from a 'core connected person' or the issuer (with an exception for securities received as part of his director's fees or pursuant to a share option scheme). A 'core connected person' is defined in Rule 1.01 as a person who is the director, supervisor (in the case of a PRC company), chief executive or substantial shareholder of the company, a subsidiary or a close associate of any of them;[27]
c. the director is a director, officer, partner or employee of a professional advisor which provided services within the last year to the company, a company within the group or a core connected person thereof or a controlling shareholder;
d. the director has a material interest or is involved in material business dealings with the company, a group company or a core connected person of the company;[28]
e. the director is on the board for the specific purpose of protecting the interests of an entity with interests different to shareholders as a whole;

[27] Due to the emphasis on controlling connected transactions in Hong Kong, these terms are all tightly defined in Rule 1.01. Generally, a close associate is a relative or, in the case of a company, a member of the same group, while a substantial shareholder owns or controls 10 per cent or more of the voting power in a company.

[28] These terms are not defined, although Rules 2.15 and 2.16 contain some guidelines in relation to material interests.

f. the director is or was connected with a director, chief executive office or substantial shareholder within two years immediately prior to appointment. The Note to this sub-section makes clear that 'connected' in this context includes a wide range of family relationships and cohabitation with or marriage to a wide range of family connections. 'Connected persons' are defined in Chapter 14A;
g. the director has been an executive (that is, any person with a management function, including the company secretary) or a director (other than an independent director) of the company, a group company or a core connected person of the company within the previous two years; or
h. the director is financially dependent on the issuer, a group company or a core connected person of the company.

A statement must be submitted to the Exchange in writing by the independent director which confirms his independence under the above eight factors, sets out any financial or other interests in the issuer, its subsidiaries or any core connected person in relation to independence and states that there are no other factors that may affect his independence. An independent director must notify the Exchange promptly of any change of circumstance that may affect his independence and provide an annual confirmation of his independence to the issuer. Similarly, the issuer must state in each annual report that it has received this confirmation and that it considers the director to be independent (Rule 3.13).

If a proposed independent director fails to meet any of these independence guidelines, the listed issuer must demonstrate to the satisfaction of the Exchange that the person is indeed independent, prior to his appointment. The reasons must be disclosed in the announcement of the appointment in the next annual report of the company (Rule 3.14).

The issue of long-serving directors and the impact that the length of service may have on independence is addressed in Code Provision A.4.3, which states that service for more than nine years may cast doubt on the independence of the director and requires that the further appointment of such a person be subject to a separate resolution to be approved by shareholders. The papers provided to the shareholders should set out the reasons why the board considers the person still to be independent. (Code Provision A.4.1 states that non-executive directors should be elected for a specific term, subject to re-election.)

3 *Duties of Independent Non-executive Directors*

An independent director is subject to the duties and responsibilities which apply to all directors (Rule 3.12). Rule 3.8 states that the board of directors of an issuer is collectively responsible for its organisation and management. The directors, collectively and individually, must satisfy 'fiduciary duties and duties of skill, care and diligence to a standard at least commensurate with the standard established by Hong Kong law'.

The fiduciary duties of directors in Hong Kong have traditionally been those set out in the common law.[29] Recent amendments to the Companies Ordinance in 2014 have endeavoured to codify and clarify the director's obligation to exercise reasonable care, skill and diligence (section 465). These duties are summarised in Rule 3.8 as: acting honestly and in good faith in the interests of the company as a whole; acting for a proper purpose; being answerable to the issuer for the application or misapplication of its assets; avoiding conflicts of interest and duty – actual and potential; disclosing fully and fairly any interests in contracts with the issuer; and applying such degree of skill, care and diligence as may reasonably be expected of a person with his experience and commensurate with his position in the company.

In addition to the general obligations of directors, Rule 3.16 provides that the issuer must ensure that the directors, collectively and individually, accept full responsibility for the issuer's compliance with the Listing Rules. Directors must also, pursuant to Rule 3.17, comply with the Model Code for Security Transactions by Directors of Issuers contained in Appendix 10, or the issuer's own code, which sets out the standards which issuers and the directors are expected to meet. Any failure to comply is considered to be a breach of the Listing Rules.

The Corporate Governance Code extends these requirements in relation to non-executive directors, which includes independent (non-executive) directors. Principle A.6 reiterates the duty of every director to know his responsibilities as a director and emphasises that all directors have the same duties of care and skill, and fiduciary duties. Code Provision A.6.1 provides that a newly appointed director should receive a suitable formal induction and subsequent training and professional development

[29] See discussion in D. Friedlander et al., 'Topic 6: Directors' Duties – International Regulatory Perspective' (University of New South Wales: 2012 Directors' Duties Seminar, 20 March 2012), 6–12, available at www.clmr.unsw.edu.au.

to ensure that he understands the issuer and his own responsibilities. Code Provision A.6.5 requires ongoing professional development for directors to ensure that their contribution remains 'informed and relevant'.

Disclosure is a very important principle of the Listing Rules and the Code generally. In relation to directors, Code Principle A.3.4 requires that an issuer must issue an explanation in relation to the resignation or retirement of any director. Code Provisions A.3.1 and A.3.2 require that the independent directors be so identified on all corporate communications identifying directors, as well as on the issuer's website.

Although non-executive directors, other than independent directors, are not required in the Listing Rules to be independent, it is clear from the Code Principles that their position as non-executive directors requires them to exercise independent judgement (Code Provision A.6.2). Code Provisions A.6.7 and A.6.8 require both independent directors and other non-executive directors to give the board and any committee the benefit of their skills, expertise and varied backgrounds, to attend shareholder meetings to 'develop a balanced understanding of the views of shareholders' and to 'make a positive contribution to the development of the issuer's strategy and policies through independent, constructive and informed comments'.

There is no requirement or expectation in the Listing Rules or the Code that independent and/or non-executive directors will constitute a majority on the board of directors. However, in addition to participating in the main board, independent directors play an important role on board committees and in relation to connected transactions.

a Audit Committee

Pursuant to Rule 3.21, a listed company is required to have an audit committee. This must be composed entirely of non-executive directors and have a minimum of three members. Of these, at least one director must be an independent director with professional qualifications and the majority of the members, including the chair, must be independent directors. The board of directors is required to compile written terms of reference for the committee under Rule 3.22. The issuer is also required to issue an announcement and rectify the matter within three months if there is no audit committee or if the issuer fails to meet these requirements. The note to Rule 3.21 refers the issuer to 'A Guide for Effective Audit Committees' published by the Hong Kong Institute of Certified Public Accountants[30]

[30] Hong Kong Institute of Certified Public Accountants (Hong Kong Society of Accountants), 'A Guide for Effective Audit Committees' (February 2002), available at www.hkicpa.org.hk.

and provides that the issuer should use the guidelines in that publication or adopt comparable terms of reference. Principle C.3 reiterates that the board should establish clear terms of reference for the audit committee. Recommended terms of reference for the audit committee are set out at Code Provision C.3.3 *et seq*. They include provisions on the relationship with the issuer's auditors, review of financial information, oversight of financial reporting system and internal controls.

b Remuneration and the Remuneration Committee

Under Rule 3.25, a listed company must have a remuneration committee. This must be chaired by an independent director, and a majority of members must be independent directors. The board of directors is required to approve and provide written terms of reference for the committee. A public announcement must be made and the position rectified if there is no such committee or if there are no written terms of reference for the committee.

The Listing Rules do not contain specific provisions relating to the terms of reference for the remuneration committee. However, Rule 13.68 (Directors' Service Contracts) provides that a service contract for a director or proposed director of the issuer or a subsidiary requires shareholder approval if it is for longer than three years or provides for termination on more than one year's notice. The relevant director may not vote on the contract. The remuneration committee, if there is one, must form a view and provide advice to the shareholders as to whether the terms of the contract are fair and reasonable, whether the contract is in the best interests of the issuer and the shareholders as a whole and as to how the shareholders should vote, provided that the committee has a majority of independent directors. If not, an independent board committee (that is, a committee of independent directors) must form the view and advise the shareholders. (An independent director with a material interest in the contract may not vote.)

Code Provisions B.1 *et seq* set out in much more detail the recommended scope of the remuneration committee. An important principle is that the remuneration committee should consult the chair of the board but must also have access to independent legal advice. The scope of responsibility of the remuneration committee should include the power to make recommendations in relation to the structure and policy of remuneration for directors and senior officers; to review and approve remuneration proposals in light of the issuer's objectives; to have delegated authority to determine remuneration packages of individual executive directors and senior managers or to make recommendations to the board on those packages; to make recommendations on remuneration of non-executive directors; to make recommendations on compensation in relation to termination and dismissal and to ensure that no director or his associates make a determination on his own remuneration.

c Nomination Committee

The Listing Rules do not make provision for a nomination committee. However, the Corporate Governance Code does provide for a nomination committee. Principle A.5 states that the nomination committee should give consideration to the principles in relation to the board addressed in Principles A.3 and A.4. Principle A.3, as discussed above, deals with the composition of the board and requires a balance of skills, experience and diversity of perspectives and a balance between executive and non-executive directors in order to obtain a strong independent element. Principle A.4 provides for a 'formal, considered and transparent procedure' for the appointment of directors, plans for succession and regular re-election of directors, with the reasons for the resignation or removal of directors to be disclosed.

Code Provision A.5.1 *et seq* provides for a nomination committee to be chaired either by the chair of the board or by an independent director and for the majority of the members to be independent directors. The committee should have terms of reference which include advising on the size of the board, identifying candidates to serve as directors and determining whether a candidate is indeed independent. Where the committee nominates a person to be elected at the next annual general meeting as an independent director, it must provide a statement of reasons to the shareholders as to why the candidate should be elected and why the committee considers that the candidate is independent.

d Connected Transactions and Conflicts of Interest

The issue of conflicts of interest is a major concern for the Hong Kong market, primarily due to the prevalence in Hong Kong listed companies of a controlling shareholder or group of controlling shareholders or substantial shareholders and the related problem of transactions between the controlling shareholder or another entity controlled by it and the issuer. The Listing Rules therefore make detailed provision for the definition of connected transactions, disclosure and voting requirements designed to protect the independent (often minority) shareholders from exploitation.

Independent directors have come to play an important role in minority protection in a number of ways.

The first of these relates to conflicts of interest on the board. Code Provision A.1.7 provides that where a substantial shareholder or director has an interest which the board considers to be material in a matter to be dealt with at board level, there must be a physical board meeting, and independent directors who have no material interest (and whose associates have no material interest) in the transaction should be present.

Pursuant to the Listing Rules, there are a number of situations where the independent shareholders[31] of the issuer must be notified or must be given the opportunity to approve or disapprove a particular transaction. In this case, it is considered that the independent shareholders should be provided with assistance, in the form of independent advice. The Listing Rules require that this be provided by an independent board committee and/or an independent financial advisor acceptable to the Exchange. Rule 13.39(6) provides that the independent board committee must be composed only of independent non-directors, excluding any independent director with a material interest in the relevant transaction. Thus the committee may consist of only one independent director if all of the others have a material interest in the transaction, and, if all of the independent directors have a material interest in the transaction or arrangement, the independent financial advisor will be responsible for making its recommendation to the shareholders directly. Otherwise the independent financial advisor makes its recommendation to the independent board committee and the shareholders.

Where the Listing Rules or Practice Note requires the approval of the independent shareholders for a transaction, the responsibility of the independent board committee under Chapter 13 (Rule 13.39(6)) is to advise shareholders whether the terms of the transaction or arrangement are 'fair and reasonable' and whether the transaction or arrangement is in the interests of the issuer and the 'shareholders as a whole'. The committee should also advise the shareholders how to vote. The advice, if required, should be set out in a separate letter from the independent board committee to the shareholders and take into account the recommendations of the independent financial advisor.

[31] The notes to Rules 13.39(6) and (7) explain that independent shareholders are shareholders other than controlling shareholders of the issuer and their affiliates or, if there are no controlling shareholders, any shareholders other than directors (but excluding the independent directors) and the chief executive of the issuer and their respective associates.

The main circumstances in which a separate vote is required are set out in Chapter 14A, which deals with connected transactions, and Practice Note 15 of the Listing Rules, relating to proposals for 'spin-offs'.

Rule 14A.01 sets out the general principle of the very complicated connected transaction rules, which is that the Rules 'ensure that the interests of shareholders as a whole are taken into account by the listed issuer when the listed issuer's group enters into a connected transaction'. The independent directors (through the independent board committee) play a major role in protecting the interests of the independent shareholders in relation to the approval of connected transactions for which an independent shareholder approval is required pursuant to Rule 14A.36 and in conducting an annual review of continuing connected transactions (Rule 14A.03). Rule 14A.40 provides for the formation of an independent board committee and repeats the provisions set out in Rule 13.39. However, in addition to the requirements that the committee advise the shareholders on the terms of the connected transaction (as set out above), the committee must also advise whether the connected transaction is on normal commercial terms or better and whether it is in the ordinary and usual course of business of the issuer's group. Their advice must be contained in the circular to shareholders.

The independent directors also play a role in annually reviewing any ongoing connected transaction (such as a supply contract), and reviewing any transaction involving an acquisition from a connected person which is supported by a guarantee from that person. Under Rule 14A.63 a failure to meet the guarantee must be disclosed in the next annual report of the issuer, with the independent directors' opinion on whether the connected person had fulfilled its obligations and whether any decision by the listed issuer's group to exercise a remedy in relation to the non-performance is fair and reasonable and in the interests of the shareholders as a whole. The independent directors are also required to provide opinions in relation to connected transactions between the listed issuer's group and a connected person at the subsidiary level which are on normal commercial terms and thus exempt from the shareholder approval requirements (Rule 14A.101),[32] as well as the grant of share options to directors, the chief executive officer or subsidiary shareholders.

Rule 17.03 requires that the shareholders approve a share option scheme. Under Rule 17.04, each grant of options to a director, chief

[32] Non-executive directors may be exempted from some or all of the connected transaction requirements if the transaction is connected only because of the director's interest and the director does not control the issuer's group or have the issuer's group as his principal business (Rule 14A.103).

executive or substantial shareholder of an issuer or any of their associates must be approved by the independent directors of the issuer (other than an independent director who is the grantee of the option). If the grant of an option to a substantial shareholder or independent director, or one of their associates would result in the cumulative grant over a 12-month period of securities representing in total over 0.1 per cent of the relevant class of securities or an aggregate value in excess of HKD 5 million, shareholder approval must be obtained. In that case, a recommendation from the independent directors, other than the grantee, must also be provided to the shareholders. This also applies to a change in the terms of options.

In addition to these various requirements in the Listing Rules, there are numerous requirements relating to disclosure and reporting which relate to the independent directors and their decisions as well as the various committees on which the independent directors serve.

4 *Background : Issues for Listed Companies in Hong Kong and the Development of the Listing Rules*

The 1990s were a very important period for the government of Hong Kong and its regulators, as well as for the Exchange. Hong Kong was recovering from the Financial Crisis which commenced in 1987, which had seen the four-day suspension of shares from trading on the Exchange, and was followed by the appointment and report of the Securities Review Committee appointed by the then Governor, Sir David Wilson (the Hay Davison Report) and the establishment of the Securities and Futures Commission in 1989.[33] The Exchange and the regulators were preparing for the hand-over of the colony to China on 1 July 1997, and coping with market response and apprehension in relation to the hand-over. The development in this period of the Chinese corporate and securities law regime, the creation and development of the Chinese stock markets[34] and the expansion of Chinese companies and business presented both opportunities and challenges.

This period also saw a rapid increase in the 're-domiciling' of Hong Kong companies listed on the Exchange,[35] despite the guarantees of

[33] 'Establishment of the Securities and Futures Commission – the Davison Report' in Securities and Futures Commission, *Securities Regulation in Hong Kong* (May 2002), ch 2 (extract), available at www.sfc.hk; Goo, 'Study Report on History of Company Incorporation in Hong Kong', 49 *et seq.*

[34] See Chapter 6 (China) at II.

[35] Goo, 'Study Report on History of Company Incorporation in Hong Kong', 49.

substantial autonomy for the Hong Kong economy and regulation in the Basic Law.[36] This may have been due to lack of confidence in the Hong Kong legal system after the hand-over or the increase in regulation of the Hong Kong market after the Hay Davison Report, or both.[37] By the end of March 1994, listings of Bermuda companies alone accounted for 46 per cent of the market capitalisation of the Exchange. By the end of 1998, there were 680 companies listed on the Exchange, of which only 200 had been incorporated in Hong Kong.[38] With the advent of Chinese companies listing directly on the Exchange, as well as companies incorporated in Bermuda, the Cook Islands and the Cayman Islands,[39] the importance of sound regulation of all listed companies, wherever incorporated, was given high priority.

The development of Chinese securities markets also made it necessary for there to be close cooperation between the Hong Kong and Chinese regulators.[40] In 1993, a Memorandum of Regulatory Cooperation ('MORC') was signed between the China Securities Regulatory Commission, the Shanghai Stock Exchange, the Shenzhen Stock Exchange, the SFO and the Exchange, requiring quarterly meetings to discuss market developments and other matters of mutual interest.[41] The scope of the MORC is broad, and provides for the exchange of information in order to protect investors, provide for fair, orderly and efficient markets and to comply with the other party's laws and regulations. The Listing Rules were amended by the introduction of Chapter 19A, relating to the listing of Chinese company securities and the ground-work was laid for the listing of the shares of Chinese-incorporated companies on the Exchange. The first Chinese company listed was Tsingdao Brewery Co, Ltd in July 1993.[42]

A major issue for Hong Kong companies has traditionally been the dominance of the controlling shareholder. Companies listed in Hong

[36] *Basic Law of the Hong Kong Special Administrative Region of the People's Republic of China.*

[37] Goo, 'Study Report on History of Company Incorporation in Hong Kong', 49.

[38] *Ibid.*, 52.

[39] Main Board Listing Rules Chapter 19A and Appendix 13. The Cook Islands was removed in 1999.

[40] L. Cha, 'The SFC's Role in Regulating Listed Companies in Hong Kong' in Securities and Futures Commission, *Securities Regulation in Hong Kong* (May 2002), ch 14, 213, 219.

[41] 'Memorandum of Co-operation on Regulatory Co-operation' (19 June 1993).

[42] Hong Kong Exchanges and Clearing Limited, 'List of H Share Companies (Main Board)' (last updated February 2015), available at www.hkex.com.hk.

Kong are often majority owned or controlled by a family grouping or group of related shareholders. The expansion of Chinese and Chinese-owned companies in the Hong Kong market, which often had a controlling shareholder in the form of a Chinese parent company, often a state-owned enterprise, increased the number of companies listed in Hong Kong in which public shareholders do not hold a controlling interest. In 2013, for example, 'mainland' enterprises accounted for 57 per cent of market capitalisation and 72 per cent of annual equity turnover value.[43]

The question of adequate shareholder protection for the public investors is therefore an important issue in the Hong Kong market, given the internationalisation of the market and the important role of foreign investors. The HKEx Fact Book 2013 indicates that overseas investors are the major contributors to market turnover value, led by investors from the United States (28 per cent of overseas investor trading), the United Kingdom (26 per cent) and the rest of Europe (14 per cent), with Asia (including China (11 per cent) and Australia (5 per cent) accounting for 27 per cent.[44] The reliance on independent directors in Hong Kong is generally regarded as being directed at the controlling shareholder issue rather than, as in other jurisdictions with more widely dispersed holdings, the agency problem presented by the dominance of management on the board.

The Cadbury Report (formally known as the 'The Report of the Committee on the Financial Aspects of Corporate Governance' issued by the London Stock Exchange)[45] was issued in 1992 and had a significant impact on corporate governance in Hong Kong. The Cadbury Report concluded that non-executive directors have two very important roles to play on the board: the first in reviewing the performance of the board and the second in dealing with conflicts of interest between executive management and the wider interests of the company (paragraphs 4.5 and 4.6). Accordingly, the Committee recommended that there be no fewer than three non-executive directors on the board of a listed company of whom two should be independent (paragraph 4.11) and the introduction of a Code of Best Practice to raise the standard of corporate governance (paragraph 2.9 *et seq*).

[43] Hong Kong Exchanges and Clearing Limited, 'HKEx Fact Book 2013', 1, available at www.hkex.com.hk.

[44] *Ibid.*, 706–707.

[45] London Stock Exchange, 'The Report of the Committee on the Financial Aspects of Corporate Governance', available at www.ecgi.org.

In 1993, the first working group was established in Hong Kong by the Exchange and other parties to consider the Cadbury Report[46] and in November 1993, a requirement was introduced into the Listing Rules that each listed company have two independent non-executive directors (Rule 3.10), with a further requirement that the Exchange be empowered to require more than two independent directors if it was of the opinion that the size of the board or other circumstances justified it (Rule 3.15). The Listing Rules did not, at that time, mandate audit or remuneration committees.[47]

The Exchange also published in 1993 a Code of Best Practice, which was a set of voluntary guidelines for boards of directors. Together with the Hong Kong Society of Accountants, the Exchange set up no fewer than five working groups to consider the recommendations of the Cadbury Report, which bore fruit over the next ten years,[48] followed by frequent public consultations regarding potential changes to the Listing Rules.

A consultation paper issued in 1998 by the Exchange[49] focused on disclosure requirements for controlling shareholders and improving the rules on connected transactions, primarily by increasing disclosure requirements and the rules relating to the approval of certain transactions by a shareholder vote where shareholders with an interest in the transactions would not be permitted to vote. As a result, independent directors were required by the new Chapter 14A to play an active role in relation to connected transactions. The consultation paper does not, however, make clear why an expanded role for independent directors will be helpful – the proposed changes are based on 'best market practices and current market conditions'[50] and a general reference to minority protection for the independent shareholders.[51] A further paper in 2000 resulted in a greater role for independent directors in relation to the share

[46] C. McKenna, 'Hong Kong', *International Financial Law Review* (12 April 2000), available at www.iflr.com.

[47] B. M. Ho, 'Restructuring the Boards of Directors of Public Companies in Hong Kong: Barking up the Wrong Tree', *Singapore Journal of International and Comparative Law*, 1 (1997), 507, 508.

[48] ACGA, 'Building Stronger Board and Companies in Asia: A Concise Report on Corporate Governance Policies and Practices' (January 2000), 8, available at www.acga-asia.org.

[49] Stock Exchange of Hong Kong Limited, *Consultation Paper: 1998 Review of the Listing Rules* (1998), available at www.hkex.com.hk.

[50] *Ibid.*, 1, Part A.

[51] *Ibid.*, 46.

options and the grant of options to directors who are themselves substantial shareholders.[52]

In 2002, the Exchange issued a further consultation paper in relation to corporate governance.[53] The reasons provided for the very detailed proposed changes provided in the paper were, however, again very brief. The paper stated that the Rules were reviewed from the point of view of prudent market governance in order to bring them up to 'international market practices'.[54] Second, the Rules should conform to international market practices after considering circumstances in Hong Kong. The Exchange considered that it was 'equally important that we should strike a balance between commercial practicability and protection of investors'.[55]

Some detail on the reasoning behind the Exchange's decisions was provided in the subsequent Consultation Conclusions,[56] in which the Exchange repeated its point on reflecting 'the characteristics of the Hong Kong market'.

In relation to independent directors, the Exchange proposed adding criteria in relation to independence and the importance of independent directors 'particularly on matters that involve conflicts of interest or connected persons or have significant impact on the issuers and shareholders'.[57] The Exchange also proposed including a requirement that independent directors constitute at least one-third of the board, with a minimum of two, to ensure a sufficient number of independent directors on the board.[58]

In the event, there was considerable resistance to this proposal.[59] Much of this appeared to be based on the idea that there was insufficient talent in the Hong Kong market and the requirement to have more independent

52 Stock Exchange of Hong Kong Limited, *Consultation Paper on Chapter 17 (Share Schemes) of the Rules Governing the Listing of Securities on the Stock Exchange of Hong Kong Limited* (May 2000), 15–16, available at www.hkex.com.

53 Hong Kong Exchanges and Clearing Limited, *Consultation Paper on Proposed Amendments to the Listing Rules Relating to Corporate Governance Issues* (January 2002), available at www.hkex.com.

54 *Ibid.*, 1.

55 *Ibid.*

56 Stock Exchange of Hong Kong Limited, *Consultation Conclusions Relating to Proposed Amendments to the Listing Rules Relating to Corporate Governance Issues* (January 2003), 4, available at www.hkex.com.

57 Hong Kong Exchanges and Clearing Limited, *Consultation Paper on Proposed Amendments to the Listing Rules Relating to Corporate Governance Issues*, 93 *et seq.*

58 *Ibid.*, 100.

59 Stock Exchange of Hong Kong Limited, *Consultation Conclusions Relating to Proposed Amendments to the Listing Rules Relating to Corporate Governance Issues*, 29.

directors would place an undue burden on smaller companies; others took the view that it would be better to improve the quality of independent directors. As a consequence, the Exchange retreated from its initial proposal and implemented, effective 31 March 2004, a requirement for a minimum of three independent directors, with a recommendation in the Code of Best Practice that at least one-third of the board should be independent.[60] Further rule changes in 2004 gave independent directors a more significant role in relation to continuing connected transactions.[61]

A consultation process was also conducted by the Exchange on the Draft Code of Corporate Governance Practices and Corporate Governance Report,[62] which, with the exception of one provision, came into effect on 1 January 2005. The Code included a number of provisions relating to the role of independent directors and board committees, the independence of independent directors and the public disclosure of their position in corporate documents, as described above. Although it was heavily based on the UK Combined Code and the principle of 'comply or explain' set out in that code,[63] it did not incorporate the UK concept of 'senior independent director' in the Code, which it did not consider warranted by the 'typical board structure' in a Hong Kong listed company.[64]

In 2011, after another round of consultations, a number of further changes were added to the Listing Rules in relation to directors and independent directors.[65] These included expanding Rule 3.08 in relation to directors' duties, adding in provisions in the Code requiring review of a director's contribution and compliance with training requirements, adding in a provision that shareholders must vote to approve the re-election of an independent director who has served for more than nine years and including the requirement that no less than one-third of the directors on the board be independent non-executive directors. The duties of the independent directors were significantly increased by the decision to bring in requirements under the Listing Rules that each issuer establish

60 *Ibid.*, 30.

61 Hong Kong Exchanges and Clearing Limited, *Consultation Paper on Review of Connected Transaction Rules* (April 2013), 100, available at www.hkex.com.hk.

62 Hong Kong Exchanges and Clearing Limited, *Exposure of Draft Code on Corporate Governance Practices and Corporate Governance Report* (January 2004), available at www.hkex.com.hk.

63 *Ibid.*, 1.

64 *Ibid.*, 44.

65 Hong Kong Exchanges and Clearing Limited, *Consultation Conclusions on Review of the Corporate Governance Code and Associated Listing Rules* (October 2011), available at www.hkex.com.hk.

a remuneration committee with a majority of independent directors as members, with an independent director as chair, and obligations under the Code that each issuer should have a nomination committee with a majority of independent directors as members, with an independent director as chair, as well as a requirement that the board take responsibility for corporate governance and that terms of reference be established for the committees.[66]

In making these proposals, the Exchange looked at practice in New York, Australia, China and the United Kingdom. It did not, however, follow the practice in those jurisdictions, without providing much in the way of explanation.

An important part of the rationale presented for the proposal that independent directors constitute one-third of the board was the amount of extra work which would be created for the independent directors as a result of the addition of duties on the committees and the consequent need for more directors. The Exchange was not, however, moved by arguments that there should be more than one-third of independent directors on the Board.[67] Even though the paper notes that international practice in New York, the United Kingdom and Australia favoured a majority of independent directors (as opposed to China and Singapore), it did not discuss the concept of requiring a majority of independent directors, or present this as an option in the questionnaire sent out for public comment.

III Discussion

It is clear that Hong Kong regulators and the Exchange have made a commitment to improving corporate governance, with some success. The World Bank ranked Hong Kong second in the world in 2014 in its 'Doing Business' rankings in relation to minority protection.[68] According to a 2012 survey, Hong Kong and Singapore are leaders in corporate governance in Asia. The Asian Corporate Governance Association, however, still takes the view that neither has a world-class system of corporate governance.[69] A more recent survey on Asian markets indicates that

[66] *Ibid.*

[67] *Ibid.*, 14.

[68] World Bank Group, 'Doing Business – Measuring Business Regulations: Ease of Doing Business in Hong Kong SAR, China' (2015), available at www.doingbusiness.org.

[69] J. Allen, 'New Developments in Corporate Governance Reform in Asia: Northern Chills, Southern Warmth' (ACGA Members' Briefing, Sydney, 25 March 2013), available at www.acga-asia.org.

respondents in Hong Kong have a generally positive view in relation to corporate governance, but still consider the level of minority protection to be weak.[70]

The consultation papers on changes to the Listing Rules show that the policy of the Exchange is to comply with international market practice, while taking Hong Kong circumstances into account. There are, as noted above, a number of factors specific to the Hong Kong market. First, it continues to be a market in which most listed companies are not incorporated in Hong Kong. According to the Webb-site Who's Who Database,[71] of the 1,549 companies listed on the main board at the beginning of 2015, only 205 or 13.23 per cent were incorporated in Hong Kong.[72] Companies incorporated in the Cayman Islands (674 or 43.51 per cent) constituted the largest group of listed companies, while there were 467 or 30.15 per cent Bermuda companies and 180 Chinese incorporated companies (11.62 per cent). Including the GEM market, Hong Kong companies (213) constituted only 12.14 per cent of the companies listed on the entire Exchange.

It is generally accepted in Hong Kong that the major corporate governance for Hong Kong listed companies arise not from agency issues, that is, the relationship between managers and shareholders, but from the concentration of ownership of companies in the Hong Kong market and the issue of the controlling shareholder – that is, a situation in which one shareholder, or a group of shareholders, owns or controls a listed company. This can be a family group or grouping, or, in the case particularly of Chinese companies, a corporate controlling shareholder. A survey published in 2011 indicates that family-owned businesses (that is, more than 20 per cent ownership) constituted 61 per cent of listed companies in Hong Kong with a market capitalisation of more than US $50 million (though only 26.2 per cent of the market overall).[73] A review of the 50

[70] CPA Australia, *CPA Australia Asia-Pacific Governance Survey* (2014), 45, available at www.cpaaustralia.com.au.

[71] Webb-site, 'Domicile of HK Main Board Listed Companies', available at webb-site.com (compiled on the basis of publicly available sources).

[72] Note, however, that in 2013, although Hong Kong incorporated companies constituted only 13.9 per cent of the total listed companies, they accounted for more than 36 per cent of market capitalisation. See Hong Kong Exchanges and Clearing, 'HKEx Fact Book 2013', chart titled 'Market Capitalisation and Trading Value of Listed Companies by Incorporation Place'.

[73] Credit Suisse, *Asian Family Business Report 2011* (October 2011), 10, available at https://publications.credit-suisse.com.

companies listed on the main Hang Seng Indices shows that only HSBC and Hong Kong Exchanges and Clearing Limited themselves have truly diverse holdings.[74] Indeed, the SFC issued 18 notices relating to listed companies in 2014, warnings that the share price could fluctuate and extreme caution should be used in dealing with the shares in view of the high concentration of shares in the hands of a small number of shareholders.[75]

Over time, the role of the independent director has expanded from the original general concept of the value of having independent non-executive directors on the board to provide an independent perspective to the allocation of specific functions to independent directors in relation to minority shareholder protection. The level and breadth of responsibility has increased commensurately.

1 *Compliance with the Independent Director Requirements*

According to Webb-site, at the beginning of 2015, of the 1,754 companies listed on the GEM and main board, in the case of 171 companies, more than half of the directors on the board were independent directors (9.7 per cent); 284 listed companies had a board of which 50 per cent were independent (16 per cent); and 36 did not comply with the requirement to have one-third independent directors on the board (2 per cent).[76]

2 *Commentary on Independent Directors: Success?*

There are mixed views on the success of the independent director rules both in dealing with the controlling shareholder issue and in relation to corporate governance of Hong Kong listed companies generally. Criticisms are directed at the theory behind the independent director rules, particularly the utility of requiring independent directors in view of the particular issues presented by the Hong Kong market. Other criticisms are directed at the content of the rules, their practicability in the Hong Kong market, their implementation and the ability or inability of

[74] Thanks to Julian Byrnes for his review of the annual reports of these companies.

[75] Securities and Futures Commission, 'High Shareholding Concentration Announcements' (13 March 2015), available at www.sfc.hk.

[76] Webb-site.com draws attention to the fact that at least one listed company appears to have received a waiver from the one-third requirement. See United Company Rusal Plc, 'Change of Directorate and Change of Composition of the Corporate Governance and Nomination Committee and the Remuneration Committee' (27 May 2013), available at www.hkexnews.hk.

the Exchange and other regulators, including the courts, effectively to police or enforce the requirements of the Rules.

In 1997, Betty Ho, a well-known Hong Kong corporate lawyer, published an article[77] strongly attacking the theory behind the introduction of independent directors in Hong Kong. She argued that the purpose of independent directors was to deal with agency issues in companies with dispersed shareholdings and was not necessary or useful in Hong Kong due to the dominance in the Hong Kong market of public companies with majority shareholders.

Meng Fangpeng subsequently expressed the view in relation to Chinese companies listed in Hong Kong that the theory behind independent directors was the wrong prescription for a market where families often control listed companies, on the basis that it is unreasonable to think that a director nominated by the controlling shareholder could be truly independent.[78]

It is clear that the independent director requirement in Hong Kong is based on the need for better minority protection. Thus, the advisory role of the independent directors in relation to connected transactions and other issues where approval of the independent shareholders is required has greatly increased in importance. Indeed, in 2008, one commentator queried whether independent directors serving on the audit committee of issuers who were censured by the Exchange were being held to a higher level of responsibility than the executive and non-independent non-executive directors of the issuer.[79]

The fundamental issue is the question of independence – how it should be defined, whether true independence can realistically be achieved and whether there are enough persons in Hong Kong with the appropriate qualifications to be appointed as independent directors. A number of commentators, of whom activist David Webb has been the most vociferous,[80] argue that a director who is elected in an election in which the controlling shareholder group can vote – and whose nomination is also

[77] Ho, 'Restructuring the Boards of Directors of Public Companies in Hong Kong: Barking up the Wrong Tree'.

[78] F. Meng, 'Legal vs Reputational Bonding: Board Independence of Chinese Companies Listed in Hong Kong', *Australian Journal of Corporate Law*, 27 (2013), 319, 340.

[79] C. K. Low, 'Is the Standard of Care of Directors Inverted in Hong Kong?', *Hong Kong Law Journal*, 38(1) (2008), 31.

[80] C. Lee, 'David Webb: Tireless Champion of Shareholder's Rights', *Financial Times*, 13 October 2009, available at www.ft.com; D. Webb, 'Hong Kong's Not So Independent Directors' (20 April 1999), available at https://webb-site.com/.

dependent on the support of the controlling shareholders – cannot ever be considered to be independent of management and controlling shareholders.[81] Support for the view that the minority shareholders should have the power to appoint one or more independent directors also comes from Arner and others in a recent report on Hong Kong as an international financial centre.[82] The Chairman of the SFC has also commented on the decision by the UK Financial Conduct Authority that separate voting for independent directors both by the shareholders as a whole and by the independent shareholders as a class should be required, though without any indication that this change is seriously under consideration in Hong Kong.[83] (These changes were implemented in the UK Listing Rules in May 2014.[84])

The Exchange has responded to some of these criticisms by increasing the number of independent directors and expanding the list of factors relevant to the assessment of independence. The result is that independent directors must show that they are themselves not major shareholders, and that they are not tied to the controlling shareholders of the issuer either, or tied in with the company through share option schemes or other incentives such as gifts.

3 *Quality of Candidates*

The discussion on the effectiveness of independent directors is inseparable from commentary on the selection, quality and performance of independent directors. It is argued that there is too much of a tendency in Hong Kong for Hong Kong managers to elect their friends to each other's boards.[85] It is also often claimed that there is a shortage of talent in Hong Kong, although it is not clear why, in a major financial centre the size of Hong Kong, there should be a shortage of suitable candidates. The issue is

[81] Webb-site, 'The Three Wise Monkeys of HK Boards' (15 February 2011), available at www.webb-site.com.

[82] D. W. Arner et al., *Assessing Hong Kong as an International Financial Centre: First Report of the Hong Kong Research Grants Council Theme-Based Research Scheme Project: Enhancing Hong Kong's Future as a Leading International Financial Centre* (April 2014), 13, available at corporateaccountability2014.com.

[83] C. Tong, 'Towards Better Corporate Governance' (Chamber of Hong Kong Listed Companies 11th Anniversary Gala Dinner, December 2013), available at www.sfc.hk.

[84] Ashurst London, 'Changes to the Listing Rules: Final Rules in Force 16 May 2014' (June 2014), available at www.ashurst.com/.

[85] M. Devereux and R. Sasanow, 'How Independent Are Independent Directors?', *Corporate Governance* (July 2008), 22–25, available at http://app1.hkicpa.org.hk.

therefore how (and from which pool) the candidates for independent directors are selected. Directors of Hong Kong companies are overwhelmingly males who are more than 50 years old, with only 9.29 per cent of independent directorships held by women.[86] In 2012, the Exchange held a market consultation exercise in relation to diversity on boards, as a result of which a recommendation – rather than a requirement – that a board should have a balance of 'diversity of perspectives' was added into Principle A.4.[87]

4 *Studies on Independent Directors*

There have been a range of studies attempting to examine the role of independent directors in Hong Kong listed companies in order to assess their effect on corporate governance and corporate management. Some of these studies accept at face value the correlation between corporate governance and the appointment of independent directors. They therefore focus on the compliance of Hong Kong listed companies with the Listing Rule requirements, emphasising those cases where companies go beyond these requirements and comply with what is said to be international best practice, for example, with independent directors constituting more than half of the directors.[88] In contrast, a poll conducted on webb-site.com in 2011 concluded by a handsome majority that the system for appointing independent directors was totally ineffective to protect investors and that the performance of independent directors was generally or totally ineffective.[89] (There were 176 participants in this study, but these were presumably drawn from regular readers of the website and this therefore does not by any means constitute an empirical study.)

Lei and Song's study in 2004[90] concluded that there is a positive correlation between corporate governance and firm valuation, using the

[86] Webb-site, 'HK-listed Directorships by Type and Gender', available at https://webb-site.com/.

[87] Hong Kong Exchanges and Clearing, *Consultation Conclusions: Board Diversity* (December 2012), available at www.hkex.com.hk.

[88] See, for example, L. Barnes and P. Lau, 'Corporate Governance of Banks in Hong Kong: A Banking Sector Governance (BGS) Perspective' (20th Australasian Finance and Banking Conference Paper, 2007) available at http://papers.ssrn.com/sol3/papers.cfm?abstract_id=1007436.

[89] Webb-site, 'Poll Results: INEDs' (2011), available at https://webb-site.com.

[90] A. Lei and F. Song, 'Corporate Governance and Firm Valuations: Evidence from Hong Kong' (China International Conference in Finance, July 2005), available at www.ccfr.org.cn.

number of independent directors as one of the factors relating to the independence of the board. Some studies indicate that there is a positive correlation between the presence of independent directors on boards and standards of corporate governance, monitoring and supervision, although a lower correlation may be apparent in the case of family-owned companies – a significant concern in a jurisdiction where many listed companies are still family owned.[91]

Other earlier studies examine whether the composition of the board is significant in investors' decisions on investment, with differing results.[92] Lei and Deng[93] found that there is a strong positive correlation between firm value and a larger number of independent directors. They concluded, in relation to directors holding multiple directorships, that 'highly engaged independent directors' increase firm value notwithstanding their 'busyness' in view of what the authors describe as a 'quality deficit' in the Hong Kong market. They therefore found a positive correlation between multiple directorships held by independent directors and firm value,[94] although again there is evidence that the effect is mitigated where the firm is family controlled.[95] Thus these studies suggest that independent directors do have a positive effect, at least on firm value, but that the quality – or perceived quality – of independent directors is a significant factor.

[91] C. Chen and B. Jaggi, 'Association between Independent Non-Executive Directors, Family Control and Financial Disclosures in Hong Kong', *Journal of Accounting and Public Policy*, 19 (2000), 285; B. Jaggi, S. Leung and F. Gul, 'Family Control, Board Independence and Earnings Management: Evidence Based on Hong Kong Firms', *Journal of Accounting and Public Policy*, 28(4) (2009), 281. See also S. Ho and K. Wong, 'A Study of the Relationship between Corporate Governance Structures and the Extent of Voluntary Disclosure', *Journal of International Accounting, Auditing and Taxation*, 10 (2001), 139; S. Cheng et al., 'The Influence of Corporate Governance Structure on Executive Pay', *Research in Business and Economics Journal*, 3 (2011), 1.

[92] Y. Cheung et al., 'Do Investors Really Value Corporate Governance? Evidence from the Hong Kong Market', *Journal of International Financial Management and Accounting*, 18(2) (2007), 86, 106.

[93] A. Lei and D. Deng, 'Do Multiple Directorships Increase Firm Value? Evidence from Independent Directors in Hong Kong', *Journal of International Financial Management and Accounting*, 25(2) (2014), 121; see also F. Cheng, 'Corporate Governance in Hong Kong: An Empirical Study of the Effects of Independent Non-Executive Directors on Voluntary Corporate Disclosures and Adoption of Best Corporate Governance Practices' (City University of Hong Kong Institutional Repository, 2011) available at http://dspace.cityu.edu.hk.

[94] Lei and Deng, 'Do Multiple Directorships Increase Firm Value? Evidence from Independent Directors in Hong Kong', 157.

[95] *Ibid.*, 168–169.

5 *Alternative Methods of Minority Protection and Enforcement*

These studies do not, however, resolve the question of independence, and issues frequently raised include the lack of experience of independent directors[96] and the risk that independent directors have strong pecuniary incentives to vote with the majority of the board.[97] A further issue related to effectiveness is the fact that the main remedy of independent directors who are dissatisfied with the actions of their board is to resign from office.[98] A listed company must provide reasons publicly in relation to the retirement of a person as an independent non-executive director, which in theory puts additional pressure on the company to ensure that the director's complaints have been addressed – but this is effective only if the director is prepared to go public with his complaints.[99]

Another way of trying to examine the effectiveness of independent directors is to examine cases and disciplinary proceedings brought by the Exchange and the SFC (as well as derivative actions brought by shareholders). To what extent are the independent directors held to account for the way in which they fulfil their role? A related question is the extent to which enforcement in relation to minority protection is actually undertaken by the SFC or shareholders themselves rather than by independent directors.

The Exchange may take action against directors and has done so relatively frequently. Disciplinary action against the independent directors of listed companies has been infrequent, but appears to be becoming more common since 2012, when the directors, including the independent directors, of Zhejiang Prospect Company Limited were censured (and ordered to undergo training) by the GEM Listing Committee for their failure to properly announce certain significant transactions.[100] There were two further cases in 2014 in which independent directors were

[96] Arner et al., *Assessing Hong Kong as an International Financial Centre: First Report of the Hong Kong Research Grants Council Theme-Based Research Scheme Project: Enhancing Hong Kong's Future as a Leading International Financial Centre*, 123, who recommend an apprentice system and the creation of a profession of corporate directors.

[97] *Ibid.*, 126.

[98] Ho, 'Restructuring the Boards of Directors of Public Companies in Hong Kong: Barking up the Wrong Tree', 523.

[99] Code Provision A.3.4; Section 8, Companies (Directors' Reports) Regulations, c. 622D.

[100] Stock Exchange of Hong Kong, 'HKEx News Release (GEM Listing Committee Censure of Zhejiang Prospect Company Limited)' (26 September 2012) available at www.hkex.com.hk.

criticised.[101] In the case of Richly Field China Development Limited at the beginning of 2015,[102] the former Chairman and executive director and another former executive director were censured, and one former executive director, two former non-executive and three former independent directors were criticised for their failure to take the appropriate action when a major issue in the company's internal controls became apparent and directed to undertake 24 hours of Listing Rule compliance training as a pre-requisite to any future appointment as a director. (In addition to directors' training, the Listing Committee often requires the appointment of a professional compliance officer, suggesting that the Exchange sees as a major problem the lack of knowledge of the directors relating to their obligations as directors of a listed company.)

The SFC can bring enforcement actions through the courts (criminal action), to the Market Misconduct Tribunal (civil action) and, under the SFO, may seek remedies essentially on behalf of affected investors, including in cases where minority protections or the protections in the Listing Rules have failed. The SFC has sweeping power under the SFO,[103] particularly sections 213 and 214 (which relate specifically to listed corporations), to bring cases to the court[104] or the Market Misconduct Tribunal alleging market misconduct.[105] Shareholders also have direct access to the courts.

Under section 213, the SFC may apply to the court for a range of orders, including restraining and restoration orders, for contraventions of the Ordinance. Similarly, section 214(1) allows the SFC to apply to the

[101] See also Stock Exchange of Hong Kong, 'HKEx News Release; Censure of Long Success International (Holdings) Limited' (18 August 2014), available at www.hkex.com.hk (censure of a former independent director for failing to cooperate with the investigation: training ordered; criticism of all other directors for passivity on the board in failing to investigate unilateral actions of one director which were potentially detrimental to the company); Stock Exchange of Hong Kong, 'HKEx News Release; Censure of Huscoke Resources Holdings Ltd' (28 January 2014), available at www.hkex.com.hk (failure to disclose company's financial condition; directors, including independent directors, criticised for breach of undertaking due to failure to use best endeavours to remain informed of company's financial situation or to act proactively: training ordered).

[102] Stock Exchange of Hong Kong, 'HKEx News Release; Censure of Richly Field China Development Limited' (21 January 2015), available at www.hkex.com.hk.

[103] Securities and Futures Ordinance, c. 571 (Hong Kong).

[104] The SFC has power to investigate, among other things, potential actions oppressive to the shareholders pursuant to Section 179, Securities and Futures Ordinance, c. 571 (Hong Kong).

[105] Section 252, Securities and Futures Ordinance, c. 571(Hong Kong).

court for a remedy in relation to a listed corporation if it considers that the business or affairs of the company have been conducted in a manner which is oppressive to its members or part thereof, which involves fraud or failure to provide information or which was unfairly prejudicial.[106]

The SFC has become increasingly active in bringing enforcement actions,[107] although its activism and choice of targets are not universally admired.[108] The ability of the SFC to enforce the return of funds to an issuer (thus protecting the interests of the shareholders) may on occasion present a strong contrast with the failures in corporate governance which resulted in the case being brought and the ability – or willingness – of the independent directors to monitor the board's activities or improve corporate governance. The recent case of *SFC v Yin and others*[109] related to the approval and signature by the executive directors of a document designed to justify a large payment to the controlling shareholder of the listed company (First China Network Limited). The independent directors at that time do not appear to have been told about the relevant transaction, although it appears several of them had resigned over the related issue of the board's handling of receivables owed to the listed company by companies connected to the controlling shareholder. When the SFC brought a case on behalf of the company to recover the funds paid to the controlling shareholder, the new independent directors approved the giving of an indemnity by the company to the directors in respect of the legal costs of defending the case. The judge described this as 'a very poor reflection of the corporate governance exercised over the company'.[110]

Part 14 of the Companies Ordinance (which extends to non-Hong Kong companies) allows the court to make any order it thinks fit if satisfied, on the application of a member or the Financial Secretary or past member that 'the company's affairs are being or have been conducted in a manner unfairly prejudicial to the interests of the members generally or of one or more members (including the member)' or

[106] Securities and Futures Commission, '2011/2012 Annual Report 40: Operational Review: Enforcement' (2012), 40–44, available at www.sfc.hk.

[107] Freshfields Bruckhaus Deringer, 'Enforcement Trends in Hong Kong: A Surge in Scrutiny' (January 2014), available at www.freshfields.com; Freshfields Bruckhaus Deringer, 'Enforcement Trends in Hong Kong: An Uptick in Scrutiny' (29 January 2015), available at www.freshfields.com.

[108] Jake Van Der Kamp, 'Securities and Futures Commission Has Spun out of Control', *South China Morning Post*, 4 January 2015, available at www.scmp.com.

[109] *Securities and Futures Commission v Yin Yingneng Richard and others* HCMP 2502/2012 (High Court of the Hong Kong SAR).

[110] *Ibid.*, [208] per Chan J.

an act, proposed act or omission of the company would be unfairly prejudicial. This extends to acts of third parties and covers derivative actions. Shareholders also retain the right to bring a common law derivative action. Cheng argues that shareholders are willing to bring cases to defend their rights in the Hong Kong courts because they have confidence in the courts and their chances of winning if their case is strong.[111] Shareholders have been quite prepared to bring both unfair prejudice cases against listed companies,[112] as well as derivative actions.[113] There must, however, be a question whether these cases cast doubt on the efficacy of the role played by the independent directors at the board level.

IV Summary and Conclusion

Since the introduction of independent directors in 1993, independent directors have become an increasingly important part of the corporate governance structure in the Hong Kong markets. Over the last 20 or so years, the Exchange, the SFC, the Hong Kong government and other Hong Kong regulators have revised laws and regulations and substantially modified the Listing Rules and listing requirements to impose a higher standard of transparency and corporate governance on listed companies in Hong Kong. The role (and numbers) of the independent directors have increased, with responsibilities ranging from the role of providing an independent voice on the board, to roles on board committees and in advising the independent shareholders of the company. Hong Kong regulators have seen the institution of independent directors as integral to the provision of minority shareholder protection.

[111] W. Cheng, 'Protection of Minority Shareholders in Hong Kong and China: Do Culture and Institutional Design Make Any Difference?', *North Ireland Legal Quarterly*, 61 (2010), 53.

[112] See Arner et al., *Assessing Hong Kong as an International Financial Centre: First Report of the Hong Kong Research Grants Council Theme-Based Research Scheme Project: Enhancing Hong Kong's Future as a Leading International Financial Centre*, 99, 127, for a summary of *Luck Continent Ltd v Cheng Chee Tock Theodore* [2012] HKEC 567, affirmed on appeal at [2013] 4 HKLRD 181.

[113] P. Kwan, 'Statutory Derivative Actions: New Hope for Minority Shareholders?' (2 April 2012), available at www.deacons.com.hk. See, for example, the failed action in *World One Investments Limited v Chow and others* [2013] 3 HKLRD 701 (company listed on the GEM Market; no fraud on the minority); *Grand Field Group Holdings Ltd v Tsang Wa Lun Wayland and others* [2010] 4 HKLRD 487 (High Court of the Hong Kong SAR).

There is, however, doubt as to their effectiveness in this role. Most of the criticisms relating to the efficacy of independent directors appear to be directed at the persons who are chosen as independent directors, with the view being taken that the guidelines relating to independence are not satisfactory; the talent pool in Hong Kong is too small; the controlling shareholders invariably choose the directors, so they cannot in fact be independent; the existing directors choose their friends and professional associates, so there is no true diversity on the board; the incentives on the board discourage true independence and best corporate governance practice is to have a majority of independent directors on the board. The Exchange has, over time, tried to deal with many of these complaints through the medium of the Listing Rules, by adding new criteria relating to independence, recommending diversity, requiring training programmes for directors and so on. However, it has not mandated gender diversity, for example, nor has it been responsive to comments that the independent shareholders should choose the independent directors or that independent directors should comprise a majority of the board of directors.

At the same time, both the Exchange and the SFC have become more active in relation to enforcement. It should be noted, however, that a court case is generally effective to remedy a relatively long-standing series of abuses, while the role of the independent directors is to monitor and prevent the abuses in the first place. The prominence of the independent directors on board committees and the need for their approval for major transactions does potentially give them a major role if that role is truly exercised in an independent fashion.

The studies certainly suggest that the success of independent directors depends on the personal qualities of independence and expertise of the persons selected to play that role. Thus, although training can certainly be helpful, the manner of selection is highly relevant. A nomination committee, which is composed of existing directors, will not necessarily look to a truly diverse range of candidates, particularly if it is chaired by the chairman of the board rather than an independent director (Code Provision A.5.1). Similarly, the controlling shareholder has little incentive to vote for or support the appointment of directors who are likely to be truly independent and therefore unpredictable. The next step in corporate governance in Hong Kong, therefore, should be to look more closely at the United Kingdom Listing Rules and the advice of a number of outside commentators and to introduce elections for independent directors by the minority shareholders. The Exchange could also consider the role of the senior independent director as it exists in the UK. Since this role appears to be to act as a sounding board for other independent directors if they find it difficult to deal with the chairman or executive and to coordinate with the major shareholders,[114] it may well be helpful in the Hong Kong context. Compulsory requirements in relation to diversity would also allow for the talent pool to be broadened and extend selection of directors beyond the group of Hong Kong friends and professional colleagues.

[114] Prism Cosec, *A Spotlight on Senior Independent Directors* (December 2011), available at www.prismcosec.com.

9

Independent Directors in Singapore

A Corporate Governance Outlier?

DAN W. PUCHNIAK AND LUH LUH LAN*

I Introduction

When Singapore needed to bolster its corporate governance in the wake of the 2001 Asian Financial Crisis, it looked to Anglo-America for solutions. Back then, the American independent director stood out as the most recognisable global symbol for good corporate governance.[1] Independent directors were (and still largely are) credited with transforming American boardrooms from inept managerial clubs into effective managerial-monitors.[2] In the UK, the London Stock Exchange was

* This chapter is a condensed version of the article: D. W. Puchniak and L. L. Lan, 'Independent Directors in Singapore: Puzzling Compliance Requiring Explanation', *American Journal of Comparative Law*, 65 (2017) (forthcoming), available at https://doi.org/10.1093/ajcl/avx023. For additional empirical data, citations, tables and arguments supporting the points made in this chapter please see the *American Journal of Comparative Law* article. Many thanks to the *American Journal of Comparative Law* for giving us permission to publish this condensed version of our article, and to the National University of Singapore Centre for Asian Legal Studies (CALS) and EW Barker Centre for Law & Business (EWBCLB) for funding this research.

[1] R. Gilson, 'Controlling Shareholders and Corporate Governance', *Harvard Law Review*, 119 (2006), 1641, 1647; R. Gilson, 'Globalizing Corporate Governance: Convergence of Form or Function', *American Journal of Comparative Law*, 49 (2001), 329, 331, but see D. W. Puchniak, 'The Japanization of American Corporate Governance? Evidence of the Never-Ending History for Corporate Law', *Asian-Pacific Law and Policy Journal*, 9 (2007), 7.

[2] J. Gordon, 'The Rise of Independent Directors in the United States, 1950–2005: Of Shareholder Value and Stock Market Prices', *Stanford Law Review*, 59 (2007), 1465. For comparative analyses see, B. R. Cheffins, 'The History of Modern U.S. Corporate

thriving as its dispersedly held American-style Berle-Means type companies embraced American-style independent monitoring boards.[3] The UK's implementation of American-style independent directors, through its market-driven 'comply or explain' Code of Corporate Governance, was the avant-garde of corporate governance reform.[4] From this perspective, Singapore's decision in 2001 to adopt American-style independent directors on a 'comply or explain' basis, appeared highly conventional. As history would have it, however, it turned out to be anything but.

This chapter reveals that Singapore's embrace of American-style independent directors made it a corporate governance outlier. As explained in section II below, the widely held belief that the American concept of the independent director has been transplanted around the world is a myth. The reality, which our review of the rules governing independent directors in 245 corporate governance codes from 87 jurisdictions reveals, is that only a handful of jurisdictions have ever adopted the American concept of the independent director (i.e., where directors who are independent from management *only* – but not substantial shareholders – are deemed to be independent). Most jurisdictions with controlling-block shareholders[5] merely adopted the term 'independent director' from the US, while requiring directors to be independent from management *and* significant shareholders (i.e., the *Un*-American concept of the independent director). This alters the core function of the 'independent director' from being a corporate governance mechanism designed to monitor management on behalf of dispersed shareholders, to one designed to monitor controlling shareholders on behalf of minority shareholders.[6]

Governance: Introduction' in B. R. Cheffins (ed.), *The History of Modern U.S. Corporate Governance* (Edward Elgar, 2012), ix–xli, xxix; P. L. Davies and K. J. Hopt, 'Corporate Boards in Europe: Accountability and Convergence', *American Journal of Comparative Law*, 61(2) (2013), 301, 323; D. W. Puchniak, 'Multiple Faces of Shareholder Power in Asia: Complexity Revealed' in J. G. Hill and R. S. Thomas (eds.), *Research Handbook on Shareholder Power* (Edward Elgar, 2015), 511, 516.

3 B. R. Cheffins, 'The History of Corporate Governance' in M. Wright et al. (eds.), *Oxford Handbook of Corporate Governance* (Oxford University Press, 2013), 5–20.

4 *Ibid.*, 19–20.

5 S. Claessens et al., 'The Separation of Ownership and Control in East Asian Corporations', *Journal of Financial Economics*, 58 (2000), 81, 82, 84; H. Huang, 'Shareholder Derivative Litigation in China: Empirical Findings and Comparative Analysis', *Banking and Finance Law Review*, 27 (2012), 619, 625, 649; R. La Porta et al., 'Corporate Ownership around the World', *Journal of Finance*, 54 (1999), 471, 472, 491–498; Puchniak, 'Multiple Faces of Shareholder Power in Asia: Complexity Revealed', 524–525.

6 Davies and Hopt, 'Corporate Boards in Europe: Accountability and Convergence', 324.

Against this backdrop, Singapore's status as a corporate governance outlier becomes glaringly visible. The vast majority of listed companies in Singapore have highly concentrated block-shareholding structures.[7] This raises the first puzzle: why would Singapore's highly-skilled regulators deviate from the seemingly logical and well-trodden path of other controlling-shareholder-dominated jurisdictions by transplanting the American concept of the independent director into Singapore's controlling-shareholder environment and maintaining it for over a decade?

Strange as this decision may be, the response of listed companies in Singapore presents an even more intriguing puzzle. Rather than shun the 2001 Code's seemingly ill-defined and functionally irrelevant American-style independent directors, listed companies in Singapore embraced them with vigour – the opposite of what agency theory and leading corporate governance scholars would have predicted.[8] Shortly after the 2001 Code went into force in 2003, an overwhelming 96 per cent of Singapore-listed companies reported full compliance with the Code's recommendation that one-third of the board be composed of American-style independent directors. Not long after that, 98 per cent of Singapore-listed companies reported full compliance, with a majority of all directors in Singapore reportedly being 'independent'.[9] These extraordinary statistics raise a second intriguing puzzle: why did listed companies in Singapore embrace seemingly functionally irrelevant American-style independent directors, and what role (if any) have these directors played in Singapore corporate governance?

To add a final twist to this bemusing regulatory tale, after more than a decade of near-perfect compliance, Singapore recently decided to abandon its support of American-style independent directors. The 2012 Code of Corporate Governance (2012 Code), which went into force in

[7] Claessens et al., 'The Separation of Ownership and Control in East Asian Corporations', 104; C. H. Tan et al., 'State-Owned Enterprises in Singapore: Historical Insights into a Potential Model for Reform', *Columbia Journal of Asian Law*, 28 (2015), 61, 66–67; L. H. Tan, 'Exploring the Question of the Separation of Ownership from Control: An Empirical Study of the Structure of Corporate Ownership in Singapore's Top Listed Companies' (Working Paper, 2011), 17, 20, 25, available at http://docs.business.auckland.ac.nz.

[8] W. Ringe, 'Independent Directors: After the Crisis', *European Business Organization Law Review*, 14(3) (2013), 401, 413–414.

[9] H. Tjio, *Principles and Practice of Securities Regulation in Singapore*, 2nd edn (LexisNexis, 2011), 326.

early 2015, requires independent directors to be independent from management and from shareholders holding more than 10 per cent of the company's shares.[10] This raises the final puzzle: why, after more than a decade of near-perfect compliance, has Singapore decided to abandon American-style independent directors; and what impact (if any) may this have on the future of corporate governance in Singapore?

This chapter offers solutions to these three puzzles and explores the comparative corporate law lessons that can be derived from the intriguing rise of independent directors in Singapore. The remainder of this chapter proceeds as follows. Section II describes how historical evidence suggests that Singapore's seemingly illogical decision to adopt and maintain American-style independent directors for over a decade was the product of effective strategic regulatory design. Section III explains how the functionality of independent directors in Singapore varies depending on the *identity* of a company's controlling shareholder, particularly for Family-Controlled Firms (Family Firms) versus the state-controlled companies (Government-Linked Companies). Section IV examines the various factors behind Singapore's recent decision to abandon the American-style independent director and its potential impact on Singapore corporate governance. Finally, although this is a Singapore story, we posit in Part V that it raises important broader questions for comparative corporate law theory.

II The Rise of American-Style Independent Directors in Singapore

1 *In the (American) Independent Director We Trust*

The genesis of the independent director as a global mechanism for good corporate governance can be traced to the US in the 1970s. Before this, American boards were seen largely as an extension of corporate management, composed of senior executives and some outsiders with deep connections to the company (e.g., bankers, lawyers or suppliers). In the 1970s, there was a paradigm shift. Scathing academic evidence of the abysmal failure of insider-dominated advisory boards and the rise of the social responsibility movement changed the way Americans viewed the

[10] Article 2.3, Code of Corporate Governance (Monetary Authority of Singapore, 2012); Monetary Authority of Singapore, 'Response to Recommendations by the Corporate Governance Council on the Code of Corporate Governance' (2012), 9, available at www.mas.gov.sg [hereinafter *Response to Recommendations 2012*].

primary function of corporate boards. The board was no longer to be a body of friendly trusted advisors to the CEO, but a group of independent monitors watching over the CEO and senior management.[11]

The concept of a 'monitoring model' was first proposed as an aspirational academic theory by Professor Melvin Eisenberg.[12] Eisenberg's academic theory became quasi-legislation when the NYSE amended its listing rules in 1977 to require all listed companies to have an audit committee composed of directors who were independent from management.[13] By the 1990s, Eisenberg's aspirational managerial-monitoring model was fully entrenched as a primary feature of American corporate governance, with a majority of directors on American boards being independent *from management.*[14]

As the story goes, the American concept of the independent director then went global. Following the collapse of the Japanese and German economies in the 1990s, the American model of corporate governance became the standard-bearer for global norms of 'good' corporate governance.[15] In the 2000s, the UK with its 'comply or explain' Combined Code of Corporate Governance (UK Code) also emerged as a leader in promoting norms of good corporate governance around the world.[16]

The US and UK were viewed as promoting similar corporate governance norms, with independent managerial-monitoring boards being a

[11] Gordon, 'The Rise of Independent Directors in the United States', 1513–1514; U. Varottil, 'Evolution and Effectiveness of Independent Directors in Indian Corporate Governance', *Hastings Business Law Journal*, 6 (2010), 281, 294; U. Velikonja, 'The Political Economy of Board Independence', *North Carolina Law Review*, 92 (2014), 855, 863–864.

[12] M. A. Eisenberg, *The Structure of the Corporation: A Legal Analysis* (Little, Brown and Company, 1976), 162–170; Gordon, 'The Rise of Independent Directors in the United States', 1518; Varottil, 'Evolution and Effectiveness of Independent Directors in Indian Corporate Governance', 295.

[13] Cheffins, 'The History of Corporate Governance', 3; Gordon, 'The Rise of Independent Directors in the United States', 1518; Velikonja, 'The Political Economy of Board Independence', 883.

[14] Velikonja, 'The Political Economy of Board Independence', 863–864. For further information on the historical development of the concept of the independent director in the US, see Chapter 1 at III.

[15] Gilson, 'Controlling Shareholders and Corporate Governance', 1647; Gilson, 'Globalizing Corporate Governance: Convergence of Form or Function', 331; Puchniak, 'The Japanization of American Corporate Governance? Evidence of the Never-Ending History for Corporate Law', 20–21.

[16] Cheffins, 'The History of Corporate Governance', 12–13, 19–20, 22; Varottil, 'Evolution and Effectiveness of Independent Directors in Indian Corporate Governance', 282, 306.

hallmark of the Anglo-American approach.[17] However, although the inaugural UK Code largely adopted the American concept of the independent director, it was amended in 2003 to require independent directors to be independent from management *and* significant shareholders.[18] That the UK subsequently abandoned the American concept of the independent director is a significant corporate governance event which has been almost entirely overlooked.[19]

As the story goes, the new millennium ushered in the global era of the American independent director, which had apparently been transplanted around the world.[20] Following Japan's lost decade (1990–2000) and the Asian Financial Crisis (1997–1999), Asian countries ostensibly took steps to shore up their maligned corporate governance systems by either heralding the arrival of American-style independent directors as evidence of 'good' corporate governance or implementing them as a forced condition of international financial aid.[21] Today, prominent academics speak of the 'unequalled [global] triumph of the concept of director independence', which ostensibly originated in the US.[22]

[17] A Google search of the term 'Anglo-American corporate governance' done on 6 July 2015 produced 11,200 results. This provides useful insight into how this term has entrenched itself in the comparative corporate governance lexicon.

[18] Section 1(A.3.1), The Combined Code on Corporate Governance (Financial Reporting Council, 2003), available at www.ecgi.org/codes/documents/combined_code_final.pdf. This was at the recommendation of D. Higgs, 'Review of the Role and Effectiveness of the Non-Executive Directors' (2003), available at www.ecgi.org/codes/documents/higgsreport.pdf [hereinafter Higgs' Report].

[19] Indeed, as Davies and Hopt astutely note, more generally, the critical point of how to define independence in the context of controlled companies has also often been overlooked (see Davies and Hopt, 'Corporate Boards in Europe: Accountability and Convergence', 320–324). For further information on the development of independent directors in the UK and Europe generally, see Chapter 1 at IV.

[20] B. R. Cheffins, 'Corporate Governance Reform: Britain as an Exporter' in David Hume Institute, *Hume Papers on Public Policy: Corporate Governance and the Reform of the Company Law* (Edinburgh University Press, 2000); D. C. Langevoort, 'The Human Nature of Corporate Boards: Law, Norms, and the Unintended Consequences of Independence and Accountability', *Georgetown Law Journal*, 89 (2001), 797, 798.

[21] For example, Japan (see D. W. Puchniak, 'The 2002 Reform of the Management of Large Corporations in Japan', *The Australian Journal of Asian Law*, 5 (2003), 42), and Korea (see H. Kim, 'Living with the IMF: A New Approach to Corporate Governance and Regulation of Financial Institutions in Korea', *Berkeley Journal of International Law*, 17 (1999), 61, 74). See Chapter 5 (South Korea) at III.1; Chapter 7 (Taiwan) at II.1; Chapter 8 (Hong Kong) at II; Chapter 10 (India) at III.

[22] Ringe, 'Independent Directors: After the Crisis', 412; R. Kraakman et al., *The Anatomy of Corporate Law: A Comparative and Functional Approach*, 2nd edn (Oxford University Press, 2009), 65.

However, leading academics have struggled to explain the driving forces behind the global rise of the independent director.[23] Despite numerous empirical studies, there is a surprising absence of empirical evidence in the US and around the world that independent directors improve corporate performance or reduce corporate wrongdoing.[24] This lack of empirical evidence has not prevented every country that we examined (87 in total) from adopting provisions to promote independent directors in all of their corporate governance codes (245 in total).[25] Despite this dearth of empirical evidence, the conventional wisdom that the American-style independent director has come to dominate corporate governance in the US and has ostensibly been transplanted around the world remains largely unquestioned.[26]

2 *The Mythical Transplant of the American Independent Director*

Over the last decade, a more nuanced story about the global rise of the American independent director has emerged. Recent scholarship has explained how attempting to transplant the American independent director into jurisdictions outside the US and UK is akin to trying to fit a square peg into a round hole. Although the primary purpose for the American independent director may be clear in America (i.e., to monitor management on behalf of dispersed shareholders who are hindered by collective action problems from monitoring management themselves),[27] this purpose evaporates quickly once it is transplanted outside of its

[23] D. C. Clarke, 'Three Concepts of the Independent Director', *Delaware Journal of Corporate Law*, 32 (2007), 73, 77; Gordon, 'The Rise of Independent Directors in the United States', 1563; Velikonja, 'The Political Economy of Board Independence', 859.

[24] For example, see S. Bhagat and B. S. Black, 'The Non-Correlation between Board Independence and Long-Term Firm Performance', *Journal of Corporation Law*, 27 (2002), 231, 239; Y. Miwa and J. M. Ramseyer, 'Who Appoints Them, What Do They Do? Evidence on Outside Directors from Japan', *Journal of Economics and Management Strategy*, 14 (2005), 299.

[25] See discussion *infra* section II.3.

[26] L. A. Bebchuk and A. Hamdani, 'The Elusive Quest for Global Corporate Governance Standards', *University of Pennsylvania Law Review*, 157 (2009), 1263, 1302–1304, 1311; Gordon, 'The Rise of Independent Directors in the United States', n. 164.

[27] Gordon, 'The Rise of Independent Directors in the United States', 1477; Puchniak, 'Multiple Faces of Shareholder Power in Asia: Complexity Revealed', 512.

dispersed shareholder environment. In almost every jurisdiction, most listed companies are dominated by controlling-block shareholders who are fully capable of monitoring management directly or managing the company themselves. The American-style independent director becomes functionally redundant in these countries, at least from the perspective of agency theory.[28]

However, this recent scholarship tends to gloss over the reality that only a handful of jurisdictions has ever attempted to fit the square-American-independent-director-peg into the round controlling-block-shareholder-jurisdiction-hole.[29] The conventional story about the global rise of the American independent director does not merely lack nuance; rather, it is a myth. As we demonstrate below, it appears that what has been portrayed as one of the most prolific legal transplants of our time is actually a legal mechanism that has not been transplanted much at all.

3 *An Outlier among the Outliers*

Our review of what is, to our knowledge, the most complete Collection of Corporate Governance Codes (the CCGC, which contains 273 codes, from 94 developed and developing jurisdictions, on six continents, from a variety of legal traditions) confirms that contrary to conventional wisdom the American-style independent director has rarely been transplanted outside of the US.[30] In fact, based on our hand-compiled Database of Independent Director Definitions (DIDD) from the CCGC, only 8.1 per cent of jurisdictions (7 out of 87) currently use the American concept of the independent director in their codes.[31] Similarly, at the time that Singapore adopted its Code in 2001, only 16.7 per cent of jurisdictions (4 out of 24) used the American definition of independence in their codes.[32] In this sense, Singapore's decision to adopt the American

[28] Puchniak, 'Multiple Faces of Shareholder Power in Asia: Complexity Revealed', 513–514; D. C. Clarke, 'The Independent Director in Chinese Corporate Governance', *Delaware Journal of Corporate Law*, 31 (2006), 125; U. Varottil, 'Independent Directors and Their Constraints in China and India', *Jindal Global Law Review*, 2 (2007), 127.

[29] See discussion *infra* section II.3; Clarke, 'Three Concepts of the Independent Director', 73–111.

[30] Puchniak and Lan, 'Independent Directors in Singapore: Puzzling Compliance Requiring Explanation', Table 1.

[31] *Ibid.*

[32] *Ibid.*, Table 2.

independent director in its 2001 Code and maintain it for over a decade makes it a corporate governance outlier.[33]

To be fair, Singapore was one of the earliest adopters of a 'comply or explain' code.[34] When Singapore adopted its inaugural Code in 2001, the first versions of the UK Code and the OECD Model Code were in force, and neither explicitly required independence from significant shareholders.[35] However, in 2003 and 2004 respectively, both codes were revised and adopted the *Un*-American definition for independence.[36] Nevertheless, when Singapore's Council on Corporate Disclosure and Governance proposed a revised Code on 14 July 2005 (2005 Code),[37] the issue to include independence from significant shareholders was expressly brought up, but explicitly rejected.[38] Singapore's decision to maintain the American independent director in its 2005 Code arguably made it even more of a corporate governance outlier, since its decision was made in the face of two influential models for corporate governance reform moving away from the American concept of the independent director.[39]

Singapore also appears to stand out even among several other prominent jurisdictions – the UK, Russia, Germany, Japan and Canada – which at some point in their histories were seen to have adopted the American concept of the independent director. Indeed, in each of these 'outlier jurisdictions' there appears to be an obvious theoretical rationale for the adoption of the American independent director, which Singapore lacks.

33 *Ibid.* When Singapore adopted its Code in 2001, 24 countries had some form of governance codes for companies, but many had no definition or an unclear definition for independence. Out of the 17 countries with Codes that defined 'independence' only four (Japan, Singapore, Sweden and the Philippines) used the 'American' definition of independence. *Ibid.* at Appendix II.

34 Only Australia (1999), South Korea (1999), Malaysia (2000), the United Kingdom (2000) and the Czech Republic (2001) preceded Singapore in this regard. *Ibid.*

35 Section 1(A.3.2), The Combined Code: Code of Best Practice (Committee on Corporate Governance, 2000); Sections V(E), V(E)(1), OECD Principles of Corporate Governance (OECD, 1999).

36 Changes inspired by the UK and OECD definitions appear to have been especially evident for countries within the EU. No code within the EU currently employs an American definition.

37 See 'Regulations and Financial Stability: Code of Corporate Governance', Monetary Authority of Singapore, available at www.mas.gov.sg.

38 The Council on Corporate Disclosure and Governance, *Consultation Paper on Proposed Revisions to the Code of Corporate Governance* (2004), available at www.acga-asia.org.

39 In 2005, only 24 per cent of jurisdictions (12 out of 50) used the American definition of independence in their codes. Puchniak and Lan, 'Independent Directors in Singapore: Puzzling Compliance Requiring Explanation', Table 3.

The fact that the UK's inaugural Code did not clearly require independence from significant shareholders could have been justified because most UK listed companies have dispersed shareholders.[40] In any event, shortly after its adoption, the UK Code was revised to explicitly include independence from significant shareholders.[41] Russia's initial failure to explicitly require independence from significant shareholders made it a corporate governance outlier in Europe.[42] At least theoretically, however, Russia's mandatory cumulative voting in large companies creates a level of independence among minority shareholder-appointed directors from controlling shareholders, regardless of how independence is defined. In any event, Russia has also recently revised its Code to explicitly require independence from significant shareholders.

In a similar vein, Germany's initial vocal resistance to requiring independence from significant shareholders had a solid theoretical basis in its co-determination system,[43] where the mandatory labour representation required on its supervisory boards creates a degree of independence from controlling shareholders.[44] In any event, similar to several of the other outlier jurisdictions, Germany has included independence from controlling shareholders in its recently amended Code. In Japan, at least in theory, a lack of large-block shareholders and lifetime-employee-controlled boards makes the shareholder–manager agency problem (rather than the majority–minority agency problem) more salient – another justification for the American independent director which Singapore lacks.[45]

[40] Puchniak, 'Multiple Faces of Shareholder Power in Asia: Complexity Revealed', 524–525.

[41] Higgs' Report, para. 9.1.

[42] B. S. Black et al., 'Russian Privatization and Corporate Governance: What Went Wrong?', *Stanford Law Review*, 52 (2000), 1731; G. Ferrarini and M. Filippelli, 'Independent Directors and Controlling Shareholders around the World' (European Corporate Governance Institute (ECGI) – Law Working Paper No. 258/2014, 2014), 17, available at http://ssrn.com/abstract=2443786.

[43] Davies and Hopt, 'Corporate Boards in Europe: Accountability and Convergence', 320–321.

[44] *Ibid.*

[45] Although Japan theoretically has a dispersed shareholding environment, the reality is far more complex, see Puchniak, 'Multiple Faces of Shareholder Power in Asia: Complexity Revealed', 524, 530. In addition, an in-depth comparative analysis of Japan's optional 'American-style' independent director regime suggests that the inaugural definition it introduced for 'independence' in 2002 neither required independence from management nor significant shareholders. In this sense, arguably the inaugural definition of 'independence' in Japan could be considered to have adopted neither an American nor un-American independent director concept, as it did not require boards that opted for the 'American-style' structure to have any directors who were independent from management or significant shareholders – it merely required outside directors. This being

In addition, the combined effect of recent amendments to Japan's listing rules, Companies Act and its 2015 Corporate Governance Code have implemented some level of independence from controlling shareholders into Japan's optional independent director regime.[46] Finally, Canada's deep economic integration with the US has often caused it to dovetail a number of its corporate governance mechanisms with the American model – a final justification for the American independent director which does not exist in Singapore.[47]

The theoretical rationales above highlight the fact that when Singapore adopted and maintained the American independent director for over a decade, there was no obvious rationale for its outlier decision. Singapore's shareholding structure was (and still is) extremely concentrated.[48] Singapore company law does not provide any provisions that hardwire a level of independence from significant shareholders into the structure of corporate boards (e.g., mandatory employee representation or cumulative voting). Singapore's deviation from the seemingly logical and well-trodden path adopted in most other controlling-shareholder jurisdictions by transplanting the American concept of the independent director into its controlling-shareholder environment is therefore puzzling.

4 *Strategic Regulatory Design: Local Constraints, Signalling and Functional Substitutes*

There are two possible logical explanations for why Singapore's regulators made their outlier decision to transplant American-style independent

said, many commentators labelled the Japanese independent director system 'American-style' and the inaugural definition clearly did not require independence from significant shareholders – which is a hallmark of the American concept of the independent director. See Chapter 3 at II.3.

46 The 2015 Japanese Corporate Governance Code does not define independence but makes reference to the listing rules, which require independent directors to be independent from management and significant block shareholders – a position which is reinforced by the definition of 'outside director' in the recently reformed Companies Act. See Chapter 3 at II.3.

47 B. Reiter, 'What Makes a Director Independent', *Lexpert*, 15 February 2010; S. Griggs, 'Are Corporate Directors Really in Charge?', *Financial Post*, 24 January 2013, available at http://business.financialpost.com.

48 Claessens et al., 'The Separation of Ownership and Control in East Asian Corporations', 104; Tan et al., 'State-Owned Enterprises in Singapore: Historical Insights into a Potential Model for Reform', 66–67; Tan, 'Exploring the Question of the Separation of Ownership from Control', 17, 20, 25.

directors into Singapore's controlling shareholder environment and maintain it for over a decade. One possibility is that Singapore's regulators were ignorant of the critical differences between the corporate governance environments in the US and Singapore. Another possibility is that they were acutely aware of the differences, but nevertheless decided to adopt the American independent director and maintain it for over a decade for strategic reasons.

Historical evidence suggests that the second possibility – strategic regulatory design – was the more likely basis for Singapore's outlier decision. Understanding the broader regulatory environment in which this specific regulatory decision was made is important here. Singapore is a small country that relies heavily on foreign inflows of capital, and has been extremely successful in attracting it.[49] One key reason for Singapore's success has been its ability to signal 'good' governance to international markets through its compliance with international standards.[50]

Singapore's regulation of its independent directors is an example of its penchant for using strategic regulatory signalling (i.e., what we coin 'halo signalling') to attract foreign investment. Over the last decade, Singapore's success in signalling 'good' corporate governance is evident in its first-place ranking in Asia for corporate governance on numerous occasions by various organisations,[51] and the high level of compliance with its corporate governance code, which itself is often seen as a proxy for good corporate governance. Singapore's relatively high number of independent directors has played an important role in its high corporate governance rankings and its high compliance rates.[52]

Singapore's strategy of attracting foreign capital through corporate governance signalling was forged in the early 2000s following the Asian Financial Crisis. The Singapore government established the

[49] Tan et al., 'State-Owned Enterprises in Singapore: Historical Insights into a Potential Model for Reform', 78–79; H. Auyong, 'Singapore Productivity Challenge Part I', Lee Kuan Yew School of Public Policy, available at http://lkyspp.nus.edu.sg.

[50] Tan et al., 'State-Owned Enterprises in Singapore: Historical Insights into a Potential Model for Reform', 65–66.

[51] Asian Corporate Governance Association (ACGA) and KPMG, *Balancing Rules and Flexibility* (2014), 19–20, available at www.accaglobal.com; Y. T. Mak (ed.), *Corporate Governance Case Studies*, Vol. II (CPA Australia, 2013), 2, available at http://governanceforstakeholders.com.

[52] Tjio, *Principles and Practice of Securities Regulation in Singapore*, 326; ACGA and KPMG, *Balancing Rules and Flexibility*, app. C, 70–77.

private-sector-led Corporate Governance Committee (CGC) in 2000 to 'attract and retain international capital' in listed companies in Singapore by making 'Singapore a financial hub of international standing'.[53] The CGC, composed of 13 highly qualified members representing a broad range of corporate stakeholders, spent a year studying 'international best practice benchmarks in corporate governance in major jurisdictions'.[54] The CGC then issued a Report and a Draft Code in 2001 proposing that Singapore adopt a UK-style 'comply or explain' code, with American-style independent directors at its core.[55]

From this perspective, the CGC's proposal for the 2001 Code makes perfect sense. By proposing the adoption of American-style independent directors as a global standard for good corporate governance in Singapore, the CGC captured the sentiment of global investors and corporate governance pundits in the early 2000s. The government accepted and maintained the CGC's suggested adoption of American-style independent directors for at least three other reasons. Interestingly, none of these three reasons appear to have anything to do with Professor Eisenberg's managerial-monitoring model, and point to the Singapore government's skilful use of strategic regulatory design to address local (often idiosyncratic) conditions.

First, adopting American-style independent directors would not risk excluding a significant percentage of Singapore's small and tight-knit pool of talented directors from sitting on the boards of listed companies. As described in section III below, quantitative and qualitative evidence suggest that a significant portion of 'independent' directors in listed companies in Singapore have strong connections with the company's controlling shareholder. By accepting the CGC's recommendation to adopt American-style independent directors, the Singapore government was able to create a system that promotes compliance of listed companies in Singapore with international standards of 'good' corporate governance, while ensuring that the talent level of directors in listed companies was not eroded by a rush to compliance.

Second, adopting American-style independent directors all but guaranteed exceptionally high compliance rates with the independent director provisions in the 2001 Code. This is because controlling shareholders

[53] Corporate Governance Committee, *Consultation Paper* (2000), 1, available at www.mas.gov.sg.

[54] *Ibid.*, 1.

[55] Corporate Governance Committee, *Report of the Committee and Code of Corporate Governance* (2001), available at www.acra.gov.sg.

could maintain control, while complying with the Code by selecting directors who were independent of management, but with whom they had a connection and could therefore trust. The ease with which listed companies could comply with the independent director requirements in the 2001 Code is evident, since two years after the 'comply and explain' regime became mandatory, 96 per cent of companies listed in Singapore complied with the one-third board requirement. After five years, compliance was at an astounding 98 per cent and a majority of directors in listed companies were reportedly independent – far exceeding the recommendation in the 2001 Code.

Indeed, a significant portion of independent directors may have in essence been 'created' purely by strategic regulatory design, as *existing directors* were defined to be 'independent'. In 2002, before the 'comply or explain' regime even became mandatory, 80 per cent of companies already complied with the requirement that one-third of their board must be American-style independent directors. It seems that the government's decision to adopt American-style independent directors merely added a visible label to directors who were already on boards to begin with.

Third, as explained in section III below, Singapore has functional substitutes that mitigate the private benefits of control which *Un*-American independent directors are designed to address. The government's decision to adopt American-style independent directors may have been partly based on the belief that American-style independent directors did not present the same corporate governance risk as they might have in other controlling shareholder environments because of these unique functional substitutes. As explained in section IV, these functional substitutes appear to have been ineffective in controlling wealth tunnelling in PRC-Controlled Firms (i.e., companies that are listed on the Singapore Exchange but whose operations and controlling shareholders are located in mainland China) – one factor which appears to have driven the eventual adoption of the *Un*-American independent director in the 2012 Code.

In sum, the historical evidence suggests that Singapore's seemingly illogical decision to adopt American-style independent directors was the product of strategic regulatory design. It also appears that the government's decision was effective, at least from the perspective of maintaining the quality of directors and sending a signal of good corporate governance. PRC-Controlled Firms aside, Singapore has had relatively few problems with controlling shareholders in listed companies abusing their power to extract private benefits of control. The government's faith in the effectiveness of functional substitutes for the *Un*-American independent director appears to have been rational – especially considering the economic success of publicly listed Government-Linked Companies and Family Firms in Singapore, which we explain below.

III The Function of American-Style Independent Directors in Singapore

1 *Understanding Why Controlling Shareholders in Singapore Have Embraced American-Style Independent Directors*

Since 1989, all companies listed in Singapore must have at least two independent directors on their boards.[56] This requirement, however, does not account for the reality that over half of the directors on the boards of listed companies in Singapore have been American-style independent directors since the 2000s.[57] Although the 2001 Code required only one-third of the board to be composed of American-style independent directors, the Code is based on a 'comply or explain' regime and the percentage of independent directors on the boards of listed companies has consistently exceeded the Code's recommendation.[58] Much of the rise of American-style independent directors in Singapore has thus occurred in an 'unregulated space'.

In this context, it is important to note that an independent director must be elected by a majority shareholder vote in order to sit on the board of a listed company in Singapore. Therefore, in Singapore's controlling shareholder environment, American-style independent directors must have the support of the company's controlling shareholder. The rise of American-style independent directors demonstrates that controlling shareholders in Singapore's listed companies strongly support having American-style independent directors on the boards of the companies they control.

To understand why controlling shareholders in Singapore have embraced American-style independent directors with such vigour, we must first consider the unique governance structure and

[56] Section 21, Companies Amendment Act, 1989, c. 40; Tjio, *Principles and Practice of Securities Regulation in Singapore*, 323.

[57] Tjio, *Principles and Practice of Securities Regulation in Singapore*, 326.

[58] *Ibid.*

regulatory architecture that shapes Family Firms and Government-Linked Companies in Singapore. Against this backdrop, the various functions that American-style independent directors perform in Family Firms and Government-Linked Companies, and the diverse incentives that drive them, become clear.

2 *The Function of American-Style Independent Directors in Family Firms: Signallers, Mediators and Advisors*

Family Firms are ubiquitous among listed companies in Singapore. According to a recent in-depth empirical study, up to 60.8 per cent of listed companies in Singapore can be classified as Family Firms. However, Family Firms tend to be smaller than non-Family Firms; despite their large numbers, they collectively represent only 33.1 per cent of Singapore's market capitalisation.[59] Nevertheless, since Family Firms account for a healthy majority of Singapore listed companies and approximately a third of Singapore's market capitalisation, understanding the role of American-style independent directors in Family Firms is essential.

There are three facts that are critical for understanding the corporate governance environment in which American-style independent directors operate in Family Firms. First, empirical evidence suggests that family members collectively hold large controlling blocks of shares in Family Firms. On average, the top five largest shareholders in Family Firms control a 65.9 per cent stake, with 38.3 per cent being directly traceable to family members. The top 20 largest shareholders also control on average an astounding 80.5 per cent stake, highlighting the extent of the concentration of shareholding in Family Firms.[60] Thus, Singapore family members often collectively enjoy actual control (either directly or indirectly) over Family Firms through their voting rights.

Second, the same study suggests that family members collectively utilise their large blocks of voting shares to dominate the corporate governance of Family Firms by controlling and entrenching themselves in the most important executive and board positions. This is illustrated by the dominance that family members have in leadership positions in Family

[59] M. Dieleman et al., *Success and Succession: A Study of SGX-Listed Family Firms* (2013), 9, available at http://bschool.nus.edu [hereinafter *Success and Succession*].

[60] *Ibid.*, 21.

Firms: 78.6 per cent of CEOs and 72.9 per cent of chairpersons are family members. In 42.8 per cent of Family Firms, the positions of CEO and chairperson are combined, in contrast to non-Family Firms where only 17.0 per cent combine the positions of CEO and chairperson. The average tenure of family member directors in Family Firms is 15.7 years (for non-founder directors) to 20.7 years (for founding directors) as compared to 7.5 years for non-family-member directors – suggesting that family members also use their controlling power to entrench themselves in those positions.

Third, the study also shows that Family Firms in Singapore have strong corporate performance and 'perform significantly better' than non-Family Firms,[61] which is impressive as Singapore's economy is one of the most competitive and dynamic in the world.[62] In sum, the available empirical evidence suggests that on average Singapore's Family Firms are relatively well governed.

Considering the clear dominance that family members have over the governance of Family Firms, it is surprising that independent directors account for a sizable 44.6 per cent of directors in Family Firms. In fact, independent directors form the largest constituency of any type of directors in Family Firms – with the remaining directors being 41.5 per cent executive directors, 12.6 per cent non-executive (non-independent) directors and 1.4 per cent alternate directors.[63] This raises two intriguing questions: (1) why would family-member-controllers, who appear to otherwise dominate the governance of Family Firms, place such a significant number of independent directors on the boards of the companies they control?; and (2) what function do these independent directors normally serve?

We begin with the second question first, as understanding the function of independent directors in Family Firms provides valuable insight into why family-member-controllers have chosen to place such a large contingent of independent directors on their boards. When viewed through the lens of agency theory, the functional utility of having such a large contingent of American-style independent directors on the boards of Family

[61] *Ibid.*, 2.

[62] C. Cram, 'The UK Can Learn a Lot from Lee Kuan Yew and Singapore', *Guardian*, 4 April 2015, available at www.theguardian.com; A. Austin, 'World's Best Economy: Australia Loses Top IAREM Ranking under Coalition', *Independent Australia*, 22 April 2015, available at https://independentaustralia.net.

[63] Dieleman et al., *Success and Succession*, 15.

Firms is puzzling. Empirical evidence suggests that American-style independent directors have strong connections with family-member-controllers,[64] which limit their ability to monitor them effectively as executives, directors or shareholders. This limitation is compounded because directors of public companies can be removed, at any time, without cause, by a majority shareholder vote.[65]

However, if we widen our lens of inquiry beyond agency theory, several possible functions of American-style independent directors on boards of Family Firms become evident.[66] Where more than one-third of the board is composed of independent directors, Family Firms are able to signal 'good' corporate governance by complying with the Code, which benefits the company and ultimately the family-member-controllers. This may be attractive because directors can be recruited from close family friends or business associates of non-executive family-member-controllers, or even from family-member-controllers themselves where Family Firms are managed by professional non-family members. The strong removal rights under Singapore company law allow family-member-controllers to retain control over the independent directors during their entire tenure.[67]

Empirical evidence confirms this hypothesis. In a comprehensive empirical study of 1,281 directors holding 2,233 independent directorships in 679 Singapore listed companies, Mak and Ng found that independent directors in family-owned companies (i.e., companies where at least 20 per cent of the ordinary shares are held by at least two generations of family members) are distinct from those in other types of companies in that a greater proportion of them are 'single board' independent directors (i.e., they sit on only one board). This is because they are normally recruited 'on account of friendship between the IDs and the family owners'.[68] This supports the claim that independent directors in Family Firms in Singapore are not elected to be the watchdog American-style monitors that Eisenberg's model contemplates, but 'family friends' that promote compliance with the Code, while allowing family members to maintain dominance over their firm's corporate governance.

64 Y. T. Mak and T. Ng, 'Independent Directors: A Well-Functioning Market', *Business Times*, 16 September 2010.

65 Section 152, Companies Act, 2006, c. 50 (Singapore).

66 W. Ng and J. Roberts, '"Helping the Family": The Mediating Role of Outside Directors in Ethnic Chinese Family Firms', *Human Relations*, 60 (2007), 285.

67 Section 152, Companies Act, 2006, c. 50 (Singapore).

68 Mak and Ng, 'Independent Directors: A Well-Functioning Market', 7.

In another study, Ng and Roberts carried out an extensive three-year qualitative investigation in the mid-2000s on a range of directors, managers and other employees in 20 listed Family Firms in Singapore.[69] Using Critical Incident Technique,[70] they found that family-friendly directors can be extremely valuable in fostering effective corporate governance in Family Firms in Singapore because they serve as effective mediators in family and firm disputes, and act as useful advisors to the family patriarch, who is normally the chairman of the board.[71]

This may explain why American-style independent directors made up a significant portion of independent directors even before the 2001 Code went into force, and why Family Firms in Singapore exceeded the recommendation in the 2001 Code that one-third of the board be American-style independent directors. It also illustrates why analysing the role of independent directors in Singapore *solely* through the narrow lens of agency theory can be misleading.[72]

However, agency theory is nevertheless helpful for identifying potential agency costs which may arise if management and/or controlling shareholders in Family Firms are not monitored properly. Agency theory raises an important question about the corporate governance of Family Firms in Singapore: considering the limited ability of American-style independent directors to monitor family-controllers effectively, what prevents the family-controllers from extracting private benefits of control from Family Firms?

We suggest that at least two factors have mitigated the problem of wealth tunnelling in Family Firms. First, Singapore culture strongly emphasises preserving and passing on Family Firms to future generations of the controlling-family. Such cultural norms intrinsically link the family's (including even the extended family's) reputation in the community to the success of the Family Firm. Although such norms tend to exist in family businesses in other parts of the world, they appear to be deeply rooted in Singapore's mainly ethnic Chinese business culture.[73]

[69] Ng and Roberts, '"Helping the Family": The Mediating Role of Outside Directors in Ethnic Chinese Family Firms', 292.

[70] As described by Ng and Roberts, *ibid.*, 311: '"Critical Incident Technique" is an interview technique in which the researcher engages the response of interviewees to publicized events or issues that are researched and then raised for discussion (Chell, 1998).'

[71] *Ibid.*, 299.

[72] Family firms also play a significant role in other Asian jurisdictions. See, for example, Chapter 7 (Taiwan) at II.4; Chapter 8 (Hong Kong) at III; Chapter 10 (India) at II.2.

[73] Ng and Roberts, '"Helping the Family": The Mediating Role of Outside Directors in Ethnic Chinese Family Firms', 287, 306–307; Dieleman et al., *Success and Succession*, 29, 31.

Admittedly, more research is required on the effectiveness of such cultural norms in mitigating wealth tunnelling in Family Firms.[74] Yet, it appears likely that this provides at least a partial functional substitute for effective monitoring of family-member-controllers by truly independent directors in Family Firms.

Second, the effectiveness of Singapore's corporate regulators appears to be another important functional substitute for truly independent directors. Singapore's government is among the most effective and efficient in the world, particularly when it comes to regulating business. Singapore is consistently ranked as a leader in the World Bank Governance Indicators based on government effectiveness, regulatory quality, rule of law and control of corruption.[75] This is supported by similar findings by a number of other international organisations.[76]

Unfortunately, the effectiveness of Singapore's regulators in preventing wealth tunnelling in Family Firms is difficult to prove definitively. Anecdotally, most Singapore family-controllers would not dare to engage in blatant wealth tunnelling because they believe they would be caught by the public regulatory authorities and heavily punished. Singapore's public regulators are well-funded and well-staffed, and Singapore's small and tight-knit business community makes it easier for public regulators to gather information and take action against abuse by family-controllers of Family Firms. Moreover, the Singapore Exchange (SGX) works closely with the public regulatory authority (The Monetary Authority of Singapore (MAS)) on regulatory issues. It has been suggested that Singapore-based listed companies largely cooperate with regulators – even when they may have engaged in wealth tunnelling – because they believe a failure to cooperate would be even more harmful to their long-term interests than essentially admitting to their malfeasance.[77]

[74] A. Wooldridge, 'Family Companies: To Have and to Hold', *The Economist*, 18 April 2015, available at www.economist.com; A. N. Licht, 'Culture and Law in Corporate Governance' (European Corporate Governance Institute (ECGI) – Law Working Paper No. 247/2014, 2014), available at http://ssrn.com/abstract=2405538.

[75] World Bank, *Worldwide Governance Indicators: Country Data Report for Singapore, 1996–2013* (2013), available at http://info.worldbank.org.pdf.

[76] World Justice Project, *Rule of Law Index* (2015), available at http://worldjusticeproject.org.

[77] This observation is based on anecdotal evidence received by the authors from Singapore regulators, and is supported by the fact that until the recent China Sky case, no firm had ever rejected a request by the SGX to appoint a special auditor. The China Sky case involved a PRC-Controlled Firm, which suggests that the corporate culture in such firms

Section IV provides novel and concrete evidence supporting this hypothesis. It explains how the importance of Singapore's regulators and culture have been illuminated by the rash of scandals in PRC-Controlled Firms. These firms fell beyond the reach of Singapore regulators and were not bound by the cultural norms of Singapore's Family Firms. Thus, they were able to exploit the gap in corporate governance created by a lack of truly independent directors and absence of Singapore's functional substitutes for keeping private benefits of control in check. The PRC-Controlled Firms scandals therefore highlight the extent to which Singapore's regulators and culture have been integral to mitigating private benefits of control in Singapore-based Family Firms.

3 *The Function of American-Style Independent Directors in Government-Linked Companies: Filling the Gap Created by Singapore's Unique Regulatory Regime*

With Singapore's international accolades for having one of the most free, dynamic and wealthy economies in the world, it is easy to forget that the most powerful shareholder in Singapore is the Singapore government.[78] The government, through its holding company Temasek Holdings Pte Ltd (Temasek), is the controlling shareholder in 23 of Singapore's largest listed companies (commonly referred to as Government-Linked Companies).[79] Collectively, these 23 Government-Linked Companies account for an astonishing 37 per cent of Singapore's total market capitalisation.[80] Singapore's Government-Linked Companies model has become an issue of global importance as the Chinese Communist Party has identified it as the model for reforming China's juggernaut State-Owned Enterprises (SOEs).[81] Understanding the role of independent directors in Singapore's Government-Linked Companies is not only essential for accurately understanding the importance of independent

differs from Singapore firms and that they are considerably more insulated from the reach of Singapore regulators. Mak, *Corporate Governance Case Studies*, Vol. II, 1–13.

78 Tan et al., 'State-Owned Enterprises in Singapore: Historical Insights into a Potential Model for Reform', 67.

79 I. Sim et al., *The State as Shareholder: The Case of Singapore* (2014), 22, available at http://bschool.nus.edu.

80 *Ibid.*, 6.

81 L. Lin and C. J. Milhaupt, 'We Are the (National) Champions: Understanding the Mechanisms of State Capitalism in China', *Stanford Law Review*, 65 (2013), 697, 754; R. J. Gilson and C. J. Milhaupt, 'Sovereign Wealth Funds and Corporate Governance: A

directors in Singapore, but may also provide useful insights into the future role of independent directors in Chinese SOEs and, in turn, in the global economy.

The government's current status as Singapore's most powerful shareholder can be traced back to Singapore's post-independence period in the late 1960s.[82] Then, the People's Action Party (PAP), which has governed Singapore since its independence, decided to intervene in a variety of sectors in the economy by investing in a wide range of companies due to Singapore's dearth of skilled entrepreneurs and lack of private capital.[83] From the outset, the PAP was acutely aware of the risks involved in the government being an active investor in the private economy.[84] It was (and still is) in the PAP's self-interest to devise and maintain a system to ensure that Government-Linked Companies were not merely government automatons guided purely by political motives, but rather incorporated (and preferably listed) companies managed in a commercially effective manner to maximise their long-term value.[85] In 1974, with a view to developing such a system, the government incorporated Temasek as an exempt private limited company under the Singapore Companies Act.[86] The government's portfolio of Government-Linked Companies was transferred to Temasek, whose sole shareholder is the Singapore Minister for Finance (MOF).[87] The government hoped that by interposing a holding company between itself and its portfolio of Government-Linked Companies, Government-Linked Companies would be insulated from any undue political influence and managed as competitive commercial companies.[88]

The obvious risk in Temasek's corporate structure is that although it is a company whose day-to-day affairs are managed by its board of

Minimalist Response to the New Mercantilism', *Stanford Law Review*, 60 (2008), 1345, 1359.

82 Tan et al., 'State-Owned Enterprises in Singapore: Historical Insights into a Potential Model for Reform', 77–80.

83 *Ibid.*, 79–83.

84 *Ibid.*, 84; K. Y. Lee, *From Third World to First: The Singapore Story: 1965–2000* (2000), 87.

85 Tan et al., 'State-Owned Enterprises in Singapore: Historical Insights into a Potential Model for Reform', 89–91; Y. N. Lee, 'Temasek's Success Down to Separation of Its Role from Govt's', *Today*, 23 September 2014, available at http://m.todayonline.com.

86 Sim et al., *The State as Shareholder: The Case of Singapore*, 6; Tan et al., 'State-Owned Enterprises in Singapore: Historical Insights into a Potential Model for Reform', 89.

87 Under the Minister for Finance (Incorporation) Act, 2014, c. 183, § 2(1) the Minister for Finance is a body corporate. See Temasek, *Temasek Annual Review 2014* (2014), 20 n. 1.

88 'FAQs: Why Was Temasek Established', Temasek, available at www.temasek.com.sg.

directors, the government (through the MOF) is its sole shareholder.[89] From this perspective, Temasek is a wholly owned subsidiary of the government, and the government is the ultimate controlling shareholder of the 23 publicly listed Government-Linked Companies in Temasek's portfolio. Although the interposition of Temasek created a level of formal legal separation between the government and Government-Linked Companies, the government's status as Temasek's sole shareholder raised the prospect of Government-Linked Companies becoming political automatons rather than successful commercial vehicles.

To mitigate this risk, the PAP constructed a highly visible and well-tailored regulatory regime, which aims to prevent the government from abusing its position as the ultimate controlling shareholder of Government-Linked Companies in four ways. First, restrictions enshrined in the Singapore Constitution[90] are placed on the MOF's shareholder rights to prevent the government from abusing its position for short-term political gain. Although the MOF is Temasek's sole shareholder, the directly elected, non-party affiliated and independent President of Singapore must concur with the appointment, reappointment or removal of Temasek's directors by the MOF.[91] Temasek's Articles of Incorporation also make it clear that its board (and not the MOF as Temasek's sole shareholder) has ultimate authority over the amount of dividends paid to the government.[92]

Second, restrictions are placed on Temasek's board to ensure that its decisions are commercially oriented. Temasek's board is accountable to the President to ensure that every disposal of an investment by Temasek is transacted at fair market value.[93] Temasek also requires approval from the President to draw on any reserves it accumulated prior to the term of the incumbent government.[94] These provide safeguards against the government using its status as Temasek's sole shareholder to engage in wealth tunnelling, or draw on past reserves for political or non-commercial reasons.

[89] Tan et al., 'State-Owned Enterprises in Singapore: Historical Insights into a Potential Model for Reform', 89.

[90] Article 22A, Constitution of the Republic of Singapore, 9 August 1965, S 1/63.

[91] Sim et al., *The State as Shareholder: The Case of Singapore*, 16; 'FAQs: How Is the President Involved with the Board of Temasek?', Temasek, available at www.temasek.com.sg.

[92] Sim et al., *The State as Shareholder: The Case of Singapore*, 16 n. 8.

[93] *Ibid.*

[94] *Ibid.*, 16; 'FAQs: How Is the President Involved in the Protection of Temasek's Past Reserves?', Temasek, available at www.temasek.com.sg.

Third, restrictions are placed on the role that Temasek plays in the management decisions of Government-Linked Companies to prevent undue government influence from trickling down through Temasek into its portfolio of Government-Linked Companies. According to the Temasek Charter,[95] as an engaged shareholder, Temasek aims to promote good corporate governance in its portfolio of Government-Linked Companies by drawing on its contacts to prepare shortlists of high calibre, experienced and diverse directorial candidates for Government-Linked Companies,[96] *without* directing the business decisions or operations of Government-Linked Companies.[97] The individual boards of Government-Linked Companies can then decide whether to include Temasek's recommendations in their final list of directorial candidates, with Temasek reserving its right to exercise its voting power in directorial elections.[98]

Fourth, Temasek subjects itself to strict audit and disclosure requirements to expose poor corporate governance and to demonstrate that it is a successful commercial company run for the benefit of Singaporeans.[99] Temasek provides annual statutory financial statements to the MOF, which are audited by an international audit firm.[100] Although Temasek is an exempt private company – which under Singapore law is not legally required to disclose any financial information to the public – it publishes a Group Financial Summary and portfolio of performance in its yearly Temasek Review since 2004.[101] Temasek's disclosure has garnered the highest possible ranking for transparency among sovereign wealth funds by the Linaburg-Maduell Transparency Index.[102]

Considering the measures taken to ensure that Temasek and its portfolio of Government-Linked Companies are successful commercial

95 Temasek Holdings, 'Temasek Charter' (25 August 2009), available at http://temasekreview.com.

96 *Ibid.*; Tan et al., 'State-Owned Enterprises in Singapore: Historical Insights into a Potential Model for Reform', 89–91. 'FAQs: Does Temasek Request Representation on the Boards of Companies in Which It Invests?', Temasek, available at www.temasek.com.sg.

97 Tan et al., 'State-Owned Enterprises in Singapore: Historical Insights into a Potential Model for Reform', 89–90; Temasek Holdings, 'Temasek Charter'.

98 'FAQs: Does Temasek Request Representation on the Boards of Companies in Which It Invests?'; 'FAQs: How Does Temasek Work with Its Portfolio Companies?', Temasek, available at www.temasek.com.sg.

99 Sim et al., *The State as Shareholder: The Case of Singapore*, 8, 16, 34.

100 *Ibid.*, 16.

101 Temasek International Private Limited, *Temasek Annual Review 2014*; Sim et al., *The State as Shareholder: The Case of Singapore*, 16.

102 Sim et al., *The State as Shareholder: The Case of Singapore*, 17.

companies, how successful have Temasek and its portfolio of Government-Linked Companies been? Almost every available metric for corporate performance points to Temasek and its Government-Linked Companies being extremely successful. Temasek's initial portfolio of Government-Linked Companies was worth S $354 million in 1974, and has grown to S $215 billion as of March 2013, with an astonishing average annual return of 16 per cent since its inception – significantly outstripping the average performance of other large and mid-sized Singapore listed companies.[103] Empirical evidence suggests that Government-Linked Companies on average are significantly more profitable, better governed and receive much higher valuations than non-Government-Linked Companies.[104]

It is clear that Temasek and its portfolio of Government-Linked Companies have been successful. In the context of this chapter, however, the critical question is: what role have independent directors played in their success? At first blush, it appears that independent directors are at the core of the Temasek model. Indeed, Temasek advertises the fact that 'the majority of [its] board members are non-executive independent private sector business leaders'.[105] It also advocates that the boards of Government-Linked Companies be 'independent of management in order to provide effective oversight and supervision of management'.[106]

To determine whether Temasek has put its American-style independent director policy into practice, we hand-collected and analysed all publicly available information on all of the independent directors currently on the boards of Temasek and its portfolio of Government-Linked Companies (the Temasek Independent Director Database (TIDD)).[107] Further, Temasek voluntarily discloses information about its board

103 *Ibid.*, 17, 20. Temasek's net portfolio value is S $266 billion, as of March 2015. See Temasek, 'Portfolio Highlights', available at www.temasek.com.sg.

104 Tan et al., 'State-Owned Enterprises in Singapore: Historical Insights into a Potential Model for Reform', 67–69.

105 Temasek, 'Board of Directors', available at www.temasek.com.sg.

106 Tan et al., 'State-Owned Enterprises in Singapore: Historical Insights into a Potential Model for Reform', 90.

107 The TIDD was prepared based on a review of information contained in the annual reports of Government Linked Companies available on the SGX website which were accessed online on 21–22 December 2014. Moreover, additional internet searches were done in January 2015 to gather as much publicly available professional information about the independent directors on the boards of Temasek and its portfolio of Government-Linked Companies as possible. D. W. Puchniak and L. L. Lan, *Temasek Independent Director Database* (2015) (unpublished manuscript on file with authors) [hereinafter TIDD].

and corporate governance practices in the Temasek Review and on its official webpage.[108] Based on our analysis of this information and the TIDD, it appears that Temasek's claim that 'the majority of [its] board members are non-executive independent private sector business leaders' is accurate.[109] Temasek's own board comprises extremely qualified, highly accomplished and widely respected Singaporean (ten) and international (three) directors who all, except for the CEO, are independent from Temasek's management. Temasek's chairman and CEO positions are held by different people and the chairman is a non-executive director who is independent from Temasek's management. The TIDD suggests that Temasek's board conforms to the American-style independent director model that it purports to follow.[110]

Turning our attention to the boards of Government-Linked Companies, our review of the most recent annual reports of the 23 Government-Linked Companies in Temasek's portfolio reveals that 64.87 per cent of directors are identified by the Government-Linked Companies as 'independent directors' – exceeding significantly the level of independence recommended by the Code.[111] Our review of the TIDD reveals that they are generally highly skilled, prominent figures in the Singapore business community, who appear to be independent from the management of their respective Government-Linked Companies.[112] Based on the publicly available information in the TIDD, it appears that Temasek has achieved its stated goal of promoting Government-Linked Companies boards that are 'independent of management in order to provide effective oversight and supervision of management'.[113]

However, merely confirming that the boards of Temasek and its portfolio of Government-Linked Companies conform to Temasek's stated policy of promoting American-style independent managerial-monitoring boards leaves a gaping hole in our analysis. Considering

[108] Temasek, *Temasek Annual Review 2014*, 50–56.

[109] Temasek, 'Board of Directors'.

[110] Sim et al., *The State as Shareholder: The Case of Singapore*, 16.

[111] The annual reports that were reviewed were those available on the SGX website, which were accessed online on 21–22 December 2014. There is a full summary of the review conducted in the TIDD.

[112] TIDD.

[113] Tan et al., 'State-Owned Enterprises in Singapore: Historical Insights into a Potential Model for Reform', 90. See also, C. C. Chen, 'Corporate Governance of State-Owned Enterprises: An Empirical Survey of the Model of Temasek Holdings in Singapore' (Singapore Management University School of Law Research Paper No. 6/2014, 2013), 22, available at http://ssrn.com/abstract=2366699.

Temasek's controlling shareholder structure and Singapore's regulatory regime, a critical question remains: are the American-style independent directors on the boards of Temasek and its portfolio of Government-Linked Companies also independent from the government? The answer to this question sheds light on the function(s) that these independent directors perform, and why they may have been elected to their respective boards.

We re-examined the TIDD to determine the extent of the connections (if any) between the Singapore government and the independent directors on the boards of Temasek and its portfolio of Government-Linked Companies. These connections appear to be extensive. Eight out of 12 of the independent directors on Temasek's board currently hold (five) and/or previously held (five) positions in the Singapore government and/or on government bodies.[114] Further, as is widely publicised, the CEO and sole executive director of Temasek, Madam Ho Ching, is married to the current Prime Minister of Singapore, Lee Hsien Loong, and was formerly a civil servant in the Singapore government.[115] There also appears to be a significant number of formal connections between the American-style independent directors on the boards of Government-Linked Companies and the Singapore government: 50 per cent of them (74 out of 148) currently hold (49) and/or previously held (41) positions in the Singapore government and/or government bodies.[116]

Without these government connections, the primary function of American-style independent directors in Temasek and its portfolio of Government-Linked Companies would be relatively clear. As explained in detail above, to insulate Government-Linked Companies from political influence, the shareholder rights of the government and Temasek to intervene in the management of Government-Linked Companies have been significantly restricted.[117] While these restrictions reduce the risk of the government and Temasek extracting private (political) benefits of control from Government-Linked Companies, they simultaneously limit the government and Temasek's abilities to monitor management effectively or manage Government-Linked Companies themselves. As such, American-style independent directors are a critical component of the

[114] TIDD.

[115] C. J. Milhaupt and K. Pistor, *Law and Capitalism: What Corporate Crises Reveal about Legal Systems and Economic Development around the World* (University of Chicago Press, 2008), 137 [hereinafter *Law and Capitalism*].

[116] TIDD.

[117] See text accompanying notes 86–102, above.

Temasek model as they fill the managerial-monitoring gap created by Singapore's unique regulatory environment. From this perspective, the high percentage of American-style independent directors on the boards of Temasek and its portfolio of Government-Linked Companies makes sense. It also reinforces the PAP's foundational policy that Government-Linked Companies should be governed as successful commercial (not political) enterprises.

However, the high proportion of American-style independent directors who hold current and/or held past positions with the Singapore government and/or government bodies injects a level of uncertainty into this analysis. At first blush, it may suggest that the government is using its influence over Temasek to elect government-connected American-style 'independent' directors to the boards of Government-Linked Companies to gain political influence over them. This suggestion fits with the views of some leading international observers who point to the deep ties between the PAP and the past and current Presidents of Singapore as evidence of the politicisation of Temasek and its portfolio of Government-Linked Companies. Similarly, some international observers suggest that the power wielded by Madam Ho Ching, as the Prime Minister's wife and Temasek's CEO, shows that politics has infiltrated the decision-making process in Temasek and its portfolio of Government-Linked Companies.[118]

Our analysis of the extent and nature of the government connections suggests that political influence does not appear to drive the appointments of independent directors for at least three reasons. First, based on the TIDD, 50 per cent of the independent directors on the boards of Government-Linked Companies have *no* present or past formal connections with the Singapore government or government bodies at all.[119] If the goal of the government is to covertly control Government-Linked Companies by electing government-connected American-style independent directors to their boards, one would expect virtually all such directors to have government connections – which appears not to be the case.

Second, a significant portion of the government connections are based solely on the independent directors holding some position (often

[118] K. J. Hatton and K. Pistor, 'Maximizing Autonomy in the Shadow of Great Powers: The Political Economy of Sovereign Wealth Funds', *Columbia Journal of Transnational Law*, 50 (2012), 1, 47–66; Milhaupt and Pistor, *Law and Capitalism*, 137.

[119] TIDD.

a part-time board or advisory appointment) related to a branch of the government that is far removed from the regulation or governance of Temasek and/or its portfolio of Government-Linked Companies. Among these independent directors who hold current and/or held past positions with the government, 59.81 per cent of the current positions and 70.73 per cent of the past positions were in statutory boards and/or agencies under a Ministry other than the MOF.[120] The remoteness of these positions suggests that they are not likely being used by the government to control the boards of Government-Linked Companies. If the MOF's goal was to circumvent the limitations on its controlling-shareholder power, one would expect it to use its influence to place mostly MOF officials or persons closely connected with the MOF on such boards – which does not appear to be the case.

Third, the government is well-known for its meritocracy, competitive remuneration and prestige,[121] and has been internationally recognised as one of the most efficient and least corrupt governments in the world.[122] Instead of being a proxy for political interference by the government in Government-Linked Companies, current or past government positions generally indicate that these directors have been selected from a talented group of Singaporeans (i.e., having a connection to the government in Singapore is often a proxy for talent). It would be surprising (and concerning) if most American-style independent directors on the boards of Temasek and its portfolio of Government-Linked Companies had no connection with the Singapore government.[123]

In sum, it appears that the primary function of American-style independent directors on the boards of Temasek and its portfolio of Government-Linked Companies is to monitor management in the interest of shareholders – a critical function given the restrictions placed on the controlling-shareholder power of the government and Temasek. We suggest that this is the main reason why such a large contingent of

[120] TIDD.

[121] Corrupt Practices Investigations Bureau, 'Transparency International', CPIB.gov, available at www.cpib.gov.sg; Transparency International, 'Corruption Perceptions Index 2014: Results', Transparency.org, available at www.transparency.org.

[122] Tan et al., 'State-Owned Enterprises in Singapore: Historical Insights into a Potential Model for Reform', 65, 87–88; Corrupt Practices Investigations Bureau, 'Transparency International'.

[123] This also applies to the current positions held by Madam Ho Ching and Tony Tan. Their professional qualifications and accomplishments suggest that their current positions are based more on merit than the politicisation of the Temasek model.

American-style independent directors have been elected to the boards of Temasek and its portfolio of Government-Linked Companies.

Finally, it is important to stress that the risk of the government and Temasek using their shareholder power to extract private benefits of control from Government-Linked Companies is limited in Singapore's regulatory environment. Such risks are limited by the restrictions placed on the controlling-shareholder power of the government and Temasek, and the nature of the Singapore civil service itself – a culture of meritocracy, carefully calibrated performance incentives and systematic monitoring. This provides another layer of protection (which does not exist for a stereotypical controlling shareholder) against the extraction of private benefits of control from Government-Linked Companies.[124] Even though Temasek and its portfolio of Government-Linked Companies have controlling shareholders, it appears that the American concept of the independent director is congruent with Singapore's unique Government-Linked Companies corporate governance model. In fact, requiring strict separation between the government and independent directors on the boards of Temasek and its portfolio of Government-Linked Companies would probably reduce the talent pool of available directors, without any significant resulting benefits.

IV Signalling Reform: American-Style Independent Directors Abandoned?

1 *The Impetus for the 2012 Reform: Shifting International Standards, PRC-Controlled Firm Scandals and Signalling*

Singapore's decision to transplant the American concept of the independent director into its controlling shareholder environment in 2001 and maintain it for over a decade was not only rational, but most likely an example of successful strategic regulatory design which, on balance, seems to have largely benefited Government-Linked Companies, Family Firms and ultimately the Singapore economy. Against this backdrop, the decision of Singapore's regulators to (ostensibly) abandon the American concept of the independent director in the 2012 Code appears puzzling: why would Singapore decide to abandon the American concept of

[124] Tan et al., 'State-Owned Enterprises in Singapore: Historical Insights into a Potential Model for Reform', 91–93.

the independent director after more than a decade of success; and what impact (if any) may this have on the future of corporate governance in Singapore?

There are three possible reasons for why Singapore's regulators decided to (ostensibly) abandon the American concept of the independent director. First, by the end of the 2000s, there was an emerging international consensus that American-style independent directors might be ill-suited for controlling shareholder environments like Singapore.[125] Considering these developments, upon the recommendation of Singapore's private sector-led CGC, MAS adopted a new definition of independence in the 2012 Code, which appears to abandon the American concept of the independent director and change the manner in which listed companies in Singapore will be governed.[126] MAS noted that this would align Singapore's corporate governance 'with international best practices' and 'enhance market confidence in the strength of the governance of listed companies in Singapore'.[127] MAS's desire to send a strong signal of Singapore's 'good' corporate governance to the market therefore played a significant role.

Second, despite Singapore's indisputable economic success throughout the 2000s, it was rocked by a litany of scandals in PRC-Controlled Firms (i.e., companies that are listed on the Singapore Exchange but whose operations and controlling shareholders are located in mainland China).[128] Both the meteoric rise of PRC-Controlled Firms and their propensity to be embroiled in egregious scandals that tunnelled wealth away from minority shareholders are astounding. In the early 2000s, immediately following the Asian Financial Crisis, PRC-Controlled Firms were virtually unheard of in Singapore. By the end of the 2000s, they accounted for approximately half of all new listings on the SGX, made up almost one-third of its total IPO value and 20 per cent of its total listings. Yet, by 2011, almost 10 per cent of PRC-Controlled Firms had been suspended from trading on the SGX due to governance or accounting related issues. This figure is even more troubling considering that

125 See Bebchuk and Hamdani, 'The Elusive Quest for Global Corporate Governance Standards', 1311; Davies and Hopt, 'Corporate Boards in Europe: Accountability and Convergence', 320–321.

126 Monetary Authority of Singapore, *Response to Recommendations 2012*, 2.

127 *Ibid.*, 3.

128 Stamford Law Corporation, 'Making SGX Attractive to PRC-Controlled Firms', Legal 500, available at www.legal500.com; J. Kwok, 'Are PRC-Controlled Firms Still a Possible Play?', *Straits Times*, 25 December 2011.

it excludes a number of PRC-Controlled Firms which had been either delisted entirely or saved by a white knight.[129] The majority of the PRC-Controlled Firm scandals involved egregious wealth tunnelling by mainland Chinese controlling-shareholders largely at the expense of minority shareholders and international investors in Singapore.[130] The damage done by the PRC-Controlled Firm scandals to Singapore's reputation for good corporate governance appears to have been another factor which drove MAS to (ostensibly) abandon the American independent director in the 2012 Code.[131]

Third, although the reformed definition of independence in the 2012 Code has been advertised as Singapore's abandonment of the American concept of the independent director to meet international best practices, it is questionable whether this is in fact the case.[132] The restrictive definition adopted in the 2012 Code, combined with Singapore's rules for electing directors and its unique shareholder structure, will most likely render the reform more of a change in the form of corporate governance in Singapore than in how it actually functions. Another possible factor which drove the reform of the 2012 Code's definition of independence is that it was crafted in such a way that Government-Linked Companies and Family Firms could signal compliance with international best practices without fundamentally altering their controlling shareholder corporate governance structures.

2 *The Un-American Definition of Independence in the 2012 Code: More of a Change in Form Than Function*

The relevant amendments in the 2012 Code state that a director is deemed to *not* be independent if she is:

> A director who is a 10% shareholder or an immediate family member of a 10% shareholder of the company; or a director who is or has been directly associated with a 10% shareholder of the company, in the current or immediate past financial year.[133]

[129] Kwok, 'Are PRC-Controlled Firms Still a Possible Play?'.

[130] Stamford Law Corporation, 'Making SGX Attractive to S-Chips'; M. Qian, 'Why S-Chip Fraud Cases Keep Cropping Up?', *Business Times*, 17 February 2012.

[131] A. Maharaj, 'New Corporate Governance Codes to Shake Up Singapore's Boardrooms', *Corporate Secretary*, 17 June 2011, available at www.corporatesecretary.com.

[132] Monetary Authority of Singapore, *Response to Recommendations 2012*, 3.

[133] Article 2.3(e)–(f), Code of Corporate Governance (Monetary Authority of Singapore, 2012).

> ['Directly associated with' means] being accustomed or under the obligation ... to act in accordance with the directions, instructions or wishes of the 10% shareholder in relation to the corporate affairs of the corporation.[134]

There are three aspects of this expanded definition of independence which suggest that it is more likely to bring about a formal than functional change in Singapore corporate governance. First, the new definition in the 2012 Code is *unlikely* to prevent most (if not all) independent directors on the boards of Government-Linked Companies from continuing to be deemed as independent directors, even if they have current or past connections with the MOF or the government. Although the MOF and the government clearly qualify as 10 per cent shareholders in all Government-Linked Companies,[135] the explicit policy of the MOF and Singapore government is to not interfere in the corporate affairs of Government-Linked Companies.[136] As such, no one connected with the government would likely qualify as a 'directly associated' person provided in the definition above. This limitation is critical because 50 per cent of independent directors in Government-Linked Companies have past or current connections with the government – the ultimate controlling shareholder of all Government-Linked Companies.[137]

Our review of the latest annual reports of Government-Linked Companies revealed that these companies uniformly appear to interpret the 2012 Code's definition of independence in the restrictive manner described above, since no annual report mentions any connection between independent directors and the Singapore government – even though many such relationships appear to exist. This does not suggest that Government-Linked Companies are contravening the 2012 Code. Rather, it confirms that such relationships do not appear to be covered by the restrictive '*Un*-American definition' of independence in the 2012 Code.

[134] Article 2.3(f) n. 6, Code of Corporate Governance (Monetary Authority of Singapore, 2012).

[135] Article 2 n. 2, Code of Corporate Governance (Monetary Authority of Singapore, 2012).

[136] K. S. Goh, 'Public Enterprises' (Speech at the NTUC Income Annual General Meeting, 20 June 1977), reproduced in Linda Low (ed.), *Wealth of East Asian Nations: Speeches and Writings by Goh Keng Swee* (Federal Publications, 1995), 122–123; S. Y. Lee, 'Public Enterprise and Economic Development in Singapore', *Malayan Economic Review*, 21(2) (1976), 49, 57; Lee, 'Temasek's Success Down to Separation of Its Role from Govt's'; Tan et al., 'State-Owned Enterprises in Singapore: Historical Insights into a Potential Model for Reform', 88, 92.

[137] TIDD; see *supra* section III.3 and text accompanying note 116, above for a discussion of what constitutes a connection.

Further, as Temasek is an unlisted private exempt company, the 2012 Code does not apply to it at all. Temasek can continue to apply the American concept of the independent director when describing the characteristics of its board. This appears to be Temasek's approach, as it describes its directors and the directors in its portfolio companies as independent with a clear focus on their independence from the management of Temasek and its portfolio companies – and not their independence from the Singapore government.[138]

Second, the amendment to the definition of independence is likely to have less of an impact on independent directors in Family Firms because it is limited to those with an interest of 'not less than 10%' of the company's voting shares.[139] As many of Singapore's Family Firms are transitioning to their third generation of family ownership, their shares are increasingly held in blocks of less than 10 per cent – even though family members collectively still maintain actual voting control in most Family Firms.[140] A friend or associate of a family member holding less than 10 per cent may still be deemed to be independent under the expanded definition of independence.

The 'directly associated' person restriction also leaves considerable room for 10 per cent shareholders in Family Firms to elect 'family friendly' independent directors, as many family friends will likely be able to claim that they are not 'accustomed' or 'under an obligation' to act in accordance with the wishes of their friends, who are also family controllers.[141] Since the *Un*-American definition in the 2012 Code is further limited to directors directly associated with a 10 per cent shareholder 'in the current or immediate past financial year', this further expands the scope for electing 'family friendly' directors in Family Firms who may have worked for a family controller in the past.[142]

Third, as directors of listed companies in Singapore can be removed, without cause, at any time, by a majority shareholder vote, the controlling shareholders in Family Firms and Government-Linked Companies will still control the fate of the '*Un*-American' independent directors in their respective companies.[143] The 2012 Code reinforces the control of

138 Temasek, 'Board of Directors'.

139 Article 2.3, Code of Corporate Governance (Monetary Authority of Singapore, 2012).

140 Dieleman et al., *Success and Succession*, 25.

141 Article 2.3(f) n. 6, Code of Corporate Governance (Monetary Authority of Singapore, 2012).

142 Monetary Authority of Singapore, *Response to Recommendations 2012*, 3.

143 H. Cai, 'An Acid Test of Board Independence', *Business Times Singapore*, 22 October 2012.

controlling shareholders over '*Un*-American' independent directors by stating that 'a director will not be considered "directly associated" with a 10 per cent shareholder by reason only of his or her appointment having been proposed by that 10% shareholder'.[144] This calls into question how '*Un*-American' the independent directors on the boards of Government-Linked Companies and Family Firms will actually be in practice under the 2012 Code.

It appears that once again Singapore's regulators will be able to signal 'good' corporate governance by complying with international best practices, because most listed companies will be able to easily comply with the new *Un*-American concept of the independent director in the 2012 Code. Directors in Government-Linked Companies who may have some form of connections with the MOF or Singapore government can still in most (if not all) cases be deemed to be independent directors. There is considerable scope for 'family friendly' directors to be elected by family-member-controllers to the boards of Family Firms as independent directors. All said, we do not in any way imply that such directors cannot be independent in their decision making. However, we are of the opinion that the changing of the definition of independent directors from the American concept to the *Un*-American one will not cause a major shift in the corporate governance of listed companies in Singapore.

3 Strategic Regulatory Design Revisited: The Rationale Behind the 2012 Code's Restrictive Definition of the Un-American Independent Director

The adoption of the *Un*-American independent director by Singapore's regulators to signal good corporate governance, while leaving Singapore's controlling shareholder corporate governance system largely intact, may prove once again to be an example of successful strategic regulatory design. This is especially likely in Government-Linked Companies, which have been largely free from corporate scandals and are effectively insulated from controlling shareholder abuse by Singapore's unique regulatory architecture. Further, requiring strict separation between independent directors in Government-Linked Companies and the Singapore government would probably reduce the talent pool of available directors.[145] It

[144] Article 2.3(f) note n. 6, Code of Corporate Governance (Monetary Authority of Singapore, 2012).

[145] V. Wee, 'Boardrooms Due for Re-calibration', *Business Times Singapore*, 12 April 2012.

appears that the 2012 Code's restrictive definition of the *Un*-American independent director is warranted in the case of Government-Linked Companies.

The situation in Family Firms appears to be somewhat less clear. Although Family Firms in Singapore have performed extremely well, some recent corporate scandals involving Family Firms suggest that *Un*-American independent directors may provide a useful additional check on private benefits of control.[146] Requiring stricter separation between the controlling shareholders and independent directors in Family Firms would not significantly reduce the talent pool of independent directors for Family Firms – which distinguishes Family Firms from Government-Linked Companies. This being said, there is still the risk that the family-based corporate culture of Family Firms may be disrupted if their boards become dominated by non-family-friendly directors, and in some cases family-friendly independent directors appear to add unique value. Although there may be a stronger rationale for promoting stricter separation between controlling shareholders and independent directors in Family Firms than Government-Linked Companies, the success of Family Firms in Singapore suggests that their controlling-shareholder-dominated model should not be entirely discarded.

It appears that Singapore's regulators have attempted to strike this difficult balance for Family Firms in the 2012 Code. Besides amending the definition for independence, the 2012 Code adds two other provisions which will probably make the boards of Family Firms more independent from family-controllers. First, directors who have been on the board for more than nine years must have their independence reviewed and the board must explain why they should be considered independent.[147] Considering the exceptionally long tenure of directors in Family Firms – especially family-member directors – this provision is likely to create greater separation between independent directors and controlling shareholders in Family Firms.

Second, companies with a chairperson who is not an independent director are required to have at least half of their boards composed of independent directors (as opposed to one-third when the chairperson is an independent director).[148] This new provision will likely have the greatest

[146] Y. T. Mak (ed.), *Corporate Governance Case Studies*, Vol. III (CPA Australia, 2013), available at www.cpaaustralia.com.

[147] Article 2.4, Code of Corporate Governance (Monetary Authority of Singapore, 2012).

[148] Article 2.2, Code of Corporate Governance (Monetary Authority of Singapore, 2012).

impact on the boards of Family Firms as they currently stand out among listed companies in Singapore in their propensity to combine the positions of CEO and chairperson.[149] While these two additional provisions will probably have a significant impact on Family Firms, they are unlikely to fundamentally change the controlling-shareholder-dominated corporate governance system in Family Firms in Singapore.

In contrast, there have been significant changes in the regulation of PRC-Controlled Firms which have gone far beyond the provisions related to independent directors in the 2012 Code. Singapore regulators have not viewed the implementation of *Un*-American independent directors as the sole solution to the PRC-Controlled Firm problem. This appears to be prudent as the PRC-Controlled Firm scandals have illuminated at least two critical distinctions between PRC-Controlled Firms and Government-Linked Companies/Family Firms that appear to warrant a more robust regulatory regime.

First, the corporate structure of PRC-Controlled Firms effectively places their corporate controllers beyond the reach of Singapore's normally effective and powerful regulators.[150] In the typical PRC-Controlled Firm, revenue generating operations and business are conducted solely in China, while a separate entity is normally incorporated in a low tax jurisdiction for the purpose of listing it on the SGX.[151] In a number of PRC-Controlled Firm scandals, the corporate controllers of the listed company used their controlling power to tunnel wealth from it back to China – where the controllers could carry on 'business as usual' under the protection of local Chinese authorities.[152] Singapore's regulators have been left with the unsatisfactory option of imposing sanctions on the hollowed out listed company – which only serves to further punish minority shareholders.

Second, the difference in corporate culture between Government-Linked Companies/Family Firms and PRC-Controlled Firms suggests that a distinct and more robust regulatory regime is warranted for PRC-Controlled Firms. In Family Firms, the desire of the controlling family to pass on their business to the next generation and to maintain the controlling family's reputation in Singapore's small and tight-knit business

[149] Dieleman et al., *Success and Succession*, 17.

[150] Stamford Law Corporation, 'Making SGX Attractive to S-Chips'; Y. T. Mak, 'Now Let's See the Practical Impact', *Business Times Singapore*, 16 June 2011.

[151] Stamford Law Corporation, 'Making SGX Attractive to S-Chips'.

[152] The standard response from local Chinese authorities has usually been that no action could be taken against these corporate controllers because they had not breached Chinese law. *Ibid.*

community helps mitigate the risk of private benefits of control.[153] In Government-Linked Companies, the meritocratic, largely corruption free and efficient culture of the Singapore civil services, combined with Singapore's distinct regulatory architecture for protecting the boards of Government-Linked Companies from politics, appears to significantly reduce the risk of private benefits of control in Government-Linked Companies. In contrast, PRC-Controlled Firms tend to lack good corporate governance because they tend to be second-class Chinese companies that have emerged from an environment where controlling shareholder abuse is rife.[154]

To mitigate the higher risk of private benefits of control in PRC-Controlled Firms, the SGX Listing Rules were amended in 2008 to require foreign issuers to have at least two independent directors who are Singapore residents on a continuing basis on their boards.[155] Unfortunately, tightening such regulations was somewhat ineffective as most reputable Singaporean directors were unwilling to take the risk of acting as a resident independent director in a PRC-Controlled Firm. The SGX also agreed to devise a dual compliance requirement with the Chinese Securities Regulatory Commission (CSRC) in 2014 for PRC-Controlled Firms that want to list on the SGX in the future.[156] If Chinese regulators play a part in the vetting process, they may be more willing to facilitate actions against rogue controllers of PRC-Controlled Firms when scandals arise *ex post*, which should provide an *ex ante* deterrent effect.

As this new 'dual compliance' system has not yet been rolled out, only time will tell whether it will solve the problem of controlling shareholder abuse that has plagued PRC-Controlled Firms in Singapore. Although most observers view the PRC-Controlled Firm scandals as a rare failure of Singapore's regulators, they also illuminate a key to Singapore's success. They suggest that the extraordinary economic performance and absence of such scandals in Government-Linked Companies and Family Firms may hinge on the effectiveness of Singapore's regulator and

[153] Ng and Roberts, '"Helping the Family": The Mediating Role of Outside Directors in Ethnic Chinese Family Firms', 287, 307.

[154] Qian, 'Why S-Chip Fraud Cases Keep Cropping Up?'; for further information on the potential exploitation of Chinese companies by their controlling shareholders, see Chapter 6 (China) at II.1.

[155] Singapore Exchange, *Listing Rule Amendments* (2006), available at http://rulebook.sgx.com.

[156] Stamford Law Corporation, 'Making SGX Attractive to S-Chips'.

its business culture – two mechanisms for mitigating private benefits of control that PRC-Controlled Firms lack.

V Uniquely Singaporean, But with Comparative Lessons That Abound

On some level, the story of the rise of the independent director in Singapore is uniquely Singaporean. Only by understanding Singapore's unique political history, regulatory architecture, institutional environment, shareholder landscape and detailed legislation can one gain an accurate picture of the rise and function of the independent director in Singapore. At least two aspects of the independent director in Singapore highlight its idiosyncratic nature.

First, our research reveals that Singapore's adoption and maintenance of the American independent director into its controlling-block shareholder environment made (and arguably still makes) it a corporate governance outlier. While this revelation provides valuable insight into a unique and important aspect of Singapore's world-leading corporate governance system, it also suggests that drawing wider comparative lessons from it may be difficult.

Second, many of the most salient aspects of the rise and function of the independent director in Singapore may not be readily generalisable. The ability of Singapore's regulators to use informal mechanisms to effectively mitigate private benefits of control in local companies has almost certainly been facilitated by the small and tight-knit nature of Singapore's business community. Singapore's small pool of talented independent directors is another distinct feature that has had a significant impact on the regulation of its independent directors. Singapore's efficient and meritocratic government has played an important role in the rise of the independent director in Singapore – an aspect that further distinguishes it from some other jurisdictions. Finally, Singapore's status as a small city state heightens the need for it to attract foreign capital, and limits its ability to set its own corporate governance standards – which create distinctive high-powered incentives for Singapore to signal compliance with international corporate governance standards.

Despite the undeniably Singaporean character of the rise and function of the independent director in Singapore, this analysis teems with comparative lessons that challenge core understandings about independent directors and comparative corporate law. First, it suggests that comparative corporate law pays insufficient attention to the *precise identity* of shareholders – not merely whether they are generally dispersed or concentrated – as a determinant of how independent directors (and, we suspect, many other corporate governance mechanisms) actually function. As demonstrated above, the function and effectiveness of independent directors in Singapore is highly contingent on whether they are on the board of a Family Firm, a Government-Linked Company or a PRC-Controlled Firm. Ultimately, this suggests that understanding the precise identity of controlling shareholders (i.e., who they are and, in turn, what drives them) is imperative for accurately understanding the function and effectiveness of independent directors and potentially many other corporate governance mechanisms.

Second, this analysis suggests that the definition of 'independence' has received far too little attention. It is surprising that some of the most often cited literature on independent directors – particularly cross-country empirical analyses – have almost entirely disregarded the critical differences in the definition of independence and/or erroneously assumed the global ubiquity of American-style independent directors.[157] The failure of prominent international organisations, such as the World Bank, to account for jurisdictional differences in the definition of independence is disconcerting.[158] The Singapore story demonstrates that the precise definition of independence is critically important and must be carefully considered.

Third, the rise of the independent director in Singapore demonstrates the importance of signalling as a driving force in the regulation and adoption of independent directors, which has largely been overlooked. Singapore has apparently been able to credibly signal 'good' corporate governance by formally adopting independent directors without fundamentally altering the manner in which its companies function. At first blush, it would seem that such 'hollow signalling' would be quickly identified by free-market forces and thus be highly ineffective as its credibility as a signal of 'good' corporate governance quickly erodes.

However, such 'hollow signalling' appears to have remained effective and credible in Singapore for a significant period of time. We suggest

[157] Gordon, 'The Rise of Independent Directors in the United States', n. 164.

[158] N. A. Chakra and H. Kaddoura, *Doing Business 2015: Measuring Business Regulations Protecting Minority Investors in [Name of Economy] 2014* (2014), available at www.doingbusiness.org; N. A. Chakra et al., *Doing Business 2016: Protecting Minority Investors* (2015), available at www.doingbusiness.org.

that this has occurred because of the unique functional substitutes that Singapore has developed to mitigate private benefits of control. Singapore's system of corporate governance kept private benefits of control in check in Government-Linked Companies and Family Firms (i.e., Singapore delivered on its promise to investors, but just not in the way that the signal suggested it would). Thus, it may be better to view Singapore's adoption of the American independent director as an example of 'halo signalling', as it was done to bolster the image of Singapore's corporate governance by leveraging on the positive image of American-cum-international norms of 'good' corporate governance (i.e., something akin to the 'halo effect').

Finally, the problems that Singapore has faced with PRC-Controlled Firms illuminate the complexity of corporate governance regulation in an increasingly globalised environment. It is now common for companies to be listed in jurisdictions that have no connection to their place of business or the domicile of their controllers. As demonstrated by PRC-Controlled Firms, such companies may disrupt otherwise effective corporate governance solutions that rely on informal regulation built on reputational capital and local business norms. This suggests that formal, transparent and standard regulatory mechanisms – similar to those implemented by Singapore to mitigate its problem with PRC-Controlled Firms – may increasingly become the norm. We suggest this with a twinge of sadness as academics who delight in uncovering idiosyncratic local corporate governance solutions that challenge conventional wisdom.

10

Board Independence in India

From Form to Function?

VIKRAMADITYA KHANNA AND UMAKANTH VAROTTIL*

I Introduction

Board independence has become a critical centrepiece in the corporate governance debate.[1] Many argue that enhancing board independence is likely to improve firm performance, reduce corporate wrongdoing and result in a host of other benefits.[2] Others suggest that the current working of the board and the definition of independence are such that

* Thanks to Hita Kumar for research assistance. Errors or omissions, however, remain ours.

[1] See J. Armour, H. Hansmann and R. Kraakman, 'What Is Corporate Law?' in R. Kraakman et al. (eds.), *The Anatomy of Corporate Law: A Comparative and Functional Approach*, 2nd edn (Oxford University Press, 2009), 31; R. C. Clark, *Corporate Law*, 2nd edn (Little, Brown and Company, 1986); W. Allen, R. Kraakman and G. Subramanian, *Commentaries and Cases on the Law of Business Organization*, 4th edn (Wolters Kluwer, 2012); D. C. Clarke, 'Three Concepts of the Independent Director', *Delaware Journal of Corporate Law*, 32 (2007), 73.

[2] See R. C. Anderson and D. M. Reeb, 'Board Composition: Balancing Family Influence in S&P 500 Firms', *Administrative Science Quarterly*, 49 (2004), 209. See also R. C. Anderson and D. M. Reeb, 'Founding-Family Ownership and Firm Performance: Evidence from the S&P 500', *Journal of Finance*, 58 (2003), 1301. See also B. Villalonga and R. Amit, 'How Do Family Ownership, Control and Management Affect Firm Value?', *Journal of Financial Economics*, 80 (2006), 385; J. Dahya, O. Dimitrov and J. J. McConnell, 'Dominant Shareholders, Corporate Boards, and Corporate Value: A Cross-Country Analysis', *Journal of Financial Economics*, 87 (2008), 73; B. E. Hermalin and M. S. Weisbach, 'The Determinants of Board Composition', *The Rand Journal of Economics*, 19 (1988), 589; B. D. Baysinger and H. N. Butler, 'Corporate Governance and the Board of Directors: Performance Effects of Changes in Board Composition', *Journal of Law, Economics and Organization*, 1 (1985), 101.

achieving these benefits is not likely to be easy or, in some instances, realistic.[3] Although these debates rage in Anglo-American scholarship, their importance has become more global as scholars and practitioners from around the world discuss whether board independence might serve a useful function in their countries. However, firms in countries outside the US and the UK tend to have very different ownership structures and institutional backgrounds than Anglo-American firms. For example, Anglo-American firms are perceived to be dispersedly held, with no controlling group, while firms in the rest of the world are thought to be largely controlled firms. Similarly, the institutional conditions in the US and the UK are considerably different than those in emerging economies. These different types of ownership structures and institutional conditions, amongst other things, raise questions about how well one can transplant the independent director concept to other parts of the world.

In this chapter we explore the application and evolution of board independence in India, what effects it has had, and how one might make the best use of the board independence concept in an environment different from the Anglo-American one. In particular, we examine how the concept of board independence came to India, how the different ownership and institutional conditions in India may influence one's views on the functioning and value of board independence, and how the definition of independence may emphasise factors differently across varying ownership and institutional conditions.

Section II begins the discussion by describing how firms in India (and much of the world) are quite different from the Anglo-American firms on which the concept of board independence was built. In particular, it lays out the different ownership and institutional conditions in India and discusses how that may influence one's views on board independence. Section III then provides a discussion of how the concept of an independent board came to be in India. It largely appears to be a result

[3] D. Yermack, 'Higher Market Valuation of Companies with a Small Board of Directors', *Journal of Financial Economics*, 40 (1996), 185; B. S. Black et al., 'Russian Privatization and Corporate Governance: What Went Wrong?', *Stanford Law Review*, 52 (2000), 1731; D. A. DeMott, 'Guests at the Table?: Independent Directors in Family-Influenced Public Companies', *Journal of Corporation Law*, 33 (2008), 819; R. J. Gilson and J. N. Gordon, 'Controlling Controlling Shareholders', *University of Pennsylvania Law Review*, 152 (2003), 785; B. S. Black et al., 'Does Corporate Governance Predict Firms' Market Values? Evidence from Korea', *Journal of Law, Economics and Organization*, 22 (2006), 366; S. Bhagat and B. S. Black, 'The Non-Correlation between Board Independence and Long-Term Firm Performance', *Journal of Corporation Law*, 27 (2002), 231.

of Indian firms and the government wishing to attract foreign investors to India. Section IV then adds to this by describing the existing empirical research on the effects of board independence both in the US and in other parts of the world. From this we can examine whether the use of independent boards has proven valuable (and why) in these contexts and what that may tell us about how best to utilise board independence in India. Indeed, thus far, the evidence does not suggest that the current rules for board independence are generating value across all firms. Moreover, the evidence in India is at best equivocal. Section V then proceeds to lay out the most recent Indian reforms in this area and notes that they appear to have moved away from the fairly formalistic conception of board independence discussed earlier and towards greater functionality by adapting the operation of the board to the environment in India. These developments augur well for the concept of board independence, but there is still much to do if it is to reach its full potential. Section VI discusses some further reforms that may facilitate more effective use of board independence in India. Section VII concludes.

Before beginning our exploration of board independence in India, we note that the concept of independence is not a self-defining one and reasonable minds might differ on what it precisely means. The simplest conception of independence is usually that the director has no financial ties (direct or indirect) to the party engaging in the putatively conflicted transaction.[4] For example, if the conflicted transaction involves a firm selling something (e.g., an apartment) to one of its executives then a director may be considered independent as long as she has no financial ties with the executive or is not dependent on the executive for something of importance. Although this may be treated as the most basic definition, there are others. The Delaware Chancery Court has held that in the context of a special independent litigation committee, independence may have a broader meaning – can a director make a decision simply based on the facts of the issue at hand and not be influenced by other considerations?[5] This expands the concept of independence from financial connections to social connections as well.[6] In yet other contexts, independence may need to include examination of the effects of other relationships (e.g., family, kinship networks) and may involve positive qualifications

[4] See, e.g., Clarke, 'Three Concepts of the Independent Director', 86–87.

[5] See *In Re Oracle Corp. Derivative Litigation*, 824 A.2d 917, 938–39 (Del. Ch. 2003).

[6] *Ibid.*

(e.g., expertise requirements).[7] We mention these different conceptions to note that independence is a malleable concept that is likely to vary with what one considers important in influencing a director's decision making and the board's perceived role in a country's corporate governance tapestry. This indicates that board independence is likely to depend on context – a point we will be underscoring throughout our analysis.

II How Might Independent Boards Be Useful to Indian Firms?

We begin with a fairly basic, but surprisingly complicated, question: what is the value of board independence to Indian firms? To explore this question we examine how board independence might be valuable in the context of Anglo-American firms – where the concept seems to have been most debated – and then discuss how it might be valuable in the, quite different, Indian context.

Much of the prior literature notes that the discussion of independent directors in the US and UK seems to assume a dispersed ownership structure at the firm (i.e., no controlling shareholder and few large shareholders).[8] Such dispersed shareholders may face a collective action problem in monitoring managers and holding them accountable. This makes it more likely that managers will be able to behave in a manner that benefits themselves at the expense of shareholders. Thus, the agency problem in these firms is between managers and shareholders *en masse*.[9] That leads to the types of issues that independent directors face most often

[7] This can be found in the examples of family business groups in India, *chaebol* in South Korea, *keiretsu* in Japan, *guanxi* (relationships) in China, Palanpuri Jains and Maghrabi Jewish merchants, to name a few. See, for example, H. Dahles and H. Wels (eds.), *Culture, Organization and Management in East Asia: Doing Business in China* (Nova Science Publishers, 2002); A. Grief, 'Family Structure, Institutions, and Growth: The Origins and Implications of Western Corporations', *American Economic Review*, 96(2) (2006), 308.

[8] See Armour et al., 'What Is Corporate Law?'; Gilson and Gordon, 'Controlling Controlling Shareholders'; R. J. Gilson, 'Controlling Shareholders and Corporate Governance: Complicating the Comparative Taxonomy', *Harvard Law Review*, 119 (2006), 1641; R. La Porta et al., 'Corporate Ownership around the World', *Journal of Finance*, 54 (1999), 471; B. Cheffins, 'Law as Bedrock: The Foundations of an Economy Dominated by Widely Held Public Companies', *Oxford Journal of Legal Studies*, 23 (2003), 1; L. A. Bebchuk and A. Hamdani, 'The Elusive Quest for Global Corporate Governance Standards', *University of Pennsylvania Law Review*, 157 (2009), 1263; V. Khanna, 'Corporate Governance Ratings: One Score, Two Scores, or More?', *University of Pennsylvania Law Review*, 158 (2009), 39.

[9] See Clark, *Corporate Law*; Allen et al., *Commentaries and Cases*; Bebchuk and Hamdani, 'The Elusive Quest for Global Corporate Standards', 1301–1302.

in the US (e.g., executive compensation, hostile takeovers and potential self-dealing with a director). Independent directors may prove useful here because these are often discrete transactions (that can be reviewed in a meeting) and these directors are thought to have sufficient 'distance' from management that they can exercise their independent judgement and oversight.

However, in many countries (e.g., India) most firms are not dispersedly held, but rather are controlled. Here the controller normally closely monitors managers. In such a situation, the concern is not that managers can simply benefit themselves at the expense of shareholders, but rather that managers will do what a controller tells them to do and that may lead to decisions benefitting the controller at the expense of non-controlling shareholders (i.e., the minority shareholders). Thus, the agency problem is between the controlling shareholder and other shareholders.[10] That leads to the following common issues – tunnelling of profits from the controlled firm to another firm, freeze out transactions and sales of control.[11]

That raises the critical question – how are independent directors useful in addressing concerns arising in these kinds of controlled transactions? The key problem is that directors are normally appointed by the controlling shareholder or group, which raises doubts about whether they can act independently from the controller.[12] Moreover, the board's primary source of information is likely to be the controller, thereby raising further doubts about their effectiveness.[13] Of course, if directors could obtain good information and felt secure that they could not be easily removed by the controller (e.g., there would be a reputational loss visited upon a controller for such a dismissal), then one might have more confidence in them. Further, if the controller does not drive the appointments process, then there may also be greater room for the director to display their independence. Indeed, judicial standards in the US, and

10 Bebchuk and Hamdani, 'The Elusive Quest for Global Corporate Standards', 1302; U. Varottil, 'Evolution and Effectiveness of Independent Directors in Indian Corporate Governance', *Hastings Business Law Journal*, 6 (2010), 281, 283.

11 M. Bertrand et al., 'Ferreting Out Tunneling: An Application to Indian Business Groups', *Quarterly Journal of Economics*, 117(1) (2002), 121, 121; V. S. Khanna and U. Varottil, 'Regulating Squeeze Outs in India: A Comparative Perspective', *American Journal of Comparative Law*, 63 (2015), 1009.

12 See Gilson and Gordon, 'Controlling Controlling Shareholders'; Varottil, 'Evolution and Effectiveness of Independent Directors in Indian Corporate Governance'; Khanna, 'Corporate Governance Ratings'.

13 Gilson and Gordon, 'Controlling Controlling Shareholders'; Varottil, 'Evolution and Effectiveness of Independent Directors in Indian Corporate Governance'; Khanna, 'Corporate Governance Ratings'.

reform efforts in many countries, seem designed to incentivise controllers to give directors the ability to obtain their own information and act more independently.[14] In spite of this, the effectiveness of these measures is very much up for debate.

Although the controlled versus dispersedly held firm is a helpful dichotomy, we argue this division may be too coarse for the purpose of evaluating, and even defining, board independence. For example, it is quite clear that all controllers are not the same. Some firms have one person who is a controlling shareholder (e.g., Larry Ellison at Oracle), but other firms have multiple people or firms that operate together as a controlling group (e.g., the founders at Google, a family business group in India). There are likely to be differences of import between these two. Further, even amongst firms with controlling groups there are likely to be differences. Some controlling groups are comprised of multi-generational family members and their group decision making is likely to involve a different constellation of factors than that of controlling groups comprised of non-family members (e.g., the common image of the Japanese *keiretsu*). Moreover, a different set of considerations likely operates when the state is the controller. Let us examine each of these separately.

1 Single Controller vs. Controlling Group

In a firm controlled by a single controller, that controller will make her decisions – for good or bad. Thus, non-controlling shareholders will focus their monitoring primarily on the behaviour of the controlling person. However, the calculus may look somewhat different if the firm is controlled by a group of shareholders. In such a firm, the controlling group may not always act as cohesively as a single controller firm. Indeed, one can imagine that a controlling group may not always act in tandem or that the issues driving the vote may not only revolve around a particular transaction, but around other seemingly unrelated issues. Further, different controlling groups may have differing levels of cohesion over time so that group decision making can be fraught with many complications.

[14] See Allen et al., *Commentaries and Cases*; Khanna and Varottil, 'Regulating Squeeze Outs'; L. Lin, 'The Effectiveness of Outside Directors as a Corporate Governance Mechanism: Theories and Evidence', *Northwestern University Law Review*, 90 (1996), 898, 914–916; M. A. Eisenberg, *The Structure of the Corporation: A Legal Analysis* (Little, Brown and Company, 1976), 144.

In light of these differences, one can imagine independent directors having a somewhat different task for single controller firms compared to firms controlled by a group. Of course, for the directors to be useful they will need to perceive that they can act independently, but even if they perceive that, their tasks will be different depending on whether the controller is one person or a group.

2 Family Controlling Group vs. Non-Family Controlling Group

However, even firms controlled by groups could differ if the group was a multi-generational family as opposed to a group of relative strangers. These two types of groups may raise differing concerns for monitoring purposes. For example, family groups may have concerns that are very long term in nature (e.g., multi-generational), whereas non-family groups seem less likely to possess such multi-generational concerns. Second, within families the internal politics are renowned for bedevilling the best of strategists.[15] In light of this, the monitoring task at family firms is likely to be substantially more complicated than at firms where the controlling group is not family. Indeed, as studies in both the US and elsewhere have suggested, being a director at a family controlled firm involves a host of complex issues not only in terms of monitoring, but also understanding one's role.[16]

In light of these different kinds of ownership structures, one might suspect that both monitoring and the role of independent directors is likely to vary substantially depending on what type of firm is at issue. One could imagine that the independent directors, non-controlling shareholders and controlling shareholders might have different expectations in these situations. This might then quite plausibly lead to a need to have different duties or nuances to duties and roles for independent directors in these kinds of firms.[17]

[15] J. Baron and R. Lachenauer, 'Surviving in a Family Business When You're Not Part of the Family', *Harvard Business Review*, 15 January 2015, available at https://hbr.org/2015/01/surviving-in-a-family-business-when-youre-not-part-of-the-family.

[16] DeMott, 'Guests at the Table?'; T. Khanna and Y. Yafeh, 'Business Groups in Emerging Markets: Paragons or Parasites?', *Journal of Economic Literature*, 45(2) (2007), 331; P. Ghemawat and T. Khanna, 'The Nature of Diversified Business Groups: A Research Design and Two Case Studies', *Journal of Industrial Economics*, 46(1) (1998), 35; C. Holderness, 'The Myth of Diffuse Ownership in the United States', *The Review of Financial Studies*, 22 (2009), 1377.

[17] One might respond that having shareholders with different time horizons or interests is something that is present even in dispersedly held firms in the US and elsewhere and

3 The State as Controlling Shareholder

In India, and in many other countries, state-owned enterprises (SOEs) continue to play an important role.[18] The state, however, is a somewhat unique controller because its incentives may differ from those of other controllers suggesting that the monitoring tasks for independent directors may be different. At one level, the state may be considered as a single controller, but that notion would be rather superficial. Unlike a single private controller, the state is not a unitary actor.[19] Different governmental bodies and agencies may carry differing interests that may be difficult to reconcile.[20] In that sense, the state's position could be akin to that of a group of controllers.

Further, the state's incentives as a controller are likely to be different from that of private controllers. In the case of private controllers, conflicts of interests and benefits of control are manifested through financial transactions. For example, one might surmise that private controllers may engage in abusive related party transactions by which they enrich themselves to the detriment of the minority shareholders.[21] We might not expect the state to engage in as much of this kind of behaviour, but it might deviate from wealth maximisation. For example, the state may pursue transactions that help achieve certain political goals that are detrimental to the financial interest of the firm (and thereby its minority shareholders).[22] For example, Indian SOEs have been subject to criticism on the ground that they have sold their products at less than market price (effectively operating as a subsidy) to achieve political goals of the

there have been few significant changes to the roles of independent directors there: so why expect (or demand) them here? One critical difference is that here we are talking about differences in the set of people who are the *controllers* of a firm, whereas in the US the shareholders with different interests are not controllers and hence have a lower likelihood of being able to actually influence corporate behaviour.

18 Several leading listed companies in India are substantially owned by the state. They are referred to as 'public sector undertakings' (PSUs). See R. Chakrabarti, W. Megginson and P. K. Yadav, 'Corporate Governance in India', *Journal of Applied Corporate Finance*, 20 (2008), 59, 66.

19 M. Kahan and E. B. Rock, 'When the Government Is the Controlling Shareholder', *Texas Law Review*, 89 (2011), 1293, 1318.

20 M. Pargendler, 'State Ownership and Corporate Governance', *Fordham Law Review*, 80 (2012), 2917, 2921.

21 Kahan and Rock, 'When the Government', 1318.

22 *Ibid.* See also, L. Lin and C. J. Milhaupt, 'We Are the (National) Champions: Understanding the Mechanisms of State Capitalism in China', *Stanford Law Review*, 65 (2013), 697.

state, thereby depriving minority shareholders of wealth maximisation through their investment.[23]

Board independence may thus take on a different hue in SOEs. The full ramifications of the role and actions of independent directors in SOEs are yet elusive, but it is clear that their position requires them to balance varying factors. To illustrate, the task of independent directors in privately controlled firms may be relatively clear-cut: related party transactions can be judged through measurable standards. However, when it comes to a state controller's actions to fulfil political goals, monitoring by independent directors is somewhat obscure. Hence, the traditional notions of board independence and what we expect from independent directors are unlikely to operate in the same manner for SOEs, which may require an alternative focus.

Although these differences in ownership structure are likely to be important, they are not the only matters of importance. Institutional conditions are also critical. For example, family controlled firms are quite common in countries with institutional environments that are quite different to the US. Indeed, taking India as an example, it is generally well acknowledged that family groups often fill certain institutional voids.[24] Further, SOEs may also be more common in certain kinds of institutional environments. Thus, the general institutional environment is likely to influence many things, including how monitoring might occur and the resultant role of independent directors. To obtain a taste of this we discuss institutional environments and family group firms.

4 *Family Groups and Institutional Environment*

Khanna and Yafeh provide a detailed overview of the literature on family groups and find that in emerging markets, the family group structure often helps to fill a number of institutional voids or weaknesses. Thus, if the court system moves slowly (as it does in India) then transacting with a family group may provide more assurances than relying on contractual promises.[25] Weak judicial enforcement is likely to lead to less weight placed on contractual promises and more weight on the reputation of

[23] V. Bajaj, 'The Children's Investment Fund Wages Battle with Coal India', *New York Times*, 19 April 2012.

[24] Khanna and Yafeh, 'Business Groups in Emerging Markets'.

[25] *Ibid.*, 340; R. J. Gilson, 'Controlling Family Shareholders in Developing Countries: Anchoring Relational Exchange', *Stanford Law Review*, 60 (2007), 633.

the parties who are transacting.[26] A family group may have years (perhaps generations) of family capital at stake in transactions.[27] Further, if the leaders of the firm are concerned about future generations they are likely to have reputational concerns that spill over into the future as well.[28] Indeed, Khanna and Yafeh refer to work where the family's ability to prevent the bankruptcy of a particular firm in a group can be viewed as a strong advantage in an institutional environment with weak credit markets and glacial bankruptcy processes.[29]

This means, however, that family norms (either society-wide or family-specific) may substitute for some of the institutional apparatus seen in the US and the UK. If so, then one might expect that when the institutional pre-conditions for the effectiveness of independent directors in the US are not present (as in many emerging markets),[30] then the optimal role of independent directors in these institutionally distinct markets is likely to be different from that in the US. Indeed, one doubts that non-controlling shareholders in India expect independent directors to operate as they do in the US and elsewhere.[31] If so, then the price they pay for their minority shares and the steps they take to protect themselves are likely to be different than similarly placed shareholders in the US.[32]

In a similar vein, Professors Black and Kraakman have argued that emerging economies face unique constraints in that the presence of controlling shareholders is coupled with weaknesses in institutional, market, cultural and legal protections.[33] Hence, what applies in the developed markets will not equally hold well in emerging markets. They propose a 'self-enforcing' model of corporate law that takes into consideration the

[26] Khanna and Yafeh, 'Business Groups in Emerging Markets', 340.

[27] *Ibid.*, 349.

[28] *Ibid.*

[29] *Ibid.*

[30] B. S. Black and R. Kraakman, 'A Self-Enforcing Model of Corporate Law', *Harvard Law Review*, 109 (1996), 1911; B. S. Black, 'The Core Institutions That Support Strong Securities Markets', *Business Lawyer*, 55 (2000), 1565.

[31] V. Khanna and S. J. Mathew, 'The Role of Independent Directors in Controlled Firms in India: Preliminary Interview Evidence', *National Law School of India Review*, 22 (2010), 35.

[32] This, of course, might result in less efficiency and wealth than if institutions were closer to the US (although there is debate on that), but at a minimum it means that we should think carefully about whether we can hold independent directors in India and other emerging markets to the same standards and expectations in the substantially different institutional and ownership environments seen in the US and the UK.

[33] Black and Kraakman, 'A Self-Enforcing Model'.

unique factors present in emerging markets and seeks to enforce corporate law through direct participation by shareholders, directors and managers with minimal reliance upon the institutional set-up within the legal system.[34] The presence of controlling shareholders would require independent directors to play a significant role, particularly in filtering significant transactions such as those with related parties. The lack of a robust institutional environment puts greater pressures on independent directors than in the more developed markets such as the US.

5 *Desirable Features of Board Independence in India*

Given the structural and institutional considerations present in India, how might one regulate board independence in India? As we have seen, controlling shareholders of varying kinds have the ability to appoint and remove independent directors. This then means that independent directors are required to monitor the controlling shareholders who decide whether to appoint or remove these same independent directors. This raises the question of how can one expect independent directors to discharge their roles when they are operating in the shadow of the immense power wielded by controlling shareholders over their appointment?

Of course, one might consider alternative appointment mechanisms. For example, the appointment of independent directors by cumulative voting or by a vote in which the controlling shareholder cannot participate (i.e., majority-of-the-minority vote) may offer some succour. Similarly, one might require detailed disclosure if an independent director is removed, resigns or is not renewed. Detailed disclosures to shareholders in this situation not only make the process transparent, but may also disincentivise controllers from acting in a manner that imposes undue influence on independent directors. Further, conferring greater powers to independent directors to approve specific transactions might also help curtail the agency problem between controllers and minority shareholders. We set out our wish list for enhancing board independence in India later,[35] but very few of them operate currently in India primarily because the regime in India on board independence is the result of a legal transplant.

[34] *Ibid.*, 1916.

[35] We discuss the desirable features of board independence in greater detail in section VI below.

If the norms and expectations governing independent directors in the US are not a good fit for India then the issue becomes what might be a better way to utilise the advantages of independent directors in the Indian institutional context. We begin exploring this in sections III through VI starting with a discussion of the key rules governing board independence in India.

Prior to that, it may be useful to note that much of the discussion thus far has focused on the board monitoring either management or the controller. However, this is not the extent of the board's functions at the firm. Generally, directors may be conceived of as engaging in at least two roles – providing strategic advice to management/the controller and monitoring the behaviour and transactions of these key players for the benefit of the firm or its shareholders.[36] Most studies of directors find that directors believe their role is primarily the former, whereas the law and other players seem to think monitoring is key. Indeed, there is some tension in these roles,[37] but in this section we abstracted away from that to focus on the critical role played by ownership structure and institutional conditions. We will come back to the monitoring and strategic roles later when we discuss reforms.

III Evolution of Norms on Board Independence in India

The initial development of independent directors in India can be traced to measures implemented soon after India's 1991 economic liberalisation. The first foray into governance reform came in 1998 in the form of a voluntary code promulgated by Indian industry – the Confederation of Indian Industry (CII) – which adopted global best practices, at that time, for governance including independent directors.[38] Only a few

[36] J. Gordon, 'The Rise of Independent Directors in the United States, 1950–2005: Of Shareholder Value and Stock Market Prices', *Stanford Law Review*, 59 (2007), 1465; Khanna and Mathew, 'The Role of Independent Directors'.

[37] At first cut, these two roles may sometimes lead in different directions – providing strategic advice requires a high level of trust and information exchange, whereas being thought of as a monitor may result in suspicion and hoarding of information. This makes engaging in both roles potentially challenging. Moreover, effective monitoring may require much more frequent engagement with the firm (e.g., meeting every week) than the standard board assignment involves (e.g., meeting once every two months). Yet, it seems clear that much of the discussion surrounding independent directors assumes that they will pursue both of these roles with vigour.

[38] V. Khanna, 'Corporate Governance in India: Past, Present and Future', *Jindal Global Law Review*, 1 (2009), 171; Chakrabarti et al., 'Corporate Governance in India'.

firms adopted this voluntary code, which led CII to lobby the securities markets regulator, the Securities and Exchange Board of India (SEBI), to enact governance reforms. SEBI constituted the Kumar Mangalam Birla Committee and it proposed governance reforms (including provisions for independent directors) that were quickly implemented by SEBI in the form of Clause 49 of the listing agreement in the year 2000.[39] In 2004 these reforms were strengthened with larger penalties for non-compliance.[40] This formed the basis for the regulation of independent directors in India.[41]

Before discussing the impact of the initial version of Clause 49, it might be useful to consider some of the factors that motivated these enhanced governance norms, particularly board independence. One factor relates to the ability of Indian companies to raise capital from international investors both in the primary markets as well as secondary markets. This required governance norms that were consistent with international standards so as to be able to raise foreign capital at attractive valuations. The other factor relates to cross-listing whereby Indian companies began listing their securities (usually depository receipts) on foreign stock exchanges. Apart from seeking capital at better valuations, overseas listings were also driven by the desire of companies to build credibility and reputation in the international markets.[42] Greater numbers of offshore listings by Indian companies compelled such companies to adhere to the corporate governance norms and practices of the markets where they listed their securities.[43] Consequently, those norms and

[39] Khanna, 'Corporate Governance in India'; B. S. Black and V. S. Khanna, 'Can Corporate Governance Reforms Increase Firm Market Values? Event Study Evidence from India', *Journal of Empirical Legal Studies*, 4 (2007), 749.

[40] See *ibid.*; D. Dharmapala and V. Khanna, 'Corporate Governance, Enforcement, and Firm Value: Evidence from India', *Journal of Law, Economics and Organization*, 29 (2013), 1056.

[41] Clause 49 has undergone a revamp in 2014, so as to bring it in line with the provisions of the Companies Act, 2013, a matter that we discuss in section V below.

[42] V. Khanna and N. C. Howson, 'Reverse Cross-Listings: The Coming Race to List in Emerging Markets and an Enhanced Understanding of Classical Bonding', *Cornell International Law Journal*, 47 (2014), 607; T. Khanna and K. G. Palepu, 'Globalization and Convergence in Corporate Governance: Evidence from Infosys and the Indian Software Industry', *Journal of International Business Studies*, 35 (2004), 484, 484.

[43] See also A. N. Licht, 'Cross-Listing and Corporate Governance: Bonding or Avoiding?', *Chicago Journal of International Law*, 4 (2003), 141, 142 (referring to this concept as the 'bonding thesis' and noting that 'cross-listing on a foreign stock market can serve as a bonding mechanism for corporate insiders to commit credibly to a better governance regime').

practices permeated into the general Indian corporate scenario, at least among the leading and more reputable companies.

Under Clause 49 the basic requirement was that publicly listed firms must have a board composed of at least one-third independent directors and if the board chair is an executive (or promoter or related thereto) of the firm then the board must be half independent directors.[44] In order for a director to qualify as 'independent', the general test was that apart from receiving director's remuneration, the person should not have any material pecuniary relationships or transactions with the company, its promoters, its directors, its senior management or its holding company, or its subsidiaries and associates which may affect independence of the director.[45] Certain additional circumstances were listed in Clause 49 where a director would be presumed not to be independent.

Although Clause 49 defined independence in a manner consistent with global standards, it did not provide guidance on the nomination and appointments process (which is thus largely run by the controller), to whom duties are owed to (thus leaving the minority with little explicit protection), or on the roles of independent directors (to monitor or be strategic advisors) except in the context of audit committees and remuneration committees – both matters of importance in US and UK firms.[46] Indeed, there was less than full compliance with these requirements (with state-run firms often being the violators) and director compensation was low by international standards (yet there are non-trivial liability risks for directors).[47] This further limits the effectiveness of independent directors.

The overall impression created is that the definition of independence and the roles of independent directors have largely been borrowed from global best standards and implemented in India with little attention paid to the Indian commercial and institutional context and with rules that have the effect of weakening some of the potential benefits of independent directors in India.[48] Perhaps the motivating factors discussed above

[44] Clause 49, Article X(1)(ii) of the Listing Agreement, available at www.nseindia.com [hereinafter Listing Agreement].

[45] This definition was initially introduced by the Kumar Mangalam Committee Report (at para. 6.5).

[46] Varottil, 'Evolution and Effectiveness of Independent Directors in Indian Corporate Governance'.

[47] N. Balasubramanian et al., 'The Relation between Firm-Level Corporate Governance and Market Value: A Study of India', *Emerging Markets Review*, 11 (2010), 319.

[48] See Varottil, 'Evolution and Effectiveness of Independent Directors in Indian Corporate Governance'; Khanna, 'Corporate Governance in India'. One cross-country study points out that the weakness in the role of independent directors in several countries indicates that board independence is introduced to accommodate investors' preference

in terms of the internationalisation of India's capital markets and cross-listing partly explain this phenomenon whereby there was great emphasis on form and less on substance or function. This then led to the sense, voiced in some research, that independent directors primarily provide some sense of assurance (or a signal) to Western investors rather than having a meaningful impact on governance in India.[49] We will explore this further in the next section, which examines empirical evidence on independent directors.

IV What Effects Do Independent Boards Have?

The most detailed research on the value of board independence has been conducted in the US. A number of scholarly studies have empirically examined the effects of board independence on a firm's performance and the likelihood of certain types of wrongdoing. The studies do not provide consistent results, although there are some trends that are emerging.

1 Empirical Studies on the Value of Board Independence

Some studies have found a negative association between board independence and firm performance, while others have found little to no effect.[50] Scholars have indicated that this may be the result of a strong background institutional environment (e.g., effective court system, active public and private enforcement and large stock markets) where the value of board independence may be hard to separate from these other institutional elements or where the added value of board independence is difficult to ascertain.[51] Further, many firms in the US may follow quite similar

for Western-style corporate governance. G. Ferrarini and M. Filipelli, 'Independent Directors and Controlling Shareholders around the World' (European Corporate Governance Institute – Law Working Paper No. 258/2014, 2014), available at http://ssrn.com/abstract=2443786. For further discussion on possible divergence in the definitions of independence, see Chapter 2 at III.2.

49 Varottil, 'Evolution and Effectiveness of Independent Directors in Indian Corporate Governance'; for similar research in the context of Singapore's independent director regime, see Chapter 9 (Singapore) at IV.

50 Clarke, 'Three Concepts'; Black et al., 'Russian Privatization'; DeMott, 'Guests at the Table?'; Gilson and Gordon, 'Controlling Controlling Shareholders'; Black et al., 'Evidence from Korea'; Bhagat and Black, 'The Non-Correlation'; Gordon, 'The Rise of Independent Directors in the United States'.

51 Black, 'The Core Institutions'; Bhagat and Black, 'The Non-Correlation'; Gordon, 'The Rise of Independent Directors in the United States'.

governance practices (at least on paper) and that may make it more difficult to discern an effect empirically.[52]

In terms of the likelihood of reducing corporate wrongdoing, many studies find that overall board independence has little effect on the likelihood of wrongdoing, but that independent directors with financial expertise are associated with lower rates of financial misstatement fraud.[53] One likely explanation for this outcome is that the studies examining the effect of financial expertise amongst independent directors were focused on a particular type of wrongdoing, financial misstatements or misreporting, where possessing financial expertise might be particularly important in deterring or preventing it. Few studies examining non-financial misstatement fraud seem to find strong effects associated with board independence, although these studies are sometimes equivocal.[54]

These mixed results have led scholars to examine more deeply the US market (looking for firms that may respond differentially to board independence, such as controlled firms versus dispersed firms) and to turn their focus to markets outside the US and the UK (e.g., China, India, Brazil, South Korea, Russia) where there is likely to be much greater heterogeneity in governance practices as well as in institutional environments (making it potentially easier to measure the effects of board independence empirically). There too results have been mixed, but with some clearer trajectories.

In family controlled firms in the US, Anderson and Reeb find that a higher degree of board independence was correlated with better firm performance.[55] Similar findings were present in a study of Hong Kong firms

52 Bhagat and Black, 'The Non-Correlation'; Gordon, 'The Rise of Independent Directors in the United States'.

53 A. Klein, 'Audit Committee, Board of Director Characteristics, and Earnings Management', *Journal of Accounting and Economics*, 33 (2002), 375; V. Khanna et al., 'CEO Connectedness and Corporate Fraud', *Journal of Finance*, 70 (2015), 1203; C. Skousen et al., 'Detecting and Predicting Financial Statement Fraud: The Effectiveness of the Fraud Triangle and SAS No. 99', *Advances in Financial Economics*, 13 (2009), 53; D. Blanchard and G. Dionne, 'Risk Management and Corporate Governance' (HEC Montreal Risk Management Chair Working Paper No. 03-04, 2003), available at http://ssrn.com/abstract=441482; P. Gompers, J. Ishii and A. Metrick, 'Corporate Governance and Equity Prices', *The Quarterly Journal of Economics*, 118 (2003), 107; L. Bebchuk, A. Cohen and A. Ferrell, 'What Matters in Corporate Governance?', *Review of Financial Studies*, 22 (2008), 783.

54 For a fuller discussion of some of these studies see V. Khanna, 'An Analysis of Internal Governance and the Role of the General Counsel in Reducing Corporate Crime', Draft (2017) [hereinafter 'Internal Governance'].

55 Anderson and Reeb, 'Board Composition'. See also Anderson and Reeb, 'Founding-Family Ownership'; Villalonga and Amit, 'How Do Family Ownership'.

(which are often family controlled).[56] Dahya, Dimitrov and McConnell also find, looking at controlled firms in 22 countries, that board independence is associated with better firm performance.[57] Others have obtained similar results as well.[58]

Although these results suggest that board independence may matter for family controlled firms, and controlled firms in general across countries, the results become more mixed once we explore studies on individual countries as well as more recent studies. Thus, studies on board independence in Brazil seem to find it is either negatively correlated, or not at all correlated, with firm performance,[59] while in South Korea board independence seems positively correlated with performance.[60]

These results suggest that to learn more about India, more in-depth inquiry into the Indian context is essential. The existence of significant ownership concentration in Indian companies has been well documented.[61] Moreover, empirical studies have identified the existence of tunnelling within corporate groups suggesting the exercise of undue influence by controlling shareholders.[62] Thus far, there are a few studies examining the effect of governance (including board independence) on firm performance in India[63] finding that the overall set of Clause 49 corporate governance reforms and enhanced sanctions had a positive impact on firm market value. However, these studies do not focus on the potential impact of board independence in India.

[56] B. Jaggi and J. Tsui, 'Insider Trading Earnings Management and Corporate Governance: Empirical Evidence Based on Hong Kong Firms', *Journal of International Financial Management and Accounting*, 18(3) (2007), 192.

[57] Dahya et al., 'Dominant Shareholders'.

[58] A. Durnev and E. H. Kim, 'To Steal or Not to Steal: Firm Attributes, Legal Environment and Valuation', *Journal of Finance*, 60 (2005), 1461.

[59] B. S. Black et al., 'Methods for Multicountry Studies of Corporate Governance: Evidence from the BRIKT Countries', *Journal of Econometrics*, 183 (2014), 230.

[60] *Ibid.*

[61] S. J. Mathew, 'Hostile Takeovers in India: New Prospects, Challenges, and Regulatory Opportunities', *Columbia Business Law Review*, 3 (2007), 800; N. Balasubramanian and R. V. Anand, 'Ownership Trends in Corporate India 2001–2011: Evidence and Implications' (Indian Institute of Management, Bangalore, Working Paper No. 419, 2013), available at http://ssrn.com/abstract=2303684. For this reason, there is no effective market for corporate control in Indian companies that operates to enhance governance by the managers in the interests of shareholders (particularly the minorities).

[62] Bertrand et al., 'Ferreting Out Tunneling'.

[63] For summaries see Khanna, 'Corporate Governance in India'; Chakrabarti et al., 'Corporate Governance in India'; Black and Khanna, 'Event Study Evidence from India' and Dharmapala and Khanna, 'Corporate Governance, Enforcement'.

For that we turn to Balasubramaniam, Black and Khanna, whose study conducted a large-scale survey of corporate governance practices at publicly traded Indian firms. Their results are based on 370 completed responses and they find little effect of board independence on firm value in India. Moreover, later studies on India[64] confirm this result in a multi-year setting.[65] One recent study finds that the presence of controlling shareholders on the board negatively correlates with firm performance (measured by Tobin's Q), and that a higher proportion of board independence or institutional ownership does not appear to mitigate that result.[66] Another study shows that non-compliance with board independence provisions by Indian SOEs did not have any effect on firm performance.[67] Here too, the empirical studies of the effects of board independence in India do not provide clear indications as to its value or how it might generate value.

Although this suggests that the current structure of independent directors in India is of somewhat uncertain value, that does not mean that the institution of independent directors could not be made more valuable in India with some reforms. After all, in other emerging markets[68] and in family-controlled firms in other countries (e.g., South Korea), board independence appears to be of some value. The question for India may well be what reforms should be considered in order to make the concept of board independence more useful in the Indian context. We turn to that issue in a moment, but prior to that it is important to learn more about the identities and backgrounds of the current crop of independent directors in India in order to have an appropriate sense as to both what they can be expected to do and what reforms may facilitate that.

2 *Information on the Current Crop of Independent Directors in India*

The surveys conducted by Balasubramanian, Black and Khanna (hereinafter BBK)[69] and by various consulting and accounting

[64] Black et al., 'Methods for Multicountry Studies'.

[65] Indeed, in Black et al., 'Methods for Multicountry Studies', there are additional results on board independence using firm fixed effects on Brazil (no effect to mildly positive effect), South Korea (positive effect) and Turkey (little to no effect).

[66] A. Jameson et al., 'Controlling Shareholders, Board Structure, and Firm Performance: Evidence from India', *Journal of Corporate Finance*, 27 (2014), 1.

[67] S. Gill, 'Rethinking the Primacy of Board Efficacy for Governance: Evidence from India', *Corporate Governance*, 13 (2013), 99.

[68] Dahya et al., 'Dominant Shareholders'.

[69] N. Balasubramanian et al., 'The Relation between Firm-Level Corporate Governance and Market Value: A Study of India', *Emerging Markets Review*, 11 (2010), 319.

organisations form the basis of our discussion on the identities and backgrounds of current directors. The first thing to note is that there has been a non-trivial amount of non-compliance with the law regarding board independence – only 87 per cent of responding firms seem to comply with the most basic part of the board independence rules.[70] Even for those firms that comply, there is a sense that a large number engage in paper compliance to satisfy regulatory requirements. One report suggests that almost 60 per cent of its respondents did not have a nominating committee or formal process for selecting independent directors.[71] Here, it appeared it was left to the discretion of the controlling shareholder in large measure. Another report indicates an even higher percentage being appointed via the controller's connections.[72]

The composition of the board also provides some interesting morsels for thought. First, roughly 30 per cent of respondents in BBK had at least one female director (though usually only one), about 40 per cent had one lawyer (usually only one), about 40 per cent had scholars or academics (often more than one) and 30 per cent had former government officials or politicians as independent directors.[73] The reliance on academics and others (e.g., former politicians), who sometimes do not have substantial business experience, raises concerns about their level of expertise. This further contributes to the paper compliance 'feel' of some of these developments in India.[74]

In terms of the working environment and other terms of appointment, the BBK survey provides a few more details. First, most independent directors are appointed for three-year terms and face little risk of being dismissed for poor performance.[75] Although many firms appear to have systems in place for evaluating CEOs and other top executives, only about a quarter have something similar for non-executive directors.[76] Moreover, even for the CEOs and other top executives one may wonder how exacting the evaluation systems are given that in the BBK

[70] *Ibid.*

[71] FICCI and Grant Thornton, 'CG Review 2009: India 101–500' (March 2009).

[72] AT Kearney, AZB & Partners and Hunt Partners, 'India Board Report – 2007: Findings, Action Plans and Innovative Strategies' (2007).

[73] Balasubramanian et al., 'A Study of India'.

[74] One should note that there has been an increase in other firms' executives being appointed to boards – thereby addressing some concerns over expertise, but raising concerns about whether they are truly independent: Varottil, 'Evolution and Effectiveness of Independent Directors in Indian Corporate Governance'.

[75] Balasubramanian et al., 'A Study of India'.

[76] *Ibid.*

survey none of the respondents had their CEO replaced by the board in the last five years.[77]

In terms of executive compensation, the levels reported in BBK did not seem excessive by global standards (indeed they appeared low) and certainly seemed lower than what might be available in the US. Although there are reports that the level of board compensation is increasing, it seems unlikely to be at the level necessary to attract the highest talent.[78] In contrast to the modest compensation levels, there is substantial liability risk for directors. For example, if the company were to breach the law or engage in other kinds of wrongdoing, the directors could conceivably be held liable[79] and directors are unlikely to benefit from indemnification in India.[80]

The expectations of independent directors are also somewhat unclear. The law does not state whether independent directors are to primarily take an active monitoring role or be strategic advisors or both. The risk of liability suggests primarily monitoring, but the selection process (which is highly dependent on the controller) seems to suggest strategic advising. Prior studies, however, suggest that the directors themselves view their role as that of strategic advisors and indeed it does not seem that monitoring has taken on a large role in their tasks.[81] Moreover, the ability of independent directors in India to take on a monitoring role depends largely on the information they have (which is not at the level necessary to engage in monitoring) and the type of training they receive before joining and while functioning as a director (which tend to be minimal).[82]

The overall impression conveyed is that being an independent director at an Indian firm involves fairly modest levels of compensation, potentially substantial liability risks, little training and guidance, little expectation to monitor the controller, a need to be well liked by the controller (because he selects independent directors) and little need to possess high-end business expertise. Of course, there are some firms where this is not

[77] *Ibid.*

[78] Varottil, 'Evolution and Effectiveness of Independent Directors in Indian Corporate Governance'.

[79] U. Varottil, 'Directors' Duties and Liabilities in the New Era', *NSE Quarterly Briefing* (2014), available at www.nseindia.com/research/content/res_QB5.pdf.

[80] Varottil, 'Evolution and Effectiveness of Independent Directors in Indian Corporate Governance'. However, certain exoneration provisions in the company law following recent reforms might come to the aid of independent directors. See section V.5 below.

[81] Khanna and Mathew, 'The Role of Independent Directors'.

[82] Note there are nominee directors in India appointed by institutional investors by way of an agreement and they largely look after the interests of those who appointed them. See Varottil, 'Evolution and Effectiveness of Independent Directors in Indian Corporate Governance'.

the case and the independent directors are world class, but at the majority of firms it appears that independent directors are not particularly well suited to play a significant monitoring role, either because of background, pay or other factors. This stands in contrast to much of the rhetoric related to independent directors (suggesting they can prevent misbehaviour) leading us to question whether this is the best way to utilise the various strengths and talents of the independent director crop in India.

However, there seems to be change in the air. In 2013 India enacted the Companies Act, 2013 (the '2013 Act') and revamped clause 49 of the listing agreement. These reforms have brought about a sea change in the role of Indian independent directors. We now discuss these reforms and their implications for board independence.

V Recent Reforms and the Increasingly Functional Approach to Board Independence

The corporate law reform process in India has been underway for nearly two decades. However, it acquired a greater sense of urgency more recently due to corporate governance scandals such as the massive fraud of over US $1 billion at Satyam Computer Services Limited, a leading company in the information technology (IT) sector.[83] The need was felt, among other things, to strengthen the corporate governance regime in India, of which board independence is an important component.

The reform process culminated in the enactment of the 2013 Act by the Parliament of India. A substantial part of the corporate governance provisions, and all of those relating to independent directors, came into effect 1 April 2014. Concurrently, India's securities regulator, SEBI, also brought about an overhaul of the corporate governance provisions contained in Clause 49 of the listing agreement, which took effect from 1 October 2014. The corporate governance provisions of the listing agreement have since been subsumed into the Securities and Exchange Board of India (Listing Obligations and Disclosure Requirements), Regulations, 2015 (the 'LODR Regulations'), which took effect from December 2015.

The recent reforms represent a turning point in the evolution of corporate governance in India and they usher in greater stringency in governance norms, accompanied by further reliance on independent directors as a key institution. The reforms elaborate on the roles, responsibilities and liabilities of independent directors and appear to be moving independent directors in India towards being more functional than formalistic. While this is

[83] For greater discussion of the Satyam scandal, see Khanna, 'Corporate Governance in India'.

welcome in many respects, these changes need to occur carefully because they risk putting large burdens on independent directors, which may in turn deter the more capable candidates from accepting these positions. After all, if our goal is to have careful and skilful people monitor controllers then we are likely to scare such people away from the position of independent director by having wide ranging liability and broad obligations on them for activities they may not be able to easily prevent or control.[84]

The new regime for independent directors, its rationale as well as its drawbacks are analysed in the remainder of this section.

1 *Transitioning to Functionality of Independent Directors*

A recent genre of literature posits that board independence acquired greater potency in the aftermath of the Global Financial Crisis.[85] The failure of monitoring boards in large corporations (particularly in the banking and finance sector) led to governance failures that resulted in both poor performance as well as collapses of major financial institutions.[86] This was followed by rapid legislative reaction that brought about much tighter regulation of these institutions. One of the methods followed was to lay greater emphasis on the role of the boards and, more particularly, independent directors, in overseeing the activities of these firms. For example, the US Dodd-Frank Act highlights the role of independent directors in risk management in financial and non-financial firms. Another reason suggested by some scholars for why board independence may be a popular measure is its utility in preventing more stringent substantive regulation.[87] According to this theory, institutional investors and managers have engaged in rent-seeking behaviour to minimise the cost of

[84] V. Khanna, 'Written Statement of Professor Vikramaditya Khanna University of Michigan Law School, Before the Committee on the Judiciary United States Senate Hearing on Evaluating the Propriety and Adequacy of the OxyContin Criminal Settlement, Tuesday, 31 July 2007' (2007), available at www.judiciary.senate.gov/imo/media/doc/Khanna%20Testimony%20073107.pdf [hereinafter Senate Written Statement].

[85] G. Ringe, 'Independent Directors: After the Crisis' (University of Oxford Legal Research Paper Series Paper No. 72/2013, 2013), available at http://ssrn.com/abstract=2293394; U. Velikonja, 'The Political Economy of Board Independence', *North Carolina Law Review*, 92 (2014), 855; L. Fairfax, 'The Uneasy Case for the Inside Director', *Iowa Law Review*, 96 (2010), 127, 136; see generally Chapter 2.

[86] Ringe, 'Independent Directors'.

[87] Velikonja, 'The Political Economy'. For an analogous argument in the context of corporate crime legislation see V. Khanna, 'Corporate Crime Legislation: A Political Economy Analysis', *Washington University Law Quarterly*, 82 (2004), 95.

regulation, as board independence is a relatively inexpensive mechanism both for the firms as well as for the regulators given its self-regulating propensity.[88]

Although moves to enhance board independence are evident in India too, these theories do not present themselves in the same manner. In India, the reasons for enhancing board independence have more to do with internal factors rather than a push coming from external factors (e.g., the Global Financial Crisis).

India was not affected to the same extent as the West by the Global Financial Crisis and the push for independent director reforms can be attributed to lessons from local governance crises such as the Satyam scandal, which received a lot of media attention as well as generating political backlash.[89] Hence, the changes in India have been brought about through internal pressures.[90] In terms of its evolution, while the initial phase of board independence (formalistic) was due to legal transplantation from the Western markets, the transition to the second phase of board independence (functional) was largely due to local factors wherein the developments in the international arena played little direct role. Of course, the international models of board independence did provide some basic forms for Indian legislators to adopt, but on this occasion the philosophy of, and motivation for, the Indian reforms were driven by the predominant governance concerns facing Indian companies – the agency problem between the controlling shareholders and the minority shareholders.

2 *Who Is an Independent Director?*

One of the criticisms of the previous regime was that it defined independence primarily with regard to the lack of any material pecuniary

[88] Velikonja, 'The Political Economy'; Khanna, 'Corporate Crime Legislation: A Political Economy Analysis'.

[89] A number of the significant reforms in strengthening board independence were introduced in the Companies Bill when it went before a Parliamentary Standing Committee on Finance, which was headed by Mr Yashwant Sinha, who was a senior member of the then opposition party, the BJP.

[90] For a discussion of the motivations behind the 2013 Act and its corporate governance provisions, see U. Varottil, 'The Evolution of Corporate Law in Post-Colonial India: From Transplant to Autochthony', *American University International Law Review* 31 (2016), 253. Contrast this with the development in Japan wherein corporate governance scandals do not seem to have directly impacted corporate governance reforms. See Chapter 4 (Japan) at II.1.c.

relationship between the director and the company or the controlling shareholder. This was a negative test (who is not independent), rather than a positive definition highlighting what sorts of factors would be helpful to have in independent directors (e.g., competencies, qualifications or experience).[91] Some of these deficiencies have now been addressed.[92]

Under the 2013 Act, directors are required to possess some qualities, albeit general in nature, before they qualify to act as independent directors. For example, the board must form an opinion that the individual 'is a person of integrity and possesses relevant expertise and experience'.[93] Moreover, the central government may prescribe additional qualifications.[94] This would hopefully ensure that only persons with the requisite positive qualities and competencies would be appointed as independent directors. It is now difficult to appoint 'friendly' or 'celebrity' directors that may have helped short change the board independence requirement under a more formal regime. Interestingly, under the new regime, a government-approved agency maintains a data bank of people who are eligible and willing to act as independent directors, and companies are free to choose from that list.[95]

One concern that persisted in India historically was the elongated tenure of directors, including independent directors. Since familiarity could affect independence and the monitoring role of directors, the reforms impose a mandatory tenure on independent directors. They are able to serve in such a role only for one term of five consecutive years, although they can be reappointed for a similar term through a special resolution that obtains a 75 per cent majority.[96] In many firms this amounts to giving the minority a veto on the re-appointment. This makes it more likely that the individuals appointed as independent directors are able to act in an impartial manner without being influenced by management or controlling shareholders.[97] Furthermore, a person can serve as an independent

[91] Varottil, 'Evolution and Effectiveness of Independent Directors in Indian Corporate Governance'.

[92] The detailed definition of an 'independent director' is set out in the statutory supplement to this chapter. See Legislative Appendix.

[93] Section 149(6)(a), Companies Act, 2013.

[94] Section 149(6)(f), Companies Act, 2013.

[95] Section 150, Companies Act, 2013.

[96] Sections 149(10), 149(11), Companies Act, 2013. They may be reappointed after a period of three years from the expiry of their term, which operates as a 'cooling off' period.

[97] Until recently, several directors continued to be treated as independent although they have served on those company boards for decades. See B. Srivastava, 'Are Long-Serving Independent Directors Truly Independent?', *The Mint*, 23 September 2012.

director in no more than seven listed companies.[98] This is to ensure that independent directors are able to devote sufficient time and attention to the boards on which they sit.

Although the identification of desirable positive traits in independent directors (e.g., expertise, competence) is a helpful development, one should note that it puts some pressure on the concept of independence. Generally speaking one gains expertise and competence not only through formal education, but also through work and other experiences. However, acquiring these experiences will often put the individual in a position where they meet and interact with many luminaries in business and other fields. If so, then these highly qualified people are likely to be known to (and to know) some of the people they are being called upon to monitor. In sectors where most players know each other (e.g., smaller, newer industries), this can lead to some questions about whether there is a tradeoff between expertise and independence.[99]

3 *Appointment of Independent Directors*

Because each director's appointment is to be voted upon individually by the shareholders by way of a majority through a separate resolution,[100] the controlling shareholders can determine the composition of the entire board, including the independent directors. Such a dominating influence extends to the removal of independent directors as well. Although independent directors are expected to monitor the actions of the controlling shareholders in light of the interests of the minority, they are unlikely to do so if they owe their allegiance (and position) to the controlling shareholders in the first place.

Given this incongruence, the recent reforms introduce the mandatory requirement of a nomination and remuneration committee for appointment of all directors, including independent directors. Such a nomination committee must itself consist of a majority of independent directors.[101] The committee's role extends to formulating 'the criteria for determining qualifications, positive attributes and independence of a director', and to

[98] LODR Regulations, reg. 25(1). In a similar vein, a full-time director in any listed company is prohibited from serving as an independent director in more than three listed companies. *Ibid.*

[99] See generally V. Khanna, 'An Analysis of the Critical Elements of Board Independence', Draft (2017).

[100] Section 162, Companies Act, 2013.

[101] Section 178(1), Companies Act, 2013.

identifying individuals to be recommended to the board for appointment and also to carrying out the evaluation of directors.[102]

While this represents an important step in introducing greater transparency in the independent director nomination and appointment process, it remains only a partial solution in addressing the agency problem between controlling shareholders and minority shareholders. First, nomination committees – even if independent – may be appointed by the controlling shareholder raising the same kinds of concerns with independent directors in controlled firms. Second, even if an independent nomination committee were to nominate candidates without the influence of the controlling shareholders or management, those candidates would ultimately have to be voted in at a shareholders' meeting where the controlling shareholders would wield significant influence. Hence, nomination committees might be compelled to function in the shadow of an ultimate shareholder decision that lies substantially in the hands of the controlling shareholders.

The opportunity has been missed to consider other methods of voting for the election of independent directors. These include (1) cumulative voting by shareholders; and (2) election by a 'majority of the minority'. At the outset, these methods may appear somewhat extreme, but their benefits may outweigh their costs. While we are not advocating the use of these methods *per se*, they are worthy of consideration for the future depending upon the experience regarding the operation of nominating committees.[103]

4 *The Role of Independent Directors*

The criticism that the previous regime neither elucidated the role of independent directors nor specified the constituency that required their attention has been addressed, to some extent, in the 2013 Act. The legislation contains an elaboration of the roles and duties of independent directors by way of both the statutory provisions as well as an extensive schedule to the Act.

a Monitoring Role; Minority Shareholder Interests

The role of independent directors includes safeguarding the interests of all stakeholders, particularly the minority shareholders, balancing the

[102] Sections 178(2), 178(3), Companies Act, 2013.

[103] Recent scholarship explores a variety of voting schemes from nineteenth-century US firms that provide a broader sense that there are many other voting options one might

conflicts among various stakeholders and also acting as a moderator or arbitrator in cases of conflicts between management and shareholders.[104] More specifically, independent directors now have a greater role to play in matters such as related party transactions wherein they are required to ensure that the board adequately deliberates over these matters and acts in the interests of the company.[105] This is even more relevant because related party transactions tend to be rampant in jurisdictions such as India with concentrated shareholding,[106] which makes their oversight and regulation crucial.

There are a number of other roles and duties set out in Schedule IV, which we do not discuss in depth, but the overall focus is clearly now on the monitoring role of independent directors. This imposes a higher onus on independent directors, and would require them to participate in the affairs of the company more closely in order to be able to discharge this monitoring role. How that might be achieved when the board meets only a handful of times a year is yet to be elucidated.[107]

Another aspect that receives clarity is that independent directors are now expressly required to pay attention to the interests of minority shareholders. This is crucial given the agency problems between the controlling and the minority shareholders. The new regime requires independent directors to take on a more active role on significant transactions such as mergers, corporate restructuring or related party transactions where the minority interests may be at stake.

b Stakeholder Interests

Not only are independent directors required to consider the interests of minority shareholders specifically, but they must also take into account the interests of other stakeholders as well. This issue is likely to raise many questions, and therefore requires some greater discussion, including background. As far as stakeholders are concerned, the Companies Act prescribes general duties for all directors, including independent directors.

It is clear that directors ought to act in good faith for the benefit of the company. Since the company is a separate legal personality, there is often the question as to who represents the interests of the company. Generally,

consider. See H. Hansmann and M. Pargendler, 'The Evolution of Shareholder Voting Rights: Separation of Ownership and Consumption', *Yale Law Journal*, 123 (2014), 100.

104 Companies Act, 2013, Schedule IV, paras. II(5),(6),(8).

105 Companies Act, 2013, Schedule IV, para. III(9).

106 Bertrand et al., 'Ferreting Out Tunneling'.

107 Khanna, 'Critical Elements of Board Independence'.

the interests of the company are said to equate with the interests of the shareholders, but the question whether other stakeholders, such as the employees, consumers, and the community and society in general, constitute the interests of the company leaves room for some controversy.

The new 2013 Act, which for the first time codifies directors' duties, provides:

> A director of a company shall act in good faith in order to promote the objects of the company for the benefit of its members as a whole, and in the best interests of the company, its employees, the shareholders, the community and for the protection of environment.[108]

This clearly reinforces the stakeholder principle into corporate law. This is also buttressed by other provisions of the 2013 Act such as those relating to corporate social responsibility while enlarging the boundaries of constituencies deserving the attention of corporate law and corporate boards.[109]

This approach could give rise to a number of practical issues that may arise in Indian boardrooms. The attempt in this section is only to set out some of these practical concerns that require further consideration.

First, directors may be confronted with a conflict between the interests of the shareholders and those of other stakeholders. In that case, whose interests ought to be preferred? For example, if a decision is made that benefits either customers or employees, then a question arises as to whether the directors have breached their duties to the company giving rise to a legal claim against them.

Such a conflict has been resolved in a different manner in the UK where the Companies Act of 2006 adopted the 'enlightened shareholder value' approach which takes the position that the ultimate objective of company law to generate maximum shareholder value is also the best

[108] Section 166(2), Companies Act, 2013.

[109] Section 135, Companies Act, 2013. The concept of corporate social responsibility (CSR) has undertaken significant overtones under the 2013 Act. While we do not deal with issues pertaining to CSR here, boards (including independent directors) are foisted with additional responsibilities to ensure compliance with these provisions. For a broader discussion on CSR, see A. Afsharipour, 'Directors as Trustees of the Nation? India's Corporate Governance and Corporate Social Responsibility Reform Efforts', *Seattle University Law Review*, 34 (2011), 995; C. Van Zile, 'India's Mandatory Corporate Social Responsibility Proposal: Creative Capitalism Meets Creative Regulation in the Global Market', *Asian-Pacific Law and Policy Journal*, 13 (2012), 269; A. Afsharipour and S. Rana, 'The Emergence of New Corporate Social Responsibility Regimes in China and India', *UC Davis Business Law Journal*, 14 (2014), 175.

means of securing protection of all stakeholders' interests.[110] Under this dispensation, it is clear that in case of conflict between various interests, the directors must prioritise shareholders' interests, which is the paramount goal.[111] On the other hand, the 2013 Act in India has preferred to adopt a pluralist approach by providing recognition to both stakeholders and shareholders, without necessarily indicating preference to either. In a more practical sense, this means that the directors carry the burden of making the difficult choices in determining the hierarchy of differing interests in a given set of circumstances.[112] Moreover, this also grants substantial discretion to directors to pick and choose which interests will be determinative in a given context with little to constrain their decision making. This may itself raise concerns because of the apparently unfettered discretion it is giving to directors.

Second, shareholders' interests are more tangible and measurable than stakeholder interests. Shareholder interests are represented largely by financial parameters of a company that indicate corporate performance (with the most common resultant indicator being the share price of a company) as well as other indicators that may represent corporate governance.[113] Conversely, stakeholder interests are somewhat more intangible and subjective in nature causing decision making to be more difficult for the board and allowing for greater discretion to the board.[114]

Finally, even if some of the aforesaid practical considerations can be addressed through focused board measures and processes, the 2013 Act does not seem to provide for remedies against breach of directors' duties to take into account stakeholder interests. Hence, their rights may not be justiciable in nature thereby questioning the extent of their efficacy, adding to some confusion on the role of the board, including independent

110 Companies Act, 2006, § 172(1).

111 C. M. Bruner, *Corporate Governance in the Common-Law World: The Political Foundations of Shareholder Power* (Cambridge University Press, 2013).

112 Indeed, there could potentially be conflicts among the interests of various stakeholders themselves. While shareholders' interests are generally homogenous (except for differences that could arise between the controlling shareholders and the minority shareholders), stakeholders could possess vastly differing interests that may require prioritisation among themselves. This results in added determination and adjudication responsibilities on the board. See S. M. Bainbridge, 'Director Primacy: The Means and Ends of Corporate Governance', *Northwestern University Law Review*, 97 (2003), 547.

113 *Ibid.*

114 Although stakeholder approaches grant much discretion to directors, even the shareholder primacy norm can leave quite a lot of discretion with directors. See Allen et al., *Commentaries and Cases.*

directors.[115] The open-ended nature of independent directors' roles and responsibilities acquire greater importance when seen in the light of their widened exposure to liability under the new regime.

5 *Liability of Independent Directors*

Independent directors may be subject to liabilities that arise under various statutes in India. However, the focus here is on liabilities arising under company law. The first set of liabilities is statutory in nature, being specifically set forth in the 2013 Act. These could be either civil liability requiring directors to make payments to victims or the state, or criminal liability resulting in fines or imprisonment.[116] The approach in the new regime has been to impose stiffer penalties for criminal offences.

The second set of liabilities could arise from claims made against the directors by either the company or the shareholders for breaches of directors' duties. These claims are quite robust in theory, but are riddled with tremendous difficulties in practice. Given the jaw dropping rates of docket explosion before the Indian courts, the ability of shareholders or the company to bring a suit, and even more, to enforce a successful claim against directors, is highly doubtful. It is not surprising that India displays a rather meagre track record of civil claims against directors that have resulted in payouts by them.[117]

In order to obviate the difficulties (particularly on the procedural count) under the pre-existing law, the 2013 Act institutes mechanisms that are novel in the Indian context. The first is the establishment of a class action mechanism that allows a group of shareholders (constituting a minimum of 100 shareholders or those holding 10 per cent shares in the company)

[115] These issues may appear somewhat esoteric to begin with, but they would have to be confronted by corporate boards to face the new reality. They would also figure more prominently if and when legal claims begin to get litigated before the courts for breach of directors' duties under the new law.

[116] For example, directors (including independent directors) will become exposed to class actions whereby shareholders can claim compensation or demand suitable action against them 'for any fraudulent, unlawful or wrongful act or omission or conduct or any likely act or omission or conduct on its or their part'. Section 245, Companies Act, 2013. Furthermore, in case of criminal liability, the approach in the new regime has been to impose stiffer penalties so as to constitute a strong deterrent on director conduct that falls short of the desired standards.

[117] V. Khanna and U. Varottil, 'The Rarity of Derivative Actions in India: Reasons and Consequences' in D. W. Puchniak et al., *The Derivative Action in Asia: A Comparative and Functional Approach* (Cambridge University Press, 2012).

to bring an action on behalf of all affected parties, which includes claims for compensation from directors for any fraudulent, unlawful or wrongful act or omission or conduct on their part.[118] More importantly, the 2013 Act devises a mechanism to sidestep the regular court system by enabling such actions to be brought before a recently constituted National Company Law Tribunal (NCLT) that is expected to be faster, more efficient and less costly.[119] Once these remedial mechanisms are in place and effective, it is likely that directors may be subject to greater scrutiny through the use of civil liability suits by companies and shareholders. Only time will tell whether the directors' liabilities regime in India would transform itself from a scenario where directors face almost no lawsuits for company law duties to one where they might, and what impact that might have on their willingness to serve on corporate boards as well as on their conduct.

At the same time, the severity of the liability provisions is softened through certain mitigating factors that operate in favour of directors. First, the 2013 Act creates a specific safe harbour provision for independent directors. An independent director is liable 'only in respect of such acts of omission or commission by a company which had occurred with his knowledge, attributable through board processes, and with his consent or connivance or where he had not acted diligently'.[120] While such a provision for limitation of liability is useful, much would depend upon the manner in which courts interpret it based on the specific facts and circumstances of individual cases. Clarity on this count is still elusive.[121]

Second, it may be possible for directors to obtain indemnities from the company. Under the 1956 Act, companies were constrained from providing such indemnities, as they are not permitted to indemnify directors for negligence, default, breach of duty and the like.[122] The 2013 Act,

[118] Section 245, Companies Act, 2013.

[119] Although the constitutional validity of the establishment of the NCLT was previously upheld by the Supreme Court of India, subject to certain conditions and modifications in *Union of India v. R. Gandhi*, [2010] 100 SCL 142 (SC), its potential establishment under the 2013 Act was challenged again before the courts, although it ultimately survived such challenge. See I. Bhan, 'What's the Role of Tribunals?', *The Financial Express*, 22 January 2014.

[120] Section 149(12), Companies Act, 2013.

[121] A detailed analysis of the safe harbour provisions may be beyond the scope of this chapter. For their more elaborate discussion, see Varottil, 'Directors' Duties'; U. Varottil, 'Director Liability under the New Regime', *IndiaCorpLaw Blog* (2014), available at http://indiacorplaw.blogspot.com/2014/06/director-liability-under-new-regime.html. For a general discussion of the impact of fear of liability on directors see Khanna, Senate Written Statement; Khanna, 'Critical Elements of Board Independence'.

[122] Section 201, Companies Act, 1956.

however, does not contain such a restriction, which may confer greater flexibility on directors to seek indemnities from the company in case they have to meet any liabilities, particularly if no fault can be attached to the directors' conduct.

Third, the practice of obtaining directors and officers (D&O) insurance has already become prevalent in Indian companies, especially among the larger ones, and is only likely to grow in view of the expansive liability regime under the new law.[123] In fact, the 2013 Act implicitly recognises the ability of the company to incur the premium expense in order to obtain D&O insurance policies.[124] While obtaining adequate levels of D&O insurance would be prudent for all boards and directors, regard must be had to the fact that policies are usually accompanied by specific exceptions for fraud, wilful misconduct and other forms of intentional criminal conduct.

The discussion in this section is confined to matters of civil liability. Directors may continue to be bound by criminal liability provisions under both the Companies Act as well as other legislation applicable to companies. In those situations, the usual principles of corporate and directorial criminal liability would apply.

6 *Reviewing the Independent Director's Position under the New Regime*

Clearly, the institution of the independent director in India has undergone a metamorphosis more recently. However, some concerns remain as to whether the reforms are excessive in nature.

First, the new regime may be considered too prescriptive. By stipulating the features of board independence in microscopic detail, it leaves much less room for independent thought and discretion to be exercised by individual directors. The invasion of corporate regulation into the boardroom might arguably increase the cost of doing business and affect entrepreneurialism and innovation. This is similar to concerns that arose in the aftermath of the Sarbanes-Oxley Act of 2002 in the US,[125] and those that might arise with the Dodd-Frank Act.

[123] M. Lea and A. Malkan, 'The Changing Environment for D&O Insurance in India', *D&O Diary* (2013), available at www.dandodiary.com/2013/03/articles/international-d-o/guest-post-the-changing-environment-for-do-insurance-in-india/.

[124] Section 197(13), Companies Act, 2013.

[125] R. Romano, 'The Sarbanes-Oxley Act and the Making of Quack Corporate Governance', *Yale Law Journal*, 114 (2005), 1521; L. E. Ribstein, 'Market v. Regulatory Responses to Corporate Fraud: A Critique of the Sarbanes-Oxley Act of 2002', *Journal of Corporation Law*, 28 (2002), 1.

Second, the higher obligations under the new legal regime might hinder competent individuals from taking up independent directorships on corporate boards. For instance, the regime makes the duties and liabilities of independent directors fairly significant. Meaningful levels of remuneration do not complement this. Since the remuneration levels for independent directors in India are considerably lower than international standards, highly skilled individuals might be unlikely to take the risk or put their reputation at stake to serve on corporate boards. The duties and liabilities may operate as a disincentive to highly skilled people, which then leads to boards being populated by individuals with less skill and greater risk tolerance. This appears the opposite of what would be desired if the goal is to enhance monitoring.[126]

Third, as a procedural matter, the implementation could give rise to difficulties although the intention of greater stringency is understandable. Corporate governance norms are dynamic in nature and require reconfiguration periodically to keep pace with the changing business climate. Usually, while the basic governance framework is dealt with by statute, the details are contained in codes of conduct that are more flexible in nature. However, the 2013 Act results in many items being made less flexible because they are contained in legislation which is more difficult to change nimbly. While this may address some immediate problems, it is bound to result in a greater amount of rigidity. Experience with the Companies Act, 2013 (which was first proposed in 2005) clearly evidences the enormous difficulties in amending companies' legislation in India, and any changes to the governance norms in the future are likely to be as cumbersome. The question remains whether there has been a knee-jerk reaction to recent scandals that may adversely impact genuine businesses during the times ahead.[127] We begin to address these concerns in the next section, which explores some potential reforms.

VI Future Prospects for Board Independence in India: Potential Reforms?

In this section, we approach the issue of board independence from a normative standpoint and explore some possible options for reforms. We

[126] Khanna, Senate Written Statement.

[127] For a discussion on the Japanese experience regarding mandatory requirements compared with the 'comply-or-explain' approach, see Chapter 4 (Japan) at III.1.c.

confine ourselves to reforms at a conceptual level that legislators and regulators in India may consider.[128]

1 *Definition and Appointment of Independent Directors*

Independent directors are defined with reference to the absence of any specific relationships with the company or its controlling shareholder (such as employment, familial or other financial relationships). However, the Indian legal regime does not take cognisance of social and other relationships, which are widely prevalent in India.[129] Unless those relationships are recognised, board independence may not serve its purpose to the extent envisioned.

Moreover, in countries like India where controlling shareholders are dominant, measures must be taken to reduce the dominant power of controllers over the appointment of independent directors. This can be achieved through alternative appointment methods such as cumulative voting or a voting by the 'majority-of-the-minority'. Of course, these methods may confer significant power in the hands of the minority shareholders and may hamper the collegiality and efficiency in decision making on the board (by creating factions), but the additional monitoring it introduces would be a countervailing benefit.

2 *Monitoring Specific Transactions*

One way in which independent directors may be able to reduce the agency costs between controllers and minorities is by having greater powers to review specific transactions such as related party transactions (the abusive forms of which would amount to tunnelling). The new corporate law regime in India does introduce greater stringency in the regulation of related party transactions, but less has been said about the role that independent directors can play. For instance, although all related party transactions are now to be approved by the board, and the material ones by a majority of the minority shareholders, the role of independent directors is unclear. One thing that could be considered is that in these (and

[128] The limitations of space do not enable us to delve into the details of the reforms, including the structuring and drafting of legislative or regulatory proposals, which could be built upon the conceptual discussion herein.

[129] More studies are finding that social connections matter. Khanna et al., 'CEO Connectedness and Corporate Fraud', provide an overview of these studies as does Khanna, 'Internal Governance'.

other significant) transactions a committee of independent directors could be required to consider the transaction after obtaining information and independent legal and financial advice from advisors specifically appointed by the committee. While such a process has been well established in the US,[130] such a culture of independent committees making decisions on interested transactions is yet to fully develop in India. We believe that vesting independent directors with such specific powers would enhance their monitoring roles in companies.

3 *Refining Independent Directors' Roles for Different Types of Controllers*

The new Companies Act, 2013 has taken some significant strides in recognising and beginning to address the controller–minority shareholder agency problem, but it is arguably still too coarse as it provides uniform treatment for all companies with controllers, irrespective of the specific type of controller. As we argued earlier in section II,[131] the roles and responsibilities of independent directors may vary considerably depending on whether a company has a single controller or a group of controllers, and also, if a group, then on the type of controlling group (i.e., whether it is a business family, the state or an unrelated group of shareholders). Board independence and how directors satisfy their duties (whether through legal measures or softer norms such as industry practice) could take into account these variations so that independent directors can be more effective monitors of the different types of controllers.

For example, in companies with a family business group as controller, the independent directors pay greater attention to issues such as related party transactions and succession planning and would often act as possible arbiters on family issues that may have an impact on the company (and consequently the minority shareholders). In SOEs, the independent directors may have to consider the interests of the minority keeping in view the larger political ramifications of decisions that the board or senior management might make. Greater emphasis on these differences among controllers will arguably introduce better value in board independence due to the specific structural, institutional and cultural conditions that are at play in India.

[130] For a recent recognition of this process as a means of sanctifying a transaction, see *Kahn v. M&F Worldwide Corp.*, 88 A.3d 635, 642 (Del. 2014).

[131] See section II above.

4 *Trade-offs between Expertise and Independence*

The current regime in India mandates that independent directors have 'relevant' expertise and experience, but at the same time be independent of management and controllers of the company. While persons with industry experience and strategic expertise would add value to the company (and consequently its financial performance), companies may find it difficult to find such individuals who also simultaneously satisfy the independence requirements (especially if these include not only financial connections, but social ones). One reason for this is that one of the key ways in which people obtain experience is by working with others and that also tends to build social and other connections.[132] This is especially the case when one is dealing with small or nascent industries or in sectors where the number of players is limited. This may well be true for many sectors in India raising concerns about whether those who are selected under this approach may be effective as monitors or strategic advisors or whether we may be trading off monitoring and strategic advising.

Future thinking on board independence may require further consideration of this concern. One possibility would be for the board to be composed of two types of independent directors, one set of directors who are recruited for their experience in business, industry and strategy, and the other who are likely to act as monitors.[133] Executives of other companies within the same industry might perform the former role, while lawyers, accountants, retired government officials or academics may perform the latter. Again, these distinctions need not be cast in stone: it is just that the specific type of director may provide greater focus on her specific type of role.

5 *Comparing Effectiveness of Board Independence with Other Players*

Finally, it is necessary to reiterate that the independent director institution is only one of the mechanisms that would enhance corporate governance in India. That institution, as we have seen, cannot work by itself.

[132] This concern largely emanates from Khanna, 'An Analysis of the Critical Elements of Board Independence'.

[133] This suggestion bears some similarity to the approach in Germany with a dual board structure – one that deals with operational matters and another that deals with monitoring (including concerns held by labour). See S. R. Foreman, 'Bored Boards: The Directorial Disengagement Dilemma', *Washburn Law Journal*, 50 (2010), 147, 157–158; L. L. Dallas, 'The Multiple Roles of Corporate Boards of Directors', *San Diego Law Review*, 40 (2003), 781, 784–785.

To be effective it would probably require a whole host of other attributes such as a stringent accounting and financial disclosure regime, whistle blowing mechanisms, a code of ethics and even perhaps an open market for corporate control, just to name a few. The role of independent directors should also be supported by other gatekeeper functionaries such as accountants, investment bankers, corporate and securities lawyers, securities analysts, rating agencies and even the business press.[134]

The effectiveness of the independent directors also depends on other systemic factors. For example, it requires courts (or a regulator of some kind)[135] in India to be in a position to rule efficaciously on corporate and securities law aspects, set precedents for lower courts to follow and create a set of principles that imbue certainty in the functioning of independent directors as emissaries of enhanced corporate governance.

Given this scenario, it is necessary to acknowledge and accept the limitations of board independence, in the sense that it is not a panacea for all ills confronting corporate governance in India. We should consider moderating our expectations from this institution, and so should regulators and courts.

VII Conclusion

Although board independence has become a mainstay in contemporary corporate governance discussion, there is yet much to learn about the concept. More particularly, its evolution and application differ across economies and legal systems. In this chapter, we find that the concept must be applied differently in countries such as India where ownership is concentrated as compared to countries such as the US and the UK where ownership is diffused (and from which systems the concept first originated). Even within countries with concentrated shareholding, there could be differences that merit varying treatments. For instance, the nature of the controller (e.g., individual, group, family, state) matters to a large extent, as do other institutional and legal factors.

[134] For a similar argument see Ministry of Finance, Government of India, New Delhi, *Report of the High Powered Expert Committee on Making Mumbai an International Financial Centre* (2007), available at: www.finmin.nic.in/mifc/mifcreport.pdf.

[135] For example, systems in jurisdictions such as the United Kingdom, Hong Kong and Singapore are driven by regulators or through self-regulation rather than by the courts. See, for example, S. C. Y. Wong, 'Developing and Implementing Corporate Governance Codes', *Private Sector Opinion*, Global Corporate Governance Forum, 10 (2008), available at www.ifc.org.

The transition in India where board independence was adopted initially in a formalistic sense, but has more recently taken more functional overtones, suggests that legislators and regulators are keen to press on with this governance mechanism by embellishing it further on a gradual basis. This is not dissimilar to several other jurisdictions, which also tend to follow the same trajectory. The arguably excessive reliance on board independence as a primary means of corporate governance may appear puzzling, but our intention in this chapter is to use India as a case study to make sense of the country-specific aspects that might help address the larger puzzle on a comparative basis.

PART III

Alternative Perspectives and Conclusions

11

The Rise and Unlikely Demise of Independent Directors in Australia

FADY AOUN AND LUKE NOTTAGE*

I Introduction

Australia enjoys a large and active share market within the Asian-Pacific region, notwithstanding its blockholder tradition.[1] As we explore in section II, since the 1990s, the concept of 'monitoring' rather than executive boards has emerged. In 2012, 73 per cent of directors in the largest 100 listed entities on the Australian Securities Exchange (ASX) were described as independent directors (IDs).

Section III considers the gradual development of IDs in Australia. The Bosch Committee, the business sector's response to a spate of corporate failures and misdeeds in the late 1980s, first emphasised the notion of IDs and its significance in 1991.[2] Concerned about shareholders in corporate groups abusing their powers, the Committee broke new ground by defining directorial independence as including not being (affiliated with) a significant shareholder. That innovative concept took root in Hong Kong in 1993. In Australia, by contrast, the ASX did not adopt the Committee's corporate governance recommendations into a mandatory or even 'comply or explain' regime for IDs in listed companies. Instead,

* This is an extensively reworked and abridged version of L. Nottage and F. Aoun, 'The Rise of Independent Directors in Australia: Adoption, Reform and Uncertainty', *University of Miami International and Comparative Law Review*, 23 (2016), 443, available at http://ssrn.com/abstract=2567504. The manuscript for this chapter was substantially completed in April 2015. We thank Matthew Barry for editorial and research assistance.

[1] R. Mitchell et al., 'Shareholder Protection in Australia: Institutional Configurations and Regulatory Evolution', *Melbourne University Law Review*, 38(1) (2014), 68; L. Nottage, 'Corporate Governance in Australia: The Evolving Blockholder Legacy' (background paper for the Berlin Conference on Independent Directors in Asia, 17–19 July 2014), available at http://tinyurl.com/lwtrwkl.

[2] Working Group of the Australian Institute of Company Directors et al., *Corporate Practices and Conduct* (May 1991) [hereinafter *Bosch Report (1st edition)*].

in 1996, the ASX Listing Rules called for an annual corporate governance statement explaining board composition, including executive versus non-executive directors. It was only in 2003, following more spectacular corporate collapses, that the Listing Rules and the ASX Corporate Governance Principles and Recommendations (ASX Principles) introduced a majority ID board requirement on an 'if not, why not' basis. Listing Rules also mandated that larger companies have audit committees comprising a majority of IDs.[3]

We consider the impact of the 2008 Global Financial Crisis on ID requirements in Australia; such requirements have become somewhat stricter through amendments in 2010 and 2014 that were partly influenced by developments abroad. While serious questions about the role of IDs in Australian companies remain, recent public discussion and law reform regarding executive remuneration and board diversity – especially with respect to increasing women representation on boards – have overshadowed these concerns.

Given Australia's strong blockholder tradition, the rise of IDs there is interesting for at least two reasons. First, blockholders theoretically have less need for ID-led managerial supervision. Secondly, since the mid-1990s, commentators have noted that introducing IDs as a corporate governance improvement measure raises practical and theoretical problems. These scholarly works refer to the limited empirical evidence (at least in the US) that IDs significantly improve overall corporate performance.[4] As summarised in section V, subsequent quantitative and qualitative studies in Australia reveal an ambivalent picture. Although subsequent research has documented more positive results, recent econometric studies have controversially asserted that the 2003 majority ID ASX requirements have led to significant negative effects on corporate performance.[5] In section VI, we consider recent queries raised by other Australian researchers as to the conventional wisdom about IDs. Further avenues for empirical and theoretical research remain, which may have an impact on ongoing policy debates. However, for better or worse, IDs are probably here to stay in Australia.

[3] This requirement has been in place since 2004. See Rule 12.7, ASX Listing Rules.

[4] H. Bird, 'The Rise and Fall of the Independent Director', *Australian Journal of Corporate Law*, 5 (1995), 235; G. Stapledon and J. Lawrence, 'Board Composition, Structure and Independence in Australia's Largest Listed Companies', *Melbourne University Law Review*, 21 (1997), 150; for a general discussion, see Chapter 2 at IV.2.

[5] P. Swan and D. Forsberg, 'Does Board "Independence" Destroy Corporate Value?' (27th Australasian Finance and Banking Conference, August 2014), available at http://ssrn.com/abstract=2312325.

II The Boards of Australia's Leading Listed Companies: Role, Size, Composition and Diversity

Scholarly debates on presumed directorial roles in listed companies' boards have raged since the early 1990s. A more expansive view – encompassing a broad range of responsibilities – was taken by a committee chaired by Henry Bosch, an eminent businessman who led the then securities regulator from 1985 to 1990. This committee produced a report in May 1991 for the Australian Institute of Company Directors,[6] updated in 1993 and 1995, with significant parallels to the Cadbury Report finalised in the UK in December 1992.[7] The broader approach has been favoured since the establishment of the Australian Stock Exchange (now ASX) Corporate Governance Council in 2002, comprising business, shareholder and industry groups. Yet others have advanced a narrower view of directors' roles and duties that mainly focuses on monitoring corporate performance. For instance, an influential judgement in 1992 suggested that contemporary boards generally set corporate objectives, appoint the CEO and monitor progress.[8] Professor Fred Hilmer also favoured this narrower view.[9]

As to 'ideal' board size and composition, a recent Credit Suisse study investigating the connection between board size and corporate performance of leading ASX 200 firms for the period 2008–2013 contends that nine to eleven board members produce the best shareholder returns for companies with a market capitalisation of AUS $5 billion. For companies

[6] *Bosch Report (1st edition).* Bosch also appeared as an influential witness at public hearings of the Senate Standing Committee on Legal and Constitutional Affairs on 'Company Directors' Duties', November 1989, [hereinafter *Cooney Report*] (Australian Government Publishing Service, Canberra, 1989).

[7] Committee on the Financial Aspects of Corporate Governance, *Cadbury Report* (December 1992) [hereinafter *Cadbury Report*]. The Committee was established in May 1991.

[8] *AWA Ltd v. Daniels* (1992) 7 ACSR 759. Instead of insisting on a clear demarcation between the roles of executive and non-executive directors, the majority of the New South Wales Court of Appeal in *Daniels v. Anderson* (1995) 37 NSWLR 438 emphasised (at 505) that a director's duty 'will vary according to the size and business of the particular company and the experience or skills that the director held himself or herself out to have in support of appointment to the office' (per Clarke and Sheller JJA). For recent case law arguably confirming a more expansive view of directors' duties, see J. Hill, 'Evolving Directors' Duties in the Common Law World' in Adolfo Paolini (ed.), *Research Handbook on Directors' Duties* (Edward Elgar, 2014), 3.

[9] Bird, 'The Rise and Fall of the Independent Director'. See also N. Dunbar, 'Role and Value of Independent Directors in Modern Australian Corporate Governance', *Company and Securities Law Journal*, 30(5) (2012), 312.

with a lower market capitalisation, the optimal number of board members lies between six and eight.[10] Unfortunately, that study is completely silent on the breakdown of non-executive directors (NEDs), IDs or executive directors, so we must look elsewhere for a conception of board composition.

In September 2013, the Australian Council of Superannuation Investors (ACSI) published its 12th Annual Research Report on 'Board Composition and Non-Executive Director Pay in the Top 200 Companies: 2012', analysing 94 qualifying largest companies in the Standard & Poors/ASX 200 Index as at 30 June 2012 (ASX 100) and 86 from the next 100 largest companies (ASX 101–200).[11] An executive recruitment firm, Korn Ferry, has also published its '2010 Board of Directors Study' based on a survey of Australia's 300 largest companies by market capitalisation as at 30 June 2010.[12] Table 11.1 summarises key results from these studies.

NEDs clearly form a large majority on boards, and most are also IDs. This is especially true in Australia's biggest companies (the ASX 100).[13] Professor Peter Swan's controversial research examining the performance of the largest 500 ASX listed companies over 2001–2011 (discussed further in section V.2 below) also reported broadly consistent findings: 75 per cent non-executive directors (NEDs), with 32 per cent IDs and 39 per cent 'grey' (non-independent NED) directors, as well as an average and median board size of six directors.[14]

The 2013 ACSI report suggests that the proportion of IDs in ASX 100 companies in 2012 (73 per cent, or 585 out of 797 directorships) has grown considerably since around 2004 (50 per cent).[15] It notes though

[10] Credit Suisse, *Optimal Board Member Numbers Produce the Best Shareholder Returns* (5 September 2014). See also *Cooney Report*, 107, Table 1, 117.

[11] ACSI, *Board Composition and Non-Executive Director Pay in the Top 200 Companies: 2012* (25 September 2013) (with earlier reports dating back to 2002).

[12] Korn Ferry Institute, *2010 Board of Directors Study: Australia and New Zealand* (2010).

[13] D. Etheridge, 'Boards of a Feather Flock Together: Board Networks among ASX Firms' (2012 Financial Markets and Corporate Governance Conference, 4 November 2011), available at http://ssrn.com/abstract=1972254, 10–11 notes that over 150 new listings were added in 2005–2006 alone, and that the number of ASC listed companies increased by 46 per cent over 2000–2007 while the number of directors only rose by 10 per cent. Nonetheless, the largest 50 listed companies represent about 70 per cent of total ASX market capitalisation (at 32).

[14] M. Fischer and P. Swan, 'Does Board Independence Improve Firm Performance? Outcome of a Quasi-Natural Experiment' (27th Australasian Finance and Banking Conference, August 2014), 2, 12–13, 49, Table 2, available at http://ssrn.com/abstract=2312325. But see Swan and Forsberg, 'Does Board "Independence" Destroy Corporate Value?'.

[15] This upward trend has continued, with the proportion of NEDs held by IDs rising slightly to 75.6 per cent of all directorships in 2013. ACSI, *Board Composition and Non-Executive Director Pay in the ASX 200 Companies: 2013* (November 2014), 10.

Table 11.1 Snapshot of Australian Board Size and Composition

	Number of directors on boards	Proportion of NEDs and IDs	Committees	CEO separate from chair	Average / median fees of non-executive directors and chairs (in AUS)
ASX 100 (2012)	8.5 (average)	83% NEDs, of which 88% IDs (so 73% IDs)	n/a	99% (93/94)	$218,434 / $203,250 (and $481,415 / $450,924)
ASX 101–200 (2012)	6.2	79%, of which 70% (so 56% IDs)	n/a	87% (75/86)	$134,981 / $115,029 (and $225,534 / $193,230)
Top 300 (2010)	4–9 (89% of firms)	77% NEDs (82% for ASX 50)	Audit (97%), Remuneration (89%), Nomination (30%)	n/a	$124,985 / $102,500 (and $241,687/ $174,000)

that the jump in proportion to 65 per cent in 2005 occurred because 'ACSI [previously] classified all directors with more than nine years' service on a board as affiliated [i.e. non-independent] and from 2005 only those directors who had spent more than 20 years on a board were considered affiliated'.[16] Comparing 2012 with 2005, therefore, the growth in proportions of IDs was less dramatic, but still noteworthy – including in 2009 where the proportion rose from 65.5 per cent in 2008 to 69 per cent.

As elaborated in sections III and IV below, Professor Swan's study also noted significant increases in large listed ASX companies adopting a majority of IDs from 2003. (This is when the ASX Principles first required this, albeit on an 'if not, why not' basis.) Specifically, his study found that, in 2003, about 19 per cent of firms had a majority of IDs (172

[16] *Ibid.*, 10, n. 6: 'the change in definition was effective from the 2nd edition of the ACSI Guidelines, released in 2005'.

of 841 firms that year), rising to 57 per cent by 2011 (551 of 969 firms), and then to 59 per cent, including firms that had a majority of IDs before 2003.[17]

Although the ASX only introduced a loose disclosure-based regime from 1996 to 2002, the largest Australian companies saw a significant increase in both NED and ID appointments and proportions on boards from 1992. This expansive trend continued in the ensuing decade.[18] The efficacy of ID monitoring, however, has been doubted. Writing in 2002, Henry Bosch suggested that: 'Since [IDs] often owe their positions to the controlling shareholders it is not unknown for them to suppress any misgivings they may have about arguments which happen to work in favour of the individual interests of controllers'.[19] Contemporaneous qualitative empirical research also documents serious problems faced by IDs in freely accessing the information necessary for the effective discharge of their duties.[20] In other words, the actual independence and impact of IDs on corporate governance seemed quite underwhelming, a problem identified also by several subsequent empirical studies in Australia, and which we further explore in section V below.

For ASX 100 companies, the 2015 ACSI report finds a general plateauing in NED (and probably therefore now ID) board representation. This result may well be due to the growth and consolidation of a cadre of 'professional NEDs', defined as directors holding more than one board seat in the sample group(s). As Table 11.2 illustrates, this proportion of multiple directorships grew from 2001 (30.6 per cent) to 2006 (45.1 per cent), although it had fallen by 2012 (33.4 per cent) and remained largely unchanged through to 2014 (34.4 per cent). Further, although smaller (ASX 101–200) listed companies have a lower proportion of NED positions held by professional NEDs (26 out of 475, or 12.4 per cent) in 2014, almost 36 per cent of 1,144 NED positions in the combined top ASX 200 companies were held by 176 professional NEDs.[21]

[17] Fischer and Swan, 'Does Board Independence Improve Firm Performance?', 10.

[18] For example, a Korn Ferry survey of 200 companies in 1992 had noted an average board size of eight (ten for large companies), comprising 75 per cent NEDs (jumping from around 50 per cent over 1982–1992), with 60 per cent appointing NEDs in 1992. Bird, 'The Rise and Fall of the Independent Director', 253–254.

[19] H. Bosch, 'The Changing Face of Corporate Governance', *UNSW Law Journal*, 25(2) (2002), 270.

[20] M. Nowak and M. McCabe, 'Information Costs and the Role of the Independent Corporate Director', *Corporate Governance: An International Review*, 11(4) (2003), 300.

[21] ACSI, *Board Composition and Non-Executive Director Pay: 2014* (30 October 2015), 13. For example, two professional NEDs (Jane Hemstritch and Gene Tilbrook) held all four of their board seats in ASX 100 companies.

Table 11.2 Snapshot of Multiple Directorships Held by NEDs

Sample group	*Year*	*Number of NEDs*	*Proportion of NED directorships held by professional NEDs*	*Held by*
ASX 200	2014	1,144	35.9%	174 persons
ASX 101–200	2014	475	12.4%	26
ASX 100	2014	669	34.4%	105
ASX 100	2012	665	33.4%	100
ASX 100	2006	626	45.1%	123
ASX 100	2001	536	30.6%	72

An analysis of the top 200 ASX companies conducted in 2012 by a leading Australian newspaper further supports this penchant for multiple directorships. It found that of 1,539 directors (executive directors as well as NEDs), 205 held positions on multiple boards. Some of 'the most interesting connections', the study revealed, 'are at one or two degrees of separation from any particular company'.[22]

The phenomenon of multiple directorships is not the exclusive domain of men. While women were generally under-represented among NEDs and EDs, the ACSI study found that women were more likely to be professional NEDs.[23] (The 2014 ACSI report supports these findings.)[24] In 2012, some notable female NEDs included: Catherine Livingstone (Non-Executive Chairman for Telstra Corporation and NED for Worley Parsons and Macquarie Group); and Carolyn Hewson (NED at BHP Billiton, Westpac Banking Corporation and Stockland).[25] Moreover, according to the 2013 ACSI report, the average tenure for female NEDs increased from 3.8 years (with a median of 2.1) in 2011 to 4.2 years (with a median of 2.8) in 2013.[26]

[22] M. Moncrieff, 'Unravelling the Ties That Connect and Direct', *Sydney Morning Herald*, 18 August 2012.

[23] ACSI, *Board Composition and Non-Executive Director Pay in the Top 200 Companies: 2012*, 14–16.

[24] ACSI, *Board Composition and Non-Executive Director Pay: 2014*, 3.

[25] Korn Ferry Institute, *Cultivating Greatness in the Boardroom* (June 2012), 9, 11.

[26] ACSI, *Board Composition and Non-Executive Director Pay in the ASX 200 Companies: 2013*, 26.

Increased gender board diversity is laudable, yet there are real concerns that the ASX's 2010 'if not, why not' disclosure rule regarding gender diversity will encourage a box-ticking exercise. A survey of 57 female directors appointed to ASX 200 boards since the 2010 change remarked that while the majority of respondents reported improvements in board culture, 22 per cent of respondents lamented the apparent fixation 'on the idea that having one woman on the board ticks the box'.[27] Those respondents therefore claim that boards have not made 'any structural or philosophical changes to attract and appoint more women'.[28]

Furthermore, improved gender diversity on boards may create unintended results. Women currently in full-time middle or senior management – already under-represented – may be lured to (part-time but lucrative) multiple ID appointments. While that might enhance corporate performance (or at least have other benefits for the other firms) there may be more far-reaching negative effects for the original firm. More worryingly, as in the US, Australia may (at least in the short term) end up with so-called 'trophy women' on boards.[29] Such trends might exacerbate broader potential problems for board independence, such as an unnatural amplification of the 'professional directors' phenomenon, increased board interlocks and IDs' board tenure'.[30]

The issue of diversity has taken on a wider import, with some commentators openly challenging the lack of cultural and ethnic diversity on Australian boards.[31] The 2010 amendments to the ASX Principles include Recommendation 3.2: the adoption of a 'diversity policy' and its disclosure, or at least a summary thereof. The commentary defines diversity as including but not limited to 'gender, age, ethnicity and cultural

[27] Korn Ferry Institute, 'Beyond If Not, Why Not: The Pathway to Directorship for Women in Leadership' (May 2014), 15.

[28] *Ibid.*, 16, Figure 5. See also A. Schetzer, 'Women Stall on Reaching Australia's Highest Rungs', *Sydney Morning Herald*, 1 November 2014.

[29] D. Branson, 'An Australian Perspective on a Global Phenomenon: Initiatives to Place Women on Corporate Boards of Directors', *Australian Journal of Corporate Law*, 27 (2012), 2, 8–9.

[30] For large firms in 2001, for example, see Z. Matolcsy et al., 'Do Independent Directors Add Value?', *Australian Accounting Review*, 14(1) (2004), 33, 37–38 (observing that firm valuation in high-growth firms was significantly negative for IDs with tenure of more than one year, and for IDs with at most two other board positions).

[31] See, for example, J. Du Plessis, I. Saenger and R. Foster, 'Board Diversity or Gender Diversity? Perspectives from Europe, Australia and South Africa', *Deakin Law Review*, 17(2) (2012), 207; Diversity Council Australia, *Capitalising on Culture: A Study of the Cultural Origins of ASX 200 Business Leaders* (2013); L. McNamara, 'Lack of Cultural Diversity a "Risk"', *The Australian*, 3 January 2013.

background'.[32] Despite this inclusive definition – expanded in the third edition of the ASX Principles[33] – measurable objectives and metrics reporting relate *only* to gender diversity.[34] As a result, there is little, if any, data collation of ethnic and cultural board diversity on ASX listed companies, and nothing by way of Australian empirical studies exploring this burgeoning issue. Anecdotal evidence nevertheless suggests that the latest 'big trend' is adding an Asian director to the board.[35] This is consistent with Australia's accelerating turn towards Asia in the twenty-first century, promoted by the then Gillard government.[36]

Thus, a relatively small group of individuals is likely to continue to dominate directorships in larger Australian companies (especially NED and ID positions). This tendency may well intensify – somewhat ironically – as the ASX and corporate sector promote gender diversity initiatives. Furthermore, limiting metrics reporting and the creation of measurable objectives to gender issues is unlikely to assist the promotion of more culturally diverse boards, notwithstanding the more expansive definition of diversity.

III Historical Milestones

Scholarly debates on corporate governance and regulatory changes dating back to the early 1990s have underpinned this growth of IDs in Australia's listed companies, particularly the larger ones.

1 *The Bosch Committee Report and the ASX's First Disclosure Regime*

Australia's stock market crash in 1987, and corporate failures in the UK and the resultant Cadbury Committee Report in 1992,[37] strongly

[32] ASX Corporate Governance Council, *Corporate Governance Principles and Recommendations with 2010 Amendments*, 2nd edn (June 2010), 24.

[33] ASX Corporate Governance Council, *Principles and Recommendations*, 3rd edn (March 2014), Box 1.5: 'diversity not only includes gender diversity but also includes matters of age, disability, ethnicity, marital or family status, religious or cultural background, sexual orientation and gender identity'.

[34] ASX Corporate Governance Council, *Corporate Governance Principles and Recommendations with 2010 Amendments*, 2nd edn, Recommendation 3.3 and 3.4; ASX Corporate Governance Council, *Corporate Governance Principles and Recommendations*, 3rd edn, Recommendation 1.5.

[35] P. Durkin, 'Meet the Directors from Hell', *Australian Financial Review*, 21 June 2012, 9.

[36] L. D'Angelo Fisher, 'Know-how in the Asian Century', *BRW*, 16 May 2013.

[37] Bird, 'The Rise and Fall of the Independent Director', 238–246; F. Clarke, G. Dean and K. Oliver, *Corporate Collapse: Accounting, Regulatory, and Ethical Failure* (Cambridge University Press, 2003).

influenced the Bosch Committee Report (May 1991, revised somewhat in 1993 and 1995). The Bosch Report recommended that Australian listed companies should have:

- boards consisting of a majority of NEDs, of whom a majority should be IDs; and
- audit, remuneration and nomination committees, each with a majority of IDs.

The Bosch Committee, which included representatives from the ASX, the Australian Institute of Company Directors (AICD) and the Law Council of Australia, envisaged independence as being freedom from both management and 'any other external influence that might detract from their ability to act in the interest of the company as a whole'.[38] Independence was presumptively satisfied if the ID was not:

- a substantial shareholder;
- employed by the company as an executive within the last few years;
- a professional advisor to the company;
- a significant customer or supplier, or
- in any significant contractual relationship with the company other than as a director.

This general definition and the Report's recommended board composition track closely the Cadbury Committee approach.[39] Interestingly, the first edition of the Bosch Report noted that while personal or professional associations with the company, its officers or shareholders should not preclude NEDs from serving as directors:[40]

> [I]t is [nevertheless] a useful safeguard to appoint to the Board at least two directors who have no [personal or professional] association with

[38] Working Group of the Australian Institute of Company Directors et al., *Corporate Practices and Conduct* (1993), 16 [hereinafter *Bosch Report (2nd edition)*].

[39] The Bosch Report recommended remuneration, nomination and audit committees, each with a majority of IDs, with sufficient IDs on the board overall so that their views could carry significant weight. While acknowledging that ID numbers would vary with board size, the Report mentioned that 'it is unlikely that less than two will be able to exercise sufficient influence and it is desirable that at least one third of the Board should be genuinely independent'. *Bosch Report (2nd edition)*, 16–17. Similarly, the Cadbury Report recommended a remuneration committee, a nomination committee (with a majority of NEDs) and an audit committee (all NEDs, with a majority of IDs), thus a minimum of three NEDs including two IDs.

[40] *Bosch Report (1st edition)*, 6 (emphasis added).

the company or its officers or *a particular shareholder*. The independence of a NED may be defined as not having:

1. A contractual relationship with the company other than the office of Director (and therefore not subject to the control or influence of any other director or group of directors); and
2. Any relationship with the company which could affect the exercise of independent judgement.

In 1993, the second edition of the Bosch Report added that independence is 'more likely to be assured' when the director is not 'a *substantial* shareholder' of the company.[41] The Cadbury Report had instead recommended that a majority of NEDs should be independent, meaning that 'apart from their director's fees *and shareholdings*, they should be independent of management and free from any business or other relationship which could materially interfere with the exercise of their independent judgement'.[42] This difference is all the more interesting given that the Bosch Committee also had an eye to American developments emphasising the importance of NEDs and IDs, such as the American Law Institute's Principles of Corporate Governance and New York Stock Exchange (NYSE) listing rules. Yet the US did not (and does not) define independence to exclude substantial shareholders.[43] Aiming to restore public faith in listed companies following a string of major Australian corporate collapses in the late 1980s, the Bosch Committee apparently adopted this stricter definition partly in response to concerns that strong individuals, often with significant shareholdings, had abused their board positions, thereby contributing to these collapses.[44]

Although the ASX acknowledged that the Bosch Report was not well-received by listed companies, it released a Discussion Paper in September 1994 that was heavily influenced by the latter. The ASX proposed a new Listing Rule requiring companies to include in their annual reports a

[41] *Bosch Report (2nd edition)*, 16 (emphasis added).

[42] *Cadbury Report*, [4.12] (emphasis added). However, the Cadbury Committee did 'regard it as good practice for [NEDs] not to participate in share option schemes'. *Cadbury Report*, [4.13].

[43] See further Chapter 1 at III.4, text accompanying note 90; Chapter 3 at II.3.

[44] Telephone interview by L. Nottage with Henry Bosch, 16 March 2015. It was only in 1995 that the Australian Investment Managers' Association (AIMA) published the first edition of what became known as its 'Blue Book' guidelines for investment decisions, including recommendations on director independence largely consistent with the Bosch Reports (including, importantly and even then somewhat controversially, independence from substantial shareholders).

statement as to whether they had followed its 'Schedule of Corporate Governance Practices' from 1996 onwards, and to explain why they had not followed specified practices. This proposal was similar to the Bosch Report's recommendation, and the 'comply or explain' approach favoured by the Cadbury Committee, and adopted in the UK since 1992. The ASX then invited public comment on the desirable Schedule benchmarks for a minimum number of NEDs and (more tentatively) IDs, as well as for audit, remuneration and nomination committees, including a majority of IDs. The ASX's cautious approach here is partly explained by the strong negative reaction to its 1992 Exposure Draft advocating a new listing rule mandating a minimum IDs requirement.[45]

Even this watered-down proposal proved controversial.[46] It referred to the Hilmer Report,[47] which identified principal board functions of monitoring and enhancing corporate performance, but argued that undue emphasis was placed on the former. Essential group interaction was supposedly compromised by board composition guidelines that confused directors as to their responsibilities. Instead of defining NED roles, the Hilmer Report urged prioritising performance responsibilities. It rejected ID requirements – except for the audit committee, where it recommended a majority of IDs have no business relationship with the company that might impede independent judgement – because the role envisaged for IDs overall, as 'quasi auditors', was perceived as unconstructive and unrealistic. One academic response to the 1994 ASX Discussion Paper identified similar 'environmental limitations' on IDs, like structural bias in (re-)appointments, intimidation by management, a lack of cohesive power, questions as to who would monitor such monitors and a lack of adequate resources and experience.[48]

Following this robust resistance, the ASX refrained from introducing even a UK-style 'comply or explain' model. Ironically, the fledgling Hong Kong Securities Commission introduced a stricter regime from 1993, through a Listing Rules requirement for IDs that excluded significant shareholders.[49] A contributing factor for this partial 'transplant' may have been a senior Commission official, Mr Robert Nottle,

45 Bird, 'The Rise and Fall of the Independent Director', 237.

46 See Chapter 4 (Japan) at III.2.a for the comparative political discussion in Japan.

47 F. G. Hilmer, *Strictly Boardroom: Improving Governance to Enhance Company Performance* (The Sydney Institute, 1993). But see section II on tensions between the broad and narrow conception of board roles.

48 Bird, 'The Rise and Fall of the Independent Director', 246–243.

49 See Chapter 13 at III, and Chapter 8 (Hong Kong) at II.4.

an Australian recruit who had earlier worked with Mr Henry Bosch at Australia's corporate regulator.[50] Mr Nottle, who later became Chairman of the Commission from 1992 to 1994, apparently kept abreast of Australian corporate governance initiatives, including the Bosch Committee consultations and Reports.[51]

Instead of adopting the UK 'comply or explain' model, ASX Listing Rule 4.10.3 required Australian companies merely to disclose their corporate governance practices for the annual reporting periods ending on or after 30 June 1996.[52] The then Appendix 4A to this Listing Rule set out a non-exhaustive list of corporate governance matters that could be considered as part of these disclosure obligations. However, as commentators pointed out soon after the promulgation of this indicative list, this Listing Rule encouraged ambivalent disclosure by failing to clearly distinguish between IDs and NEDs or between non-executive and independent chairs.[53] The new ASX disclosure appears to have had limited direct impact, notwithstanding corporate governance practice in the early 1990s had witnessed an increase in NEDs, and by the late 1990s, larger listed companies tended to appoint significantly more IDs as well as NEDs.[54]

Australia was then hit by another wave of corporate collapses in some ways worse than the corporate failures of the late 1980s. Poor corporate governance and inadequate regulation[55] as opposed to general share market and economic downturns drove corporate failures from 2001. One such dramatic failure involved One.Tel, a newer telecom company, which

[50] B. Potter, 'Crosby Quits Job as NCSC Officer', *Sydney Morning Herald* (Business), 5 May 1989, 27.

[51] Telephone interview by L. Nottage with Henry Bosch, 16 March 2015.

[52] 'The rationale for the rule was that it would result in the release of more information of greater relevance to the market compared with a rule requiring specific corporate governance practices to be adopted by all listed companies': see Commonwealth Treasury, Corporate Law Economic Reform Program Proposals for Reform, Paper No. 3: *Directors' Duties and Corporate Governance*, 62.

[53] I. Ramsey and R. Hoad, 'Disclosure of Corporate Governance Practices by Australian Listed Companies', *Company and Securities Law Journal*, 15(8) (1997), 454.

[54] Bosch, 'The Changing Face of Corporate Governance'. See also G. Kiel and G. Nicholson, 'Board Composition and Corporate Performance: How the Australian Experience Informs Contrasting Theories of Corporate Governance', *Corporate Governance: An International Review*, 11(3) (2003), 189; H. Kang et al., 'Corporate Governance and Board Composition: Diversity and Independence of Australian Boards', *Corporate Governance: An International Review*, 15(2) (2007), 194; I. Bonn et al., 'Effects of Board Structure on Firm Performance: A Comparison between Japan and Australia', *Asian Business Management*, 3 (2004), 105.

[55] F. Clarke and G. Dean, *Indecent Disclosure: Gilding the Corporate Lily* (Cambridge University Press, 2007).

collapsed in May 2001. News Limited and PBL were large blockholders, with Lachlan Murdoch and James Packer (respectively heirs to those large family-controlled companies) appointed NEDs of One.Tel.[56] Both Murdoch and Packer claimed they were 'profoundly misled'[57] by executives regarding the company's true financial position, although PBL and News executives were regularly briefed on One.Tel[58] and Packer was substantially involved in its daily operations. Curiously, in evidence to the court, both Packer and Murdoch suffered from serious memory lapses.[59] The Australian Securities and Investments Commission (ASIC) did not bring proceedings against these NEDs, but only the non-executive chair and three other executive directors. Two accepted settlements, but the New South Wales Supreme Court ultimately exonerated the other two directors.[60] Packer and Murdoch later settled their long-running disputes with One.Tel's creditors by paying them AUS $40 million.[61]

Another spectacular collapse was HIH, then Australia's second largest insurer. It owed:[62]

> [D]ebts of about [AUS] $5.3 billion, which Ray Williams and his cohorts achieved through gross mismanagement, largely charging too little for premiums and failing to put away enough to pay out claims. They concealed this by under-reserving (which boosts profits) and using 'financial reinsurance' contracts to turn losses into gains. Williams, the chief executive, distracted the investment community with a string of takeovers, culminating in paying [AUS] $300 million for Rodney Adler's FAI Insurances in 1998.

The biggest corporate failure in Australian history led to a Royal Commission, chaired by Justice Neville Owen, which cost AUS $40 million and reported in April 2003 after an 18-month inquiry. In addition to highlighting HIH's corporate governance failures and recommending various improvements,

[56] P. Barry, *Rich Kids* (Random House, 2003).

[57] E. Knight, 'You've Come a Long Way since the One.Tel Days, Packer', *Sydney Morning Herald* (Business), 15 April 2014.

[58] A. Lampe, 'One.Tel Kept PBL Briefed, Court Told', *Sydney Morning Herald* (Business), 5 October 2005, 25.

[59] These dramatic memory losses extended to PBL's Chief Financial Officer, Geoff Kleeman, described as 'PBL's eyes and ears' at One.Tel: see V. Carson, 'Packer Man Blanks out Pivotal 3 Weeks', *The Australian*, 7 October 2005, 21.

[60] *ASIC v Rich* [2009] NSWSC 1229; Hill, 'Evolving Directors' Duties in the Common Law World'.

[61] 'Packer, Murdoch Stump up $40m for One.Tel', *Sydney Morning Herald*, 17 April 2014.

[62] M. Saville, 'HIH: The Inside Story of Australia's Biggest Corporate Collapse', *Sydney Morning Herald*, 15 March 2003, reviewing M. Westfield, *HIH: The Inside Story of Australia's Biggest Corporate Collapse* (John Wiley, 2003).

the Report led to ASIC bringing largely successful civil and criminal proceedings against Williams and others.[63] Justice Owen nevertheless expressed reservations about IDs functioning as a governance panacea:[64]

> The weight of current opinion is that it is desirable to have a majority of independent directors on a public company board. The board of HIH had several 'independent' directors but this provided little protection against the folly of management. I am not convinced that a mandatory requirement for boards to have a majority of non-executive directors is either necessary or desirable. In most cases it will be desirable (assuming the non-executive directors are truly independent) but flexibility ought to be maintained to enable corporations to be structured in a way that best suits their circumstances. Nonetheless, the trend in the prescription of codes of conduct seems to assume the premise. My recommendations have been developed accordingly.

One problem was that executives did not pass on sufficient information to the Board; another was the lack of auditor independence, and insufficient independence on the company's audit committee set up to appoint them. Legislation strengthening auditor independence was later passed, albeit not to the levels witnessed in the US following the Enron debacle.[65]

2 *The ASX's 'If Not, Why Not' Disclosure Regime since 2003*

In March 2003, arguably to pre-empt more extensive legislative intervention, the ASX unveiled the first edition of the ASX Principles. These generally adopted a UK-style 'if not, why not' approach,[66] especially as it relates to the recommendation that the NED only audit committees and majority ID-led boards.[67] However, for (larger) companies on the Standard & Poors (S&P)/ASX All Ordinaries index, the ASX also adopted a new Listing Rule (presently Rule 12.7) mandating such an

[63] J. Hill, 'Takeovers, Poison Pills and Protectionism in Comparative Corporate Governance' (Sydney Law School Research Paper No. 10/120, November 2010), available at http://ssrn.com/abstract=1704745.

[64] Commonwealth, Royal Commission of Inquiry into the Failure of HIH Insurance, *Final Report* (2003), 112 [6.2.6].

[65] Nottage, 'Corporate Governance in Australia: The Evolving Blockholder Legacy' with further references.

[66] However, the Chair of the ASX Corporate Governance Council (since November 2011) had earlier suggested that the Australian '*if not*, why not' approach may be somewhat less directive than the UK '*comply* or explain' approach, which he sees as instead implicating a presumption that companies will comply with the recommendations: A. Cameron, 'How Do Directors Sleep at Night?' in R. Austin and A. Bilski (eds.), *Directors in Troubled Times* (Ross Parsons Centre for Commercial, Corporate and Taxation Law, 2009), 115, 118.

[67] See Chapter 4 (Japan) at II.1.c for corresponding developments in Japan a decade later.

audit committee without exception.[68] Recommendation 2.1 of the ASX Principles also required all listed companies to have a majority of IDs on an 'if not, why not' basis, and it largely adopted the criteria for independence first outlined in the Bosch Report.[69]

The ASX Principles included general comments somewhat reminiscent of statements in Justice Owen's Report and the Hilmer Report as to the need for boards to retain appropriate diversity:[70]

> What constitutes good corporate governance will evolve with the changing circumstances of a company and must be tailored to meet those circumstances. Best practice must also evolve with developments both in Australia and overseas.
>
> There is no single model of good corporate governance. This document articulates 10 core principles that the ASX Corporate Governance Council [formed in 2002] believes underlie good corporate governance. Each principle is explained in detail, with implementation guidance in the form of best practice recommendations.
>
> Although the Council's recommendations are not mandatory and cannot, in themselves, prevent corporate failures or mistakes in corporate decision-making, they can provide a reference point for enhanced structures to minimize problems and optimize performance and accountability.

The second edition of the ASX Principles adopted in August 2007 (in effect from 2008)[71] took a similar approach. As explained further in

[68] ASX Corporate Governance Council, *Principles of Good Corporate Governance and Best Practice Recommendations*, 1st edn (March 2003), Recommendations 4.2 and 4.3. But consider the extent to which the ASX grants 'waivers' to its Listing Rules. One commentator (Professor Jennifer Hill) suggests they are rather pervasive: see E. Sexton, 'ASX Merger Plan Raises Questions of Governance', *The Age*, 29 October 2010. However, the extent of waivers as they relate to minimum ID requirements (if at all) deserves further empirical study.

[69] Recommendation 2.2 of the ASX Principles added that the chair should be an ID, with Recommendation 2.3 splitting the roles of chair and CEO. ASX Corporate Governance Council, *Principles of Good Corporate Governance and Best Practice Recommendations*, 1st edn; J. J. Du Plessis, A. Hargovan and M. Bagaric, *Principles of Contemporary Corporate Governance*, 2nd edn (Cambridge University Press, 2011), Part 4.4.2, also notes parallels between the ASX Principles' criteria for IDs and those set out in the Investment and Financial Services Association (IFSA, now the Financial Services Council) 'Blue Book' (*Guidance Note No 2:00: Corporate Governance: A Guide for Fund Managers and Corporations*, December 2002); and that the UK Higgs Report (released in January 2003) had for the first time defined IDs in great detail. However, the Bosch Committee recommendations seem to have influenced institutional investors rather than the other way around: Telephone interview by L. Nottage with Henry Bosch, 16 March 2015.

[70] ASX Corporate Governance Council, *Principles of Good Corporate Governance*, 1st edn, 3.

[71] ASX Corporate Governance Council, *Corporate Governance Principles and Recommendations*, 2nd edn, 4, largely repeats the paragraph above (although instead mentioning more succinctly that the recommendations are 'a reference point for companies about their corporate governance structures and practices').

section IV below, this edition made relatively minor changes overall and with respect to ID requirements.[72] These ASX Principles reiterated that:[73]

> The Recommendations are not prescriptions, they are guidelines, designed to produce an outcome that is effective and of high quality and integrity. This document does not require a 'one size fits all' approach to corporate governance. Instead, it states suggestions for practices designed to optimise corporate performance and accountability in the interests of shareholders and the broader economy. If a company considers that a Recommendation is inappropriate to its particular circumstances, it has the flexibility not to adopt it – a flexibility tempered by the requirement to explain why – the 'if not, why not' approach.

Analyses by the ASX over 2004–2007 found that just under half of listed firms complied with Recommendation 2.1 (a majority of IDs on boards), although larger companies reported higher compliance.[74]

Another ambiguous development for IDs in 2004 was the National Australia Bank's boardroom brawl that erupted following a foreign exchange trading scandal. One ID, Catherine Walter, challenged the board's decision to commission an investigative report by PwC, citing alleged conflicts of interest. Following the intervention of institutional investors, a compromise was reached: Walter and others involved in the dispute resigned.[75] This led to mixed reactions: some supported Walter's independent approach, whereas others warned of the risks of fragmenting boards. Some companies considered introducing 'prenuptial agreements' for NEDs that would allow the board to review their 'performance' every two years and remove them if it was deemed unsatisfactory. ASIC and some commentators declared that this would contravene the shareholders' non-derogable right to remove directors of public companies pursuant to s 203E of the Corporations Act 2001,[76] which then caused (some) companies to water down such agreements with directors.[77]

[72] *Ibid.*, Recommendations 2.1–2.3.

[73] *Ibid.*, 5 (with note 2 noting however the mandatory audit committee requirement still exists/applies for larger ASX companies), largely repeating the first edition at 5. The third edition tones down this message, although still mentioning that they constitute a disclosed-based regime that allows for flexibility (at 5).

[74] A. Veljanovski et al., 'Independent Directors and Australia's Corporate Governance Model. A Survey of Independent Directors' Views', *Australian Journal of Corporate Law*, 24 (2009), 33, 40, with further references.

[75] Ultimately, the fallout from this scandal led to the resignation of six NEDs and the Chairman, Graeme Kraehe, as part of a 'board renewal' process: ABC AM, 'Ex NAB Board Member Catherine Walter Speaks Out', 1 September 2004.

[76] Corporations Act No. 50, 2001 as amended.

[77] Hill, 'Takeovers, Poison Pills and Protectionism in Comparative Corporate Governance', 30–38. However, ASIC regularly issues reminders opposing this practice of director 'pre-nuptial agreements', emphasising that directors are ultimately accountable to

3 *Developments Following the Global Financial Crisis*

By mid-2008, the Global Financial Crisis had reached Australia's shores, but, for various reasons, its impact was far less severe than in most other major world economies.[78] Lingering concerns over excessive managerial risk taking and executive pay were firmly in the crosshairs of post-Crisis Australian policymakers. While space constraints prevent a fuller discussion of these regulatory responses,[79] a few salient points may be made. First, in April 2010, the ASX responded to growing disquiet regarding executive pay by releasing an exposure draft of further proposed amendments to the ASX Principles. Subsequent amendments to the ASX Principles clarified the roles of the remuneration committee; but reaffirmed its long-held recommendation since the first edition of the ASX Principles that an ID should chair the remuneration committee, which should have a majority of IDs, and at least three directors. Listing Rule 12.8, was subsequently introduced, and further mandated that an entity listed in the S&P/ASX 300 Index at the beginning of its financial year should have a remuneration committee comprised solely of NEDs, like the audit committee, for the entire duration of that financial year.[80]

In addition, the 2010 amendments to the ASX Principles introduced new disclosure requirements concerning board diversity, prompted particularly by concerns over a persistent lack of women directors in listed companies.[81] At the behest of the newly elected Rudd Government (September 2008), the Corporations and Markets Advisory Committee (CAMAC) inquired into board diversity. Its Report of March 2009 included (more limited) recommendations for the ASX Principles. CAMAC noted that the proportion of women directors in the ASX 200 companies had remained around 8 per cent since 2002, with those in executive management around

shareholders. See, for example, ASIC Media Release, *04-40 Removal of Directors of Public Companies*, 17 August 2004. It may be that directors forced to resign do not kick up a fuss because they are keen to avoid reputational damage. On directors caring about their reputations generally, see especially R. Masulis and S. Mobbs, 'Independent Director Incentives: Where Do Talented Directors Spend Their Limited Time and Energy?', *Journal of Financial Economics*, 111(2) (2014), 406.

[78] J. G. Hill, 'Why Did Australia Fare So Well in the Global Financial Crisis?' in E. Ferran et al. (eds.), *The Regulatory Aftermath of the Global Financial Crisis* (Cambridge University Press, 2012), 203; R. Garnaut, *Dark Days: Australia after the Boom* (Black Inc, 2013), 7.

[79] Nottage and Aoun, 'The Rise of Independent Directors in Australia: Adoption, Reform and Uncertainty', with further references.

[80] Productivity Commission, *Executive Remuneration* (Inquiry Report No. 49, 2009), also suggested amendments along these lines.

[81] Etheridge, 'Boards of a Feather Flock Together: Board Networks Among ASX Firms', 35–36 (observing that diversity had *diminished* somewhat over 2004–2007).

11–12 per cent over 2004–2008 (with only half in line management, considered a valuable precursor to board appointments).[82]

Further discussion about IDs (and NEDs more generally) surfaces sporadically throughout a third significant report from CAMAC, which emerged soon after the Global Financial Crisis.[83] In August 2009, the Government sought CAMAC's views on whether and how Australia might benefit from more guidance to both executive directors and NEDs in light of guidance or codes of conduct available to directors abroad, such as the Higgs Report and the revised Corporate Governance Code in the UK. After examining various official and non-official sources of guidance available in Australia, the UK, North America and internationally (especially from the Organisation for Economic Co-operation and Development and Basel Committee on Banking Supervision), CAMAC concluded that it did 'not see a need for the development of a new code of conduct or best practice guidance by a regulator', but that (*inter alia*) it would be 'timely for the ASX Corporate Governance Council to review its principles and recommendations in light of international developments'.[84] CAMAC also noted:[85]

> The overriding responsibility of directors is to act in the best interests of the company. This can be a difficult and demanding task. It includes, but goes beyond, an understanding of compliance and other legal issues. First and foremost, it requires directors to focus on the business of the company and direct it towards success.

It then argued that directors should not become 'subject to licensing or other requirements that could be employed to administer or enforce a mandatory code or best practice principles', although the Australian Prudential Regulation Authority (APRA) enforced these criteria for its regulated financial institutions, and that in general:[86]

> There are dangers too in moving to a more prescriptive approach that attempts to codify the large volume of existing regulation. It could result in inflexibility or complexity or a focus on formal compliance rather than in helping to bring about substantive improvements in governance

[82] Corporation and Markets Advisory Committee, Australian Parliament, *Diversity on Boards of Directors* (2009), 26–28. In Australia's largest 100 companies in 1995, women held 3.6 per cent of 889 board seats, with most (29 out of 32 seats) held by women in non-executive positions: Stapledon and Lawrence, 'Board Composition, Structure and Independence in Australia's Largest Listed Companies', 186.

[83] Corporations and Markets Advisory Committee, Australian Parliament, *Guidance for Directors* (April 2010), 73.

[84] *Ibid.*

[85] *Ibid.*

[86] *Ibid.*, 80.

> practices and behaviour. It could also have the effect of imposing new or enhancing obligatory standards on directors in complying with their current statutory and common law duties and responsibilities. Furthermore, it may give the misleading impression that particular matters are more settled, or less open to further development, than may in fact be the case.

Over 2012–2013, the ASX Council duly reviewed the ASX Principles and commenced a public consultation on a third edition, which was finalised in March 2014.[87] The new edition added recommendations establishing a risk committee, either standalone or as part of an audit committee, also needing a majority of IDs, or otherwise disclosing the company's risk management practices, and disclosing whether and how it evaluates economic, environmental and social sustainability risks. It amended slightly the diversity-related recommendations, such as to those with disabilities, and elevated some practices or disclosures hitherto mentioned in the Commentary on the ASX Principles into actual Recommendations (triggering the 'if not, why not' disclosure obligations), while allowing several more flexible alternatives for smaller listed companies. The third edition also made minor amendments to the provisions on IDs. For example, the Commentary on 'close family ties' as indicia of a lack of independence was elevated into 'the Box'. Throughout the Council's consultation paper, references were made and comparisons drawn:[88]

> [T]o the corporate governance codes operating elsewhere, including those in the UK, Singapore, Hong Kong, South Africa, Canada, NYSE's Corporate Governance Rules, and the International Corporate Governance Network's Global Corporate Governance Guidelines (Revised 2009). These codes were chosen on the basis that they apply to major and comparable markets to the Australian market and are written in English.

Other differences from the earlier editions include: bringing the (somewhat confusing) reporting recommendations into the substantive recommendations themselves; rewriting some of the general commentary to give it more of a 'directive' tone; and the significant expansion in footnote references.

The latest ASX changes documented above occurred against the backdrop of government reviews, such as the 2004 Jackson Inquiry Report, legislative enactments and significant developments in Australian corporate law. The Jackson Inquiry further prompted two governmental reports investigating whether existing law required directors and officers to only protect the interests of shareholders (i.e., not other

[87] ASX Corporate Governance Council, *Corporate Governance Principles and Recommendations*, 3rd edn.
[88] *Ibid.*, 5 (citations omitted).

stakeholders). Subsequent reports from CAMAC[89] and a Parliamentary Joint Committee on Corporations and Financial Services[90] found that Australian corporate law permits a broader stakeholder perspective, notwithstanding the scant case law (especially as a corporation approaches or becomes insolvent). As a result, they did not recommend legislative reform along the lines of s 176 of the Companies Act 2006 (UK).[91]

There were also meaningful developments in case law regarding directors' duties of care and diligence, with ASIC realising a high measure of success in enforcement proceedings.[92] In the 2011 case of *ASIC v Healey*, the Federal Court of Australia held that both executives and NEDs of Centro breached their statutory duty of care and diligence by, for example, approving Centro's financial statements that erroneously classified AUS $2 billion of current liabilities as non-current.[93] This breach held firm although Middleton J found the directors 'intelligent, experienced and conscientious people',[94] and despite sound corporate governance practices, such as an audit committee with IDs and auditing reports from a major accounting firm.

The Commentary on Recommendation 2.6 (on induction for new directors and professional development opportunities) for the third edition of the ASX Principles cites *ASIC v Healey* as a cautionary tale of the minimum duties expected regarding financial literacy:[95]

> In *ASIC v Healey* … the Federal Court held that it is the duty of every director of an entity subject to section 344 of the Corporations Act … to read the financial statements of the entity carefully and to consider whether what they disclose is consistent with the director's own knowledge of the entity's affairs. It is important that a listed entity's board have a diverse range of skills and experience and this necessarily means that not all directors will have the same level of accounting skills and experience. Nevertheless, it is in the

89 Corporations and Markets Advisory Committee, Australian Parliament, *The Social Responsibility of Corporations* (December 2006), available at www.camac.gov.au.

90 Parliamentary Joint Committee on Corporations and Financial Services, *Inquiry into Corporate Responsibility* (June 2006), available at www.aph.gov.au.

91 Hill, 'Evolving Directors' Duties in the Common Law World', 32–41.

92 *ASIC v. Healey & Ors (No 2)* (2011) 196 FCR 430 and *ASIC v. Hellicar* (2012) CLR 286 501, but see, *ASIC v. Rich* (2009) 236 FLR 1. For a discussion of these cases, see Hill, 'Evolving Directors' Duties in the Common Law World', 18–30; G. Golding, 'Tightening the Screws on Directors: Care, Delegation and Reliance', *UNSW Law Journal*, 35(1) (2012), 266; H. Glasbeek, 'The James Hardie Directors: A Case of Missing Directors and Misdirections by Law', *Australian Journal of Corporate Law*, 28 (2013), 107.

93 *ASIC v. Healey & Ors (No 2)*, 430.

94 *ASIC v. Healey & Ors (No 2)*, 434.

95 ASX Corporate Governance Council, *Corporate Governance Principles and Recommendations*, 3rd edn, 18 n. 22.

> interests of a listed entity and its security holders (and also in the personal interests of the director concerned) that each director of the entity has an appropriate base level of understanding of accounting matters.

Although the current edition adds several footnote references to statutory provisions and ASX Listing Rules (and other material) compared to the two earlier editions, this is the only judgement cited.

IV Defining Independent Directors

Unlike the US or Japan,[96] there are no legislative provisions concerning board composition and definition of independence in Australia. Instead, 'soft law' instruments buttress the Australian regulatory framework. As mentioned in section III, the emergence of IDs as a centrepiece of Australian corporate governance practices traces its roots to these ASX initiatives, especially around 2003 when it first introduced the ASX Principles and Recommendations on an 'if not, why not' basis. Although the first and second editions are similar, the third edition contains significant modifications.

Recommendation 2.1 in the first and second editions requires a majority of the board to be IDs. The Commentary views IDs as separate from management and any business or other relationship that could 'materially interfere with – or could reasonably be perceived to materially interfere with' – the exercise of their independent judgement.[97] Because the Commentary (especially in the second edition) also highlights that all directors should bring an independent judgement to bear on board decisions, and because separation from management is a characteristic shared by all NEDs, the distinguishing feature of IDs logically must be matters which (actually or reasonably) 'materially interfere' with their exercise of independent judgement.[98]

Importantly, the Commentary lists in 'Box 2.1'[99] various relationships that 'define' a lack of independence (according to the first edition) or that 'may affect independent status' (according to the second edition).[100] All NEDs should provide any information relevant to their independence, with the board then identifying in the annual report's corporate governance

[96] See Chapter 1 at III for developments in the US and Chapter 4 (Japan) for Japan.

[97] The first edition of the ASX Principles adds a reference to 'unfettered and independent judgement'. ASX Corporate Governance Council, *Principles of Good Corporate Governance and Best Practice Recommendations*, 1st edn (note 68 above), 19.

[98] In many ways, this is consistent with the Bosch Committee's views introduced above at III.1.

[99] See Table 11.3.

[100] ASX Corporate Governance Council, *Corporate Governance Principles and Recommendations*, 2nd edn, 16. This also differs slightly from the first edition by adding to

statement those directors it considers to be IDs. If the board considers those directors 'independent' notwithstanding the existence of relationships listed in Box 2.1, it should provide reasons in support of this conclusion. The second (and third) edition states that such relationships should then be disclosed in the annual report. Despite the board's ultimate discretion to declare those directors affected by the Box 2.1 relationship factors as 'independent', these relationships have had a significant impact on corporate practice. In making such assessments, the Commentary to both the first and second editions emphasises the importance of boards evaluating 'materiality thresholds from the perspective of both the company and its directors, and to disclose these'. A footnote to that text provides one example.[101]

The third edition omits this specific example of a materiality threshold, reordering and rephrasing the Recommendations and commentary, but essentially retains the same approach as the earlier editions. Recommendation 2.3 calls for the company to identify those directors adjudged as IDs, and to disclose if and why that assessment has been made notwithstanding the existence of a Box 2.3 factor. It also requires disclosure of 'the length of service of each director'.[102] The 'materiality' of the relationship is retained, but in the Box itself (detailing the list of interests or relationships that 'might cause doubts' about a director's independence) rather than in the Commentary itself. The assessment depends on the extent of interference with the director's capacity for exercising independent judgement 'and to act in the best interests of the entity and its security holders generally'.[103] The Commentary also talks about IDs not being 'allied with the interests of management, a substantial security holder or other relevant stakeholder', and cautions how this 'appellation … gives great comfort to security holders and [is] not one that should be applied lightly'.[104] Table 11.3

Commentary on Principle 2 that generally ('structure the board to add value') the board should be structured so it 'encourages enhanced performance of the company', as well as exercising independent judgement, reviewing and challenging management, and properly understanding and dealing with current and emerging business issues.

101 Repeated in *Ibid.*, 16, with note 11 stating: 'For example, a board may decide that affiliation with a business which accounts for, say, less than X% of the company's revenue is, as a category, immaterial for the purpose of determining independence. If the company discloses the standard it follows and makes a general statement that the relevant director meets that standard, investors are better informed about the board's reasoning.'

102 ASX Corporate Governance Council, *Corporate Governance Principles and Recommendations*, 3rd edn, 16. The average and median tenure of NEDs, which is significantly higher for men than women, increased for ASX 100 companies from 5.6 in 2011 to 5.8 years in 2012 (median 4.7), as well as for ASX 101–200 companies. ACSI, *Board Composition and Non-Executive Director Pay in the ASX 200 Companies: 2013*.

103 ASX Corporate Governance Council, *Corporate Governance Principles and Recommendations*, 3rd edn, Box 2.3.

104 *Ibid.*, 16. The Commentary adds (at 17) a duty on candidates for directorships – seemingly not just for NED positions – to 'disclose to the company all relationships or

Table 11.3 Changes in ASX Principles and Recommendations Regarding IDs

1st edition (2003) Box 2.1[a]	**2nd edition (2007) Box 2.1**	**3rd edition (2014) Box 2.3**
1. substantial shareholder of the company or an officer of, or otherwise associated directly with, a substantial shareholder of the company	1. [same as the 1st edition]	1. [similar to the 2nd edition, but omits being '*directly*' associated with 'security holder', rather than 'shareholder']
2. within the last three years has been employed in an executive capacity by the company or another group member, *or been a director after ceasing to hold such employment*	2. [essentially the same: 'is employed, or has previously been employed in an executive capacity by the company or another group member, and there has not been a period of at least three years between ceasing such employment and serving on the board']	2. [very similar, but refers to the company's 'child entities' rather than a 'group member']
3. has within the last three years been a principal of a material professional advisor or a material consultant to the company or another group member, or an employee materially associated with the service provided	3. [same]	3. [similar, but refers to 'partner, director *or senior employee* of a provider of material professional services to the entity or any of its child entities']
4. is a material supplier or customer of the company or other group member, or an officer of or otherwise associated directly or indirectly with a material supplier or customer	4. [same]	4. [quite similar, but adds having 'been *within the last three years*' in a 'material business relationship (e.g. as a supplier or customer')]

5. has a material contractual relationship with the company or another group member other than as a director of the company	5. [same]	5. [very similar, but refers to the company's 'child entities' rather than a 'group member']
6. *has served on the board for a period which could, or could reasonably be perceived to, materially interfere with the director's ability to act in the best interests of the company*	[omitted]	6. *has been a director of the entity for such a period that his or her independence may have been compromised*
7. *is free of any interest and any business or other relationship which could, or could reasonably be perceived to, materially interfere with the director's ability to act in the best interests of the company*	[not listed in the Box, but Principle commentary defines independence to exclude interests etc. materially interfering with independent judgement]	[similar to 2007, but adds that independence also means acting in the best interests of the corporation and its security holders generally]
		7. has close family ties with any person who falls within any of the categories described above

[a] Only the first edition lists these relationships in the negative, defining an ID to be an NED ('not a member of management') which is not a substantial shareholder, an employee, etc.

summarises the relevant considerations that may compromise a director's independence, thus calling for board assessment.

This comparative analysis, with different editions' provisions italicised for emphasis, demonstrates strong similarities over time, but the third edition reflects tightened criteria.[105] That is particularly evident with respect to associations with professional services providers and business partners of the company. The third edition also incorporates 'close family ties' into the Box. This is yet another example of a relationship that 'might cause doubts' about the director's independence, thus triggering the disclosure and reporting obligations discussed above. The earlier editions merely set out Commentary that: 'Family ties and cross-directorships may be relevant in considering interests and relationships which affect independence, and should be disclosed by directors to the board.'[106] The elevation of 'family ties' in the third edition into the Box, however, appears qualified. A careful reading reveals that the third edition only refers to 'close' family ties. More curiously it is silent on any reference to potential problems with cross-directorships.[107] Arguably, such relationships may be captured by the catch-all definition in the Commentary.[108]

A broad reference to directors' tenure – conspicuously absent from the second edition – resurfaces in the third edition, and in contradistinction to the first edition, is reworded to focus on its possible detrimental impact on independence. The Commentary to the first edition mentions: 'The UK Higgs report nominates 10 years in relation to director tenure considerations, but [this] has not yet been adopted in the UK. The Council will continue to monitor developments in other jurisdictions

interests that may bear on independence', which in turn should be disclosed to shareholders in materials for board elections.

105 For a broader comparison of changes between the second and third edition, see ASX Corporate Governance Council, 'Translation Table: Corporate Governance Council Recommendations (New to Old)', available at www.asx.com.au.

106 ASX Corporate Governance Council, *Corporate Governance Principles and Recommendations*, 2nd edn, 17 (restating this observation).

107 Moncrieff, 'Unravelling the Ties That Connect and Direct'; Kiel and Nicholson, 'Board Composition and Corporate Performance'; Etheridge, 'Boards of a Feather Flock Together: Board Networks Among ASX Firms'.

108 However, although the Box itself has not included a catch-all since the first edition: see Item 7, Table 11.3.

in this area.'[109] The 2013 ASX Corporate Governance Council's public Consultation Paper for the third edition noted that 'Tenure was subsequently dropped from Box 2.1 in the third edition'[110] (without elaboration), but that subsequently 'the UK, Singapore, South Africa and Hong Kong codes have all been amended to recommend that there should be a rigorous review of the independence of those directors who have served more than 9 years'.[111]

This controversial '9-year' tenure featured in an early draft of the third edition, but soon disappeared. The Council was evidently aware of the controversy this was likely to engender as the accompanying review tentatively suggested the nine-year service period as a possible 'indicator'[112] militating against independence. The third edition now simply refers to a director serving 'for such a period that his or her independence may have been compromised'.[113] Although the ASX Principles eschew specified tenure limits as indicative of compromised independence, the Commentary explains that 'the board should [nevertheless] regularly assess whether that might be the case for any director who has served in that position for more than 10 years'.[114]

This compromise may well be in response to the stiff opposition from directors' lobbies and other interest groups. For instance, the AICD, which has long opposed the ASX's indicative list of factors informing the question of directorial independence, is particularly critical of the re-emergence of tenure as a factor that *might* inform the question

[109] ASX Corporate Governance Council, *Principles of Good Corporate Governance and Best Practice Recommendations*, 1st edn, 21.

[110] ASX Corporate Governance Council, *Review of the Corporate Governance Principles and Recommendations: Consultation Paper*, 16 August 2013, 11 [41].

[111] *Ibid.*, 11–12 (omitting citations, e.g., to the Singapore Code Guideline 2.4 [maximum of nine years] and Hong Kong Code Provision A.4.3 [nine years]); T. Ritchie, 'Independent Directors: Magic Bullet or Band-Aid?', *Bond University Corporate Governance eJournal* (2007), n. 21, available at http://epublications.bond.edu.au. Ritchie remarks that the ASX's Consultation Paper in 2006 had suggested that length of service should be viewed as an issue relating to succession, not independence of the board. He also notes that US and European models around that time, the first edition of the ASX Principles were also distinctive in having a catch-all provision and stricter criteria regarding employment with a company consultant, but looser criteria regarding being an employee in that only those working 'in an executive capacity' may lack independence.

[112] ASX Corporate Governance Council, *Review of the Corporate Governance Principles and Recommendations: Consultation Paper*, 2 [9].

[113] ASX Corporate Governance Council, *Corporate Governance Principles and Recommendations*, 3rd edn, Box 2.3.

[114] *Ibid.*, 17.

of directorial independence. In its submission to the ASX Corporate Governance Council, the AICD was particularly scathing of any references to 'arbitrary time limits'. The submission also warned that the ASX's approach here 'fails to acknowledge the benefits' of long-serving directors, including: continuity of organisation-specific knowledge (particularly important in complex industries); greater board stability; and improved board dynamics and collegiality.[115]

Although it is tempting (and too convenient) to characterise this concession as a panicky capitulation to the strong resistance by director lobbies and other vested interests, there may be more at stake here. The status quo in fact may reflect efforts to accommodate the significant increase in ID numbers brought about by the ASX corporate governance initiatives since 2003. Put another way, the ASX's retreat may be tacit acknowledgement of the lack of supply of appropriately qualified directors. Of course, these reforms together with the stark reality of a (supposedly) thin director labour supply market combine to generate a large group of incumbents – including a significant cohort of 'professional IDs' – who may be resistant to the idea of tenure informing their perceived independence.[116]

We turn next to the 'substantial shareholder' relationship as potentially compromising independence. While this relationship is mentioned in all three editions of the ASX Principles (as in the original Bosch Report of 1991), the third edition no longer includes a footnote cross-reference to the 5 per cent definition in the Corporations Act 2001.[117] It also adds the following new Commentary:[118]

> In relation to the fourth example in Box 2.3 (being or being an associate of a substantial security holder), the holding of securities in the entity may help to align the interests of a director with those of other security holders, and such holdings are therefore not discouraged. The example simply reflects that a director holding or representing a substantial stake

[115] Australian Institute of Company Directors, *Submission on Revised Corporate Governance Principles and Recommendations*, 14 November 2013, 6–7.

[116] See section II, and further Nottage and Aoun, 'The Rise of Independent Directors in Australia: Adoption, Reform and Uncertainty'.

[117] ASX Corporate Governance Council, *Corporate Governance Principles and Recommendations*, 2nd edn, 13 n. 13, referring to s 9 of the Corporations Act (still otherwise applicable and defining 'substantial holding' as 5 per cent or more of the total number of votes attached to voting shares).

[118] ASX Corporate Governance Council, *Corporate Governance Principles and Recommendations*, 3rd edn, 17.

> in the entity is likely to be seen as having a different interest to security holders with smaller stakes.

The Council here appears mindful of critiques from financial economists such as Professor Peter Swan, arguing that the 'if not, why not' approach of the ASX Principles towards requiring a majority of IDs has caused a decline in corporate performance.[119] Swan, a trenchant critic of the ASX Principles on ID 'requirements', is especially critical of the 5 per cent 'substantial shareholder' (or their associates) 'rule' (see section V below). These criticisms, it seems, have served as a catalyst for ACSI's first collation of director shareholdings in ASX-listed companies. That study reports that 11.5 per cent of NEDs of ASX 100 companies had 'no skin in the game' (i.e., no shares in the companies they govern), described as a 'concerning statistic'.[120]

A final subtle difference in the third edition is that it no longer footnotes the fact that its Box factors have been 'adapted' from the definition given in guidance for fund managers (and others) from their peak body in Australia, the so-called 'Blue Book' developed by the Investment and Financial Services Association.[121] The Association is now called the Financial Services Council, and still promotes a Blue Book. Its definition for IDs bears close parallels to the current ASX Principles.[122] Investors may also wish to consider the guidance offered by another major peak association, ACSI, which has recently outlined indicia for assessing independence.[123]

On their face, the ACSI criteria are more detailed and stringent than the ASX factors. For length of tenure, however, there is no formal threshold. Nevertheless, in ACSI's 2013 board composition survey, 20-plus years seems to be used as one outer limit for determining whether directors

[119] Fischer and Swan, 'Does Board Independence Improve Firm Performance?'.

[120] ACSI, *Board Composition and Non-Executive Director Pay in the ASX 200 Companies: 2013*, 3, 33–35. Twenty-one per cent of ASX 101–200 NEDs had no shares.

[121] ASX Corporate Governance Council, *Corporate Governance Principles and Recommendations*, 2nd edn, 17 n. 12.

[122] IFSA, *Corporate Governance: A Guide for Fund Managers and Corporations*, 18. This 'Blue Book' refers to 'direct or indirect' associations with a substantial shareholder, or having been an 'employee' – not even a 'senior employee' – of a material professional advisor or consultant to the company. Multiple directorships are also addressed, though IDs are not the sole focus. See also Commentary on Recommendation 2.1, ASX Corporate Governance Council, *Corporate Governance Principles and Recommendations*, 3rd edn.

[123] ACSI, *ACSI Governance Guidelines: A Guide for Superannuation Funds to Monitor Listed Australian Companies* (July 2013), 15.

are 'affiliated' as opposed to being independent.[124] That study went on to explain that this was:[125]

> [B]ased on the classification by ACSI of directors, which can differ from that of the company. For example, Woodside in its 2012 annual report classifies as independent former Shell executive Christopher Haynes, who retired in 2011, despite Shell owning 23 per cent of the company's shares and having nominated Haynes to the board. ACSI classified Haynes as affiliated. These cases illustrate that the ASX Council's guidelines on assessing director independence, unlike the rules of foreign stock exchanges such as the NYSE, allow for considerable exercise of judgement by company boards when assessing director independence.

V Quantitative and Qualitative Research into the Impact and Roles of IDs

Whether or not the gradual increase in IDs on the boards of publicly listed Australian companies, especially since 2003, has led to corporate governance improvements remains an open question. When the ASX first proposed a mandatory requirement in 1992 and then a UK-style 'comply or explain' regime in 1994, many commentators queried whether IDs would make any practical difference. Critics highlighted the ambiguous US empirical evidence regarding the impact of IDs on overall corporate performance.[126] The ASX later compromised by introducing a more relaxed disclosure regime in 1996, as outlined in section III above. Naturally, it took several years for the emergence of Australia-specific empirical research on the efficacy of IDs.

First, *quantitative* studies investigating the (in)efficacy of IDs have produced ambivalent results. Table 11.4 sets out a selective assortment of econometric studies investigating the impact of IDs on corporate performance in Australia.

Generally speaking, this evidence from Australia does not strongly support the proposition that IDs are responsible for improvements in

[124] ACSI, *Board Composition and Non-Executive Director Pay in the ASX 200 Companies: 2013*, 9–10 ('Prior to 2005, ACSI classified all directors with more than nine years' service on a board as affiliated and from 2005 only those directors who had spent more than 20 years on a board were considered affiliated (the change in definition was effective from the second edition of the ACSI Guidelines, released in 2005)').

[125] *Ibid.*, 11 (citation omitted).

[126] Bird, 'The Rise and Fall of the Independent Director', 255–258.

Table 11.4 ID Impact on Corporate Performance in Australia

Study	*Sample size (and year)*	*Definition of directors*	*Firm performance*	*Impact*
Muth and Donaldson (1998)	largest 145 from 550 sampled from 1,173 listed ASX companies (1992)	composite 'board independence'[a]	1993–1994	**negative** for composite shareholder wealth (ROA and ROE) and sales growth
Lawrence and Stapledon (1999)	ASX 100 (1995)	IDs (as per AIMA / IFSA in 1997)	1985–1995	**Nil**
Cotter et al. (2003)	ASX 200 (1997)	IDs (as per AIMA)	1997	**Nil**
Kiel and Nicholson (2003)	348 from ASX 500 (1996, excluding banks and mining firms)	NEDs	1996–1998 (averages)	**positive** for Tobin's Q but **negative** for ROA
Hutchison (2002)	229 from ASX 500 (1998)	NEDs		**negative**
Matolcsy et al. (2004)	306 from sample of largest 507 companies (2001)	outside NEDs (including 'grey directors' with 'potential links to the managers … such as bankers or lawyers')	1999–2001	**positive** for composite Market Value but only for firms with above-average 'growth options' (market to book value)
Bonn et al. (2004)	104 manufacturing firms from the top 500 companies (1998)	NEDs	1999	**positive** only for ROA (contrasting Japan: nil for Market to Book value)

Table 11.4 (*cont.*)

Study	*Sample size (and year)*	*Definition of directors*	*Firm performance*	*Impact*
Setja-Atmaja (2009)	316 from ASX (1998, excluding banks)	IDs (but not as per ASX Principles 2003)	2000–2005	**positive** for closely-held firms, and overall (greater impact for closely-held firms or those paying low dividends)[b]
Pham et al. (2012)	136 largest ASX (excluding financial and utility companies)	NEDs (not current or former employees, or related by family to executive directors or with business dealings)	1994–2003	**positive** for cost of capital
Fischer and Swan (2013)	ASX 500 (2001–2011, so 969 distinct firms)		2001–2011	**negative** (and other effects summarised below)
Swan and Forsberg (2014)	ASX 200 (2002–2012), so 430 distinct firms		2002–2012	**negative** (and other effects summarised below)

[a] Proportion of NEDs; interest alignment (relationships with executives, suppliers etc., significant shareholders, family members and founders); CEO duality; board size; average age.

[b] Closely-held companies here (i.e., those with a 20 per cent + shareholding) preferred fewer IDs and underperformed widely-held companies, suggesting 'rent extraction' from other shareholder(s).

overall corporate performance or value.[127] However, there are various methodological difficulties with these studies, including:

- some studies only focus on NEDs, while others distinguish between IDs and NEDs, albeit with varying definitions;
- time periods and sample sizes for firms are generally limited, thus impacting on robustness of the results;
- studies often do not refer to earlier research, perhaps because they were published too close together or simply overlooked, often resulting in different control variables – exacerbating difficulties in comparing studies; and
- all econometric studies may have serious limitations regarding measurement of key variables (including measures of corporate performance, such as Return on Assets or ROA, as the dependent variable),[128] and especially endogeneity between the independent and dependent variables (including the extent of IDs).

Endogeneity is particularly troublesome because companies that do poorly tend to appoint more IDs, and vice versa. Testing for causation under such circumstances, requires a mandatory rule change that compels all companies (good and bad performers) to adopt IDs. The ASX Principles and Listing Rules, as outlined above in section II, instead leave scope for board and company discretion, at least regarding the 'majority of IDs' requirement. While Listing Rules mandate IDs for audit committees since 2004, and remuneration committees since 2011 for certain listed companies, designing a convincing econometric study is proving particularly difficult. Consequently, none have been published in Australia.[129]

The endogeneity problem remains serious for the large-scale econometric study of ASX listed company performance publicised in 2013 under the leadership of Professor Peter Swan. The fact that the introduction of the first edition of the ASX Principles constituted only a 'quasi-natural experiment' weakens, without completely destroying, the impact of his controversial key conclusions:[130]

[127] See Chapter 2 at IV.2 for a general discussion of the empirical studies.

[128] Tobin Q, for example, is a theoretical concept requiring approximation. It assumes that current market prices are an effective measure of corporate value. Following the Global Financial Crisis, this proposition is more debatable, even though the allure of the associated 'efficient markets hypothesis' remains remarkably strong. See, for example, J. Quiggin, *Zombie Economics: How Dead Ideas Still Walk among Us* (Princeton University Press, 2010).

[129] We thank Professor Ron Masulis for helpful discussion regarding these methodological issues.

[130] Fischer and Swan, 'Does Board Independence Improve Firm Performance?', 9. This estimated 'cost', however, should be contextualised in light of the ASX's current market capitalisation of around AUS $1.5 trillion.

> [M]ajority board independence reduces firm performance regardless of whether the criterion is shareholder value in terms of the Tobin's *Q* or Market-to-Book ratios, or accounting performance as measured by the industry-adjusted ROA. We also find that boards once they become dominated by independent directors are far poorer at replacing a relatively under-performing CEO, pay poorly performing CEOs significantly more, and take home significantly higher director fees. ... We estimate the dollar cost of these treatment effects over the period 2003–2011 conservatively at AUS $69 billion, making it one of the most costly and disastrous regulatory changes ever implemented in Australia by a private regulator.

Despite revisions,[131] this study remains particularly critical of the ASX Principles' view that independence could be compromised by associations with a major shareholder.[132] The original study received mixed reactions. Initial reports were favourable, yet commentators soon expressed concern over the possible agency costs between directors with large shareholdings and minority shareholders should there be a change to the status quo.[133]

Perhaps due to the strong vested interest now among incumbent IDs (anecdotally referred to as the 'chosen ones')[134] as well as peak bodies like the AICD that became increasingly involved in training them and promoting their interests over the 1990s,[135] the ASX Council decided

[131] Swan and Forsberg, 'Does Board "Independence" Destroy Corporate Value?', 30. In this latest study, Swan has yet again revised downwards the supposed destruction of 'shareholder value' attributable to majority ID-led board contending that ASX 200 companies with majority ID-led boards have 'destroyed between AUS $30.7 billion and AUS $51.6 billion of shareholder value over the period 2002–2012'. See also P. Swan, *Submission to (Australian Government's) Financial System Inquiry*, 31 March 2014 (estimating AUS $85 billion over the period 2002–2012).

[132] G. Smith et al., 'Institutional Investor Monitoring and the Structure of Corporate Boards', Draft (2 October 2007). Curiously, the authors of this article had previously noted that institutional influence was negatively related to board size and positively related to board independence, with institutions working to remove inside directors (thus increasing the proportion of NEDs and IDs) if firms performed badly.

[133] A. Creighton, 'Shareholders Suffer as Independent Directors Pay Fat Cats', *The Australian*, 28 August 2013; A. Creighton, 'ASX, Directors Dispute Claims Execs to Blame', *The Australian*, 29 August 2013, 27. For details, see Nottage and Aoun, 'The Rise of Independent Directors in Australia: Adoption, Reform and Uncertainty'.

[134] Parliamentary Joint Committee on Corporations and Financial Services, Australian Parliament, *Better Shareholders – Better Company Shareholder Engagement and Participation in Australia* (2008), [4.76] (arguing more generally that 'board patronage and dominance by an entrenched few is unhealthy for good corporate governance' and urging that processes for electing directors in Australia could be 'substantially improved'). See also J. Spigelman, 'Institutional Shareholders and Corporate Governance', *Companies and Securities Law Journal*, 28(4) (2010), 235–242.

[135] See generally *Bosch Report, 3rd edition*, 281–282 (also noting the emergence of a significant board consulting industry).

against relaxing ID disclosure requirements in the third edition of the ASX Principles. If anything, the requirements were slightly tightened. However, Commentary was added about the possibility of shareholder links with directors instead creating some positive benefits, along with some more flexible disclosure provisions especially for smaller listed companies (e.g., regarding audit committees).

Another dimension to the corporate governance contributions offered by IDs lies in the evaluation of their performance in crisis situations, especially in moderating the likelihood of corporate collapses. Unfortunately, such counter-factuals cannot be proved. Though case study research may be illuminating here in suggesting a positive contribution, little work has been done in Australia. In fact, some prominent corporate failures offer ambivalent results. As mentioned above in section III, the failed HIH group was notionally an 'early adopter' and appeared to have a majority of IDs, even before the first edition of the ASX Principles was introduced, as did the Centro group, which almost failed in 2007.[136]

Broader *qualitative* research in Australia has also been limited. One study published in 2008, based on interviews of 30 directors, with multiple appointments, including 24 only with NED positions and five with NED and executive director positions, as well as 16 Australian fund manager executives in Australia, reported that IDs should have the following qualities:

- demonstrate independence of mind, information, relationships with the company and income;
- be responsible to shareholders; and
- be available, allocating sufficient time for board duties, and appointed for a limited time.[137]

Another survey identified 684 IDs from the top 200 ASX listed companies in 2006, with an average of 3.4 directors per company, but merely secured 143 responses (22.5 per cent response rate). Most respondents (85 per cent) had more than five years' experience as an ID and 41 per

[136] D. F. Jackson Q. C., Commissioner, 'Report of the Special Commission of Inquiry into the Medical Research and Compensation Foundation' (2004). The HIH board had 13 directors, five of whom were executive and eight were NEDs, of which only two were truly IDs: see Chapter 12 at II.

[137] One respondent remarked that IDs 'should not remain on the board of a particular company for too long … we have said ten years is ample': M. McCabe and M. Nowak, 'The Independent Director on the Board of Company Directors', *Managerial Auditing Journal*, 23(6) (2008), 545, 558.

cent had served on boards for over ten years, with 66 per cent also having served on more than five boards over these periods.[138] Most (81 per cent) had executive experience in one or more companies, and many (61 per cent) viewed themselves as 'professional directors'.

Unfortunately, such 'sample bias' somewhat undermines the respondents' views on appropriate ID roles and features, and Australian corporate governance generally. It is unsurprising, therefore, that 95 per cent thought that IDs strengthen corporate governance! More interestingly, questionnaire responses were evenly split on whether having IDs would lead to conservative decision making. Thirty per cent thought there was need for a UK-style 'senior ID' and only 26 per cent thought that international business experience was needed to be an effective ID.[139] Most (90 per cent) preferred the 'self-regulatory' approach of the ASX Principles to mandatory requirements especially in light of diverse needs of companies, the flexibility of guidelines and crucially, because independence was dependent on the character or state of mind and is something that could be legislated.[140] The respondents generally favoured the ASX Principles' indicia of (non-)independence,[141] and rejected any prohibition on multiple directorships, but they differed over issues such as 'common' directorships, the pool of directorial talent and tenure limits.

Given such results, it is unsurprising that the third edition of the ASX Principles makes relatively few changes regarding IDs, which we explored in section IV. But much more research – qualitative and quantitative – could have been and should be done in Australia.

VI Conclusions

Although ID requirements, in comparison to other jurisdictions, were slowly introduced and mainly on an 'if not, why not' basis, IDs are now a very prominent and entrenched part of the Australian corporate landscape. Despite the regulatory developments canvassed above, there is still

[138] Veljanovski et al., 'Independent Directors and Australia's Corporate Governance Model', 44. Regrettably, the authors do not mention the average tenure of those directors sitting on the same board.

[139] *Ibid.*, 47–49. See also J. How et al., 'Internationalisation and Corporate Governance: Australian Evidence', *Asia Pacific Journal of Economics and Business*, 6(1) (2002), 42–63 (showing that the degree of a firm's internationalisation in Australia had a significant impact on the proportion of IDs with international experience).

[140] *Ibid.*, 45–47, 51.

[141] *Ibid.*, 50.

only weak Australian empirical evidence regarding the positive effects of a majority-independent board on risk management and overall corporate performance. Indeed, a controversial and well-publicised Australian econometric study published in 2013 boldly maintained that over AUS $69 billion in corporate value had been destroyed over 2003–2011 by the (largely) 'if not, why not' ASX requirement for a majority of independent directors on listed company boards.[142] The authors were particularly critical of the ASX's stance that major shareholders (or nominees etc.) would lack the necessary independence as directors, arguing that they instead have stronger incentives to monitor management than independent directors without 'skin in the game'.[143] This aspect of the research has received support from former NSW Supreme Court Justice, Bob Austin. Writing in an editorial piece for Australia's leading financial newspaper, he argues that it is 'time for us to revisit the definition of independence … to permit and encourage independent directors to have more skin in the game'.[144] Seemingly frustrated with the almost Frankenstein-like expansion of the ASX Corporate Governance Council's conception of independence, Dr Austin reminds us that 'investor independence is a different kind of independence and a difference governance strategy, which has been bolted on to the management independence idea'.[145]

Such concerns are not novel. For example, Justice Owen in the 2003 HIH Royal Commission Report doubted 'why a substantial shareholding in the company should be regarded as compromising independence. Such a shareholding, [he maintained] may provide greater incentive to bring the interests of the company to bear'.[146] Contributing very recently to the strongest critique against the 'independence from ownership' ID

142 Fischer and Swan, 'Does Board Independence Improve Firm Performance?'.

143 See, for example, P. Swan and S. Honeine, 'Is Company Performance Dependent on Outside Director "Skin in the Game"?' (2010), available at http://ssrn.com/abstract=1746536, finding a significant positive relationship between NED ownership and firm performance, especially during the Global Financial Crisis (where endogeneity effects might arguably be less).

144 B. Austin, 'Directors Should Have More Skin in the Game', *Australian Financial Review*, 31 July 2014, 55. Austin maintains that 'investor independence is not necessary in order to achieve the board's independence from management', but he seemingly diverges from Swan by declaring that the 'majority of the board should be independent from management'.

145 *Ibid.*

146 Commonwealth, Royal Commission of Inquiry into the Failure of HIH Insurance, *Final Report* (2003), 113 [6.2.6]. See also Stapledon and Lawrence, 'Board Composition, Structure and Independence in Australia's Largest Listed Companies', 161.

requirement since its adoption a decade ago, Hanrahan and Bednall suggest relaxing the ASX definition of IDs (excluding 'significant' (5 per cent and more) shareholders or affiliates) to cover only those who are (or are affiliated with) '*controlling*' shareholders insufficiently constrained by other corporate law rules governing conflict of interest situations for directors.[147]

Notwithstanding these rumblings, it is hard to see even the compromise approach of Hanrahan and Bednall gaining traction in the short term, given that the substantial shareholding criterion was not changed significantly in the third edition of the ASX Principles. This was perhaps due to real concerns that relaxation might disproportionately benefit large over smaller shareholders. Their proposed reforms are also unlikely to eventuate over the medium term given the quite restrictive definition of IDs which is also already found in many other parts of the Asian region and worldwide. In addition, longer-standing critiques of IDs, from Australian professors of accountancy who argue that this institution diverts attention from the real problem of inadequate financial reporting especially in groups of companies,[148] are even more unlikely to find much traction as reforms in the latter respect would be very disruptive to conventional wisdom and entrenched interests.

[147] P. Hanrahan and T. Bednall, 'Independence of Directors Affiliated with Substantial Shareholders: Issues of Law and Corporate Governance', *Companies and Securities Law Journal*, 33 (2015), 239.

[148] F. Clarke, G. Dean and M. Egan, *The Unaccountable and Ungovernable Corporation: Companies' Use-by Dates Close In* (Routledge, 2014).

12

Case Studies of Independent Directors in Asia

BRUCE ARONSON

I Introduction

This book challenges the popular idea that the role of independent directors is essentially the same everywhere, i.e., that the model of director independence developed in the United States (US) and the United Kingdom (UK) is directly applicable to the functioning of independent directors in Asian countries.[1] As noted in both the theoretical introductory chapters and in the country-specific chapters, context counts. Many jurisdictions in Asia have controlling shareholders, whether governments or families, which immediately raises the fundamental question of 'independence from whom?' Similarly, the focus in Asia remains on the management model of the board of directors, even though the monitoring model is receiving increased attention.

Given the strong presence of controlling shareholders, one might be tempted to leap to the conclusion that the 'true' role of independent directors in Asia should be to protect the interests of minority shareholders against the acquisition of private benefits by the majority shareholder. However, as discussed in the prior chapters, independent directors may still potentially play a positive role on behalf of minority shareholders without formally opposing the majority shareholder. There are also other valuable functions that could be played by independent directors in the Asian context that are not directly related to such conflicts of interest.

As noted throughout the book, defining a single 'function' for independent directors is no easy task. Rather, this book sets forth a number of useful approaches to consider functionality. One could consider the role of independent directors in important board functions, i.e., hiring

[1] See Chapters 1, 3, and 13.

and firing of the company president, executive compensation, strategic decision making, conflicts between management and shareholders, conflicts between majority and minority shareholders and compliance.[2] One could move beyond the agency model altogether, and consider independent director functions such as market signalling, acting as advisor to the controller and acting as a mediator between the controller and other shareholders/stakeholders.[3] One could also consider the role of substitutes for independent directors, as well as the desirability of directors who are independent of the controller but accountable to other stakeholders.[4]

The purpose of this chapter is to draw lessons about the functionality of independent directors from individual case studies and thus provide an additional lens through which to understand independent directors in Asia. This chapter presents case studies from six countries in Asia to examine the actual functioning of independent directors at specific companies in these jurisdictions. Although every country has its corporate governance scandals, the case studies represent a mix of negative and positive examples designed to provide concrete illustrations of how independent directors may function in the Asian context.

The first two case studies look at the issue of the role of independent directors in the case of deliberate fraud conducted by a majority shareholder. The Australian case study (HIH) considers the question of nominal independence in the context of a seemingly 'Western' corporate governance system, and is reminiscent of the well-known Enron case in the United States. The Taiwan case study (AIBT) looks at the difficulty of both independent directors and independent supervisors (a would-be substitute for independent directors in some jurisdictions such as Taiwan and Japan) to prevent and counter deliberate fraud, even when the individuals involved appear to have sufficient independence and seem prepared to use it.

The third, and longest, case study in Japan examines the question of form versus function. The number or percentage of directors who qualify as independent directors has been a big issue in Asia. However, a comparison of Japan's leading companies with very different corporate governance structures that either rely on (Sony) or in the past have excluded

[2] See Chapter 1 at I.3; Chapter 13 at I.
[3] See Chapter 3 at II.4.
[4] See Chapter 2 at I.

(Toyota) independent directors suggests that both types of companies can encounter serious corporate governance issues and are also capable of meaningful reform. In addition, a brief examination of an emerging voluntary 'hybrid' structure (Asahi Glass) and a recent corporate governance failure by a hybrid company (Toshiba) provides further evidence that leading companies are beginning to focus more on the practical desire to utilise independent directors to facilitate effective board functioning rather than on the theoretical merits or demerits of alternative governance structures that either do or do not require a substantial number of independent directors.

The fourth case study in India (Suzuki) examines the role of independent directors from a different, practical perspective: rather than expecting independent directors to be aggressive change agents in improving corporate governance, which may be an overoptimistic view of their role, this case study examines how independent directors react to external pressure from shareholders. As much pressure for change in corporate governance is externally generated, either by institutional investors or changes in law, it is important to consider whether independent directors react positively to encourage their company to adapt to such change or whether they tend to react negatively and seek to insulate management from external pressure.

The fifth case study in China (Keda Group) focuses on the important issue of enforcement of the obligations of independent directors. This is another case of deliberate fraud by a controlling shareholder and the difficulty of independent directors to prevent and counter such misbehaviour. Here, however, the focus is on the standard for the conduct of independent directors and for sanctions against them. Although in many (but not all) jurisdictions in Asia the fiduciary duties of independent directors are similar to those of inside directors despite the outsiders' general lack of information and personal connections and other handicaps, this case study illustrates how a mechanical application of a legally provided standard of conduct has the potential to lead to harsh results.

The final two case studies in Singapore highlight both the potential positive contributions and pitfalls of independent directors in the case of controlling shareholders, and demonstrate that the independent director's function in Asia looks substantially different from the monitoring role anticipated under agency theory in the US and the UK. One study (Minco) looks at family-controlled SMEs and finds that independent directors can serve useful functions as mediators and advisors to the controlling family. The second case study (China Sky) acts as a counterexample to the perceived success of many Government-Linked Companies in Singapore. It examines a case where a mainland Chinese company listed in Singapore (an 'S chip' company, also known as 'PRC-Controlled Firms') runs into serious regulatory problems despite the presence of independent directors. The controlling shareholder of this S-chip company resists informal enforcement practices by Singapore authorities. The presence of independent directors by itself proves insufficient to avoid serious governance issues, but through their resignation the independent directors ultimately play a significant role in obtaining the company's compliance with Singapore's standards.

II Australia: The Cautionary Tale of HIH and the Problem of Nominal Independence: 'Independent' Directors as Lemons[5]

The implosion of HIH Insurance Ltd (HIH) in 2001 was arguably Australia's worst corporate collapse, generating much soul-searching and a large literature.[6] Shareholders lost billions of dollars, employees and insurance policy holders suffered, and Chief Executive Officer (CEO)/director Ray Williams and another senior executive were jailed. Justice Neville Owen's three-volume Royal Commission report summarised HIH's deep-rooted problems as follows:[7]

> There was blind faith in a leadership that was ill-equipped for the task. There was insufficient ability and independence of mind in and associated with the organisation to see what had to be done and what had to be stopped or avoided. Risks were not properly identified and managed. Unpleasant information was hidden, filtered or sanitised. And there was a lack of sceptical questioning and analysis when and where it mattered.

The Report also highlighted the dysfunctional board, which nominally included a majority of 'independent' directors. As of mid-1999,

[5] This case study was provided by the authors of Chapter 11 (Australia), Fady Aoun and Luke Nottage, summarising their Appendix in 'The Rise of Independent Directors in Australia: Adoption, Reform and Uncertainty', *University of Miami International and Comparative Law Review*, 23 (2016), 433.

[6] See, for example, R. Tomasic, 'Corporate Collapse, Crime and Governance', *Australian Journal of Corporate Law*, 14 (2002), 183; M. De Martinis, 'Do Directors, Regulators, and Auditors Speak, Hear, and See No Evil? Evidence from the Enron, HIH, and One.Tel Collapses', *Australian Journal of Corporate Law*, 15 (2002), 1.

[7] Commonwealth, Royal Commission of Inquiry into the Failure of HIH Insurance, *Final Report* (2003), Vol. 1, xvii (elaborated at xxxiii–xliii).

the 13 directors included eight non-executives. Yet four of those were insider directors (including the chair, Geoffrey Cohen), two might have been characterised as outside directors (including Justin Gardener), leaving only two who met UK Higgs Report standards of independence – Alexander Gorrie and Neville Head, who had resigned by the end of 1999.

Several major lessons can be drawn from this sorry story. The problems of an anaemic board, in the face of a dictatorial CEO hurtling down a path of business expansion, are evident. Concerns were raised belatedly by Gardener (to Williams) and by Head (to Cohen), but swept away at a meeting convened by Williams of non-executive directors (when Head was abroad). The chair and the board also failed to maintain an effective system to manage conflict of interests, exemplified by Cohen denying any conflict from serving also as chair of HIH's audit committee while retaining a personal consultancy agreement with the company's outside auditors.

While there was a 'semblance of standard corporate governance mechanisms at work',[8] HIH's collapse resulted from poor corporate governance structures combined with disastrous mismanagement. The scandal contributed to the Australian Stock Exchange issuing in March 2003 its first Corporate Governance Principles, including independent director requirements – albeit mostly on a 'comply or explain' ('if not, why not') basis.

III Taiwan: The ABIT Case: Can Truly Independent Directors Prevent and Detect Deliberate Fraud?[9]

1 *Factual Background and History of the Case*

ABIT Computer Corporation (ABIT) was founded on 25 September 1989 by Mao-Hsiung Chu. Mr Chu served as the chairman until 2000 when he was succeeded by Yi-Tsun Lu. The company's core businesses included design, manufacture and sale of motherboards for microcomputers, interface cards and computer components. However, the company later started relocating all of the motherboard manufacturing machines and equipment in the Guishan Factory in Taoyuan, Taiwan to Suzhou,

[8] *Ibid.*, 101.

[9] This case study was provided by the authors of Chapter 7 (Taiwan), Hsin-Ti Chang, Yu-Hsin Lin and Ying-Hsin Tsai.

China. As of the end of 2002, the company did not have any production line remaining in Taiwan and conducted only brand management and group management activities there. ABIT's shares started trading on the Taiwan Stock Exchange (TWSE) in 2000. Prior to the incident, the company was making an average monthly revenue of NTD 1.5 billion to NTD 2.0 billion. In December 2004, ABIT and Kobian of Singapore started facing questions regarding a suspected fraudulent deal between the two companies worth NTD 18 billion. In addition, on 16 December 2004 TWSE issued to ABIT a notice on eight questionable facts regarding its business practice, and the Securities and Futures Bureau reclassified ABIT's shares as full-cash delivery stock. When the company's auditor subsequently stated it was 'unable to express an opinion' regarding the semi-annual financial statements for the first half of 2005, ABIT's shares were ordered to be removed from the exchange and terminated from trading.

A criminal proceeding against the responsible person, Yi-Tsun Lu, and relevant parties was commenced on 21 May 2007. Lu was sentenced to imprisonment under decisions by the Taiwan District Court on 31 August 2011 and the Taiwan High Court on 8 January 2012.[10] A separate criminal and civil procedure was commenced and accepted at the Taiwan Shi-Lin District Court.[11] On 5 September 2011, the court ruled that the supplementary civil action in criminal procedure was transferred to the Civil Court, and the civil action was withdrawn on 16 February 2012. Furthermore, the Securities and Futures Investors Protection Center[12] filed an independent civil action at the Taiwan Shi-Lin District Court on behalf of 2,398 investors to claim NTD 1,167,479,000 in damages from ABIT. The ruling for this action was given in Taiwan Shi-Lin District Court 2 May 2011.[13] The court ruled that the suspected criminal activities of Yi-Tsun Lu and relevant parties would influence the ruling of the said civil action and therefore this civil action should be suspended.

In the above court cases, Yi-Tsun Lu, chairman of ABIT, and relevant parties were found to be in violation of Section 171, paragraph I, subsection

[10] Judgement by Taiwan Shi-Lin District Court 96-Year-Jin-Chong-Su-Zi-2 dated 31 August 2011 and Judgement by Taiwan High Court 101-Year-Jin-Shang-Chong-Su-Zi-5 dated 8 January 2012.

[11] Judgement by Taiwan Shi-Lin District 96-Year-Chong-Fu-Min-Zi-19.

[12] For a brief summary of the role of the Securities and Futures Investors Protection Center, see Chapter 7 (Taiwan) at III.1.b.

[13] Judgement by Taiwan Shi-Lin District Court 95-Year-Du-Jin-Zi-22 dated 2 May 2011.

(2) of the Securities and Exchange Act causing the company to conduct transactions to its disadvantage and not in the normal course of business.

2 *Role of Independent Directors and Supervisors*

Before the illegal activities in ABIT set forth above were exposed, Professor Chen-En Ko of National Taiwan University (NTU) was invited to serve as an independent director and Professor Tsun-Siou Lee as an independent supervisor in early 2004. Chen-En Ko is a professor in the Department of Accounting of NTU and Tsun-Siou Lee in the Department of Finance of NTU. Both professors are prominent scholars with substantial experience in the US, as Ko received a PhD in accounting from the University of Minnesota and Lee earned a PhD in finance at the University of California, Berkeley.

Both professors were also active in corporate governance activities, as Ko is a member of the Executive Yuan's Taskforce for Reforming Corporate Governance and served as the chairman of the Taiwan Corporate Governance Association between 2004 and 2008. Lee served as the director of the Asia Pacific Corporate Governance Research Center of the College of Management of NTU between August 2003 and January 2005. The two professors agreed to serve as the company's independent director/supervisor because Yi-Tsun Lu studied under them when he attended the Executive Master of Business Administration programme at NTU. It is assumed that both prominent professors intended to act independently and would not knowingly be involved in illegal or questionable activities on behalf of their former student.

As noted above, in December 2004 TWSE announced that it was reclassifying the company's shares as full-cash delivery stock based on suspected embezzlement at ABIT. Professor Ko had resigned from his position as a director on 28 October 2004 before the scandal occurred, while Professor Lee resigned from his position as a supervisor at ABIT as well as his positions as a director/supervisor at five other TWSE/Over-The-Counter listed companies at the end of 2004 after the scandal occurred. However, in order to show accountability, he exercised the right of a supervisor for one last time before his resignation. He appointed a Certified Public Accountant to re-audit ABIT's financial statements and commissioned a well-known foreign accounting firm to audit ABIT's overseas subsidiaries. When he became aware of the problem at ABIT, Lee went to Hong Kong by himself to bring back accounting records. This exercise of his rights as a supervisor was unprecedented among listed companies, and he was praised by TWSE as the most responsible supervisor. Neither professor was prosecuted in the criminal case. However, the Securities and Futures Investors Protection Center included their names in the list of defendants in the civil case. That case is still ongoing.

This case study illustrates that even highly qualified and truly independent outside directors and supervisors find it difficult to prevent or detect deliberate fraud.[14] This is likely to be particularly true in the case of a controlling shareholder who engages in various business activities, including related party transactions and the purchase and sale of the company's securities without disclosing such activities to the board of directors or supervisors. On a more positive note, the actions of the two independent director/supervisors following initial disclosure of the problem contributed to its resolution.

IV Japan: Function over Structure – Toyota vs. Sony and Hybrid Structures

1 Background

Japan represents the biggest clash between traditional views that extolled the virtues of a managing board model and the views of corporate governance reformers and global investors who advocated a change to a monitoring board model. The most controversial issue for some 15 years was whether to require listed Japanese companies to have outside/independent directors. The monitoring function in the traditional Japanese system ('Company with Auditors') is largely performed by internal corporate auditors (*kansayaku* or 'company auditor'),[15] who emphasise compliance with law by all employees, rather than by independent directors who monitor the performance of the CEO and top corporate management.[16]

In a major corporate law reform in 2002, a proposal to require every corporation to have at least one outside director was defeated, but a new

[14] Professors have proven to be popular candidates in Taiwan to serve as independent directors due to their image of independence. See Chapter 7 (Taiwan) at II.2.b. However, both their independence and competence have been called into question. *Ibid.* at 15. This case study is significant in that it illustrates the limits of independent director functioning, even in the case of qualified and independent directors, in preventing corporate governance problems in the absence of appropriate information disclosure by the controller.

[15] Further details on the functions of *kansayaku* are provided in Chapter 4 (Japan) at I and II.1.

[16] See generally Chapter 4 (Japan).

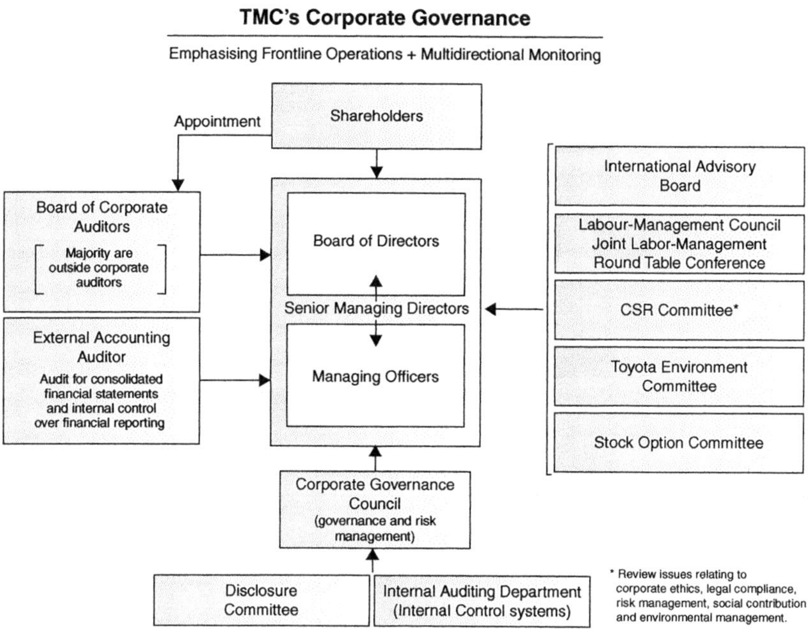

Figure 12.1 Toyota's Corporate Governance Structure

Source: Excerpt from English translation of corporate governance report (dated 13 November 2009) submitted by Toyota to the Tokyo Stock Exchange, current version available on Toyota's website at www.toyota.co.jp.

board committee system ('Company with Committees') was added as an optional alternative corporate structure.[17] This new board committee system separates the functions of officers and directors and replaces the traditional German-inspired positions of representative director and company auditor with American-derived positions of representative officer and the audit committee of the board of directors (compare the traditional system of Toyota in Figure 12.1 with the board committee system of Sony in Figure 12.2). However, very few Japanese companies (roughly 2.2 per cent of listed companies) adopted this new committee structure.

The debate over board function and structure and the role of independent directors was epitomised by a popular comparison between Toyota and Sony. The chairman of Toyota, the champion of traditional

[17] See Chapter 4 (Japan) at II.1.a. See also R. J. Gilson and C. J. Milhaupt, 'Choice as Regulatory Reform: The Case of Japanese Corporate Governance', *The American Journal of Comparative Law*, 53(2) (2005), 343.

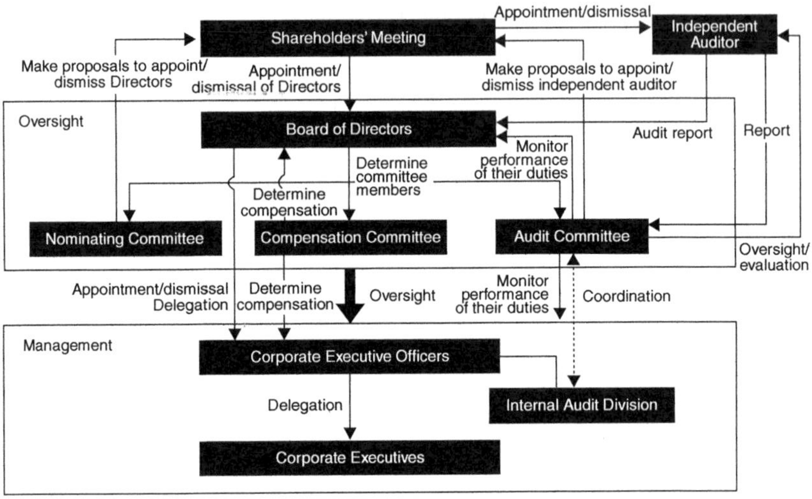

Figure 12.2 Sony's Corporate Governance Structure

Source: Excerpt from corporate governance section of Sony's website, current version available at www.sony.net/.

Japanese manufacturers, stated at a conference of the International Corporate Governance Network in 2001 that Toyota would stick to its own well-established system that did not include any outsiders.[18] Sony, the first company to introduce executive officers separate from directors in 1996, was an early adopter of the new 'American-style' board committee system. Some commentators have attributed the gradual and voluntary nature of Japanese corporate governance during the 2000s to a 'Toyota effect' – the well-publicised economic success of Toyota under the traditional governance system, in contrast to the struggles of Sony, acting as a disincentive for Japanese companies to increase the number of outside directors or adopt the new board committee structure.[19]

However, the following case studies of Toyota and Sony illustrate that either corporate governance structure can encounter difficulties, and that actual board and management functioning is arguably more important than board structure. In addition, focusing on contrasting board structures can result in oversimplification, since both companies have

[18] S. M. Jacoby, 'Principals and Agents', *Journal of Japanese Law*, 12(27) (2007), 23, 31–32.

[19] C. J. Milhaupt, 'A Lost Decade for Japanese Corporate Governance Reform?: What's Changed, What Hasn't, and Why' in M. Blomstrom and S. La Croix (eds.), *Institutional Change in Japan* (Routledge, 2006), 97–119, 111.

adapted over time to improve their board functioning in response to corporate governance issues. In addition, the structural argument is blurred by recent voluntary reforms leading to a 'hybrid' form of corporate structure at a number of leading Japanese large companies to address functionality more directly. Finally, an amendment to Japan's Companies Act in 2014 introduced yet another structural alternative: a 'one-committee' system in which the traditional board of audit composed of company auditors is replaced by a new audit committee of the board of directors.[20]

2 *Toyota*[21]

Toyota is Japan's largest company by revenue, a substantial employer and arguably the most respected corporation in Japan. It is emblematic of Japanese manufacturing quality, with practices such as 'just in time' and 'lean' manufacturing being rendered in Japanese simply as the 'Toyota Production System (Toyota kanban hoshiki)'. The traditional board structure of all directors being experienced insiders representing different departments of the company is highlighted in Toyota's case by its emphasis on the role of senior managing directors (one from each department) acting as 'bridges' connecting the board and management (see Figure 12.1). This traditional structure did gradually evolve by, for example, a reduction in the number of directors in 2003.

The big impetus for more substantial reform was Toyota's recall problem related to unintended sudden acceleration that began in 2009. Toyota failed to report as required to US authorities for over four months following quality concerns raised in Europe in the autumn of 2009. In February 2010 problems with sudden unintended acceleration and other issues resulted in a recall of over 6 million vehicles in the United States and over 8 million worldwide within a two-week period. During that same month Akio Toyoda, the President of Toyota Motor Corporation, was summoned to testify before a US congressional committee, where he attributed the mounting problems to the company's excessive emphasis on growth and profits in recent years at the expense of its traditional focus on quality and product safety.[22]

[20] See Chapter 4 (Japan) at II 1 c.

[21] The main source for this case study is B. E. Aronson, 'Learning from Toyota's Troubles: The Debate on Board Oversight, Board Structure, and Director Independence in Japan', *Journal of Japanese Law*, 15(30) (2010), 67.

[22] For the full text of Mr Toyoda's testimony, see 'TEXT-Full Text of Toyota President's Testimony', *Reuters*, 24 February 2010, available at http://uk.reuters.com.

There was extensive fallout, including additional recalls (totalling 10 million vehicles in the US and 14 million worldwide), a dramatic drop in car sales, halts in vehicle production, investigations and enforcement actions by the National Highway Traffic Safety Administration, including the largest civil fine in the agency's history (US $16.375 million) and a spate of private lawsuits. A resulting criminal suit in the US against Toyota was settled in 2014 for a payment of US $1.2 billion.[23] Toyota eventually recovered economically, aided, like all major exporters, by a weaker yen as a result of aggressive Bank of Japan easing of monetary policy as part of Abenomics.

Ensuing corporate governance reforms, announced in March 2011 and March 2013, included both executive and organisational changes.[24] Outside directors were added to Toyota's board for essentially the first time in the company's history. Of the three new outside directors (among a total of 16 directors), one was a non-Japanese who came from General Motors and had previously worked with Toyota at a joint venture in California. A number of senior executives were retired, which marked a generational change. Organisationally, Toyota condensed its businesses into four main units and promoted a number of non-Japanese to oversee regional businesses, including elevating an American who already led Toyota Motor Sales in the US to be head of North American operations. This action was presumably in response to the lack of authority by local US executives in 2010 to deal cooperatively and quickly with governmental investigations and other recall-related issues.

In 2015 Toyota also began to internationalise its top management team by promoting three non-Japanese to senior managing officer positions within Toyota Motor Corporation itself rather than merely in overseas subsidiaries: an executive vice-president of the company (in France); a managing officer in charge of legal affairs (US); and an American woman as chief communications officer in Tokyo. This effort suffered a very public setback when the new chief communications officer was arrested in Japan and resigned shortly thereafter due to the illegal import (under Japanese law) of a prescription opioid pain reliever.[25]

[23] See, for example, C. Levinson, J. Bennett and D. Barrett, 'Toyota to Pay $1.2 Billion to Settle US Probe', *Wall Street Journal*, 19 March 2014, available at www.wsj.com.

[24] Y. Takahashi and Y. Koh, 'Toyota Overhauls Management', *Wall Street Journal*, 6 March 2015, available at www.wsj.com. For the company's announcement see Toyota Motor Corporation, 'TMC Announces New Organizational Structure and Executive Changes', 6 March 2013, available at www2.toyota.co.jp.

[25] K. Inagaki and J. Thompson, 'Toyota Executive Julie Hamp Resigns after Drug Arrest', *Financial Times*, 1 July 2015, available at www.ft.com; C. Trudell and Y. Hagiwara,

3 *Sony*

Hopes were high for Sony when it became one of the early adopters of Japan's new, optional 'American-style' board committee system of governance in 2003.[26] In addition to a majority of outside directors, Sony announced early on that it would voluntarily conform to the New York Stock Exchange's definition of independence in determining its outside directors. Strengthening the monitoring function by the use of outside directors was the goal emphasised by foreign investors. But an equal, and perhaps more important, goal for Japanese companies was to formally introduce an executive officer system. This would speed up decision making by delegating authority for daily operations from the board to officers, add transparency by moving authority formerly held by the president to the three committees, and make it easier for large multinational Japanese companies who have global networks to more readily manage their overseas operations.

Sony's biggest business challenge began in the early 2000s. All of Japan's formerly successful household electronics companies began facing increasing pressures as the rise of low-cost competitors in Asia made their traditional lines of business, such as the manufacture of television sets, unprofitable. Japanese companies generally found it difficult to undertake aggressive restructuring of fading business divisions. At the same time, Sony also faced the difficult challenge of whether it could de-emphasise its heretofore successful technology in favour of a new effort to digitalise its products and make them internet compatible. A 30 per cent reduction in Sony's profit forecast in 2003 resulted in a 'Sony shock', with its stock price declining to less than one-quarter of its value in the year 2000.[27]

For over a decade Sony's management was not up to the challenge. Sony was widely criticised for operating in 'silos', i.e., each division worrying about its own products and employment without regard to overall corporate goals or strategy. Sony appointed a non-Japanese CEO, Howard Stringer, to lead the company from 2007 to 2012, to no avail.

A number of governance issues were raised with respect to Sony's board and the performance of its majority of independent directors. First is the failure to monitor performance, as the CEO and management team

'Loss of Toyota's First Female Executive Is Blow to Japan's Diversity Drive', *Bloomberg*, reprinted in *Japan Times*, 2 July 2015, available at www.japantimes.co.jp.

[26] For the legislative history, see Chapter 4 (Japan) at II.1.a.

[27] 'Chronology of Events Leading to Sony's Shake-up', *Financial Times*, 7 March 2005, available at www.ft.com.

were not held accountable for ongoing losses and failures in their business plans. Second, unsuccessful executives were, in fact, rewarded for poor performance, i.e., they were given positions with generous compensation packages and were, in effect, allowed to designate their successors[28] – a serious problem at traditional Japanese companies that the committee structure, with its nomination committee dominated by independent directors, was designed to avoid. Finally, some challenged the role of independent directors at Sony more directly. As of 2012, only one of ten independent directors had any relevant industry experience, only one independent director was new to the board (the others joining between 2005 and 2010) despite ongoing failures, and seven of the ten independent directors were also on at least three other boards, which raises the issue of their time for, and commitment to, monitoring Sony's operations.[29]

Sony saw no immediate improvement under its new CEO, Kazuo Hirai, who assumed his post in 2012. And the following year Sony's situation attracted an investment by an activist hedge fund manager, Daniel Loeb, of Third Point. He advocated continuing cost-cutting in Sony's traditional electronics business and a spinoff to capture the value of its successful entertainment business.[30] To the extent that this development represented an opportunity for Sony's board, and particularly its majority of independent directors to rethink Sony's existing strategy, such opportunity was not taken. Sony was relieved when Loeb sold off his investment in 2014 at a substantial profit to him, but without any spinoff or other restructuring or any increase in the share price for general shareholders.[31] Sony's own turnaround plans may have finally begun to pay off, as it returned to profitability in 2015.[32]

4 *Traditional Hybrid: Asahi Glass*

As noted above, when Japanese corporate law provided companies with an alternative 'American-style' company with committees structure in

[28] S. Yonekura, 'Poor Corporate Governance Fueled Sony's Meltdown', 23 April 2014, available at www.nippon.com.

[29] D. Rallis, 'At Sony Corporation It's the Same Old Sony', *GMI*, 10 October 2012, available at http://tremulous23.rssing.com.

[30] M. Saito, 'Sony Rejects Loeb's Proposal to Spin Off Entertainment Unit', *Reuters*, 6 August 2013, available at www.reuters.com.

[31] A. Sakoui, 'Loeb Exit Leaves Sony's Hirai with Bigger Challenges', *Bloomberg*, 22 October 2014, available at www.bloomberg.com.

[32] T. Mochizuki and M. Negishi, 'Sony Bullish on PlayStation as It Swings to Profit', *Wall Street Journal*, 29 October 2015, available at www.wsj.com.

2002, a mere 2 per cent of listed companies adopted that structure.[33] However, a fair number of Japan's leading large companies proceeded to voluntarily modify their corporate governance structure and processes to streamline decision making at large, complex companies, including greater separation of the management and supervisory roles of the board of directors.

Asahi Glass Corporation is one of the well-known examples of such a 'mixed' or hybrid system in which traditional Japanese companies voluntarily add a number of outside directors in an effort to combine insiders' information with outsiders' independence to achieve more effective board functioning.[34] Although there is no clear definition of a 'hybrid' system in Japan, it typically applies to a traditional Company with Auditors that has several independent directors and at least one board committee, in particular a nomination committee (see Figure 12.3).

One of the major methods Japanese companies have adopted to address the issue of board function is to utilise the equivalent of intermediate 'holding' companies. Occasionally this is accomplished by the use of operating subsidiaries and actual holding companies. However, this division also often occurs within the same corporation as major product lines are divided into a number of internal business units (in Japanese they generally use the English term 'company' to describe such internal business units) (see Figure 12.3). Most day-to-day decisions are made by each 'company' with respect to its business.

Delegating daily management to 'company' leaders permits the board to focus more on strategic issues, such as capital allocation, business plans and global operations. It also adds to the functioning of independent directors, since the board discussion no longer focuses as much on detailed operational issues which Japanese generally believe require substantial experience within the corporation and knowledge of the corporate culture. This makes it easier for outsiders who lack knowledge of the internal working of the corporation to make a substantial contribution to corporate decision making and substantially broadens the pool of potential candidates for independent director positions.

[33] See Chapter 4 (Japan) at II.1.a.

[34] For a discussion of the emergence of a hybrid form of corporate governance among large companies in Japan, see, e.g., B. E. Aronson, 'Japanese Corporate Governance Reform: A Comparative Perspective', *Hastings Business Law Journal*, 11(1) (2015), 85, 103–110; B. E. Aronson, 'The Olympus Scandal and Corporate Governance Reform: Can Japan Find a Middle Ground between the Board Monitoring Model and Management Model?', *Pacific Basin Law Journal*, 30(1) (2012), 93, 140–147.

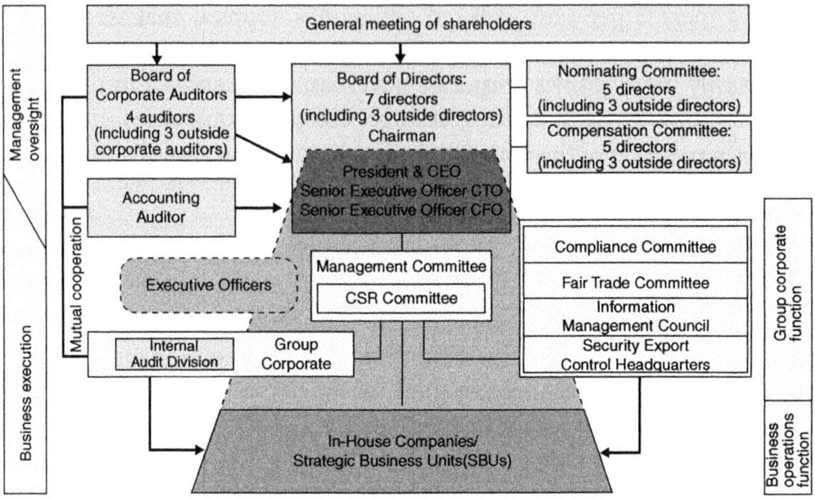

Figure 12.3 Asahi Glass's Hybrid Corporate Governance Structure

Source: Company website, current version available at www.agc.com.

Japan's new corporate governance code (effective 1 June 2015)[35] may act to reinforce this trend in favour of a hybrid form of the Company with Auditors structure. The code is premised on the reality that the vast majority of Japanese companies operate under the Company with Auditor structure, but its clearest, most significant provision is a recommendation that every listed company have a minimum of two independent directors.[36] A Company with Auditors with two independent directors is already on its way to becoming a hybrid. The code further encourages this 'hybridisation' of the Company with Auditor structure through a number of provisions, such as the provision relating to advice of independent directors on nomination and compensation issues.[37]

35 Tokyo Stock Exchange, Japan's Corporate Governance Code, 1 June 2015, available at www.jpx.co.jp. The Tokyo Stock Exchange and Financial Services Agency jointly formed a Council of Experts concerning the Corporate Governance Code, which issued a final proposal on 5 March 2015. That proposal was adopted by the Tokyo Stock Exchange as an 'Exhibit' to its Securities Listing Regulations. For details, see Chapter 4 (Japan) at II.1.d.

36 Principle 4.8, Japan Corporate Governance Code.

37 Supplementary Principle 4.10.1, Japan Corporate Governance Code.

5 'American-style' Hybrid: Toshiba Corporation[38]

Toshiba Corporation has occupied an interesting place in Japanese corporate governance by essentially developing an alternative hybrid system based on the 'American-style' Company with Committees structure. It is intended as a 'best of both worlds' system that made the committee structure more practical and effective for Japanese companies.[39] For over a decade half of the Toshiba board (currently totalling 16 directors) consisted of 'insider' executive directors and the other half of non-executive directors. The latter were equally divided between former senior company officials, to help ensure that the board had sufficient experience, expertise and information, and independent directors. As of mid-2015 there were four independent directors and they were reported to have been truly independent and to have participated actively in open board discussions.[40]

In mid-2015 a new major corporate governance scandal emerged at Toshiba. A third-party investigative report released on 20 July 2015[41] found that Toshiba Corporation had padded its profits by US $1.2 billion (150 billion yen) over the past six years. The current and two past presidents and half the board of directors have resigned from their positions. Once again Japan was faced with the questions of how good are Japanese corporate governance practices and how might they be improved.

The Toshiba case was shocking news, even compared to other recent Japanese corporate governance scandals such as the Olympus case in 2011, for two reasons. First, as noted above, Toshiba was well-known

[38] Part of this case study is based on B. E. Aronson, 'The Toshiba Corporate Governance Scandal: How Can Japanese Corporate Governance be Fixed?', *Commentary on Jurist Online*, 10 August 2015, available at http://jurist.org/forum/2015/08/bruce-aronson-toshiba-scandal.php.

[39] For a description and discussion of Toshiba's corporate governance structure, see Aronson, 'The Olympus Scandal and Corporate Governance Reform: Can Japan Find a Middle Ground between the Board Monitoring Model and Management Model?', 145.

[40] Toshiba's formal structure is typical of the Company with Committees system, and is similar to Sony's structure depicted in Figure 12.2. For a similar figure for Toshiba, see its website at www.toshibatec.co.jp. The biggest feature of Toshiba's system was its insistence on the important role of former company officials (who do not formally qualify as independent or even as 'outside' directors) to interact with truly independent directors to monitor management and cause effective board functioning. Toshiba satisfied the Company Act requirement that Companies with Committees have a majority of outside directors for each of the required committees, but unlike Sony, Toshiba did not have a majority of outside directors on the board as a whole.

[41] In English see Independent Investigation Committee for Toshiba Corporation, 'Investigation Report, Summary Version' (20 July 2015), available at www.toshiba.co.jp [hereinafter Investigation Report].

for its efforts in the corporate governance area and its 'Company with Committees hybrid' structure. Second, Toshiba is very much a part of Japan's business establishment. Two of the past four presidents have been vice-chairmen of the main big business lobby (*Keidanren*), and a number of its top executives have served on cabinet level committees charged with improving Japan's economic growth. This major failure at Toshiba arguably undermined the government's effort under Abenomics to show improvement in Japan's corporate governance as part of structural reform to attract foreign investment and spur economic growth.

A year after the scandal's outbreak, fallout from the Toshiba case is still ongoing. Toshiba was assessed a record-setting fine of 7.3 billion yen (US $59.9 million at the time of announcement), its former top executives are still under investigation for possible prosecution in a criminal case, and disgruntled shareholders have filed civil litigation against it.[42] Toshiba has also engaged in major asset sales to deal with the economic losses and to prevent any need for further bank borrowing to shore up its financial position.[43]

How did things go so wrong despite this apparently sophisticated corporate governance structure? The third-party investigative report criticised Toshiba's 'corporate culture' under which operational managers 'couldn't refuse' challenging profit targets demanded by top management.[44] However, this is an incomplete explanation for bad practices that continued for six years during the terms of three company presidents.

Board functioning, as opposed to structure, and the role of independent directors on the board may be of far greater importance. Specifically, commentators have focused on the role of the audit committee.[45] As part of its 'American-style' board committee system, Toshiba had an audit committee of the board with a majority of outside directors, an arrangement which experts generally regard as superior to Japan's traditional

[42] 'Toshiba Scandal: Securities Watchdog Inches Toward Criminal Case', *Asia Nikkei*, 15 December 2015, available at www.asia.nikkei.com.

[43] M. Yamazaki and R. Ando, 'Toshiba in $5.9 Billion Asset Sale, Shares Hit by Report of U.S. Probe', *Reuters*, 17 March 2016, available at www.reuters.com.

[44] 'Investigation Report', 68: 'A corporate culture existed at Toshiba whereby employees could not act contrary to the intent of their superiors.'

[45] 'Toshiba Shock: Failure of Governance Gives Abenomics a Rude Awakening', *Nikkei Asian Review*, 23 July 2015, available at http://asia.nikkei.com (noting that 'The presence of a Toshiba insider, rather than an outside director, at the head of its audit committee had raised questions about the body's ability to exercise proper oversight'). See also 'Investigation Report', 73 (concluding that 'internal control by the Audit Committee did not function').

internal corporate auditor system.[46] However, as part of Toshiba's modification of the committee structure, the head of the audit committee was an inside director and two of the independent directors on the committee were ex-diplomats with little business experience. It does not appear to have functioned effectively. In addition, sceptics have claimed that Toshiba deliberately appointed independent directors to the audit committee who were both unqualified and unwilling to act as effective monitors with respect to the preparation of financial statements. In response to its corporate governance problems, Toshiba essentially gave up on its much-publicised hybrid corporate structure and reverted to a typical 'American-style' committee structure similar to that of Sony.[47]

In addition to the above internal issues, more general weaknesses in Japan's corporate governance system that contributed to the Olympus scandal still remain today. These include relatively weak regulation and little risk of liability for external auditors who act as 'gatekeepers' or financial intermediaries between companies and financial markets with respect to the accuracy of financial statements, a relatively ineffective whistle-blower system, and a general lack of public and private enforcement to provide incentives for both disclosure and monitoring.

This is not to suggest that accounting problems at Toshiba condemn the entire system of Japanese corporate governance. Japan's household electronics companies may be something of a special case – they all have faced tremendous problems for two decades as the rise of low-cost competitors in Asia has decimated their traditional lines of business such as the manufacture of television sets. Sony, an industry rival, has been a particularly popular lightning rod for Japanese criticism of the ineffectiveness of the 'American-style' board committee system of governance.

[46] ACGA, 'The Roles and Functions of *Kansayaku* Boards Compared to Audit Committees' (November 2013), at 3, available at www.acga-asia.org (concluding that 'a genuinely independent and well-run Audit Committee has the potential to strengthen board governance and oversight of management more effectively than the *Kansayaku* system'; also noting, however, that audit committees under the Japanese Company with Committee structure may be less effective than audit committees in other markets).

[47] For a description of Toshiba's hybrid structure prior to this scandal, see note 40 above, and accompanying text. Following the scandal Toshiba revamped its board to consist of 11 members (as of 30 September 2015): four 'insider' executive directors and seven non-executive directors, with all of the latter group qualifying as outside directors, in accordance with Toshiba's new policies of maintaining a majority of outside directors on the board and having its three board committees 'composed, in principle, only of independent Outside Director members'. See www.toshiba.co.jp.

Sony's board, with a majority of independent directors, also functioned poorly as it was unable either to shut down failing divisions or hold poorly performing management to account for over a decade.

Problems with Toshiba's seemingly well-considered 'hybrid' approach to governance clearly illustrate the tension and difficult trade-offs between insider and outsider perspectives. Director independence is important for monitoring management; however, failures by American companies during the 2008 Financial Crisis have also indicated the limits of independence and resulted in a renewed call for director competence. Toshiba made an effort to utilise the knowledge and experience of former insiders, in combination with independent directors, to ensure effective monitoring of management. However, in this case, what it assumed was a strength proved to be a double-edged sword, as the audit committee apparently failed to function with sufficient independence.

V India: Maruti Suzuki and the Response of Independent Directors to Activist Pressure[48]

Generally, case studies involving independent directors tend to be critical about their role in the companies' governance, and that has not been different in India going by the high-profile Satyam scandal.[49] But, here we focus on a recent instance in India where independent directors have made a positive difference, albeit through pressure applied by institutional investors. This instance demonstrates that independent directors can indeed be effective when supported by active investors.

Maruti Suzuki India Limited (MSIL), which began operations in 1983, has played a significant role in the growth of the automotive industry in India. Currently, it is a subsidiary of Suzuki Motor Corp, Japan (Suzuki Japan), which holds 56.2 per cent, with the remaining 43.8 per cent held by public shareholders, including prominent institutional investors. In terms of board independence, four out of its 12 directors are listed as independent, thereby satisfying the compliance requirements. Even though independent directors constitute only a third of the board, they are individuals with stellar reputations, including an accountant,

[48] This case study was provided by the authors of Chapter 10 (India), Vikramaditya Khanna and Umakanth Varottil.

[49] U. Varottil, 'Evolution and Effectiveness of Independent Directors in Indian Corporate Governance', *Hastings Business Law Journal*, 6 (2010), 281; V. Khanna, 'Corporate Governance in India: Past, Present and Future?', *Jindal Global Law Review*, 1 (2009), 171.

corporate lawyer, industry expert and retired bureaucrat, all leaders in their respective fields.

MSIL's governance practices came under a significant cloud when on 28 January 2014 it announced that its board approved a transaction with Suzuki Motor Gujarat Private Limited (Suzuki Gujarat), a wholly owned subsidiary of Suzuki Japan.[50] Under this arrangement, instead of establishing its own additional manufacturing facility, MSIL will lease land in Gujarat to Suzuki Gujarat, which will manufacture and supply cars to MSIL at cost of production plus incremental capital expenditure. Suzuki Gujarat would manufacture vehicles exclusively for MSIL and in accordance with its requirements.

The proposal was severely resisted by MSIL's institutional investors, who were amply supported by the advice of the three proxy advisory firms in India. Not only were there concerns about the transfer of value and future business potential from MSIL to Suzuki Gujarat so as to make it a largely marketing concern with limited prospects that pays short shrift to the minority shareholders of MSIL, but also questions were raised regarding transparency given that this was a related party transaction requiring closer scrutiny. Suspicion arose on account of the timing of the transaction since it was announced months before the new Companies Act, 2013 was to take effect on 1 April 2014, which would impose the requirement of obtaining the approval of the public shareholders of MSIL (i.e., a 'majority-of-the-minority' (MoM) vote). The collective support of leading institutional investors led to their active protests to the company against the proposal and also a representation to the Securities and Exchange Board of India (SEBI).

The fervent reaction of the institutional investors caused the board to review the proposal, with press reports indicating that the independent directors of MSIL played the lead role in the reconsideration.[51] From an operational standpoint, MSIL's board clarified that Suzuki Gujarat would operate on the basis that while it would not make any losses, it would also not accumulate any cash surpluses.[52] This is perhaps a measure to

[50] Maruti Suzuki India Limited, 'Maruti Suzuki Board Decision on Gujarat Project', Press Release (28 January 2014).

[51] N. Inamdar, 'Have Independent Directors Finally Found Their Voice?', *Business Standard*, 12 March 2014; P. Doval and Sidhartha, 'Suzuki's Gujarat Plan Splits Maruti Board', *The Times of India*, 13 March 2014; 'Maruti Blinks in Gujarat Plant Standoff', *The Telegraph*, 16 March 2014.

[52] Maruti Suzuki India Limited, 'Information on Gujarat Project', Press Release (26 February 2014).

prevent the perceived transfer of value out of MSIL. Other adjustments to the structure included that upon expiry of the arrangement the assets of Suzuki Gujarat would be transferred to MSIL at 'book value' rather than 'fair value'. The company also provided greater details of the arrangement to the investing public. The independent directors also sought greater details on the impact of taxation on the proposed arrangement for MSIL. More importantly, the board decided that even though the law did not yet require it, as a 'measure of good governance' it would seek the MoM vote.[53]

At one level, it might be possible to criticise the role of MSIL's board for according its approval to the transaction in the first place. It is only the powerful (and perhaps less expected) response of the institutional shareholders that caused the directors to go back to the drawing board. At the same time, this is a story where the board, led by the independent directors, lent their ears to investor sentiments rather than ignore them. Reactive as the board's approach may have been, the directors were willing to review their decision in the light of a more activist approach adopted by shareholders. What might have caused the board, particularly the independent directors, to act in the manner they did? We proffer a number of factors.

First, previous corporate governance crises in India have put the reputation of certain independent directors at stake and also raised doubts about the utility of the institution more generally. One can only surmise that MSIL's independent directors, acting in the shadow of bleak historical experience, may have been keen to avoid similar fallout. Second, one can attribute such an attitude to the sea change in corporate law and governance regulations. The Companies Act, 2013 and the revised governance norms prescribed by SEBI have reinforced their reliance on board independence as a means to good governance. This is represented by detailed prescription of the requirements of conduct and performance of independent directors. The failure of such directors to meet with the standards is met with stiff measures such as civil and criminal liability, which act as a strong disincentive against both shirking as well as wrongful conduct. An enabling enforcement regime (for example one that now expressly recognises shareholder class actions) coupled with an increasingly activist investor community may propel independent directors to play a more significant role on their boards.

[53] Maruti Suzuki India Limited, 'Information on Gujarat Project', Press Release (15 March 2014).

The MSIL case may very well represent the dawning of a new era in board independence in India. However, this is not the end of the MSIL story. As of this writing, the shareholders' meeting to seek a MoM vote is yet to be convened. How the shareholders may respond remains to be seen. In addition, in mid-2015 an activist hedge fund, Third Point, took a position in Suzuki Motor on the theory its shares were undervalued since they did not reflect the success and profitability of Maruti Suzuki in the Indian market.[54]

VI China: Keda Group and Enforcement of Independent Director Requirements (Duties)[55]

1 *China's Securities Law and Administrative Sanctions for Violations by Independent Directors*

China's current Securities Law provides that directors, supervisors and senior management of a listed company shall *ensure* that the information disclosed by the company is truthful, accurate and complete.[56] Securities issuers or listed companies which breach their disclosure obligations (i.e., by making false statements, misleading statements or statements with material omissions) are subject to penalties (fines and warnings) issued by China's securities market regulator, the China Securities Regulatory Commission (CSRC). The CSRC may also give warnings and fines (RMB 30,000 to 300,000) to the 'persons directly in charge' and 'other persons directly responsible' for such wrongdoings.[57]

Based on the Decisions on Administrative Penalties published by the CSRC, from 1 April 2004 to 30 November 2014, the regulatory agency has issued 74 decisions on administrative penalties relating to independent directors, sanctioning 218 independent directors in total. Almost all of the administrative penalties involving independent directors related to violations of information disclosure rules governing the listed companies they worked in. Among the independent directors who were punished, 108 independent directors were subject to both warnings and fines and the other 109 independent directors received warnings only.[58]

[54] Y. Kubota, 'Suzuki to Rev Up Value after Loeb's Third Point Discloses Stake', *Wall Street Journal*, 3 August 2015, available at www.wsj.com.

[55] This case study was provided by the author of Chapter 6 (China), Xin Tang.

[56] § 68.3, Securities Law.

[57] § 193.1, Securities Law. For the central role of the CSRC, see Chapter 6 (China) at IV.1.

[58] See the relevant column on the official website of the CSRC, available at www.csrc.gov.cn.

In the cases of administrative penalties related to independent directors, all of the independent directors were punished as 'other persons directly liable'. The 'persons directly in charge' sanctioned by the CSRC were normally the president, CEO, chief financial officer (CFO) or sometimes the secretary of the board of directors in listed companies.[59]

From April 2004 to the end of November 2014, there were only three cases in which the independent directors were exempted from administrative liabilities or at least were given lesser punishment compared with 'other persons directly liable' after having signed publicly disclosed documents with illegal contents.[60] Among these cases, the Keda Group case described below is the only one in which one of the independent directors was found 'not guilty' while the other independent directors were still sanctioned.

2 *The Keda Group and Securities Law Violations by Insiders*

Keda Group Co., Ltd (the 'Keda Group' or 'the Company') is a company established in Dongying City of Shandong Province, China, engaging primarily in the construction and management of highways. The Company publicly issued 30,000,000 shares on 9 April 2004 and the shares have been listed on the main board of the Shanghai Stock Exchange since 26 April 2004. By 31 December 2005, Keda Group's share capital was 140,000,000. The original controlling shareholder of the Company was Keda Industrial Company, holding 44.91 per cent of the outstanding shares, while the original *de facto* controller was the local town government. In 2005, 72.08 per cent of the shares in the company were 'non-circulating shares' (only tradable pursuant to privately negotiated agreements), while the other 27.92 per cent were 'circulating shares' (tradable in the auction market). By the end of 2009, the share capital of the Company amounted to 335,000,000, the controlling shareholder changed to Shandong Keda Group, holding 18.37 per cent of the outstanding shares, and the *de facto* controller was then an individual, Mr A. Keda Group completed its 'Split Share Structure Reform' by 2009, and after that all the outstanding shares of the company were circulating shares.

[59] Articles 58(2) and 58(3), Measures for the Administration of Information Disclosure by Listed Companies, CSRC (2007).

[60] The three cases are: China Securities Regulatory Commission Administrative Sanction Decision ([2010] No. 10), China Securities Regulatory Commission Administrative Sanction Decision ([2011] No. 38) and China Securities Regulatory Commission Administrative Sanction Decision ([2014] No. 69).

The CSRC found that, from 2006 to 2009, Keda Group did not disclose a series of significant transactions, including the transfer of valuable land use rights and major affiliated transactions with the controlling shareholder. This lack of disclosure led to material omissions and false statements in its annual reports, semi-annual reports and interim reports. As such, Keda Group violated the Securities Law which requires the disclosure of true, accurate and complete information. The CSRC held that Mr A, the president of Keda Group, was 'the person directly in charge of' the wrongdoings. In addition, the CSRC found the CEO, CFO and several other directors (including independent directors), the board secretary and the statutory supervisors as 'other persons directly responsible', and intended to impose administrative penalties upon them.

Mr A, the president of Keda Group at the relevant time, claimed that he was mainly responsible for the strategic decision making, rather than the financial issues; he also asked for a reduced punishment by claiming that he had recognised the seriousness of the problem before the scheduled sanctions, and then had resigned from the chairmanship of the Company's board of directors. Mr B, serving as a director and the CEO of the Company at the relevant time, claimed that he was only supposed to supervise the management of the Company with respect to its daily production and operations (and not the financial workings of the Company). He further claimed that he could not reasonably be expected to identify illegal conduct in the Company due to his limited knowledge about the Company's financial issues. Moreover, he claimed that he had already resigned from the Company and asked for a lesser punishment. The CSRC rejected all of these arguments.

3 *Liability of Independent Directors and Statutory Supervisors*

C, D, E, F and G, all served as independent directors in the Company at the relevant time and claimed that: (1) they did not organise, plan or participate in any of the illegal conduct, were ignorant of the violations and should not be blamed for the ignorance; and (2) in spite of their diligence the violations were very difficult to discover. The evidence supporting their claim that they were reasonably diligent included: participating diligently in the board meetings and shareholder meetings; giving professional advice concerning the company's construction projects; questioning the board secretary and even the president when noticing negative reports of the company in the media; and supervising the company on corporate governance related issues.

E, one of the above independent directors and an accounting professor, claimed further that she had personally examined construction projects in which the company had invested and proposed that the feasibility of an investment project needed to be investigated. In addition, she claimed that when she found the financial statements of the company showed some signs of 'out of the ordinary changes', she immediately questioned and even warned the president and CFO to avoid possible illegalities. She often communicated with the CFO at each general meeting and board meetings. She urged the CFO to explain the suspicious changes in the company's cash flow report, and asked if these changes were the outcome of the Company's capital misallocated to its controlling shareholders or other affiliated parties. She communicated with the certified public accountants who provided auditing services to the Company, discussed the auditing plan and other important issues with them. She conducted tracking evaluations of the company's investment projects. She reminded and urged the Company to recover funds embezzled by the controlling shareholder in a timely manner.

The CSRC held that E had fulfilled her obligations as an independent director and, as such, should not face any sanctions. In contrast, the CSRC found that independent directors C, D, F and G only partially fulfilled their duties. This finding was based on the evidence that they: (1) failed to take further measures to research the actual problems facing the Company; (2) did not pressure the Company to correct its irregularities after the media released negative reports; and (3) only proposed, but did not insist, that the Company rectify its wrongdoings after the commencement of the CSRC's formal investigation. Therefore, the CSRC held that C, D, F and G did not perform their duties with full loyalty and diligence. However, as a result of a number of mitigating factors (i.e., that these four independent directors were not directly involved in the wrongdoings of the Company, that their ignorance was caused by the intentional concealment of the insiders and that they acted positively in urging the rectification of the company's wrongdoings), the CSRC exempted them from fines but still sanctioned them with a warning.

Similarly, H and I, the statutory supervisors of the company, asked for an exemption from any sanctions. They based their claim on the following facts: (1) that they diligently attended the board meetings and shareholder meetings; (2) that they reviewed the Company's periodical reports and commented on the reports; (3) that they checked the Company's financial situation periodically, wrote reports and requested rectification based on the problems they identified; (4) that they were unaware of any of the relevant violations; and (5) that they were no longer statutory supervisors of the company. The CSRC ultimately found that these two individuals had performed some of their supervising duties, did not participate in the company's illegal conduct intentionally, were unaware of the violations due to the concealment of the insiders and that they had urged the Company to correct its wrongdoings after the commencement of the CSRC's investigation. Therefore, CSRC decided not to impose fines on them.

4 *CSRC Decision and Discussion*

Eventually in 2011, the CSRC decided to issue warnings and impose fines against the related parties as follows: (1) the Keda Group was given a warning and a fine of RMB 600,000; (2) Mr A was given a warning and a fine of RMB 300,000; (3) Mr B and a vice-general manager were given warnings and fines of RMB 150,000 and RMB 100,000 respectively; (4) the CFO was given a warning and a fine of RMB 100,000; (5) the other inside directors were given warnings and each a fine of RMB 30,000; (6) the independent directors C, D, F and G and the statutory supervisors were given only warnings; and (7) independent director E was exempted from all penalties.

As illustrated in its Decision on Administrative Penalties against Keda Group and other responsible persons, the CSRC has been disciplining independent directors in China's listed companies according to the Securities Law, the Administrative Punishment Law and the agency's rules, including *Measures for the Administration of Information Disclosure by Listed Companies* (2007) and *Rules on Determining Administrative Liability for Illegal Information Disclosure* (2011) (hereinafter referred to as 'The Rules for Determining Liability'). In terms of the Rules for Determining Liability, the CSRC has tried to accurately define key terms such as 'persons directly in charge', 'other persons directly responsible', 'having false records', 'having misleading statements' and 'having major omissions' provided for under the Securities Law.[61] The Rules for Determining Liability go further by making clear the evidence that an accused person can use to prove that they are not at fault, that they mitigated their liability or that they should even be exempted from any liability.[62] The Rules for Determining Liability also list the situations

[61] §§ 15, 17, 18, 19, 7, 8, 9, Rules on Determining Administrative Liability for Illegal Information Disclosure, CSRC.

[62] *Ibid.*, §§ 20, 21, 22.

in which heavier punishments shall be imposed on the accused.[63] With regard to the detailed clauses in The Rules for Determining Liability, the CSRC has developed a sophisticated and nuanced approach towards sanctioning directors, statutory supervisors and senior officers in cases concerning breaches of information disclosure.

This case study again highlights the difficulties of independent directors fulfilling their duties in cases of deliberate fraud by controlling shareholders. Here the focus is on the enforcement phase. Specifically, the CSRC rules and sanction cases arguably need to do a better job in fine-tuning the distinction among different types of accused persons, especially with respect to independent directors, other outside directors, senior officers other than the CEO/CFO and supervisors. Since it is almost impossible for even the most diligent independent director to prevent their listed company from breaching their disclosure obligations, it may be wise to evaluate the liability of independent directors based on how they perform their basic (day-to-day) duties – although admittedly it may be difficult to evaluate the performance of such duties. In this regard, the newly drafted *Duty Performance Guidelines for the Independent Directors of Listed Companies* should be helpful.[64] In practice, the obligation under the Securities Law that directors (especially independent directors) of listed companies shall *ensure* compliance with the company's information disclosure obligations should be applied with more caution; the CSRC needs to permit more independent directors who successfully prove their reasonable diligence to fulfil their general duties to be exempt from liability.

VII Singapore: Family-Controlled Companies and the China Sky (S-Chip) Case

As noted in Chapter 9, the role of independent directors in Singapore varies sharply depending on the identity of the controlling shareholder. Singapore is best known for its Government-Linked Companies which are controlled by Temasek Holdings Pte Ltd, a holding company that is wholly owned by the Government of Singapore. Temasek's successes in placing independent directors in companies it controls to monitor

[63] *Ibid.*, § 23.

[64] China Association For Public Companies, *Duty Performance Guidelines for the Independent Directors of Listed Companies* (2014).

management from a business performance perspective without any governmental political interference has increased the importance of state-owned enterprises generally and is a model that has inspired other countries such as China.[65]

The other class of controlling shareholder in Singapore is the traditional family-controlled small and medium enterprises. Here the role of independent director is often to act as a mediator and advisor to the principal shareholder rather than to act 'independently' of him. The reported successes in this area are not as well-known as the Government-Linked Companies and are also of great instructional value to other jurisdictions in Asia and to comparative corporate law generally.

This chapter does not include a case study of a successful Government-Linked Company, as this is already a well-known story.[66] Rather, we proceed with a case study of the role of independent directors in a family-controlled company (Minco). This is followed by a case study of a so-called S-chip company or 'PRC-Controlled Firm' (China Sky), i.e., a holding company often incorporated in an offshore haven such as Bermuda, with its business activities (i.e., operating subsidiaries) in mainland China and its stock listing in Singapore. Serious and frequent corporate governance problems at such companies, such as tunnelling by mainland Chinese principal owners at the expense of minority shareholders in Singapore, have resulted in significant regulatory changes. The most striking change, noted in Chapter 9, was a revision of the definition of independent director under Singapore's code of corporate governance in 2012 to require independence from block shareholders as well as from management.

[65] However, transplanting such a model to China or elsewhere may prove to be difficult. See C. Tan et al., 'State-Owned Enterprises in Singapore: Historical Insights into a Potential Model for Reform', *Columbia Journal of Asian Law*, 28(2) (2015), 61 (arguing that Singapore's model of Government-Linked Companies is 'closely intertwined with Singapore's idiosyncratic history and unique regulatory culture').

[66] For empirical studies on performance see two studies cited in Tan et al., 'State-Owned Enterprises in Singapore', n. 20–21 (showing that Government-Linked Companies in Singapore show higher valuations than other listed companies), for Temasek's success in promoting corporate governance, see C. Chen, 'Corporate Governance of State-Owned Enterprises: An Empirical Survey of the Model of Temasek Holdings in Singapore' (Working Paper, 30 September 2013), available at http://ssrn.com/abstract=2366699 (showing that companies in which Temasek has a direct stake have more independent directors and are more likely to have an independent director as chairman than other listed companies).

1 *Family-Controlled Companies (Minco)*[67]

Minco is a first generation family-controlled manufacturer of industrial chemicals founded in 1964. From the beginning the family directors appointed outside non-executive directors (NEDs) who were well-connected Singaporeans with professional skills. The NEDs were utilised as unofficial business advisors to the family directors, usually in informal one-on-one settings rather than at board meetings. In any case, the family directors saw no real difference between an NED's informal role of personal advisor to family directors and formal role as an outside director on the board.

Two factors caused a reconsideration of the role of NEDs: (1) during the 1980s the Singaporean government removed market protection from the domestic chemical industry and opened it up to international competition; and (2) beginning in the second half of the 1990s various government committees began emphasising the role of NEDs on the board of directors, including advocating board committees with a majority of NEDs and formal board meetings as the locus of decision making.

Matters came to a head when the founder's eldest son (the company's executive director) initiated a joint venture in China to manufacture artificial rubies in 1997 and the joint venture collapsed amidst fraud by the Chinese partner. The press and the stock exchange demanded explanations and investigation. Two new NEDs appointed in 2000 went beyond the traditional role of advising the family directors in private to assume a role of facilitating more formal board interaction and greater responsiveness to regulatory and public concerns. While being careful to emphasise that they were working on behalf of the interests of the family and the firm, they were able to arrange for both withdrawal from the ruby business and the resignation of the eldest son as executive director (although he remained a director).

2 *China Sky*[68]

China Sky Chemical Fibre Co Ltd is a so-called S-chip (or 'PRC-Controlled Firm') with its business activities on the Chinese mainland

[67] This case study is based on W. Ng and J. Roberts, '"Helping the Family": The Mediating Role of Outside Directors in Ethnic Chinese Family Firms', *Human Relations*, 60 (2007), 285, available at http://hum.sagepub.com/content/60/2/285.

[68] This case study is based on M. Teen, 'Sky's the Limit: The China Sky Saga' in M. Teen (ed.), *Corporate Governance Case Studies*, Vol. 2 (CPA Australia, 2013), 1–13, available at http://governanceforstakeholders.com/wp-content/uploads/2013/05/CPA-CG-Case-Studies-Vol2-0410.pdf.

but its stock listing in Singapore. It was incorporated (in Grand Cayman) in 2005 and listed in Singapore the same year. Its main business is the production of high-end nylon fibres. The largest shareholder (37.8 per cent), Mr Huang, was an executive director on the board. The board had six directors, three executive directors and three NEDs. Among the latter were two independent directors from Singapore.

Beginning in 2010 the stock exchange sent a number of inquiries to China Sky concerning its financial statements, independent directors, compensation, interested party transactions and other issues. The chair of the audit committee, Mr Lai, headed his own accounting firm. His firm provided substantial accounting services to China Sky, including services related to review of internal accounting controls and financial statements. Despite this obvious conflict of interest, the company continued to assert Mr Lai's independence in the company's corporate governance report.

In November 2011 the Singapore Exchange (SGX) ordered China Sky to appoint a special auditor to investigate the above conflict of interest and certain property investments in China, and the following day a suspension in the trading of its shares began at the company's request. However, a month later China Sky issued a statement that it would not appoint such a special auditor since it was not necessary and not in the company's best interests. The Monetary Authority of Singapore (MAS) also publicly supported the SGX directive. China Sky announced a reshuffling of committee chairs, with Mr Lai moving from the audit committee to the nominating committee, but it did not say whether it would comply with the SGX directive.

As a result of China Sky's failure to appoint a special auditor in accordance with the SGX directive, all three independent directors resigned at once on 5 January 2012, and the following day the SGX commenced a rare lawsuit against China Sky to enforce its directive. However, the suit was withdrawn ten days later, as the parties entered into negotiations. The major shareholder, Mr Huang and the financial controller also resigned on 7 February, and a criminal investigation began the following week. In April MAS requested a court order restraining Mr Huang from any further transfer of monies out of his Singapore bank account.

China Sky's external audit firm (Deloitte and Touche LLP) resigned on 23 April 2012 since there were no independent directors (and, accordingly, no independent members of the audit committee) since January. Eventually China Sky relented, appointing new management in September and a special auditor in October 2012.

The company proposed a resumption of trading in its shares in May 2014. It reached a civil settlement with the SGX in the litigation pending with Mr Huang in February 2015, under which he, the principal shareholder, will pay a civil fine and will surrender 10 per cent of his shareholdings to the company in order to increase the net asset value per share of other shareholders. The SGX then stated it would permit the resumption of share trading once China Sky fulfilled a number of conditions.[69] In a filing with the SGX dated 9 September 2015 the company announced that it believed it had fulfilled all of the SGX's conditions and stated that it expects the resumption of trading in its shares.[70]

Following a number of corporate governance scandals at S-chip companies, the SGX suspended such listings in 2012 and announced the creation of a new direct listings framework in cooperation with the securities regulator in mainland China, the CSRC, in 2013.[71] A Chinese company would need to first obtain approval from the CSRC before applying for a listing in Singapore. To the extent that the SGX was unable to sufficiently influence China-based companies through its informal regulation and guidance, it can now potentially harness the authority of the CSRC to help ensure compliance by Chinese companies.

VIII Discussion

The case studies illustrate the variety and subtlety of the functions of independent directors in Asia.[72] One clear conclusion that can be drawn from the case studies is that independent directors in Asia do not function in the same manner as envisioned in the US/UK model. Although the US model of independent directors, aided by investment-related activities of global institutional investors, has become a popular export in terms of form, the same cannot be said with respect to function. In general terms, independent directors are not change agents who represent general shareholders and challenge management. Rather, as discussed below, independent directors in Asia tend to work cooperatively with management and shareholders.

[69] SGX, News and Updates, 'Trading of China Sky Shares Will Resume after Company's Board Complies with SGX Conditions' (12 February 2015), available at www.sgx.com.

[70] China Sky Chemical Fibre Co., Ltd, 'Miscellaneous: Trading Resumption', filing with SGX dated 9 September 2015, available at http://infopub.sgx.com.

[71] J. M. Watts, 'Singapore to Allow Mainland Chinese Listings', *Wall Street Journal*, 27 November 2013, available at http://blogs.wsj.com.

[72] See also Chapter 3 at II and III, and Chapter 13 for a general discussion.

The most obvious cause of this difference between the US model and Asian practice is the widespread presence of controlling shareholders in most Asian jurisdictions. This shifts the main corporate governance problem from one of agency costs (protecting shareholders from management) to one of controlling shareholders (protecting minority shareholders from the majority shareholder). However, as noted above, the primary function of independent directors in Asia in practice is not an aggressive representation of minority shareholders as might be expected from comparative corporate governance theory.

The first question is the meaning of 'independence' in a controlling shareholder context. The HIH case study from Australia demonstrates that a US definition of independence from management (i.e., a focus on excluding economic or financial ties and disregarding personal relationships) is not useful in the case of a controlling shareholder. Nominally independent directors are unlikely to function effectively unless the controlling shareholder accepts that their function, however defined, can contribute meaningfully to the company.

A related question is the ability of even truly independent and competent directors to work in the best interests of the corporation in the case of tunnelling or other actions by a controlling shareholder to obtain private benefits from the corporation. The case studies from Taiwan and China (and the Toshiba example in Japan) indicate that it is usually not possible for independent directors to prevent or detect deliberate fraud by a controlling shareholder or management. This is unsurprising in that the same result has generally held true in the US and other countries even in the absence of a controlling shareholder.

The Japan case studies provide a further indication that importing the form of independent director from the US will not result in a similar function in Asia. For over 15 years, active debate in Japan focused heavily on the form of the board of directors, and particularly on the questions of a possible legal requirement for outside directors and the value of 'independence' of outside directors. Opposition to a legal requirement for outside/independent directors was based precisely on the view that any such requirement constituted an emphasis on form over function with great uncertainty as to how the proposed outside/independent directors would work in the Japanese context. Ultimately, companies were given a choice of corporate forms (as was also the case in Taiwan).

However, no corporate form has proven to be immune to serious corporate governance problems, as illustrated by the troubles at both the 'traditional' champion, Toyota, and the 'American-style' leader, Sony.

A major effort to combine the 'best of both worlds' at Toshiba eventually led to the worst corporate governance scandal of the last few years in Japan. In sum, the Japanese case studies reinforce an important theme of the book, i.e., that we have devoted too much time, effort and thought to corporate form and the desirability of a requirement for independent directors, and not given sufficient consideration to the actual function of independent directors.

If the above negative case studies highlight the difficulties of attempting to import the US model of independent directors, what do the more positive case studies tell us about the actual functioning of independent directors in Asia?

Although the actual functioning of independent directors depends heavily on local context, we can nevertheless generalise by saying that, compared to their role in corporate governance theory, independent directors in Asia play a 'lesser', but somewhat unexpected and positive role. This is a result not only of shareholder structure and the widespread presence of controlling shareholders in Asian jurisdictions. The primary function of the board itself in Asia is more often seen as that of a managing board rather than of a monitoring board. Expectations concerning the role of independent directors in Asia may also be lower than in the US due in part to a number of substitutes for some of the functions typically associated with independent directors in the US

The result, as noted above, is that independent directors in Asia tend to have a cooperative relationship with controlling shareholders/management rather than challenging them on behalf of general shareholders. The case studies indicate a number of specific positive functions. First, independent directors can still have some monitoring function as illustrated by the role of independent directors on the nomination committee and other board committees in Japan. Unlike the US where such board committees are composed entirely of independent directors to circumvent all management influence, in Japan independent directors serving on these committees generally review management recommendations. This limited vetting function is designed, for example in the case of nomination committees, to prevent outlier nominations (e.g., a personal friend of the CEO who is clearly unqualified for the position in question) rather than to assume control of the nomination process.

Examples of independent directors in Asia playing a partial or limited monitoring role apart from the nomination committee would include similar functions on other board committees (i.e., remuneration issues on the compensation committee and financial issues on the audit committee), strategic decision making and compliance matters. To the extent that board function in Asian jurisdictions is gradually incorporating a larger element of the monitoring model, the board's significant role in daily management would likely be reduced. A greater board emphasis on strategic planning and decision making would, in turn, expand the potential contribution and role of independent directors who are less familiar with the details of daily operations but may have background and experience that is relevant to overall strategy.

The main function of independent directors in a number of the case studies is to act as an advisor to the controlling shareholder/management and, even more importantly, as a mediator between the controlling shareholder/management and general shareholders and public markets. Even in the US there is theoretical work in support of a mediating role for the board,[73] even if it is not commonly accepted in a system of widely dispersed shareholders and high expectations of a more aggressive role for independent directors.

One Singapore case study (Minco) illustrates the advisor/mediator role clearly in family-controlled companies, as the independent directors help the family members to respond and adapt to changing societal demands and improve their company's corporate governance over time. Similarly, the Indian case study shows how independent directors can play an important role as mediators by acting as the board members who respond most effectively to the demands of general shareholders, market pressure and government regulators (even though they do not necessarily initiate corporate governance change or reform). The Korean chapter also cites its own examples of how independent directors can mediate with the controlling shareholder behind the scenes without visibly fulfilling the role of independent director as envisioned in the US model.[74]

The contribution of independent directors to enforcement is a little explored function to date. The case studies from Taiwan and China provide examples of how conscientious independent directors, even if they are not successful in preventing fraud, can nevertheless contribute after the fact through additional investigation and, ultimately, through timely resignation. The Singapore China Sky case further illustrates how corporate governance issues and a company's failure to respond to regulators' concerns can make it difficult for independent directors to continue

[73] M. Blair and L. Stout, 'Director Accountability and the Mediating Role of the Corporate Board', *Washington University Law Quarterly*, 79(2) (2001), 403.

[74] See Chapter 5 (South Korea) at II.3 and IV.

to function in even nominal roles. In either case, resignation and other actions by independent directors act to 'raise the stakes' and substantially increase pressure on the company to remedy corporate governance problems. Although director resignation may, at first blush, sound like an extreme and unlikely response by independent directors in Asia, the case studies illustrate a number of such instances in the real world.

An additional function of independent directors may be to act as a signalling device. A number of case studies (such as Sony and traditional hybrid companies like Asahi Glass in Japan) include instances where companies voluntarily add additional independent directors that are not required by law or regulation. In such cases, these companies may be sending a signal to capital markets that they are sensitive to the concerns of general shareholders (including foreign investors) and welcome their participation in the company. Such signalling (particularly if it results in an increase in foreign investment) can create higher expectations for the role of independent directors and added pressure for the company to meet such expectations. The same signalling function may also operate at the national (rather than the company) level, as an increasing number of jurisdictions in Asia have created a legal requirement for a minimum number or percentage of independent directors for listed companies.

Finally, it is worth noting that despite the 'lesser' positive role of independent directors in a number of the case studies, it remains unclear if Asian jurisdictions have developed effective substitutes for some independent director functions. One of the best known substitutes is the role of supervisors, particularly the *kansayaku* in Japan. There is no indication, at least in these case studies, that such supervisors were effective as monitoring 'replacements' for 'US-style' independent directors. Rather, such supervisors seemed to face concerns that were similar to those applicable to independent directors: were they truly independent (i.e., functioning of the selection process); and were they provided with sufficient information and other tools and an operating environment to function effectively? The answer would presumably be the same – either positive or negative – for both independent supervisors and independent directors in a particular company. The Taiwan case study included a supervisor who went to extraordinary measures after a corporate governance problem occurred, but like the independent directors was not in a position to prevent or detect the fraud beforehand.

On the other hand, the China Sky case study in Singapore suggests that informal government regulation might act as a kind of substitute for independent directors. The corporate governance issues at S-chip companies from China and their resistance to the suggestions of regulators in Singapore eventually led to the Singapore authorities taking unusual formal enforcement action against China Sky. More importantly, it also led to a regulatory agreement between the Singapore regulators and the CSRC in China under which the Chinese regulators screen Chinese companies seeking to list in Singapore and presumably use their influence to aid in enforcing corporate governance standards. This clearly illustrates that authorities in Singapore believed their informal regulation was important in maintaining corporate governance standards and would not permit Chinese S-chip companies listed in Singapore to ignore the regulators' suggestions.

In sum, the case studies indicate that independent directors in Asian jurisdictions can and do play a positive role, although not necessarily the role assumed by the US model.[75] Instead, the presence of controlling shareholders and other local conditions have encouraged independent directors to adapt and, for example, to contribute to monitoring functions without being directly in charge of such functions. More importantly, independent directors have acted creatively to earn the trust of controlling shareholders and help them to adapt to changing social demands on businesses through advice and mediation between the company and outsiders. Such a role for independent directors is a logical reaction to local context, even if not predicted by the US model, and also constitutes a positive contribution to corporate governance in Asia.

[75] See also Chapter 13 at IV.

13

Independent Directors in Asia

Theoretical Lessons and Practical Implications

SOUICHIROU KOZUKA AND LUKE NOTTAGE*

I Proliferating Independent Director Requirements

As the chapters in this book show, the institution of the independent director has rapidly become common in Asia, within a mere quarter of a century since the Cadbury Report in the United Kingdom (UK) brought independent director requirements to the centre of the global corporate governance debate.[1] At first blush, this trend appears to support the view that independent directors have contributed to improvements in corporate governance, making corporate management more efficient and more focused on shareholder interests. This perception of independent directors undergirds the OECD's Principles of Corporate Governance; the preamble in its most recent edition declares that 'good corporate governance will reassure shareholders and other stakeholders that their rights are protected and make it possible for corporations to decrease the cost of capital and to facilitate their access to the capital market'.[2]

* We thank Kym Sheehan (University of Sydney), Wataru Tanaka (University of Tokyo) and Akio Hoshi (Gakushuin University) for helpful information on institutional investment patterns; as well as Harald Baum, Vivienne Bath, Vikramaditya Khanna and Umakanth Varottil for comments on an earlier version of this chapter, which was substantially completed in April 2016. Any errors or misconceptions remain our own.

1 See Chapter 1 at IV.1; Chapter 11 (Australia) at II.

2 Organisation for Economic Cooperation and Development, *G20/OECD Principles of Corporate Governance* (OECD Publishing, 2015), 10. Siems and Alvarez-Macotela make an interesting analysis about the nature of this instrument: M. S. Siems and O. Alvarez-Macotela, 'The OECD Principles of Corporate Governance in Emerging Markets: A Successful Example of Networked Governance?' in M. Fenwick et al. (eds.), *Networked Governance, Transnational Business and the Law* (Springer, 2014), 257.

The prevailing view is that independent directors are necessary to address agency problems within public companies. Agency problems arise in situations where the interests of one party (principal) are affected by the behaviour of another party (agent).[3] In public companies with dispersed shareholders, the most serious agency problem exists between shareholders (principals) and managers (agents). Independent directors have been touted as a corporate governance solution to this agency problem. Specifically, independent directors are supposed to monitor the management on behalf of dispersed, powerless shareholders to prevent or redress the harm that the management can cause to the shareholders. Independent director requirements therefore function as a 'guarantee' of good corporate governance for investors seeking worthy targets. The apparent popularity of independent directors in Asia suggests that regulatory competition remains robust; many jurisdictions may have adopted such requirements to avoid 'losing out' in the global competition for investors.[4]

However, a closer look at the Asian jurisdictions under study reveals that there is more diversity than uniformity.[5] First, the definition of independence is not uniform; but in most jurisdictions independent directors are expected to monitor substantial shareholders and should thus be independent from them. The treatment of functional substitutes has been uneven as well. In Japan, for example, 'statutory auditors' remain a popular alternative to independent directors, especially since they may perform similar functions.[6]

[3] R. Kraakman et al., *The Anatomy of Corporate Law*, 2nd edn (Oxford University Press, 2009), 35.

[4] See Chapter 3 at II.4.

[5] See also Chapter 3 at II. Nonetheless, some overall formal and even partial functional convergence arguably can be observed, including trends to introduce independent director requirements from around 2000 and to gradually tighten criteria, especially for larger listed companies. See L. Nottage and F. Aoun, 'Independent Director Requirements in Australia and the Asian Region', *Company and Securities Law Journal*, 34 (2016), 631, 636–637.

[6] See Chapter 4 (Japan) at I; Chapter 3 at III.2 (discussing functional substitutes generally); and B. E. Aronson, 'Japanese Corporate Governance Reform: A Comparative Perspective', *Hastings Business Law Journal*, 11 (2015), 85, 98–102 (pointing out the limited empirical studies on roles played by statutory auditors). For a succinct outline of the evolving corporate law and contemporary governance structures in Japan, see B. E. Aronson et al., 'Corporate Law' in P. Haghirian (ed.), *Handbook of Japanese Business and Management* (Routledge, 2016), 103–113.

Second, substantial diversity exists in the enforcement of independent director requirements.[7] While several jurisdictions rely primarily on the non-binding 'comply or explain' requirement, especially common law jurisdictions such as Singapore and Australia, independent directors are mandatory for listed companies in Hong Kong as well as certain companies in South Korea.[8] China even has a governmental organisation tasked with ensuring compliance.[9] Even among countries with a 'comply or explain' regime, some apply slightly stronger pressure on companies to 'comply', as is exemplified by Japan's requirement for companies to disclose 'the reason why an independent director is not appropriate for the company'. In contrast, Australia's 'if not, why not' regime takes a more relaxed approach towards compliance.[10]

Third, in practice, the identity of independent directors varies considerably.[11] Unlike in the US, a considerable number of former government officials, and even academics, serve as independent directors in countries in Northeast Asia (Japan, China, South Korea and Taiwan)[12] as well as India. India is also an outlier, given that women represent a substantial proportion of independent directors, even before the 2013 Companies Act amendments imposed a requirement for at least one woman to be present on the board (although she did not necessarily need to be an independent director).[13] In Hong Kong, concerns have been raised as to the tendency for directors to elect their friends to each other's boards; further, controlling shareholders can still impede the emergence of

[7] See Chapter 3 at II.3 (discussing variations in 'comply or explain' and mandatory requirements across jurisdictions in the context of board composition).

[8] See Chapter 5 (South Korea) at III.2.a; Chapter 8 (Hong Kong) at II.1; in Singapore a minimum number of two independent resident directors is required for foreign issuers by the SGX Listing Rules, see Chapter 9 (Singapore) at II.3; in Australia the ASX Listing Rules demand an audit committee for all listed companies but comprising a majority of IDs for large (ASX 300) companies, see Chapter 11 (Australia) at III.2. See also Chapter 3 at II.3.

[9] See Chapter 6 (China) at II.2.

[10] See Chapter 11 (Australia).

[11] See Chapter 3 at II.3 and II.4 (discussing the diverse and idiosyncratic forms and functions of independent directors across jurisdictions).

[12] See Chapter 7 (Taiwan) at II.2.b.

[13] Section 149(1), second proviso of the Companies Act, 2013 of India. N Balasubramanian and Nirmal Mohanty, *Gender Diversity on Boards* (NSE Quarterly Briefing No. 10, July 2015), available at www.nseindia.com/research/content/res_QB10.pdf. However, the new rules (in effect from 1 April 2015) do not require the female director to be independent, and data is unclear as to whether women directors on Indian listed companies so far are in fact independent.

effective independence as long as directors must be appointed by majority shareholder vote.[14]

These derogations from the original independent director concept may not be surprising, given that significant block shareholdings exist in almost every Asian jurisdiction (and indeed Australia).[15] One might argue that convergence should be found in the function, if not in the form, of legal institutions.[16] However, the expected roles or functions of independent directors do not appear to be uniform across countries either.[17] It is doubtful that an ex-government official or academic as independent director can effectively monitor managerial performance of managers and protect shareholders' interests. But these independent directors may still serve other purposes: they can effectively liaise with regulatory authorities on the company's behalf or provide useful advice based on their unique expertise.[18] As long as the institutional design or expected functions of independent directors differ, the seeming prevalence of independent director requirements in Asia cannot be taken as the result of simple regulatory competition. Further, there is not even a guarantee that the differences among jurisdictions appropriately reflect the specific problems that each jurisdiction faces.

These observations invite us to depart from the simple theory that perceives independent directors as a useful corporate governance mechanism for public companies. In reality, independent director requirements may be primarily driven by lawmakers or other interest groups, who may have different motivations from investors, managers or other stakeholders in the company.[19] The phenomenon of independent directors in Asia

[14] See Chapter 8 (Hong Kong) at III.2 and III.3.

[15] Most of the jurisdictions surveyed in this book are dominated by companies with concentrated ownership. See Chapter 5 (South Korea) at II.3; Chapter 6 (China) at I and II.1; Chapter 7 (Taiwan) at II.4; Chapter 8 (Hong Kong) at II.4; Chapter 9 (Singapore) at I; Chapter 10 (India) at II.3.

[16] R. Gilson, 'Globalizing Corporate Governance: Convergence of Form or Function', *American Journal of Comparative Law*, 49 (2001), 329.

[17] See Chapter 3 at II.4.

[18] It is widely accepted that the board of directors anyway has the role of advising management, besides the role of monitoring. See generally J. R. Macey, *Corporate Governance: Promises Kept, Promises Broken* (Princeton University Press, 2008), 53; and Chapter 10 (India) at III and IV.2. The question here is whether ex-government officials or academics have enough experience and competence to serve as monitors, not merely as advisors.

[19] See Chapter 3 at III.2 (discussing the six key factors driving varieties of independent directors in Asia).

also has implications for longstanding debates in comparative corporate law, including the debate about convergence (section II) and legal transplants (section III), which in turn provide indications regarding the future of independent directors in the region (section IV).

II Reassessing Convergence

As discussed above, the apparent general prevalence of independent director regimes, combined with significant diversity in their specific requirements raises intriguing issues in the longstanding debate on convergence in corporate governance.[20] Hansmann and Kraakman ignited this debate 15 years ago,[21] by arguing that the contemporary US shareholder-centric model would prevail worldwide over the previous manager-centric model of corporate law in the US, as well as the stakeholder model associated with continental Europe and Asian jurisdictions. Some scholars responded by emphasising the ongoing importance of path dependence on legal, political, social and economic structures.[22] This included more coordinated market economies in Europe and Asia, traditionally populated by concentrated shareholder structures, where the protection of shareholder interests required greater emphasis on legal mechanisms to restrain exploitation by controlling shareholders. By contrast, liberal market economies with more dispersed shareholdings, such as the US, focused on mechanisms designed to facilitate shareholder control over management of listed companies.[23] Another response was that interjurisdictional competition might instead lead to a regulatory 'race to the bottom' to attract incorporations.[24]

20 Gilson, 'Globalizing Corporate Governance: Convergence of Form or Function', 329; D. Clarke, '"Nothing but the Wind?" The Past and Future of Comparative Corporate Governance', *American Journal of Comparative Law*, 59 (2011), 75, 96–103; D. Cabrelli and M. Siems, 'Convergence, Legal Origins, and Transplants in Comparative Corporate Law: A Case-Based and Quantitative Analysis', *American Journal of Comparative Law*, 63 (2015), 109, 113–117.

21 H. Hansmann and R. Kraakman, 'The End of History for Corporate Law', *Georgetown Law Journal*, 89 (2001), 439.

22 T. Clarke, *International Corporate Governance: A Comparative Approach* (Routledge, 2008).

23 Cf. e.g., L. Nottage, 'Japanese Corporate Governance at a Crossroads: Variation in "Varieties of Capitalism"', *The North Carolina Journal of International Law and Commercial Regulation*, 27 (2001), 255, with further references.

24 P. Rose, 'EU Company Law Convergence Possibilities after Centros', *Transnational Law and Contemporary Problems*, 11 (2001), 121.

It is evident that some convergence is broadly apparent from the emergence of independent director requirements across the Asian jurisdictions under study, which have built on developments in other economies in Asia and on the Pacific Rim such as the US and Australia, as well as further afield.[25] This should be a welcome development for many 'legal origins' theorists, in that it supports their provocative argument that better shareholder protections (allegedly characteristic of common law jurisdictions) promote dispersed shareholdings, vibrant financial markets and economic growth.[26]

On the other hand, a striking feature of independent director requirements in Asia is that they generally diverge from the US model, which allows substantial shareholders to qualify as independent directors.[27] This divergence seemingly recognises, and is a better fit with, the concentrated shareholder environment in most Asian jurisdictions – and even in Australia, where this expanded definition first originated.[28] Yet, there is little evidence that careful analysis has been undertaken as to the relative benefits and drawbacks of adopting a narrower definition of independence, let alone about calibrating it to the typical shareholding structures and the corporate governance regimes in such jurisdictions.[29] Instead, different jurisdictions have adopted varying percentages or thresholds restricting substantial shareholders from qualifying as independent directors. Some may have modelled their requirements on existing definitions used for other corporate law issues, without further consideration as to whether such thresholds limit possible abuse by controlling shareholders while incentivising directors to enhance corporate value.[30]

[25] See Chapter 1 at V.

[26] See, for example, R. La Porta et al., 'Investor Protection and Corporate Governance', *Journal of Financial Economics*, 58 (2000), 3. For various critiques, see Cabrelli and Siems, 'Convergence, Legal Origins, and Transplants in Comparative Corporate Law: A Case-Based and Quantitative Analysis', 121–123. See also Chapter 3 at III.2 and IV.

[27] See Chapter 3 at II.4.

[28] See Chapter 11 (Australia) at IV. Highlighting the formal or functional lack of dispersed shareholdings still in Asian economies, see also D. W. Puchniak, 'Multiple Faces of Shareholder Power in Asia: Complexity Revealed' in J. Hill and R. Thomas (eds.), *Research Handbook on Shareholder Power* (Edward Elgar, 2015), 511, 523–526.

[29] See generally Chapter 2. See also Japan's 2014 amendments to disqualify a director, officer or employee of the parent company as well as a controlling person (which includes a controlling shareholder, but also an individual who controls the management without holding a share) as outside director, despite the fact that shareholdings in Japan are relatively dispersed.

[30] For example, Australia has recently proposed raising the threshold from 5 per cent (used in other corporate law contests) to 20 per cent (the threshold used to trigger takeover

Jurisdictions also adopt a variety of other indicia to define independence, such as family relationships and (less commonly) director tenure.[31] Some jurisdictions in Asia have adopted a UK-style 'comply or explain' regime for independent directors on boards generally, as opposed to US-style mandatory rules. Yet, compliance is high among most listed companies in Asia, and the 'comply or explain' regimes are often supplemented by mandatory requirements for specific issues (e.g., audit committees).[32] Thus, to the extent there is some general convergence with respect to independent director requirements across Asia, it is still a far cry from 'Americanisation'.[33]

Singapore is yet another interesting case study in the convergence debate: it originally adopted a US-style definition in 2001 that allowed substantial shareholders to qualify as independent directors, as required on a 'comply or explain' basis.[34] Singapore's relaxed approach enabled it to 'signal' compliance with global best practices, without substantially altering corporate governance structures in its many government-linked and family companies. This definition was only tightened in 2012, and came into force from 2015 onwards; nevertheless, its requirements remain comparatively relaxed, in that it only requires independent directors to be independent from management and from shareholders holding more than 10 per cent of the company's shares.[35] The three-year transition period also gave Singapore listed companies ample time to adjust their board compositions accordingly, which may account for the continued

bid regulation), instead of some other percentage: see P. Hanrahan and T. Bednall, 'Independence of Directors Affiliated with Substantial Shareholders: Issues of Law and Corporate Governance', *Company and Securities Law Journal*, 33 (2015), 239.

31 See, e.g., Chapter 8 (Hong Kong) at II.2 (Hong Kong's stricter approach to family relationships), compared to Chapter 10 (India) at V.2 (the absence of such restrictions in India, although its 2013 reforms have limited tenure in principle to five years).

32 See, e.g., Chapter 11 (Australia) at III.2; Chapter 10 (India) at IV.2, noting only 87 per cent compliance (at least prior to significant 2013 amendments) despite mandatory requirements being introduced from 2001 (with stronger penalties from 2004); Chapter 3 at II.3 (discussing the interaction between 'comply or explain' and mandatory requirements generally).

33 Other studies have also observed that the US is a comparative law outlier; see Cabrelli and Siems, 'Convergence, Legal Origins, and Transplants in Comparative Corporate Law: A Case-Based and Quantitative Analysis', 152. Cf. generally, e.g., D. Kelemen and E. Sibbett, 'The Americanization of Japanese Law', *Pennsylvania Journal of International Economic Law*, 23 (2002), 269.

34 Chapter 9 (Singapore) at II.3.

35 See, e.g., Chapter 8 (Hong Kong) at II.2 (under Listing Rule 3.13, the Exchange 'is more likely' to question independence if the director holds more than 1 per cent of

high rate of compliance following these amendments. Yet, even if the initial and more recent requirements could not theoretically be expected to have any major impact on restricting controlling shareholder behaviour, especially vis-à-vis minority shareholders, the Singaporean experience shows that these independent directors perform different functions.[36] In particular, they help mediate background family disputes among the controlling shareholder bloc(s), a phenomenon that may also be present in India.[37] Similarly, independent directors appointed pursuant to the mandatory independent director requirements imposed in South Korea following the Asian Financial Crisis include a large proportion of former government officials. Their functions appear to be primarily directed at managing the company's relationship with public authorities (e.g., when tax audits are involved).[38] Thus, derogations from the Anglo-American model in Asia do not restrict or diminish the importance of independent directors in such jurisdictions.

The unexpected roles of independent directors are intriguing from a comparative corporate law perspective, and indeed comparative law more generally. First, such developments highlight the limitations of legal convergence; similar observations have been made by recent corporate law studies of Asian jurisdictions.[39] Nevertheless, independent director requirements may have proliferated across jurisdictions, and even serve some of their intended functions (i.e., constraining professional managers, but also controlling shareholders, at least to some

shareholdings, and a director holding more than 5 per cent 'normally will not be considered to be independent'); Chapter 11 (Australia) at IV (5 per cent). In India, under section 149(6)(e)(iii) of the Companies Act, 2013, any person holding (along with relatives) more than 2 per cent of the total voting power of the company would not be considered as an independent director.

36 See Chapter 3 at II.4.

37 Chapter 10 (India) at VI.3. See generally the concept of the 'mediating' board (rather than the 'monitoring' board), as elaborated in M. Blair, 'Boards of Directors and Corporate Performance under a Team Production Model' in J. Hill and R. Thomas (eds.), *Research Handbook on Shareholder Power* (Edward Elgar, 2015), 249.

38 Chapter 5 (South Korea) at IV.4. See also Chapter 10 (India) at IV.2, noting also a significant proportion of former politicians. Cf. the earlier 'resource dependency' theory of corporate governance, predicting that directors will be appointed to bring in outside 'resources' or connections: G. Kiel and G. Nicholson, 'Board Composition and Corporate Performance: How the Australian Experience Informs Contrasting Theories of Corporate Governance', *Corporate Governance: An International Review*, 11 (2003), 189.

39 Finding even more limited convergence, see D. W. Puchniak, H. Baum and M. Ewing-Chow (eds.), *The Derivative Action in Asia: A Comparative and Functional Approach*

extent).[40] However, such requirements may also play additional roles that reflect and reinforce persistent significant differences in corporate governance regimes across jurisdictions.[41] Second, novel roles identified in some jurisdictions should remind practitioners of 'functional' comparative law[42] to be imaginative and open-minded when defining and redefining the various functions that are hypothesised to be needed in the respective jurisdictions.[43]

III Complex Transplants

The preceding analysis suggests that some convergence is occurring, but fulfilling (at least to some extent) *multiple* expected functions as well as some *unexpected* ones, and certainly has not resulted in a straightforward US-style corporate law regime focused on maximising shareholder value.[44] On the one hand, the relationship between independent director requirements and shareholding patterns in Asian jurisdictions undermine Watson's 'legal transplant' theory,[45] at least with respect to the strong form of his 'insulation thesis', which posits that the development of private law can be explained without any reference to economic, social or political factors. The links even go against the weaker form of his argument, which argues that such factors are largely unimportant.[46]

(Cambridge University Press, 2012). More generally, see also Puchniak, 'Multiple Faces of Shareholder Power in Asia: Complexity Revealed'.

40 See Chapter 9 (Singapore) at III.3 (observing that this is the case in Singapore Government-Linked Companies); Chapter 10 (India) at V (observing that the 2013 reforms rendered independent director requirements distinctly more 'functional' than 'formal').

41 See generally, M. Siems, 'The Curious Case of Overfitting Legal Transplant' in M. Adams and D. Thilbaut (eds.), *The Method and Culture of Comparative Law* (Hart, 2014), 133, 141 (calling this a type of 'over-fitting' legal transplant, which is *more* effective in the destination country than the original).

42 On other methodological challenges with this approach, see R. Michaels, 'The Functional Method of Comparative Law' in M. Reimann and R. Zimmermann (eds.), *Oxford Handbook of Comparative Law* (Oxford University Press, 2005).

43 See, e.g., Clarke, '"Nothing but the Wind?" The Past and Future of Comparative Corporate Governance', 109.

44 See Chapter 3 at II.4 and IV.

45 See, e.g., A. Watson, *Legal Transplants: An Approach to Comparative Law* (University of Georgia Press, 1993) and generally J. Fedtke, 'Legal Transplants' in J. Smits (ed.), *Encyclopedia of Comparative Law* (Edward Elgar, 2012), 550.

46 W. Ewald, 'Comparative Jurisprudence (II): The Logic of Legal Transplants', *American Journal of Comparative Law*, 43 (1995), 489, 500–501.

On the other hand, it cannot be said that such factors and the broader culture in the receiving jurisdiction render the very concept of the independent director utterly different in meaning, or unintelligible, compared to the source jurisdiction. In contrast to this 'culturalist' view of legal transplants associated with Legrand,[47] which argues that such transplants are impossible, the fine-grained analysis undertaken in this volume favours the 'contextualist' critique of Watson's theory about the ubiquity and ease of legal transplants.[48] Independent director requirements have indeed been widely transplanted in a relatively standardised form, but with variations and adjustments in relation to the complex contexts of the recipient jurisdictions.[49]

As part of such context, the main motivations of those responsible for 'importing' independent director requirements may help explain the timing and features of divergences associated with this overall phenomenon in Asia. In this respect, Miller suggests a general typology of transplants: externally dictated; cost-saving; entrepreneurial; and legitimacy-generating transplants.[50] In post-colonial times, it is rare to find *externally dictated* transplants. However, a contemporary example may be the introduction of independent director requirements in Korea, as part of a broader suite of corporate governance and other systematic legal reforms accompanying the bailout led by the International Monetary Fund, following the Asian Financial Crisis in 1997.[51]

More often nowadays, transplants are motivated by *cost-savings*, given their prior development in other jurisdictions, and because these transplants may also be aimed at promoting economic efficiency in the receiving jurisdiction. This type of transplant could be present in Hong Kong in several respects. First, its requirement for at least two independent directors, introduced in 1993 (when it was still a British colony), largely tracked the recommendations of the 1992 Cadbury Report. However, instead of adopting a UK-style 'comply or explain' regime, Hong Kong made it mandatory for companies to comply with the stipulated minimum

47 P. Legrand, 'What "Legal Transplants"?' in D. Nelken and J. Feest (eds.), *Adapting Legal Cultures* (Hart, 2001), 57.

48 Cabrelli and Siems, 'Convergence, Legal Origins, and Transplants in Comparative Corporate Law: A Case-Based and Quantitative Analysis', 124–125.

49 See Chapter 3 at II.3 and IV.

50 J. Miller, 'A Typology of Legal Transplants: Using Sociology, Legal History and Argentine Examples to Explain the Transplant Process', *American Journal of Comparative Law*, 51 (2013), 839.

51 See Chapter 5 (South Korea) at III.1.

number of independent directors,[52] so the transplant was only partial. Second, Hong Kong adopted from the outset a definition that excluded in principle shareholders holding up to 1 per cent of shares from qualifying as independent directors,[53] unlike the Cadbury Report. Therefore, Hong Kong follows the *concept* originally proposed by the Bosch Committee from 1991 in Australia. However, it should be noted that the definition of a 'substantial' shareholder eventually introduced in Australia from 2003 specifically refers to a person with shareholdings of only 5 per cent or more.[54] The Committee's chair, Mr Henry Bosch, has suggested that the Australian (rather than British) approach may have attracted attention in Hong Kong because his former colleagues when he was leading Australia's securities regulator, notably Mr Robert Nottle, moved to work for the fledgling Hong Kong Securities and Futures Commission from 1989, and kept abreast of the Bosch Committee consultations and eventual recommendations.[55] However, it remains conceivable that Hong Kong policymakers independently came up with an approach similar to Australia, as the former also had a tradition of concentrated shareholdings in listed companies, making it more sensible to adopt a more stringent definition than in the UK (at that time) as well as the US.

The *entrepreneurial transplant* is instead primarily motivated by material or political advantages for the norm entrepreneurs in the destination country. Japan is a possible example, in that the ruling conservative party presently perceives political advantages in trying new types of 'structural reform' for their ailing economy.[56] What is less obvious is that independent director requirements appear to be politically attractive across jurisdictions as a signal that policymakers are highly responsive to corporate collapses, and will take action to prevent

[52] Chapter 8 (Hong Kong) at II.1.

[53] B. Ho, 'Restructuring the Boards of Public Companies in Hong Kong: Barking Up the Wrong Tree', *Singapore Journal of International and Comparative Law*, 1 (1997), 507, 528 (noting that under Listing Rule 1.01, even smaller shareholders would tend to be disqualified 'where the director has received those shares as a gift from or by means of other financial assistance from a connected person', such as a director, chief executive or substantial (10 per cent) shareholder of the company or any of its subsidiaries or his associate).

[54] Chapter 11 (Australia) at IV.

[55] Telephone interview by Luke Nottage with Henry Bosch, 16 March 2015. A senior investigator in the Australian regulator also moved to the Hong Kong regulator six months after Mr Nottle: 'Crosby Quits Job as NCSC Officer', *Sydney Morning Herald*, 5 May 1989. Mr Nottle eventually became Chairman of the Hong Kong regulator, over 1992–1994.

[56] See Chapter 4 (Japan) at III.2.b.

future scandals. This point has been forcefully argued in Australia,[57] where requirements were introduced in 2003 after the failure of HIH, but this pattern of reform can also be observed in several other Asian jurisdictions.[58] It coincides with observations in Europe that corporate governance codes have primarily spread with the aim of assuring investors that the corporate governance in local markets is credible.[59] Similar regulatory changes in Australia were also favourable to organisations that provide training for directors and to a lesser extent the proxy advisors who emerged from around 2000 to service institutional investors, especially US investors subject to heightened fiduciary duties on voting matters.[60]

The *legitimacy-generating transplant* is driven by the prestige offered by the foreign transplant. Hong Kong's law reformers may have had this motivation in mind when they sought guidance from Australia, a fellow common law jurisdiction; the same may have been true for India's law reformers as well. As the US's influence grew over the 1990s, a broader 'Anglo-American'[61] concept of independent directors probably enhanced the legitimacy of introducing such requirements in China and Taiwan. In Singapore, the fact that the US-style definition for independence allowed substantial shareholders to be classified as independent directors was used to enhance the introduction of a similar approach, although it was subsequently altered in 2012. This was perhaps a result of declining US prestige, but more likely due to the growing sophistication and diversification of foreign institutional investors, especially after the 2008 Global Financial Crisis.[62]

[57] F. L. Clarke and G. W. Dean, *Indecent Disclosure: Gilding the Corporate Lily* (Cambridge University Press, 2007).

[58] Chapter 11 (Australia) at III.1; Chapter 10 (India) at V (referring to the Satyam scandal as the motivation for the 2013 reforms, in contrast to the introduction of requirements a decade earlier in order to promote cross-border investment).

[59] P. L. Davies and K. J. Hopt, 'Corporate Boards in Europe: Accountability and Convergence', *American Journal of Comparative Law*, 61 (2013), 301, 326.

[60] Regulatory developments in the late 1980s in the US resulted in institutional investors overwhelmingly conducting their voting through a separate internal voting system or outside proxy advisors, almost always adopting 'one-size-fits-all voting policies based on perceived corporate governance best practices, without reference to the particulars of each company's situation': Latham & Watkins LLP, 'The Parallel Universes of Institutional Investing and Institutional Voting', *Corporate Governance Commentary* (March 2010), available at www.lw.com/upload/pubContent/_pdf/pub3446_1.pdf.

[61] See Chapter 6 (China) at II.2; Chapter 7 (Taiwan) at II.1.

[62] For an alternative explanation of Singapore's change in regulatory approach, see Chapter 9 (Singapore) at IV.

This book's analysis of the proliferation of independent director requirements across Asia also reinforces the 'IKEA' theory of legal transplants.[63] The argument suggests that legal transplantation is actually a process by which elements and concepts of a legal system are de-contextualised and stored in a global intellectual reservoir – just like IKEA products – and then reassembled by the importing jurisdiction without much interest in how they functioned in the original jurisdiction.

Admittedly, the independent director requirements were partly triggered by a 'bilateral' transfer from Australia to Hong Kong in the early 1990s. At least this was true with respect to the definition of independent directors that excluded substantial shareholders, which were potentially more useful in Asian jurisdictions with a tradition of more concentrated shareholdings, even though the broad concept of independent directors was influenced by developments in the US and elsewhere. However, from the late 1990s, the concept had been largely de-contextualised, standardised and globalised – like IKEA furniture. The broad notion of independent director requirements has now been promoted by international organisations like the OECD, IMF and World Bank as an 'Anglo-American' development that could be and was being adopted by jurisdictions following civil law or socialist traditions.[64] As such, independent director requirements joined a global reservoir or toolkit of corporate governance 'best practices' available for jurisdictions to import. When they boomeranged back to Australia and were introduced from 2003,[65] independent director requirements (including the exclusion of substantial shareholders) were no longer seen as something from Hong Kong or even originating from Australia.

The risk with such highly standardised solutions is that they may fail to take root when transferred into novel environments.[66] Even with looser instruments to promote legal harmonisation, Arvind points out that this

[63] See originally G. Frankenberg, 'Constitutional Transfer: The Ikea Theory Revisited', *Journal of International Constitutional Law*, 8 (2010) 563.

[64] It should be noted that the US and UK origins of the independent director are arguably more complex than this label suggests: see Chapter 3 at II.2.

[65] This phenomenon is also intriguing, and seemingly quite rare, from a broader comparative law perspective: namely, (a) a law reform proposal made in one country (Australia) but (b) instead taken up first in another (Hong Kong), before being implemented in the source country. Cf., e.g., Siems, 'The Curious Case of Overfitting Legal Transplant', 133, 142 (giving the example of (a) law reform proposals by German corporate law professor Karsten Schmidt, not adopted in his home country in 1998, (b) implemented from 2007 in Austria – but, not, so far (c) similar reforms being introduced in Germany).

[66] See generally Fedtke, 'Legal Transplants', 551–552.

may occur when informal institutions are not imported or adjusted at the same time.[67] A similar problem may be seen in India, China and Taiwan, where extensive independent director requirements were introduced relatively early without new options for training and support to develop a professional cadre of directors. Another problem identified by Arvind arises where the global instrument is promoted by a small group within the new country: the majority may impede its operation, either in good faith (to maintain the integrity of the existing system) or to protect their vested interests.[68]

However, Michaels persuasively identifies some advantages of the IKEA model of standardised transplants,[69] which might be applicable also to our field. First, this model allows for a 'good enough' solution, and thus one available to those without adequate resources to seek out and implement the 'best solution'. Second, the formal aspect of the rule – de-contextualised from a particular legal system, for the global inventory – can actually open it up productively to multiple meanings when it comes to be re-contextualised in the new jurisdiction. Third, the rule may fit well (or well enough) with other aspects of the global inventory. It may also trigger further transformations in the new jurisdiction, at least some of which may be beneficial. Close and ongoing observation of the actual performance and characteristics of independent directors is essential for each jurisdiction, and across the region,[70] to see whether these more optimistic aspects prevail over the more pessimistic outlook presented by Arvind.

IV Future Perspectives

Miller's four-fold typology of legal transplants, arguably evident across the various Asian jurisdictions examined in this volume, may also help provide insights into the observed and likely ongoing presence of

[67] T. T. Arvind, 'The "Transplant Effect" in Harmonization', *International and Comparative Law Quarterly*, 59 (2010), 65, 82. This seems particularly likely with cost-saving, externally dictated or legitimacy-generating transplants.

[68] *Ibid.*, 83–84. This seems particularly likely with entrepreneurial transplants.

[69] R. Michaels, '"One Size Can Fit All": On the Mass Production of Legal Transplants' in G. Frankenberg (ed.), *Order from Transfer: Studies in Comparative (Constitutional) Law* (Edward Elgar, 2013), 56.

[70] Chapter 12 is based on cross-jurisdictional case studies (including some hybrid structures emerging in Japan), and is generally more optimistic. According to Chapter 10 (India), India's national regime has been significantly more 'functional' since the 2013

independent director requirements in the region. Thus, the transmogrification of an Anglo-Australian model into an 'Anglo-American' model, and more recently a 'global best practice' approved by international organisations such as the OECD, insulates independent director requirements from significant roll-back even if the US corporate governance model has suffered from some declining *legitimacy* after the 2008 Global Financial Crisis.[71] Secondly, the vagaries of politics may indeed have an impact on more *entrepreneurial transplants*; but as independent director requirements persist over time, the material gains for other groups (such as director-training institutes) continue to grow, thus also diminishing the potential for major change. Thirdly, *external pressures* from major international organisations may have receded in the aftermath of the Global Financial Crisis, but the worldwide economic influence of Anglo-American institutional investors persists.[72] Fourthly, for transplants driven primarily by *cost-savings*, Miller remarks that it is only transaction costs that 'limit changes in the model if lawmakers determine that the model is inefficient'.[73] Yet such costs are now significant, given the various interests associated with independent director requirements. In addition, empirical research cited in this volume[74] shows that it is hard to prove positively that they are inefficient – even if their benefits may have been overstated, or at least too readily assumed in the early years of adoption.

reforms, but still faces significant challenges, primarily due to the fact that independent directors must still be elected by majority shareholder vote: see Chapter 10 (India) at V.1.

71 Some of the lustre has come off the American approach to corporate governance due to strong critiques from within the US itself, including against the 'fetish for independence': see S. M. Bainbridge, *Corporate Governance after the Financial Crisis* (Oxford University Press, 2012), Chapter 3.

72 D. Das, 'Growth, Integration and Trends in Equity Markets in Asia', *Asia-Pacific Business Review*, 20 (2014) 286, 291. More generally, on the large and growing proportion of traditional institutional investors, namely pension funds, mutual funds and insurance companies, see generally M. Issakson and S. Çelik, 'Who Cares? Corporate Governance in Today's Equity Markets' (OECD Corporate Governance Working Papers, No. 8, 2013), 29–30 (also pointing out potential misalignment of incentives). Pension funds investment has continuously grown in both OECD and non-OECD countries: see OECD, *Pension Markets in Focus, 2015 edition*, available at www.oecd.org/finance/private-pensions/globalpensionstatistics.htm. Interestingly, the growth rate has remained rather modest in Japan, where this volume has found the least enthusiasm about introducing independent director requirements. See also generally J. Buchanan, D. Heesang Chai and S. Deakin, *Hedge Fund Activism in Japan: The Limits of Shareholder Primacy* (Cambridge University Press, 2012).

73 Miller, 'A Typology of Legal Transplants', 885.

74 See, e.g., Chapter 11 (Australia) at V; Chapter 10 (India) at IV.1; Chapter 8 (Hong Kong) at III.4. See also the studies cited by Blair, 'Boards of Directors and Corporate Performance

Thus, it is most likely that the independent directors will continue to be the norm in Asian countries, notwithstanding that academics are becoming increasingly critical about their usefulness.[75] It is also likely that the varieties of independent directors found among jurisdictions will not diminish.[76] Indeed, they may even expand given that the legal regimes often make adaptations for the local market and address (intentionally or otherwise) the problems unique to those markets.

The transformation that a globally generated norm experiences in the phase of local implementation may look familiar to observers of law reform in emerging market countries – what Halliday conceptualised as its 'recursivity'.[77] This refers to the dynamic process by which law reform initiated by global actors gets compromised, when implemented locally; this may frustrate the aim of the reform. If the frustration is severe enough, the dynamic process returns to the starting point and the global actors start putting pressure on the local actors to commence another round of reform. However, in the case of independent director requirements, the local adaptation is seldom avoidance or compromise of the aimed reform. Rather, independent directors often find unintended roles, but locally meaningful ones, in Asian jurisdictions. It is closer to what the IKEA theory of legal transplants presents as re-contextualisation of 'neutral' concepts taken out of the global reservoir.[78]

After all, the background of corporate governance reform differs from the assumption of Halliday's theory. While he assumes that global actors suggest (or push) law reform to address the problems identified with the specific country, corporate governance reform does not always follow the finding of a structural problem. In many cases, big corporate scandals trigger calls for reform, a phenomenon typically observed in the US but also increasingly across the Asian region.[79] However, even in such cases, whether a scandal is in fact anecdotal or instead rooted in a structural problem is seldom examined – still less, whether independent directors are the best solution to cure the alleged problem. If the reform is an

Under a Team Production Model', 252–253, finding little evidence of positive impacts on financial performance from director independence requirements.

[75] Outlining various academic critiques, see Chapter 2 at IV.2.

[76] See Chapter 3 at III (explaining the driving forces behind the varieties of independent directors in Asia).

[77] T. C. Halliday and B. G. Carruthers, *Bankrupt: Global Lawmaking and Systemic Financial Crisis* (Stanford University Press, 2009).

[78] Michaels, '"One Size Can Fit All": On the Mass Production of Legal Transplants'.

[79] See Chapter 1 at III; Chapter 12 at VIII.

entrepreneurial transplant or legitimacy-generating transplant, there is often no identification of a specific problem that requires the introduction or enhancement of independent director requirements other than the vague reference to global recognition of independent directors as a key to effective corporate governance.

Where there is no identification of a problem, the target or goal of the reform becomes unclear. The requirement of independent directors as exported from a reservoir of global concepts conveniently fits such a situation. Because of global recognition, the government can send a signal to investors that its policymakers and market actors are taking corporate governance seriously. As there is already considerable diversity in the design of independent director requirements, strict compliance with the universally established model is not required (unlike, for example, the legal framework for arbitration, highlighted by Arvind).[80] There is also room for adaptations to meet the demands of local actors, when necessary. Once introduced, independent directors can find roles meaningful in the local market, which in turn contributes to the general acceptance of independent directors. The apparent proliferation of independent directors requirement in Asia, notwithstanding large varieties in institutional and functional settings in each jurisdiction, may reflect the absence of a common and specific problem as well as the vagueness of the goals for reform.

Thus, for the foreseeable future, the process of formulation, decontextualisation and storage in the global reservoir of corporate governance tools, followed by re-contextualisation to adapt to the local market, will continue with independent director requirements in Asia (and probably elsewhere). Instead of convergence in the narrow sense, we will witness continued reform of corporate governance involving constant adjustment to the independent director requirements, ever-growing variety (rather than convergence) in such requirements and occasional intercourse between global and local ideas. It will remain a dynamic process with no distinct common objective, yet an important part of the 'corporate governance obsession' that has arguably paralleled the decline of the state since the 1990s.[81]

[80] Arvind, 'The "Transplant Effect" in Harmonization'.

[81] M. Pargendler, 'The Corporate Governance Obsession' (Stanford Law and Economics Olin Working Paper No. 470, 2015), available at http://ssrn.com/abstract=2491088.

APPENDIX A

Comparative Timelines of Key Developments Relating to Independent Director Requirements in Asia

Chapter 4

Japan's Gradual Reception of Independent Directors: An Empirical and Political-Economic Analysis

Gen Goto, Manabu Matsunaka and Souichirou Kozuka

Chronological list of major regulatory and corporate governance events related to the development/evolution of independent directors

1989–1992	Structural Impediments Initiative
June 1993	Commercial Code amendments, requiring at least one outside *kansayaku* on a large company as mandatory.
1996	Sony introduces senior officers to downsize the board of directors.
December 2001	Amendments to the Special Rules Act, requiring half or more of the *kansayaku* board to be outside *kansayaku*.
May 2002	Amendments to the Special Rules Act, introducing committee-type structure as an option for a large company.
June 2005	Companies Act enacted, Commercial Code's Book II on Corporations abolished.
August 2007	Supreme Court decision on Bulldog Sauce case: upholding the defensive measure against hostile takeover if the measure is introduced by the majority decision at the shareholder meeting.
June 2009	Ministry of Economy, Trade and Industry Study Group on Corporate Governance report on independent directors.

June 2009	FSA Financial System Council, Sectional Committee on Finance report on independent directors.
August 2009	DPJ comes to power in general election.
December 2009	TSE Listing Rules Amendments, requiring at least one independent member on either the board of directors or board of *kansayaku*.
February 2010	The Legislative Council commences deliberations on the amendments to the Companies Act.
November 2011	Olympus scandal revealed.
May 2012	TSE Listing Rules amendments enacted, provide strong recommendation for companies to have at least one independent director.
September 2012	The Legislative Council concludes the deliberations with the adoption of the 'Outline' of the amendments: no mandatory requirement of outside directors.
December 2012	LDP returns to power in general election.
2013	Bill to amend the Companies Act drafted, after having been modified in a few respects by the LDP members: duty to explain 'the reason why having an outside director is inappropriate' at the general shareholders' meeting introduced.
June 2014	Diet approves the Companies Act amendments.
August 2014	Expert group on Corporate Governance Code commences deliberations.
June 2015	Amendments to the Companies Act enter into force; Corporate Governance Code becomes part of the listing requirements, introducing 'comply or explain' rule on having at least two independent directors.
September 2015	FSA sets up the Council of Experts Concerning the Follow-up of Japan's Stewardship Code and Japan's Corporate Governance Code.
January 2016	Ministry of Justice starts unofficial preliminary discussions for the next round of amendments of the Companies Act.

Chapter 5

Korea's Mandatory Independent Directors: Expected and Unexpected Roles

Kyung-Hoon Chun

Chronological list of major regulatory and corporate governance events related to the development/evolution of independent directors

1997–1999	Asian Financial Crisis
February 1998	'Korea: Memorandum on Economic Program' attached to the Letter of Intent between Korean government and the IMF dated 7 February 1998 requires 'listed companies on the Korea Stock Exchange to have at least one outside director'.
February 1998	Securities Listing Rules of the Korea Stock Exchange are amended to require listed companies to have outsiders constitute at least a quarter of their board members.
May 1998	'Updated Memorandum on the Economic Program for the Second Quarterly Review' attached to the 2 May 1998 Letter of Intent between Korean government and the IMF requires 'listed companies on the Korean Stock Exchange to have at least one-fourth of Board of Directors to be outsiders from FY 1999'.
21 January 2000 (Effective from 1 April 2000)	Securities Exchange Act is amended to require that all the listed companies fill at least a quarter of their board seats with the outside directors satisfying certain independence criteria ('independent directors') and that the listed companies with total assets exceeding 2 trillion Won ('large listed companies') have at least three independent directors, and fill at least a half of their board seats with such independent directors. The same amendment also required that the large listed companies establish an audit committee in lieu of the statutory auditor and that at least two-thirds of the audit committee members be independent directors. Further, large listed companies are required to establish 'independent director nomination committees'.

31 December 2003 (Effective from 1 April 2004)	Securities Exchange Act is further amended to require large listed companies to have a majority (as opposed to 'at least a half') of their board members be independent directors. The same amendment also required at least one of the audit committee members to be an expert in accounting or finance, and that the chairperson of the audit committee be an independent director.
30 January 2009 (Effective from 4 February 2009)	Provisions on the independent directors are moved from the Securities Exchange Act to the Korean Commercial Code, with little change in substance. Further, certain independence criteria were provided in the Korean Commercial Code for independent directors of unlisted companies, although it still remained optional for the unlisted companies to have independent directors or not.

Chapter 6

Independent Directors in China: Facts and Reform Proposals

Xin Tang

Chronological list of major regulatory and corporate governance events related to the development/evolution of independent directors

1993	Qingdao Brewery Co., a Mainland China company listed on the Hong Kong Stock Exchange, recruited two independent directors to meet the listing requirements.
1997	The China Securities Regulatory Commission ('CSRC') released the *Guidelines for the Articles of Association of Listed Companies*, which encouraged the listed companies to establish an independent director system.
1999	The National Economic and Trade Commission and the CSRC jointly issued the *Opinions on the Promotion of Overseas Listed Companies on Standardizing Operation and Deepening Reform*, urging the companies listed overseas to establish and gradually improve the outside director and independent director system.

2001	The CSRC issued the *Guiding Opinions on the Establishment of Independent Director System in Listed Companies* ('*CSRC Guiding Opinions*'),that explicitly mandated the establishment of an independent director system in all listed companies. The CSRC also required independent directors to comprise at least one-third of the total directors on the board by 30 June 2003.
2002	The CSRC and the National Economic and Trade Commission issued the *Code of Corporate Governance of Listed Companies*, which reinforced the role of the independent directors in decision making of the board of directors.
2004–2015	From 1 April 2004 to 31 December 2015, the CSRC issued 82 decisions on administrative penalties relating to independent directors, sanctioning a total of 245 independent directors.
2005	The revised *Company Law* confirmed that listed companies have to appoint independent directors.
2006	The CSRC revised the *Guidelines for the Articles of Association of Listed Companies*, and extended the definition of the duties of independent directors.
2008	The No. 1 Intermediate People's Court of Beijing upheld an administrative sanction made by the CSRC against an outside director, addressing the duty of care for directors of listed companies.
2010	Shanghai Stock Exchange released the *Working Guidelines for the Filing and Training of Independent Directors of Listed Companies.*
2011	Shenzhen Stock Exchange released the *Measures for Record-Filing of Independent Directors.*
2014	The China Association for Public Companies released the *Guidelines for the Exercise of Duties of Independent Directors of Public Companies*, that provide detailed provisions on the duties, authorities and exercise of duties of independent directors.

Chapter 7

From Double Board to Unitary Board System: Independent Directors and Corporate Governance Reform in Taiwan

Hsin-Ti Chang, Yu-Hsin Lin and Ying-Hsin Tsai

Chronological list of major regulatory and corporate governance events related to the development/evolution of independent directors

28 March 2006	TSE-listed and OTC-traded companies with paid-up capital of NTD 50 billion (US $1.6 billion) and public companies in the financial industry, such as a financial holding company, bank, securities firm, insurance company and integrated securities firm of TSE-listed or OTC-traded or the financial holding company's subsidiaries, shall appoint independent directors in accordance with its articles of incorporation.
1 November 2006	The Securities and Exchange Act provides that a company that has issued stock may appoint independent directors in accordance with its articles of incorporation.
1 November 2006	The Securities and Exchange Act provides that the establishment of an audit committee is not mandatory, but if it is adopted, it must be composed entirely of independent directors.
24 November 2010	Mandatory requirements for TSE-listed and OTC-traded companies to establish a remuneration committee are enacted.
18 March 2011	The Securities and Exchange Act provides that TSE-listed and OTC-traded companies shall establish a remuneration committee in accordance with these Regulations by 30 September 2011, and shall convene at least one meeting by 31 December 2011 at the latest. However, a company with paid-in capital of less than NTD 10 billion, may establish the committee by 31 December 2011.

22 March 2011 — The Financial Supervisory Commission issued an order requiring TSE-listed and OTC-traded companies with paid-in capital of NTD 10 billion (US $330 million) and public companies in the financial industry, such as a financial holding company, bank, securities firm, insurance company, integrated securities firm and TSE-listed or OTC-traded futures commission merchants, to appoint independent directors in accordance with their articles of incorporation.

20 February 2013 — The Financial Supervisory Commission issued an order requiring TSE-listed and OTC-traded companies with paid-in capital of NTD 50 billion (US $1.6 billion) and public companies in the financial industry, such as a financial holding company, bank, securities firm, insurance company, integrated securities firm and TSE-listed or OTC-traded futures commission merchants, to establish an audit committee to replace the statutory supervisors in accordance with its articles of incorporation.

31 December 2013 — The Financial Supervisory Commission issued an order requiring TSE-listed, OTC-traded companies and public companies in the financial industry, such as banks, insurance companies, securities firms, investment trust enterprises, integrated securities firms, TSE-listed and OTC-traded futures commission merchants to appoint at least two independent directors on the board, and not less than one-fifth of the total number of directors.

Further, in accordance with Article 181-2 of the Securities and Exchange Act, the said order applied to TSE-listed and OTC-traded companies with paid-in capital not more than NTD 10 billion (US $330 million) from the time of expiration of the term currently being served by the directors or statutory supervisors; the order could also be applied after the expiration of the term of being elected in 2014, if the term of current directors or statutory supervisors expires in 2014.

This order superseded the previous order issued by the Financial Supervisory Commission on 22 March 2011.

31 December 2013	The Financial Supervisory Commission issued an order requiring: (A)TSE-listed and OTC-traded companies with paid-in capital over NTD 10 billion (US $330 million) and public companies in the financial industry (except for the wholly owned subsidiaries of a financial holding company), such as banks, insurance companies, securities firms, investment trust enterprises, integrated securities firms, together with TSE-listed and OTC-traded futures commission merchants to establish an audit committee to replace their statutory supervisors; (B)TSE-listed and OTC-traded companies with paid-in capital between NTD 2 billion (US $60 million) to 10 billion (US $330 million) were required to establish the audit committee from 1 January 2017. Further, in accordance with Article 181-2 of the SEA, if the term of current directors and statutory supervisors has not expired, the order is provided as follows: (A)If the term of current directors and statutory supervisors expires in 2014, this order will not apply until the term of the 2014-elected directors and statutory supervisors ends. If companies are TSE-listed and OTC-traded non-financial companies with paid-in capital more than NTD 10 billion (US $330 million) but not more than NTD 50 billion (US $1.6 billion), investment trust enterprises, integrated securities firms that are non-TSE-listed or non-OTC-traded companies or are not the subsidiaries of a financial holding company, or TSE-listed and OTC-traded futures commission merchants, this order will not apply until the expiration of the term of current directors and statutory supervisors; and (B)For TSE-listed and OTC-traded non-financial companies with paid-in capital more than NTD 2 billion (US $66 million) but not more than NTD 10 billion (US $330 million), if the term of current directors and statutory supervisors will not expire before 2017, this order will not apply until the expiration of the term. This order superseded the previous order issued by the Financial Supervisory Commission on 20 February 2013.

Chapter 8

Independent Directors in Hong Kong

Vivienne Bath

Chronological list of major regulatory and corporate governance events related to the development/evolution of independent directors

October 1987	Hong Kong Stock Market and Futures Markets closed for four days as a result of a widespread market crash.
November 1987; May 1988	A Securities Review Committee is appointed to review the Hong Kong Stock and Futures Exchange and regulatory bodies. The Report of the Securities Review committee is presented in May 1988 (the Hay Davison Report).
May 1989	The Securities and Futures Commission (SFC) was established pursuant to the Securities and Futures Ordinance.
April 1990	The Basic Law of the Hong Kong Special Administrative Region is adopted by the National People's Congress of the People's Republic of China.
December 1992	The Cadbury Report was issued, followed by significant developments to corporate governance.
June 1993	A Memorandum of Regulatory Cooperation is signed between the China Securities Regulatory Commission, the Shanghai Stock Exchange, the Shenzhen Stock Exchange, the Securities and Futures Exchange and the Stock Exchange of Hong Kong.
July 1993	The first listing of a Chinese company on the Stock Exchange of Hong Kong occurs – Tsingdao Brewery Co Ltd.
November 1993	A requirement is introduced into the Listing Rules that each listed company have two independent non-executive directors (Rule 3.10), with a further requirement that the Exchange be empowered to require more than two independent directors if it is of the opinion that the size of the board or other circumstances justify it (Rule 3.15).
December 1993	The Exchange publishes a Code of Best Practice, which was a set of voluntary guidelines for the board of directors.

1 July 1997	Hong Kong becomes a Special Administrative Region of the People's Republic of China.
July 1997	Asian Financial Crisis triggered by collapse of Thai currency.
June 1998	The Exchange issues a consultation paper focused on disclosure requirements for controlling shareholders and improving the rules on connected transactions.
January 2002	The Exchange issues a further consultation paper in relation to corporate governance.
March 2004	The Exchange requires that a board of a listed company have at least three independent directors.
January 2005	The Corporate Governance Code comes into effect.
October 2011	The Listing Rules are changed to require that one-third of the board be constituted by independent directors, effective 1 January 2012.
March 2014	New Companies Ordinance comes into effect, incorporating provisions related to the duties of directors.

Chapter 9

Independent Directors in Singapore: A Corporate Governance Outlier?

Dan W. Puchniak and Luh Luh Lan

Chronological list of major regulatory and corporate governance events related to the development/evolution of independent directors

1989	The Companies Act is amended to required all listed companies in Singapore to have an audit committee with at least three members, a majority of whom must be independent from the company's executive directors and exercise independent judgement. No definition for 'independence' is provided.
1997–1999	Asian Financial Crisis
2000	The government establishes the private-sector-led Corporate Governance Committee (CGC) to review global corporate governance standards and suggest corporate governance reforms.
	CGC proposes draft UK-style 'comply or explain' code suggesting that American-style independent directors make up one-third of the board in listed companies.

2001	Code of Corporate Governance (2001 Code) that was proposed by the CGC is accepted by the government.
2002	The Council of Corporate Disclosure and Governance (CCDG) is set up to enhance the corporate governance framework and prescribe accounting standards in Singapore.
	S-chips start listing on the SGX.
2003	Comply or explain regime under the 2001 Code becomes mandatory for all listed companies.
2005	The CCDG undertakes a review of the 2001 Code and a revised Code (2005 Code) was issued – but the government rejected the CCDG's proposal to tighten the definition of independence to require independence from the controlling shareholder.
2007	CCDG is dissolved and the task of overseeing corporate governance of listed companies is transferred to MAS and the SGX.
	170 S-chips listed on the SGX.
2008	SGX amends its listing rules to require foreign issuers to have at least two independent directors who are Singapore residents on a permanent basis.
2008–2009	First wave of S-chip scandals.
2010	Corporate Governance Council is established.
2010–2011	Second wave of S-chip scandals.
2011	Corporate Governance Council recommends tightening the definition of independence to require independence from shareholders holding 5 per cent or more of the company's shares.
2012	Government issues a revised code (2012 Code) which tightens the definition of independence by requiring independence from shareholders holding 10 per cent or more of the company's shares – other aspects of independent director system also strengthened in the 2012 Code.
2013	SGX and CSRC institute Direct Listing Framework for Chinese companies that requires a 'double-vetting process' which is aimed to solve S-chip problem.
2015	All listed companies must 'comply or explain' under the new definition of independence in the 2012 Code requiring independence from shareholders holding 10 per cent or more of the company's shares.

Chapter 10

Board Independence in India: From Form to Function?

Vikramaditya Khanna and Umakanth Varottil

Chronological list of major regulatory and corporate governance events related to the development/evolution of independent directors

1998	A voluntary code on 'Desirable Corporate Governance' recommended by the Confederation of Indian Industry (CII) that introduced independent directors in India for the first time.
2000	The report of the Kumar Mangalam Birla Committee recommended adoption of corporate governance norms (including board independence) through regulation.
2000	Clause 49 introduced into the listing agreement mandating board independence for large listed companies.
2003	Committee on Corporate Governance headed by Narayana Murthy recommended tightening the corporate governance norms, including aspects relating to independent directors.
2004	Clause 49 amended to make board independence more stringent, although these amendments took effect only in 2006.
2005	Expert Committee on Company Law headed by J. J. Irani recommended a new companies' legislation in place of the Companies Act, 1956.
2008–2009	A new Companies Bill was presented in Parliament.
2009	The occurrence of a major corporate governance scandal at Satyam Computers that generated greater debate on governance norms in India.
2011	Another version of the Companies Bill introduced in Parliament after substantial debate, which included extensive provisions on independent directors.
2013	Companies Act, 2013 enacted.
2014	The provisions relating to independent directors in Companies Act, 2013 came into force (1 April 2014).
2014	Clause 49 of the listing agreement amended to bring it substantially in line with the Companies Act, 2013 (with effect from 1 October 2014).
2014	Companies (Appointment and Qualification of Directors) Rules, 2014 promulgated under the Companies Act, 2013.

Chapter 11

The Rise and Unlikely Demise of Independent Directors in Australia

Fady Aoun and Luke Nottage

Chronological list of major regulatory and corporate governance events related to the development/evolution of independent directors

May 1991	Following corporate failures in the late 1980s, the Bosch Committee Report recommends that listed companies have independent directors on their boards as well as their audit, remuneration and nomination committees.
September 1994	The ASX proposes a new Listing Rule requiring companies to 'comply or explain' with its 'Schedule of Corporate Governance Practices'. The ASX invites public comment on Schedule requirements for independent directors.
1996	Following negative responses to the 'comply or explain' regime, the ASX settles on a weaker disclosure regime, requiring listed companies merely to disclose their corporate governance practices.
2001	Australia experiences another wave of corporate failures, including One.Tel and HIH. The collapse of HIH is the largest corporate failure in Australian history.
August 2002	The ASX Corporate Governance Council is formed, bringing together 21 groups 'to develop an industry-wide, supportable and supported framework for corporate governance which could provide a practical guide for listed companies, their investors, the wider market and the Australian community'.
March 2003	The first edition of the ASX's Corporate Governance Principles is released (applicable in the listed company's first financial year commencing after 1 January 2003). Under Listing Rule 4.10, on an 'if not, why not' basis, all listed companies must disclose in their annual reports whether and how they have followed these Principles. They recommend that a majority (and the chair) of the board should be independent directors, and that nomination, remuneration and audit committees be established with a majority of independent directors. However, a new Listing Rule 12.7 makes such audit committees mandatory for companies listed on the S&P/ASX All Ordinaries Index.

April 2003	The Royal Commission into the collapse of HIH hands down its report. The chair of the Commission, Justice Neville Owen, expresses reservations about the necessity and desirability of independent directors.
2006	APRA requires banks and other financial institutions to comply with ASX criteria for director and committee independence without the leeway of an 'if not, why not' approach.
August 2007	The ASX releases the second edition of its Corporate Governance Principles, making only minor changes to independent director requirements.
December 2009	The Productivity Commission publishes its final report on executive remuneration, recommending a 'two strikes and re-election resolution'. A version of the recommendation is implemented by legislation in June 2011.
April 2010	The ASX responds to concerns about executive remuneration by releasing a draft of amendments to its Corporate Governance Principles, as well as revised Listing Rules. Listing Rule 12.8 mandates that an entity listed in the S&P/ASX 300 Index must have a remuneration committee comprised solely of non-executive directors (of whom a majority must be independent, under the 'if not, why not' basis required by the ASX Principles).
April 2010	CAMAC releases a report entitled *Guidance for Directors*. The report concludes that there is no need for a new code of conduct for directors, but that the ASX should review its principles and recommendations in light of international developments.
July 2010	APRA requires Australian financial institutions to have a Capital Board Remuneration Committee with a majority of independent directors and an independent director as chair.
2013	A controversial econometric study co-authored by Professor Peter Swan concludes that over AUS $69 billion in corporate value was destroyed between 2003 and 2011 because of independent director requirements.

Appendix B

Legislative Appendix: Key Provisions Relating to Independent Director Requirements in Asia

Chapter 4 – Japan

Article 2 of the Company Act (Definitions)

For the purposes of this Act, the meaning of the term mentioned in the following items shall be as defined in the respective item.

(15) Outside director means a director of a joint stock company that:

a. is not an executive director (which means here and hereinafter a director of a company that meets either of the items under Article 363, Paragraph 1, or other director that engages in the execution of the company's business), executive officer or *Prokura* or other employee (hereinafter as 'executive director etc.') of the company or its subsidiary, or has never been an executive director etc. of the company or its subsidiary during the ten years before becoming director;

b. had, if the person has ever been a director, accounting advisor (in case an incorporated firm is an accounting advisor, its member in charge of the service), or statutory auditor of the company or its subsidiary (excluding a person that has ever been its executive director etc.), never been an executive director etc. of the company or its subsidiary during the ten years before becoming director, accounting advisor or statutory auditor;

c. is not a parent company etc. (only applicable to a natural person) or director, executive officer or *Prokura* or other employee of the parent company etc.;

d. is not an executive director etc. of the subsidiary etc. of the company's parent company etc. (excluding the company itself and its subsidiary); or

e. is not a spouse or a relative within the second degree of a director, executive officer or *Prokura* or other senior employee of the company or its parent company etc. (only applicable to a natural person).

(16) Outside statutory auditor means a statutory auditor of a joint stock company that:
   a. has never been a director, accounting advisor (in case an incorporated firm is an accounting advisor, meaning its member in charge of the service here and in item b), executive officer or *Prokura* or other employee of the company or its subsidiary during the ten years before becoming a statutory auditor;
   b. had, if the person has ever been a statutory auditor of the company or its subsidiary during the ten years before becoming an outside statutory auditor, never been a director, accounting advisor, executive officer, or *Prokura* or other employee of the company or its subsidiary during the ten years before becoming statutory auditor;
   c. is not a parent company etc. (only applicable to a natural person) or director, statutory auditor, executive officer or *Prokura* or other employee of the parent company etc.;
   d. is not an executive director etc. of the subsidiary etc. of the company's parent company etc. (excluding the company itself and its subsidiary); or
   e. is not a spouse or a relative within the second degree of a director or *Prokura* or other senior employee of the company or its parent company etc. (only applicable to a natural person).

Article 326 of the Company Act (Organs Other Than the Shareholders' Meeting)

(1) A joint stock company shall have one or more director(s).
(2) A joint stock company may, by so providing in the articles of incorporation, have a board of directors, accounting advisor, statutory auditor, board of statutory auditors, accounting auditor, audit and supervisory committee and nomination and other committees.

Article 327-2 of the Company Act (Disclosure of the Reason Why There Is No Outside Director)

If a company with board of statutory auditors (only applicable to a public company that is a large company) that must file an annual securities report with the Prime Minister's Office with respect to the shares that it issues pursuant to Article 24, Paragraph 1, of the Financial Products and Exchanges Act has no outside director, its director shall explain the reason why it is inappropriate to have an outside director at the annual shareholders' meeting.

Article 328 of the Company Act (The Duty of a Large Company to Have a Board of Statutory Auditors etc.)

(1) A large company (excluding one that is not a public company, a company with audit and supervisor committee and a company with nomination and other committees) shall have a board of statutory auditors and an accounting auditor.
(2) A large company that is not a public company shall have an accounting auditor.

Article 331 of the Company Act (Qualifications of Directors)

(6) In a company with audit and supervisory committee, there shall be three or more directors serving as member of the audit and supervisory committee, majority of which shall be outside directors.

Article 335 of the Company Act (Qualifications of Statutory Auditor)

(3) In a company with the board of statutory auditors, there shall be three or more statutory auditors, half or more of which shall be outside statutory auditors.

Article 400 of the Company Act (Appointment of Committee Members)

(1) A nomination committee, audit committee or remuneration committee (in this article, the following article and Article 911, Paragraph 3, item 23, lit.b, as 'each committee') comprises of three or more members.
(2) Members of each committee are appointed by the decision of the board of directors from among the directors.
(3) The majority of each committee shall be outside directors.

Article 25 of Law No. 90 of 2014 (Review)

After two years of entry into force of this law, the government shall review the regulations on corporate governance, considering the changes in social and economic situations, including how outside directors are appointed, and, if found necessary, introduce mandatory requirement of outside directors or otherwise take appropriate measures.

Rule 436-2 of the Tokyo Stock Exchange's Securities Listing Regulations (Securing Independent Director(s)/Auditor(s))

(1) For the protection of general investors, an issuer of listed domestic stocks must secure at least one independent director/auditor (meaning an outside director (meaning an entity falling under an outside director prescribed in Article 2, Item 15 of the Companies Act who is an outside director/auditor prescribed in Article 2, Paragraph 3, Item 5 of the Ordinance for Enforcement of the Companies Act (the Ordinance of the Ministry of Justice No. 12 of 2006)) or outside auditor (meaning an entity falling under an outside auditor prescribed in Article 2, Item 16 of the Companies Act who is an outside director/auditor prescribed in Article 2, Paragraph 3, Item 5 of the Ordinance for Enforcement of the Companies Act) who is unlikely to have conflicts of interest with general investors; hereinafter the same).
(2) The Exchange shall specify the necessary items for securing an independent director(s)/auditor(s) in the Enforcement Rules.
(3) Notwithstanding the provisions of Paragraph 1, a JASDAQ-listed domestic company in the Growth sub-division (hereinafter referred to as a 'Growth-listed domestic company') shall secure at least 1 independent director/auditor by the day of the general shareholders meeting pertaining to the first fiscal year that closes for the first time after the listing.

Rule 445-4 of the Tokyo Stock Exchange's Securities Listing Regulations (Securing Independent Directors/Auditors as Directors on the Board)

An issuer of listed domestic stocks must make efforts to secure at least one independent director/auditor as a member of its board of directors.

Guideline III.5 of the Guidelines Concerning Listed Company Compliance by the Tokyo Stock Exchange (Measures against Violation of Code of Corporate Conduct)

In the case of a violation by a listed company of the provisions of Chapter 4, Section 4, Sub-section 1 of the Regulations, a decision on public announcement pursuant to the provisions of Rule 508, Paragraph 1 of the Regulations, as well as a decision on whether or not to impose the listing agreement violation penalty pursuant to the provisions of Rule 509 of the Regulations, shall be made in comprehensive consideration of (i) the matters prescribed in the classifications referred to in the following (1) to (8) and (ii) the details, the background, the cause, and the actual state of affairs relating to said violation, as well as the state of implementation of measures such as a regulatory action taken by the Exchange in response to said violation and any other circumstances.

Guideline III.5.(3)-2 of the Guidelines Concerning Listed Company Compliance by the Tokyo Stock Exchange (The Provisions of Rule 436-2 of the Regulations)

The status of a person(s) who is reported to the Exchange as being an independent director(s)/auditor(s) by the issuer of a listed domestic stock pursuant to the provisions of Rule 436-2 of the Enforcement Rules when such person falls under any of the following a. to e.;

a. A person who executes business of the parent company or fellow subsidiary of said company;
b. A person for which said company is a major client or a person who executes business for such person, or a major client of said company or a person who executes business for such client;
c. A consultant, accounting professional or legal professional (in the case of a group such as a juridical person or association, including persons belonging to such group) who receives a large amount of money or other asset other than remuneration for directorship/auditorship from said company; or
d. A person who has recently fallen under any of a. to the preceding c.;
e. A close relative of a person referred to in any of the following (a) to (c) (excluding those of insignificance);
   (a) A person referred to in a. to the preceding d.;
   (b) A person who executes business of said company or its subsidiary (including directors who do not execute business or accounting advisors (when any of such accounting advisors is a juridical person, including any member thereof who is in charge of such advisory affairs) in the case where said company designates its outside auditor(s) as an independent auditor(s)); or
   (c) Persons who have recently fallen under the preceding (b).

Chapter 5 – Korea

Article 382 of the Korean Commercial Code (Appointment of Directors, Relationship with Company and Outside Directors)

(1) Directors shall be appointed at a general shareholders' meeting.
(2) [omitted]
(3) Outside directors are directors who are not engaged in the regular business of the relevant company, and do not correspond to any of the following subparagraphs. Where any outside director falls under any of the following subparagraphs, he/she shall be removed from office:
   1. Directors, executive directors and employees who are engaged in the regular business of the relevant company, or directors, auditors, executive directors and employees who have engaged in the regular business of the relevant company within the latest two years;
   2. The principal, his/her spouse, lineal ascendants, and lineal descendants, in cases where the largest shareholder is a natural person;
   3. Directors, auditors, executive directors and employees of the corporation, in cases where the largest shareholder is a corporation;
   4. The spouses, lineal ascendants, and lineal descendants of directors, auditors and executive directors;
   5. The directors, auditors, executive directors and employees of a parent company or a subsidiary company of the relevant company;
   6. Directors, auditors, executive directors and employees of a corporation which has a significant interest in the relevant company, such as business relations with the company;
   7. Directors, auditors, executive directors and employees of another company for which directors, executive directors and employees of the relevant company serve as directors and executive directors.

Article 542-8 of the Korean Commercial Code (Appointment of Outside Directors)

(1) A listed company shall ensure that outside directors comprise no less than one fourth of the total number of directors except in cases determined by Presidential Decree in light of the scale of assets; Provided, That listed companies determined by Presidential Decree

based on the scale of assets, etc., shall appoint three or more outside directors and the number of outside directors shall account for more than half of the total directors.

(2) No outside director of a listed company shall fall under any of the following subparagraphs as well as any subparagraph of Article 382 (3), and if he/she falls under any of the following subparagraphs, he/she shall be removed from his/her office:

1. A minor, incompetent, or quasi-incompetent;
2. A person adjudicated bankrupt and who has not yet reinstated;
3. A person for whom two years have not yet elapsed since his or her imprisonment without prison labor or a heavier punishment was completely executed or exempted;
4. A person for whom two years have not yet elapsed since he was dismissed or removed from office after he/she violated an Act separately determined by Presidential Decree;
5. In cases where a shareholder of the listed company and persons who have a special relationship with the shareholder as prescribed by Presidential Decree (hereinafter referred to as 'specially related persons') own the largest number of shares, based on the total number of issued and outstanding shares other than nonvoting shares, such shareholder (hereinafter referred to as the 'largest shareholder') and his/her specially related persons;
6. A shareholder who owns more than 10 percent of the total number of issued and outstanding shares other than nonvoting shares for his/her own account regardless of in whose name the shares are held, or exerts *de facto* influence on important matters related to the management of the listed company, including the appointment and dismissal of directors, executive directors or auditors, and his/her spouse, lineal ascendants and lineal descendants (hereinafter referred to as a 'major shareholder');
7. A person determined by Presidential Decree, who has difficulty faithfully performing any of his/her duty as an outside director, or who may have an influence on the management of the listed company.

(3) In cases where the number of outside directors does not meet the quorum required for the establishment of the board of directors under paragraph (1) due to any cause such as resignation or death of any outside director, a listed company under paragraph (1) shall appoint outside directors at the first general meeting of shareholders

convened after such cause has occurred, to satisfy the requirements prescribed in paragraph (1).

(4) A listed company under the proviso to paragraph (1) shall establish a committee referred to in Article 393-2 (hereafter referred to as the 'committee for recommending candidates for outside directors' in this Article) to recommend candidates for outside directors. In such cases, the committee shall ensure that outside directors comprises a majority of the total number of committee members.

(5) When a listed company under the proviso to paragraph (1) intends to appoint outside directors at a general meeting of shareholders, the company shall appoint outside directors from among candidates recommended by the committee for recommending candidates for outside directors. In such cases, when the committee recommends candidates for outside directors, the candidates recommended by a shareholder who is eligible to exercise the rights provided for in Article 363-2 (1), 542-6 (1) and (2) six weeks prior to the date set for a general meeting of shareholders (in cases of an ordinary general meeting of shareholders, referring to the date of the relevant year that corresponds to the date of an ordinary general meeting of shareholders of the immediately preceding year) shall be included.

Article 542-11 of the Korean Commercial Code (Audit Committees)

(1) A listed company determined by Presidential Decree in light of the scale of assets, etc. shall establish an audit committee.

(2) The audit committee of a listed company under paragraph (1) shall meet the requirements of Article 415-2 (2) and the following subparagraphs:

1. One or more members of the committee shall be an accounting or financing expert as determined by Presidential Decree;
2. The representative of the committee shall be an outside director.

(3) No person who falls under any of the subparagraphs of Article 542-10 (2) shall be a member of the audit committee who is not an outside director of a listed company under paragraph (1), and he/she shall be removed from office when falling under any of such cases.

(4) In cases where the number of outside directors fails to meet the quorum required for the establishment of an audit committee set forth in the following subparagraphs due to any cause such as resignation or death of any outside director as member of the audit committee, a listed company shall ensure that the requirements are met at the

first general meeting of shareholders convened after such cause has occurred;

1. Requirements set forth in the subparagraphs of paragraph (2) and Article 415-2 (2), in cases where the listed company has established the audit committee under paragraph (1);
2. Requirements set forth in Article 415-2 (2), in cases where the listed company has established the audit committee under Article 415-2 (1).

Article 542-12 of the Korean Commercial Code (Constitution, etc. of Audit Committees)

(1) In cases of a listed company under Article 542-11 (1), notwithstanding the provisions of Article 393-2, a general meeting of shareholders shall have the authority to appoint or dismiss members of an audit committee.

(2) A listed company under Article 542-11 (1) shall appoint members of its audit committee from among directors appointed by a general meeting of shareholders.

(3) In cases where the total amount of voting stocks of a listed company held by the largest shareholder, his/her specially related persons, and other persons determined by Presidential Decree exceeds three percent of the total number of shares issued and outstanding, excluding nonvoting stocks, such shareholder may not exercise his/her voting rights on the stocks in excess when appointing or dismissing members of the audit committee who are neither auditors nor outside directors: Provided, That a lower ratio of holding shares may be determined in the articles of association.

(4) Any shareholder who has stocks in excess of three percent of the total number of issued stocks other than nonvoting rights of a listed company determined by Presidential Decree, may not exercise his/her voting rights on the stocks in excess when appointing members of the audit committee as outside directors: Provided, That a lower ratio of holding shares may be determined in the articles of association.

(5) When a listed company intends to submit a proposal on appointment or remuneration of auditors as an agenda item for a general meeting of shareholders, the company shall propose and resolve the

proposal separately from a proposal on appointment or remuneration of directors.

(6) Any auditor of a listed company and an audit committee, notwithstanding the provisions of Article 447-4 (1), may submit an audit and inspection report to directors at least one week prior to the date set for a general meeting of shareholders.

Chapter 6 – China

Article 122 of the Company Law

A listed company shall have independent directors, who shall be subject to any specific measures of the State Council.

Preface to the Guidelines for the Establishment of an Independent Directors System by Listed Companies

The following guiding opinions on the establishment of a system of independent outside directors (Independent Directors) by listed companies are put forward in order to further improve the corporate governance structures and promote the standardized operation of listed companies:

Article 1 of the Guidelines for the Establishment of an Independent Directors System by Listed Companies (Listed Companies Shall Establish an Independent Director System)

1. The term 'Independent Director of a listed company' means a director who does not hold any position in the company other than director and who has no relationship with the listed company engaging him or its principal shareholders that could hinder his making independent and objective judgments.
2. An Independent Director has a fiduciary obligation and an obligation of diligence toward the listed company and all its shareholders. An Independent Director shall, pursuant to the requirements of the relevant laws and regulations, these Guiding Opinions and the company's articles of association, conscientiously perform his duties and responsibilities, safeguard the company's overall interests and, in particular, pay attention that the lawful rights and interests of small and medium shareholders are not prejudiced. An

Independent Director shall perform his duties and responsibilities independently, without the interference of the principal shareholders or the persons in actual control of, or other entities or individuals that have a material interest in, the listed company. In principle, an Independent Director shall not simultaneously hold the position of Independent Director in more than five listed companies and he shall ensure that he has sufficient time and energy to effectively perform his duties and responsibilities as an Independent Director.

3. Each listed company in China shall amend its articles of association and engage suitable persons as Independent Directors in accordance with the requirements hereof. At least one of the Independent Directors shall be a professional accountant … (A)t least one-third of the members of the board of directors shall be Independent Directors. …

Article 2 of the Guidelines for the Establishment of an Independent Directors System by Listed Companies (An Independent Director Shall Have the Qualifications Required to Exercise His Functions and Powers as Such)

A person holding the position of Independent Director shall fulfill the basic conditions set forth below:

1. Having the qualifications to hold the position of Independent Director in a listed company in accordance with laws, administrative regulations and other relevant regulations;
2. Being independent as required herein;
3. Having a basic knowledge of the operation of listed companies and being familiar with related laws, administrative regulations and rules;
4. Having not less than five years' experience in the law or economics or other work experience required for performing the duties and responsibilities of an Independent Director; …

Article 3 of the Guidelines for the Establishment of an Independent Directors System by Listed Companies (Independent Directors Must Be Independent)

The following persons may not hold the position of Independent Director:

1. Persons holding a position in the listed company or a subsidiary thereof and their lineal relatives and major social relations (the term 'lineal relatives' meaning spouses, parents, children, etc.; and the term 'major social relations' meaning siblings, parents-in-law, children-in-law, siblings' spouses, spouse's siblings, etc.);
2. Natural person shareholders who directly or indirectly hold not less than 1% of the issued shares of the listed company or who rank in the top ten shareholders of the listed company, and their lineal relatives;
3. Persons who hold positions in entities that directly or indirectly hold not less than 5% of the issued shares of the listed company or that rank in the top five shareholders of the listed company, and their lineal relatives;
4. persons who, at some time in the previous year, have fallen into one of the three categories listed above;
5. Persons who provide financial, legal, consultancy or other such services to the listed company or its subsidiaries;
6. Other persons specified in the company's articles of association;
7. Other persons determined by the CSRC.

Article 4 of the Guidelines for the Establishment of an Independent Directors System by Listed Companies (The Nomination, Election and Replacement of Independent Directors Shall Be Conducted in a Legal and Standardised Manner)

1. A listed company's board of directors, supervisory board and shareholders who individually or together hold not less than 1% of the shares in the listed company may nominate candidates for Independent Director. Such directors will be decided through election by the shareholders' general meeting.
2. [omitted]
3. A listed company shall simultaneously submit the relevant materials on all the nominees to the CSRC, the CSRC agency of the place where the company is located and the stock exchange where the company is listed before the holding of a shareholders' general meeting at which an Independent Director is to be elected. …
4. The term of office of Independent Directors will be the same as that of the other directors of the listed company. At the expiration of their

terms, they may continue to serve if re-elected, but the additional time in office may not exceed six years.

5. [omitted]

Article 5 of the Guidelines for the Establishment of an Independent Directors System by Listed Companies (Listed Companies Shall Put the Functions of Independent Directors into Full Play)

In order that the advantage of having Independent Directors is fully exploited, in addition to the functions and powers granted directors under the Company Law and other relevant laws and regulations, listed companies shall grant Independent Directors the following special functions and powers:

1. Major related-party transactions (namely proposed related-party transactions between the listed company and a connected person with a total value of more than CNY 3 million or more than 5% of the listed company's most recently audited net asset value) shall be submitted to the board of directors for deliberation after the approval of the Independent Directors:
   (1) Before rendering their judgment, Independent Directors may engage an intermediary organization to issue an independent financial consultant report for use as a basis for rendering their judgment;
   (2) Proposing the engagement or dismissal of an accounting firm to the board of directors;
   (3) Proposing to the board of directors the convening of an extraordinary shareholders' general meeting;
   (4) Proposing the convening of a meeting of the board of directors;
   (5) Independently engaging external auditing institutions and consultancies; and
   (6) Openly soliciting shareholders' voting rights before the holding of a shareholders' general meeting;
2. Independent Directors shall obtain the consent of at least half of all the Independent Directors before exercising the afore-mentioned functions and powers.
3. [omitted]

Article 6 of the Guidelines for the Establishment of an Independent Directors System by Listed Companies (Independent Directors Shall Express Independent Opinions on Material Matters of the Listed Company)

1. In addition to performing the duties and responsibilities mentioned above, an Independent Director shall express his independent opinion to the board of directors or the shareholders' general meeting on the following matters:
   (1) The nomination, appointment and removal of directors;
   (2) The engagement or dismissal of senior management personnel;
   (3) The remuneration of the company's directors and senior management personnel;
   (4) Existing or new loans totaling more than CNY 3 million or more than 5% of the listed company's most recently audited net asset value extended to the listed company by its shareholders, persons in actual control or affiliates [or similar transactions between these] …
   (5) matters that may, in an Independent Director's opinion, prejudice the rights and interests of small and medium shareholders …
2. [omitted]

Article 7 of the Guidelines for the Establishment of an Independent Directors System by Listed Companies (Listed Companies Shall Provide the Necessary Conditions to Ensure That the Independent Directors Effectively Exercise Their Functions and Powers)

1. Listed companies shall ensure that their Independent Directors enjoy the same right-to-know as other directors. For any matters that require the decision of the board of directors, listed companies must give Independent Directors prior notice by the statutory deadline and provide them sufficient information. If an Independent Director is of the opinion that the information provided is insufficient, he may ask for further information. If two or more Independent Directors are of the opinion that the information provided is insufficient or the arguments made are unclear they may jointly propose to the board of directors in writing that the meeting of the board or the deliberations on the matter in question be postponed. The board of directors shall accept such a proposal. …
2. Listed companies shall provide the working conditions necessary for their Independent Directors to perform their duties and responsibilities. …
3. When an Independent Director is exercising his functions and powers, the relevant personnel of the listed company shall actively cooperate with him and may not refuse to do so, hinder him, conceal

information from him or interfere with his independently exercising his functions and powers.

4. The expenses incurred by Independent Directors when engaging intermediary organizations … shall be borne by the listed company.
5. Listed companies shall provide an appropriate allowance to their Independent Directors. …
6. Listed companies may establish necessary Independent Director liability insurance systems in order to mitigate the risks that may arise in the normal performance by Independent Directors of their duties and responsibilities.

Article 49 of the Code of Corporate Governance for Listed Companies

A listed company shall introduce independent directors to its board of directors in accordance with relevant regulations. Independent directors shall be independent from the listed company that employs them and the company's major shareholders. An independent director may not hold any other position apart from independent director in the listed company.

Article 50 of the Code of Corporate Governance for Listed Companies

The independent directors shall bear the duties of good faith and due diligence toward the listed company and all the shareholders. They shall … protect the overall interests of the company, and shall be especially concerned with protecting the interests of minority shareholders from being infringed. Independent directors shall carry out their duties independently and shall not subject themselves to the influence of the company's major shareholders, actual controllers, or other entities or persons who are interested parties of the listed company.

Article 51 of the Code of Corporate Governance for Listed Companies

Relevant laws and regulations shall be complied with for matters such as the qualifications, procedure of election and replacement, and duties of independent directors.

Article 70 of the Code of Corporate Governance for Listed Companies

The evaluation of the directors and management personnel shall be conducted by the board of directors or by the remuneration and appraisal committee of the board of directors. The evaluation of the performance of independent directors and supervisors shall be conducted through a combination of self-review and peer review.

Summary of the Guidelines for the Exercise of Duties of Independent Directors of Public Companies

This self-regulatory organization guideline consists of 48 articles divided in six chapters, covering detailed provisions on the general principles, duties, authorities and exercise of duties of independent directors, conditions required to be met for independent directors to participate in board meetings, and supplementary provisions. The Guidelines set out explicit provisions on the duties and authorities of the listed company independent directors.

Summary of the Working Guidelines for the Filing and Training of Independent Directors of Listed Companies on Shanghai Stock Exchange

These Guidelines stipulate the duty for companies listed on the Shanghai Stock Exchange to inform the exchange before the election of an independent director. If the Shanghai Stock Exchange raises objections against the candidate she may not be elected.

Chapter 7 – Taiwan

Article 14-2 of the Securities and Exchange Act (Appointment and Qualification of Independent Directors)

A company that has issued stock in accordance with this Act may appoint independent directors in accordance with its articles of incorporation. The Competent Authority, however, shall as necessary in view of the company's scale, shareholder structure, type of operations, and other essential factors, require it to appoint independent directors, not less than two in number and not less than one-fifth of the total number of directors.

Independent directors shall possess professional knowledge and there shall be restrictions on their shareholdings and the positions they may concurrently hold. They shall maintain independence within the scope of their directorial duties, and may not have any direct or indirect interest in the company. Regulations governing the professional qualifications, restrictions on shareholdings and concurrent positions held, assessment of independence, method of nomination, and other matters for compliance with respect to independent directors shall be prescribed by the Competent Authority.

Given any of the following circumstances, a person may not act as an independent director, or if already acting in such capacity, shall be dismissed:

1. Any circumstance set out in a subparagraph of Article 30 of the Company Act.
2. The director is a government agency, juristic person, or representative thereof, and was elected in accordance with Article 27 of the Company Act.
3. The person fails to meet the qualifications for independent director set forth in the preceding paragraph.

Transfer of an independent director's shareholdings is not subject to the provisions of the latter part of paragraph 1 or of paragraph 3, Article 197, of the Company Act.

When an independent director is dismissed for any reason, resulting in a number of directors lower than that required under paragraph 1 or the company's articles of incorporation, a by-election for independent director shall be held at the next following shareholders meeting. When all independent directors have been dismissed, the company shall convene a special shareholders meeting to hold a by-election within 60 days from the date on which the situation arose.

Article 14-3 of the Securities and Exchange Act (Matters Required to Be Submitted to Board of Directors for Resolution and Adoption)

When a company has selected independent directors as set forth in paragraph 1 of the preceding article, then the following matters shall be submitted to the board of directors for approval by resolution unless approval has been obtained from the Competent Authority; when an independent director has a dissenting opinion or qualified opinion, it shall be noted in the minutes of the directors meeting:

1. Adoption or amendment of an internal control system pursuant to Article 14-1.
2. Adoption or amendment, pursuant to Article 36-1, of handling procedures for financial or operational actions of material significance, such as acquisition or disposal of assets, derivatives trading, extension of monetary loans to others, or endorsements or guarantees for others.
3. A matter bearing on the personal interest of a director.

4. A material asset or derivatives transaction.
5. A material monetary loan, endorsement, or provision of guarantee.
6. The offering, issuance, or private placement of any equity-type securities.
7. The hiring or dismissal of an attesting CPA, or the compensation given thereto.
8. The appointment or discharge of a financial, accounting, or internal auditing officer.
9. Any other material matter so required by the Competent Authority.

Article 14-4 of the Securities and Exchange Act (Establishment of Either Audit Committee or Supervisor)

A company that has issued stock in accordance with this Act shall establish either an audit committee or a supervisor. The Competent Authority may, however, in view of the company's scale, type of operations, or other essential considerations, order it to establish an audit committee in lieu of a supervisor; the relevant regulations shall be prescribed by the Competent Authority.

The audit committee shall be composed of the entire number of independent directors. It shall not be fewer than three persons in number, one of whom shall be convener, and at least one of whom shall have accounting or financial expertise.

For a company that has established an audit committee, the provisions regarding supervisors in this Act, the Company Act, and other laws and regulations shall apply mutatis mutandis to the audit committee.

The following provisions of the Company Act shall apply mutatis mutandis with regard to independent directors who are members of the audit committee: Article 200; Articles 213 – 215; Article 216, paragraphs 1, 3, and 4; Article 218, paragraphs 1 and 2; Article 218-1; Article 218-2, paragraph 2; Article 220; Articles 223 – 226; the proviso of Article 227; and Article 245, paragraph 2.

Regulations governing exercise by the audit committee and its independent director members of the powers set out in the preceding two paragraphs, and matters related thereto, shall be prescribed by the Competent Authority.

A resolution of the audit committee shall have the concurrence of one-half or more of all members.

Article 14-5 of the Securities and Exchange Act (Matters Requiring Consent of Audit Committee)

For a company that has issued stock in accordance with this Act and established an audit committee, the provisions of Article 14-3 shall not apply to the following matters, which shall be subject to the consent of one-half or more of all audit committee members and be submitted to the board of directors for a resolution:

1. Adoption or amendment of an internal control system pursuant to Article 14-1.
2. Assessment of the effectiveness of the internal control system.
3. Adoption or amendment, pursuant to Article 36-1, of handling procedures for financial or operational actions of material significance, such as acquisition or disposal of assets, derivatives trading, extension of monetary loans to others, or endorsements or guarantees for others.
4. A matter bearing on the personal interest of a director or supervisor.
5. A material asset or derivatives transaction.
6. A material monetary loan, endorsement, or provision of guarantee.
7. The offering, issuance, or private placement of any equity-type securities.
8. The hiring or dismissal of an attesting CPA, or the compensation given thereto.
9. The appointment or discharge of a financial, accounting, or internal auditing officer.
10. Annual and semi-annual financial reports.
11. Any other material matter so required by the company or the Competent Authority.

With the exception of subparagraph 10, any matter under a subparagraph of the preceding paragraph that has not been approved with the consent of one-half or more of all audit committee members may be undertaken upon the consent of two-thirds or more of all directors, without regard to the restrictions of the preceding paragraph, and the resolution of the audit committee shall be recorded in the minutes of the directors meeting.

A company that has established an audit committee is not subject to the provisions of Article 36-1 requiring that its financial reports be recognized by a supervisor.

'All audit committee members' as used in paragraph 1 and the preceding article's paragraph 6, and 'all directors' as used in paragraph 2, shall mean the actual number of persons currently holding those positions.

Article 1 of the Regulations Governing Appointment of Independent Directors and Compliance Matters for Public Companies (Statutory Authority)

These Regulations are adopted pursuant to Article 14-2, paragraph 2, of the Securities and Exchange Act (the 'Act').

Article 2 of the Regulations Governing Appointment of Independent Directors and Compliance Matters for Public Companies (Qualification of Independent Directors)

An independent director of a public company shall meet one of the following professional qualification requirements, together with at least five years work experience:

1. An instructor or higher in a department of commerce, law, finance, accounting, or other academic department related to the business needs of the company in a public or private junior college, college, or university;
2. A judge, public prosecutor, attorney, certified public accountant, or other professional or technical specialist who has passed a national examination and been awarded a certificate in a profession necessary for the business of the company.
3. Have work experience in the area of commerce, law, finance, or accounting, or otherwise necessary for the business of the company.

A person to whom any of the following circumstances applies may not serve as an independent director, or if already serving in such capacity, shall ipso facto be dismissed:

1. Any of the circumstances in the subparagraphs of Article 30 of the Company Act.
2. Elected in the capacity of the government, a juristic person, or a representative thereof, as provided in Article 27 of the Company Act.
3. Any violation of the independent director qualification requirements set out in these Regulations.

Article 3 of the Regulations Governing Appointment of Independent Directors and Compliance Matters for Public Companies (Disqualification of Independent Directors)

During the two years before being elected or during the term of office, an independent director of a public company may not have been or be any of the following:

1. An employee of the company or any of its affiliates.
2. A director or supervisor of the company or any of its affiliates. The same does not apply, however, in cases where the person is an independent director of the company, its parent company, or any

subsidiary in which the company holds, directly or indirectly, more than 50 percent of the voting shares.

3. A natural-person shareholder who holds shares, together with those held by the person's spouse, minor children, or held by the person under others' names, in an aggregate amount of one percent or more of the total number of issued shares of the company or ranking in the top 10 in holdings.
4. A spouse, relative within the second degree of kinship, or lineal relative within the third degree of kinship, of any of the persons in the preceding three subparagraphs.
5. A director, supervisor, or employee of a corporate shareholder that directly holds five percent or more of the total number of issued shares of the company or that holds shares ranking in the top five in holdings.
6. A director, supervisor, officer, or shareholder holding five percent or more of the shares, of a specified company or institution that has a financial or business relationship with the company.
7. A professional individual who, or an owner, partner, director, supervisor, or officer of a sole proprietorship, partnership, company, or institution that, provides commercial, legal, financial, accounting services or consultation to the company or to any affiliate of the company, or a spouse thereof, provided that this restriction does not apply to any member of the remuneration committee who exercises powers pursuant to Article 7 of the Regulations Governing the Establishment and Exercise of Powers of Remuneration Committees of Companies Whose Stock is Listed on the TWSE or Traded on the GTSM.

The requirement of the preceding paragraph in relation to 'during the two years before being elected' does not apply where an independent director of a public company has served as an independent director of the company or any of its affiliates, or of a specified company or institution that has a financial or business relationship with the company, as stated in subparagraph 2 or 6 of the preceding paragraph, but is currently no longer in that position.

The term 'specified company or institution' as used in paragraph 1, subparagraph 6, means a company or institution that has one of the following relationships with the company:

1. It holds 20 percent or more and no more than 50 percent of the total number of issued shares of the public company;

2. It holds shares, together with those held by any of its directors, supervisors, and shareholders holding more than 10 percent of the total number of shares, in an aggregate total of 30 percent or more of the total number of issued shares of the public company, and there is a record of financial or business transactions between it and the public company. The shareholdings of any of the aforesaid persons include the shares held by the spouse or any minor child of the person or by the person under others' names.
3. It, together with any of its affiliates, serves as a source of 30 percent or more of the operating revenue of the public company.
4. It, together with any of its affiliates, serves as a source of 50 percent or more of the total volume or total purchase amount of principal raw materials (those that account for 30 percent or more of total procurement costs, and are indispensable and key raw materials in product manufacturing) or principal products (those accounting for 30 percent or more of total operating revenue) of the public company.

For the purposes of paragraph 1 and the preceding paragraph, the terms 'parent' and 'affiliate' shall have the meaning given in Statement of Financial Accounting Standards Nos. 5 and 7 issued by the Accounting Research and Development Foundation of the Republic of China.

Article 4 of the Regulations Governing Appointment of Independent Directors and Compliance Matters for Public Companies (Restriction of Concurrent Service as Independent Directors)

No independent director of a public company may concurrently serve as an independent director of more than three other public companies.

Article 5 of the Regulations Governing Appointment of Independent Directors and Compliance Matters for Public Companies (Election of Independent Directors)

The election of independent directors at a public company is subject to the provisions of Article 192-1 of the Company Act in that a candidate nomination system shall be adopted, that such system shall be expressly stated in the articles of incorporation of the company, and that shareholders shall elect independent directors from among the those listed in the slate of independent director candidates.

The public company shall, prior to the book closure date before the convening of the shareholders' meeting, publish a notice specifying a period for receiving nominations of independent director candidates, the number of independent directors to be elected, the place for receiving such nominations, and other necessary matters; the period for receiving nominations shall be not less than 10 days.

The public company may present a slate of independent director candidates nominated by the methods set out below, and, upon evaluation by the board of directors that all candidates so nominated are qualified independent director candidates, submit it to the shareholders' meeting for elections:

1. A shareholder holding one percent or more of the total number of issued shares may present a slate of independent director candidates in writing to the company; the number of nominees may not exceed the number of independent directors to be elected.
2. The board of directors presents a slate of independent director candidates; the number of nominees may not exceed the number of independent directors to be elected.
3. Otherwise as designated by the competent authority.

When providing a recommended slate of independent director candidates under the preceding paragraph, a shareholder or the board of directors shall include in the documentation attached thereto each nominee's name, educational background, work experience, a written undertaking indicating the nominee's consent to serve as an independent director if elected as such, a written statement that none of the circumstances in Article 30 of the Company Act exists, and other relevant documentary proof.

When calling a shareholders' meeting for the purpose of independent director elections, the board of directors, or other person having the authority to call a shareholders' meeting, shall review the qualifications of each independent director nominee; except under any of the following circumstances, all qualified nominees shall be included in the slate of independent director candidates:

1. Where the nominating shareholder submits the nomination at a time not within the published period for receiving nominations.
2. Where the shareholding of the nominating shareholder is less than one percent at the time of book closure by the company under Article 165, paragraph 2 or 3 of the Company Act.
3. Where the number of nominees exceeds the number of independent directors to be elected.

4. Where the relevant documentary proof required under the preceding paragraph is not attached.

The directors of the public company shall be elected in accordance with Article 198 of the Company Act, with independent and non-independent directors elected at the same time, but in separately calculated numbers. If the public company has established an audit committee under the Act, at least one of its independent directors is required to have accounting or financial expertise.

Article 6 of the Regulations Governing Appointment of Independent Directors and Compliance Matters for Public Companies (Prohibition of Independent Director Status Change)

If an independent director elected at a shareholders' meeting, or appointed by a financial holding company, the government, or a corporate shareholder under Article 7, is required to be dismissed during the term of office for reason of a violation of Article 2 or 3, it is prohibited to change the status of the person from independent director to non-independent director. A non-independent director elected at a shareholders' meeting, or appointed by a financial holding company, the government, or a corporate shareholder under Article 7, likewise may not be arbitrarily changed from a non-independent director to an independent director during the term of office.

Article 7 of the Regulations Governing Appointment of Independent Directors and Compliance Matters for Public Companies (Exception of Financial Holding Company or a One-Man Company Constituted by the Government or by One Sole Corporate Shareholder)

In the case of a subsidiary whose issued shares are held entirely by the parent financial holding company, or a public company constituted by the government or by one sole corporate shareholder, the independent directors of the company may be appointed by the financial holding company, government, or corporate shareholder, as the case may be, provided that such appointment shall be made in compliance with the provisions of these Regulations, excluding Article 5.

Article 8 of the Regulations Governing Appointment of Independent Directors and Compliance Matters for Public Companies (Managing Directors)

Where a company that has created independent director positions under the Act has also created managing director positions on the board of directors, vthe managing directors shall include not less than one independent director member, and not less than one-fifth of the managing director seats shall be held by independent directors.

Article 9 of the Regulations Governing Appointment of Independent Directors and Compliance Matters for Public Companies (Excuse from Application of the Provisions)

A public company that has created independent director positions under the Act is excused from application of the provisions hereof before the expiration of the term of office of the incumbent directors.

Article 10 of the Regulations Governing Appointment of Independent Directors and Compliance Matters for Public Companies (Effective Date)

These Regulations shall enter into force from 1 January 2007.

The amendments to these Regulations shall enter into force from the date of issuance.

Chapter 8 – Hong Kong

Section 465 of the Companies Ordinance (Duty to Exercise Reasonable Care, Skill and Diligence)

(1) A director of a company must exercise reasonable care, skill and diligence.
(2) Reasonable care, skill and diligence mean the care, skill and diligence that would be exercised by a reasonably diligent person with –
    (a) the general knowledge, skill and experience that may reasonably be expected of a person carrying out the functions carried out by the director in relation to the company; and
    (b) the general knowledge, skill and experience that the director has.
(3) The duty specified in subsection (1) is owed by a director of a company to the company.
(4) The duty specified in subsection (1) has effect in place of the common law rules and equitable principles as regards the duty to exercise reasonable care, skill and diligence, owed by a director of a company to the company.
(5) This section applies to a shadow director as it applies to a director.

(6) For the purposes of subsection (5), a body corporate is not to be regarded as a shadow director of any of its subsidiaries by reason only that the directors, or a majority of the directors, of the subsidiary are accustomed to act in accordance with its direction or instructions.

Rule 3.08 of the Rules Governing the Listing of Securities on the Growth Enterprise Market of the Stock Exchange of Hong Kong Limited

The board of directors of an issuer is collectively responsible for its management and operations. The Exchange expects the directors, both collectively and individually, to fulfil fiduciary duties and duties of skill, care and diligence to a standard at least commensurate with the standard established by Hong Kong law. This means that every director must, in the performance of his duties as a director: –

(a) act honestly and in good faith in the interests of the company as a whole;
(b) act for proper purpose;
(c) be answerable to the issuer for the application or misapplication of its assets;
(d) avoid actual and potential conflicts of interest and duty;
(e) disclose fully and fairly his interests in contracts with the issuer; and
(f) apply such degree of skill, care and diligence as may reasonably be expected of a person of his knowledge and experience and holding his office within the issuer.

Directors must satisfy the required levels of skill, care and diligence. Delegating their functions is permissible but does not absolve them from their responsibilities or from applying the required levels of skill, care and diligence. Directors do not satisfy these required levels if they pay attention to the issuer's affairs only at formal meetings. At a minimum, they must take an active interest in the issuer's affairs and obtain a general understanding of its business. They must follow up anything untoward that comes to their attention. Directors are reminded that if they fail to discharge their duties and responsibilities, they may be disciplined by the Exchange and may attract civil and/or criminal liabilities under Hong Kong law or the laws of other jurisdictions.

Note: These duties are summarised in 'A Guide on Directors' Duties' issued by the Companies Registry. In addition, directors are generally expected by the Exchange to be guided by the Guidelines for Directors and the Guide for Independent Nonexecutive Directors published by the Hong Kong Institute of Directors (www.hkiod.com). In determining whether a director has met the expected standard of care, skill and diligence, courts will generally consider a number of factors. These include the functions that are to be performed by the director concerned, whether he is a fulltime executive director or a part-time non-executive director and his professional skills and knowledge.

Rule 3.09 of the Rules Governing the Listing of Securities on the Growth Enterprise Market of the Stock Exchange of Hong Kong Limited

Every director of a listed issuer must satisfy the Exchange that he has the character, experience and integrity and is able to demonstrate a standard of competence commensurate with his position as a director of a listed issuer. The Exchange may request further information regarding the background, experience, other business interests or character of any director or proposed director of a listed issuer.

Rule 3.10 of the Rules Governing the Listing of Securities on the Growth Enterprise Market of the Stock Exchange of Hong Kong Limited

Subject to the transitional provisions in rule 3.19,

(1) every board of directors of a listed issuer must include at least three independent non-executive directors; and
(2) at least one of the independent non-executive directors must have appropriate professional qualifications or accounting or related financial management expertise.

Note: With regard to 'appropriate accounting or related financial management expertise', the Exchange would expect the person to have, through experience as a public accountant or auditor or as a chief financial officer, controller or principal accounting officer of a public company or through performance of similar functions, experience with internal controls and in preparing or auditing comparable financial statements or experience reviewing or analysing audited financial statements of public companies. It is the responsibility of the board to determine on a case-by-case basis whether the candidate is suitable for the position. In making its decision, the board must evaluate the totality of the individual's education and experience.

Rule 3.10A of the Rules Governing the Listing of Securities on the Growth Enterprise Market of the Stock Exchange of Hong Kong Limited

An issuer must appoint independent non-executive directors representing at least one-third of the board.

Note: The issuer must comply with this rule by 31 December 2012.

Rule 3.11 of the Rules Governing the Listing of Securities on the Growth Enterprise Market of the Stock Exchange of Hong Kong Limited

An issuer shall immediately inform the Exchange and publish an announcement containing the relevant details and reasons if at any time the number of its independent non-executive directors falls below:

(1) the minimum number required under rule 3.10(1) or at any time it has failed to meet the requirement set out in rule 3.10(2) regarding qualification of the independent non-executive directors; or
(2) one-third of the board as required under rule 3.10A.

The issuer shall appoint a sufficient number of independent non-executive directors to meet the minimum number required under rule 3.10(1) or 3.10A or appoint an independent non-executive director to meet the requirement set out in rule 3.10(2) within three months after failing to meet the requirement(s).

Rule 3.12 of the Rules Governing the Listing of Securities on the Growth Enterprise Market of the Stock Exchange of Hong Kong Limited

In addition to fulfilling the requirements and continuing obligations of rules 3.08, 3.09 and 3.13, every independent non-executive director must satisfy the Exchange that he has the character, integrity, independence and experience to fulfil his role effectively. The Exchange may stipulate a minimum number of independent non-executive directors which is higher than three if, in the opinion of the Exchange, the size of the board or other circumstances of the listed issuer justify it.

Rule 3.13 of the Rules Governing the Listing of Securities on the Growth Enterprise Market of the Stock Exchange of Hong Kong Limited

In assessing the independence of a non-executive director, the Exchange will take into account the following factors, none of which is necessarily conclusive. Independence is more likely to be questioned if the director: –

(1) holds more than 1% of the total issued share capital of the listed issuer;

Notes:

1. A listed issuer wishing to appoint an independent non-executive director holding an interest of more than 1% must satisfy the Exchange, prior to such appointment, that the candidate is independent. A candidate holding an interest of 5% or more will normally not be considered independent.
2. When calculating the 1% limit set out in rule 3.13(1), the listed issuer must take into account the total number of shares held legally or beneficially by the director, together with the total number of shares which may be issued to the director or his nominee upon the exercise of any outstanding share options, convertible securities and other rights (whether contractual or otherwise) to call for the issue of shares.

(2) has received an interest in any securities of the listed issuer as a gift, or by means of other financial assistance, from a core connected person or the listed issuer itself. However, subject to Note 1 to rule 3.13(1), the director will still be considered independent if he receives shares or interests in securities from the listed issuer or its subsidiaries (but not from core connected persons) as part of his director's fee or pursuant to share option schemes established in accordance with Chapter 17;

(3) is a director, partner or principal of a professional advisor which currently provides or has within one year immediately prior to the date of his proposed appointment provided services, or is an employee of such professional advisor who is or has been involved in providing such services during the same period, to:

(a) the listed issuer, its holding company or any of their respective subsidiaries or core connected persons; or

(b) any person who was a controlling shareholder or, where there was no controlling shareholder, any person who was the chief executive or a director (other than an independent non-executive director), of the listed issuer within one year immediately prior to the date of the proposed appointment, or any of their close associates;

(4) has a material interest in any principal business activity of or is involved in any material business dealings with the listed issuer, its holding company or their respective subsidiaries or with any core connected persons of the listed issuer;

(5) is on the board specifically to protect the interests of an entity whose interests are not the same as those of the shareholders as a whole;

(6) is or was connected with a director, the chief executive or a substantial shareholder of the listed issuer within two years immediately prior to the date of his proposed appointment;

Note: Without prejudice to the generality of the foregoing, any person cohabiting as a spouse with, and any child, step-child, parent, step-parent, brother, sister, step-brother and step-sister of, a director, the chief executive or a substantial shareholder of the listed issuer is, for the purpose of rule 3.13(6), considered to be connected with that director, chief executive or substantial shareholder. A father-in-law, mother-in-law, son-in-law, daughter-in-law, grandparent, grandchild, uncle, aunt, cousin, brother-in-law, sister-in-law, nephew and niece of a director, the chief executive or a substantial shareholder of the listed issuer may in some circumstances also be considered to be so connected. In such cases, the listed issuer will need to provide the Exchange with all relevant information to enable the Exchange to make a determination.

(7) is, or has at any time during the two years immediately prior to the date of his proposed appointment been, an executive or director (other than an independent non-executive director) of the listed issuer, of its holding company or of any of their respective subsidiaries or of any core connected persons of the listed issuer; and

Note: An 'executive' includes any person who has any management function in the company and any person who acts as a company secretary of the company.

(8) is financially dependent on the listed issuer, its holding company or any of their respective subsidiaries or core connected persons of the listed issuer.

An independent non-executive director shall submit to the Exchange a written confirmation which must state:

(a) his independence as regards each of the factors referred to in rule 3.13(1) to (8);

(b) his past or present financial or other interest in the business of the issuer or its subsidiaries or any connection with any core connected person (as such term is defined in the Exchange Listing Rules) of the issuer, if any; and

(c) that there are no other factors that may affect his independence at the same time as the submission of his declaration and undertaking in Form B or H of Appendix 5.

Each independent non-executive director shall inform the Exchange as soon as practicable if there is any subsequent change of circumstances which may affect his independence and must provide an annual confirmation of his independence to the listed issuer. The listed issuer must confirm in each of its annual reports whether it has received such confirmation and whether it still considers the independent non-executive director to be independent.

Note: The factors set out in rule 3.13 are included for guidance only and are not intended to be exhaustive. The Exchange may take account of other factors relevant to a particular case in assessing independence.

Rule 3.14 of the Rules Governing the Listing of Securities on the Growth Enterprise Market of the Stock Exchange of Hong Kong Limited

Where a proposed independent non-executive director fails to meet any of the independence guidelines set out in rule 3.13, the listed issuer must demonstrate to the satisfaction of the Exchange, prior to the proposed appointment, that the person is independent. The listed issuer must also disclose the reasons why such person is considered to be independent in the announcement of his appointment as well as in the next annual report published after his appointment. In cases of doubt, the listed issuer must consult the Exchange at an early stage.

Rule 3.15 of the Rules Governing the Listing of Securities on the Growth Enterprise Market of the Stock Exchange of Hong Kong Limited

Independent non-executive directors who were appointed by listed issuers on or before 31 March 2004 shall submit to the Exchange a written confirmation in respect of the factors set out in rule 3.13 concerning their independence no later than 30 September 2004.

Rule 3.16 of the Rules Governing the Listing of Securities on the Growth Enterprise Market of the Stock Exchange of Hong Kong Limited

A listed issuer must ensure that its directors accept full responsibility, collectively and individually, for the listed issuer's compliance with the Exchange Listing Rules.

Rule 3.17 of the Rules Governing the Listing of Securities on the Growth Enterprise Market of the Stock Exchange of Hong Kong Limited

Every director shall comply with the Model Code set out in Appendix 10 or the listed issuer's own code on no less exacting terms. The Model Code sets out the required standard which the Exchange requires all listed issuers and their directors to meet and any breach of such required standard will be regarded as a breach of the Exchange Listing Rules. A listed issuer may adopt its own code on terms no less exacting than those set out in the Model Code. Any breach of its own code will not be regarded as a breach of the Exchange Listing Rules provided that the required standard under the Model Code is met.

Rule 3.20 of the Rules Governing the Listing of Securities on the Growth Enterprise Market of the Stock Exchange of Hong Kong Limited

Every director of a listed issuer shall provide to the Exchange, immediately upon his resignation as a director of the listed issuer, his up-to-date contact information, including his address for correspondence from and service of notices and other documents by the Exchange and telephone number.

Provision A.1.7 of the Corporate Governance Code and Corporate Governance Report

If a substantial shareholder or a director has a conflict of interest in a matter to be considered by the board which the board has determined to be material, the matter should be dealt with by a physical board meeting rather than a written resolution. Independent non-executive directors who, and whose close associates, have no material interest in the transaction should be present at that board meeting.

Provision A.2.7 of the Corporate Governance Code and Corporate Governance Report

The chairman should at least annually hold meetings with the non-executive directors (including independent non-executive directors) without the executive directors present.

Provision A.3 of the Corporate Governance Code and Corporate Governance Report (Board Composition)

Principle: The board should have a balance of skills, experience and diversity of perspectives appropriate to the requirements of the issuer's business. It should ensure that changes to its composition can be managed without undue disruption. It should include a balanced composition of executive and non-executive directors (including independent non-executive directors) so that there is a strong independent element on the board, which can effectively exercise independent judgement. Non-executive directors should be of sufficient calibre and number for their views to carry weight.

Provision A.3.1 of the Corporate Governance Code and Corporate Governance Report

The independent non-executive directors should be identified in all corporate communications that disclose the names of directors.

Provision A.3.2 of the Corporate Governance Code and Corporate Governance Report

An issuer should maintain on its website and on the Exchange's website an updated list of its directors identifying their role and function and whether they are independent non-executive directors.

Provision A.4 of the Corporate Governance Code and Corporate Governance Report (Appointments, Re-election and Removal)

Principle: There should be a formal, considered and transparent procedure for the appointment of new directors. There should be plans in place for orderly succession for appointments. All directors should be subject to re-election at regular intervals. An issuer must explain the reasons for the resignation or removal of any director.

Provision A.4.1 of the Corporate Governance Code and Corporate Governance Report

Non-executive directors should be appointed for a specific term, subject to re-election.

Provision A.4.2 of the Corporate Governance Code and Corporate Governance Report

All directors appointed to fill a casual vacancy should be subject to election by shareholders at the first general meeting after appointment. Every director, including those appointed for a specific term, should be subject to retirement by rotation at least once every three years.

Provision A.4.3 of the Corporate Governance Code and Corporate Governance Report

Serving more than 9 years could be relevant to the determination of a non-executive director's independence. If an independent non-executive director serves more than 9 years, his further appointment should be subject to a separate resolution to be approved by shareholders. The papers to shareholders accompanying that resolution should include the reasons why the board believes he is still independent and should be re-elected.

Provision A.6 of the Corporate Governance Code and Corporate Governance Report (Responsibilities of Directors)

Principle: Every director must always know his responsibilities as a director of an issuer and its conduct, business activities and development. Given the essential unitary nature of the board, non-executive directors have the same duties of care and skill and fiduciary duties as executive directors.

Provision A.6.1 of the Corporate Governance Code and Corporate Governance Report

Every newly appointed director of an issuer should receive a comprehensive, formal and tailored induction on appointment. Subsequently he should receive any briefing and professional development necessary to ensure that he has a proper understanding of the issuer's operations and business and is fully aware of his responsibilities under statute and common law, the Exchange Listing Rules, legal and other regulatory requirements and the issuer's business and governance policies.

Provision A.6.2 of the Corporate Governance Code and Corporate Governance Report

The functions of non-executive directors should include:

(a) participating in board meetings to bring an independent judgement to bear on issues of strategy, policy, performance, accountability, resources, key appointments and standards of conduct;

(b) taking the lead where potential conflicts of interests arise;
(c) serving on the audit, remuneration, nomination and other governance committees, if invited; and
(d) scrutinising the issuer's performance in achieving agreed corporate goals and objectives, and monitoring performance reporting.

Provision A.6.3 of the Corporate Governance Code and Corporate Governance Report

Every director should ensure that he can give sufficient time and attention to the issuer's affairs and should not accept the appointment if he cannot do so.

Provision A.6.4 of the Corporate Governance Code and Corporate Governance Report

The board should establish written guidelines no less exacting than the Model Code for relevant employees in respect of their dealings in the issuer's securities. 'Relevant employee' includes any employee or a director or employee of a subsidiary or holding company who, because of his office or employment, is likely to possess inside information in relation to the issuer or its securities.

Provision A.6.5 of the Corporate Governance Code and Corporate Governance Report

All directors should participate in continuous professional development to develop and refresh their knowledge and skills. This is to ensure that their contribution to the board remains informed and relevant. The issuer should be responsible for arranging and funding suitable training, placing an appropriate emphasis on the roles, functions and duties of a listed company director.
Note: Directors should provide a record of the training they received to the issuer.

Provision A.6.6 of the Corporate Governance Code and Corporate Governance Report

Each director should disclose to the issuer at the time of his appointment, and in a timely manner for any change, the number and nature of offices held in public companies or organisations and other significant commitments. The identity of the public companies or organisations and an indication of the time involved should also be disclosed. The board should determine for itself how frequently this disclosure should be made.

Provision A.6.7 of the Corporate Governance Code and Corporate Governance Report

Independent non-executive directors and other non-executive directors, as equal board members, should give the board and any committees on which they serve the benefit of their skills, expertise and varied backgrounds and qualifications through regular attendance and active participation. They should also attend general meetings and develop a balanced understanding of the views of shareholders.

Provision A.6.8 of the Corporate Governance Code and Corporate Governance Report

Independent non-executive directors and other non-executive directors should make a positive contribution to the development of the issuer's strategy and policies through independent, constructive and informed comments.

Chapter 9 – Singapore

Section 2 of the 2001 Corporate Governance Code (Board Composition and Balance)

Principle 2:

There should be a strong and independent element on the Board, which is able to exercise objective judgement on corporate affairs independently, in particular, from Management. No individual or small group of individuals should be allowed to dominate the Board's decision making.

Guideline 2.1:

An 'independent' director is one who has no relationship with the company, its related companies or its officers that could interfere, or be reasonably perceived to interfere, with the exercise of the director's independent business judgement with a view to the best interests of the company. Examples of such relationships, which would deem a director not to be independent, include:

a) A director being employed by the company or any of its related companies for the current or any of the past three financial years;
b) A director who has an immediate family member who is, or has been in any of the past three financial years, employed by the company or any of its related companies as a senior executive officer whose remuneration is determined by the remuneration committee;

c) A director accepting any compensation from the company or any of its related companies other than compensation for board service for the current or immediate past financial year; or
d) A director being a substantial shareholder of or a partner in (with 5% or more stake), or an executive officer of, any for-profit business organisation to which the company made, or from which the company received, significant payments in the current or immediate past financial year. As a guide, payments aggregated over any financial year in excess of S$200,000 should generally be deemed significant.

Guideline 2.2:

The four relationships set out above are not intended to be exhaustive, and are examples of situations which would deem a director to be not independent. If the company wishes, in spite of the existence of one or more of these relationships, to consider the director as independent, it should disclose in full the nature of the director's relationship and bear responsibility for explaining why he should be considered independent.

Section 4 of the 2001 Corporate Governance Code (Board Membership)

Principle 4:

There should be a formal and transparent process for the appointment of new directors to the Board. As a principle of good corporate governance, all directors should be required to submit themselves for re-nomination and re-election at regular intervals.

Guideline 4.1:

The Nominating Committee ('NC') should comprise at least three directors, a majority of whom, including the chairman, should be independent.

Section 7 of the 2001 Corporate Governance Code (Procedures for Developing Remuneration Policies)

Principle 7:

There should be a formal and transparent procedure for fixing the remuneration packages of individual directors. No director should be involved in deciding his own remuneration.

Guideline 7.1:

The Board should set up a remuneration committee ('RC') comprising a majority of non-executive directors who are independent of Management and free from any business or other relationships, which may materially interfere with the exercise of their independent judgement.

Guideline 7.2:

The RC should be chaired by an independent non-executive director, and have at least one member who is knowledgeable in the field of executive compensation, failing which the committee should have access to expert advice inside and/or outside the company.

Section 11 of the 2001 Corporate Governance Code (Audit Committee)

Principle 11:

The Board should establish an Audit Committee ('AC') with written terms of reference which clearly set out its authority and duties.

Guideline 11.1:

The AC should comprise at least three directors, all non-executive, the majority of whom, including the chairman, should be independent.

Guideline 11.2:

At least two members should have accounting or related financial management expertise or experience, as the Board interprets such qualification in its business judgement.

Section 2 of the 2005 Corporate Governance Code (Board Composition and Guidance)

Principle 2:

There should be a strong and independent element on the Board, which is able to exercise objective judgement on corporate affairs independently, in particular, from Management. No individual or small group of individuals should be allowed to dominate the Board's decision making.

Guideline 2.1:

An 'independent' director is one who has no relationship with the company, its related companies or its officers that could interfere, or be reasonably perceived to interfere, with the exercise of the director's independent business judgement with a view to the best interests of the company. Examples of such relationships, which would deem a director not to be independent, include:

(a) a director being employed by the company or any of its related companies for the current or any of the past three financial years;
(b) a director who has an immediate family member who is, or has been in any of the past three financial years, employed by the company or any of its related companies as a senior executive officer whose remuneration is determined by the remuneration committee;
(c) a director, or an immediate family member, accepting any compensation from the company or any of its subsidiaries other than compensation for board service for the current or immediate past financial year; or
(d) a director, or an immediate family member, being a substantial shareholder of or a partner in (with 5% or more stake), or an executive officer of, or a director of any for-profit business organisation to which the company or any of its subsidiaries made, or from which the company or any of its subsidiaries received, significant payments in the current or immediate past financial year. As a guide, payments aggregated over any financial year in excess of S$200,000 should generally be deemed significant.

Guideline 2.2:

The relationships set out above are not intended to be exhaustive, and are examples of situations which would deem a director to be not independent. If the company wishes, in spite of the existence of one or more of these relationships, to consider the director as independent, it should disclose in full the nature of the director's relationship and bear responsibility for explaining why he should be considered independent.

Guideline 2.4:

The Board should comprise directors who as a group provide core competencies such as accounting or finance, business or management experience, industry knowledge, strategic planning experience and customer-based experience or knowledge.

Section 3 of the 2005 Corporate Governance Code (Chairman and Chief Executive Officer)

Principle 3:

There should be a clear division of responsibilities at the top of the company – the working of the Board and the executive responsibility of the company's business – which will ensure a balance of power and authority, such that no one individual represents a considerable concentration of power.

Guideline 3.1:

The Chairman and chief executive officer ('CEO') should in principle be separate persons, to ensure an appropriate balance of power, increased accountability and greater capacity of the Board for independent decision making. The division of responsibilities between the Chairman and CEO should be clearly established, set out in writing and agreed by the Board. In addition, companies should disclose the relationship between the Chairman and CEO where they are related to each other (i.e., be of the same immediate family, as defined in footnote 2 [which defines family member 'to mean the spouse, child, adopted child, step-child, brother, sister and parent'].)

Section 4 of the 2005 Corporate Governance Code (Board Membership)

Principle 4:

There should be a formal and transparent process for the appointment of new directors to the Board.

Guideline 4.1:

The Nominating Committee ('NC') should comprise at least three directors, a majority of whom, including the Chairman, should be independent. The NC Chairman should be a director who is not, or who is not directly associated with, a substantial shareholder (with interest of 5% or more in the voting shares of the company). [At footnote 4, '[a] director will be considered "directly associated" to a substantial shareholder when the director is accustomed or under an obligation, whether formal or informal, to act in accordance with the directions, instructions or wishes of the substantial shareholder'.]

Section 7 of the 2005 Corporate Governance Code (Procedures for Developing Remuneration Policies)

Principle 7:

There should be a formal and transparent procedure for developing policy on executive remuneration and for fixing the remuneration packages of individual directors. No director should be involved in deciding his own remuneration.

Guideline 7.1:

The Board should set up a Remuneration Committee ('RC') comprising entirely of non-executive directors, the majority of whom, including the Chairman, should be independent.

Section 11 of the 2005 Corporate Governance Code (Audit Committee)

Principle 11:

The Board should establish an Audit Committee ('AC') with written terms of reference which clearly set out its authority and duties.

Guideline 11.1:

The AC should comprise at least three directors, all non-executive, the majority of whom, including the Chairman, should be independent.

Guideline 11.2:

At least two members should have accounting or related financial management expertise or experience, as the Board interprets such qualification in its business judgement.

Section 2 of the 2012 Corporate Governance Code (Board Composition and Guidance)

Principle 2:

There should be a strong and independent element on the Board, which is able to exercise objective judgement on corporate affairs independently, in particular, from Management and 10% shareholders. No individual or small group of individuals should be allowed to dominate the Board's decision making.

Here, the term '10% shareholder' shall refer to a person who has an interest or interests in one or more voting shares in the company and the total votes attached to that share, or those shares, is not less than 10% of the total votes attached to all the voting shares in the company. 'Voting shares' exclude treasury shares.

Guideline 2.1:

There should be a strong and independent element on the Board, with independent directors making up at least one-third of the Board.

Guideline 2.2:

The independent directors should make up at least half of the Board where:

(a) the Chairman of the Board (the 'Chairman') and the chief executive officer (or equivalent) (the 'CEO') is the same person;
(b) the Chairman and the CEO are immediate family members;
(c) the Chairman is part of the management team; or
(d) the Chairman is not an independent director.

Guideline 2.3:

The Board should identify in the company's Annual Report each director it considers to be independent. The Board should determine, taking into account the views of the Nominating Committee ('NC'), whether the director is independent in character and judgement and whether there are relationships or circumstances which are likely to affect, or could appear to affect, the director's judgement. Directors should disclose to the Board any such relationship as and when it arises. The Board should state its reasons if it determines that a director is independent notwithstanding the existence of relationships or circumstances which may appear relevant to its determination, including the following:

(a) a director being employed by the company or any of its related corporations for the current or any of the past three financial years;
(b) a director who has an immediate family member who is, or has been in any of the past three financial years, employed by the company or any of its related corporations and whose remuneration is determined by the remuneration committee;
(c) a director, or an immediate family member, accepting any significant compensation from the company or any of its related corporations for the provision of services, for the current or immediate past financial year, other than compensation for board service;
(d) a director:
    (i) who, in the current or immediate past financial year, is or was; or
    (ii) whose immediate family member, in the current or immediate past financial year, is or was,

a 10% shareholder of, or a partner in (with 10% or more stake), or an executive officer of, or a director of, any organisation to which the company or any of its subsidiaries made, or from which the company or any of its subsidiaries received, significant payments or material services (which may include auditing, banking, consulting and legal services), in the current or immediate past financial year. As a guide, payments aggregated over any financial year in excess of S$200,000 should generally be deemed significant;

(e) a director who is a 10% shareholder or an immediate family member of a 10% shareholder of the company; or

(f) a director who is or has been directly associated with a 10% shareholder of the company, in the current or immediate past financial year.

The relationships set out above are not intended to be exhaustive, and are examples of situations which would deem a director to be not independent. If the Board wishes, in spite of the existence of one or more of these relationships, to consider the director as independent, it should disclose in full the nature of the director's relationship and bear responsibility for explaining why he should be considered independent.

Guideline 2.4:

The independence of any director who has served on the Board beyond nine years from the date of his first appointment should be subject to particularly rigorous review.

Guideline 2.6:

The Board and its board committees should comprise directors who as a group provide an appropriate balance and diversity of skills, experience, gender and knowledge of the company. They should also provide core competencies such as accounting or finance, business or management experience, industry knowledge, strategic planning experience and customer-based experience or knowledge.

Section 3 of the Corporate Governance Code 2012 (Chairman and Chief Executive Officer)

Principle 3:

There should be a clear division of responsibilities between the leadership of the Board and the executives responsible for managing the company's business. No one individual should represent a considerable concentration of power.

Guideline 3.1:

The Chairman and the CEO should in principle be separate persons, to ensure an appropriate balance of power, increased accountability and greater capacity of the Board for independent decision making. The division of responsibilities between the Chairman and the CEO should be clearly established, set out in writing and agreed by the Board. In addition, the Board should disclose the relationship between the Chairman and the CEO if they are immediate family members.

Guideline 3.3

Every company should appoint an independent director to be the lead independent director where:

(a) the Chairman and the CEO is the same person;
(b) the Chairman and the CEO are immediate family members;
(c) the Chairman is part of the management team; or
(d) the Chairman is not an independent director.

The lead independent director (if appointed) should be available to shareholders where they have concerns and for which contact through the normal channels of the Chairman, the CEO or the chief financial officer (or equivalent) (the 'CFO') has failed to resolve or is inappropriate.

Section 4 of the Corporate Governance Code 2012 (Board Membership)

Principle 4:

There should be a formal and transparent process for the appointment and re- appointment of directors to the Board.

Guideline 4.2:

The Board should establish a NC to make recommendations to the Board on all board appointments, with written terms of reference which clearly set out its authority and duties. The NC should comprise at least three directors, the majority of whom, including the NC Chairman, should be independent. The lead independent director, if any, should be a member of the NC. The Board should disclose in the company's Annual Report the names of the members of the NC and the key terms of reference of the NC, explaining its role and the authority delegated to it by the Board.

Section 7 of the 2012 Corporate Governance Code (Procedures for Developing Remuneration Policies)

Principle 7:

There should be a formal and transparent procedure for developing policy on executive remuneration and for fixing the remuneration packages of individual directors. No director should be involved in deciding his own remuneration.

Guideline 7.1:

The Board should establish a Remuneration Committee ('RC') with written terms of reference which clearly set out its authority and duties. The RC should comprise at least three directors, the majority of whom, including the RC Chairman, should be independent. All of the members of the RC should be nonexecutive directors. This is to minimise the risk of any potential conflict of interest. The Board should disclose in the company's Annual Report the names of the members of the RC and the key terms of reference of the RC, explaining its role and the authority delegated to it by the Board.

Section 12 of the 2012 Corporate Governance Code (Audit Committee)

Principle 12:

The Board should establish an Audit Committee ('AC') with written terms of reference which clearly set out its authority and duties.

Guideline 12.1:

The AC should comprise at least three directors, the majority of whom, including the AC Chairman, should be independent. All of the members of the AC should be non-executive directors. The Board should disclose in the company's Annual Report the names of the members of the AC and the key terms of reference of the AC, explaining its role and the authority delegated to it by the Board.

Guideline 12.2:

The Board should ensure that the members of the AC are appropriately qualified to discharge their responsibilities. At least two members, including the AC Chairman, should have recent and relevant accounting or related financial management expertise or experience, as the Board interprets such qualification in its business judgement.

Section 201B of the 1989 Companies Act (Audit Committees)

(1) Every listed company shall, within 12 months of the commencement of the Companies (Amendment) Act 1989 or such further period as the Registrar may, in any particular case, allow, have an audit committee.
(2) An audit committee shall be appointed by the directors from among their number (pursuant to a resolution of the board of directors) and

shall be composed of not fewer than 3 members of whom a majority shall not be –

(a) executive directors of the company or any related corporation;
(b) a spouse, parent, brother, sister, son or adopted son or daughter or adopted daughter of an executive director of the company or of any related corporation; or
(c) any person having a relationship which, in the opinion of the board of directors, would interfere with the exercise of independent judgment in carrying out the functions of an audit committee.

(3) The members of an audit committee shall elect a chairman from among their number who is not an executive director or employee of the company or any related corporation.

Section 201B of the 2006 Companies Act (Audit Committees)

(1) Every listed company shall have an audit committee.
(2) An audit committee shall be appointed by the directors from among their number (pursuant to a resolution of the board of directors) and shall be composed of not fewer than 3 members of whom a majority shall not be –
  (a) executive directors of the company or any related corporation;
  (b) a spouse, parent, brother, sister, son or adopted son or daughter or adopted daughter of an executive director of the company or of any related corporation; or
  (c) any person having a relationship which, in the opinion of the board of directors, would interfere with the exercise of independent judgment in carrying out the functions of an audit committee.
(3) The members of an audit committee shall elect a chairman from among their number who is not an executive director or employee of the company or any related corporation.
(11) Any reference in this section to a director who is not an executive director of a company is a reference to a director who is not an employee of, and does not hold any other office of profit in, the company or in any related corporation of that company in conjunction with his office of director and his membership of any audit committee, and any reference to an executive director shall be read accordingly.

Chapter 10 – India

Section 149 of the Companies Act, 2013 (Company to Have Board of Directors)

(4) Every listed public company shall have at least one-third of the total number of directors as independent directors and the Central Government may prescribe the minimum number of independent directors in case of any class or classes of public companies.

Explanation. – For the purposes of this sub-section, any fraction contained in such one-third number shall be rounded off as one.

(5) Every company existing on or before the date of commencement of this Act shall, within one year from such commencement or from the date of notification of the rules in this regard as may be applicable, comply with the requirements of the provisions of sub-section (4).

(6) An independent director in relation to a company, means a director other than a managing director or a whole-time director or a nominee director, –

(a) who, in the opinion of the Board, is a person of integrity and possesses relevant expertise and experience;

(b) (i) who is or was not a promoter of the company or its holding, subsidiary or associate company;

(ii) who is not related to promoters or directors in the company, its holding, subsidiary or associate company;

(c) who has or had no pecuniary relationship with the company, its holding, subsidiary or associate company, or their promoters, or directors, during the two immediately preceding financial years or during the current financial year;

(d) none of whose relatives has or had pecuniary relationship or transaction with the company, its holding, subsidiary or associate company, or their promoters, or directors, amounting to two per cent. or more of its gross turnover or total income or fifty lakh rupees or such higher amount as may be prescribed, whichever is lower, during the two immediately preceding financial years or during the current financial year;

(e) who, neither himself nor any of his relatives –

(i) holds or has held the position of a key managerial personnel or is or has been employee of the company or its holding, subsidiary or associate company in any of the three financial years immediately preceding the financial year in which he is proposed to be appointed;

(ii) is or has been an employee or proprietor or a partner, in any of the three financial years immediately preceding the financial year in which he is proposed to be appointed, of –

(A) a firm of auditors or company secretaries in practice or cost auditors of the company or its holding, subsidiary or associate company; or

(B) any legal or a consulting firm that has or had any transaction with the company, its holding, subsidiary or associate company amounting to ten per cent. or more of the gross turnover of such firm;

(iii) holds together with his relatives two per cent. or more of the total voting power of the company; or

(iv) is a Chief Executive or director, by whatever name called, of any non-profit organisation that receives twenty-five per cent. or more of its receipts from the company, any of its promoters, directors or its holding, subsidiary or associate company or that holds two per cent. or more of the total voting power of the company; or

(f) who possesses such other qualifications as may be prescribed.

(7) Every independent director shall at the first meeting of the Board in which he participates as a director and thereafter at the first meeting of the Board in every financial year or whenever there is any change in the circumstances which may affect his status as an independent director, give a declaration that he meets the criteria of independence as provided in sub-section (6).

Explanation. – For the purposes of this section, 'nominee director' means a director nominated by any financial institution in pursuance of the provisions of any law for the time being in force, or of any agreement, or appointed by any Government, or any other person to represent its interests.

(8) The company and independent directors shall abide by the provisions specified in Schedule IV.

(9) Notwithstanding anything contained in any other provision of this Act, but subject to the provisions of sections 197 and 198, an independent director shall not be entitled to any stock option and may receive remuneration by way of fee provided under sub-section (5) of section 197, reimbursement of expenses for participation in the

Board and other meetings and profit related commission as may be approved by the members.

(10) Subject to the provisions of section 152, an independent director shall hold office for a term up to five consecutive years on the Board of a company, but shall be eligible for reappointment on passing of a special resolution by the company and disclosure of such appointment in the Board's report.

(11) Notwithstanding anything contained in sub-section (10), no independent director shall hold office for more than two consecutive terms, but such independent director shall be eligible for appointment after the expiration of three years of ceasing to become an independent director:

Provided that an independent director shall not, during the said period of three years, be appointed in or be associated with the company in any other capacity, either directly or indirectly.

Explanation. – For the purposes of sub-sections (10) and (11), any tenure of an independent director on the date of commencement of this Act shall not be counted as a term under those sub-sections.

(12) Notwithstanding anything contained in this Act, –

(i) an independent director;

(ii) a non-executive director not being promoter or key managerial personnel

shall be held liable, only in respect of such acts of omission or commission by a company which had occurred with his knowledge, attributable through Board processes, and with his consent or connivance or where he had not acted diligently.

(13) The provisions of sub-sections (6) and (7) of section 152 in respect of retirement of directors by rotation shall not be applicable to appointment of independent directors.

Section 150 of the Companies Act, 2013 (Manner of Selection of Independent Directors and Maintenance of Databank of Independent Directors)

(1) Subject to the provisions contained in sub-section (5) of section 149, an independent director may be selected from a data bank containing names, addresses and qualifications of persons who are eligible and willing to act as independent directors, maintained by any body, institute or association, as may be notified by the Central

Government, having expertise in creation and maintenance of such data bank and put on their website for the use by the company making the appointment of such directors:

Provided that responsibility of exercising due diligence before selecting a person from the data bank referred to above, as an independent director shall lie with the company making such appointment.

(2) The appointment of independent director shall be approved by the company in general meeting as provided in sub-section (2) of section 152 and the explanatory statement annexed to the notice of the general meeting called to consider the said appointment shall indicate the justification for choosing the appointee for appointment as independent director.

(3) The data bank referred to in sub-section (1), shall create and maintain data of persons willing to act as independent director in accordance with such rules as may be prescribed.

(4) The Central Government may prescribe the manner and procedure of selection of independent directors who fulfil the qualifications and requirements specified under section 149.

Section 152 of the Companies Act, 2013 (Appointment of Directors)

(5) A person appointed as a director shall not act as a director unless he gives his consent to hold the office as director and such consent has been filed with the Registrar within thirty days of his appointment in such manner as may be prescribed:

Provided that in the case of appointment of an independent director in the general meeting, an explanatory statement for such appointment, annexed to the notice for the general meeting, shall include a statement that in the opinion of the Board, he fulfils the conditions specified in this Act for such an appointment.

Section 166 of the Companies Act, 2013 (Duties of Directors)

(1) Subject to the provisions of this Act, a director of a company shall act in accordance with the articles of the company.

(2) A director of a company shall act in good faith in order to promote the objects of the company for the benefit of its members as a whole, and in the best interests of the company, its employees, the shareholders, the community and for the protection of environment.

(3) A director of a company shall exercise his duties with due and reasonable care, skill and diligence and shall exercise independent judgment.
(4) A director of a company shall not involve in a situation in which he may have a direct or indirect interest that conflicts, or possibly may conflict, with the interest of the company.
(5) A director of a company shall not achieve or attempt to achieve any undue gain or advantage either to himself or to his relatives, partners, or associates and if such director is found guilty of making any undue gain, he shall be liable to pay an amount equal to that gain to the company.
(6) A director of a company shall not assign his office and any assignment so made shall be void.
(7) If a director of the company contravenes the provisions of this section such director shall be punishable with fine which shall not be less than one lakh rupees but which may extend to five lakh rupees.

Section 177 of the Companies Act, 2013 (Audit Committee)

(1) The Board of Directors of every listed company and such other class or classes of companies, as may be prescribed, shall constitute an Audit Committee.
(2) The Audit Committee shall consist of a minimum of three directors with independent directors forming a majority:

Provided that majority of members of Audit Committee including its Chairperson shall be persons with ability to read and understand, the financial statement.

Section 178 of the Companies Act, 2013 (Nomination and Remuneration Committee and Stakeholder Relationship Committee)

(1) The Board of Directors of every listed company and such other class or classes of companies, as may be prescribed shall constitute the Nomination and Remuneration Committee consisting of three or more non-executive directors out of which not less than one-half shall be independent directors:

Provided that the chairperson of the company (whether executive or non-executive) may be appointed as a member of the Nomination and Remuneration Committee but shall not chair such Committee.

Section 197 of the Companies Act, 2013 (Overall Maximum Managerial Remuneration and Managerial Remuneration in Case of Absence or Inadequacy of Profits)

(5) A director may receive remuneration by way of fee for attending meetings of the Board or Committee thereof or for any other purpose whatsoever as may be decided by the Board:

Provided that the amount of such fees shall not exceed the amount as may be prescribed:

Provided further that different fees for different classes of companies and fees in respect of independent director may be such as may be prescribed.

(6) A director or manager may be paid remuneration either by way of a monthly payment or at a specified percentage of the net profits of the company or partly by one way and partly by the other.

(7) Notwithstanding anything contained in any other provision of this Act but subject to the provisions of this section, an independent director shall not be entitled to any stock option and may receive remuneration by way of fees provided under sub-section (5), reimbursement of expenses for participation in the Board and other meetings and profit related commission as may be approved by the members.

Schedule IV of the Companies Act, 2013 [see Section 149(8)] – Code for Independent Directors

The Code is a guide to professional conduct for independent directors. Adherence to these standards by independent directors and fulfilment of their responsibilities in a professional and faithful manner will promote confidence of the investment community, particularly minority shareholders, regulators and companies in the institution of independent directors.

Provision I of the Code for Independent Directors (Guidelines of Professional Conduct)

An independent director shall:

(1) uphold ethical standards of integrity and probity;

(2) act objectively and constructively while exercising his duties;

(3) exercise his responsibilities in a bona fide manner in the interest of the company;

(4) devote sufficient time and attention to his professional obligations for informed and balanced decision making;

(5) not allow any extraneous considerations that will vitiate his exercise of objective independent judgment in the paramount interest of the company as a whole, while concurring in or dissenting from the collective judgment of the Board in its decision making;
(6) not abuse his position to the detriment of the company or its shareholders or for the purpose of gaining direct or indirect personal advantage or advantage for any associated person;
(7) refrain from any action that would lead to loss of his independence;
(8) where circumstances arise which make an independent director lose his independence, the independent director must immediately inform the Board accordingly;
(9) assist the company in implementing the best corporate governance practices.

Provision II of the Code for Independent Directors (Role and Functions)

The independent directors shall:
(1) help in bringing an independent judgment to bear on the Board's deliberations especially on issues of strategy, performance, risk management, resources, key appointments and standards of conduct;
(2) bring an objective view in the evaluation of the performance of board and management;
(3) scrutinise the performance of management in meeting agreed goals and objectives and monitor the reporting of performance;
(4) satisfy themselves on the integrity of financial information and that financial controls and the systems of risk management are robust and defensible;
(5) safeguard the interests of all stakeholders, particularly the minority shareholders;
(6) balance the conflicting interest of the stakeholders;
(7) determine appropriate levels of remuneration of executive directors, key managerial personnel and senior management and have a prime role in appointing and where necessary recommend removal of executive directors, key managerial personnel and senior management;
(8) moderate and arbitrate in the interest of the company as a whole, in situations of conflict between management and shareholder's interest.

Provision III of the Code for Independent Directors (Duties)

The independent directors shall –

(1) undertake appropriate induction and regularly update and refresh their skills, knowledge and familiarity with the company;
(2) seek appropriate clarification or amplification of information and, where necessary, take and follow appropriate professional advice and opinion of outside experts at the expense of the company;
(3) strive to attend all meetings of the Board of Directors and of the Board committees of which he is a member;
(4) participate constructively and actively in the committees of the Board in which they are chairpersons or members;
(5) strive to attend the general meetings of the company;
(6) where they have concerns about the running of the company or a proposed action, ensure that these are addressed by the Board and, to the extent that they are not resolved, insist that their concerns are recorded in the minutes of the Board meeting;
(7) keep themselves well informed about the company and the external environment in which it operates;
(8) not to unfairly obstruct the functioning of an otherwise proper Board or committee of the Board;
(9) pay sufficient attention and ensure that adequate deliberations are held before approving related party transactions and assure themselves that the same are in the interest of the company;
(10) ascertain and ensure that the company has an adequate and functional vigil mechanism and to ensure that the interests of a person who uses such mechanism are not prejudicially affected on account of such use;
(11) report concerns about unethical behaviour, actual or suspected fraud or violation of the company's code of conduct or ethics policy;
(12) acting within his authority, assist in protecting the legitimate interests of the company, shareholders and its employees;
(13) not disclose confidential information, including commercial secrets, technologies, advertising and sales promotion plans, unpublished price sensitive information, unless such disclosure is expressly approved by the Board or required by law.

Provision IV of the Code for Independent Directors (Manner of Appointment)

(1) Appointment process of independent directors shall be independent of the company management; while selecting independent directors the Board shall ensure that there is appropriate balance of skills, experience and knowledge in the Board so as to enable the Board to discharge its functions and duties effectively.

(2) The appointment of independent director(s) of the company shall be approved at the meeting of the shareholders.
(3) The explanatory statement attached to the notice of the meeting for approving the appointment of independent director shall include a statement that in the opinion of the Board, the independent director proposed to be appointed fulfils the conditions specified in the Act and the rules made thereunder and that the proposed director is independent of the management.
(4) The appointment of independent directors shall be formalised through a letter of appointment, which shall set out:
  (a) the term of appointment;
  (b) the expectation of the Board from the appointed director; the Board-level committee(s) in which the director is expected to serve and its tasks;
  (c) the fiduciary duties that come with such an appointment along with accompanying liabilities;
  (d) provision for Directors and Officers (D and O) insurance, if any;
  (e) the Code of Business Ethics that the company expects its directors and employees to follow;
  (f) the list of actions that a director should not do while functioning as such in the company; and
  (g) the remuneration, mentioning periodic fees, reimbursement of expenses for participation in the Boards and other meetings and profit related commission, if any.
(5) The terms and conditions of appointment of independent directors shall be open for inspection at the registered office of the company by any member during normal business hours.
(6) The terms and conditions of appointment of independent directors shall also be posted on the company's website.

Provision V of the Code for Independent Directors (Re-appointment)

The re-appointment of independent director shall be on the basis of report of performance evaluation.

Provision VI of the Code for Independent Directors (Resignation or Removal)

(1) The resignation or removal of an independent director shall be in the same manner as is provided in sections 168 and 169 of the Act.
(2) An independent director who resigns or is removed from the Board of the company shall be replaced by a new independent director

within a period of not more than one hundred and eighty days from the date of such resignation or removal, as the case may be.

(3) Where the company fulfils the requirement of independent directors in its Board even without filling the vacancy created by such resignation or removal, as the case may be, the requirement of replacement by a new independent director shall not apply.

Provision VII of the Code for Independent Directors (Separate Meetings)

(1) The independent directors of the company shall hold at least one meeting in a year, without the attendance of non-independent directors and members of management;
(2) All the independent directors of the company shall strive to be present at such meeting;
(3) The meeting shall:
 (a) review the performance of non-independent directors and the Board as a whole;
 (b) review the performance of the Chairperson of the company, taking into account the views of executive directors and non-executive directors;
 (c) assess the quality, quantity and timeliness of flow of information between the company management and the Board that is necessary for the Board to effectively and reasonably perform their duties.

Provision VIII of the Code for Independent Directors (Evaluation Mechanism)

(1) The performance evaluation of independent directors shall be done by the entire Board of Directors, excluding the director being evaluated.
(2) On the basis of the report of performance evaluation, it shall be determined whether to extend or continue the term of appointment of the independent director.

Rule 4 of the Companies (Appointment and Qualification of Directors) Rules, 2014 (Number of Independent Directors)

The following class or classes of companies shall have at least two directors as independent directors –

(i) the Public Companies having paid up share capital of ten crore rupees or more; or

(ii) the Public Companies having turnover of one hundred crore rupees or more; or

(iii) the Public Companies which have, in aggregate, outstanding loans, debentures, deposits, exceeding fifty crore rupees:

Provided that in case a company covered under this rule is required to appoint a higher number of independent directors due to composition of its audit committee, such higher number of independent directors, shall be applicable to it:

Provided further that any intermittent vacancy of an independent director shall be filled-up by the Board at the earliest but not later than immediate next Board meeting or three months from the date of such vacancy, whichever is later:

Provided also that where a company ceases to fulfil any of three conditions laid down in sub-rule (1) for three consecutive years, it shall not be required to comply with these provisions until such time as it meets any of such conditions;

Explanation. – For the purposes of this rule, it is hereby clarified that, the paid up share capital or turnover or outstanding loans, debentures and depositors, as the case may be, as existing on the last date of latest audited financial statements shall be taken into account:

Provided that a company belonging to any class of companies for which a higher number of independent directors has been specified in the law for the time being in force shall comply with the requirements specified in such law.

Rule 5 of the Companies (Appointment and Qualification of Directors) Rules, 2014 (Qualifications of Independent Director)

An independent director shall possess appropriate skills, experience and knowledge in one or more fields of finance, law, management, sales, marketing, administration, research, corporate governance, technical operations or other disciplines related to the company's business.

Rule 6 of the Companies (Appointment and Qualification of Directors) Rules, 2014 (Creation and Maintenance of Data Bank of Persons Offering to Become Independent Directors)

(1) Any body, institute or association (hereinafter to be referred as 'the agency'), which has been authorised in this behalf by the Central Government shall create and maintain a data bank of persons willing and eligible to be appointed as independent director and such data bank shall be placed on the website of the Ministry of Corporate

Affairs or on any other website as may be approved or notified by the Central Government.

(2) The data bank referred to in sub-rule (1) shall contain the following details in respect of each person included in the data bank to be eligible and willing to be appointed as independent director –

(a) DIN (Director Identification Number);
(b) the name and surname in full;
(c) [omitted];
(d) the father's name;
(e) the date of Birth;
(f) gender;
(g) the nationality;
(h) the occupation;
(i) full address with PIN Code (present and permanent);
(j) phone number;
(k) e-mail id;
(l) the educational and professional qualifications;
(m) experience or expertise, if any;
(n) any legal proceedings initiated or pending against such person;
(o) the list of limited liability partnerships in which he is or was a designated partner along with –

(i) the name of the limited liability partnership;
(ii) the nature of industry; and
(iii) the duration – with dates;

(p) the list of companies in which he is or was director along with –

(i) the name of the company;
(ii) the nature of industry;
(iii) the nature of directorship – Executive or Non-executive or Managing Director or Independent Director or Nominee Director; and
(iv) duration – with dates.

(3) A disclaimer shall be conspicuously displayed on the website hosting the databank that a company must carry out its own due diligence before appointment of any person as an independent director and 'the agency' maintaining the databank or the Central Government shall not be held responsible for the accuracy of information or lack of suitability of the person whose particulars form part of the databank.

(4) Any person who desires to get his name included in the data bank of independent directors shall make an application to 'the agency'.

(5) The agency may charge a reasonable fee from the applicant for inclusion of his name in the data bank of independent directors.
(6) Any person who has applied for inclusion of his name in the data bank of independent directors or any person whose name appears in the data bank, shall intimate to the agency about any changes in his particulars within fifteen days of such change.
(7) The databank posted on the website shall –
  (a) be accessible at the specified website;
  (b) be substantially identical to the physical version of the data bank;
  (c) be searchable on the parameters specified in sub-rule (2);
  (d) be presented in a format or formats convenient for both printing and viewing online; and
  (e) contain a link to obtain the software required to view or print the particulars free of charge.

Article II.A of Clause 49 of the Listing Agreement (Composition of Board)

1. The Board of Directors of the company shall have an optimum combination of executive and non-executive directors with at least one woman director* and not less than fifty percent of the Board of Directors comprising non-executive directors.
(*As per SEBI circular dated September 15, 2014 (appointment of woman director shall be applicable with effect from April 01, 2015)
2. Where the Chairman of the Board is a non-executive director, at least one-third of the Board should comprise independent directors and in case the company does not have a regular non-executive Chairman, at least half of the Board should comprise independent directors.

Provided that where the regular non-executive Chairman is a promoter of the company or is related to any promoter or person occupying management positions at the Board level or at one level below the Board, at least one-half of the Board of the company shall consist of independent directors.

Explanation: For the purpose of the expression 'related to any promoter' referred to in sub-clause (2):

i. If the promoter is a listed entity, its directors other than the independent directors, its employees or its nominees shall be deemed to be related to it;

ii. If the promoter is an unlisted entity, its directors, its employees or its nominees shall be deemed to be related to it.

Article II.B of Clause 49 of the Listing Agreement (Independent Directors)

1. For the purpose of the clause A, the expression 'independent director' shall mean a non-executive director, other than a nominee director of the company:
   a. who, in the opinion of the Board, is a person of integrity and possesses relevant expertise and experience;
   b. (i) who is or was not a promoter of the company or its holding, subsidiary or associate company;

(ii)who is not related to promoters or directors in the company, its holding, subsidiary or associate company;

   c. apart from receiving director's remuneration, has or had no material pecuniary relationship with the company, its holding, subsidiary or associate company, or their promoters, or directors, during the two immediately preceding financial years or during the current financial year;
   d. none of whose relatives has or had pecuniary relationship or transaction with the company, its holding, subsidiary or associate company, or their promoters, or directors, amounting to two per cent. or more of its gross turnover or total income or fifty lakh rupees or such higher amount as may be prescribed, whichever is lower, during the two immediately preceding financial years or during the current financial year;
   e. who, neither himself nor any of his relatives –

a. holds or has held the position of a key managerial personnel or is or has been employee of the company or its holding, subsidiary or associate company in any of the three financial years immediately preceding the financial year in which he is proposed to be appointed;
b. is or has been an employee or proprietor or a partner, in any of the three financial years immediately preceding the financial year in which he is proposed to be appointed, of –

i. a firm of auditors or company secretaries in practice or cost auditors of the company or its holding, subsidiary or associate company; or

ii. any legal or a consulting firm that has or had any transaction with the company, its holding, subsidiary or associate company amounting to ten per cent or more of the gross turnover of such firm;

c. holds together with his relatives two per cent or more of the total voting power of the company; or

d. is a Chief Executive or director, by whatever name called, of any non-profit organisation that receives twenty-five per cent or more of its receipts from the company, any of its promoters, directors or its holding, subsidiary or associate company or that holds two per cent or more of the total voting power of the company;

e. is a material supplier, service provider or customer or a lessor or lessee of the company;

f. who is not less than 21 years of age.

Explanation: For the purposes of the sub-clause (1):

i. 'Associate' shall mean a company which is an 'associate' as defined in Accounting Standard (AS) 23, 'Accounting for Investments in Associates in Consolidated Financial Statements', issued by the Institute of Chartered Accountants of India.

ii. 'Key Managerial Personnel' shall mean 'Key Managerial Personnel' as defined in section 2(51) of the Companies Act, 2013.

iii. 'Relative' shall mean 'relative' as defined in section 2(77) of the Companies Act, 2013 and rules prescribed there under.

2.Limit on number of directorships

a. A person shall not serve as an independent director in more than seven listed companies.

b. Further, any person who is serving as a whole time director in any listed company shall serve as an independent director in not more than three listed companies.

3. Maximum tenure of Independent Directors

The maximum tenure of Independent Directors shall be in accordance with the Companies Act, 2013 and clarifications/ circulars issued by the Ministry of Corporate Affairs, in this regard, from time to time.

4. Formal letter of appointment to Independent Directors

a. The company shall issue a formal letter of appointment to independent directors in the manner as provided in the Companies Act, 2013.

b. The terms and conditions of appointment shall be disclosed on the website of the Company.

5. Performance evaluation of Independent Directors

a. The Nomination Committee shall lay down the evaluation criteria for performance evaluation of independent directors.
b. The company shall disclose the criteria for performance evaluation, as laid down by the Nomination Committee, in its Annual Report.
c. The performance evaluation of independent directors shall be done by the entire Board of Directors (excluding the director being evaluated).
d. On the basis of the report of performance evaluation, it shall be determined whether to extend or continue the term of appointment of the independent director.

6. Separate meetings of the Independent Directors
   a. The independent directors of the company shall hold at least one meeting in a year, without the attendance of non-independent directors and members of management. All the independent directors of the company shall strive to be present at such meeting.
   b. The independent directors in the meeting shall, inter-alia:
   i. review the performance of non-independent directors and the Board as a whole;
   ii. review the performance of the Chairperson of the company, taking into account the views of executive directors and non-executive directors;
   iii. assess the quality, quantity and timeliness of flow of information between the company management and the Board that is necessary for the Board to effectively and reasonably perform their duties.
7. Familiarisation programme for Independent Director
   a. The company shall familiarise the independent directors with the company, their roles, rights, responsibilities in the company, nature of the industry in which the company operates, business model of the company, etc., through various programmes.
   b. The details of such familiarisation programmes shall be disclosed on the company's website and a web link thereto shall also be given in the Annual Report.

Article II.B of Clause 49 of the Listing Agreement (Non-Executive Directors' Compensation and Disclosures)

All fees / compensation, if any paid to non-executive directors, including independent directors, shall be fixed by the Board of Directors and shall require previous approval of shareholders in general meeting. The shareholders' resolution shall specify the limits for the maximum number of stock options that can be granted to non-executive directors, in any financial year and in aggregate.

Provided that the requirement of obtaining prior approval of shareholders in general meeting shall not apply to payment of sitting fees to non-executive directors, if made within the limits prescribed under the Companies Act, 2013 for payment of sitting fees without approval of the Central Government.

Provided further that independent directors shall not be entitled to any stock option

Article II.D of Clause 49 of the Listing Agreement (Other Provisions as to Board and Committees)

4. An independent director who resigns or is removed from the Board of the Company shall be replaced by a new independent director at the earliest but not later than the immediate next Board meeting or three months from the date of such vacancy, whichever is later.
5. Provided that where the company fulfils the requirement of independent directors in its Board even without filling the vacancy created by such resignation or removal, as the case may be, the requirement of replacement by a new independent director shall not apply.

Article II.E of Clause 49 of the Listing Agreement (Code of Conduct)

3. The Code of Conduct shall suitably incorporate the duties of Independent Directors as laid down in the Companies Act, 2013.
4. An independent director shall be held liable, only in respect of such acts of omission or commission by a company which had occurred with his knowledge, attributable through Board processes, and with his consent or connivance or where he had not acted diligently with respect of the provisions contained in the Listing Agreement.

Article III.A of Clause 49 of the Listing Agreement (Qualified and Independent Audit Committee)

A qualified and independent audit committee shall be set up, giving the terms of reference subject to the following:

1. The audit committee shall have minimum three directors as members. Two-thirds of the members of audit committee shall be independent directors. …
3. The Chairman of the Audit Committee shall be an independent director;

Article IV of Clause 49 of the Listing Agreement (Nomination and Remuneration Committee)

A. The company through its Board of Directors shall constitute the nomination and remuneration committee which shall comprise at least three directors, all of whom shall be non-executive directors and at least half shall be independent. Chairman of the committee shall be an independent director.

Provided that the chairperson of the company (whether executive or non- executive) may be appointed as a member of the Nomination and Remuneration Committee but shall not chair such Committee.

Article V of Clause 49 of the Listing Agreement (Subsidiary Companies)

A. At least one independent director on the Board of Directors of the holding company shall be a director on the Board of Directors of a material non-listed Indian subsidiary company.

Chapter 11 – Australia

Recommendation 2.1 of the ASX Corporate Governance Principles and Recommendations (3rd edition 2014)

The board of a listed entity should:

(a) have a nomination committee which:
  (1) has at least three members, a majority of whom are independent directors; and
  (2) is chaired by an independent director, …

(b) if it does not have a nomination committee, disclose that fact and the processes it employs to address board succession issues and to ensure that the board has the appropriate balance of skills, knowledge, experience, independence and diversity to enable it to discharge its duties and responsibilities effectively.

Recommendation 2.3 of the ASX Corporate Governance Principles and Recommendations (3rd edition 2014)

A listed entity should disclose:

(a) the names of the directors considered by the board to be independent directors;

(b) if a director has an interest, position, association or relationship of the type described in Box 2.3 but the board is of the opinion that it does not compromise the independence of the director, the nature of the interest, position, association or relationship in question and an explanation of why the board is of that opinion; and

Recommendation 2.4 of the ASX Corporate Governance Principles and Recommendations (3rd edition 2014)

A majority of the board of a listed entity should be independent directors.

Recommendation 2.5 of the ASX Corporate Governance Principles and Recommendations (3rd edition 2014)

The chair of the board of a listed entity should be an independent director and, in particular, should not be the same person as the CEO of the entity.

Recommendation 4.1 of the ASX Corporate Governance Principles and Recommendations (3rd edition 2014)

The board of a listed entity should:

(a) have an audit committee which:

(1) has at least three members, all of whom are non-executive directors and a majority of whom are independent directors; and

(2) is chaired by an independent director, who is not the chair of the board, …

(b) if it does not have an audit committee, disclose that fact and the processes it employs that independently verify and safeguard the integrity of its corporate reporting, including the processes for the appointment and removal of external auditor and the rotation of the audit engagement partner.

Recommendation 7.1 of the ASX Corporate Governance Principles and Recommendations (3rd edition 2014)

The board of a listed entity should:

(a) have a committee or committees to oversee risk, each of which:
   (1) has at least three members, a majority of whom are independent directors; and
   (2) is chaired by an independent director, …

(b) if it does not have a risk committee or committees that satisfy (a) above, disclose that fact and the processes it employs for overseeing the entity's risk management framework.

Recommendation 8.1 of the ASX Corporate Governance Principles and Recommendations (3rd edition 2014)

The board of a listed entity should:

(a) have a remuneration committee which:
   (1) has at least three members, a majority of whom are independent directors; and
   (2) is chaired by an independent director, …

(b) if it does not have a remuneration committee, disclose that fact and the processes it employs for setting the level and composition of remuneration for directors and senior executives and ensuring that such remuneration is appropriate and not excessive.

ASX Listing Rule 4.10: Additional Information to Be Included by All Entities

An entity must include the following information in its annual report. …
4.10.3 Either of the following

- •A corporate governance statement that meets the requirements of this rule;…
- The corporate governance statement must disclose the extent to which the entity has followed the recommendations set by the ASX Corporate Governance Council during the reporting period. If the entity has not followed a recommendation for any part of the reporting period, its corporate governance statement must separately identify that recommendation and the period during which it was not followed and state its reasons for not following the recommendation and what (if any) alternative governance practices it adopted in lieu of the recommendation during that period.

BOX 2.3: FACTORS RELEVANT TO ASSESSING THE INDEPENDENCE OF A DIRECTOR

Examples of interests, positions, associations and relationships that might cause doubts about the independence of a director include if the director:

- is, or has been, employed in an executive capacity by the entity or any of its child entities and there has not been a period of at least three years between ceasing such employment and serving on the board;
- is, or has within the last three years been, a partner, director or senior employee of a provider of material professional services to the entity or any of its child entities;
- is, or has been within the last three years, in a material business relationship (eg as a supplier or customer) with the entity or any of its child entities, or an officer of, or otherwise associated with, someone with such a relationship;
- is a substantial security holder of the entity or an officer of, or otherwise associated with, a substantial security holder of the entity;
- has a material contractual relationship with the entity or its child entities other than as a director;
- has close family ties with any person who falls within any of the categories described above; or
- has been a director of the entity for such a period that his or her independence may have been compromised.

In each case, the materiality of the interest, position, association or relationship needs to be assessed to determine whether it might interfere, or might reasonably be seen to interfere, with the director's capacity to bring an independent judgment to bear on issues before the board and to act in the best interests of the entity and security holders generally.

BIBLIOGRAPHY

第4回 産業競争力会議 議事要旨 [The Summary of the Discussions at the 4th Meeting of the Industrial Competitiveness Council], held on 15 March 2013, available at www.kantei.go.jp.

会社法制の見直しに関する要綱案　（第一次案） [The First Draft of the Outline for the Companies Act Reform], available at www.moj.go.jp.

法制審議会　第152回会議　議事概要　[The Summary of the Discussions at the 152nd Meeting of the Legal Council], available at www.moj .go.jp.

法制審議会　会社法制部会 第1回会議議事録 [The Minutes of the 1st Meeting of the Companies Act Working Group of the Legislative Council], held on 28 April 2010, available at www.moj.go.jp.

法制審議会　会社法制部会 第2回会議議事録 [The Minutes of the 2nd Meeting of the Companies Act Working Group of the Legislative Council], held on 26 May 2010, available at www.moj.go.jp.

法制審議会　会社法制部会 第3回会議議事録 [The Minutes of the 3rd Meeting of the Companies Act Working Group of the Legislative Council], held on 23 June 2010, available at www.moj.go.jp.

法制審議会　会社法制部会 第4回会議議事録 [The Minutes of the 4th Meeting of the Companies Act Working Group of the Legislative Council], held on 25 August 2010, available at www.moj.go.jp.

法制審議会　会社法制部会 第9回会議議事録 [The Minutes of the 9th Meeting of the Companies Act Working Group of the Legislative Council], held on 26 January 2011, available at www.moj.go.jp.

法制審議会　会社法制部会　第23回会議議事録　[The Minutes of the 23rd Meeting of the Companies Act Working Group of the Legislative Council], held on 18 July 2012, available at www.moj.go.jp.

Acer Group, 'Corporate Governance', available at www.acer-group.com.

Adams, R. B., 'Governance and the Financial Crisis', *International Review of Finance*, 12 (2012), 7.

Adams, R. B., Hermalin, B. E., and Weisbach, M. S., 'The Role of Boards of Directors in Corporate Governance: A Conceptual Framework and Survey', *Journal of Economic Literature*, 48 (2010), 58.

Afsharipour, A., 'Directors as Trustees of the Nation? India's Corporate Governance and Corporate Social Responsibility Reform Efforts', *Seattle University Law Review*, 34 (2011), 995.

Afsharipour, A., and Rana, S., 'The Emergence of New Corporate Social Responsibility Regimes in China and India', *UC Davis Business Law Journal*, 14 (2014), 175.

Ahmadjian, C. L., 'Corporate Governance and Business Systems in Asia' in G. Redding and M. A. Witt (eds.), *The Oxford Handbook of Asian Business Systems* (Oxford University Press, 2014).

Allen, J., 'New Developments in Corporate Governance Reform in Asia: Northern Chills, Southern Warmth' (ACGA Members' Briefing, Sydney, 25 March 2013), available at www.acga-asia.org.

Allen, W., Kraakman, R., and Subramanian, G., *Commentaries and Cases on the Law of Business Organization*, 4th edn (Wolters Kluwer, 2012).

Aman, H., and Nguyen, P., 'The Size and Composition of Corporate Boards in Japan', *Asian Business and Management*, 11(4) (2012), 425.

Anabtawi, I., 'Explaining Pay without Performance: The Tournament Alternative', *Emory Law Journal*, 54 (2005), 1557.

Anderson, R. C., and Reeb, D. M., 'Founding-Family Ownership and Firm Performance: Evidence from the S&P 500', *Journal of Finance*, 58 (2003), 1301.

Anderson, R. C., and Reeb, D. M., 'Board Composition: Balancing Family Influence in S&P 500 Firms', *Administrative Science Quarterly*, 49 (2004), 209.

Aoun, F., and Nottage, L., 'The Rise of Independent Directors in Australia: Adoption, Reform and Uncertainty', *University of Miami International and Comparative Law Review*, 23 (2016), 433.

Aoyagi, C., and Ganelli, G., 'Unstash the Cash! Corporate Governance Reform in Japan' (International Monetary Fund Working Paper, 2014), available at www.imf.org.

Armour, J., Hansmann, H., and Kraakman, R., 'What Is Corporate Law?' in R. Kraakman et al. (eds.), *The Anatomy of Corporate Law: A Comparative and Functional Approach*, 2nd edn (Oxford University Press, 2009).

Armour, J. et al., 'Shareholder Protection and Stock Market Development: An Empirical Test of the Legal Origins Hypothesis', *Journal of Empirical Legal Studies*, 6 (2009), 343.

Arner, D. W. et al., *Assessing Hong Kong as an International Financial Centre: First Report of the Hong Kong Research Grants Council Theme-Based Research Scheme Project: Enhancing Hong Kong's Future as a Leading International Financial Centre* (April 2014), available at corporateaccountability2014.com.

Aronson, B. E., 'The Toshiba Corporate Governance Scandal: How Can Japanese Corporate Governance be Fixed?', *Commentary on Jurist Online*, 10 August 2015, available at http://jurist.org.

Aronson, B. E. 'Learning from Toyota's Troubles: The Debate on Board Oversight, Board Structure, and Director Independence in Japan', *Journal of Japanese Law*, 15(30) (2010), 67.

Aronson, B. E., 'The Olympus Scandal and Corporate Governance Reform: Can Japan Find a Middle Ground between the Board Monitoring Model and Management Model?', *Pacific Basin Law Journal*, 30(1) (2012), 93.

Aronson, B. E., 'Japanese Corporate Governance Reform: A Comparative Perspective', *Hastings Business Law Journal*, 11(1) (2015), 85.

Aronson, B. E., Kozuka, S., and Nottage, L., 'Corporate Legislation in Japan' in P. Haghirian (ed.), *Routledge Handbook of Japanese Business and Management* (Routledge, 2016).

Arvind, T. T., 'The "Transplant Effect" in Harmonization', *International and Comparative Law Quarterly*, 59 (2010), 65.

Ashurst London, 'Changes to the Listing Rules: Final Rules in Force 16 May 2014' (June 2014), available at www.ashurst.com.

Asian Corporate Governance Association, 'Building Stronger Board and Companies in Asia: A Concise Report on Corporate Governance Policies and Practices' (January 2000), available at www.acga-asia.org.

Asian Corporate Governance Association, 'Rules and Recommendations on the Number of Independent Directors in Asia', available at www.acga-asia.org.

Asian Corporate Governance Association, 'White Paper on Corporate Governance in Japan' (2008), available at www.acga-asia.org.

Asian Corporate Governance Association, *The Roles and Functions of Kansayaku Boards Compared to Audit Committees* (November 2013), available at www.acga-asia.org.

Asian Corporate Governance Association and KPMG, *Balancing Rules and Flexibility* (2014), available at www.accaglobal.com.

ASX Corporate Governance Council, *Principles of Good Corporate Governance and Best Practice Recommendations*, 1st edn (March 2003).

ASX Corporate Governance Council, *Corporate Governance Principles and Recommendations*, 2nd edn (August 2007).

ASX Corporate Governance Council, *Corporate Governance Principles and Recommendations with 2010 Amendments*, 2nd edn (June 2010).

ASX Corporate Governance Council, *Corporate Governance Principles and Recommendations*, 3rd edn (March 2014).

ASX Corporate Governance Council, *Review of the Corporate Governance Principles and Recommendations: Consultation Paper*, 16 August 2013.

AT Kearney, AZB & Partners and Hunt Partners, 'India Board Report – 2007: Findings, Action Plans and Innovative Strategies' (2007).

Austin, A., 'World's Best Economy: Australia Loses Top IAREM Ranking under Coalition', *Independent Australia*, 22 April 2015, available at https://independentaustralia.net.

Austin, B., 'Directors Should Have More Skin in the Game', *Australian Financial Review*, 31 July 2014.

Australian Council of Superannuation Investors, *Board Composition and Non-Executive Director Pay in the Top 200 Companies: 2012* (25 September 2013).

Australian Council of Superannuation Investors, *ACSI Governance Guidelines: A Guide for Superannuation Funds to Monitor Listed Australian Companies* (July 2013).

Australian Council of Superannuation Investors, *Board Composition and Non-Executive Director Pay: 2013* (2014).

Australian Council of Superannuation Investors, *Board Composition and Non-Executive Director Pay in the ASX 200 Companies* (November 2014).

Australian Council of Superannuation Investors, *Board Composition and Non-Executive Director Pay: 2014* (2015).

Australian Institute of Company Directors, *Submission on Revised Corporate Governance Principles and Recommendations* (14 November 2013).

Auyong, H., 'Singapore Productivity Challenge Part I', Lee Kuan Yew School of Public Policy, available at http://lkyspp.nus.edu.sg.

'Back to the Drawing Board', *The Economist*, 3 November 2012, 68.

Bainbridge, S. M., 'Director Primacy: The Means and Ends of Corporate Governance', *Northwestern University Law Review*, 97 (2003), 547.

Bainbridge, S. M., 'Director Primacy and Shareholder Disempowerment', *Harvard Law Review*, 119 (2006), 1735.

Bainbridge, S. M., 'Dodd-Frank: Quack Federal Corporate Governance Round II', *Minnesota Law Review*, 95 (2011), 1779.

Bainbridge, S. M., *Corporate Governance after the Financial Crisis* (Oxford University Press, 2012).

Bainbridge, S. M., 'Director Versus Shareholder Primacy in New Zealand Company Law as Compared to U.S.A. Corporate Law' (2014), available at http://ssrn.com/abstract_id=2416449.

Bainbridge, S. M., and Henderson, M. T., 'Boards-R-Us: Reconceptualizing Corporate Boards', *Stanford Law Review*, 66 (2014), 1051.

Bajaj, V., 'The Children's Investment Fund Wages Battle with Coal India', *New York Times*, 19 April 2012.

Balasubramanian, N., and Anand, R. V., 'Ownership Trends in Corporate India 2001–2011: Evidence and Implications' (Indian Institute of Management, Bangalore, Working Paper No. 419, 2013), available at http://ssrn.com/abstract=2303684.

Balasubramanian, N., Black, B. S., and Khanna,V., 'The Relation between Firm-Level Corporate Governance and Market Value: A Study of India', *Emerging Markets Review*, 11 (2010), 319.

Barca, F., and Becht, M., *The Control of Corporate Europe* (Oxford University Press, 2001).

Barnes, L., and Lau, P., 'Corporate Governance of Banks in Hong Kong: A Banking Sector Governance (BGS) Perspective' (20th Australasian Finance and Banking Conference Paper, 2007), available at http://papers.ssrn.com/sol3/papers.cfm?abstract_id=1007436.

Baron, J., and Lachenauer, R., 'Surviving in a Family Business When You're Not Part of the Family', *Harvard Business Review*, 15 January 2015.

Barry, P., *Rich Kids* (Random House, 2003).

Basel Committee on Banking Supervision, *Principles for Enhancing Corporate Governance* (2010), available at www.bis.org.

Baum, H., 'Emulating Japan?' in H. Baum (ed.), *Japan: Economic Success and Legal System* (De Gruyter, 1997), 1.

Baum, H., and Takahashi, E., 'Commercial Law and Corporate Law in Japan: Legal and Economic Developments after 1868', in W. Röhl (ed.), *A History of Law in Japan Since 1868* (Brill, 2005).

Baysinger, B. D., and Butler, H. N., 'Corporate Governance and the Board of Directors: Performance Effects of Changes in Board Composition', *Journal of Law, Economics and Organization*, 1 (1985), 101.

Bebchuk, L. A., 'The Case for Increasing Shareholder Power', *Harvard Law Review*, 118 (2005), 833.

Bebchuk, L. A., and Hamdani, A., 'The Elusive Quest for Global Corporate Governance Standards', *University of Pennsylvania Law Review*, 157 (2009), 1263.

Bebchuk, L. A., and Spamann, H., 'Regulating Bankers' Pay', *Georgetown Law Journal*, 98 (2010), 247.

Bebchuk, L. A., and Weisbach, M. S., 'The State of Corporate Governance Research', *Review of Financial Studies*, 23 (2010), 939.

Bebchuk, L., Brav, A., and Jiang, W., 'The Long-Term Effects of Hedge Fund Activism', *Columbia Law Review*, 115 (2015), 1085.

Bebchuk, L., Cohen, A., and Ferrell, A., 'What Matters in Corporate Governance?', *Review of Financial Studies*, 22 (2008), 783.

Belcredi, M., Bozzi, S., and Di Noia, C., 'Board Elections and Shareholder Activism: The Italian Experiment' in M. Belcredi and G. Ferrarini (eds.), *Boards and Shareholders in European Listed Companies* (Cambridge University Press, 2013).

Beleya, P. et al., 'Independent Directors and Stakeholders Protection: A Case of Sime Darby', *International Journal of Academic Research in Business and Social Sciences*, 2 (2012), 422.

Beltratti, A., and Stulz, R. M., 'The Credit Crisis around the Globe: Why Did Some Banks Perform Better?', *Journal of Financial Economics*, 105 (2012), 1.

Berle, A. A., and Means, G. C., *The Modern Corporation and Private Property* (Commerce Clearing House, 1932).

Bertrand, M., Mehta, P., and Mullainathan, S., 'Ferreting Out Tunneling: An Application to Indian Business Groups', *Quarterly Journal of Economics*, 117(1) (2002), 121.

Bhagat, S., and Black, B. S., 'The Uncertain Relationship between Board Composition and Firm Performance', *Business Lawyer*, 54 (1999), 921.

Bhagat, S., and Black, B. S., 'The Non-Correlation between Board Independence and Long-Term Firm Performance', *Journal of Corporation Law*, 27 (2002), 232.

Bhan, I., 'What's the Role of Tribunals?', *The Financial Express*, 22 January 2014.

Bird, H., 'The Rise and Fall of the Independent Director', *Australian Journal of Corporate Law*, 5 (1995), 235.

Black, B. S., 'Shareholder Passivity Reexamined', *Michigan Law Review*, 89 (1990), 520.

Black, B. S., 'The Core Institutions That Support Strong Securities Markets', *Business Lawyer*, 55 (2000), 1565.

Black, B. S., and Khanna, V. S., 'Can Corporate Governance Reforms Increase Firm Market Values? Event Study Evidence from India', *Journal of Empirical Legal Studies*, 4 (2007), 749.

Black, B. S., and Kim, W., 'The Effect of Board Structure on Firm Value: A Multiple Identification Strategies Approach Using Korean Data', *Journal of Financial Economics*, 104 (2012), 203.

Black, B. S., and Kraakman, R., 'A Self-Enforcing Model of Corporate Law', *Harvard Law Review*, 109 (1996), 1911.

Black, B. S., Cheffins, B. R., and Klausner, M., 'Outside Director Liability', *Stanford Law Review*, 58 (2006), 1055.

Black, B. S., Cheffins, B. R., and Klausner, M., 'Outside Director Liability: A Policy Analysis', *Journal of Institutional and Theoretical Economics*, 162 (2006), 5.

Black, B. S., Cheffins, B. R., and Klausner, M., 'Shareholder Suits and Outside Director Liability: The Case of Korea' in Young-Jae Lim (ed.), *Corporate Governance and the Capital Market in Korea* (Korea Development Institute, 2006).

Black, B. S., Jang, H., and Kim, W., 'Does Corporate Governance Predict Firms' Market Values? Evidence from Korea', *Journal of Law, Economics, and Organization*, 22 (2006), 366.

Black, B. S. et al., 'Russian Privatization and Corporate Governance: What Went Wrong?', *Stanford Law Review*, 52 (2000), 1731.

Black, B. S. et al., 'Corporate Governance in Korea at the Millennium: Enhancing International Competitiveness', *Journal of Corporation Law*, 26 (2001), 537.

Black, B. S. et al., 'Methods for Multicountry Studies of Corporate Governance: Evidence from the BRIKT Countries', *Journal of Econometrics*, 183 (2014), 230.

Black, B. S. et al., 'Corporate Governance Indices and Construct Validity' (ECGI Finance Working Paper No. 483/2016, September 2016), 21 Table 2, available at https://papers.ssrn.com/sol3/papers.cfm?abstract_id=2838273.

Blair, M., 'Boards of Directors and Corporate Performance under a Team Production Model' in J. Hill and R. Thomas (eds.), *Research Handbook on Shareholder Power* (Edward Elgar, 2015), 249–268.

Blair, M., and Stout, L., 'A Team Production Theory of Corporate Law', *Virginia Law Review*, 85 (1999), 247.

Blair, M., and Stout, L., 'Director Accountability and the Mediating Role of the Corporate Board', *Washington University Law Quarterly*, 79 (2001), 403.

Blanchard, D., and Dionne, G., 'Risk Management and Corporate Governance' (HEC Montreal Risk Management Chair Working Paper No. 03-04, 2003), available at http://ssrn.com/abstract=441482.

Bonn, I., Yoshikawa, T., and Phan, P. H., 'Effects of Board Structure on Firm Performance: A Comparison between Japan and Australia', *Asian Business Management*, 3 (2004), 105.

Bosch, H., 'The Changing Face of Corporate Governance', *UNSW Law Journal*, 25(2) (2002), 270.

Branson, D., 'An Australian Perspective on a Global Phenomenon: Initiatives to Place Women on Corporate Boards of Directors', *Australian Journal of Corporate Law*, 27 (2012), 2.

Brown, J. R., Jr., 'The Demystification of the Board of Directors' (University of Denver Sturm College of Law, Legal Research Paper Series, Working Paper No. 14–37, 2014), available at http://ssrn.com/abstract= 2474394.

Brudney, V., 'The Independent Director: Heavenly City or Potemkin Village?', *Harvard Law Review*, 95 (1982), 597.

Bruner, C. M., *Corporate Governance in the Common-Law World: The Political Foundations of Shareholder Power* (Cambridge University Press, 2013).

Buchanan, J., Heesang Chai, D., and Deakin, S., *Hedge Fund Activism in Japan: The Limits of Shareholder Primacy* (Cambridge University Press, 2012).

Cabrelli, D., and Siems, M., 'Convergence, Legal Origins, and Transplants in Comparative Corporate Law: A Case-Based and Quantitative Analysis', *American Journal of Comparative Law*, 63 (2015), 109.

Cai, H., 'An Acid Test of Board Independence', *Business Times Singapore*, 22 October 2012.

Cai, W., 'The Dilemmas of Independent Directors in China: An Empirical and Comparative Study', *European Business Organization Law Review*, 18 (2017), 123, available at SSRN: http://ssrn.com/abstract=2758519.

Capital Market Research Institute of Shanghai Securities Exchange, 年度沪市上市公司治理专题调查和研究报告 [Special Survey and Research Report on Corporate Governance of Companies Listed on Shanghai Securities Exchange 2012], 上海证券报 [Shanghai Securities], 23 October 2013.

Carlile, L. E., 'The Labor Movement' in A. Gaunder (ed.), *The Routledge Handbook of Japanese Politics* (Routledge, 2011).

Carlin, W., and Mayer, C., 'Finance, Investment and Growth', *Journal of Financial Economics*, 69 (2003), 191.

Cha, L., 'The SFC's Role in Regulating Listed Companies in Hong Kong' in Securities and Futures Commission, *Securities Regulation in Hong Kong* (May 2002).

Chakra, N. A., and Kaddoura, H., 'Doing Business 2015: Measuring Business Regulations, Protecting Minority Investors in [Name of Economy]' (World Bank, 2014), available at www.doingbusiness.org.

Chakra, N. A. et al., 'Doing Business 2016: Protecting Minority Investors' (World Bank, 2015), available at www.doingbusiness.org.

Chakra, N. A. et al., 'Doing Business 2017: Equal Opportunity for All' (World Bank, 2016), available at www.doingbusiness.org.

Chakrabarti, R., Megginson, W., and Yadav, P. K., 'Corporate Governance in India', *Journal of Applied Corporate Finance*, 20 (2008), 59.

Chandler, A. D., *The Visible Hand: The Managerial Revolution in America*, 16th edn (Belknap Press of Harvard University Press, 2002).

Chang, H. T., '薪資報酬委員會獨立性與專業性再思考' [Rethinking of the Independence and Expertise Requirements of the Remuneration Committee in Taiwan], *The Taiwan Law Review*, 233 (October 2014), 129.

Chang, S. J., *Financial Crisis and Transformation of Korean Business Groups: The Rise and Fall of Chaebols* (Cambridge University Press, 2006).

Cheffins, B. R., 'Corporate Governance Reform: Britain as an Exporter' in David Hume Institute, *Hume Papers on Public Policy: Corporate Governance and the Reform of the Company Law*, Vol. VIII (Edinburgh University Press, 2000).

Cheffins, B. R., 'Law as Bedrock: The Foundations of an Economy Dominated by Widely Held Public Companies', *Oxford Journal of Legal Studies*, 23 (2003), 1.

Cheffins, B. R., 'Did Corporate Governance "Fail" during the 2008 Stock Market Meltdown? The Case of the S&P 500', *Business Lawyer*, 65 (2009), 1.

Cheffins, B. R., 'The History of Modern U.S. Corporate Governance: Introduction' in B. R. Cheffins (ed.), *The History of Modern U.S. Corporate Governance*, Vol. I (Edward Elgar, 2012).

Cheffins, B. R., 'The History of Corporate Governance' (ECGI Law Working Paper No. 184/2012, 2012) available at http://ssrn.com/ abstract=1975404.

Cheffins, B. R., 'The History of Corporate Governance' in M. Wright et al. (eds.), *Oxford Handbook of Corporate Governance* (Oxford University Press, 2013).

Cheffins, B. R., 'Delaware and the Transformation of Corporate Governance' (The University of Cambridge Faculty of Law Legal Studies Research Paper Series, Paper No. 64/2014, November 2014), available at: http://ssrn.com/abstract=2531640.

Cheffins, B. R., 'Corporate Governance Since the Managerial Capitalism Era', *Business History Review* (forthcoming) (University of Cambridge Faculty of Law Research Paper No. 39/2015, 2015), available at http://ssrn.com/abstract=2618480.

Cheffins, B. R., 'The Rise of Corporate Governance in the UK: When and Why', *Current Legal Problems*, 68 (2015), 387, available at http://dx.doi.org/10.1093/clp/cuv006.

Cheffins, B. R., and Black, B. S., 'Outside Director Liability across Countries', *Texas Law Review*, 84 (2006), 1385.

Chen, C. C., 'Corporate Governance of State-Owned Enterprises: An Empirical Survey of the Model of Temasek Holdings in Singapore' (Singapore Management University School of Law Research Paper No. 6/2014, 2013), available at http://ssrn.com/abstract=2366699.

Chen, C., and Jaggi, B., 'Association between Independent Non-Executive Directors, Family Control and Financial Disclosures in Hong Kong', *Journal of Accounting and Public Policy*, 19 (2000), 285.

Cheng, F., 'Corporate Governance in Hong Kong : An Empirical Study of the Effects of Independent Non-Executive Directors on Voluntary Corporate Disclosures and Adoption of Best Corporate Governance Practices' (City University of Hong Kong Institutional Repository, 2011), available at http://dspace.cityu.edu.hk.

Cheung, Y. et al., 'Do Investors Really Value Corporate Governance? Evidence from the Hong Kong Market', *Journal of International Financial Management and Accounting*, 18(2) (2007), 86.

China Association for Public Companies, 'Guideline for the Exercise of Duties of Independent Directors of Public Companies', available at www.capco.org.cn.

China Association for Public Companies, 上市公司独立董事履职情况报告 [Report of Duty Performance of Independent Directors in the Listed Companies] (16 January 2014), available at www.capco.org.cn.

China Association for Public Companies Research Team on Drafting the Guidelines for Exercise of Duties of Independent Directors of Public Companies, 独立董事作用显著 提升空间仍较大 [Effects of Independent Directors Are Significant, While Promotion Space Is Still Big], 中国证券报 [China Securities News], 16 January 2014.

China Credit Information Service Ltd, *Business Groups in Taiwan* (2014).

China Sky Chemical Fibre Co., Ltd, 'Miscellaneous: Trading Resumption' (filing with SGX dated 9 September 2015), available at http://infopub.sgx.com.

Choi, J. J., Park, S. W., and Yoo, S. S., 'The Value of Outside Directors: Evidence from Corporate Governance Reform in Korea', *Journal of Financial and Quantitative Analysis*, 42 (2007), 941.

'Chronology of Events Leading to Sony's Shake-up', *Financial Times*, 7 March 2005, available at www.ft.com.

Chun, K. H. et al., *Corporations and Partnerships in South Korea* (Wolters Kluwer, 2014).

Cioffi, J. W., *Public Law and Private Power: Corporate Governance Reform in the Age of Finance Capitalism* (Cornell University Press, 2010).

Claessens, S., and Fan, J. P. H., 'Corporate Governance in Asia: A Survey', *International Review of Finance*, 3 (2002), 71.

Claessens, S. et al., 'The Separation of Ownership and Control in East Asian Corporations', *Journal of Financial Economics*, 58 (2000), 81.

Clarke, D. C., 'The Independent Director in Chinese Corporate Governance', *Delaware Journal of Corporate Law*, 31 (2006), 125.

Clarke, D. C., 'Three Concepts of the Independent Director', *Delaware Journal of Corporate Law*, 32 (2007), 73.

Clarke, D. C., '"Nothing but Wind"? The Past and Future of Comparative Corporate Governance', *American Journal of Comparative Law*, 59 (2011), 75.

Clark, R. C., 'The Four Stages of Capitalism: Reflections on Investment Management Treatises', *Harvard Law Review*, 94 (1981), 561.

Clark, R. C., *Corporate Law*, 2nd edn (Little, Brown and Company, 1986).

Clarke, F., and Dean, G., *Indecent Disclosure: Gilding the Corporate Lily* (Cambridge University Press, 2007).

Clarke, F., Dean, G., and Egan, W., *The Unaccountable and Ungovernable Corporation: Companies' Use-By-Date Closes In* (Routledge, 2014).

Clarke, F., Dean, G., and Oliver, K., *Corporate Collapse: Accounting, Regulatory, and Ethical Failure* (Cambridge University Press, 2003).

Clarke, T., *International Corporate Governance: A Comparative Approach* (Routledge, 2008).

Coffee, J. C., Jr., 'What Went Wrong? An Initial Inquiry into the Causes of the 2008 Financial Crisis', *Journal of Corporate Law Studies*, 9 (2009), 1.

Cole, R. A., Berkman, H., and Fu, J., 'Expropriation through Loan Guarantees to Related Parties: Evidence from China', *Journal of Banking and Finance*, 33 (2009), 141.

Commission Staff Working Document, Report on the Application by the Member States of the EU of the Commission Recommendation on the Role of Non-executive or Supervisory Directors of Listed Companies and on the Committees of the (Supervisory) Board, 13 July 2007, SEC (2007) 1021.

Committee on the Financial Aspects of Corporate Governance, *Cadbury Report* (December 1992).

Commonwealth, Royal Commission of Inquiry into the Failure of HIH Insurance, *Final Report* (2003).

Companies Registry, 'A Guide on Directors' Duties' (March 2014), available at www.sfc.hk/web/EN/files/ER/eGuide%201301.pdf.

Companies Registry, The Government of the Hong Kong Special Administrative Region, 'CR – About Us', available at www.cr.gov.hk.

Corporate Governance Committee, *Consultation Paper* (2000), available at www.mas.gov.sg.

Corporate Governance Committee, *Report of the Committee and Code of Corporate Governance* (2001), available at www.acra.gov.sg.

Corporate Governance Service, *CGS Report*, 45 (January 2014).

Corporations and Markets Advisory Committee, Australian Parliament, *Diversity on Boards of Directors* (2009), available at www.camac.gov.au.

Corporations and Markets Advisory Committee, Australian Parliament, *Guidance for Directors* (2010), available at www.camac.gov.au.

Corporations and Markets Advisory Committee, Australian Parliament, *The Social Responsibility of Corporations* (December 2006), available at www.camac.gov.au.

Corrupt Practices Investigations Bureau, 'Transparency International', CPIB.gov, available at www.cpib.gov.sg.

Council on Corporate Disclosure and Governance, *Consultation Paper on Proposed Revisions to the Code of Corporate Governance* (2004), available at www.acga-asia.org.

CPA Australia, *CPA Australia Asia-Pacific Governance Survey* (2014), available at www.cpaaustralia.com.au.

Cram, C., 'The UK Can Learn a Lot from Lee Kuan Yew and Singapore', *The Guardian*, 4 April 2015, available at www.theguardian.com.

Credit Suisse, *Asian Family Business Report 2011* (October 2011), available at https://publications.credit-suisse.com.

Credit Suisse, *Optimal Board Member Numbers Produce the Best Shareholder Returns* (5 September 2014).

Creighton, A., 'Shareholders Suffer as Independent Directors Pay Fat Cats', *The Australian*, 28 August 2013, available at www.theaustralian.com.au.

Creighton, A., 'ASX, Directors Dispute Claims Execs to Blame', *The Australian*, 29 August 2013.

Culpepper, P. D., *Quiet Politics and Business Power: Corporate Control in Europe and Japan* (Cambridge University Press, 2011).

Cunningham, L. A., 'Rediscovering Board Expertise: Legal Implications of the Empirical Literature', *University of Cincinnati Law Review*, 77 (2008), 465.

Dahles, H., and Wels, H. (eds.), *Culture, Organization and Management in East Asia: Doing Business in China* (Nova Science Publishers, 2002).

Dahya, J., and McConnell, J., 'Board Composition, Corporate Performance, and the Cadbury Committee Recommendation', *Journal of Financial and Quantitative Analysis*, 42 (2007), 535.

Dahya, J., Dimitrov, O., and McConnell, J. J., 'Dominant Shareholders, Corporate Boards, and Corporate Value: A Cross-Country Analysis', *Journal of Financial Economics*, 87 (2008), 73.

Dallas, L. L., 'Developments in US Boards of Directors and the Multiple Roles of Corporate Boards' in J. Sarra (ed.), *Corporate Governance in Global Capital Markets* (UBC Press, 2003).

Dallas, L. L., 'The Multiple Roles of Corporate Boards of Directors', *San Diego Law Review*, 40 (2003), 781.

Dallas, L. L., 'Short-Termism, the Financial Crisis, and Corporate Governance', *Journal of Corporation Law*, 37 (2012), 265.

D'Angelo Fisher, L., 'Know-How in the Asian Century', *BRW*, 16 May 2013, available at www.brw.com.au.

Das, D., 'Growth, Integration and Trends in Equity Markets in Asia', *Asia-Pacific Business Review*, 20 (2014), 286.

Davies, P. L., *Gower's Principles of Modern Company Law*, 6th edn (Sweet and Maxwell, 1997).

Davies, P. L., 'Corporate Boards in the United Kingdom' in P. L. Davies et al. (eds.), *Boards in Law and Practice* (Oxford University Press, 2013).

Davies, P. L., 'Shareholders in the United Kingdom' (ECGI Working Paper No. 280/2015, 2015).

Davies, P. L., and Hopt, K. J., 'Control Transactions' in R. Kraakman et al. (eds.), *The Anatomy of Corporate Law: A Comparative and Functional Approach*, 2nd edn (Oxford University Press, 2009).

Davies, P. L., and Hopt, K. J., 'Boards in Europe: Accountability and Convergence', *American Journal of Comparative Law*, 61 (2013), 301.

Davies, P. L., and Worthington, S., *Gower and Davies' Principles of Modern Company Law*, 9th edn (Sweet and Maxwell, 2012).

Davies, P. L. et al., 'Boards in Law and Practice: A Cross-Country Analysis in Europe' in P. L. Davies et al. (eds.), *Boards in Law and Practice* (Oxford University Press, 2013).

DBS Group Holdings, 'Annual Report 2015 – Board of Directors', available at www.dbs.com.

De Martinis, M., 'Do Directors, Regulators, and Auditors Speak, Hear, and See No Evil? Evidence from the Enron, HIH, and One.Tel Collapses', *Australian Journal of Corporate Law*, 15 (2002), 1.

Deakin, S., 'What Directors Do (and Fail to Do): Some Comparative Notes on Board Structure and Corporate Governance', *New York Law School Law Review*, 55 (2010/11), 525.

DeMott, D. A., 'Guests at the Table?: Independent Directors in Family-Influenced Public Companies', *Journal of Corporation Law*, 33 (2008), 819.

Devereux, M., and Sasanow, R., 'How Independent Are Independent Directors?', *Corporate Governance* (July 2008), available at http://app1.hkicpa.org.hk.

Dharmapala, D., and Khanna, V., 'Corporate Governance, Enforcement, and Firm Value: Evidence from India', *Journal of Law, Economics and Organization*, 29 (2013), 1056.

Dieleman, M. et al., *Success and Succession: A Study of SGX-Listed Family Firms* (2013), available at http://bschool.nus.edu.

Diversity Council Australia, *Capitalising on Culture: A Study of the Cultural Origins of ASX 200 Business Leaders* (2013), available at http://dca.org.au.

Douglas, W. O., 'Directors Who Do Not Direct', *Harvard Law Review*, 47 (1934), 1305.

Doval, P., and Sidhartha, 'Suzuki's Gujarat Plan Splits Maruti Board', *The Times of India*, 13 March 2014.

Druey, J. N., 'Unabhängigkeit als Gebot des allgemeinen Unternehmensrechts' in S. Kalss, C. Nowotny and M. Schauer (eds.), *Festschrift Peter Doralt* (Manz, 2004).

Du, W., '英美民事证据开示若干问题研析' [Research on the (Evidence) Disclosure Procedure under Anglo-American Law], *证据科学* [*Evidence Science*], 16 (2008), 713.

du Plessis, J. J., and Saenger, I., 'The Supervisory Board as Company Organ' in J. J. du Plessis et al. (eds.), *German Corporate Governance in International and European Context*, 2nd edn (Springer, 2012).

du Plessis, J. J., and Saenger, I., 'An overview of the Corporate Governance Debate in Germany' in J. J. du Plessis et al. (eds.), *German Corporate Governance in International and European Context*, 2nd edn (Springer, 2012).

du Plessis, J., Hargovan, A., and Bagaric, M. (eds.), *Principles of Contemporary Corporate Governance*, 2nd edn (Cambridge University Press, 2014).

du Plessis, J., Saenger, I., and Foster, R., 'Board Diversity or Gender Diversity? Perspectives from Europe, Australia and South Africa', *Deakin Law Review*, 17(2) (2012), 207.

du Plessis, J. J. et al., 'An Overview of German Business or Enterprise Law and the One-Tier and Two-Tier Board Systems Contrasted' in J. J. du Plessis et al. (eds.), *German Corporate Governance in International and European Context*, 2nd edn (Springer, 2012).

Duchin, R., Matsusaka, J. G., and Ozbas, O., 'When Are Outside Directors Effective?', *Journal of Financial Economics*, 96(2) (2010), 195.

Dunbar, N., 'The Role and Value of Independent Directors in Modern Australian Corporate Governance', *Company and Securities Law Journal*, 30(5) (2012), 312.

Durkin, P., 'Meet the Directors from Hell', *Australian Financial Review*, 21 June 2012, available at www.afr.com.

Durnev, A., and Kim, E. H., 'To Steal or Not To Steal: Firm Attributes, Legal Environment and Valuation', *Journal of Finance*, 60 (2005), 1461.

Eckbo, B. E. et al., 'Efficiency of Share-Voting Systems: Report on Italy' (ECGI Law Working Paper 174/2011, 2011), available at http://ssrn.com/abstract=1431733.

Edelman, P., Thomas, R., and Thompson, R., 'Shareholder Voting in the Age of Intermediary Capitalism', *Southern California Law Review*, 87 (2014), 1359.

Eisenberg, M. A., *The Structure of the Corporation: A Legal Analysis* (Little, Brown and Co., 1976).

Emerging Markets Committee of the International Organisation of Securities Commissions, 'Corporate Governance Practices in Emerging Markets' (2007), available at www.iosco.org.

Enriques, L., 'EC Company Law Directives and Regulations: How Trivial Are They?', *University of Pennsylvania Journal of International Economic Law*, 27 (2006), 1.

Enriques, L., Hansmann, H., and Kraakman, R., 'The Basic Governance Structure; Minority Shareholders and Non-Shareholder Constituencies' in R. Kraakman et al. (eds.), *The Anatomy of Corporate Law: A Comparative and Functional Approach*, 2nd edn (Oxford University Press, 2009).

Enriques, L., Hansmann, H., and Kraakman, R., 'The Basic Governance Structure: The Interests of Shareholders as a Class' in R. Kraakman et al. (eds.), *The Anatomy of Corporate Law: A Comparative and Functional Approach*, 2nd edn (Oxford University Press, 2009).

Enriques, L., Hertig, G., and Kanda, H., 'Related-Party Transactions' in R. Kraakman et al. (eds.), *The Anatomy of Corporate Law: A Comparative and Functional Approach*, 2nd edn (Oxford University Press, 2009).

Erkens, D. H., Hung, M., and Matos, P., 'Corporate Governance in the 2007–2008 Financial Crisis: Evidence from Financial Institutions Worldwide', *Journal of Corporate Finance*, 18 (2012), 389.

Etheridge, D., 'Boards of a Feather Flock Together: Board Networks Among ASX Firms' (2012 Financial Markets and Corporate Governance Conference, 4 November 2011), available at http://papers.ssrn.com/sol3/papers.cfm?abstract_id=1972254.

European Commission, *Green Paper: Corporate Governance in Financial Institutions and Remuneration Policies* (COM (2010) 284), available at http://ec.europa.eu.

European Commission, *Green Paper: The EU Corporate Governance Framework* (COM (2011) 164), available at http://ec.europa.eu.

European Corporate Governance Forum, *Statement of the European Corporate Governance Forum on Director Remuneration* of 23 March 2009, available at http://ec.europa.eu.

European Model Company Act Group, *The European Model Company Act (EMCA) Draft 2015*, available at http://law.au.dk.

Ewald, W., 'Comparative Jurisprudence (II): The Logic of Legal Transplants', *American Journal of Comparative Law*, 43 (1995), 489.

Fairfax, L. M., 'The Uneasy Case for the Inside Director', *Iowa Law Review*, 96 (2010), 127.

Faleye, O., Hoitash, R., Hoitash, U., 'The Costs of Intense Board Monitoring', *Journal of Finance Economy*, 101 (2011), 160.

Fang, G., and Liu, X., '董事会结构对行为影响的实证分析' [An Empirical Analysis of the Impact of Board Structure on Board Behaviours], *北京工商大学学报(社会科学版)* [*Journal of Beijing Technology and Business University (Social Science)*], 28(5) (2013), 28.

Fedtke, J., 'Legal Transplants' in J. Smits (ed.), *Encyclopedia of Comparative Law* (Edward Elgar, 2012).

Fernandes, N., 'EC: Board Compensation and Firm Performance: The Role of "Independent" Board Members', *Journal of Multinational Financial Management*, 18 (2008), 30.

Ferrarini, G. A., and Filippelli, M., 'Independent Directors and Controlling Shareholders around the World' (European Corporate Governance Institute (ECGI) Law Working Paper No. 258/2014, 2014), available at http://ssrn.com/abstract=2443786.

Ferreira, D., and Kirchmaier, T., 'Corporate Boards in Europe: Size, Independence and Gender Diversity' in M. Belcredi and G. Ferrarini (eds.), *Boards and Shareholders in European Listed Companies: Facts, Context and Post-Crisis Reforms* (Cambridge University Press, 2013).

Ferreira, D., Kirchmaier, T., and Metzger, D., 'Boards of Banks' (ECGI Finance Working Paper No. 289/2010, 2010), available at http://ssrn.com/abstract=1620551.

Ferris, S. P. et al., 'Too Busy to Mind the Business? Monitoring by Directors with Multiple Board Appointments', *Journal of Finance*, 58 (2003), 1087.

FICCI and Grant Thornton, 'CG Review 2009: India 101–500' (March 2009).

Financial Conduct Authority, 'Feedback on CP12/25: Enhancing the Effectiveness of the Listing Regime and Further Consultation' (CP13/15, November 2013).

Financial Conduct Authority, 'PS 14/8: Response to CP13/15: Enhancing the Effectiveness of the Listing Regime' (May 2014), available at www.fca.org.uk.

Financial Reporting Council, 'Developments in Corporate Governance and Stewardship 2011: The Impact and Implementation of the UK Corporate Governance and Stewardship Codes' (Financial Reporting Council, 2011), available at www.frc.org.uk.

Financial Reporting Council, *The UK Corporate Governance Code* (September 2014), available at http://frc.org.uk.

Financial Reporting Council, 'Developments in Corporate Governance and Stewardship 2015' (Financial Reporting Council, 2016), available at www.frc.org.uk.

Financial Services Authority, 'Enhancing the Effectiveness of the Listing Regime and Feedback on CP12/2: Supplementary Consultation on Proposed Changes to the Listing Rules Resulting from the Implementation of the Alternative Investment Fund Managers Directive' (CP12/25, October 2012).

Financial Supervisory Commission, 'Regulations Governing Appointment of Independent Directors and Compliance Matters for Public Companies', available at http://law.fsc.gov.tw.

Findlaw, 'SEC Approves NYSE and NASDAQ Proposals Relating to Director Independence' (23 March 2006), available at http://corporate.findlaw.com.

Finlay, J. R., 'Outrage of the Week: Leadership Fiddles While Bear Stearns Burns' (blog entry, 14 March 2008), available at http://finlayongovernance.com.

Fischer, M., and Swan, P., 'Does Board Independence Improve Firm Performance? Outcome of a Quasi-Natural Experiment' (27th Australasian Finance and Banking Conference, August 2014), available at http://ssrn.com/abstract=2312325.

Fleckner, A. M., 'Adam Smith on the Joint Stock Company' (Max Planck Institute for Tax Law and Public Finance Working Paper 2016–01, 2016), available at www.tax.mpg.de.

Fleckner, A. M., and Hopt, K. J. (eds.), *Comparative Corporate Governance: A Functional and International Analysis* (Cambridge University Press, 2013).

Florstedt, T., 'Die Unabhängigkeit des Aufsichtsratsmitglieds vom kontrollierenden Aktionär', *Zeitschrift für Wirtschaftsrecht*, 337 (2013).

Fockenbrock, D., 'Strengers Kampf für Unabhängigkeit', *Handelsblatt*, 22 February 2013, 22.

Fogel, E. M., and Geier, A. M., 'Strangers in the House: Rethinking Sarbanes-Oxley and the Independent Board of Directors', *Delaware Journal of Corporate Law*, 32 (2007), 33.

Foreman, S. R., 'Bored Boards: The Directorial Disengagement Dilemma', *Washburn Law Journal*, 50 (2010), 147.

Formoy, R. R., *The Historical Foundations of Modern Company Law* (Sweet and Maxwell, 1923).

Forum Europaeum Corporate Group Law, 'Corporate Group Law for Europe', *European Business Organization Law Review*, 1 (2000), 165.

Francis, B. B., Hasan, I., and Wu, Q., 'Do Corporate Boards Matter during the Current Financial Crisis?', *Review of Financial Economics*, 21 (2012), 39.

Frankenberg, G., 'Constitutional Transfer: The Ikea Theory Revisited', *Journal of International Constitutional Law*, 8 (2010), 563.

Freshfields Bruckhaus Deringer, 'Enforcement Trends in Hong Kong: A Surge in Scrutiny' (January 2014), available at www.freshfields.com.

Freshfields Bruckhaus Deringer, 'Enforcement Trends in Hong Kong: An Uptick in Scrutiny' (29 January 2015), available at www.freshfields.com.

Friedlander, D. et al., 'Topic 6: Directors' Duties – International Regulatory Perspective' (University of New South Wales, 2012 Directors' Duties Seminar, 20 March 2012), available at www.clmr.unsw.edu.au.

Fujisue, K., '株主至上主義との決別' [Farewell to Shareholder Primacy], *日経テクノロジーオンライン*, 1 July 2010, available at http://techon.nikkeibp.co.jp.

Gao, L., and Zhang, J., '公司治理、机构投资者与盈余管理' [Corporate Governance, Institutional Investors, and Earnings Management], *会计研究* [Accounting Review], 9 (2008), 64.

Garnaut, R., *Dark Days: Australia after the Boom* (Black Inc, 2013).

Gay, S., and Denning, S. C., 'Corporate Governance Principal-Agent Problem: The Equity Cost of Independent Directors' (Working Paper 2014), available at http://ssrn.com/abstract=2468942.

Gevurtz, F. A., 'The European Origins and the Spread of Corporate Board of Directors', *Stetson Law Review*, 33 (2004), 925.

Gevurtz, F. A., 'The Historical and Political Origins of Corporate Board of Directors' (2004), available at http://ssrn.com/ abstract=546296.

Ghemawat, P., and Khanna, T., 'The Nature of Diversified Business Groups: A Research Design and Two Case Studies', *Journal of Industrial Economics*, 46(1) (1998), 35.

Gill, S., 'Rethinking the Primacy of Board Efficacy for Governance: Evidence from India', *Corporate Governance*, 13 (2013), 99.

Gilson, R. J., 'Globalizing Corporate Governance: Convergence of Form or Function', *American Journal of Comparative Law*, 49 (2001), 329.

Gilson, R. J., 'Controlling Shareholders and Corporate Governance: Complicating the Comparative Taxonomy', *Harvard Law Review*, 119 (2006), 1642.

Gilson, R. J., 'Controlling Family Shareholders in Developing Countries: Anchoring Relational Exchange', *Stanford Law Review*, 60 (2007), 633.

Gilson, R. J., and Gordon, J. N., 'Controlling Controlling Shareholders', *University of Pennsylvania Law Review*, 152 (2003), 785.

Gilson, R. J., and Gordon, J. N., 'The Agency Costs of Agency Capitalism: Activist Investors and the Revaluation of Governance Rights', *Columbia Law Review*, 113 (2013), 863.

Gilson, R. J., and Kraakman, R., 'Reinventing the Outside Director: An Agenda for Institutional Investors', *Stanford Law Review*, 43 (1991), 863.

Gilson, R. J., and Milhaupt, C. J., 'Choice as Regulatory Reform: The Case of Japanese Corporate Governance', *The American Journal of Comparative Law*, 53(2) (2005), 343.

Gilson, R. J., and Milhaupt, C. J., 'Sovereign Wealth Funds and Corporate Governance: A Minimalist Response to the New Mercantilism', *Stanford Law Review*, 60 (2008), 1345.

Glasbeek, H., 'The James Hardie Directors: A Case of Missing Directors and Misdirections by Law', *Australian Journal of Corporate Law*, 28 (2013), 107.

Goh, K. S., 'Public Enterprises' (Speech at the NTUC Income Annual General Meeting, 20 June 1977), reproduced in Linda Low (ed.), *Wealth of East Asian Nations: Speeches and Writings by Goh Keng Swee* (Federal Publications, 1995).

Golding, G., 'Tightening the Screws on Directors: Care, Delegation and Reliance', *UNSW Law Journal*, 35(1) (2012), 266.

Goldman, D., '"Goodbye and Good Riddance" AIG Directors!', cnnmoney.com, 30 June 2009, available at http://money.cnn.com.

Goldman, E., Rocholl, J., and So, J., 'Do Politically Connected Boards Affect Firm Value?', *The Review of Financial Studies*, 22 (2009), 2331.

Gompers, P., Ishii, J., and Metrick, A., 'Corporate Governance and Equity Prices', *The Quarterly Journal of Economics*, 118 (2003), 107.

Goo, S. J., 'Study Report on History of Company Incorporation in Hong Kong' (July 2013), available at www.cr.gov.hk.

Gopal, T., 'Japan: A Closer Look at Governance Reforms' (ISS, 2015), available at www.issgovernance.com.

Gordon, J. N., 'The Rise of Independent Directors in the United States, 1950–2005: Of Shareholder Value and Stock Market Prices', *Stanford Law Review*, 59 (2007), 1465.

Goto, G., 'The Outline for the Companies Act Reform in Japan and Its Implications', *Journal of Japanese Law*, 35 (2013), 13.

Goto, G., 'Legally "Strong" Shareholders of Japan', *Michigan Journal of Private Equity and Venture Capital Law*, 3(2) (2014), 125.

Greenfeld, K., 'The Third Way: Beyond Shareholder or Board Primacy', *Seattle University Law Review*, 37 (2014), 749.

Grief, A., 'Family Structure, Institutions, and Growth: The Origins and Implications of Western Corporations', *American Economic Review*, 96(2) (2006), 308.

Griggs, S., 'Are Corporate Directors Really in Charge?', *Financial Post*, 24 January 2013, available at http://business.financialpost.com/.

Guo, L., and Masulis, R. W., 'Board Structure and Monitoring: New Evidence from CEO Turnover', *Review of Financial Studies*, 28 (2015), 2770.

Guo Jing, J., and Wu, N., '论建立独立董事间接薪酬制度' [On Establishing Rules of Indirect Payment for the Independent Directors], *管理评论* [Management Review], 16 (2004), 24.

Gutiérrez, M., and Sáez, M., 'Deconstructing Independent Directors', *Journal of Corporate Law Studies*, 13 (2013), 63.

Hall, P. A., and Soskice, D. (eds.), *Varieties of Capitalism: The Institutional Foundations of Comparative Advantage* (Oxford University Press, 2001).

Hanrahan, P., and Bednall, T., 'Independence of Directors Affiliated with Substantial Shareholders: Issues of Law and Corporate Governance', *Company and Securities Law Journal*, 33 (2015), 239.

Hansen, J. L., 'On the Independence of Directors in the Nordic Countries: Where the Shareholder Is King' in P. Krüger Andersen, N. Jul Clausen and R. Skog (eds.), *Shareholder Conflicts* (Thomson, 2006).

Hansen, J. L., 'Active Owners and Accountable Directors' in H. S. Birkmose, M. Neville and K. E. Sørensen (eds.), *Boards of Directors in European Companies: Reshaping and Harmonising Their Organisation and Duties* (Kluwer Law International, 2013).

Hansmann, H., and Kraakman, R., 'The End of History for Corporate Law', *Georgetown Law Journal*, 89 (2001), 439.

Hansmann, H., and Pargendler, M., 'The Evolution of Shareholder Voting Rights: Separation of Ownership and Consumption', *Yale Law Journal*, 123 (2014), 100.

Harris, R., 'The English East India Company and the History of Company Law' in E. Gepken-Jager, G. van Solinge and L. Timmerman (eds.), *VOC 1602–2002: 400 Years of Company Law* (Kluwer Legal Publishers, 2005).

Hatton, K. J., and Pistor, K., 'Maximizing Autonomy in the Shadow of Great Powers: The Political Economy of Sovereign Wealth Funds', *Columbia Journal of Transnational Law*, 50 (2012), available at http://ssrn.com/abstract=1787565.

Hau, H., and Thum, M., 'Sub-prime Crisis and Board (In-)Competence: Private Versus Public Banks in Germany', *Economic Policy*, 24 (2009), 701.

Heidrick & Struggles, *Corporate Governance Report 2009: Boards in Turbulent Times* (2009).

Heritage Foundation, '2015 Index of Economic Freedom: Country Rankings', Heritage.org, available at www.heritage.org.

Hermalin, B. E., and Weisbach, M. S., 'The Determinants of Board Composition', *The Rand Journal of Economics*, 19 (1988), 589.

Higgs, D., 'Review of the Role and Effectiveness of the Non-Executive Director', Department of Trade and Industry (2003).

Hill, J., 'Takeovers, Poison Pills and Protectionism in Comparative Corporate Governance' (Sydney Law School Research Paper No. 10/120, November 2010), available at http://papers.ssrn.com/sol3/papers.cfm?abstract_id=1704745.

Hill, J., 'Centro and the Monitoring Board: Legal Duties Versus Aspirational Ideals in Corporate Governance', *University of New South Wales Law Journal*, 35(1) (2012), 341.

Hill, J., 'Why Did Australia Fare So Well in the Global Financial Crisis?' in E. Ferran et al. (eds.), *The Regulatory Aftermath of the Global Financial Crisis* (Cambridge University Press, 2012).

Hill, J., 'Evolving Directors' Duties in the Common Law World' in Adolfo Paolini (ed.), *Research Handbook on Directors' Duties* (Edward Elgar, 2014).

Ho, B. M., 'Restructuring the Boards of Directors of Public Companies in Hong Kong: Barking up the Wrong Tree', *Singapore Journal of International and Comparative Law*, 1 (1997), 507.

Ho, S., and Wong, K., 'A Study of the Relationship between Corporate Governance Structures and the Extent of Voluntary Disclosure', *Journal of International Accounting, Auditing and Taxation*, 10 (2001), 139.

Hoffmann-Becking, M., 'Unabhängigkeit im Aufsichtsrat', *Neue Zeitschrift für Gesellschaftsrecht* (2014), 801.

Holderness, C., 'The Myth of Diffuse Ownership in the United States', *The Review of Financial Studies*, 22 (2009), 1377.

Hommelhoff, P., 'Protection of Minority Shareholders, Investors and Creditors: The Strengths and Weaknesses of German Corporate Group Law', *European Business Organization Law Review*, 2 (2001), 61.

'Hong Kong Exchanges and Clearing: Down Market?', *The Economist*, 24 June 2017, available at www.economist.com.

Hong Kong Exchanges and Clearing Limited, 'About HKEx', available at www.hkex.com.hk.

Hong Kong Exchanges and Clearing Limited, 'Company Profile', available at www.hkex.com.hk.

Hong Kong Exchanges and Clearing Limited, *Consultation Paper on Proposed Amendments to the Listing Rules Relating to Corporate Governance Issues* (January 2002), available at www.hkex.com.hk.

Hong Kong Exchanges and Clearing Limited, *Exposure of Draft Code on Corporate Governance Practices and Corporate Governance Report* (January 2004), available at www.hkex.com.hk.

Hong Kong Exchanges and Clearing Limited, *Consultation Conclusions on Review of the Corporate Governance Code and Associated Listing Rules* (October 2011), available at www.hkex.com.hk.

Hong Kong Exchanges and Clearing Limited, *Consultation Conclusions: Board Diversity* (December 2012), available at www.hkex.com.hk.

Hong Kong Exchanges and Clearing Limited, *Consultation Paper on Review of Connected Transaction Rules* (April 2013), available at www.hkex.com.hk.

Hong Kong Exchanges and Clearing Limited, 'HKEx Fact Book 2013', available at www.hkex.com.hk.

Hong Kong Exchanges and Clearing Limited, 'HKEx News Release; Censure of Long Success International (Holdings) Limited' (18 August 2014), available at www.hkex.com.hk.

Hong Kong Exchanges and Clearing Limited, 'List of H Share Companies (Main Board)' (last updated February 2015), available at www.hkex.com.hk.

Hong Kong Institute of Certified Public Accountants (Hong Kong Society of Accountants), 'A Guide for Effective Audit Committees' (February 2002), available at www.hkicpa.org.hk.

Hopt, K. J., 'Comparative Corporate Governance: The State of the Art and International Regulation', *American Journal of Comparative Law*, 59 (2011), 1.

Hopt, K. J., 'Corporate Governance of Banks after the Financial Crisis' in E. Wymeersch, K. J. Hopt and G. Ferrarini (eds.), *Financial Regulation and Supervision: A Post-Crisis Analysis* (Oxford University Press, 2012).

Hopt, K. J., 'Corporate Governance of Banks and Other Financial Institutions after the Financial Crisis', *Journal of Corporate Law Studies*, 13 (2013), 219.

Hopt, K. J., 'Law and Corporate Governance: Germany within Europe', *Journal of Applied Finance*, 27 (2015), 8.

Hopt, K. J., 'The German Law of and Experience with the Supervisory Board' (ECGI Working Paper No. 305/2016, 2016), available at http://ssrn.com/abstract=272270.

Hopt, K. J., and Wiedemann, H. (eds.), *Großkommentar Aktiengesetz*, 2nd edn (De Gruyter, 2005).

How, J. et al., 'Internationalisation and Corporate Governance: Australian Evidence', *Asia Pacific Journal of Economics and Business*, 6(1) (2002), 42.

Huang, H., 'Shareholder Derivative Litigation in China: Empirical Findings and Comparative Analysis', *Banking and Finance Law Review*, 27 (2012), 648.

Hüffer, U., and Koch, J., *Aktiengesetz*, 11th edn (C. H. Beck, 2014).

Hwang, B. H., and Kim, S., 'It Pays to Have Friends', *Journal of Financial Economics*, 93 (2009), 138.

Ibrahim, H., and Samad, F. A., 'Corporate Governance Mechanisms and Performance of Public-Listed Family-Ownership in Malaysia', *International Journal of Economics and Finance*, 3 (2011), 105.

Icahn, C., 'Corporate Boards That Do Their Job', *Washington Post*, 16 February 2009, A 15.

Inagaki, K., and Thompson, J., 'Toyota Executive Julie Hamp Resigns after Drug Arrest', *Financial Times*, 1 July 2015, available at www.ft.com.

Inamdar, N., 'Have Independent Directors Finally Found Their Voice?', *Business Standard*, 12 March 2014.

Independent Investigation Committee for Toshiba Corporation, 'Investigation Report, Summary Version' (20 July 2015), available at www.toshiba.co.jp.

International Monetary Fund, *Global Financial Stability Report: Risk Taking, Liquidity, and Shadow Banking – Curbing Excess While Promoting Growth* (October 2014).

Investment and Financial Services Association, *Corporate Governance: A Guide for Fund Managers and Corporations* (2009).

ISS, 'Board Independence at a Glance' (2016), available at www.isscorporatesolutions.com.

Issakson, M., and Çelik, S., 'Who Cares? Corporate Governance in Today's Equity Markets' (OECD Corporate Governance Working Papers No. 8, 2013).

Jackson, D. F., Q. C., Commissioner, 'Report of the Special Commission of Inquiry into the Medical Research and Compensation Foundation' (2004).

Jacoby, S. M., 'Principals and Agents', *Journal of Japanese Law*, 12(27) (2007), 23.

Jaggi, B., and Tsui, J., 'Insider Trading Earnings Management and Corporate Governance: Empirical Evidence Based on Hong Kong Firms', *Journal of International Financial Management and Accounting*, 18(3) (2007), 192.

Jaggi, B., Leung, S., and Gul, F., 'Family Control, Board Independence and Earnings Management: Evidence Based on Hong Kong Firms', *Journal of Accounting and Public Policy*, 28(4) (2009), 281.

Jameson, A., Prevost, A., and Puthenpurackal, J., 'Controlling Shareholders, Board Structure, and Firm Performance: Evidence from India', *Journal of Corporate Finance*, 27 (2014), 1.

'Japan Revitalization Strategy: Japan Is Back' (14 June 2013), available at www.kantei.go.jp.

Jiang, G., Lee, C., and Yue, H., 'Tunneling through Inter-corporate Loans: The China Experience', *Journal of Financial Economics*, 98 (2010), 1.

Jiang, W., Wan, H., and Zhao, S., 'Reputation Concerns of Independent Directors: Evidence from Individual Director Voting' (1 November 2013) (American Finance Association 2014 Philadelphia Meetings Paper), available at http://ssrn.com/abstract=2023146.

Jin, Z., and Yu, P., '上市公司高管犯罪问题研究' [Researches on Crimes of Executives in the Listed Companies], *证券法苑* [*Securities Law Review*], 10 (2010).

Jiyu Minshu-to (Liberal Democratic Party), Homu Bukai, Zaimu Kinyu Bukai, Keizai Sangyo Bukai, Kigyo/Shihon-shijyo Hosei Purojekuto Chi-mu and Kigyo-Kaikei Sho-i'inkai (Judicial Affairs Division, Treasury and Finance Division, Economy, Trade and Industry Division, Project Team on Corporate and Capital Market Law and Working Group on Corporate Accountings), 企業統治改革案について[On Reform Plan of Corporate Governance], 1 April 2012, available at www.y-shiozaki.or.jp.

Johanson, D., and Østergren, K., 'The Movement Toward Independent Directors on Boards: A Comparative Analysis of Sweden and the UK', *Corporate Governance: An International Review*, 18 (2010), 527.

Johnson, J. L., Daily, C. M., and Ellstrand, A. E., 'Board of Directors: A Review and Research Agenda', *Journal of Management*, 22(3) (1996), 411.

Johnson, K. N., 'Addressing Gaps in the Dodd-Frank Act: Directors' Risk Management Oversight Obligations', *University of Michigan Journal of Law Reform*, 45 (2011), 55.

Jones, R. M., and Welsh, M. A., 'Toward a Public Enforcement Model for Directors' Duty of Oversight', *Vanderbilt Journal of Transnational Law*, 45 (2012), 343.

Kahan, M., and Rock, E. B., 'Hedge Funds in Corporate Governance and Corporate Control', *University of Pennsylvania Law Review*, 155 (2007), 1021.

Kahan, M., and Rock, E., 'Embattled CEOs', *Texas Law Review*, 88 (2010), 997.

Kahan, M., and Rock, E. B., 'When the Government Is the Controlling Shareholder', *Texas Law Review*, 89 (2011), 1293.

Kahan, M., and Rock, E., 'Symbolic Corporate Governance Politics', *Boston University Law Review*, 94 (2014), 1997.

Kang, H., Cheng, M., and Gray, S., 'Corporate Governance and Board Composition: Diversity and Independence of Australian Boards', *Corporate Governance: An International Review*, 15(2) (2007), 194.

Karmel, R. S., 'Is the Independent Director Model Broken?' (Brooklyn Law School Legal Studies Research Papers; Accepted Paper Series; Research Paper No. 348, July 2013), available at http://ssrn.com/abstract=1972057.

Katelouzou, D., and Siems, M., 'Disappearing Paradigms in Shareholder Protection: Leximetric Evidence for 30 Countries, 1990–2013', *Journal of Corporate Law Studies*, 15 (2015), 127.

Kelemen, D., and Sibbett, E., 'The Americanization of Japanese Law', *Pennsylvania Journal of International Economic Law*, 23 (2002), 269.

Khanna, T., and Palepu, K. G., 'Globalization and Convergence in Corporate Governance: Evidence from Infosys and the Indian Software Industry', *Journal of International Business Studies*, 35 (2004), 484.

Khanna, T., and Yafeh, Y., 'Business Groups in Emerging Markets: Paragons or Parasites?', *Journal of Economic Literature*, 45(2) (2007), 331.

Khanna, V., 'Corporate Crime Legislation: A Political Economy Analysis', *Washington University Law Quarterly*, 82 (2004), 95.

Khanna, V., 'Written Statement of Professor Vikramaditya Khanna University of Michigan Law School, Before the Committee on the Judiciary United States Senate Hearing on Evaluating the Propriety and Adequacy of the OxyContin Criminal Settlement', 31 July 2007, available at www.judiciary.senate.gov.

Khanna, V., 'Corporate Governance in India: Past, Present and Future', *Jindal Global Law Review*, 1 (2009), 171.

Khanna, V., 'Corporate Governance Ratings: One Score, Two Scores, or More?', *University of Pennsylvania Law Review*, 158 (2009), 39.

Khanna, V., 'An Analysis of Internal Governance and the Role of the General Counsel in Reducing Corporate Crime', Draft (2017).

Khanna, V., 'An Analysis of the Critical Elements of Board Independence', Draft (2015).

Khanna, V., and Howson, N. C., 'Reverse Cross-listings: The Coming Race to List in Emerging Markets and an Enhanced Understanding of Classical Bonding', *Cornell International Law Journal*, 47 (2014), 607.

Khanna, V., and Mathew, S. J., 'The Role of Independent Directors in Controlled Firms in India: Preliminary Interview Evidence', *National Law School of India Review*, 22 (2010), 35.

Khanna, V., and Varottil, U., 'The Rarity of Derivative Actions in India: Reasons and Consequences' in D. W. Puchniak, H. Baum and M. Ewing-Chow (eds.), *The Derivative Action in Asia: A Comparative and Functional Approach* (Cambridge University Press, 2012).

Khanna, V., and Varottil, U., 'Regulating Squeeze Outs in India: A Comparative Perspective', *American Journal of Comparative Law*, 63 (2015), 1009.

Khanna, V., Kim, E. H., and Lu, Y., 'CEO Connectedness and Corporate Fraud', *Journal of Finance*, 70 (2015), 1203.

Kiel, G. and Nicholson, G., 'Board Composition and Corporate Performance: How the Australian Experience Informs Contrasting Theories of Corporate Governance', *Corporate Governance: An International Review*, 11(3) (2003), 189.

Kim, H. J., 'Living with the IMF: A New Approach to Corporate Governance and Regulation of Financial Institutions in Korea', *Berkeley Journal of International Law*, 17 (1999), 63.

Kim, K. S., 'Transplanting Audit Committees to Korean Soil: A Window into the Evolution of Korean Corporate Governance', *Asian-Pacific Law and Policy Journal*, 9 (2007), 165.

Kirkpatrick, G., 'The Corporate Governance Lessons from the Financial Crisis', *OECD Journal: Financial Market Trends*, 96 (2009), 61.

Klein, A., 'Audit Committee, Board of Director Characteristics, and Earnings Management', *Journal of Accounting and Economics*, 33 (2002), 375.

Koellner, P. 'The Democratic Party of Japan' in A. Gaunder (ed.), *The Routledge Handbook of Japanese Politics* (Routledge, 2011).

Korea Exchange, Press release (1 February 2016) (available in Korean).

Korea Listed Companies Association, 'Status of Outside Directors of Listed Companies' (April 2012).

Korn Ferry Institute, *2010 Board of Directors Study: Australia and New Zealand* (2010), available at www.kornferryinstitute.com.

Korn Ferry Institute, *Cultivating Greatness in the Boardroom* (June 2012), available at www.kornferryinstitute.com.

Korn Ferry Institute, 'Beyond If Not, Why Not: The Pathway to Directorship for Women in Leadership' (May 2014), available at www.kornferryinstitute.com.

Kozuka, S., 'Reform after a Decade of the Companies Act: Why, How, and to Where?', *Journal of Japanese Law*, 37 (2014), 39.

Kozuka, S., and Lee, J., 'The New Japanese Insurance Act: Comparisons with Europe and Korea', *Journal of Japanese Law*, 14(28) (2009), 73.

Kraakman, R. et al., *The Anatomy of Corporate Law: A Comparative and Functional Approach*, 2nd edn (Oxford University Press, 2009).

Kubota, Y., 'Suzuki to Rev Up Value after Loeb's Third Point Discloses Stake', *Wall Street Journal*, 3 August 2015, available at www.wsj.com.

Kumpan, C., *Der Interessenkonflikt im deutschen Privatrecht* (Mohr Siebeck, 2014).

Kwan, P., 'Statutory Derivative Actions: New Hope for Minority Shareholders?' (2 April 2012), available at www.deacons.com.hk.

Kwok, J., 'Are S-Chips Still a Possible Play?', *Straits Times*, 25 December 2011.

La Porta, R., Lopez-de-Silanes, F., and Shleifer, A., 'Corporate Ownership around the World', *Journal of Finance*, 54 (1999), 471.

La Porta, R. et al., 'Investor Protection and Corporate Governance', *Journal of Financial Economics*, 58 (2000), 3.

Lai, Y. Z., *最新證券交易法解析* [*The Newest Analysis of Securities Exchange Act*], 2nd edn (2009).

Langevoort, D. C., 'The Human Nature of Corporate Boards: Law, Norms, and the Unintended Consequences of Independence and Accountability', *Georgetown Law Journal*, 89 (2001), 797.

Latham & Watkins LLP, 'The Parallel Universes of Institutional Investing and Institutional Voting', *Corporate Governance Commentary* (March 2010), available at www.lw.com/upload/pubContent/_pdf/pub3446_1.pdf.

Lau, K. L. A., Jiang, J., and An, G., 'An Overview of the Independent Director System in China', *Company Lawyer*, 34 (2013), 321.

Lawley, P., 'Panacea or Placebo? An Empirical Analysis of the Effect of the Japanese Committee System Corporate Governance Law Reform', *Asian-Pacific Law and Policy Journal*, 9 (2007), 105.

Lawley, P., 'Panacea or Placebo? An Empirical Analysis of the Effect of the Japanese Committee System on Corporate Governance Law Reform' in L. Nottage, L. Wolff and K. Anderson (eds.), *Corporate Governance in the 21st Century: Japan's Gradual Transformation* (Edward Elgar, 2008).

Le Mire, S., and Gilligan, G., 'Independence and Independent Company Directors', *Journal of Corporate Law Studies*, 13 (2013), 443.

Lea, M., and Malkan, A., 'The Changing Environment for D&O Insurance in India', *D&O Diary* (2013), available at www.dandodiary.com.

Lee, C., 'David Webb: Tireless Champion of Shareholder's Rights', *Financial Times*, 13 October 2009, available at www.ft.com.

Lee, K. Y., *From Third World to First: The Singapore Story: 1965–2000* (2000).

Lee, S. Y., 'Public Enterprise and Economic Development in Singapore', *Malayan Economic Review*, 21(2) (1976), 49.

Lee, Y. Y., 'Temasek's Success Down to Separation of Its Role from Govt's', *Today*, 23 September 2014, available at http://todayonline.com.

Legrand, P., 'What "Legal Transplants"?' in D. Nelken and J. Feest (eds.), *Adapting Legal Cultures* (Hart, 2001).

Lei, A., and Deng, J., 'Do Multiple Directorships Increase Firm Value? Evidence from Independent Directors in Hong Kong', *Journal of International Financial Management and Accounting*, 25(2) (2014), 121.

Lei, A., and Song, F., 'Corporate Governance and Firm Valuations: Evidence from Hong Kong' (China International Conference in Finance, July 2005), available at www.ccfr.org.cn.

Lekvall, P. (ed.), *The Nordic Corporate Governance Model* (sns förlag, 2014).

Lenovo, 'Corporate Governance – Board of Directors', available at www.lenovo.com.

'Letter of Intent from the Government of Korea, 2 May 1998', International Monetary Fund, available at www.imf.org.

Levinson, C., Bennett, J., and Barrett, D., 'Toyota to Pay $1.2 Billion to Settle US Probe', *Wall Street Journal*, 19 March 2014, available at www.wsj.com.

Leyens, P. C., 'Aufsichtsrat: Terra incognita des englischen Gesellschaftsrechts?', in S. Grundmann et al. (eds.), *Unternehmen, Markt und Verantwortung. Festschrift für Klaus J. Hopt zum 70. Geburtstag am 24. August 2010*, Vol. 2 (De Gruyter, 2010).

Li, J., '论我国独立董事产生机制的重构' [Restructuring the Independent Director Production Mechanism in China], *法律科学* [*Legal Science*], 2 (2004), 67.

Li, Q., '对央企控股上市公司实施独立董事间接薪酬制的质疑' [Challenging the Proposed Indirect Payment System for Independent Directors in SASAC Controlled Listed Companies], *经济纵横* [*Economic Review*], 6 (2011), 110.

Li, W. and Li, B., '机构投资者介入公司治理效果的实证研究——基于CCGINK的经验研究' [An Empirical Study on the Effect of Institutional Investors Participating in Corporate Governance: Based on the Data of 2004–2006 CCGINK], *南开管理评论* [*Nankai Business Review*], 1 (2008), 4.

Li, W., and Xu, J., '董事会独立性、总经理继任与战略变化幅度——独立董事有效性的实证研究' [Board's Independence, CEO Succession and the Scope of Strategic Change: An Empirical Research on the Effectiveness of Independent Directors'], *南开管理评论* [*Nankai Business Review*], 17 (2014), 4.

Licht, A. N., 'Culture and Law in Corporate Governance' in J. Gordon and W.-G. Ringe (eds.), *The Oxford Handbook of Corporate Law and Governance* (Oxford University Press, 2017).

Liebman, B. L., and Milhaupt, C. J., 'Reputational Sanctions in China's Securities Market', *Columbia Law Review*, 108 (2008), 929.

Lin, L., 'The Effectiveness of Outside Directors as a Corporate Governance Mechanism: Theories and Evidence', *Northwestern University Law Review*, 90 (1996), 898.

Lin, L., and Milhaupt, C. J., 'We Are the (National) Champions: Understanding the Mechanisms of State Capitalism in China', *Stanford Law Review*, 65 (2013), 697.

Lin, Y. H., 'Modeling Securities Class Action Outside the United States: The Role of Nonprofits in the Case of Taiwan', *New York University Journal of Law and Business*, 4 (2007), 143.

Lin, Y. H., 'Overseeing Controlling Shareholders: Do Independent Directors Constrain Tunneling in Taiwan?', *San Diego International Law Journal*, 12 (2011), 363.

Lin, Y. H., *How Public Regulation Changes Corporate Governance Practice–Corporate Board Reform in Taiwan* (Edward Elgar, 2012).

Lin, Y. H., 'Do Social Ties Matter in Corporate Governance? The Missing Factor in Chinese Corporate Governance Reform', *George Mason Journal of International Commercial Law*, 5 (2013), 60.

Lin, Y. H., '公開發行公司經營者薪酬決定機制之實證分析—兼論薪資報酬委員會新制' [Shareholder Primacy or Director Primacy? Who Decides Director and Executive Compensation in Taiwanese Public Companies?], *Academia Sinica Law Journal*, 14 (2014), 245.

Lin., Y., and Tan, J., '机构投资者与公司治理：文献评述与研究框架' [Institutional Investors and Corporate Governance: Literature Review and Research Framework], *会计与经济研究* [*Accounting and Economics Research*], 5 (2013), 72.

Lipton, M., and Lorsch, J. W., 'A Modest Proposal for Improved Corporate Governance', *Business Lawyer*, 48 (1992), 59.

Lipton, P., 'The Evolution of the Joint Stock Company to 1800: A Study of Institutional Change' (Monash University, Department of Business Law and Taxation, Working Paper No. 19, 2009), available at http://ssrn.com/abstract=1413502.

Liu, C., and Yang, J., '独立董事的社会关系与监管功能' [Social Relation and Supervision Function of Independent Directors: Evidence from Forced CEO Turnover], *财经研究* [*Journal of Finance and Economics*], 39 (2013), 16.

Liu, C., Liu, J., and Uchida, K., 'Do Independent Boards Effectively Monitor Management? Evidence from Japan during the Financial Crisis' in W. Sun, J. Stewart and D. Pollard (eds.), *Corporate Governance and the Global Financial Crisis: International Perspectives* (Cambridge University Press, 2011).

Liu, J., '我国公司法移植独立董事制度的思考' [Thoughts about Chinese Company Law's Transplanting the Institution of Independent Director], *政法论坛* [*Tribune of Political Science and Law*], 21 (2003), 48.

Liu, L. Y., '現行上市上櫃公司獨立董事制度之檢討暨改進方案—從實證面觀察' [A Study of the Regime of Independent Directors of Listed Companies in Taiwan: An Empirical Approach], *ChengChi Law Review*, 114 (April 2010), 53.

Liu, L. et al., *选任独立董事与公司治理* [*The Election of Independent Directors and Corporate Governance*] (元照出版公司 [Angle Publishing Co.], 2013).

Liu, S., Sun, P., and Liu, N., '终极产权论、股权结构及公司绩效' [The Ultimate Ownership and Its Shareholding Structure: Does It Matter for Corporate Performance?], *经济研究* [*Economic Research Journal*], 4 (2003), 51.

Liu, Y., '建立我国独立董事间接薪酬制度的思考' [Deliberation on Establishing Indirect Payment System for Independent Directors in China], *管理科学文摘* [*Digest of Management Science*], 1 (2005), 46.

London Stock Exchange, 'Listing Regime', available at www.londonstockexchange.com.

Low, C. K., 'Is the Standard of Care of Directors Inverted in Hong Kong?', *Hong Kong Law Journal*, 38(1) (2008), 31.

Lutter, M., 'Der Aufsichtsrat im Wandel der Zeit: von seinen Anfängen bis heute' in W. Bayer and M. Habersack (eds.), *Aktienrecht im Wandel*, Vol. 2: *Grundsatzfragen des Aktienrechts* (Mohr Siebeck, 2007).

McCabe, M., and Nowak, M., 'The Independent Director on the Board of Company Directors', *Managerial Auditing Journal*, 23(6) (2008), 545.

Mace, M. L., *Directors: Myth and Reality* (Division of Research, Graduate School of Business Administration, Harvard University, 1971).

Macey, J. R., *Corporate Governance: Promises Kept, Promises Broken* (Princeton University Press, 2008).

McKenna, C., 'Hong Kong', *International Financial Law Review*, 12 April 2000, available at www.iflr.com.

McNamara, L., 'Lack of Cultural Diversity a "Risk"', *The Australian*, 3 January 2013, available at www.theaustralian.com.au.

Maharaj, A., 'New Corporate Governance Codes to Shake up Singapore's Boardrooms', *Corporate Secretary*, 17 June 2011, available at www.corporatesecretary.com.

Mak, Y. T., 'Now Let's See the Practical Impact', *Business Times Singapore*, 16 June 2011.

Mak, Y. T. (ed.), *Corporate Governance Case Studies*, Vol. II (CPA Australia, 2013), available at http://governanceforstakeholders.com.

Mak, Y. T. (ed.), *Corporate Governance Case Studies*, Vol. III (CPA Australia, 2013), available at www.cpaaustralia.com.au.

Mak, Y. T., and Ng, T., 'Independent Directors: A Well-Functioning Market', *Business Times*, 6 September 2010.

Manns, J., 'Building Better Bailouts: The Case for a Long-Term Investment Approach', *Florida Law Review*, 63 (2011), 1349.

Market Misconduct Tribunal, 'Home', available at www.mmt.gov.hk.

'Maruti Blinks in Gujarat Plant Standoff', *The Telegraph*, 16 March 2014.

Maruti Suzuki India Limited, 'Maruti Suzuki Board Decision on Gujarat Project', Press Release (28 January 2014).

Maruti Suzuki India Limited, 'Information on Gujarat Project', Press Release (26 February 2014).

Maruti Suzuki India Limited, 'Information on Gujarat Project', Press Release (15 March 2014).

Masulis, R. W., and Mobbs, S., 'Independent Director Incentives: Where Do Talented Directors Spend Their Limited Time and Energy?', *Journal of Financial Economics*, 111 (2014), 406.

Mathew, S. J., 'Hostile Takeovers in India: New Prospects, Challenges, and Regulatory Opportunities', *Columbia Business Law Review*, 3 (2007), 800.

Matolcsy, Z., Stokes, D., and Wright, A., 'Do Independent Directors Add Value?', *Australian Accounting Review*, 14(1) (2004), 33.

Mayer, C., *Firm Commitment: Why the Corporation Is Failing Us and How to Restore Trust in It* (Oxford University Press, 2013).

Mehran, H., Morrison, A., and Shapiro, J., 'Corporate Governance and Banks: What Have We Learned from the Financial Crisis?' (Federal Reserve Bank of New York Staff Reports No. 502, June 2011).

Mehrotra, S., 'Corporate Board Structure in the United States and India: A Comparative View', *Indian Journal of Corporate Governance*, 8 (2015), 166.

Meng, F., 'Legal vs Reputational Bonding: Board Independence of Chinese Companies Listed in Hong Kong', *Australian Journal of Corporate Law*, 27 (2013), 319.

Merkt, H., 'Germany. Internal and External Corporate Governance', in Fleckner, A. M., and Hopt, K. J. (eds.), *Comparative Corporate Governance: A Functional and International Analysis* (Cambridge University Press, 2013).

Michaels, R., 'The Functional Method of Comparative Law' in M. Reimann and R. Zimmermann (eds.), *Oxford Handbook of Comparative Law* (Oxford University Press, 2005).

Michaels, R., '"One Size Can Fit All": On the Mass Production of Legal Transplants' in G. Frankenberg (ed.), *Order from Transfer: Studies in Comparative (Constitutional) Law* (Edward Elgar, 2013).

Milhaupt, C. J., 'A Lost Decade for Japanese Corporate Governance Reform?: What's Changed, What Hasn't, and Why' in M. Blomstrom and S. La Croix (eds.), *Institutional Change in Japan* (Routledge, 2006).

Milhaupt, C. J., and Pistor, K., *Law and Capitalism: What Corporate Crises Reveal about Legal Systems and Economic Development around the World* (University of Chicago Press, 2008).

Milhaupt, C. J., and Zheng, W., 'Beyond Ownership: State Capitalism and the Chinese Firm', *Georgetown Law Journal*, 103 (2015), 669.

Miller, J., 'A Typology of Legal Transplants: Using Sociology, Legal History and Argentine Examples to Explain the Transplant Process', *American Journal of Comparative Law*, 51 (2013), 839.

Ministry of Finance, Government of India, New Delhi, *Report of the High Powered Expert Committee on Making Mumbai an International Financial Centre* (2007), available at www.finmin.nic.in/mifc/mifcreport.pdf.

Ministry of Justice, 選択的夫婦別氏制度（いわゆる選択的夫婦別姓制度）について [On the Use of Different Surnames by a Married Couple], available at www.moj.go.jp.

Minton, B. A., Taillard, J. P. A., and Williamson, R., 'Financial Expertise of the Board, Risk Taking and Performance: Evidence from Bank Holding Companies', *Journal of Financial and Quantitative Analysis*, 49 (2014), 351.

Mitchell, L. E., 'The Trouble with Boards' in F. C. Kieff and T. A. Paredes (eds.), *Perspectives on Corporate Governance* (Cambridge University Press, 2010).

Miwa, Y., and Ramseyer, J. M., 'Who Appoints Them, What Do They Do?: Evidence on Outside Directors from Japan', *Journal of Economics and Management Strategy*, 14(2) (2005), 299.

Miyajima, H., and Kuroki, F., 'The Unwinding of Cross-Shareholding in Japan: Causes, Effects, and Implications' in M. Aoki, G. Jackson and H. Miyajima (eds.), *Corporate Governance in Japan* (Oxford University Press, 2007).

Miyajima, H., and Nitta, K., '株式所有構造の多様化とその帰結' [Diversification of Share-Ownership Structure and Its Consequences: Unwinding and "Revival" of Cross-Shareholdings and the Role of Foreign Investors] in

H. Miyajima (ed.), *日本の企業統治: その再設計と競争力の回復に向けて* [*Corporate Governance in Japan: Toward Redesigning Corporate Governance and Recovering Competitiveness*] (Toyo Keizai, 2011).

Miyajima, H., and Ogawa, R., '日本企業の取締役会構成の変化をいかに理解するか?: 取締役会構成の決定要因と社外取締役の導入効果' [Understanding Change in Board Composition: Determinants of Board Composition and Effects of Outside Directors] (RIETI Policy Discussion Paper Series 12-P-013, 2012), available at www.rieti.go.jp.

Miyajima, H. et al., '日本型コーポレート・ガバナンスはどこへ向かうのか (上):「日本企業のコーポレート・ガバナンスに関するアンケート」調査から読み解く' [Where Is the Japanese Corporate Governance Oriented?: Analysing the Results of 'Questionnaire on Corporate Governance of Japanese Corporations' (1 of 2)], *商事法務*, 2008 (2013), 4.

Mochizuki, T., and Negishi, M., 'Sony Bullish on PlayStation as It Swings to Profit', *Wall Street Journal*, 29 October 2015, available at www.wsj.com.

Moncrieff, M., 'Unravelling the Ties That Connect and Direct', *Sydney Morning Herald*, 18 August 2012, available at www.smh.com.au.

Monetary Authority of Singapore, 'Response to Recommendations by the Corporate Governance Council on the Code of Corporate Governance' (2012), available at www.mas.gov.sg.

Morita, A., *会議の政治学* [*Politics of Governmental Councils*] (Jigakusha, 2006).

Morita, H., 'Reforms of Japanese Corporate Law and Political Environment', *Journal of Japanese Law*, 37 (2014), 25.

MSCI, 'ESG Ratings', available at www.msci.com.

Murphy, M. E., 'Assuring Responsible Risk Management in Banking: The Corporate Governance Dimension', *Delaware Journal of Corporate Law*, 36 (2011), 121.

Muth, M., and Donaldson, L., 'Stewardship Theory and Board Structure: A Contingency Approach', *Corporate Governance: An International Review*, 6(1) (1998), 5.

Nader, R., Green, M., and Seligman, J., *Taming the Giant Corporation* (Norton, 1976).

National Tax Service, *Statistical Yearbook of National Tax* (Seoul, 2016).

Neville, M., 'The Many Roles of Boards in SMEs' in H. S. Birkmose, M. Neville and K. E. Sørensen (eds.), *Boards of Directors in European Companies: Reshaping and Harmonising Their Organisation and Duties* (Kluwer Law International, 2013).

New South Wales, Special Commission of Inquiry into the Medical Research and Compensation Foundation, Report (September 2004).

Ng, W., and Roberts, J., '"Helping the Family": The Mediating Role of Outside Directors in Ethnic Chinese Family Firms', *Human Relations*, 60 (2007), 285.

Nichols, M., 'Warren Buffett, Bill Gates Ask Billionaires to Give Away Wealth', *Reuters*, 16 June 2010.

Nihon Keizai Shinbun, '民主、社外取締役の積極活用提言　義務化明記せず' [DPJ Proposes Active Use of Outside Directors, Does Not Clearly State Introduction of Mandatory Appointment] (12 April 2012), available at www.nikkei.com.

Niu, Y., 'A Brief Analysis of the Defects and Countermeasures of the Independent Director System in China', *International Journal of Law and Management*, 51 (2009), 260.

Nolan, R., 'The Legal Control of Directors' Conflicts of Interest in the United Kingdom: Non-Executive Directors Following the Higgs Report', in J. Armour and J. McCahery (eds.), *After Enron: Improving Corporate Law and Modernising Securities Regulation in Europe and the US* (Hart Publishing, 2006).

Nordberg, D., 'Corporate Governance and the Board' in S. O. Idowu and C. Louche (eds.), *Theory and Practice of Corporate Social Responsibility* (Springer, 2011).

Nottage, L., 'Japanese Corporate Governance at a Crossroads: Variation in "Varieties of Capitalism"?', *The North Carolina Journal of International Law and Commercial Regulation*, 27 (2001), 255.

Nottage, L., 'Perspectives and Approaches: A Framework for Comparing Japanese Corporate Governance' in L. Nottage, L. Wolff and K. Anderson (eds.), *Corporate Governance in the 21st Century: Japan's Gradual Transformation* (Edward Elgar, 2008).

Nottage, L., 'Corporate Governance in Australia: The Evolving Blockholder Legacy' (Paper for the Berlin Conference on Independent Directors in Asia, 17–19 July 2014), available at http://tinyurl.com/lwtrwkl; abridging and updating Nottage, L., 'Corporate Governance and M&A in Australia: An Overview for Assessing Japan and the 'Americanisation' (Thesis, Sydney Law School Research Paper No. 08/28, March 2008), available at http://papers.ssrn.com/sol3/papers.cfm?abstract_id=1105639.

Nottage, L., and Aoun, F., 'Independent Director Requirements in Australia and the Asian Region', *Company and Securities Law Journal*, 34 (2016), 631.

Nowak, M., and McCabe, M., 'Information Costs and the Role of the Independent Corporate Director', *Corporate Governance: An International Review*, 11(4) (2003), 300.

O'Donnell, C., 'Origins of the Corporate Executive', *Bulletin of the Business Historical Society*, 26 (1952), 55.

OECD, 'Corporate Governance: A Survey of OECD Countries' (OECD, 2004), available at www.oecd.org.

OECD, *Corporate Governance and the Financial Crisis: Key Findings and Main Messages* (OECD, June 2009).

OECD, *Better Policies for Board Nomination in Asia* (OECD Publishing, 2013), available at http://dx.doi.org/10.1787/9789264204386-en.

OECD, 'OECD Principles of Corporate Governance, Draft for Public Comment – November 2014' (OECD, 2014/2015), available at www.oecd.org.

OECD, *G20/OECD Principles of Corporate Governance* (OECD Publishing, 2015), available at http://dx.doi.org/10.1787/9789264236882-en.

Okubo, Tsutomu, '経済産業事務次官の発言に関する質問主意書' [Question on a Remark by the Vice-Minister of Economy, Trade and Industry], available at www.sangiin.go.jp.

Organization Department of the Central Committee of the Communist Party of China, '关于进一步规范党政领导干部在企业兼职(任职)问题的意见' [Opinion on Further Standardizing the Party and Government Leading Cadres' Taking Offices in Enterprise], 19 October 2013.

Organization Department of the Central Committee of the Communist Party of China, '独立董事辞职潮再现的背后' [Behind the Reappearance of Resign Tide of the Independent Directors], 中国经济时报 [China Economic Times], 30 October 2014.

Pacces, A. M., 'Controlling the Corporate Controller's Misbehaviour', *Journal of Corporate Law Studies*, 11 (2011), 177.

'Packer, Murdoch Stump Up $40m for One.Tel', *Sydney Morning Herald*, 17 April 2014, available at http://news.smh.com.au.

Page, A., 'Unconscious Bias and the Limits of Director Independence', *University of Illinois Law Review* (2009), 237.

Pan, E. J., 'Rethinking the Board's Duty to Monitor: A Critical Assessment of the Delaware Doctrine', *Florida State University Law Review*, 38 (2011), 209.

Pargendler, M., 'State Ownership and Corporate Governance', *Fordham Law Review*, 80 (2012), 2917.

Pargendler, M., 'The Corporate Governance Obsession' (Stanford Law and Economics Olin Working Paper No. 470, 2015), available at http://ssrn.com/abstract=2491088.

Parliamentary Joint Committee on Corporations and Financial Services, Australian Parliament, *Better Shareholders – Better Company Shareholder Engagement and Participation in Australia* (2008).

Parliamentary Joint Committee on Corporations and Financial Services, Australian Parliament, *Inquiry into Corporate Responsibility* (June 2006), available at www.aph.gov.au.

Paschos, N., and Goslar, S., 'Unabhängigkeit von Aufsichtsratsmitgliedern nach den neuesten Änderungen des Deutschen Corporate Governance Kodex', *Neue Zeitschrift für Gesellschaftsrecht* (2012), 1361.

Peltzer, M., 'Für einen schlankeren Kodex! Kritische Evaluierung der Stellungnahme des Handelsrechtsausschusses des Deutschen Anwaltsvereins zu den Reformvorschlägen der DCGK für den Kodex', *Neue Zeitschrift für Gesellschaftsrecht* (2012), 368.

Peng, W. Q., Wei, K. C. J., and Yang, Z., 'Tunneling or Propping: Evidence from Connected Transactions in China', *Journal of Corporate Finance*, 17(2) (2011), 306.

Prabowo, M., and Simpson, J., 'Independent Directors and Firm Performance in Family Controlled Firms: Evidence from Indonesia', *Asian Pacific Economic Literature*, 25 (2011), 121.

Prism Cosec, *A Spotlight on Senior Independent Directors* (December 2011), available at www.prismcosec.com.

Pritchard, A. C., 'Monitoring of Corporate Groups by Independent Directors', *Journal of Korean Law*, 9(1) (2009), 5.

Productivity Commission, Parliament of Australia, *Executive Remuneration in Australia* (2009), available at www.pc.gov.au.

Puchniak, D. W., 'The 2002 Reform of the Management of Large Corporations in Japan: A Race to Somewhere?', *The Australian Journal of Asian Law*, 5 (2003), 42.

Puchniak, D. W., 'The Japanization of American Corporate Governance? Evidence of the Never-Ending History for Corporate Law', *Asian-Pacific Law and Policy Journal*, 9 (2007), 7.

Puchniak, D. W., 'The Derivative Action in Asia: A Complex Reality', *Berkeley Business Law Journal*, 9 (2013), 1.

Puchniak, D. W., 'Multiple Faces of Shareholder Power in Asia: Complexity Revealed' in J. G. Hill and R. S. Thomas (eds.), *Research Handbook on Shareholder Power* (Edward Elgar, 2015).

Puchniak, D. W., and Lan, L. L., 'Temasek Independent Director Database', unpublished manuscript (on file with authors).

Puchniak, D. W., and Lan, L. L., 'Independent Directors in Singapore: Puzzling Compliance Requiring Explanation', *American Journal of Comparative Law*, 65 (2017).

Qian, M., 'Why S-Chip Fraud Cases Keep Cropping Up?', *Business Times*, 17 February 2012.

Quiggin, J., *Zombie Economics: How Dead Ideas Still Walk among Us* (Princeton University Press, 2010).

Rallis, D., 'At Sony Corporation It's the Same Old Sony', GMI, 10 October 2012, available at http://tremulous23.rssing.com.

Ramsey, I., and Hoad, R., 'Disclosure of Corporate Governance Practices by Australian Listed Companies', *Company and Securities Law Journal*, 15(8) (1997), 454.

Reflection Group on the Future of EU Company Law, Report of 5 April 2011, available at http://ec.europa.eu.

Regierungskommission Deutscher Corporate Governance Kodex, Press comment (26 January 2015), available at www.dcgk.de/.

'Regulations and Financial Stability: Code of Corporate Governance', Monetary Authority of Singapore, available at www.mas.gov.sg.

Reiter, B., 'What Makes a Director Independent', *Lexpert*, 15 February 2010.

Ren, Z., '中国董事的勤勉义务标准研究' [A Study on the Criterion of the Director's Duty of Diligence], *中国法学* [*China Legal Science*], 6 (2008), 89.

Ribstein, L. E., 'Market vs. Regulatory Responses to Corporate Fraud: A Critique of the Sarbanes-Oxley Act of 2002', *Journal of Corporation Law*, 28 (2002), 1.

Ribstein, L. E., 'Bubble Laws', *Houston Law Review*, 40 (2003), 77.

Ringe, W. G., 'Changing Law and Ownership Patterns in Germany: Corporate Governance and the Erosion of Deutschland AG' (University of Oxford, Legal Research Paper Series, Paper No. XX/2014, 2014), available at http://ssrn.com/abstract=2457431.

Ringe, G., 'Independent Directors: After the Crisis' (University of Oxford Legal Research Paper Series Paper No. 72/2013, 2013), available at http://ssrn.com/abstract=2293394.

Ringleb, H. M. et al., 'Die Kodex-Änderungen vom Mai 2012', *Neue Zeitschrift für Gesellschaftsrecht* (2012), 1081.

Ringleb, H. M. et al. (eds.), *Kommentar zum Deutschen Corporate Governance Kodex*, 5th edn (C. H. Beck, 2014).

Ritchie, T., 'Independent Directors: Magic Bullet or Band-Aid?', *Bond University Corporate Governance eJournal* (2007), available at http://epublications.bond.edu.au.

Rock, E. B., 'The Logic and (Uncertain) Significance of Institutional Shareholder Activism', *Georgetown Law Journal*, 79 (1991), 445.

Rock, E. B., 'Adapting to the New Shareholder-Centric Reality', *University of Pennsylvania Law Review*, 161 (2013), 1907.

Rodrigues, U., 'The Fetishization of Independence', *Journal of Corporation Law* 33 (2008), 447.

Roe, M. J., 'A Political Theory of American Corporate Finance', *Columbia Law Review*, 91 (1991), 54.

Rose, P., 'EU Company Law Convergence Possibilities after Centros', *Transnational Law and Contemporary Problems*, 11 (2001), 121.

Rose, P., 'Regulating Risk by "Strengthening Corporate Governance"', *Connecticut Insurance Law Journal*, 17 (2010), 1.

Roth, M., 'Unabhängige Aufsichtsratsmitglieder', *Zeitschrift für das gesamte Handels- und Wirtschaftsrecht*, 175 (2011), 605.

Roth, M., 'Corporate Boards in Germany' in P. L. Davies et al. (eds.), *Boards in Law and Practice* (Oxford University Press, 2013).

Saito, M., 'Sony Rejects Loeb's Proposal to Spin off Entertainment Unit', *Reuters*, 6 August 2013, available at www.reuters.com.

Saito, T., 'Boards with and without Outside Directors: An Empirical Comparison' (Working Paper, 2010).

Saito, T., '日本企業による社外取締役の導入の決定要因とその効果' [Determinants of Appointment of Outside Directors and Their Effects in Japanese

Firms] in H. Miyajima (ed.), *日本の企業統治: その再設計と競争力の回復に向けて* [*Corporate Governance in Japan: Toward Redesigning Corporate Governance and Recovering Competitiveness*] (Toyo Keizai, 2011).

Saito, T., 'The Determinants of Board Composition When Managers Control Director Selection: Evidence from Japan' (Working Paper, 2011).

Sakamoto, S. et al., '平成二六年改正会社法の解説(I) ' [Official Commentary on the 2014 Amendments to the Companies Act], *商事法務*, 2040 (2014), 28.

Sakoui, A., 'Loeb Exit Leaves Sony's Hirai with Bigger Challenges', *Bloomberg*, 22 October 2014, available at www.bloomberg.com.

Samuel, H. B., *Shareholders' Money* (Pitman, 1933).

Samsung, 'Board of Directors', available at www.samsung.com.

Sandrock, O., and du Plessis, J. J., 'The German System of Supervisory Codetermination by Employees' in J. J. du Plessis et al. (eds.), *German Corporate Governance in International and European Context*, 2nd edn (Springer, 2012).

Santos, A. O., 'Integrated Ownership and Control in the GCC Corporate Sector' (International Monetary Fund Working Paper, 2015), available at www.imf.org.

Saville, M., 'HIH: The Inside Story of Australia's Biggest Corporate Collapse', *Sydney Morning Herald*, 15 March 2003, available at www.smh.com.au.

Schetzer, A., 'Women Stall on Reaching Australia's Highest Rungs', *Sydney Morning Herald*, 1 November 2014, available at www.smh.com.au.

Schmitthoff, M., 'The Origin of the Joint-Stock Company', *The University of Toronto Law Journal*, 3 (1939), 74.

Schnatter, J., 'Where Were the Boards? Accountability Shouldn't End with the CEO', *The Wall Street Journal*, 25 October 2008, A 11.

'SEC Approves NYSE and NASDAQ Proposals Relating to Director Independence', *FindLaw*, 23 March 2006, available at http://corporate.findlaw.com.

SEC Staff Study of the Financial Collapse of the Penn Central Co.: Summary (1972–73 Transfer Binder), Fed. Se. L. Rep. (CCH) ¶ 78,931 (1972).

Securities and Futures Appeals Tribunal, Financial Services and the Treasury Bureau, 'About Us', available at www.sfat.gov.hk.

Securities and Futures Commission, 'Our Role | Securities and Futures Commission of Hong Kong', available at www.sfc.hk.

Securities and Futures Commission, 'Establishment of the Securities and Futures Commission – the Davison Report' in Securities and Futures Commission, *Securities Regulation in Hong Kong* (May 2002).

Securities and Futures Commission, '2011/2012 Annual Report 40: Operational Review: Enforcement' (2012), available at www.sfc.hk.

Securities and Futures Commission, 'High Shareholding Concentration Announcements' (13 March 2015), available at www.sfc.hk.

Securities and Futures Commission and the Stock Exchange of Hong Kong Limited, 'Joint Policy Statement Regarding the Listing of Overseas Companies' (27 September 2013), available at www.hkex.com.hk.

Securities and Futures Investors Protection Center, News Release of SFIPC (8 April 2011), available at www.sfipc.org.tw.

Securities and Futures Investors Protection Center, News Release of SFIPC (14 April 2011), available at www.sfipc.org.tw.

Seibert, U., 'Frauenförderung durch Gesellschaftsrecht – Die Entstehung des Frauenfördergesetzes', *Neue Zeitschrift für Gesellschaftsrecht* (2016), 1.

Setia-Atmaja, L., 'Governance Mechanisms and Firm Value: The Impact of Ownership Concentration and Dividends', *Corporate Governance: An International Review*, 17(6) (2009), 694.

Sexton, E., 'ASX Merger Plan Raises Questions of Governance', *The Age*, 29 October 2010, available at www.theage.com.au.

SGX, News and Updates, 'Trading of China Sky Shares Will Resume after Company's Board Complies with SGX Conditions', 12 February 2015, available at www.sgx.com.

Sharpe, N. F., 'Rethinking Board Function in the Wake of the 2008 Financial Crisis', *Journal of Business and Technology Law*, 5 (2010), 99.

Shen, S., and Jia, J., 'Will the Independent Director Institution Work in China', *Loyola of Los Angeles International and Comparative Law Review*, 27 (2005), 223.

Shi, C., '独立董事选聘程序的完善——基于代理理论的视角' [Improving the Nomination and Election of Independent Directors: From the Perspective of Agency Theory], *财会通讯* [*Communication of Finance and Accounting*], 10 (2010), 85.

Shoji Homu Kenkyu-kai, '「会社法研究会」の審議状況' [Discussions at the Companies Act Study Group], available at www.shojihomu.or.jp.

Shui, P., '独立董事该由谁委派' [Who Shall Appoint the Independent Directors], 中华工商时报 [China Securities News], 11 May 2006.

Siems, M., 'Shareholder Protection around the World ("Leximetric II")', *Delaware Journal of Corporate Law*, 33 (2008), 111.

Siems, M., 'The Curious Case of Overfitting Legal Transplant' in M. Adams and D. Thilbaut (eds.), *The Method and Culture of Comparative Law* (Hart, 2014).

Siems, M., and Alvarez-Macotela, O., 'The OECD Principles of Corporate Governance in Emerging Markets: A Successful Example of Networked Governance?' in M. Fenwick et al. (eds.), *Networked Governance, Transnational Business and the Law* (Springer, 2014).

Sim, I. et al., *The State as Shareholder: The Case of Singapore* (2014), available at http://bschool.nus.edu.

Singapore Exchange, Listing Rule Amendments (2006), available at http://rulebook.sgx.com.

Skousen, C., Smith, K. R., and Wright, C. J., 'Detecting and Predicting Financial Statement Fraud: The Effectiveness of the Fraud Triangle and SAS No. 99', *Advances in Financial Economics*, 13 (2009), 53.

Smith, A., *An Inquiry into the Nature and Courses of the Wealth of Nations*, ed. E. Cannan (Modern Library, 1937).

Smith, G., Swan, P., and Gallagher, D., 'Institutional Investor Monitoring and the Structure of Corporate Boards', Draft (2 October 2007), available at http://papers.ssrn.com/sol3/papers.cfm?abstract_id=939441.

Solomon, L. D., 'Restructuring the Corporate Board of Directors: Fond Hope – Faint Promise?', *Michigan Law Review*, 76 (1978), 581.

Song, O. R., 'The Legacy of Controlling Minority Structure: A Kaleidoscope of Corporate Governance Reform in Korean Chaebol', *Law and Policy in International Business*, 34 (2002), 183.

Sony, 'Corporate Governance', available at www.sony.com.

Spigelman, J., 'Institutional Shareholders and Corporate Governance', *Companies and Securities Law Journal*, 28(4) (2010), 235.

Sprague, R., and Lyttle, A. J., 'Shareholder Primacy and the Business Judgment Rule: Arguments for Expanded Corporate Democracy', *Stanford Journal of Law, Business and Finance*, 16 (2010), 1.

Srivastava, B., 'Are Long-Serving Independent Directors Truly Independent?', *The Mint*, 23 September 2012.

Stamford Law Corporation, 'Making SGX Attractive to S-Chips', *Legal 500*, available at www.legal500.com.

Stock Exchange of Hong Kong Limited, *Consultation Paper: 1998 Review of the Listing Rules* (1998), available at www.hkex.com.hk.

Stock Exchange of Hong Kong Limited, *Consultation Paper on Chapter 17 (Share Schemes) of the Rules Governing the Listing of Securities on the Stock Exchange of Hong Kong Limited* (May 2000), available at www.hkex.com.hk.

Stock Exchange of Hong Kong Limited, *Consultation Conclusions Relating to Proposed Amendments to the Listing Rules Relating to Corporate Governance Issues* (January 2003), available at www.hkex.com.hk.

Stock Exchange of Hong Kong Limited, 'HKEx Listing Decision HkEx-LD104-1' (September 2010), available at www.hkex.com.hk.

Stock Exchange of Hong Kong Limited, 'HKEx News Release: GEM Listing Committee Censure of Zhejiang Prospect Company Limited' (26 September 2012), available at www.hkex.com.hk.

Stock Exchange of Hong Kong Limited, 'HKEx News Release: Censure of Richly Field China Development Limited' (21 January 2015), available at www.hkex.com.hk.

Stock Exchange of Hong Kong Limited, 'Listing Decisions', available at www.hkex.com.hk.

Stock Exchange of Hong Kong Limited, 'List of Acceptable Overseas Jurisdictions' (last updated July 2014), available at www.hkex.com.hk.

Stockwinn, J. A. A., *Governing Japan: Divided Politics in a Resurgent Economy*, 4th edn (Wiley-Blackwell, 2008).

Stulz, R., and Fahlenbrach, R., 'Bank CEO Incentives and the Credit Crisis', *Journal of Financial Economics*, 99 (2011), 11.

Swan, P., *Submission to (Australian Government's) Financial System Inquiry*, 31 March 2014.

Swan, P., and Forsberg, D., 'Does Board "Independence" Destroy Corporate Value?' (27th Australasian Finance and Banking Conference, August 2014), available at http://papers.ssrn.com/sol3/papers.cfm?abstract_id=2312325.

Swan, P., and Honeine, S., 'Is Company Performance Dependent on Outside Director "Skin in the Game"?' (2010), available at http://ssrn.com/abstract=1746536.

Swiss Financial Market Supervisory Authority (FINMA), *Board of Directors of Banks and Securities Dealers* (28 August 2012), available at www.finma.ch.

Taiwan Stock Exchange, 'Corporate Governance Best-Practice Principles for TWSE-Listed and OTC-Traded Companies', TWSE, available at http://eng.selaw.com.tw.

Takahashi, Y., and Koh, Y., 'Toyota Overhauls Management', *Wall Street Journal*, 6 March 2015, available at www.wsj.com.

Tan, C. H., 'Corporate Governance and Independent Directors', *Singapore Academy of Law Journal*, 15 (2003), 355.

Tan, C. H. et al., 'State-Owned Enterprises in Singapore: Historical Insights into a Potential Model for Reform', *Columbia Journal of Asian Law*, 28(2) (2015), 61.

Tan, L. H., 'Exploring the Question of the Separation of Ownership from Control: An Empirical Study of the Structure of Corporate Ownership in Singapore's Top Listed Companies' (Working Paper, 2011), available at http://docs.business.auckland.ac.nz.

Tanaka, W., '立法事実と実証分析の利用: 齋藤報告へのコメント' [An Empirical Analysis of Board Structure of Japanese Firms: Comment on Saito], *ソフトロー研究*, 20 (2012), 43.

Tanaka, W., '株式保有構造と会社法: 「分散保有の上場会社のジレンマ」を越えて' [Share-Ownership Structure and Corporate Law: Beyond the Dilemma of Dispersedly-Held Listed Corporations], *商事法務*, 2007 (2013), 30.

Tanaka, W., 会社法 [Company Law] (2016).

Tang, J., Li, Y., and Lu, J., '股权结构、董事会特征与大股东掏空——来自民营上市公司的经验证据' [Equity Ownership Structure, the Characteristics of Board and Tunneling: Empirical Evidence from China's Private-Owned Listed Companies], *经济评论* [Economic Review], 1 (2013), 88.

Tata Steel, 'Board of Directors', available at www.tatasteel.com.

Technical Committee of the International Organisation of Securities Commissions, 'Board Independence of Listed Companies: Final Report' (2007), available at www.iosco.org.

Temasek, 'FAQs: Does Temasek Request Representation on the Boards of Companies in Which It Invests?', Temasek, available at www.temasek.com.sg.

Temasek, 'FAQs: How Does Temasek Work with Its Portfolio Companies?', Temasek, available at www.temasek.com.sg.

Temasek, 'FAQs: How Is the President Involved in the Protection of Temasek's Past Reserves?', Temasek, available at www.temasek.com.sg.

Temasek, 'FAQs: How Is the President Involved with the Board of Temasek?', Temasek, available at www.temasek.com.sg.

Temasek, 'FAQs: Why Was Temasek Established?', Temasek, available at www.temasek.com.sg.

Temasek Holdings, 'Temasek Charter', available at http://temasekreview.com.sg.

Temasek, 'Board of Directors', available at http://temasekreview.com.sg.

Temasek, *Temasek Annual Review 2014* (2014).

Tencent, 'Board', available at www.tencent.com.

'TEXT-Full Text of Toyota President's Testimony', *Reuters*, 24 February 2010, available at http://uk.reuters.com.

Tjio, H., *Principles and Practice of Securities Regulation in Singapore*, 2nd edn (LexisNexis, 2011).

Tokyo Stock Exchange, *TSE-Listed Companies White Paper on Corporate Governance 2011* (2011).

Tokyo Stock Exchange, *2012 Share Ownership Survey, Share Distribution Survey* § 2–5 (2012), available at www.tse.or.jp.

Tokyo Stock Exchange, *TSE-Listed Companies White Paper on Corporate Governance 2013* (2013).

Tokyo Stock Exchange, *TSE-Listed Companies White Paper on Corporate Governance 2015* (2015).

Tokyo Stock Exchange, *Appointment of Outside Directors by TSE-Listed Companies [Confirmed report]* (29 July 2015), available at www.jpx.co.jp.

Tomasic, R., 'Corporate Collapse, Crime and Governance', *Australian Journal of Corporate Law*, 14 (2002), 183.

Tong, C., 'Towards Better Corporate Governance' (Chamber of Hong Kong Listed Companies 11th Anniversary Gala Dinner, December 2013), available at www.sfc.hk.

'Toshiba Scandal: Securities Watchdog Inches toward Criminal Case', *Asia Nikkei*, 15 December 2015, available at www.asia.nikkei.com.

'Toshiba Shock: Failure of Governance gives Abenomics a Rude Awakening', *Nikkei Asian Review*, 23 July 2015, available at http://asia.nikkei.com.

Toyota Motor Corporation, 'TMC Announces New Organizational Structure and Executive Changes' (6 March 2013), available at www2.toyota.co.jp.

Transparency International, 'Corruption Perceptions Index 2014: Results', Transparency.org, www.transparency.org.

Trudell, C., and Hagiwara, Y., 'Loss of Toyota's First Female Executive Is Blow to Japan's Diversity Drive', *Bloomberg*, reprinted in *Japan Times*, 2 July 2015, available at www.japantimes.co.jp.

Tseng, W. R., '半套公司治理移植經驗—以審計委員會與特別委員會為例' [An Analysis of Taiwan's Alterations and Misconceptions during Transplantation of Foreign Laws Regarding Corporate Governance: An Exploration of Taiwan's Audit Committee and Special Committee], *Cross-Strait Law Review*, 43 (2014), 33.

Tseng, W. R., and Wen, W., 'Derivative Actions in Taiwan: Legal and Cultural Hurdles with a Glimmer of Hope for the Future' in D. W. Puchniak, H. Baum and M. Ewing-Chow (eds.), *The Derivative Action in Asia: A Comparative and Functional Approach* (Cambridge University Press, 2012).

Uchida, K., 'Does Corporate Board Downsizing Increase Shareholder Value? Evidence from Japan', *International Review of Economics and Finance*, 20(4) (2011), 562.

Uchida, K., '社外取締役割合の決定要因とパフォーマンス' [Determinants of Ratio of Outside Directors on Firms' Board and Their Performance], *証券アナリストジャーナル*, 50(2) (2012), 8.

Uchida, K., '日本企業の取締役会の進化と国際的特徴' [Development and Characteristics of Board of Directors of Japanese Firms in the International Context], *商事法務*, 2007 (2013), 41.

UNData, 'Data', available at data.un.org.

United Company Rusal Plc, 'Change of Directorate and Change of Composition of the Corporate Governance and Nomination Committee and the Remuneration Committee' (27 May 2013), available at www.hkexnews.hk.

US Securities Exchange Commission, 'NASD and NYSE Rulemaking: Relating to Corporate Governance' (Release No. 34-48745, 2003), available at www.sec.gov.

Van Der Kamp, Jake, 'Securities and Futures Commission Has Spun out of Control', *South China Morning Post*, 4 January 2015, available at www.scmp.com.

Van Zile, C., 'India's Mandatory Corporate Social Responsibility Proposal: Creative Capitalism Meets Creative Regulation in the Global Market', *Asian-Pacific Law and Policy Journal*, 13 (2012), 269.

Varottil, U., 'Independent Directors and Their Constraints in China and India', *Jindal Global Law Review*, 2 (2007), 127.

Varottil, U., 'Evolution and Effectiveness of Independent Directors in Indian Corporate Governance', *Hastings Business Law Journal*, 6 (2010), 281.

Varottil, U., 'Director Liability under the New Regime', *IndiaCorpLaw Blog* (2014), available at http://indiacorplaw.blogspot.com.

Varottil, U., 'Directors' Duties and Liabilities in the New Era', *NSE Quarterly Briefing* (2014), available at www.nseindia.com.

Varottil, U., 'The Evolution of Corporate Law in Post-Colonial India: From Transplant to Autochthony', *American University International Law Review* 31 (2016), 253.

Varriale, G., 'What New London Listing Rules Mean for EM Companies', *International Financial Law Review*, 12 (2013).

Vasudev, P. M., 'Independent Directors Sank Nortel', *Financial Post*, 22 October 2014, available at http://business.financial post.com.

Velikonja, U., 'The Political Economy of Board Independence', *North Carolina Law Review*, 92 (2014), 855.

Veljanovski, A., Brooks, A., and Oliver, J., 'Independent Directors and Australia's Corporate Governance Model: A Survey of Independent Directors' Views', *Australian Journal of Corporate Law*, 24 (2009), 33.

Villalonga, B., and Amit, R., 'How Do Family Ownership, Control and Management Affect Firm Value?', *Journal of Financial Economics*, 80 (2006), 385.

Wachtell, Lipton, Rosen & Katz, *Compensation Committee Guide* (2014), available at www.wlrk.com.

Walker, D., *A Review of Corporate Governance in UK Banks and Other Financial Industry Entities* (2009), available at www.hm-treasury.gov.uk.

Wang, W., 公司法論 [Corporate Law], 4th edn (元照 [Yuan Chao], 2008).

Wang, W., 'Ownership Structure of the Chinese Growth Enterprise Market' (1 December 2012), available at http://ssrn.com/abstract=2223989.

Wang, W., 'Independent Directors and Corporate Performance in China: A Meta-Empirical Study' (27 March 2014), available at http://ssrn.com/abstract=2417078.

Watson, A., *Legal Transplants: An Approach to Comparative Law* (University of Georgia Press, 1993).

Watts, J. M., 'Singapore to Allow Mainland Chinese Listings', *Wall Street Journal*, 27 November 2013, available at http://blogs.wsj.com.

Webb-site, 'Hong Kong's Not So Independent Directors' (20 April 1999), available at https://webb-site.com.

Webb-site, 'Poll Results: INEDs' (2011), available at https://webb-site.com.

Webb-site, 'The Three Wise Monkeys of HK Boards' (15 February 2011), available at https://webb-site.com.

Wee, V., 'Boardrooms Due for Re-calibration', *Business Times Singapore*, 12 April 2012.

Weil, Gotshal & Manges LLP, *Comparative Study of Corporate Governance Codes Relevant to the European Union and Its Member States: Final Report* (2002), available at http://ec.europa.eu.

Weil, Gotshal & Manges LLP, *Public Company Advisory Group, Requirements for Public Company Boards: Including IPO Transition Rules* (2013), available at www.weil.com.

Wiethölter, R., *Interessen und Organisation der Aktiengesellschaft im amerikanischen und deutschen Recht* (C. F. Müller, 1961).

'Winds of Change: The Prospects for Shaking Up Japanese Firms Have Never Looked So Good', *The Economist*, 6 June 2015.

Winter, J., 'The Financial Crisis: Does Good Corporate Governance Matter and How to Achieve it?' in E. Wymeersch, K. J. Hopt and G. Ferrarini (eds.), *Financial Regulation and Supervision: A Post-Crisis Analysis* (Oxford University Press, 2012).

Wong, S. C. Y., 'Developing and Implementing Corporate Governance Codes', *Private Sector Opinion*, Global Corporate Governance Forum, 10 (2008), available at www.ifc.org.

Wooldridge, A., 'Family Companies: To Have and to Hold', *The Economist*, 18 April 2015, available at www.economist.com.

Working Group of the Australian Institute of Company Directors et al., *Corporate Practices and Conduct* (1991).

Working Group on Corporate Practices and Conduct, *Corporate Practices and Conduct* (1993).

World Bank Group, *Worldwide Governance Indicators: Country Data Report for Singapore, 1996–2013* (2013), available at http://info.worldbank.org.

World Bank Group, *Doing Business 2015: Going beyond Efficiency* (October 2014), available at www.doingbusiness.org.

World Bank Group, 'Doing Business – Measuring Business Regulations: Ease of Doing Business in Hong Kong SAR, China' (2015), available at www.doingbusiness.org.

World Federation of Exchanges, 'Monthly Reports' (last updated December 2014), available at www.world-exchanges.org.

World Justice Project, *Rule of Law Index* (2015), available at http://worldjusticeproject.org.

Wu, G., and Ye, Y., '股权集中度、行业特征与企业绩效——基于中国上市公司的实证分析' [Ownership Concentration, Industrial Characteristics and Corporate Performance: Based on Empirical Analysis of China's Listed Companies], *北京工商大学学报（社会科学版）* [Journal of Beijing Technology and Business University (Social Science)], 28 (2013), 92.

Wu, X., and Zhai, M., '上市公司股权结构对现金股利政策的影响' [Empirical Study on Influence of Ownership Structure on Dividend Policy: Based on Ownership Structure Changes after the Split Share Structure Reform], *山西财经大学学报* [Journal of Shanxi Finance and Economics University], 35 (2013), 89.

Xiao, W., Wang, Z., and Duan, Y., '大股东存在下的独立董事对公司业绩的影响: 基于内生视角的审视' [The Impact of Major Stake-holding, Independent Directors to Company Performance: An Endogenous Perspective], *南开管理评论* [Nankai Business Review], 12(2) (2009), 90.

Xie, C., '股份公司独立董事任免制度研究' [Study on the Mechanism of Appointment and Removal of Independent Direction in Stock Corporations], *河北法学* [Hebei Law Science], 22 (2004), 3.

Yamada, Y., 'ステイク・ホルダーと会社法' [Stakeholders and Corporate Law] in M. Nakahigashi and H. Matsui (eds.), 『会社法の選択–新しい社会の会社法を求めて』 [Choices Made by the Corporate Law: In Search of the Corporate Law for the New Society] (Shoji Homu, 2010).

Yamazaki, M., and Ando, R., 'Toshiba in $5.9 Billion Asset Sale, Shares Hit by Report of U.S. Probe', *Reuters*, 17 March 2016, available at www.reuters.com.

Yang, L. and Lu, R., '独立董事与高管薪酬———基于中国证券市场的经验证据' [Independent Director and Executive Salary: Empirical Evidences from China's Security Market], *当代财经* [Contemporary Finance and Economics], 5 (2009), 110.

Yeh, Y. H., and Ko, C. E., *The Law and Practice of Independent Directors, Audit Committees and Other Functional Committees in Germany, Japan, the US, and Korea* (Financial Supervisory Commission of Taiwan, 2006).

Yeh, Y. H., Tsun, S. L., and Woidtke, T., 'Family Control and Corporate Governance: Evidence from Taiwan', *International Review of Finance*, 2 (2001), 21.

Yermack, D., 'Higher Market Valuation of Companies with a Small Board of Directors', *Journal of Financial Economics*, 40 (1996), 185.

Yonekura, S., 'Poor Corporate Governance Fueled Sony's Meltdown', 23 April 2014, available at www.nippon.com.

Yoshii, T., 'Japan's Corporate Auditor System', *Journal of Japanese Law*, 9 (2004), 39.

Yuan, J., 'Formal Convergence or Substantial Divergence? Evidence from Adoption of the Independent Director System in China', *Asian-Pacific Law and Policy Journal*, 9 (2007), 72.

Yuan, Z., 'Independent Directors in China: The Path in Which Direction?', *International Company and Commercial Law Review*, 22 (2011), 352.

Zhao, J., 'Comparative Study of U.S. and German Corporate Governance: Suggestions on the Relationship between Independent Directors and the Supervisory Board of Listed Companies in China', *Michigan State Journal of International Law*, 18 (2010), 495.

Zhao, L., Tang, X., and Ding, G., '走出困境——独立董事的义务、职责和责任' [The Way Out: The Role, Tasks, and Responsibilities of the Independent Director], *法律出版社* [Law Press China] (2010), 39.

Zhao, Y., *Corporate Governance and Directors' Independence* (Kluwer Law International, 2011).

INDEX